FILM

A Montage of Theories

RICHARD DYER MACCANN was born in Wichita, Kansas, in 1920, and attended the University of Kansas, where he received his B.A. in Political Science in 1940. After an M.A. at Stanford University in 1942 and three-years' service in the U.S. and Europe during World War II, he completed a Ph.D. in Government at Harvard in 1951. His dissertation, *Documentary Film and Democratic Government,* led him to a growing concern about communication and public opinion in the democratic process and to a special interest in the motion picture. He accepted a position as a staff correspondent in Los Angeles for the *Christian Science Monitor,* specializing in film and television reporting from 1951 to 1957. As Assistant Professor of Cinema at the University of Southern California from 1957 to 1962, he continued a weekly Hollywood column for the *Monitor* for three years, while teaching courses in documentary film, film writing, and cinema and society. In 1963, Dr. MacCann was an adviser and teacher, on a U.S. State Department grant, for the Korean National Film Production Center in Seoul. The following year he was a producer in the program department of Subscription Television, Inc., in Santa Monica, California. From 1965-70 Dr. MacCann taught at the University of Kansas, where he was Professor of Speech and Journalism and Director of the Center for Film Studies. In 1970 he joined the faculty of the University of Iowa as professor in charge of the Ph.D. program in film in the Department of Speech and Dramatic Art. He is a member of the University Film Association, the Writers Guild of America, and Phi Beta Kappa. Dr. MacCann is editor of *Cinema Journal,* the semi-annual publication of the national Society for Cinema Studies. His articles have appeared in *Yale Review, Film Quarterly, Films and Filming,* and *Encyclopedia Americana.* He is also the author of *Hollywood in Transition* (1962) and *Film and Society* (1964).

FILM

A Montage of Theories

BY

Richard Dyer MacCann

A Dutton  Paperback

NEW YORK

E. P. DUTTON & CO., INC.

ACKNOWLEDGMENTS

Grateful acknowledgment is made to the following for permission
to quote from copyright material:

V. I. PUDOVKIN: "The Plastic Material." Excerpts reprinted from
Film Technique and Film Acting by V. I. Pudovkin by permission
of Vision Press Limited, London.

SERGEI EISENSTEIN: "Collision of Ideas." Excerpts reprinted from
"The Cinematographic Principle and the Ideogram" in *Film Form*
by Sergei M. Eisenstein, edited by Jay Leyda, by permission of
Harcourt, Brace & World, Inc. Copyright, 1949, by Harcourt,
Brace & World, Inc.

RENÉ CLAIR: "The Art of Sound." Excerpts reprinted from *Reflec-
tions on the Cinema* by René Clair by permission of Editions
Gallimard, Paris, and William Kimber & Co. Limited, London.
Copyright, ©, 1951 by Editions Gallimard.

GAVIN LAMBERT: "Sight and Sound." Reprinted from *Sequence*,
Summer 1950, by permission of Gavin Lambert.

ALFRED HITCHCOCK: "Direction." Excerpts reprinted from *Footnotes to the Film*, edited by Charles Davy, by permission of Peter
Davies Limited, London.

ALEXANDER KNOX: "Acting and Behaving." Excerpts reprinted from "Acting and Behaving" by Alexander Knox in *Hollywood Quarterly* (now *Film Quarterly*), Vol. 1, No. 3, Spring 1946, by permission of The Regents of the University of California and the author. Copyright, 1946, by The Regents of the University of California.

DUDLEY NICHOLS: "The Writer and the Film." Excerpts reprinted from "The Writer and the Film" by Dudley Nichols in *Great Film Plays*, edited by John Gassner and Dudley Nichols by permission of Crown Publishers, Inc. Copyright, ©, 1959, by Crown Publishers, Inc.

VACHEL LINDSAY: "Sculpture-in-Motion." Reprinted from *The Art of the Moving Picture* by Vachel Lindsay, New York, Macmillan, 1922, by permission of The Estate of Vachel Lindsay.

PARKER TYLER: "Movies and the Human Image." Reprinted from *The Three Faces of the Film* by Parker Tyler by permission of Thomas Yoseloff. Copyright, ©, 1960, by A. S. Barnes & Company, Inc.

HOLLIS ALPERT: "The Film is Modern Theatre." Reprinted by permission of the author.

ALLARDYCE NICOLL: "Film and Theatre." Excerpts reprinted from "Film Reality: The Cinema and the Theatre" in *Film and Theatre* by Allardyce Nicoll by permission of Thomas Y. Crowell Company. Copyright, 1936, by Thomas Y. Crowell Company, publishers; copyright, ©, 1964, by Allardyce Nicoll.

RUDOLF ARNHEIM: "Epic and Dramatic Film." Reprinted from *Film Culture*, Vol. 3, No. 1, 1957, by permission of Jonas Mekas.

ROBERT NATHAN: "A Novelist Looks at Hollywood." Reprinted from *Hollywood Quarterly* (now *Film Quarterly*), Vol. 1, No. 2, 1945, by permission of The Regents of the University of California and the author. Copyright, 1945, by The Regents of the University of California.

GEORGE BLUESTONE: "Novels Into Film." Excerpts reprinted from "The Limits of the Novel and the Limits of the Film" in *Novels Into Film* by George Bluestone by permission of The Johns Hopkins Press. Copyright, ©, 1957, by The Johns Hopkins Press.

INGMAR BERGMAN: "Film Has Nothing To Do With Literature." Excerpts reprinted from the "Introduction" by Ingmar Bergman in *Four Screenplays of Ingmar Bergman*, New York, Simon and Schuster, 1960, by permission of Janus Films, Incorporated, Cambridge, Mass.

BÉLA BALÁZS: "The Faces of Men." Reprinted from *The Theory of Film* by Béla Balázs by permission of the publishers, Dennis Dobson, London.

RALPH BLOCK: "Not Theatre, Not Literature, Not Painting." Reprinted from *The Dial*, January 1927, by permission of the author.

MACK SENNETT: "Cloud-Cuckoo Country." Reprinted from *King of Comedy* by Mack Sennett, New York, Doubleday & Company, Inc., 1954, by permission of Raymond Rohauer.

HERBERT READ: "Towards a Film Aesthetic." Excerpts reprinted from *A Coat of Many Colours* by Sir Herbert Read by permission of Routledge & Kegan Paul, Ltd., London, and the author.

SLAVKO VORKAPICH: "Toward True Cinema." Reprinted from *Film Culture*, March 1959, by permission of Jonas Mekas.

HANS RICHTER: "The Film as an Original Art Form." Reprinted from *Film Culture*, Vol. 1, No. 1, January 1955, by permission of Jonas Mekas.

ARNOLD HAUSER: "Space and Time in the Film." Excerpts reprinted from *The Social History of Art* (Vintage Edition, 4 Vols.) by Arnold Hauser by permission of Alfred A. Knopf, Inc., New York, and Routledge & Kegan Paul, Ltd., London. Copyright, ©, 1958, by Arnold Hauser.

SUSANNE LANGER: "A Note on the Film." Reprinted from *Feeling and Form* by Susanne Langer, pp. 411–415, by permission of Charles Scribner's Sons. Copyright, 1953, by Charles Scribner's Sons.

JOHN GRIERSON: "First Principles of Documentary." Reprinted from *Grierson on Documentary*, edited by Forsyth Hardy, New York, Harcourt, Brace & World, Inc., 1947, by permission of the author.

CESARE ZAVATTINI: "Some Ideas on the Cinema." Reprinted from *Sight and Sound*, October 1953, by permission of the author.

Hugo Mauerhofer: "Psychology of Film Experience." Reprinted from *Penguin Film Review #8*, London, 1949, by permission of Penguin Books Ltd.

Elizabeth Bowen: "Why I Go to the Cinema." Excerpts reprinted from *Footnotes to the Film*, edited by Charles Davy, by permission of Peter Davies Limited, London.

Siegfried Kracauer: "Theory of Film." Excerpts reprinted from *Theory of Film: The Redemption of Physical Reality* by Siegfried Kracauer by permission of Oxford University Press, Inc. Copyright, ©, 1960, by Oxford University Press, Inc.

Michael Roemer: "The Surfaces of Reality." Reprinted from *Film Quarterly*, Vol. XVIII, No. 1, Fall 1964, by permission of The Regents of the University of California and the author. Copyright, ©, 1964, by The Regents of the University of California.

Gideon Bachmann, Robert Drew, Richard Leacock, D. A. Pennebaker: "The Frontiers of Realist Cinema." Reprinted from *Film Culture,* No. 22–23, Summer 1961, by permission of Jonas Mekas.

A. William Bluem: "Television and the Documentary Quest." Excerpts reprinted from *Documentary in American Television* by A. William Bluem by permission of Hastings House, Publishers, Inc. Copyright, ©, 1965, by A. William Bluem.

Carl Dreyer: "Thoughts on My Craft." Reprinted from *Sight and Sound*, Winter 1955–1956, by permission of the author.

Charles Barr: "CinemaScope: Before and After." Excerpts reprinted from "CinemaScope: Before and After" by Charles Barr in *Film Quarterly*, Vol. XVI, No. 4, Summer 1963, by permission of The Regents of the University of California and the author. Copyright, ©, 1963, by The Regents of the University of California.

Stan VanDerBeek: "Compound Entendre." Reprinted from *8: Newsletter of 8mm. Film in Education* (July 1965), edited by Joan Rosengren Forsdale, and published by the Project in Educational Communication of the Horace Mann-Lincoln Institute of School Experimentation, Teachers College, Columbia University.

JONAS MEKAS: "Notes on the New American Cinema." Excerpts reprinted from *Film Culture*, No. 24, Spring 1962, by permission of the author.

PAULINE KAEL: "Are Movies Going to Pieces?" Reprinted from *I Lost It at the Movies* by Pauline Kael by permission of Atlantic —Little, Brown and Co. Copyright, ©, 1964, by Pauline Kael.

PENELOPE HOUSTON: "Towards a New Cinema." Reprinted from *The Contemporary Cinema* by Penelope Houston by permission of Penguin Books Ltd. Copyright, ©, 1963, by Penelope Houston.

FRANÇOIS TRUFFAUT: "We Must Continue Making Progress." Excerpts reprinted from "François Truffaut—An Interview" In *Film Quarterly*, Fall 1963, by permission of *Cahiers du Cinéma* and The Regents of the University of California. Copyright, ©, 1963, by The Regents of the University of California.

FEDERICO FELLINI: "The Road Beyond Neorealism." Reprinted from "Federico Fellini: An Interview" by Gideon Bachmann in *Film: Book I*, edited by Robert Hughes, New York, Grove Press, 1959, by permission of Gideon Bachmann and Robert Hughes. Copyright, ©, 1959, by Robert Hughes.

The author wishes to express his appreciation to Erik Barnouw, Henry Breitrose, Jack Ellis, and Arthur Knight for encouragement and advice in making the selections for this book. Professor Ellis was particularly helpful in suggesting the kind of material to include in the last section.

R.D.M.

CONTENTS

9

Dream and Reality   205

Illustrations   269

An Evolving Art   287

LIST OF ILLUSTRATIONS

(Grouped together following page 269)

11

INTRODUCTION

The art of the film is always in a tortured state of crisis, tension, hope, and despair—racked by technical, financial, and political demands; buffeted by critical whirlwinds; choked by human pride and vulgar display. Film is praised and attacked by many who do not know what it is, and equally tormented by those who claim to love and understand.

In America, the traditional middle-class view is that a movie is merely entertainment. This seems to carry with it two conflicting attitudes. On the one hand, it does not occur to most people to include film among the arts at all. The early reluctance to think of motion pictures as belonging within the Lincoln Center in New York or the Kennedy Center in Washington represents a familiar American blindness to the only art we can call our own. On the other hand, when the motion picture does demand attention by trying to move or disturb us on moral or social grounds, it may suddenly become an object of censorship. Still defined as merely entertainment, the film nevertheless is thought to have mysterious powers of persuasion, for good, perhaps, but certainly for ill. Thus, by the general run of busy "opinion leaders," film is alternately ignored and feared.

Among the informed and intellectual observers of the cinema there are extremists of other kinds. There are those who concentrate their praise on films about abortion or racial violence or some other controversy, because such subjects are thought to be daring, important, and annoying to conservatives. The stereotyped liberal is too busy hating the censors to love the film. On the other hand, there are the "in" critics who have decided that primitivism is freedom. They see no point in going on with recognizable cinematic forms, but demand that young directors wipe the slate clean of traditional dramatic structure and start over. Thus film's best friends tear it apart with ever-narrowing demands.

13

This book is for film makers, of course, and for critics and teachers and students of the film. It is also for fans, whose enthusiasm for star or story may actually be related to deeper sources of satisfaction in the art of the film. I hope that the occasional moviegoer, too, will want to cope with this kind of book, for he may then be able to place the art of the film in better perspective as part of his knowledge of contemporary civilization.

The theories conflict. Those who love movies should not be upset by the fact that there seem to be deep contradictions. What kind of aesthetic theory can reconcile realism and fantasy, entertainment and education, mysteries and musicals, slapstick and spectacle? The true philosopher of film is interested in every new artistic event. He will admit any subject, any style, any function for film, setting up his standards of excellence and noting his personal tastes within the wide range of these alternatives.

There can no more be a final theory of film than there can be a definitive theory of what to put in a book. The medium and its limits can be described, differentiated from other media, found to possess unique characteristics. But after that, the storm over style and content will rage forever.

Theory should be stimulating, liberating. It should not be so inflexible that it drops a negative pall on the artist, limiting his areas of effort. Theory should lead to something. It should open up debate and controversy, leading in turn to new theory, or to experiment and action.

Watch the young man of talent. When works of theory or criticism are available, he will sit in a corner and devour them. He may not be able to tell you everything he has read. He has nevertheless gone through an experience of comparative judgements which has informed him, stirred him, shaken him. Sometime later, after he has worked a while with film, he may come to rest at a point in the spectrum of theory where he feels comfortable. He will have a passion and a position, rooted in knowledge. He will not be embarrassed to accept an already accepted theory—nor driven to be "different" in order to be noticed. He will have a sense of the best that has been thought and said about film.

The notion that pragmatic Americans don't like theory is a notion that blocks progress in both science and art. Theory rallies enthusiasm and starts achievement. In the history of

European motion pictures, training schools and film magazines have been crucially important. Eisenstein and Pudovkin moved back and forth from film making to the state film school in Moscow; they also published important contributions to film theory. Luigi Chiarini, the first director of the Centro Sperimentale in Rome, and founder of the critical magazine *Bianco e Nero*, was a prominent film director. In France, the "new wave" directors were the ones who had earlier watched films at the Cinématheque or worked on student productions at the Institut des Hautes Études Cinématographiques; François Truffaut and Jean-Luc Godard wrote for *Cahiers du Cinéma*. In England, Tony Richardson, Karel Reisz, and Lindsay Anderson wrote articles for *Sequence* and for *Sight and Sound* before they directed films.

It is not to be expected that all of the most interesting directors, now or later, will also be profound thinkers. By the very nature of their medium and the skills needed to master that medium, it is certain that many of the best artists will always be somewhat inarticulate about what they do. The important thing is for those who work at the art to be exposed to the arguments, *pro* and *con*, to know what alternative cries have been raised.

In theory, and sometimes in practice, the cinema is an art.

In practice, the motion picture director cannot work alone. He must dominate an enormous tangle of technical and economic apparatus and a baffling variety of people. He must understand what editing can do, since the art of editing is basic to the art of the film. He must know the oldest truths about acting, the newest capabilities of the laboratories. He must evaluate the set designer's skills, meet the production manager's schedule, watch for the script clerk's reminders about matching yesterday's shots. He must be able to control the camera and the cameraman without being awed by the demands of the machinery.

Directing involves both collaboration and domination. Even Eisenstein, who was "all for the collective method of work," confessed that "there are cases when a director's 'iron heel' is not only justified but absolutely necessary." The process is not a matter of balancing all the elements evenly and democratically. In film, as in life, justice consists of more than simple equality. Within the checks and balances of technical and artistic advice, the presidential leadership of the director must firmly guide the actors, choose the shots, demand a tempo, decide the over-all shape of the outcome. In the clamor of the sound stage, in the loneliness of the cutting room, he must hold to his vision.

Jean Renoir once told an interviewer that in the studios the camera has become almost a god, "fixed on its tripod or crane, which is just like a heathen altar; and about it are the high priests—the director, cameraman, assistants—who bring victims before the camera, like burnt offerings." Mere mastery of physical arrangements leaves out the life of film.

Methodical men are always dreaming that the arts can be planned, organized, produced, and distributed according to a prearranged set of technical skills, one of which is called "talent." The prerequisite for a good film is no such combination of measurable quantities. It is something altogether unprecedented, unpredictable, intangible, and indescribable. It is a spark of electricity which fuses the elements, creating a brand-new thing in the world.

The notion that there can be mechanical combinations resulting in a work of art is a fable wrapped up in a myth. Only a scientist or engineer or businessman would give himself up to such wishful woolgathering. Art comes from encounters and inspirations, often by chance, usually without warning. Most of this has to take place before the film writer or director begins his work. It is his total life preparation. James Thurber put it clearly: "Yes, madam, I'm sure your son is better at drawing than I am. But he hasn't been through as much."

The mechanics of motion pictures must be thoroughly understood—not merely theoretically, but through practical experience—before a film maker can adequately express himself as an artist. But the wise director knows that technical knowledge is the smallest part of his equipment. After he understands it, he should be able to leave most of it to others. He should be thinking, instead, of the orchestration of emotion and mood, duration and rhythm, conflict and climax.

The director who is concerned with the film as an art is very clear about what film is made of. It is not a mechanical sandwich composed of a script, a lot of settings and actors, and a great many careful skills like photography and editing. It is a magical fusion of light, movement, and sound. It is not a simple combination of techniques. It is, as Dudley Nichols says, "a stream of images."

The motion picture is not an art of repose.

Parker Tyler has compared film to Galatea, who responded to Pygmalion's prayer, gave up being a statue, and moved. The moment she moved, she became a problem.

The first essential of the motion picture is motion. Film seeks action, and not only action but conflict. Some sort of violent change is almost inherent in its expectations. Movie-conscious audiences all over the world are pleased when one thing more in a James Bond film blows up. It is no accident that Americans—so loath to wait, so eager for something to happen—quickly grasped and developed the film as their favorite storytelling medium. The western, the chase, the detective story, the war story—these have become the staples of the screen for the most natural and intrinsic reasons.

War, ever since Aeschylus, has been a stimulus for drama. Film loves war—and is puzzled by peace. This is part of its problem, an aspect of its art that has social implications. Fear and disaster are filmic. Hope is a civilized, static concept, needing no outward action to maintain its identity or to prove itself. The film maker who seeks to convey the quiet virtues of hope, peace, and wise solutions is working against the tendencies of his medium. He may sometimes succeed, and he may deserve our blessing, but his obstacles are severe.

It is true, of course, that movement does not require a constant succession of vehicles, knives, or bodies whirling past the camera. The opening of a door, a hand, or an eye can bring about a climax as thrilling as a crash of locomotives, if it is properly prepared for in the story and on the screen. Yet the medium's need for movement and the story's need for conflict—from D. W. Griffith's *Intolerance* to William Wyler's *The Friendly Persuasion*—have combined to force the most dedicated director into firing up his theme with the western formula. Films "for peace," as Robert Hughes soberly showed us in his *Film: Book 2*, are rare in quantity and almost invariably violent in style. Persuasion by drama is a risky business. Film's contributions to social stability and orderly change have come most often from the documentary, with its steady informational base and its appeal to reason. Narration in the documentary is a civilizing brake on the action, a restraint on the dramatic forces and the restless movement inherent in the motion picture.

The second essential aspect of the motion picture is its physical nature. The camera must photograph material objects or persons or events. It cannot photograph thought (Griffith to the contrary notwithstanding). Thought must be revealed by an action or an eyebrow, a title or words spoken. This is a prime limitation on the art of motion as a direct source of ideas or inspiration.

Film is concerned with experience, not inference. The revelation of large meanings and great truths put film under a fearful strain. There is no such thing as religion on film; there can only be a film about human behavior as it responds to religious feeling or understanding. The basis of film is its visibility, its reproduction of a material image. Religion is concerned with that which is invisible. The cinema is so frequently the target of censorship precisely because its nature is to reveal the physical aspects of life: it is found far more often in the bedroom than in the chancel. It loves to pry; it is uncomfortable with dignity and righteousness.

The physical nature of film does not mean that its visual art is unable to transmit symbolic and spiritual meanings. The linking of objects with ideas—from Pudovkin's *Mother* to John Ford's *The Informer*—has been a notable aspect of the motion picture's communicative power. Robert Flaherty's remark helps us here: "You can't say as much as you can in writing, but you can say what you say with great conviction."

Most of the performing arts have similar limitations to challenge the artist. Film has more elements to work with than music, ballet, drama, or even literature. But its physical basis gives it a tone of literal realism even when it is trying hardest to be experimental. For this reason, as Sir Herbert Read suggests, the poet in film has been slow to appear. When the poet simply describes, with whatever metaphor, he is not unlike a painter or photographer; but when he reaches through abstraction to philosophic thought, the poet's words cannot be made directly visible.

The third essential aspect of the motion picture is the effect of film editing: it demolishes the traditional dramatic unities of place and time. This is film's chief weapon against its realistic bonds. Time and space are subordinate to imagination: the viewer can be whisked from here to there, from now to then, without warning. Cost alone can keep the film from going where it pleases and summoning up any part of the past or future that can be shown effectively by shapes, by light and dark. This is the wonderful infinity and eternity of the filmic universe.

This persistence of present time, without limit of place or period, also gives film its ambivalence between dream and reality. It abolishes the unities of logic as well as of drama. Every shot is a separate realistic image, yet the total edited effect can be much more than a physical report. It can become a dream or a lie. It can give us a vivid rush of excitement, a stream of images with a roller-coaster effect. This means that the jaded or style-centered film editor may often be tempted to prefer giddy action to meaningful content. The nature of film encourages him. Its underlying tendency is to strain against order, against logic.

Recent experiments with filmic time (*Last Year at Marienbad* is an example) have taken us beyond the dizziness of edited action, beyond the free association of ideas, into a self-conscious maze of irrationality. Some observers find this a sign of creative advance, a suitable reflection of what they consider the meaningless nature of existence. They are not attracted especially to the lighthearted, freewheeling wildness of *Hallelujah the Hills* or *A Hard Day's Night*, but rather to the cool denial of reason in Godard or Antonioni. One critic, tired of the logic of plots, declares that "exposition belongs to an age when we thought people did things for reasons." In this view, dream is no longer escape: it has become more real than reality. Editing, egged along by Freud, has been substituted for life.

Arnold Hauser contends, and I think rightly, that "all art is a game with and a fight against chaos." The film that simply says life is chaos is a film which has not undertaken the battle of art.

The danger today, as always, is to suppose that everything important has been said, and technique is the only frontier. Music must become electronic; painting must do without content; literature must take leave of language; movies must become something altogether different from the works already known.

Yet the heart of any film is its contact with life, its concern with humanity, connecting creator and audience. If the artist of the film keeps close to the common life, he will not find it necessary to leave it out of his work. If he abstracts, it will be to achieve communication, not to thwart it. If he refines the language, it will be to say the old things in a way that may reach us at last and move us to see his vision of life. And if he decides to come back to the age-old themes within the old-fashioned rules of construction, his work may still be art and still be creative.

There is a sense in which Marshall McLuhan's now famous dictum is true: "The medium is the message." The way film works does have effects apart from particular stories or themes. But if we leave it at that and let the film pursue relentlessly its own uniqueness, we shall be lost on a roller coaster without a destination.

It is essential to understand the theory of film. But if we allow ourselves to be bemused by the inner springs of this machine-art of our time, we may then be tempted to say that only certain subjects are truly "filmic." This would lead us sooner or later to aesthetic worship of the motorcycle, the strip tease, and the nightmare.

The great film maker uses his knowledge of the film medium as he uses the knowledge of technical tools—with respect, understanding, and an "iron heel." Because he is concerned with humanity, not with pure theory, he presses hard against the limitations of his art. He makes them work in his favor. He has something to tell us that finds the film a congenial medium but ultimately transcends the medium.

Theorists may analyze the essentials of film—its movement, its materiality, its freedom in space and time. But no mere theory of image-making can contain the work and thought of Ford, Renoir, De Sica, or Kurosawa. The artist who shows us the human condition shows us the true transparency of film.

RICHARD DYER MACCANN

The Plastic Material

V. I. PUDOVKIN

The Plastic Material*

"To show something as everyone sees it is to have accomplished *nothing*."

Direct, succinct, sensible, the great Russian director of silent films, V. I. Pudovkin, explains his view that film is "not shot, but built, built up from the separate strips of celluloid that are its raw material." His emphasis on editing as "the foundation of film art" has sometimes been exaggerated to mean that the editor needs no one else. A fuller reading of his essays and lectures reveals the importance he also attributed to the scenario writer and the director—so long as they thought of the film from an editing standpoint.

Pudovkin was the director of Mother *(1925),* End of St. Petersburg *(1927), and* Storm Over Asia *(1928), as well as the sound film* Deserter *(1933). He was also a teacher at the state cinema school in Moscow. He is especially wise and helpful in describing the nature of the scenarist's concern, not with words, but with "plastic material" the cameraman can photograph. He also explains the basic shots by which the film maker directs the attention of the spectator, and the ways the film has of adjusting space and time, as it "forces itself, ever striving, into the profoundest deeps of life."*

FROM THE INTRODUCTION TO THE
GERMAN EDITION

The foundation of film art is *editing*. Armed with this watchword, the young cinema of Soviet Russia commenced its progress, and it is a maxim that, to this day, has lost nothing of its significance and force.

* V. I. Pudovkin, *On Film Technique*. Translated and annotated by Ivor Montagu. London, Vision Press, Ltd., 1950. Pp. 15–16, 50–54, 79–82, 83–84, 84–85, 88–89, 91–94.

It must be borne in mind that the expression "editing" is not always completely interpreted or understood in its essence. By some the term is naïvely assumed to imply only a joining together of the strips of film in their proper time-succession. Others, again, know only two sorts of editing, a fast and a slow. But they forget—or they have never learnt—that rhythm (i.e., the effects controlled by the alternation in cutting of longer or shorter strips of film) by no means exhausts all the possibilities of editing.

To make clear my point and to bring home unmistakably to my readers the meaning of editing and its full potentialities, I shall use the analogy of another art-form—literature. To the poet or writer separate words are as raw material. They have the widest and most variable meanings which only begin to become precise through their position in the sentence. To that extent to which the word is an integral part of the composed phrase, to that extent are its effect and meaning variable until it is fixed in position, in the arranged artistic form.

To the film director each shot of the finished film subserves the same purpose as the word to the poet. Hesitating, selecting, rejecting, and taking up again, he stands before the separate takes, and only by conscious artistic composition at this stage are gradually pieced together the "phrases of editing," the incidents and sequences, from which emerges, step by step, the finished creation, the film.

The expression that the film is "shot" is entirely false, and should disappear from the language. The film is not *shot*, but *built*, built up from the separate strips of celluloid that are its raw material. . . .

THE PLASTIC MATERIAL

The scenario-writer must bear always in mind the fact that every sentence he writes must appear plastically upon the screen in some visible form. Consequently, it is not the words he writes that are important, but the externally expressed plastic images that he describes in these words. As a matter of fact, it is not so easy to find such plastic images. They must, before anything else, be clear and expressive. Anyone familiar with literary work can well represent to himself what is an expressive word, or an expressive style; he knows that there are such things as telling, expressive words, as vividly expressive word-constructions—sentences. Similarly, he knows that the involved, obscure style of an inexperienced writer, with a multitude of superfluous words, is the consequence of his inability to select and control them. What is here said of literary work is entirely applicable to the work of the scenarist, only the word is replaced by the plastic image. The scenarist must know how to find and to use plastic (externally expressive) material: that is to say, he must know how to discover and how to select, from the limitless mass of material provided by life and its observation, those forms and movements that shall most clearly and vividly express the *whole content* of his idea.

Let us quote certain illustrative examples.

In the film *Tol'able David* there is a sequence in which a new character—an escaped convict, a tramp—comes into the action. The type of a thorough scoundrel. The task of the scenarist was to give his characteristics. Let us analyse how it was done, by describing the series of following shots.

1. The tramp—a degenerate brute, his face overgrown with unshaven bristles—is about to enter a house, but stops, his attention caught by something.

2. Close-up of the face of the watching tramp.

3. Showing what he sees—a tiny, fluffy kitten asleep in the sun.

4. The tramp again. He raises a heavy stone with the transparent intention of using it to obliterate the sleeping little beast, and only the casual push of a fellow, just then carrying objects into the house, hinders him from carrying out his cruel intention.

In this little incident there is not one single explanatory title, and yet it is effective, clearly and vividly. Why? Because the plastic material has been correctly and suitably chosen. The sleeping kitten is a perfect expression of complete innocence and freedom from care, and thus the heavy stone in the hands of the huge man immediately becomes the symbol of absurd and senseless cruelty to the mind of the spectator who sees this scene. Thus the end is attained. The characterisation is achieved, and at the same time its abstract content wholly expressed, with the help of happily chosen plastic material.

Another example from the same film. The context of the incident is as follows: misfortune is come upon a family of peasants—the eldest son has been crippled by a blow with a stone; the father has died of a heart-attack; the youngest son (the hero of the film), still half a boy, knows who is responsible for all their ills—the tramp, who had treacherously attacked his brother. Again and again in the course of the picture the youngster seeks to be revenged upon the blackguard. The weapon of revenge—an old flint-lock. When the disabled brother is brought into the house, and the family, dazed with despair, is gathered round his bed, the boy, half crying, half gritting his teeth, secretly loads the flint-lock. The sudden death of the father and the supplications of the mother, clinging in despair to the feet of her son, restrain his outbreak. The boy remains the sole hope of the family. When, later, he again reaches secretly for the flint-lock and takes it from the wall, the voice of his mother, calling him to go and buy soap, compels him to hang the gun up again and run out to the store. Note with what mastery the old, clumsy-looking flint-lock is here employed. It is as if it incarnated the thirst for revenge that tortures the boy. Every time the hand reaches for the flint-lock the spectator knows what is passing in the mind of the hero. No titles, no explanations are necessary. Recall the scene of soap fetched for the mother just described. Hanging up the flint-lock and running to the store implies forgetfulness of self for the sake of another. This is a perfect characterisation, rendering on the one hand the naïve directness of the man still half a child, on the other his awakening sense of duty.

Another example, from the film *The Leather Pushers*. The incident is as follows. A man sitting at a table is waiting for his friend. He is smoking a cigarette, and in front of him on the table stand an ash-tray and a glass half-empty of liquid, both filled with an enormous number of cigarette ends. The spectator immediately visualises the great space of time the man has been waiting and, no less, the degree of excitement that has made him smoke nearly a hundred cigarettes.

From the examples quoted above it will be clear what is to be understood by the term: expressive plastic material. We have found here a kitten, a tramp, a stone, a flint-lock, some cigarette ends, and not one of these objects or persons was introduced by chance; each constitutes a visual image, requiring no explanation and yet carrying a clear and definite meaning.

Hence an important rule for the scenarist: in working out each incident he must carefully consider and select each visual image; he must remember that for each concept, each idea, there may be tens and hundreds of possible means of plastic expression, and that it is his task to select from amongst them the clearest and most vivid. Special attention, however, must be paid to the special part played in pictures by objects. Relationships between human beings are, for the most part, illuminated by conversations, by words; no one carries on conversation with objects, and that is why work with them, being expressed by visual action, is of special interest to the film technician, as we have just seen in these examples. Try to imagine to yourself anger, joy, confusion, sorrow, and so forth, expressed not in words and the gestures accompanying them, but in action connected with objects, and you will see how images saturated with plastic expression come into your mind. Work on plastic material is of the highest importance for the scenarist. In the process of it he learns to imagine to himself what he has written as it will appear upon the screen, and the knowledge thus acquired is essential for correct and fruitful work.

One must try to express one's concepts in clear and vivid visual images. Suppose it be a matter of the characterisation of some person of the action—this person must be placed in such conditions as will make him appear, by means of some action or movement, in the desired light (remember the tramp and the kitten). Suppose it be a matter of the representation of some event—those scenes must be assembled that most vividly emphasise visually the essence of the event represented. . . .

THE METHODS OF THE FILM

The *Americans* were the first to discover in the film-play the presence of peculiar possibilities of its own. It was perceived that the film can not only make a simple record of the events passing before the lens, but that it is in a position to reproduce them upon the screen by special methods, proper only to itself.

Let us take as example a demonstration that files by upon the street. Let us picture to ourselves an observer of that demonstration. In order to receive a clear and definite impression of the demonstration, the observer must perform certain actions. First he must climb upon the roof of a house, to get a view from above of the procession as a whole and measure its dimensions; next he must come down and look out through the first-floor window at the inscriptions on the banners carried by the demonstrators; finally, he must mingle with the crowd, to gain an idea of the outward appearance of the participants.

Three times the observer has altered his viewpoint, gazing now from nearer, now from farther away, with the purpose of acquiring as complete and exhaustive as possible a picture of the phenomenon under review. The Americans were the first to seek to replace an active observer of this kind by means of the *camera*. They showed in their work that it was not only possible to record the scene shot, but that by manœuvring with the camera itself—in such a way that its position in relation to the object shot varied several times—it was made possible to reproduce the same scene in far clearer and more expressive form than with the lens playing the part of a theatre spectator sitting fast in his stall. The camera, until now a motionless spectator, at last received, as it were, a charge of *life*. It acquired the possibility of proper movement, and transformed itself from a *spectator* to an active *observer*. It followed that the camera, controlled by the director, could not only enable the spectator to see the object shot, but could induce him to apprehend it.

It was at this moment that the concepts *close-up*, *mid-shot*, and *long-shot* first appeared in cinematography, concepts that later played an enormous part in the creative craft of editing, the basis of the work of film direction. Now, for the first time, became apparent the difference between the theatrical producer and his colleague of the film. In the beginning the material with which both theatrical producer and film director worked was *identical*. The same actors playing through in their same sequence the same scenes, which were but shorter, and, at the most, unaccompanied by words. The technique of acting for the films differed in no respect from that of stage-acting. The only problem was the replacement, as comprehensibly as possible, of words by gestures. That was the time when the film was rightly named "a substitute for the stage."

FILM AND REALITY

But, with the grasping of the concept *editing*, the position became basically altered. The real material of film-art proved to be not those actual scenes on which the lens of the camera is directed. The theatrical producer has always to do only with *real* processes—they are his material. His finally composed and created work—the scene produced and played upon the stage—is equally a real and actual process that takes place in obedience to the laws of *real space* and *real time*. When a stage-actor finds himself at one end of the stage, he cannot cross to the other without taking a certain necessary number of paces. And crossing and intervals of this kind are a thing indispensable, conditioned by the laws of real space and real time, with which the theatrical producer has always to reckon and which he is never in a position to overstep. In fact, in work with real processes, a whole series of *intervals* linking the separate significant points of action is unavoidable.

If, on the other hand, we consider the work of the film director, then it appears that the active raw material is no other than those *pieces of celluloid* on which, from various viewpoints, the separate movements of the action have been shot. From nothing but these pieces is created those appearances upon the screen that form the filmic representation of the action shot. And thus the material of the film director consists not of real processes happening in real space and real time, but of those pieces of celluloid on which these processes have been recorded. This celluloid is entirely subject to the will of the director who edits it. He can, in the composition of the filmic form of any given appearance, eliminate all points of interval, and thus concentrate the action in time to the highest degree he may require. . . .

Between the natural event and its appearance upon the screen there is a marked difference. It is *exactly this difference that makes the film an art*. Guided by the director, the camera assumes the task of removing every superfluity and directing the attention of the spectator in such a way that he shall see only that which is significant and characteristic. When the demonstration was shot, the camera, after having viewed the crowd from above in the long-shot, forced its way into the press and picked out the most characteristic details. These details were not the result of chance, they were selected, and, moreover, selected in such a way that from their sum, as from a sum of separate elements, the image of the whole action could be assembled. . . .

FILMIC SPACE AND TIME

Created by the camera, obedient to the will of the director— after the cutting and joining of the separate pieces of cel- luloid—there arises a new *filmic* time; not that real time embraced by the phenomenon as it takes place before the camera, but a new *filmic* time, conditioned only by the speed of perception and controlled by the number and duration of the separate elements selected for filmic representation of the action.

Every action takes place not only in time, but also in space. Filmic time is distinguished from actual in that it is dependent only on the lengths of the separate pieces of celluloid joined together by the director. Like time, so also is filmic space bound up with the chief process of film-making, editing. By the junction of the separate pieces the director builds a filmic space entirely his own. He unites and compresses separate elements, that have perhaps been recorded by him at differing points of real, actual space, into one *filmic* space. By virtue of the possibility of eliminating points of passage and interval, that we have already analysed and that obtains in all film- work, filmic space appears as a synthesis of real elements picked out by the camera. . . .

When we wish to apprehend anything, we always begin with the general outlines, and then, by intensifying our exami- nation to the highest degree, enrich the apprehension by an ever-increasing number of details. The particular, the detail, will always be a synonym of intensification. It is upon this that the strength of the film depends, that its characteristic speciality is the possibility of giving a clear, especially vivid representation of detail. The power of filmic representation lies in the fact that, by means of the camera, it continually strives to penetrate as deeply as possible, to the mid-point of every image. The camera, as it were, forces itself, ever striv- ing, into the profoundest deeps of life; it strives thither to penetrate, whither the average spectator never reaches as he glances casually around him. The camera goes deeper; any- thing it can see it approaches, and thereafter eternalises upon the celluloid. When we approach a given, real image, we must spend a definite effort and time upon it, in advancing from the general to the particular, in intensifying our attention to that point at which we begin to remark and apprehend details. By the process of editing, the film removes, eliminates, this effort. The film spectator is an ideal, perspicuous observer. And it is the director who makes him so. In the discovered, deeply embedded detail there lies an element of perception, the creative element that characterises as art the work of man, the sole element that gives the event shown its final worth.

To show something as everyone sees it is to have accomplished *nothing*. Not that material that is embraced in a first, casual, merely general and superficial glance is required, but that which discloses itself to an intent and searching glance, that can and will see deeper. This is the reason why the greatest artists, those technicians who feel the film most acutely, deepen their work with details. To do this they discard the general aspect of the image, and the points of interval that are the inevitable concomitant of every natural event. The theatrical producer, in working with his material, is not in a position to remove from the view of the spectator that background, that mass of general and inevitable outline, that surrounds the characteristic and particular details. He can only underline the most essential, leaving the spectator himself to concentrate upon what he underlines. The film technician, equipped with his camera, is infinitely more powerful. The attention of the spectator is entirely in his hands. The lens of the camera is the eye of the spectator. He sees and remarks only that which the director desires to show him, or, more correctly put, that which the director himself sees in the action concerned.

ANALYSIS

We now perceive that the work of the film director has a double character. For the construction of filmic form he requires proper material; if he wishes to work filmically, he cannot and must not record reality as it presents itself to the actual, average onlooker. To create a filmic form, he must select those elements from which this form will later be assembled. To assemble these elements, he must first find them. And now we hit on the necessity for a special process of analysis of every real event that the director wishes to use in a shot. For every event a process has to be carried out comparable to the process in mathematics termed "differentiation"—that is to say, dissection into parts or elements. Here the technique of observation links up with the creative process of the selection of the characteristic elements necessary for the future finished work. In order to represent the woman in the court scene, Griffith probably imagined, he may even have actually seen, dozens of despairing women, and perceived not only their heads and hands, but he selected from the whole images only the smile through tears and the convulsive hands, creating from them an unforgettable filmic picture.

Another example. In that filmically outstanding work *The Battleship "Potemkin,"* Eisenstein shot the massacre of the mob on the great flight of steps in Odessa. The running of the mob down the steps is rendered rather sparingly and is not especially expressive, but the perambulator with the baby, that, loosed from the grip of the shot mother, rolls down the steps, is poignant in its tragic intensity and strikes with the force of a blow. This perambulator is a detail, just like the boy with the broken skull in the same film. Analytically dissected, the mass of people offered a wide field for the creative work of the director, and details correctly discovered in editing resulted in episodes remarkable in their expressive power.

Another example, simpler, but quite characteristic for film-work: how should one show a motor-car accident?—a man being run over.

The real material is thoroughly abundant and complex. There are the street, the motor-car, the man crossing the street, the car running him down, the startled chauffeur, the brakes, the man under the wheels, the car carried forward by its impetus, and, finally, the corpse. In actuality everything occurs in unbroken sequence. How was this material worked out by an American director in the film *Daddy*? The separate pieces were assembled on the screen in the following sequence:

1. The street with cars in movement: a pedestrian crosses the street with his back to the camera; a passing motor-car hides him from view.

2. Very short flash: the face of the startled chauffeur as he steps on the brake.

3. Equally short flash: the face of the victim, his mouth open in a scream.

4. Taken from above, from the chauffeur's seat: legs, glimpsed near the revolving wheels.

5. The sliding, braked wheels of the car.

6. The corpse by the stationary car.

The separate pieces are cut together in short, very sharp rhythm. In order to represent the accident on the screen, the director dissected analytically the whole abundant scene, unbroken in actual development, into component parts, into elements, and selected from them—sparingly—only the six essential. And these not only prove sufficient, but render exhaustively the whole poignancy of the event represented.

In the work of the mathematician there follows after dissection into elements, after "differentiation," a combination of the discovered separate elements to a whole—the so-called "integration."

In the work of the film director the process of analysis, the dissection into elements, forms equally only a point of departure, that has to be followed by the assemblage of the whole from the discovered parts. The finding of the elements, the details of the action, implies only the completion of a preparatory task. It must be remembered that from these parts the complete work is finally to emerge, for, as said above, the real motor-car accident might be dissected by the onlooker into dozens, perhaps indeed hundreds, of separate incidents. The director, however, chooses only six of them. He makes a selection, and this selection is naturally conditioned in advance by that filmic image of the accident—happening not in reality but on the screen—that, of course, exists in the head of the director long before its actual appearance on the screen. . . .

SERGEI EISENSTEIN

Collision of Ideas*

"Montage is conflict."

Circuitous, elaborate, intellectual, Sergei Eisenstein, most famous of the Russian film directors, presents his view that montage is not built up by linkage of shots, as Pudovkin suggests, but by collision, like atoms in experimental physics. He compares it to "the series of explosions of an internal combustion engine, driving forward its automobile or tractor: for, similarly, the dynamics of montage serve as impulses driving forward the total film." Even the single frame may be a "particular, as it were, molecular case of montage" within which there may be conflicts of masses, movement, and light.

Eisenstein was the director of Potemkin *(1925),* Ten Days That Shook the World *(1928),* Old and New *(1929),* Alexander Nevsky *(1938), and* Ivan the Terrible *(Parts I and II, 1944–1948). He also taught at the state cinema school in Moscow. In this selection, he claims that his friend Pudovkin reached agreement with him, but a study of their films reveals that each continued to go his own way.*

The shot is by no means an *element* of montage.

The shot is a montage *cell*.

Just as cells in their division form a phenomenon of another order, the organism or embryo, so, on the other side of the dialectical leap from the shot, there is montage.

By what, then, is montage characterized and, consequently, its cell—the shot?

By collision. By the conflict of two pieces in opposition to each other. By conflict. By collision.

*Sergei Eisenstein, from "The Cinematographic Principle and the Ideogram," *Film Form*, New York, Harcourt, Brace, 1949. Reprinted in paperback by Meridian Books, 1957. Pp. 37–40.

In front of me lies a crumpled yellowed sheet of paper. On it is a mysterious note:

"Linkage—P" and "Collision—E."

This is a substantial trace of a heated bout on the subject of montage between P (Pudovkin) and E (myself).

This has become a habit. At regular intervals he visits me late at night and behind closed doors we wrangle over matters of principle. A graduate of the Kuleshov school, he loudly defends an understanding of montage as a *linkage* of pieces. Into a chain. Again, "bricks." Bricks, arranged in series to *expound* an idea.

I confronted him with my viewpoint on montage as a *collision*. A view that from the collision of two given factors *arises* a concept.

From my point of view, linkage is merely a possible *special* case.

Recall what an infinite number of combinations is known in physics to be capable of arising from the impact (collision) of spheres. Depending on whether the spheres be resilient, non-resilient, or mingled. Amongst all these combinations there is one in which the impact is so weak that the collision is degraded to an even movement of both in the same direction.

This is the one combination which would correspond with Pudovkin's view.

Not long ago we had another talk. Today he agrees with my point of view. True, during the interval he took the opportunity to acquaint himself with the series of lectures I gave during that period at the State Cinema Institute. . . .

So, montage is conflict.

As the basis of every art is conflict (an "imagist" transformation of the dialectical principle). The shot appears as the *cell* of montage. Therefore it also must be considered from the viewpoint of *conflict*.

Conflict within the shot is potential montage, in the development of its intensity shattering the quadrilateral cage of the shot and exploding its conflict into montage impulses *between* the montage pieces. As, in a zigzag of mimicry, the *mise-en-scène* splashes out into a spatial zigzag with the *same* shattering. As the slogan, "All obstacles are vain before Russians," bursts out in the multitude of incident of *War and Peace*.

If montage is to be compared with something, then a phalanx of montage pieces, of shots, should be compared to the series of explosions of an internal combustion engine, driving forward its automobile or tractor: for, similarly, the dynamics of montage serve as impulses driving forward the total film.

Conflict within the frame. This can be very varied in character: it even can be a conflict in—the story. As in that "prehistoric" period in films (although there are plenty of instances in the present, as well), when entire scenes would be photographed in a single, uncut shot. This, however, is outside the strict jurisdiction of the film-form.

These are the "cinematographic" conflicts within the frame:

Conflict of graphic directions.

>   (*Lines—either static or dynamic*)

Conflict of scales.

Conflict of volumes.

Conflict of masses.

>   (*Volumes filled with various intensities of light*)

Conflict of depths.

And the following conflicts, requiring only one further impulse of intensification before flying into antagonistic pairs of pieces:

Close shots and long shots.

Pieces of graphically varied directions. Pieces resolved in volume, with pieces resolved in area.

Pieces of darkness and pieces of lightness.

And, lastly, there are such unexpected conflicts as:

Conflicts between an object and its dimension—and conflicts between an event and its duration.

These may sound strange, but both are familiar to us. The first is accomplished by an optically distorted lens, and the second by stop-motion or slow-motion.

The compression of all cinematographic factors and properties within a single dialectical formula of conflict is no empty rhetorical diversion.

We are now seeking a unified system for methods of cinematographic expressiveness that shall hold good for all its elements. The assembly of these into series of common indications will solve the task as a whole.

Experience in the separate elements of the cinema cannot be absolutely measured.

Whereas we know a good deal about montage, in the theory of the shot we are still floundering about amidst the most academic attitudes, some vague tentatives, and the sort of harsh radicalism that sets one's teeth on edge.

To regard the frame as a particular, as it were, molecular case of montage makes possible the direct application of montage practice to the theory of the shot.

And similarly with the theory of lighting. To sense this as a collision between a stream of light and an obstacle, like the impact of a stream from a fire-hose striking a concrete object, or of the wind buffeting a human figure, must result in a usage of light entirely different in comprehension from that employed in playing with various combinations of "gauzes" and "spots."

Thus far we have one such significant principle of conflict: *the principle of optical counterpoint.*

And let us not now forget that soon we shall face another and less simple problem in counterpoint: *the conflict in the sound film of acoustics and optics.*

RENÉ CLAIR

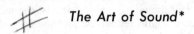

The Art of Sound*

"The talking film is not everything. There is also the sound film."

René Clair began directing films in France just before the arrival of sound. He made the transition himself successfully and smoothly. Le Million *(1931) and* A Nous la Liberté *(1931) are still favorite comedies at film-society showings. He also added some permanent contributions to the thinking of film theorists with his characteristically witty reviews of films of the day.*

He objected to the "hundred per cent talkie," which he felt was "not a very exhilarating prospect." He saw little advance in the art when "pale faces in the night exchanged stentorian confidences." Clair reminded film makers, too, that the triumphant achievement of precise sound effects for every single thing seen in the picture were becoming hackneyed and tiresome. He was pleased by Broadway Melody *(1929), in which "we hear the noise of a door being slammed and a car driving off while we are shown Bessie Love's anguished face watching from a window." In this way, the sound "has replaced the shot."*

"The talking film exists, and those sceptics who prophesy a short reign for it will die themselves long before it's over.

"It is too late for those who love the art of moving pictures to deplore the effects of this barbaric invasion. All they can do is try to cut their losses.

"The talking film is not everything. There is also the sound film—on which the last hopes of the advocates of the silent film are pinned. They count on the sound film to ward off the

* René Clair, *Reflections on the Cinema*. Translated by Vera Traill. London, Kimber, 1953. Pp. 90–92, 93–96, 96–97.

danger represented by the advent of talkies, in an effort to convince themselves that the sounds and noises accompanying the moving picture may prove sufficiently entertaining for the audience to prevent it from demanding dialogue, and may create an illusion of 'reality' less harmful for the art than the talking film.

"However, we have grounds to fear that this solution will only half-satisfy the public. If there is almost universal agreement over the improvisations of a cinema orchestra, opinions vary as far as noises accompanying the action are concerned. The usefulness of such noises is often questionable. If at first hearing they are surprising and amusing, very soon they become tiresome. After we have heard a certain number of sound films, and the first element of surprise has worn off, we are led to the unexpected discovery that the world of noises seems far more limited than we had thought. . . ."

1950. Although these remarks were written over twenty years ago, they are just as valid at the present day. The cinema and the radio do nothing more than reproduce the sound effects discovered during the first experimental period. While *organized* sounds (music or voice) lend themselves to countless new combinations, the number of *raw* sounds which can be employed for dramatic ends is negligible.

The makers of the first sound films registered very nearly every sound could be captured by the microphone. But it was soon observed that direct reproduction of reality created a completely unreal effect, and that sounds had to be *selected* as carefully as photographed objects. (If you find yourself engrossed in conversation in a busy street, your ear will pay as little attention to the noise of passing cars as your eye will to their shapes.)

It is that relative paucity of the catalogue of noises that accounts for the fact that in sound films music is so frequently, and, we must admit it, so arbitrarily used. There again, the progress accomplished in twenty years is very modest. One could have hoped that the sound film would give birth to a completely new style of music, designed for the microphone and the loud-speaker and linked so closely to the film as to become almost inseparable from it. And yet we must admit that with a few very rare exceptions nothing of the kind has occurred, and that music composed for films does not show any fundamental originality. In *Entr'acte*, made in 1924, the score composed by Erik Satie for the accompaniment of a silent film is more "cinematic" than any number of scores written to-day for sound films.

1929. ". . . Although the talkies are still in their first, experimental stage, they have already, surprisingly enough, produced stereotyped patterns. We have barely 'heard' about two dozen of these films, and yet we already feel that the sound effects are hackneyed and that it is high time to find new ones. Jazz, stirring songs, the ticking of a clock, a cuckoo singing the hours, dance-hall applause, a motor car engine or breaking crockery—all these are no doubt very nice, but become somewhat tiresome after we have heard them a dozen times in a dozen different films.

"We must draw a distinction here between those sound effects which are amusing only by virtue of their novelty (which soon wears off), and those that help one to understand the action, and which excite emotions which could not have been roused by the sight of the pictures alone. The visual world at the birth of the cinema seemed to hold immeasurably richer promise. . . . However, if *imitation* of real noises seems limited and disappointing, it is possible that an *interpretation* of noises may have more of a future in it. Sound cartoons, using 'real' noises, seem to point to interesting possibilities.

"Unless new sound effects are soon discovered and judiciously employed, it is to be feared that the champions of the sound film may be heading for a disappointment. We shall find ourselves left with the 'hundred per cent talkie,' as they say here, and that is not a very exhilarating prospect.

"In London we can see that the Americans were not exaggerating when they spoke of the extraordinary attraction exercised on the public by the talking films. From noon till eleven o'clock at night people pour in successive waves into the crowded cinemas. A few months ago Londoners laughed at the sound of American slang but to-day nobody seems surprised and to-morrow London speech may be affected by it.

"In the course of the past month three theatres have closed down and been transformed into cinemas presenting sound films. (In one of these I watched a very bad film, and however little affection I may feel for the theatre, I could not help regretting the brightness of the footlights, the sight of

the empty orchestra pit covered with flowers like a coffin and
of the dim screen—that lugubrious setting where pale faces
in the night exchanged stentorian confidences.)" . . .

1929. ". . . We need not give too much attention to inferior
talkies, which are no rarity, and of which *Give and Take* and
Strange Cargo are typical examples. In these two films the
visual content is reduced to the role of a mere gramophone
record, the whole spectacle aiming only at the closest possible
'cinematographic' reproduction of the stage play. Three or
four sets form the décor for interminable spoken scenes,
boring for those who do not understand English, and unbear-
able for those who do. The witticisms which adorn the dialogue give us a foretaste of what French films will become
in the hands of those of our directors who have already, in
the silent days, shown their attachment to the lowest form
of theatre.

"To these last, if they were not in fact incorrigible, we
would have strongly recommended, before they start on
French sound film production, to go and see *Broadway
Melody*, a hundred per cent talkie, and *Show Boat*, which is
partly a talkie, as well as those extraordinary sound cartoons
which represent to-day the least contestable achievement of
the new cinema."

London, May, 1929. "Of all the films now showing in London, *Broadway Melody* is having the greatest success. This
new American film represents the sum total of all the progress
achieved in sound films since the appearance of *Jazz Singer*
two years ago. For anyone who has some knowledge of the
complicated technique of sound recording, this film is a mar-
vel. Harry Beaumont, the director, and his collaborators (of
whom there are about fifteen, mentioned by name in the
credit titles, quite apart from the actors) seem to delight in
playing with all the difficulties of visual and sound recording.
The actors move, walk, run, talk, shout and whisper, and their
movements and voices are reproduced with a flexibility which
would seem miraculous if we did not know that science and
meticulous organization have many other miracles in store
for us. In this film, nothing is left to chance. Its makers have
worked with the precision of engineers, and their achievement
is a lesson to those who still imagine that the creation of a

film can take place under conditions of chaos known as inspiration.

"In *Broadway Melody*, the talking film has for the first time found an appropriate form: it is neither theatre nor cinema, but something altogether new. The immobility of planes, that curse of talking films, has gone. The camera is as mobile, the angles are as varied as in a good silent film. The acting is first-rate, and Bessie Love talking manages to surpass the silent Bessie Love whom we so loved in the past. The sound effects are used with great intelligence, and if some of them still seem superfluous, others deserve to be cited as examples.

"For instance, we hear the noise of a door being slammed and a car driving off while we are shown Bessie Love's anguished face watching from a window, the departure which we do not see. This short scene in which the whole effect is concentrated on the actress's face, and which the silent cinema would have had to break up in several visual fragments, owes its excellence to the 'unity of place' achieved through sound. In another scene we see Bessie Love lying thoughtful and sad; we feel that she is on the verge of tears; but her face disappears in the shadow of a fade out, and from the screen, now black, emerges a single sob.

"In these two instances the sound, at an opportune moment, has replaced the shot. It is by this economy of means that the sound film will most probably secure original effects.

"We do not need to *hear* the sound of clapping if we can *see* the clapping hands. When the time of these obvious and unnecessary effects will have passed, the more gifted film-makers will probably apply to sound films the lesson Chaplin taught us in the silent films, when, for example, he suggested the arrival of a train by the shadows of carriages passing across a face. (But will the public, and, above all, the film-makers, be satisfied with such a discreet use of sound? Will they not prefer an imitation of *all* the noises to an intelligent selection of a few useful ones?)

"Already in the films we are shown at present, we often feel that in a conversation it is more interesting to watch the listener's rather than the speaker's face. In all likelihood American directors are aware of this, for many of them have used the device quite often and not unskilfully. This is important, for it shows that the sound film has outgrown its first stage, during which directors were intent on demonstrating, with childish persistence, that the actor's lips opened at exactly the same moment as the sound was heard—in short, that their mechanical toy worked beautifully.

"It is the *alternative*, not the simultaneous, use of the visual subject and of the sound produced by it that creates the best effects. It may well be that this first lesson taught us by the birth-pangs of a new technique will to-morrow become this same technique's law.

"*Close Harmony*, a younger brother of *Broadway Melody*, also presents the back-stage life of a music hall (and not the last we are destined to see—*Sonore oblige . . .*). It is an average film, containing nothing of outstanding interest, except, perhaps, a fight in a dance hall, where the two antagonists remain invisible (hidden by the people who have crowded to watch them) and the fight is suggested by shouts and noises.

"As in *Broadway Melody*, the acting is very good. Charles Rogers talks, dances, sings and plays all the instruments which make up a jazz band. The other actors show remarkable flexibility, and their acting with speech is as natural as was their silent acting in earlier films. The total lack of theatrical affectation in their voices makes one think that film actors who have never spoken before may prove more suitable for sound films than stage actors. But it is chiefly in music hall—if we are to judge by American examples—that the talking film will find its best interpreters.

"Both these films are 100 per cent talking. *Show Boat* is somewhat different, however. Originally it was probably not meant to be a talking film. But in the twelve months it took to shoot, the success of talkies became so apparent that *Show Boat* was adapted to the fashion of the day. The result is a hybrid film in which silent scenes, with the characters expressing themselves through written sub-titles, alternate with singing and dancing episodes. The mixture, however, is not as shocking as one might expect (although theoretically, the formula is as indefensible as that of comic opera), and it has produced two excellent scenes.

"The first takes place in the little theatre on the show boat. An actor and an actress are on stage. They declaim their lines in solemn voices, and at the same time, in whispers, exchange declarations of love and arrange to meet after the show. All this takes place in full view of the spectators, deeply moved by the play, and of the producer who, in the wings, is imitating the song of a nightingale. One can imagine what a skilful director has been able to achieve with that alternation of the affected declamation and the sincere whispering, with the interplay of long shots and close-up. Neither the silent cinema nor the theatre could have created the same effect.

"Later in the film, a woman singer, miserably dressed, is singing in a little café. The director's intention was to show us by a short cut, the singer's rise to fame. As the song proceeds, the singer becomes invisible, and a series of swift flashes take us to a large concert hall where the same woman, in an evening gown, is singing the last bars of the theme song.

"Skilful cutting, and a proper, flexible utilization of a new medium—two fine achievements. . . ."

1929. ". . . Whenever the most faithful devotees of the silent cinema undertake an impartial study of talking films, they inevitably lose some of their assurance right at the start, for, at its best, the talkie is no longer photographed theatre. It is itself. Indeed, by its variety of sounds, its orchestra of human voices, it does give an impression of greater richness than the silent cinema. But are such riches not in fact quite ruinous to it? Through such 'progressive' means the screen has lost more than it has gained. It has conquered the world of voices, but it has lost the world of dreams. I have observed people leaving the cinema after seeing a talking film. They might have been leaving a music hall, for they showed no sign of the delightful numbness which used to overcome us after a passage through the silent land of pure images. They talked and laughed, and hummed the tunes they had just heard. *They had not lost their sense of reality.*"

GAVIN LAMBERT

Sight and Sound*

"The basic principles of the cinema do not end with the
Odessa steps sequence in *Potemkin*."

*Now a novelist and screenwriter, Gavin Lambert was from
1950–1956 editor of the British film quarterly* Sight and
Sound, *and was earlier one of the founders of the film magazine* Sequence. *For one of the last issues of this short-lived
publication, he wrote this perceptive article about the differences between silent and sound films.*

*He chides the critics who "had their ideas and standards
formed and fixed by silent cinema," pointing out that film is
still growing and developing, but adds that no doubt it is
harder to work out theoretical essentials in a medium so fast-
growing and involving so many aspects. Using Dovzhenko's*
Earth *as an example, he suggests that a silent film may be
described as a "poem," but sound films, by their very advantages, diffuse the concentrated essence of communication that
the earlier art offered. Sound films may nevertheless have a
"poetic" feeling: René Clair has demonstrated that "the audible need not inhibit the natural flow of the visible." John
Ford's* The Grapes of Wrath, *for example, tends to be "human
and intimate in approach rather than epic." Indeed, "sound
and dialogue give us a closer, more immediate impression of
life than images alone."*

1

One may justly observe, I think, that the senior generation
of film theorists in this country—Rotha, Lindgren, Manvell,
to name the leading ones—had their ideas and standards
formed and fixed by the silent cinema, by the rich and vital
period between, say, *Intolerance* and *Earth*. For them, one

* Gavin Lambert, "Sight and Sound," *Sequence*, Summer 1950.
Pp. 3–7.

feels, no later activity in the cinema has been as exciting or
appealing. In the revised edition of *The Film Till Now*, Rotha
let his twenty-year old strictures on the dialogue film stand,
and left the additional survey of the sound period to an
American critic, Richard Griffith. And *Movie Parade*, ostensibly brought up to date by Rotha and Manvell, devotes less
care, less space—less sympathy, perhaps—to the last fifteen
years.

Such critics do not actively underrate later films; but the
coming of sound seems to represent to them more an unresolved theoretical problem than a sum of individual achievements. The sound film as an entity is compared to the silent,
and the general feeling is that the peak of the silent film period
had a completeness and purity which the sound cinema has
not yet equalled. As a result of this, one feels the lack not
only of any attempts to reassess this major problem in the
light of recent years, but of any theoretical approach to the
sound film equivalent to the massive volumes of the early
thirties. There seems, in fact, to be a kind of unwritten law that
if you are a theoretical film critic, as opposed to a reviewer,
you must go back to the silent film to rediscover basic principles. Of course, you must—but without staying there. The
basic principles of the cinema do not end with the Odessa
steps sequence in *Potemkin* or the milk-separator sequence
in *The General Line*, admirable as they are. The cinema is a
living organism, still growing and developing; nor is it enough,
when an undisputed contemporary masterpiece arrives, like
Bicycle Thieves or *Louisiana Story*, to pay homage to it as if
nothing had happened to the cinema since *La Passion de
Jeanne d'Arc*.

It has become increasingly difficult for a critic who came
to the cinema in the late thirties to realise the feelings of one
whose memories and impressions were fixed first of all by the
best of Griffith or Eisenstein or Dreyer. The masters acclima-
tised themselves to sound no more satisfactorily than their
iconographers, and this may be held to strengthen the case for
silent supremacy. The sound cinema has produced no figures
of such impregnable stature—it may be that in twenty years'
time Ford or Renoir will be equally recognised, but to stake
a major claim for them to-day would not go unchallenged.
Part of the trouble is, perhaps, that some people do not see
enough of the contemporary cinema, and others fail to make

the effort to study silent films. What is called "Film Appreciation" has sometimes seemed to be stuck in the milk-separator sequence; on the other hand, the contemporary reviewer is occasionally guilty of patronising the past. Anyone who listened to the fantastically imperceptive discussion of Stroheim's *Queen Kelly* by the critics on the B.B.C. will realise that even a silent film to-day is by no means sure of a just estimation. The quick, manifold and uneven development of the cinema seems to have overthrown the worked-out standards and grasp of essentials so impressive to rediscover in a book like *The Film Till Now*.

The last few months in London, however, have provided an unusual number of rewards for film-goers in the way of private programmes, and opportunities not only to catch up on films unavailable or unseen before, to consolidate, but to compare and contrast—to find a microcosm of the cinema. The programmes of the London Film Club and the New London Film Society, the weekly repertory season of the British Film Institute, have all proved of great interest and variety. Weekly Press shows provide a mirror of the contemporary, but a distorted one: nothing of interest for three weeks, then perhaps two important films on the same day. These other programmes have been carefully filtered; nearly everything has a context, and even the most unmitigated failure can be constructive.

Silent film directors whose work has been included in these programmes are Griffith (*Intolerance, Hearts of the World*), Dovzhenko (*Earth*), Dreyer (*Jeanne d'Arc*), Lang (*Siegfried*), Pabst (*Pandora's Box, Joyless Street*), Stroheim (*Queen Kelly*); sound films have taken in Pabst (*Dreigroschenoper*), Lang (*You Only Live Once*), Clair (*Le Million*), Renoir (*La Règle du Jeu, La Grande Illusion*), Mamoulian (*City Streets*), John Huston (*The Maltese Falcon*). Although a few important later names—notably Carné and Ford—are not represented, it can be said that even if the best films of these two had been included, the greatest impression of all would still have been left by *Earth* and *Jeanne d'Arc*. I would not like to say which of these two silent films is, as it stands, superior to the other, but there is one extremely interesting point of comparison: *Earth* could never have gained by being a sound film, but Jeanne d'Arc is practically a sound film without dialogue. The addition of music to Dovzhenko's film

can reinforce its essential power, but many silent films were
conceived to be shown with musical accompaniment. Dreyer's
film, however, while it still retains an extraordinary intensity,
does so in spite of the limitations of its medium. One is conscious that the subtitles, though unavoidable, are too numerous; it is the passion behind the whole film, its slow arresting
rhythm, the revelatory use of close-ups, that make this striving
to go beyond the medium only a minor distraction. But if
Jeanne d'Arc had been made a year or two later as a sound
film, what then? Logically, it could have been that much
better, but one comes up against the fact that in *Day of
Wrath*, nearly fifteen years later, Dreyer showed that he still
had not really understood the dramatic fusion of sound and
image. Other things apart, the sound-film technique of *Day of
Wrath* is awkward and primitive.

It must be that for reasons which do not stop at technique
the progression from silent to sound cinema is not always
possible. It would, after all, be impertinent to suggest that
Eisenstein or Dreyer failed to make satisfactory sound films
simply because the technical grasp was beyond them. In the
same way, Eisenstein's original pronouncement on sound—
that it had a future only in non-realistic use, that synchronised
dialogue was against all principles of good cinema—which
is reflected by Rotha in *The Film Till Now*, does not hold
good either. The early-thirties Clair or Hitchcock, the best of
Ford, even *The Third Man*, are all superbly valid as cinema.
One must also beware, I think, of those who point out, wherever a sizeable wordless sequence occurs in a film to-day, that
the silent cinema is coming back into its own, that directors
are beginning to realise the value of images on their own, etc.,
etc.—as if good directors had always thought that unremitting
dialogue was *de rigueur*. ("Le cinéma sonore," Robert Bresson
remarked, "a surtout inventé le silence.") The technical antithesis between silent and sound ceased to be of major importance as soon as Clair demonstrated in *Sous les Toits de Paris*
and *Le Million* that the audible need not inhibit the natural
flow of the visible.

Beyond the textbook standards of what constitutes good or
bad cinema, one becomes aware of a more profound antithesis. Such a film as *Earth* confounds the orthodox theories:
its only element of virtuosity is its imaginative power—without words, with very little camera movement, with nothing of

the quick eye for detail and subtle switching of emphasis that
we like to pick out to-day, the whole burden of the film is on
each image. One knows from many silent films, particularly
German films, how tedious fine images uninformed by feeling
can be, but *Earth* is not a succession of striking shots, it is
the communication in great intensity of a personal vision. The
film is heroic and idealistic in mood, and the mood is expressed through massive self-contained images. This absolute-
ness of fusion, this concentration, makes of *Earth* a poem.
But when an image speaks, the pure concentration is lost. Its
force is diffused, we have to take in words as well as pictures;
the distilled self-containment that makes a poem is no longer
there. For this reason, perhaps, we may describe a dialogue
film as "poetic" in feeling but never—as might be said of
Earth and for the same reason of *Jeanne d'Arc*—as a "poem."
Sound and dialogue of themselves diffuse the essence of concentration with which silent images may be filled. They have
many other advantages, of course—they can incorporate a
mass of detail which in a silent film would appear pedestrian,
they can extend and fill out characterisation, they can create
more variety, more subtleties of dramatic presentation—but
they do not retain the original intensity of the medium. They
also throw the emphasis more on dramatic narrative; how
little plot has *Earth* compared with a feature film to-day—
and compare, too, for sheer plot value, Dreyer's *Jeanne d'Arc*
with Walter Wanger's. The one brings Jeanne completely alive
through the last (and dramatically least varied) hours of her
life, her trial, and the other starts practically at the beginning,
with voices at Domremy, battle scenes and every contemporary notability. The difference lies not only in the fact that
Wanger is not an artist and Dreyer is; but in the antithetical
silent and sound approaches. In one, the emphasis is on narrative, incident, the diffusions of life; in the other, on concentration, essence, poetry.

2

The antithesis between silent and sound cinema is emphasised
when we consider some sound films that attain a considerable
degree of concentration—by swiftness and compression of
narrative and a hard, direct impact. A film like *The Maltese
Falcon* has hardly a single image that is powerful in itself.

The tight structure, analytical control and shaping of the story, atmosphere created by character and incident rather than descriptive pictorial effect, add up to a notable intensity —but it is an intensity not from within, but imposed by a vigorous method of story-telling and firm excision of inessentials. The fact is that the sound cinema obliged a great many film-makers to look at character far more closely: the "psychological" approach was rare in silent cinema—one finds it in Pabst, in *Pandora's Box*, where curiously enough the method is much closer to sound cinema than in *Jeanne d'Arc*, although in the latter one is more conscious of the absence of dialogue. Pabst was a superb silent film technician. By focusing on the players rather than the décor, by filling his scenes with incident and dexterous observation, he caught the mood of a decadent society in the German twenties perfectly in *Pandora's Box*. But in his sound film, *Die Dreigroschenoper*, he concentrated unexpectedly on décor. Andreyev's formalised sets, the *Gassen* of Soho (in the heart of dockland) are undoubtedly most remarkable, but the visual style of the film, brilliantly clever as it is, exists in a vacuum. There is no dramatic use of sound at all. The cynical, satirical flavour of Brecht and Weill is almost gone, not only because Pabst probably misapprehended it, but because the visual style is much too elaborate for it. Unlike Pabst, Clair not only quickly understood how to fuse music and dialogue with images, but worked with a cameraman, Georges Périnal, who used lighter tones and a simpler texture to maintain the dramatic balance. The images were not so weighted as to make sound almost superfluous. This question of "inflated" visuals is very important to sound cinema, when we see films also like *Day of Wrath*, *Ivan the Terrible* or *The Fugitive*—all of which in effect depend too much on the devices of silent cinema. Not necessarily because their directors use sound inexpertly, but because the visual style is much too heavy, attempting the kind of enlarged, self-contained effects that have dramatic significance only in silent cinema. The techniques used by Gregg Toland with Ford and Wyler in *The Grapes of Wrath* and *The Best Years of Our Lives* might appear distinctly underdone in a silent film, but in their actual context they could not have been more effective. Dramatically as well as visually, they are far more expressive than the over-composed frames of Figueroa in *The Fugitive*, which again exist in a vacuum. *The Fugitive* was no doubt aiming at "poetry"; but *The Grapes of Wrath* is actually a far more poetic film. The notion that luscious visuals can make a sound film poetic seems, in fact, rather naïve. The real poetic films of the last fifteen years—films like *The Grapes of Wrath, Le Jour se Lève, L'Atalante, Louisiana Story*—are those that are true to character, and bring out visually the character of places and people rather than make formal designs of them. Because sound and dialogue give us a closer, more immediate impression of life than images alone, these films have been human and intimate in approach rather than epic, like *Jeanne d'Arc* or *Earth*. An image without sound is in itself a formalisation; an image with sound is a natural combination and makes a formalised style more difficult to achieve.

Mamoulian in *City Streets* (1931) made an interesting attempt at imposing an emphatic, slightly florid visual style on realistic material. It is a gangster story, told not in the *Scarface* manner—of which *The Maltese Falcon*, equally terse and objective, is a successor—but in a faintly impressionist way, with calculated camera mobility and a few passages of Russian-style montage, where cut-in shots of objects heighten an emotional situation. The most notable of these is a scene in which a series of shots of ornamental statues of cats in a woman's room comment on her jealous disposition. Although uneven, this is a very rewarding film; historically, one may view it as a rather self-conscious reaction against the passive naturalism of photographed plays in the early sound period, but it can also be looked at in another perspective. The direct personal comment, through symbols or visual similes, has become almost extinct in sound films. Lang experimented with it—rather crudely in *Fury*, where he cut in to a scene of gossiping townspeople a shot of cackling hens, and very effectively in *You Only Live Once*, where the frogs croaking in the lily pond provide an ominous chorus to the lovers' meeting at night. More recently, Thorold Dickinson, in *Queen of Spades*, made fine symbolic use of a spider's web. This kind of experiment is comparatively rare in the sound film—partly because (remembering the emphasis on narrative) symbolic imagery in itself is seldom dramatic, partly because the use of it is apt to look self-conscious or stylistically inappropriate in a medium of which the keynote has been realism, whether superficial or true. It remains the prerogative of a certain kind

of stylist; Mamoulian may be a very minor artist, but his early
films had a liberating influence on sound cinema in America,
as Clair's did in France, and a particular value of *Queen of
Spades* is that it reasserts many plastic and rhythmic refinements of cinema neglected in the general streamlining of narrative by sound. So great is the apparatus of illusion now, so
deceptive can the surface be, that the creative core is more
difficult to reach—and, while the demands of life itself in the
cinema grow more insistent and the pioneering spirit is most
acclaimed in directors like de Sica who explore human reality
with a new passion and honesty, it may seem trivial or perverse to suggest that the demands of cinema itself are in
danger of being overlooked. But the future of the cinema lies
in the hands of directors who recognise the richness and
variety of their medium as well as of life.

3

The future of the cinema depends on the films that are made,
and not on theories. Like any other art, the cinema is subject
to a dual pressure—that of its own expressive potentialities,
and of external forces such as popular taste or exploitation.
The external pressure has been increasingly in the direction
of collective rather than individual style. Simply as a commercial undertaking, the sound cinema is far more expensive
than the silent, and its sheer material costliness to-day is a
further obstacle to individual experiment. While box-office
standards are uncertain, as they were in the early days of
sound, some experiment within the industrial framework is
permissible because necessary. The increasing confidence and
power of showmen make for formula rather than experiment.
The most notable individualists in the cinema over the last
fifteen years—directors like Vigo, Carné, Flaherty, de Sica,
Sucksdorff—have worked either in the face of opposition or
have found a way somehow to make films outside the usual
framework. A few others, like Welles, gain a short run of
freedom until they lose too much money or, like Ford, seize
opportunities intermittently. It is hopelessly escapist not to
take practical conditions into account, because their influence,
negative and positive, is an inseparable part of the achievement of the cinema.

ALFRED HITCHCOCK

*Direction**

"The best screen actor is the man who can do nothing extremely well."

*Alfred Hitchcock has often told friends, reporters, and
movie stars that actors are puppets. He is such a famous
and successful director that he can say such things and still
get important stars to work for him. But it is not comforting
for actors to be told, as Hitchcock says in this article: "Film
work hasn't much need for the virtuoso actor who gets his
effects and climaxes himself. . . . He has to submit himself
to be used by the director and the camera. Mostly, he is
wanted to behave quietly and naturally."*

*Perhaps it is because Hitchcock is so fond of suspense
stories that he takes this position. He directed* The 39 Steps
(1935), The Lady Vanishes *(1938),* Rebecca *(1940),* Strangers
on a Train *(1951),* Psycho *(1960), and many others. Different
purposes might call for more sustained creative effort by the
actors. But he declares that the thriller is the best kind of
story for the film medium, and certainly "the screen ought
to speak its own language freshly coined." He is not an advocate of the importance of editing, either. As a director, he
does his editing before he starts shooting: "Working on the
script is the real making of the film, for me."*

Many people think a film director does all his work in the
studio, drilling the actors, making them do what he wants.
That is not at all true of my own methods, and I can write
only of my own methods. I like to have a film complete in
my mind before I go on the floor. Sometimes the first idea one

* Alfred Hitchcock, "Direction," from Charles Davy (ed.),
Footnotes to the Film. Lovat Dickson & Thompson, Ltd., London,
1937. Pp. 3–12, 13, 14, 15.

has of a film is of a vague pattern, a sort of haze with a certain shape. There is possibly a colourful opening developing into something more intimate; then, perhaps in the middle, a progression to a chase or some other adventure; and sometimes at the end the big shape of a climax, or maybe some twist or surprise. You see this hazy pattern, and then you have to find a narrative idea to suit it. Or a story may give you an idea first and you have to develop it into a pattern.

Imagine an example of a standard plot—let us say a conflict between love and duty. This idea was the origin of my first talkie, *Blackmail*. The hazy pattern one saw beforehand was duty—love—love versus duty—and finally either duty or love, one or the other. The whole middle section was built up on the theme of love versus duty, after duty and love had been introduced separately in turn. So I had first to put on the screen an episode expressing duty.

I showed the arrest of a criminal by Scotland Yard detectives, and tried to make it as concrete and detailed as I could. You even saw the detectives take the man to the lavatory to wash his hands—nothing exciting, just the routine of duty. Then the young detective says he's going out that evening with his girl, and the sequence ends, pointing on from duty to love. Then you start showing the relationship between the detective and his girl: they are middle-class people. The love theme doesn't run smoothly; there is a quarrel and the girl goes off by herself, just because the young man has kept her waiting a few minutes. So your story starts; the girl falls in with the villain—he tries to seduce her and she kills him. Now you've got your problem prepared. Next morning, as soon as the detective is put on to the murder case, you have your conflict—love versus duty. The audience know that he will be trying to track down his own girl, who has done the murder, so you sustain their interest: they wonder what will happen next.

The blackmailer was really a subsidiary theme. I wanted him to go through and expose the girl. That was my idea of how the story ought to end. I wanted the pursuit to be after the girl, not after the blackmailer. That would have brought the conflict on to a climax, with the young detective, ahead of the others, trying to push the girl out through a window to get her away, and the girl turning round and saying: "You can't do that—I must give myself up." Then the rest of the police arrive, misinterpret what he is doing, and say, "Good man, you've got her," not knowing the relationship between them. Now the reason for the opening comes to light. You repeat every shot used first to illustrate the duty theme, only now it is the girl who is the criminal. The young man is there ostensibly as a detective, but of course the audience know he is in love with the girl. The girl is locked up in her cell and the two detectives walk away, and the older one says, "Going out with your girl to-night?" The younger one shakes his head. "No. Not to-night."

That was the ending I wanted for *Blackmail*, but I had to change it for commercial reasons. The girl couldn't be left to face her fate. And that shows you how the films suffer from their own power of appealing to millions. They could often be subtler than they are, but their own popularity won't let them.

But to get back to the early work on a film. With the help of my wife, who does the technical continuity, I plan out a script very carefully, hoping to follow it exactly, all the way through, when shooting starts. In fact, this working on the script is the real making of the film, for me. When I've done it, the film is finished already in my mind. Usually, too, I don't find it necessary to do more than supervise the editing myself. I know it is said sometimes that a director ought to edit his own pictures if he wants to control their final form, for it is in the editing, according to this view, that a film is really brought into being. But if the scenario is planned out in detail, and followed closely during production, editing should be easy. All that has to be done is to cut away irrelevancies and see that the finished film is an accurate rendering of the scenario.

Settings, of course, come into the preliminary plan, and usually I have fairly clear ideas about them; I was an art student before I took up with films. Sometimes I even think of backgrounds first. *The Man Who Knew Too Much* started like that; I looked in my mind's eye at snowy Alps and dingy London alleys, and threw my characters into the middle of the contrast. Studio settings, however, are often a problem; one difficulty is that extreme effects—extremes of luxury or extremes of squalor—are much the easiest to register on the screen. If you try to reproduce the average sitting-room in Golders Green or Streatham it is apt to come out looking like nothing in particular, just nondescript. It is true that I have tried lately to get interiors with a real lower-middle-class atmosphere—for instance, the Verlocs' living-room in *Sabotage*—but there's always a certain risk in giving your audience humdrum truth.

However, in time the script and the sets are finished somehow and we are ready to start shooting. One great problem that occurs at once, and keeps on occurring, is to get the players to adapt themselves to film technique. Many of them, of course, come from the stage; they are not cinema-minded at all. So, quite naturally, they like to play long scenes straight ahead. I am willing to work with the long uninterrupted shot: you can't avoid it altogether, and you can get some variety by having two cameras running, one close up and one farther off, and cutting from one to the other when the film is edited. But if I have to shoot a long scene continuously I always feel I am losing grip on it, from a cinematic point of view. The camera, I feel, is simply standing there, *hoping* to catch something with a visual point to it. What I like to do always is to photograph just the little bits of a scene that I really need for building up a visual sequence. I want to put my film together on the screen, not simply to photograph something that has been put together already in the form of a long piece of stage acting. This is what gives an effect of life to a picture—the feeling that when you see it on the screen you are watching something that has been conceived and brought to birth directly in visual terms. The screen ought to speak its own language, freshly coined, and it can't do that unless it treats an acted scene as a piece of raw material which must be broken up, taken to bits, before it can be woven into an expressive visual pattern.

You can see an example of what I mean in *Sabotage*. Just before Verloc is killed there is a scene made up entirely of short pieces of film, separately photographed. This scene has to show how Verloc comes to be killed—how the thought of killing him arises in Sylvia Sidney's mind and connects itself with the carving knife she uses when they sit down to dinner. But the sympathy of the audience has to be kept with Sylvia Sidney; it must be clear that Verloc's death, finally, is an accident. So, as she serves at the table, you see her unconsciously serving vegetables with the carving knife, as though her hand were keeping hold of the knife of its own accord. The camera

cuts from her hand to her eyes and back to her hand; then
back to her eyes as she suddenly becomes aware of the knife
making its error. Then to a normal shot—the man uncon-
cernedly eating; then back to the hand holding the knife. In
an older style of acting Sylvia would have had to show the
audience what was passing in her mind by exaggerated facial
expression. But people to-day in real life often don't show
their feelings in their faces: so the film treatment showed the
audience her mind through her hand, through its unconscious
grasp on the knife. Now the camera moves again to Verloc—
back to the knife—back again to his face. You see him seeing
the knife, realising its implication. The tension between the
two is built up with the knife as its focus.

Now when the camera has immersed the audience so closely
in a scene such as this, it can't instantly become objective
again. It must broaden the movement of the scene without
loosening the tension. Verloc gets up and walks round the
table, coming so close to the camera that you feel, if you are
sitting in the audience, almost as though you must move back
to make room for him. Then the camera moves to Sylvia
Sidney again, then returns to the subject—the knife.

So you gradually build up the psychological situation, piece
by piece, using the camera to emphasise first one detail, then
another. The point is to draw the audience right inside the
situation instead of leaving them to watch it from outside,
from a distance. And you can do this only by breaking the
action up into details and cutting from one to the other, so
that each detail is forced in turn on the attention of the audience and reveals its psychological meaning. If you played the
whole scene straight through, and simply made a photographic record of it with the camera always in one position,
you would lose your power over the audience. They would
watch the scene without becoming really involved in it, and
you would have no means of concentrating their attention on
those particular visual details which make them feel what the
characters are feeling.

This way of building up a picture means that film work
hasn't much need for the virtuoso actor who gets his effects
and climaxes himself, who plays directly on to the audience
with the force of his talent and personality. The screen actor
has got to be much more plastic; he has to submit himself to
be used by the director and the camera. Mostly he is wanted

to behave quietly and naturally (which, of course, isn't at all easy), leaving the camera to add most of the accents and emphases. I would almost say that the best screen actor is the man who can do nothing extremely well.

One way of using the camera to give emphasis is the reaction shot. By the reaction shot I mean any close-up which illustrates an event by showing instantly the reaction to it of a person or a group. The door opens for someone to come in, and before showing who it is you cut to the expressions of the persons already in the room. Or, while one person is talking, you keep your camera on someone else who is listening. This over-running of one person's image with another person's voice is a method peculiar to the talkies; it is one of the devices which help the talkies to tell a story faster than a silent film could tell it, and faster than it could be told on the stage.

Or, again, you can use the camera to give emphasis whenever the attention of the audience has to be focussed for a moment on a certain player. There is no need for him to raise his voice or move to the centre of the stage or do anything dramatic. A close-up will do it all for him—will give him, so to speak, the stage all to himself.

I must say that in recent years I have come to make much less use of obvious camera devices. I have become more commercially-minded; afraid that anything at all subtle may be missed. I have learnt from experience how easily small touches are overlooked.

The other day a journalist came to interview me and we spoke about film technique. "I always remember," he said, "a little bit in one of your silent films, *The Ring*. The young boxer comes home after winning his fight. He is flushed with success—wants to celebrate. He pours out champagne all round. Then he finds that his wife is out, and he knows at once that she is out with another man. At this moment the camera cuts to a glass of champagne; you see a fizz of bubbles rise off it and there it stands untasted, going flat. That one shot gives you the whole feeling of the scene." Yes, I said, that sort of imagery may be quite good: I don't despise it and still use it now and then. But is it always noticed? There was another bit in *The Ring* which I believe hardly any one noticed.

The scene was outside a boxing-booth at a fair, with a barker talking to the crowd. Inside the booth a professional is taking on all-comers. He has always won in the first round. A man comes running out of the booth and speaks to the barker: something unexpected has happened. Then a cut straight to the ringside: you see an old figure 1 being taken down and replaced by a brand-new figure 2. I meant this single detail to show that the boxer, now, is up against some-one he can't put out in the first round. But it went by too quickly. Perhaps I might have shown the new figure 2 being taken out of a paper wrapping—something else was needed to make the audience see in a moment that the figure for the second round had never been used before.

The film always has to deal in exaggerations. Its methods reflect the simple contrasts of black-and-white photography. One advantage of colour is that it would give you more inter-mediate shades. I should never want to fill the screen with colour: it ought to be used economically—to put new words into the screen's visual language when there's a need for them. You could start a colour film with a board-room scene: sombre panelling and furniture, the directors all in dark clothes and white collars. Then the chairman's wife comes in, wearing a red hat. She takes the attention of the audience at once, just because of that one note of colour. Or suppose a gangster story: the leader of the gang is sitting in a café with a man he suspects. He has told his gunman to watch the table. "If I order a glass of port, bump him off. If I order green chartreuse, let him go."

This journalist asked me also about distorted sound—a device I tried in *Blackmail* when the word "knife" hammers on the consciousness of the girl at breakfast on the morning after the murder. Again, I think this kind of effect may be justified. There have always been occasions when we have needed to show a phantasmagoria of the mind in terms of visual imagery. So we may want to show someone's mental state by letting him listen to some sound—let us say church bells—and making them clang with distorted insistence in his head. But on the whole nowadays I try to tell a story in the simplest possible way, so that I can feel sure it will hold the attention of any audience and won't puzzle them. I know there are critics who ask why lately I have made only thrillers. Am I satisfied, they say, with putting on the screen the equiva-lent merely of popular novelettes? Part of the answer is that I am out to get the best stories I can which will suit the film medium, and I have usually found it necessary to take a hand in writing them myself. . . .

I choose crime stories because that is the kind of story I can write, or help to write, myself—the kind of story I can turn most easily into a successful film. It is the same with Charles Bennett, who has so often worked with me; he is essentially a writer of melodrama. I am ready to use other stories, but I can't find writers who will give them to me in a suitable form. . . .

To-day you can put over scenes that would have been ruled out a few years ago. Particularly towards comedy, nowadays, there is a different attitude. You can get comedy out of your stars, and you used not to be allowed to do anything which might knock the glamour off them.

In 1926 I made a film called *Downhill*, from a play by Ivor Novello, who acted in the film himself, with Ian Hunter and Isabel Jeans. There was a sequence showing a quarrel between Hunter and Novello. It started as an ordinary fight; then they began throwing things at one another. They tried to pick up heavy pedestals to throw and the pedestals bowled them over. In other words I made it comic. I even put Hunter into a morning coat and striped trousers because I felt that a man never looks so ridiculous as when he is well dressed and fighting. This whole scene was cut out; they said I was guying Ivor Novello. It was ten years before its time.

I say ten years, because you may remember that in 1936 M.G.M. showed a comedy called *Libelled Lady*. There is a fishing sequence in it: William Powell stumbles about in the river, falls flat and gets soaked and catches a big fish by accident. Here you have a star, not a slapstick comedian, made to do something pretty near slapstick. In *The Thirty-nine Steps*, too, a little earlier, I was allowed to drag Madeleine Carroll over the moors handcuffed to the hero; I made her get wet and untidy and look ridiculous for the purpose of the story. I couldn't have done that ten years ago.

I foresee the decline of the individual comedian. Of course, there may always be specially gifted comedians who will have films written round them, but I think public taste is turning to like comedy and drama more mixed up; and this is another move away from the conventions of the stage. In a play your divisions are much more rigid; you have a scene—then curtain, and after an interval another scene starts. In a film you keep your whole action flowing; you can have comedy and drama running together and weave them in and out. Audiences are much readier now than they used to be for sudden changes of mood; and this means more freedom for a director. The art of directing for the commercial market is to know just how far you can go. In many ways I am freer now to do what I want to do than I was a few years ago. I hope in time to have more freedom still—if audiences will give it to me.

ALEXANDER KNOX

Acting and Behaving*

"I believe that as the industry matures the contribution of the
actor will become more important."

*This prediction by Alexander Knox has come true, in part,
largely for irrelevant reasons. The change toward so-called
independent production in Hollywood has often placed top
box-office stars in control of new production companies, and
this dominant financial position has enabled them to rewrite
scripts as well as decide whether or not to perform.*

*Knox is best known, perhaps, for his portrayal of Woodrow
Wilson in 1944. Here, he is concerned to persuade us that the
actor is often the key element in film drama: "A film, like a
novel or a play, shows character in action. Anything that gets
in the way of the action of that character is dramatically
bad. . . . Too often, in film making, trickiness is used not as
a help to the actor but as a substitute for acting." He specifically objects to some symbolic photography in the Hitchcock
film* Spellbound.

*While not discounting altogether the kind of performance
in many popular films which he calls "behaving," Knox feels
that the actor of depth and versatility can not only accom-
plish roles that are "far away" from his own personality (to
use an Actors Studio phrase) but can contribute imagination
and nobility to drama on the screen.*

In this paper[1] I propose to discuss actors, and to discuss them
as if they had a contribution to make to the joy of living and
to society. On the stage and on the screen there are two

* Alexander Knox, "Acting and Behaving," *Hollywood Quarterly*, Vol. I, No. 3, Spring 1946. Pp. 260, 262–263, 263–269.
    [1] A paper from the program of the Motion Picture Panel of the
Conference on American-Russian Cultural Exchange, at the University of California, Los Angeles, December 8, 1945.

kinds of actors—actors who *behave* and actors who *act*. I hope to convince you that there is a difference between acting and behaving on the screen, and that acting is richer than behaving.

I start off under a certain difficulty: I am an actor myself; and the most powerful critic in the country, Mr. George Jean Nathan, has admitted that no one can have respect for a man who always has to go to his work up an alley. It is of stage actors, whom he respects, that he makes this unkind comment, and he declares that a screen performance bears the same relation to a stage performance that a hiccup bears to Camille's tuberculosis. If I make any attempt to answer back, Nathan asserts with finality: "Coquelin is the only actor who ever lived who proved that he had a critical mind in the appraisal of acting." However, the published words of Minnie Maddern Fiske and William Gillette, and some of the comments of George Arliss, Ellen Terry, and others, seem to me to indicate that Nathan's statement is a trifle sweeping, so I will not allow it to scare me into silence. . . .

Behaving is a form of acting which is much admired in Hollywood and elsewhere, mainly on the grounds that it holds the mirror up to nature. It is natural. But two very good critics have uttered certain warnings about behaving. Every young and revolutionary group of actors in the history of the theatre—and I think this applies with equal force in the shorter history of the movies—has seemed more natural than its predecessors. I have no doubt that, as John Mason Brown says, "Burbage would have thought Betterton too mild, that Betterton would have missed strength in Garrick, that Garrick would have been disappointed in Kean, Kean in Irving, Irving in Gielgud, and Booth in Barrymore."

John Mason Brown's word of warning about "behaving" begins, "Actors are commonly supposed to be good actors if they do not seem to be acting at all," and he continues, later, "To admire their performances as being the kind of art which conceals art is one thing, and a just cause for admiration. But to mistake their acting for not being acting, to applaud them for this very reason, is not only to insult the actors in question but to commit the final insanity of slovenly thinking. One of the pleasantest sensations they can afford us is for them to make us feel, however mildly, that what is done is done with a reason and by people who know what they are doing, so

that no one mistakes the mirror that is held up to nature for
nature herself."

And Mr. Bernard Shaw, another good critic, puts the same
point more concisely. "The one thing not forgivable in an
actor is *being* the part instead of *playing* it."

These two strong statements are in direct opposition to a
great deal of Hollywood thinking. The men who made the
statements are neither of them thoughtless men, nor are they
men who enjoy the dreadful scent of old boiled Ham.

Behaving, at its best, is the kind of art which conceals art.
Edward Dmytryk, a brilliant director who has helped a number of actors to give excellent performances, has complained
bitterly about Hollywood Ham-worship, which he alleges to
be rife, and he says, "If a man hasn't quite perfected the technique of naturalness, we say he underplays, but when he has
perfected the technique we say he is only playing himself."
To some, it may seem that Mr. Dmytryk is tilting against a
straw man, since the point he makes is fairly well accepted
and a number of actors who have perfected the technique of
naturalness in Hollywood get a great deal of credit.

In fact, behaving, when it is perfectly done, has always
been the most profitable form of acting, and the form which
inspires most confidence. Behaving makes use of intelligent
observation and an alert contemporary mind. Its power is the
power of reality, and without it no mummer has the right to
call himself an actor.

But behaving is capable of abuse. Behaving is a form of
acting which can be used to display the same kind of empty
idealizations that fill some of the popular magazines and pass
for human beings. The result is that a completely unreal creation, a man who never did exist on land or sea, is made real
by the misuse of an actor's skill. The process is one of selection. Whatever imaginary type happens to be the wishful
dream of society at the moment is built up of segments
of a human psyche, and all those which would contradict or
make diffuse the single effect of the whole are conveniently
omitted. . . .

Is acting any different? What is it? What can it do? Acting
seems to me to be *behaving plus interpretation*. The difference between acting and behaving is the difference between
Menuhin and the first violin, the difference between Van
Gogh and Sargent, between William Shakespeare and Ben

Jonson. The ability to paint photographically is probably a necessary part of a painter's equipment, but it does not make a painter. The ability to play every note in perfect pitch, volume, and tempo is a necessary part of a violinist's equipment, but it does not make a Menuhin. The ability to be just like the man next door is a necessary part of an actor's equipment, but it does not make a Chaplin.

Now I am going to attempt the impossible. I am going to try to tell you what I think acting is. I'm going to hang onto the beard of the prophet Shaw till I find my balance. Shaw is speaking about Henry Irving, whom he did not like. He says, "Irving was utterly unlike anyone else: he could give importance and nobility to any sort of drivel that was put into his mouth; and it was this nobility, bound up with an impish humour, which forced the spectator to single him out as a leading figure with an inevitability that I never saw again in any actor until it rose from Irving's grave in the person of a nameless cinema actor who afterwards became famous as Charlie Chaplin. Here, I felt, is something that leaves the old stage and its superstitions and staleness completely behind, and inaugurates a new epoch."

This is a comment by Shaw on Duse. He is explaining to Ellen Terry how to become an actress—an occupation most men would have thought rather impertinent, but Shaw didn't mind, and neither did Miss Terry. "At first you try to make a few points and don't know how to make them. Then you do know how to make them, and you think of a few more. Finally the points all integrate into one continuous point, which is the whole part in itself. I have sat watching Duse in Camille, analyzing all her play into the million or so of points of which it originally consisted, and admiring beyond expression the prodigious power of work that built it all up. *Now* the actress seems to make no points at all. This rare consummation Duse has reached."

Here is the poet W. B. Yeats speaking of a performance of Björnson's *Beyond Human Power* by Mrs. Patrick Campbell: "Your acting had the precision and delicacy and simplicity of every art at its best. It made me feel the unity of the arts in a new way."

Charles Lamb wrote of Bensley, "He seized the moment of passion with the greatest truth, he seemed to come upon the stage to do the poet's message simply—he threw over the part an air of loftiness which one catches only a few times in a lifetime."

Samuel Taylor Coleridge said of Kean, "To see Kean act is like reading Shakespeare by flashes of lightning."

And Hazlitt, one of the most objective and astute of critics, who held that Shakespeare needed no actors, that his own imagination was sufficient, when he had seen Mrs. Siddons and Kean at different times, admitted that each of them had "raised our imagination of the parts they acted." And some time later, when Kean played Hamlet, he declared that certain scenes in the production were "the finest commentary that was ever made on Shakespeare."

I have chosen these quotations because they understate the case. There are many more fulsome comments on actors of the past and present, many comments which are foolish in their abandonment to a momentary enthusiasm. The comments I have quoted were made by men of taste, each superb in his own profession, each critical, and each well provided with standards of comparison, and I suggest that these comments were made on an art which is *more than behaving*—an art which has the power to shock and to excite, an art which has a function and a life and a purpose of its own, an art which is difficult to understand and even to detect because of its evanescent nature, an art which is a deep intellectual and emotional experience, and which leaves the psyche of the person who has been in contact with it subtly changed.

And if this seems to be a spasm of mystical nonsense, I would suggest that whoever feels that way about it should suspend judgment until he has tried to define for himself the higher reaches of some other art as well. It is not easy.

The inevitable comment will now be made: "These actors were stage actors. Even supposing there is a certain amount of validity in your mystical nonsense, how does that apply to the screen?"

And I have to confess that, with the exception of Chaplin, I have not seen a sustained performance on the screen to which I would be inclined to apply similar words. But although sustained performances on this level may not exist on the screen, we have all seen short bits of film in which "acting" in this high sense has been caught and held. And when we think of acting in this way, it is well to remember that at best it is an interpretative art, and is dead the year after next; it is dead because the manners of the people have changed. It is dead, but that does not mean it has never been alive.

I can, from my own memory of films, list a number in which there were passages of great beauty created solely by the actor. There is not time to go into these in detail. Many of you will remember them also. There were superb moments of performance in Cagney's *Yankee Doodle*, and in an inferior film, *Dr. Jekyll and Mr. Hyde*, Spencer Tracy had moments of peculiar effectiveness. Greta Garbo in *Camille*, Rosalind Russell in *Craig's Wife*, Laurence Olivier in *Wuthering Heights*, a scene of curious terror in *Alice Adams*, where Miss Katharine Hepburn was trying to entertain *you* at dinner as well as the boy in the film. Several sustained passages in Paul Muni's two fine performances, *Zola* and *Pasteur*. Barrymore's *Bill of Divorcement*, Raimu in *La Femme du boulanger*, Nikolai Cherkasov-Sergeyev in *General Suvarov*, and a scene in the same film where an actor whose name I do not know—he plays an old soldier—by telling a lying story of his old campaigns creates the kind of excitement that acting alone can give.

Miss Patricia Collinge played in *The Little Foxes* in New York, and she played the same part in the film version with Miss Bette Davis. Miss Davis' performance was excellent, but the fact that interested me concerns the scene, almost a monologue, where Birdie (Miss Collinge) lets her niece know that she has been a secret drinker for some years. It is a ticklish scene, sometimes on the verge of laughter. I saw the film three times, at long intervals, and each time there was a curious attempt at scattered applause at the end of that scene. The performance was exquisitely skillful, and in a strange way the film suddenly spoke with unusual eloquence and I felt that I was watching and listening to something very close to a "great moment."

The last of these recollections of mine is more recent, and you will probably all recall it. This performance, which, in my opinion, more nearly touched the quality of the Keans and the Duses than most, was given by Barry Fitzgerald in *Going My Way*. I saw Mr. Fitzgerald give this performance, in its beginnings, about fifteen years ago, and it was a great performance then. I am told that Mr. McCarey, whose skill is unrivaled, told Mr. Fitzgerald on many occasions that the camera would keep on turning until he finished acting, that he was to do what he felt like, and that he was not to worry about wasting film. I imagine there are few people who saw the film who will not carry with them for the rest of their lives some vivid recollection of Mr. Fitzgerald.

The point about this long recital of memorable bits is an answer to the widely held belief that acting may be valuable on the legitimate stage, but only behaving is useful in movies.

Is acting of any use to the screen?

It seems obvious to me that the high qualities of fine actors of the past are not confined to the past; it is equally obvious that the essential quality that is acting has too seldom been caught in any sustained way on film. But it *has been caught*. If it can be caught in bits, there seems to me no good reason why it should not be caught more often as a sustained performance.

If it is to be caught, it will have to be caught as acting, not as behaving. I believe that a thorough study of the customs and techniques of the sound stage might indicate the reasons for the somewhat disproportionate preponderance of behaving. To refer again to John Mason Brown's warning against slovenly thinking, one form of slovenly thinking, which is particularly difficult to combat, I have noticed more frequently in some of the younger writers and directors who are vastly impressed with the power of their medium but whose occasional comments indicate that they literally don't know how an actor works. The present custom of preventing writers from working on the set and from meeting actors has something to do with this, but it is not the whole reason. Pride in the power of the medium persuades many people to think that the contribution of an actor is very slight, and anyone who knows the history of the movies at all can point to certain fine films in which the contribution of an actor was almost nonexistent. But the fact that such films have been made does not suggest that no other kind of film can be made, and I believe that as the industry matures the contribution of the actor will become more important.

Great plays provide great parts, great parts discover great actors. There are no great parts without passion, and there is no passion without belief. Passion is the emotional expression of a deep conviction. Without conviction, which is partly intellectual, passion becomes hysteria. Hysteria and the absence of emotion cannot substitute for passion and restraint.

In the complicated mechanism of a film studio, in the tremendous costs of production, it is at present impossible to give the necessary time to acting. Behaving, when an actor has practiced it for years, becomes a finished product, a performance that can be turned on and off with less nervous strain than acting, which must always give what William Gillette called "the impression of the first time." But if the distinction between acting and behaving is understood, I believe it is possible that improved techniques of the camera may make acting a steadily more valuable component of films.

Mr. Edward Dmytryk, whom I quoted before, said he had never seen anyone succeed in changing himself into a different individual on the screen. "The insecurity of the actor," he continues, "trying to portray an individual who springs from a completely unfamiliar environment, is sure to be picked up by the searching eye of the camera. Result, a self-conscious performance."

If this is true, it may be due to a number of causes. Mr. Charles Laughton played Captain Bligh one year and Ruggles of Red Gap another. I did not find the performances self-conscious. I thought each fitted its frame about as perfectly as anyone has a right to ask. Nikolai Cherkasov played Gorki in *Lenin* and Alexander Nevsky in the film of that name. Gorki seemed to me a beautifully simple and subtle performance, with a curious and telling awkwardness of movement which helped to make me believe that the actor was the man. M. Cherkasov played Nevsky in a wide, heroic manner, impossible for an untrained actor, as if he were a Russian Galahad. The effect was not one of either insecurity or self-consciousness.

I have met Mr. Charles Chaplin, Mr. Barry Fitzgerald, and M. Raimu, and I have not found them "just like" any of the parts I have seen them play in films. Many of the parts I have seen them play were characters which sprang from a completely unfamiliar environment; but the camera did not record any insecurity, it recorded fragments of what to me was a fine and sensitive work of imaginative creation. Some of these "characterizations" take years to perfect; some take minutes, just as Van Gogh spent a month on one of his self-portraits and a day on one of the canvases of "A Garden at Arles"; but the time required to do the work has little to do with its quality. The fact is, the "searching eye of the camera" picks up what is there, and if a self-conscious performance takes place in front of it, that's what it records. It is the job of the writer and the director and the actor to see that the performance is not insecure or self-conscious. It is a special ability of the actor, if he has suitable material, to provide, first, "the illusion of the first time," and second, a sense of physical, intellectual, and emotional life which is more vivid than life itself.

One could cite examples of acting for hours, but I am reasonably cer′ in that the trouble is not with the ability of the actor, but with the mechanism of the studio.

The most powerful barrier against acting on the screen rises from the fact that film is only about forty years old, and the happy writers, cameramen, and directors are still discovering new things about it. This will be, in the long run, all to the good, but just at present it makes it awkward for the actor. Tricky cinematography, from writers, cameramen, and directors, can destroy illusion faster than anything else I know.

A film, like a novel or a play, shows character in action. Anything that gets in the way of the action of that character is dramatically bad, but the boys who are expert at cinematography delight in yanking the audience off to contemplate a mountain or a goat, the immediate symbolic meaning of which is clear to everyone, but the dramatic value of which is not clear to anyone. These tricks are evidences of growing pains, but they are definitely *pains* nonetheless.

Actors are frequently asked questions such as, "Don't you find tricks of direction, photography, writing, and cutting helpful to the character you are playing?" And the answer must be a strong affirmative. But there is a great difference between clarifying a "character" and helping the actor. The invention of the tractor was a great help to the plowhorse—it put him out of work. Too often, in film making, trickiness is used not as a help to the actor but as a substitute for acting, and the man who knows his craft is therefore deprived of the advantages which he has a right to assume that knowledge of his craft will give him.

Actually, most of the tricks of the kind I mean are well conceived and add tremendously to the effectiveness of film, but there are some which are not well conceived, and add

only to confusion. The difficulty is traceable, as are most difficulties, to the economic necessities of the industry and the
present stage of mechanical development. Film will always be
predominantly an intellectual medium. It consists in the fitting
together of various pieces, one by one. This is done by means
of the intellect, but it should be constantly subject to emotional suggestion. Unless the writer and the director treat film
first emotionally, and then proceed to rationalize, we shall
always see scenes such as the one in which Lenin, admirably
played by Boris Shchukin, finishes ordering the execution of
a batch of bread-hoarders and proving to Gorki that his
harshness was warranted, and then meets a lost child in the
corridor and proceeds to teach her to draw. The object of
this scene was to show that Lenin was kind to children, but
it succeeded in convincing me that the writer was writing his
film from his mind and not his heart. If the two scenes had
followed each other in a play, the first rehearsal would have
convinced the author that the juxtaposition was too sudden,
that a short transition was required. Lenin would not have
been required awkwardly to truncate his emotions about
bread-hoarders and be kind to the child. Or, if he were, he
would have been aware of the awkwardness. The sequence,
as it was cut together, prompted people to groan "propaganda" when, if the emotions of a man in that situation had
been more thoroughly explored by the *emotions* of the writer
and not by his *mind*, the very abruptness of the juxtaposition
could have been made effective.

Another bit of trickiness which irritated me and many
others recently came in the very successful picture *Spellbound*. Miss Bergman kissed the doctor, and shortly afterward
a series of three doors opened, apparently without help from
human hands. This, my reason told me, symbolized the dawn
of love in Miss Bergman, the beginning of brighter things—
the opening of doors—a literal translation of a literary cliché
to the screen. Personally, I have complete faith in Miss Bergman's ability to convince me that doors are opening in her
soul, if she is given adequate material to do it with, and,
frankly, I'd rather look at her opening the doors than see Mr.
Hitchcock do it—or see them open by themselves.

These are just a few of the things that make acting difficult
on the screen, and, correspondingly, make behaving easy.
Actors, as George Jean Nathan says, are popinjays, but they

have something to contribute. Does anyone want that contribution? If the films can use it, I have no doubt they will,
but it will need quite a bit of careful study. Acting will never
bring in the money that behaving will bring in, and acting
is many times more expensive to buy.

DUDLEY NICHOLS

*The Writer and the Film**

"If the ultimate film is to have any significant content, throwing some new glint of light on life, it is the writer who will have to create it."

Dudley Nichols was perhaps the best known of all Hollywood screen writers, largely because of his work with the American director, John Ford. He wrote, among others, The Informer *(1935),* Stagecoach *(1939),* The Long Voyage Home *(1940). He makes clear in this article the importance of the screen writer. But he lays even greater stress on the inherent collaborative nature of film-making, and as part of this argument he gives us a revealing description of the many technical stages a film goes through. He seems to be saying that the writer may be primary but the director must be dominant. He doesn't even mention the role of the producer: this is probably a carefully calculated oversight.*

During the course of his advice for screenwriters, Nichols strikes off several memorable phrases about the nature of the film. He defines the screen as not so much a vehicle for action as "the medium of reaction." He says "it is not so much the actors on the screen who are in motion as the viewer, comfortably seated and quite unaware of riding this witch's broom, which darts him in at one instant to peer into an actor's face or at some person or object at which the actor looks, the next instant jerking him far back to look at the ensemble, or racing him along in airplane, train, or car."

1

Trite.

Ours is the age of the specialist. In older times, before the Machine, men did specialize of course in the various arts and

* Dudley Nichols, "The Writer and the Film," from John Gassner and Dudley Nichols (eds.), *Great Film Plays*. New York, Crown, 1959. Pp. ix–xiv, xiv, xv–xvii.

crafts—but those arts and crafts were not themselves sub-divided into specialized functions. The man who painted did the whole job himself: he was a painter. So with the silver-smith and the shoemaker and the sculptor. But the Machine changed all that. The painter today has his materials prepared by other people, by specialized craftsmen or tradesmen, and only wields those materials in the final function of creating pictures. The etcher buys his copper plates already prepared and seldom pulls his own prints. The sculptor models in clay and leaves to others the pouring of the mold or the work of the pointing machine. The writer no longer turns out beautiful manuscripts that may be passed from hand to hand: he pounds out a script on the typing machine and passes it on to his publisher's printing factories. In science and art we have become specialized, narrowing our fields of study and work because those fields have grown too enormous for the single mind to embrace. We are all specialized, for better or worse, and it is only natural that the one new art form which the Machine has produced should be the most highly special-ized of all. For the motion picture *is* an art form, whether it be so regarded or not.

By rights this new art form should be controlled by indi-viduals who include all functions in themselves. They should be film-makers. But the functions are too diversified and com-plex to be handled by the creative energy of one individual. So we break them down into separate crafts—writing, directing, photography, scenic designing, optical printing and camera effects, cutting and assembly of film, composing music, re-cording, mixing and re-recording, the making of *dissolves* and *fades* and other transitions—into an immense field of works which require the closest and most harmonious collaboration to produce excellent results.

This in effect is a detriment to film as an art form and an obstacle to the development of artists who wish to work in film. It is too much the modern factory system—each man working on a different machine and never in an integrated creation. It tends to destroy that individuality of style which is the mark of any superior work of art. Individual feeling gets lost in the complicated process, and standardized products come off the assembly line. I make these remarks by way of preface to point out that there is only one way to overcome the impediments—and that is to learn the whole process, to be a master craftsman within the factory system; to be, in short, a film-maker first and a writer or director or whatever-you-will afterwards.

Of course, this poses a dilemma: one cannot under our present system make films without first learning to make films; and the only way to learn film-making is by making films. Hence by subterfuge of one sort or another one must enter the field as a specialized apprentice and try to learn all the other specialized functions, so that the individual may return to his specialty with the full equipment of an artist. A screenwriter should have knowledge of direction, of cutting, of all the separate functions, before his imagination and talent can be geared effectively and skillfully to his chosen line of work. Unfortunately we are none of us so competent as we might be, if for no other reason than that Hollywood is too bent on turning out films to take the time to train its artisans to the top of their bent. As a result, there is always room for the interested new worker. A writer can find a place, even without knowing much about film-making, and if he has a secret star he may glitter into sudden prominence even without knowing the slightest thing about film-making.

Hollywood is used to taking works of fiction in other forms and translating them into film; and for this and other reasons the talented writer does not feel encouraged to write directly for the screen. This is to be regretted because the screenplay might easily become a fascinating new form of literature, provided the studio heads acquired sufficient taste to recognize and desire literary quality. Yet there have been, there are, and there will continue to be written, screenplays of quality and sincerity—if only because of the dogged efforts of writers and directors who set themselves high goals and persist frequently against their own material interests.

There is one other circumstance which makes it difficult for the screenplay to be enjoyed as a literary form in itself: It is not and never can be a finished product. It is a step, the first and most important step, in the process of making a film. One might also say that a play is not a finished product for the theatre; yet a play relies entirely on the word; idea, character, and action are projected by means of the word; and a skillful playreader can enjoy wonderful performances within the theatre of his own imagination. The screenplay is far less a completed thing than the play, for the skilled screenwriter is thinking continuously in terms of film as well as the word. The filmwriter must be a film-maker at heart, and a film-maker thinks and lives and works in film. That is the goal, the end result—eight or ten thousand feet of negative patched together to reproduce, upon its unreeling, an illusion of a particular kind and quality. It is that illusion which the film-maker—and in this instance the filmwriter—is pursuing when he begins to gather together his first nebulous conception.

The truth is that a motion picture undergoes a series of creations. First it is a novel, a short story, or a conception in the mind of the screenwriter. That is the point of departure. Next the filmwriter takes the first plunge toward the finished negative by building the story in screenplay form. This rough draft, at least in the case of the present writer, will undergo two or three revisions, each nearer to the peculiar demands of cinema. With luck the director, who must have an equal sympathy for the drama to be unfolded, will be near at hand during the groundwork, contributing cinematic ideas here and there, many of which will not appear in the script but will be remembered or recorded in other notes to be used when the time comes.

Ordinarily, when all ideas of cinematic treatment have been unearthed and the final draft completed, the writer's work is ended and the creation of the projected film moves on into the hands of the director and other specialists; this is most unfortunate for the writer, for his education ceases in the middle of an uncompleted process. Let us, however, follow along with the writer who is able to follow the progress toward film. The second creation of the film is in its casting, which can help or hinder the designed illusion. The novelist is a fortunate artist who creates his characters out of the flesh and spirit of his own imagination; they need never be distorted by being embodied by living beings who necessarily have other traits and characteristics. But the playwright and the filmwriter must have real people to present their characters—and identity is not to be found. There have been ideal casts, but even the most perfect will alter indefinably the shape and mood and meaning of an imagined drama. Now each of the actors chosen must create his part of the film; and

✶ HOW EXCRUCIATING TO SEE A BAD CASTING.

the sum of their parts create another phase of the film. Implicated in this is the personality of the director, who creates the film by combining (in his own style, which may not be the style of the writer) the contributions of the writer and actors.

It is at this point that a peculiar thing occurs, which must be understood to discriminate between the stage and screen. I have never seen this pointed out before, even by film-workers, and it needs to be set down: Stage and screen are entirely different media because the audience participates in quite opposite ways. The theatre—and I use the term to embrace both stage and screen—demands an audience. It is not complete without its audience and even derives much of its power from its audience. Every stage actor knows this and has experienced it. The audience identifies itself with the actor, its collective emotions rush out in sympathy or buffet against him with antipathy like an unseen electric discharge—which increases the actor's potential, so to speak, permitting him to give back his feelings with increased power, which again returns to him, like the oscillating discharge of an electric machine. It is these heightened moments that create unforgettable experiences in the theatre when the drama is great both in its literary power and in its acting. Here the relationship between the actor and the audience is direct and the intelligent actor can grow by what he experiences, just as the audience does.

Now, curiously, this phenomenon does not exist at all in the cinema; but it does exist at the stage of cinema-making we are discussing. On the stage of a film studio the actor still has an audience, though a small one: the half-hundred people who comprise "the crew"—grips, juicers, cameramen, script girl, and all the familiar others. But if he acts in such a style as to affect this audience solely he is lost, for his actual audience is miles away and they will see him only through the uncaring single eye of the camera that looks on like a tripod man from Mars. The significant thing is that at this point there is an invisible transition taking place that will break all the rules of the stage and impose new ones of the screen.

The actors are creating a film, not a stageplay, even though it appears they are making a stageplay. We are not cameras, we are living beings, and we cannot see things with the detachment of a lens. In the early days of sound-film I observed many failures because this was not understood. The action seemed good on the sound-stage, but it did not come off on the screen.

The reason is that the audience, the film-theatre audience, participates in an entirely different way with the projected images of a film. This is not so strange if we remember that a motion-picture film will give just as good a performance in an empty theatre as in a full one. It will not, of course, be so moving or so amusing to a single spectator as it will to that same spectator in a crowded theatre: Members of an audience need each other to build up laughter, sorrow, and joy. But the film is unaffected; it does not in itself participate as do the actors on a stage. It is a complete illusion, as in a dream, and the power of identification (which you must have in any form of theatre) must be between audience and the visually projected re-actor.

Unthinking people speak of the motion picture as the medium of "action"; the truth is that the stage is the medium of action while the screen is the medium of reaction. It is through identification with the person *acted upon* on the screen, and not with the person acting, that the film builds up its oscillating power with an audience. This is understood instinctively by the expert film-makers, but to my knowledge it has never been formulated. At any emotional crisis in a film, when a character is saying something which profoundly affects another, it is to this second character that the camera instinctively roves, perhaps in close-up; and it is then that the hearts of the audience quiver and open in release, or rock with laughter or shrink with pain, leap to the screen and back again in swift-growing vibrations. The great actors of the stage are actors; of the screen, re-actors.

If anyone doubts this, let him study his own emotions when viewing a good film; an experienced film-maker can do this automatically at the first showing of a film, but very likely others will have to go a second time, or check it over in mental review. I once did this with some lay friends after a showing of Noel Coward's *In Which We Serve*, and it was illuminating to find out that they had been most deeply moved by reactions, almost never by actions: the figure of a woman when she gets news her husband has been lost at sea, the face of an officer when told his wife has died. (And how cunningly Noel Coward had that officer writing a letter to his wife when the radioman entered with the news; the reaction then was continued to the point where the officer goes on deck and drops the letter into the sea, a reaction extended into action, so to speak.) In the same film one of the most affecting scenes was the final one where the captain bids good-by to the remainder of his crew; and while this appears to be action, the camera shrewdly presented it as reaction: It is the faces of the men, as they file past, that we watch, reaction to the whole experience even in their laconic voices in the weary figure of the captain.

It is because the film can, at any moment of high emotional tension, pull an entire audience close to the faces of the actors, that reaction exerts more powerful effects on the screen than on the stage. Thus, in the final climax of *The Bridge on the River Kwai* (to name a more recent film), we *see* the anguished bewilderment of the Colonel, played by Alec Guinness, as he realizes what is actually occurring; and this reaction goads him to the final enigmatic action which blows up the bridge. The intention behind this final act remains ambiguous, but the dramatic moment is the Colonel's realization of his terrible dilemma, which realization we read in his face. On the stage, this mental process would have to be projected in speech. On the screen, where nothing is so eloquent as the silent image, any utterance would be fatal.

Despite the importance of reaction in cinema, the film is regarded as a medium of action, or at least of motion, and we fail to perceive that *it is the audience which is in motion*. In the stage-theatre (the so-called legitimate theatre), each member of the audience sits in a fixed chair and is free to observe this character or that, or the ensemble; he is free to make his own montage or accumulation of impressions; in short, he sees through his own untrammeled eyes. But in the film-theatre, though he sits in a seemingly fixed chair, he can see only *through the roving eye of the camera* and must continually shift his position and point of view at the command of the camera.

Paradoxically, it is not so much the actors on the screen who are in motion as the viewer, comfortably seated and quite unaware of riding this witch's broom, which darts him in at one instant to peer into an actor's face or at some person or object at which the actor looks, the next instant jerking him far back to look at the ensemble, or racing him along in airplane, train, or car to watch the actions and reactions of actors and share their emotions and excitement. The viewer of a film is no longer an autonomous individual as in the stage-theatre. He can see only what the film-maker commands. It is this absolute control over the audience which makes the cinema essentially different from the traditional theatre and its plays. It is also, triumphantly, the very source of the art of the film.

This is not to say that the two theatre forms, stage and screen, are opposed. Stagecraft has borrowed many things (the flashback, for instance) from cinema, just as filmcraft has borrowed from the stage. And long before film was dreamed of, the Elizabethan stage, by leaving location and background to the imagination and continually shifting scenes, anticipated aspects of the technique of film. In any case, bearing these fundamental principles of film-writing and direction in mind, we initiate a film, working first with the pen and next with the camera.

This brings us to the next phase in the making of a film, or next "creation" if you prefer. I have said that a film ensues from a series of consecutive creations, which were enumerated from the first stage of concept to the point where the first recording on film is made. The director, the actors, the art director, the cameraman, the whole crew in fact, have followed after a fashion (but with many inevitable departures in which the writer, if he is fortunate, has collaborated) the final draft of the screenplay. Now you have perhaps a hundred thousand feet of film, the negative of which is safely tucked away in the laboratory while you have for your study a "work print." Now the film is in the cutting room, in a thousand strips or rolls, some strips perhaps only a few feet long, some four or five hundred. Every foot-and-a-half is a second of time in the projection room, and you do not want your finished film to be one second longer than is determined by dramatic necessity. Every good artist, every good workman, has a passion for economy; if you can do a thing in one stroke, don't use two; if a certain mood or atmosphere is essential to the illusion you are after and it requires a hundred strokes, use them. By elimination and rough assembly the cutter patches together a work print, say, fourteen thousand feet long: two or three miles of strips of film, assembled con-secutively on seventeen or eighteen reels. That is the first creation of the cutter.

Now another job begins, one of the most delicate and sensitive jobs of all. Rough cutting was determined by the screenwriter, but this did not and could not include the interior cutting of the director and cameraman. Since terminology is not yet standardized in film-making, I designate the cutting of the director on the set the "montage," using a word which the Russians apply for all cutting or editing. It is determined by the style of the director, his feeling for photographed images, the way he rests the eye of the audience or gives it sudden pleasures, moving in at different angles on his scenes and characters. Had the writer attempted to anticipate the director and set down all this montage on paper, his script would have become a useless mess, for this interior cutting cannot be determined precisely (though many attempt to do so) before arriving on the set. The manner of shooting and handling the camera must be guided by spontaneous feeling and by discoveries made on the set. I for one have no patience with the growing method of having every camera shot sketched beforehand so that director, cameraman, and actors can work by rote. It destroys that spontaneity of feeling which is the essence of film art; though of course many films are so unimportant that it does not matter how they are shot: they never were alive at any moment.

To continue following our film through to its finish, you now have a rough assembly which is far overlength, the cutting of which was largely determined by the script and direction. But this is only a provisional arrangement. Everything depends on the final cutting, elimination, and rearrangement. And the only compass to guide you in this final orchestration of images is your own feeling. The final test is to project the film on the screen and see how the arrangement you have made affects you. By this time you have grown weary of every foot of the film but you doggedly keep your feeling fresh as the only touchstone, until you have wearily said, "That's the best we can make of it." And I promise you disappointment in every film, for it is far removed from the perfection of imagination, as is everything that is realized.

Yet you have not finished with this scratched and tattered work print, which now looks as tired as yourself. There are two final stages, sound and music recording, and finally the re-recording of the whole thing. Sound is a magic element, and part of your design as a screenwriter or director has been the effect of sound. In the case of *This Land Is Mine*, which was directed by a great film-maker, Jean Renoir, one of the focal points of the drama was a railroad yard, and as we could not shoot the action in an actual railroad yard we determined to create it largely by sound. We spent endless days gathering sound tracks and trying to orchestrate our sounds as carefully as if they were music. And finally came the scoring of the music itself, not a great deal of it but every bar important: choosing Mendelssohn here, Méhul there, original composition for the rest, and getting it re-recorded in a harmonious whole.

At last you have, say, nine or ten thousand feet of image film and a second sound film of the same length synchronized to the split second. Every frame of both films is numbered, corresponding with the thousands of feet of negative in the laboratory. You send your final work prints to the laboratory, the negative is cut, the sound track printed alongside—and you receive your first composite print. And, if the composite print checks, your work is finished and the negative is shipped, ready for countless prints to be made and released through the theatres of the world. This is what you set out to make— or rather help to make—when you began writing your rough draft of a screenplay. And this is what you had to keep in mind all the wearisome while.

2

. . . screen plays are . . . not complete works in themselves; they are blueprints of projected films. Many factors may have intervened to make the finished films different from the designed illusion, for better or worse.

The most noticeable feature of a skillful screenplay is its terseness and bareness. This is because the eye is not there, the eye which fills and enriches. Nor does the screenwriter waste time with much descriptive matter or detailing of photographic moods. These have all been discussed at length with the director, art director, and others. It is the writer's job to invent a story in terms of cinema or to translate an existing story into terms of cinema. He creates an approximate continuity of scenes and images, suggesting cinematic touches where he can. He will write "close-up" of a character without setting down the most important thing, which is what that character is feeling during that close-up, because the text clearly shows what the character is supposed to be experiencing. The director will take care of that. If he is an artist, the director will submit the actor to that experience while photographing the close-up, by playing the actual scene out of range of the camera.

Writing for the screen, if long practiced, also seduces one to write dialogue in a synoptic fashion, which may show itself to the eye when printed on a page, but should never reveal itself to the ear when spoken from the screen. Stage dialogue, no matter how wonderful in quality, cannot be directly shifted to the screen; it must be condensed, synopsized. The reason is obvious: on the stage the actor depends for projection upon the word; on the screen he relies upon visual projection. And it is hard to describe visual projection in a screenplay; that must be left to the director and cast. . . .

. . . almost everyone who is seriously interested in the cinema has seen *The Informer* on the screen, and as the film projects the screenplay with great fidelity I am prompted by Mr. Gassner to explain the method by which I translated Mr. O'Flaherty's novel into the language of film. In 1935 this was in a certain sense an experimental film; some new method had to be found by which to make the psychological action photographic. At that time I had not yet clarified and formulated for myself the principles of screenwriting, and many of my ideas were arrived at instinctively. I had an able mentor as well as collaborator in the person of John Ford and I had begun to catch his instinctive feeling about film. I can see now that I sought and found a series of symbols to make visual the tragic psychology of the informer, in this case a primitive man of powerful hungers. The whole action was to be played out in one foggy night, for the fog was symbolic of the groping primitive mind; it is really a mental fog in which he moves and dies. A poster offering a reward for information concerning Gypo's friend became the symbol of the evil idea of betrayal, and it blows along the street, following Gypo; it will not leave him alone. It catches on his leg and he kicks it off. But still it follows him, and he sees it like a phantom in the air when he unexpectedly comes upon his fugitive friend.

So it goes all through the script; some of the symbolism is obvious, much of it concealed except from the close observer. The officer uses a stick when he pushes the blood money to Gypo at headquarters, symbolic of contempt. The informer encounters a blind man in the dark fog outside and grips his throat in sudden guilt. The blind man is a symbol of the brute conscience, and Gypo releases him when he discovers the man cannot see. But as Gypo goes on to drown his conscience in drink, the tapping of the blind man's stick follows him; we hear it without seeing the blind man as Gypo hears his guilt pursuing him in his own soul. Later, when he comes face to face with his conscience for a terrifying moment, he tries to buy it off—by giving the blind man a couple of pounds, a lordly sum. . . . But I shall not continue this account of a screenplay that cannot be presented in this book. Sufficient to say that the method of adaptation in this instance was by a cumulative symbolism, to the very last scene where Gypo addresses the carven Christ, by which the psychology of a man could be made manifest in photographic terms. In this case I believe the method was successful. I might add that I transferred the action of the drama from its original, rather special setting to a larger and more dramatic conflict which had national connotations. Whether that was any gain I do not know. Size of conflict in itself I hold to be unimportant. It is the size of characters within a conflict and how deeply they are probed that matters.

So much for an adaptation. For the problems of writing an *original* screenplay I can only rely on my personal experiences. It is not easy to trace the origin of a story. It is easier to say that a work of fiction happens. But that is not exact, for a story comes into existence because of some inner necessity of the individual. Every human being contains creative energy; he wants to make something. A man may make a chair, or a pair of shoes, a masterpiece of painting, or a pulp-magazine story; precisely what he makes is dictated by his imagination, temperament, experience, and training. But the act of creation is dictated by desire. I should imagine this runs through the universe as a law, since it is so with man, and man is a part of the universe. If the Supreme Will desires to build a Universe, the Universe will "happen." It is all a matter of the degree of intensity of desire. A storyteller is passionately interested in human beings and their endless conflicts with their fates, and he is filled with desire to make some intelligible arrangement out of the chaos of life, just as the chairmaker desires to make some useful and beautiful arrangement out of wood. Frustrate those creative desires in man, and his forces will be turned toward destruction; for energy cannot remain unexpended, it is not static, it must swing one way or another.

Stories for the purpose of entertainment alone are commonplace fiction and can be redeemed only by a dazzling style, a sheer delight in the materials of storytelling, a touch of the poet. The cinema is only in its infancy as an art form, and its usual fate so far has been to be used only for entertainment and making money. Because it is a very costly medium it will continue to be employed for making money until money ceases to be the great desire of the people of the world. Most motion pictures are mere entertainment, and accordingly the screenwriter can work with only half of himself; his satisfaction must usually be in artistry of manner, skill in the way he accomplishes his work, without much regard for the content of the film. For this reason the story of serious intention can rarely be written within a film studio; and for this reason serious writers in other fields, novelists and dramatists, have given great aid to the development of the cinema. For the powers-that-be will buy the film rights of a serious novel if it seems to have enough readers, and though the contents of the novel are sometimes perverted by film censorship or bad taste, enough remains to make a notable motion picture. But the screenwriter who desires to make an original story has no readers, at least not for the projected story. If the story proposes to make a serious statement beyond mere entertaining, it will seem off the beaten track and the writer will very likely meet opposition. It is for this reason and this reason alone that so few stories of any account *originate* within Hollywood. In France, before World War II, the film-makers were largely their own entrepreneurs and for this reason produced many brilliant original works. They were storytellers functioning freely in the new medium of film.

Nevertheless the serious film-writer cannot resign himself to Hollywood's barriers against original work designed for the screen. The average Hollywood entrepreneur is an intelligent man, and it is up to writers and directors to prove to him that films which probe into the chaos of life can be successful.

John Ford made *The Informer* in spite of studio resistance;
even after its completion it was held to be a failure and a
waste of money by certain entrepreneurs. But the film did go
out and make a profit. There *was* an audience for the realistic
film. In spite of this and other instances I will say in all
fairness that usually the studio heads have been right and
the film-makers wrong—because usually the film-makers
have not measured up to their task and their responsibilities when granted freedom. They have not measured up
or they have wanted both money and freedom, which are in-
compatible. It is an axiom that no one will pay you to be a
free artist. You are hired for profit—that is common sense.
Very well, then, you must stop working for salary; you must
devote yourself to the task in hand as do the novelist and
dramatist, and only be recompensed if the film makes a profit.
Economically I believe the writer and director will fare even
better with this arrangement than under the salary system.
Spiritually they will become whole men and work with integrity.

I have not attempted to explain the secrets of screenwriting
—because there are no secrets. There are certain prescribed
forms, but the forms are not final. Others will come along and
do better work as we come to understand more clearly the
peculiar demands of cinema. Meanwhile, those people who
may become interested in screenwriting as a vocation must
study the best examples of screenplays available and then have
a try at it themselves. I do not touch on technical jargon, such
as *fade*, *lap dissolve*, *dolly*, or *pan*, because they are quite unnecessary to the craft. And no matter where you write them
into your script, the completed film will make its own demands in the cutting room and very likely change your imagined plan. This terminology can safely be ignored; it is merely
a convenience. disagree - good to see how a director organizes
a film

We try to formulate a classical form for the cinema but
there are no final rules. Film continuity can be as broken and
erratic as a dream, if it is a potent dream and by some inner
need requires that sort of continuity. There are really no rules,
in spite of what Hollywood will tell you. A film in its continuity is a stream of images, and if they combine into an
exciting, intelligible whole you have accomplished your purpose. Most film technique today is very imperfect, as we are
still groping for the pure form. The cinema is still a giant in

chains, and a giant who has not even yet stood up and shaken his chains. Those chains are censorship, commercialism, monopoly, specialization—all the faults that are indigenous to industrial society and not just characteristic of the cinema. If control of film production should fall into the hands of government, any government, the old chains will be struck off only to be replaced by heavier ones. And because of the potent propaganda effect of film, that is a danger. No art, including the wonderful medium of sound film, can serve one set of ideas—it must be free or perish.

In conclusion, I hope that in sketching the successive steps of making a film I have not underrated the importance of the screenplay. It is, in my opinion, pre-eminent in the field of film-making. It is the writer who is the dreamer, the imaginer, the shaper. He works in loneliness with nebulous materials, with nothing more tangible than paper and a pot of ink; and his theatre is within his mind. He must generate phantoms out of himself and live with them until they take on a life of their own and become, not types, but characters working out their own destinies. If the ultimate film is to have any significant content, throwing some new glint of light on life, it is the writer who will have to create it. Yet it is the director who has always dominated the field and will no doubt continue to dominate it, for various good reasons. It is the director who must *realize* the imagined people on film, who must know all the technological processes, and command the extravagantly costly tools of film art. Writing costs are negligible by comparison. The film-writer can afford to bow to the director; and if it be one of the world's few great directors, he can do so with pride and gratitude. For there are few satisfactions to match seeing a story you have created, or even re-created in terms of film, come to a powerful life on the screen—a new creation with all the writing washed invisibly away.

Film and the Other Arts

VACHEL LINDSAY

Sculpture-in-Motion*

"I desire in motion pictures, not the stillness, but the majesty
of sculpture."

*With the zest of a fan and the skill of a poet, Vachel
Lindsay urges the film maker to notice how much he can
learn from statues. "I do not advocate for the photoplay the
mood of the Venus of Milo," he says; but look rather at
the Victory of Samothrace, and "when you are appraising
a new film, ask yourself: 'Is this motion as rapid, as godlike,
as the sweep of the wings of the Samothracian?'" Why should
we not expect, in time, to find a Michelangelo or a Rodin or
even a Borglum of the films? "Whoever is to photograph
horses, let him study the play of light and color and muscle-
texture" in Gutzon Borglum's Mares of Diomedes.*

*The troubadour author of The Congo (1914) and The Chi-
nese Nightingale (1917), who toured the South selling drawings and poems for pennies, is not so snobbish as to suppose
that the comparisons go only one way. He clips illustrations
from movie magazines of that early day and alerts us to the
sculptural value of a group awaiting a villain, of "a scene of
storm and stress in an office," in which "the eye travels without weariness, as it should do in sculpture, from the hero to
the furious woman, then to the attorney behind her." In his
book there are comparisons with other arts; Lindsay does not
expect everything filmic to be in high relief. There are times,
however, when sculpture is a valid study: "Even in a simple
chase-picture, the speed must not destroy the chance to enjoy
the modelling."*

The sculptor George Gray Barnard is responsible for none of
the views in this discourse, but he has talked to me at length
about his sense of discovery in watching the most ordinary

* Vachel Lindsay, "Sculpture in Motion," from *The Art of the
Moving Picture*. New York, Macmillan, 1922. Pp. 84–96.

motion pictures, and his delight in following them with their
endless combinations of masses and flowing surfaces.

The little far-away people on the old-fashioned speaking
stage do not appeal to the plastic sense in this way. They are,
by comparison, mere bits of pasteboard with sweet voices,
while, on the other hand, the photoplay foreground is full of
dumb giants. The bodies of these giants are in high sculptural
relief. Where the lights are quite glaring and the photography
is bad, many of the figures are as hard in their impact on the
eye as lime-white plaster-casts, no matter what the clothing.
There are several passages of this sort in the otherwise beautiful Enoch Arden, where the shipwrecked sailor is depicted on
his desert island in the glaring sun.

What materials should the photoplay figures suggest? There
are as many possible materials as there are subjects for pictures and tone schemes to be considered. But we will take for
illustration wood, bronze, and marble, since they have been
used in the old sculptural art.

There is found in most art shows a type of carved wood
gargoyle where the work and the subject are at one, not only
in the color of the wood, but in the way the material masses
itself, in bulk betrays its qualities. We will suppose a moving-
picture humorist who is in the same mood as the carver. He
chooses a story of quaint old ladies, street gamins, and fat
aldermen. Imagine the figures with the same massing and
interplay suddenly invested with life, yet giving to the eye a
pleasure kindred to that which is found in carved wood, and
bringing to the fancy a similar humor.

Or there is a type of Action Story where the mood of the
figures is that of bronze, with the æsthetic resources of that
metal: its elasticity; its emphasis on the tendon, ligament, and
bone, rather than on the muscle; and an attribute that we will
call the panther-like quality. Hermon A. MacNeil has a
memorable piece of work in the yard of the architect Shaw,
at Lake Forest, Illinois. It is called "The Sun Vow." A little
Indian is shooting toward the sun, while the old warrior,
crouching immediately behind him, follows with his eye the
direction of the arrow. Few pieces of sculpture come readily
to mind that show more happily the qualities of bronze as
distinguished from other materials. To imagine such a group
done in marble, carved wood, or Della Robbia ware is to
destroy the very image in the fancy.

The photoplay of the American Indian should in most instances be planned as bronze in action. The tribes should not move so rapidly that the panther-like elasticity is lost in the riding, running, and scalping. On the other hand, the aborigines should be far from the temperateness of marble.

Mr. Edward S. Curtis, the super-photographer, has made an Ethnological collection of photographs of our American Indians. This work of a life-time, a supreme art achievement, shows the native as a figure in bronze. Mr. Curtis' photoplay, *The Land of the Head Hunters* (World Film Corporation), a romance of the Indians of the North-West, abounds in noble bronzes.

I have gone through my old territories as an art student, in the Chicago Art Institute and the Metropolitan Museum, of late, in special excursions, looking for sculpture, painting, and architecture that might be the basis for the photoplays of the future.

The Bacchante of Frederick MacMonnies is in bronze in the Metropolitan Museum and in bronze replica in the Boston Museum of Fine Arts. There is probably no work that more rejoices the hearts of the young art students in either city. The youthful creature illustrates a most joyous leap into the air. She is high on one foot with the other knee lifted. She holds a bunch of grapes full-arm's length. Her baby, clutched on the other hand, is reaching up with greedy mouth toward the fruit. The bacchante body is glistening in the light. This is joy-in-bronze as the Sun Vow is power-in-bronze. This special story could not be told in another medium. I have seen in Paris a marble copy of this Bacchante. It is as though it were done in soap. On the other hand, many of the Renaissance Italian sculptors have given us children in marble in low relief, dancing like lilies in the wind. They could not be put into bronze.

The plot of the Action Photoplay is literally or metaphorically a chase down the road or a hurdle-race. It might be well to consider how typical figures for such have been put into carved material. There are two bronze statues that have their replicas in all museums. They are generally one on either side of the main hall, towering above the second-story balustrade. First, the statue of Gattamelata, a Venetian general, by Donatello. The original is in Padua. Then there is the figure of Bartolommeo Colleoni. The original is in Venice. It is by

Verrocchio and Leopardi. These equestrians radiate authority. There is more action in them than in any cowboy hordes I have ever beheld zipping across the screen. Look upon them and ponder long, prospective author-producer. Even in a simple chase-picture, the speed must not destroy the chance to enjoy the modelling. If you would give us mounted legions, destined to conquer, let any one section of the film, if it is stopped and studied, be grounded in the same bronze conception. The Assyrian commanders in Griffith's Judith would, without great embarrassment, stand this test.

But it may not be the pursuit of an enemy we have in mind. It may be a spring celebration, horsemen in Arcadia, going to some happy tournament. Where will we find our precedents for such a cavalcade? Go to any museum. Find the Parthenon room. High on the wall is the copy of the famous marble frieze of the young citizens who are in the procession in praise of Athena. Such a rhythm of bodies and heads and the feet of proud steeds, and above all the profiles of thoroughbred youths, no city has seen since that day. The delicate composition relations, ever varying, ever refreshing, amid the seeming sameness of formula of rider behind rider, have been the delight of art students the world over, and shall so remain. No serious observer escapes the exhilaration of this company. Let it be studied by the author-producer though it be but an idyl in disguise that his scenario calls for: merry young farmers hurrying to the State Fair parade, boys making all speed to the political rally.

Buy any three moving-picture magazines you please. Mark the illustrations that are massive, in high relief, with long lines in their edges. Cut out and sort some of these. I have done it on the table where I write. After throwing away all but the best specimens, I have four different kinds of sculpture. First, behold the inevitable cowboy. He is on a ramping horse, filling the entire outlook. The steed rears, while facing us. The cowboy waves his hat. There is quite such an animal by Frederick MacMonnies, wrought in bronze, set up on a gate to a park in Brooklyn. It is not the identical color of the photoplay animal, but the bronze elasticity is the joy in both.

Here is a scene of a masked monk, carrying off a fainting girl. The hero intercepts him. The figures of the lady and the monk are in sufficient sculptural harmony to make a formal sculptural group for an art exhibition. The picture of the hero, strong, with well-massed surfaces, is related to both. The fact that he is in evening dress does not alter his monumental quality. All three are on a stone balcony that relates itself to the general largeness of spirit in the group, and the semi-classic dress of the maiden. No doubt the title is: The Morning Following the Masquerade Ball. This group could be made in unglazed clay, in four colors.

Here is an American lieutenant with two ladies. The three are suddenly alert over the approach of the villain, who is not yet in the picture. In costume it is an everyday group, but those three figures are related to one another, and the trees behind them, in simple sculptural terms. The lieutenant, as is to be expected, looks forth in fierce readiness. One girl stands with clasped hands. The other points to the danger. The relations of these people to one another may seem merely dramatic to the superficial observer, but the power of the group is in the fact that it is monumental. I could imagine it done in four different kinds of rare tropical wood, carved unpolished.

Here is a scene of storm and stress in an office where the hero is caught with seemingly incriminating papers. The table is in confusion. The room is filling with people, led by one accusing woman. Is this also sculpture? Yes. The figures are in high relief. Even the surfaces of the chairs and the littered table are massive, and the eye travels without weariness, as it should do in sculpture, from the hero to the furious woman, then to the attorney behind her, then to the two other revilers, then to the crowd in three loose rhythmic ranks. The eye makes this journey, not from space to space, or fabric to fabric, but first of all from mass to mass. It is sculpture, but it is the sort that can be done in no medium but the moving picture itself, and therefore it is one goal of this argument.

But there are several other goals. One of the sculpturesque resources of the photoplay is that the human countenance can be magnified many times, till it fills the entire screen. Some examples are in rather low relief, portraits approximating certain painters. But if they are on sculptural terms, and are studies of the faces of thinking men, let the producer make a pilgrimage to Washington for his precedent. There, in the rotunda of the capitol, is the face of Lincoln by Gutzon Borglum. It is one of the eminently successful attempts to get at the secret of the countenance by enlarging it much, and concentrating the whole consideration there.

The photoplay producer, seemingly without taking thought,

is apt to show a sculptural sense in giving us Newfoundland fishermen, clad in oilskins. The background may have an unconscious Winslow Homer reminiscence. In the foreground our hardy heroes fill the screen, and dripping with sea-water become wave-beaten granite, yet living creatures none the less. Imagine some one chapter from the story of Little Em'ly in *David Copperfield*, retold in the films. Show us Ham Peggotty and old Mr. Peggotty in colloquy over their nets. There are many powerful bronze groups to be had from these two, on to the heroic and unselfish death of Ham, rescuing his enemy in storm and lightning.

I have seen one rich picture of alleged cannibal tribes. It was a comedy about a missionary. But the aborigines were like living ebony and silver. That was long ago. Such things come too much by accident. The producer is not sufficiently aware that any artistic element in his list of productions that is allowed to go wild, that has not had full analysis, reanalysis, and final conservation, wastes his chance to attain supreme mastery.

Open your history of sculpture, and dwell upon those illustrations which are not the normal, reposeful statues, but the exceptional, such as have been listed for this chapter. Imagine that each dancing, galloping, or fighting figure comes down into the room life-size. Watch it against a dark curtain. Let it go through a series of gestures in harmony with the spirit of the original conception, and as rapidly as possible, not to lose nobility. If you have the necessary elasticity, imagine the figures wearing the costumes of another period, yet retaining in their motions the same essential spirit. Combine them in your mind with one or two kindred figures, enlarged till they fill the end of the room. You have now created the beginning of an Action Photoplay in your own fancy.

Do this with each most energetic classic till your imagination flags. I do not want to be too dogmatic, but it seems to me this is one way to evolve real Action Plays. It would, perhaps, be well to substitute this for the usual method of evolving them from old stage material or newspaper clippings.

There is in the Metropolitan Museum a noble modern group, the Mares of Diomedes, by the aforementioned Gutzon Borglum. It is full of material for the meditations of a man who wants to make a film of a stampede. The idea is that Hercules, riding his steed bareback, guides it in a circle. He is fascinating the horses he has been told to capture. They are held by the mesmerism of the circular path and follow him round and round till they finally fall from exhaustion. Thus the Indians of the West capture wild ponies, and Borglum, a Far Western man, imputes the method to Hercules. The bronze group shows a segment of this circle. The whirlwind is at its height. The mares are wild to taste the flesh of Hercules. Who ever is to photograph horses, let him study the play of light and color and muscle-texture in this bronze. And let no group of horses ever run faster than these of Borglum.

An occasional hint of a Michelangelo figure or gesture appears for a flash in the films. Young artist in the audience, does it pass you by? Open your history of sculpture again and look at the usual list of Michelangelo groups. Suppose the seated majesty of Moses should rise, what would be the quality of the action? Suppose the sleeping figures of the Medician tombs should wake, or those famous slaves should break their bands, or David again hurl the stone. Would not their action be as heroic as their quietness? Is it not possible to have a Michelangelo of photoplay sculpture? Should we not look for him in the fulness of time? His figures might come to us in the skins of the desert island solitary, or as cave men and women, or as mermaids and mermen, and yet have a force and grandeur akin to that of the old Italian.

Rodin's famous group of the citizens of Calais is an example of the expression of one particular idea by a special technical treatment. The producer who tells a kindred story to that of the siege of Calais, and the final going of these humble men to their doom, will have a hero-tale indeed. It will be not only sculpture-in-action, but a great Crowd Picture. It begins to be seen that the possibilities of monumental achievement in the films transcend the narrow boundaries of the Action Photoplay. Why not conceptions as heroic as Rodin's Hand of God, where the first pair are clasped in the gigantic fingers of their maker in the clay from which they came?

Finally, I desire in moving pictures, not the stillness, but the majesty of sculpture. I do not advocate for the photoplay the mood of the Venus of Milo. But let us turn to that sister of hers, the great Victory of Samothrace, that spreads her wings at the head of the steps of the Louvre, and in many an art gallery beside. When you are appraising a new film, ask

yourself: "Is this motion as rapid, as godlike, as the sweep of
the wings of the Samothracian?" Let her be the touchstone
of the Action Drama, for nothing can be more swift than the
winged Gods, nothing can be more powerful than the oncoming of the immortals.

PARKER TYLER

Movies and the Human Image*

"Human identity in art was given a new meaning through its
additional element: Kinesis."

*Parker Tyler, a "difficult" writer partly because he comes
to film criticism with the equipment and bibliography of a
social critic and an art critic as well, is here concerned with
tracing the attitudes of historic schools of painting toward the
human figure. He proposes that "classical" traditions of art
assumed "the moral preëminence of Man—man as a theoretically or 'rationally,' perfectible if not perfect being." Even
some of the most modern schools—surrealism, for example—
attacked only the complacency or the sterile aspects of preceding schools, not the basic tenet of concern with humanity.*

*Abstract painting, on the contrary, he says, was a direct
challenge to the human image, a break in the cultural tradition. And at this very moment, when the older tradition was
turning into dull academism and "twentieth century painting
was girding itself to make a complete break with representationalism, the 'representational' movies came into being and
cast their universal public spell." Film is therefore "a positive
antidote to this extreme convention of modern painting" because it is basically a medium of content, a mirror of the world
of man.*

One wonders if photography competes with art in the way
that—as E. E. Cummings once poignantly noted—poetry
competes with elephants and El Greco. The consciousness
of such a hypothesis may depend on the development of
one's competitive sense. Intellectually, our more or less re-

* Parker Tyler, "Movies and the Human Image," from *The
Three Faces of the Film.* New York, Thomas Yoseloff, 1960.
Pp. 139–144. Reprinted from *Forum* magazine, 1958.

mote ancestors had to deal, when deciding any great moral issue (including the aesthetic), with fewer factors than we. A "global" community of nations has meant, whatever the specific problem, that more factors must be considered, all at once, on parallel levels. So asking the question "Have the movies prolonged the life of the classic human image?" I am aware that one might attack the problem by many routes, some deceptively simple and yet all really devious. One presumes that the issue is vital, if not to the movies, at least to art. Perhaps the movies—aside from the avant-garde ranks, which are very, very small—don't care whether their imagery has an aesthetic status, so-called, and perhaps abstract artists, for their part, are by now so convinced of their canon's public and financial triumph that the notion of the movies' doing anything in our time to revive the prestige of the classic human image seem frivolous—if not downright irrelevant.

Merely to equate the terms in my formulation brings up startling contradictions within the formulation. First of all: Is an equivalence between photography and classical art not far more "statistical" and "documentary" than aesthetic? For instance, what vital, artistically critical relation has the conventional image of the movies to an antique sculptural frieze or to Poussin's version of such a frieze? This objecting query might emanate from the admirers of Poussin as well as from true film devotées, who would urge that the photographic image per se is what holds the movies back. Indeed, to consider the atmospheric effects possible to modern photography, as well as the distortion possible through objective and laboratory means, is to conclude that an equation of photography with "classic" form represents an old-fashioned prejudice for which commercial filmdom alone is to blame. Through sheer movement—with its attendant blur of instantaneous imagery and the rapidity producing a purely psychic "blur"—highly expressionistic, no less than surrealistic, effects have been, and are, obtained by imaginative movie-makers.

Where does this reflection leave the present equation between photography and classic art? Just about no place inevitable. Granting that, with imaginative photography and its increasing technical resources, a highly realistic, stylized imagery is obtainable for the film screen, a stubborn element persists in the aesthetic equation I have proposed: an element against the grain. Abstract painting of the non-objective kind seriously differs from all filmic imagery except that which (sometimes without photography) exactly and exclusively imitates such painting; that is, non-objective painting disposes of literal and unmistakable referents to human experience. A seeming paradox naturally follows: howsoever, this is not to say that non-objective abstractionism is an art wholly *outside* human experience. An important point is to be observed of extreme abstract painting from Mondrian to Rothko, Reinhardt and company: it tends to offer viewers not, precisely speaking, a *picture*, but rather a *creative décor* of the mural type.

A Mondrian or a late Rothko, purified of figure and primarily "inactive," remains pure design—though design-atmosphere would be a better term—because late Rothkos look like tranquilly pulsing atmospheres of color. This pure design is intended as the modulation of a wall, whether private or museum wall, and is the *dernier cri* of interior design. Its pretension to being art, rather than mere decoration, is based on a quite simple idea: an aesthetic image need not be a statement concerning something external to itself; it may "state" itself as any other object does. This theoretical position has animated the practice of pure-abstract art from the beginning, when Kandinsky, Mondrian, Pevsner, Gabo, Malevich and Delaunay talked like philosophers and advocated, in one respect or another, a new "realism." Non-objective art ("extreme" or "pure" abstraction) is a statement *period* (.) Supposedly, it evokes a "mood," a psychic vibration of some kind. But, thus, it enters life like any other motivation, cause or visual happening—as would a meteor from outer space or a perfect stranger on the doorstep. The said meteor and the said stranger may affect one's life or not affect it at all. Like Kilroy, it "was here," and sometimes one remembers it, encounters its mark, or prefers to keep it, even falling in love with it. . . .

Now the only sensible, irreducible and unavoidable thing to say about this conception of the work of art as a "non-objective" phenomenon, which is really objective after all, is that it produces a gaping hole in the tradition of human culture—which it tries to fill up exactly as though it had made an actual hole in a wall. In my aforesaid proposition, therefore, the issue concerning the photographic in relation to the classic human image devolves not upon the question of style, or so-called distortion in art, but upon the question of humanity's ability to produce and assess works of art through conscious means having nothing to do with the necessary dependence of form upon content; nothing to do with the classic aesthetic dualism of form united with its content. By its nature, photography possesses a highly prejudiced standpoint on this issue. As many have already observed, the aesthetic character of the movies *begins* by being so naturalistic, so "documentary," as a notation of life that, among all the arts, the movies evoke the most urgent sense of comparison and contrast with life itself. Film is the art—and this is a pivotal definition—where the finished "form" is the most easily soluble into raw "content" or ingredients of meaning. Both psychologically and technically, the photographic lens is a mirror, even if a sometimes flattering one. For this reason, the relation of photography to the classic human image is simple and direct. Classic Western art evolved through the aesthetic desire to come as close to nature (or "content") as possible while in the same act "idealizing" it: giving it a flattering look (or "form").

Now, if, in time, the idealism of the ancient Greeks produced the aesthetic coldness of Neo-Classicism and its remoteness from common experience—something that was radically challenged by nineteenth-century artists—this became true not because Poussin and David failed to be great painters, but because what they painted, and to some extent how they painted it, became irrelevant and objectionable to a vital social experience composed of various new moral factors: the congruent rise of individualism and the bourgeoisie, the French Revolution, and so on. Yet soon a reaction set in against the nineteenth-century "revolution" in painting. When the Impressionists came along, they seemed quite as disinterested in violent feelings as they were in violent actions. And if the Post-Impressionists, carrying forward Van Gogh's violence through the Fauves, returned to activized brushes and activized feelings, theirs was simply a reaction to a reaction. In fact, when the twentieth-century began, painting was a more or less restless heap of "school" reactions, a heap both topped and toppled, temporally speaking, by the chaotic nihilism of the Dadaists and Surrealists.

All the same, in artists such as Giorgio de Chirico, Jacques Lipchitz and Marcel Duchamp, this century has produced heroic figures who have used art—however debonairly as in the case of the Dada-nurtured Duchamp—as a highly organized aesthetic instrument both creating and criticizing human values. André Breton, the best-known theorist of Surrealism, is notable for his classical poise and his equally classical literary style. After all, nothing in the tradition of classical humanism interdicts violent or positive feelings; all artistic discipline, indeed, requires initiative and decisiveness, which cannot exist without their own driving power. Chirico's art is proof-simple that the style-atmosphere of Greek classicism, the mainstay of the humanist tradition, had a twentieth-century application: was convertible into a new art idiom; his art displays the most serious use of the Surrealist postulate of synthetic vision: the "psychological" as opposed to the "natural" landscape. But when has the painted landscape ever been quite "natural"? Romanticism once had its psychological landscape, and as for the Baroque before that, its landscapes were nothing if not "theatrical."

It may be time to insert the question of why we tend to equate our cultural history with man as specifically the "classic human image." The essence of Christian-pagan idealism is necessarily philosophic and therefore "humanist" in the widest possible as well as the narrowest sense. In this specifically humanist role of classicism, the aesthetic tradition has actually subsumed all "revolutions" and "reactions," Neo-Classicism, Romanticism and Cubism alike. Historically, classicism is nothing but the moral preëminence of Man—man as a theoretically, or "rationally," perfectible if not perfect being. Preferably and conventionally, man is inspired by God, but at least he is given his basic meaning by the ability to reason, to relate himself to gods, other men, and nature as well as to art. All the aesthetic revolutions of "schools," even some in the twentieth century, have tacitly assumed this "classic" tenet of art.

The Dada-Surrealists, in their animosity against the "conventional" image of man and his world—what roughly may be called the *photographic* image—were attacking not the means of art, but its end; not the image of man and nature in all its variety and possibility, but the lack of imaginative energy with which the classical-humanist tradition was being preserved by the pictorial and literary arts. Even Futurism's violent conversion of the Cubist schema to machine imagery did not suit the Dadaists' revolt; this was because they could sense the academic future of so systematic a formal procedure as Cubism proposed; surely enough, today abstract art has arrived at its own rigid, sterile academism.

It was, then, in behalf of the inherent vitality of classical-humanism that the Dada-Surrealist spirit proceeded with its kudos, its tricks, its shocks and its chef-d'oeuvres—of which certainly Duchamp's great glass, *The Bride Denuded* (*etc.*), owned by the Philadelphia Museum since it acquired the Arensburg Collection, is one of the most important: a combined trick, shock, kudo and chef-d'oeuvre. Here man is insect, mannikin, hieroglyph, and even "thing." What, exactly, does *The Bride* "say"? It says that man exists by showing how very *specially* he *can* exist. . . . On the other hand non objective art is actually pre-human if post-humanist: the world-without-man—the world that, like original nature, could exist, and did exist, before man; it is a world, moreover, not necessarily implying that crucial evolutionary movement of nature that brought man into being—man, one should add, with all his astonishing ability to transform and "distort" himself and the world around him. . . .

Accordingly, something most significant lies in the fact that, at the same moment that twentieth-century painting was girding itself to make a complete break with representationalism, the "representational" movies came into being and cast their universal public spell. If Surrealist painting and collage, with its supreme dislocation, its fragmented and as it were "para-plegic" world of the senses, was to attack classical humanism, it was to attack its complacency, not its historical roots in man. On the contrary, in embracing the non-representational world, abstract art ultimately took the most radical step possible against human and social consciousness as the cradle, critic and creator of aesthetic values. Hence, automatically, while in a prejudiced and deceptive way, the movies adopted a hostile position toward abstract art, though on a moral rather than an artistic basis; in this distinction within the character of the movies' opposition to abstract art lies the "rub" of complexity and vagueness about the issue I have proposed: whether *as an art* they have prolonged the life of the classical human image. For, as I have said, they can be, and have been, as expressionistic, as highly "formal," even as abstract as they please; the obstacle in the way of their being as much so as they please is not technical limitation, but simply the arbitrary premises of filmdom's highly organized—if now wobbly—commercial art.

One need not stress why these premises are so "arbitrary." The point at issue is why, commercially or not, the movies may be said to take the *aesthetic* side of the classic human image. Let me point out the naïve "magic of effect" that clings to the junkiest movie. The movies' hallucination of reality is a theme to which I have devoted many thousands of words, and always with the assumption that the terms of the formulation, "reality" and "hallucination," have an equal and reflexive weight. *Reality* in the movies reasserts "content" in the classic aesthetic dualism, *hallucination* reasserts "form." What made the timing of the movies' advent so significant was exactly that the whole tradition which a painter such as Ingres had inherited from the Renaissance, and the super-photographic perfection he gave that tradition, was swiftly turning into dull academism, which seemed to the Romantics, and finally the Expressionists and the Cubists, to have a static, unbearably complacent look.

Just at this moment of greatest peril for the classic human image, the mechanism of photography intervened to mock the accumulated craft of the hand and the pencil, the hand and the brush. One might argue that photography—despite its early motives both "aesthetic" and "romantic"—killed academic art; well and good, but suppose it also killed the classic human image? If I think that photography did not do this, but the opposite, *revived* the classic human image, it is only because photography began to move: became the *movies*. Suddenly man's representational image was galvanized, and in this sense human identity in art was given a new meaning through its additional element: *kinesis*. Painting and sculpture "move" in a quite different sense from the cinema. It is instructive that not until after the movies were invented, and had progressed in technique, did the artist's eye, through Futurism, dedicate itself to an isolated "aesthetic" of movement; to a plastic which, in substance, was merely the analysis of optical mechanism made possible by the camera.

Of course, movement in the movies is already—largely owing to the requirements of the commercial product—a monotonous, by no means sufficiently aesthetic, cult. Yet one finds serious theorists of the film almost automatically insisting on the value of movement as such: on broad panoramas and swift changes of the centers of action. To be sure, this is only one of the aesthetic conditioned reflexes of a still young art, an art still naïvely inflamed by the extent to which it surpasses stage action in narrative scope and significance. On one side, the movies challenge the novel in this scope and significance, while on the other they have the literal vision of the stage (and of painting) and at last has assimilated the stage's oral dialogue. But it is fatal to dwell on the achievements of the movies as a "great" synthetic art. Among the manifold attempts to reproduce famous novels and "expand" famous plays on the screen, merely a handful have lacked the most disastrous flaws, and even with these, it would be dangerous to try to prove they deserve to be compared with the originals.

My object here is not to exalt specimens of the film but to hail the movies as the probable savior of the classic human image in our age—certainly, as an aesthetic force which has specifically "prolonged" the life of that image. What academic painting had shown as overrefined and static, the movies began to present as crude if refinable nature and as notably fluid. No art medium can convey so immediate a *sensation* of time in its changes, its whims and provocative shifts, as the movies. And yet, because basically photography remains a mirror (something it is very hard for it not to remain), the world of man, with man as the chief actor, is incontestably the abiding subject of this sensationally mirrored flux. To exclude man and nature as organic surfaces, as the actual contexture of the social world, would be, for the movies, simply to give movement not to life as such, but to the canon which non-objective art has bestowed on life; to the non-mirroring wall-décor of extreme abstractionism . . . where man is not his own spectacle and where the only "recognizable" elements are atmosphere and geometric form.

Shall it be asked, now, whether it is necessary *for man to be his own spectacle?* Maybe human self-consciousness, for all its supposed glories, is actually a handicap; maybe it is not only unnecessary, maybe it is undesirable! Do not the moral disquisitions of the new existentialist schools of philosophy hint as much? Maybe human *existence* was a pretentious and arrogant error. Maybe, too, all that is the bad conscience of idealism itself—of man as consciously the perfectible being. I wish to suggest, nevertheless, that in failing to report man in the fluid grip of his historic fate as man, non-objectivism has created a gap in the texture of consciousness itself, which only the absolute withdrawal of the individual from the world can adequately mend. This is doubtless a prejudiced, though not necessarily an inflexible, view of the values of non-objective painting. Possibly there should be, as there are and have been, moments of *human* as well as *individual* self-negation. But is not such self-negation always the function of thought itself?—and does not the crude experience of the world supply it aside from all reaching toward aesthetic feelings and artistic creation? Maybe the "gap" is inherent in consciousness. But objectively, blank walls and the void have always supplied this gap, and oftener than one may like; philosophy is its traditional antidote, art its traditional mirror. Maybe non-objective paintings are so many portraits of the void in its fluid and static moods. . . . But such a "portrait art"—a mirror of its own—would seem, in comparison with the whole of human experience, both narrow and tending to barrenness. I suggest that the lowly movies are, after all, a positive antidote to this extreme convention of modern painting; that even the banes of commercial films, the superspectacle and the mad melodrama, are athletic fields where the classic human image continues to prove its eligibility in the Olympiad of the art forms.

HOLLIS ALPERT

The Film Is Modern Theatre*

"Whether a story is presented to us on a screen or on a stage,
it is still a theatrical presentation."

*If sound and film had arrived together, as Edison originally
intended, there would have been far less mystique about the
art of the silent film. This, Hollis Alpert insists, would have
been a very good thing. It would have kept us from thinking
that the motion picture is something separate and aloof from
theatre and that it is somehow at its best when it does not
speak.*

*It is a larger step from this position to the standpoint that
"the film is not so much an art form as it is modern theatre."
Without discussing the documentary and experimental traditions, Alpert centers his attention on the mass audience, interested in movies only for their dramatic stories. He says that
movies often do the job better than the theatre because they
have "the freedom of the novelist" to replace dialogue with
flashback or photographic revelation.*

*Alpert is a novelist and short-story writer, and was associate
fiction editor of* The New Yorker *magazine from 1950–1956.
He has written about films in* The Dreams and the Dreamers
(1962) and has been a motion-picture critic for the Saturday
Review *since 1950.*

There is a school of thought that the movies as a possible art
form came to a halt when the soundtrack was invented. The
cinematic medium thereafter proceeded to limp along, im-
peded and cluttered by this thing called words. In some circles,
which consider the theatre to be a privileged (and embattled)
sanctuary, movies have never been admitted to be a branch

* Hollis Alpert, "The Film Is Modern Theatre," article prepared
for U.S. Information Service for use by newspapers, magazines,
and radio stations abroad, December, 1957.

of the drama. Theatre geared to a stream of words was to be found only on the stage.

But movies refused to stay silent, and now and then they can be found talking very well indeed. It's even time to consider the possibility that the film, with its newly expanded screen and its superior resources for staging, is not only a form of theatre, but—in almost all ways—by far the best form.

This, however, is seldom admitted. One film historian upon being asked recently to list the ten best movies of all time quickly named ten pictures made before 1928. The list was a familiar one, including such movies as *The Cabinet of Dr. Caligari*, *City Lights*, and *Variety*. Nothing made after the era of sound came into being seemed, in his view, the equal of these silent classics. There are little cinema societies, all across the land, which meet periodically to worship before the altar of the silent screen. The prints are dark, scratched, nearly eroded away, but still they flicker on for rapt audiences of ten or twenty.

The theory held by many who attend these showings is that the cinema, first and last, is a visual medium and that its primary language is movement. The movement is created by a change in the image, or by a succession of images. The images can be made meaningful by clever juxtaposition, and by technical tricks such as the dissolve.

Movies did not talk from the very beginning because they did not know how to. It is true that a silent-movie technique developed and that it was often used beautifully, but why should silence be the language of the movies for all time? The reason the movies developed a language separate from speech was the need for a substitute. That movies have been enriched as a result goes without question, but to confine the movies to the silent technique would be like confining acting to pantomime.

To stay with the theoretical a bit longer—the movie camera does not necessarily take moving pictures, nor is the taking of moving pictures its prime function. The camera is but one step in an operation that has the object of deceiving the eye and creating an illusion. The reason that fifty or sixty million Americans go each week to the movies is not to have their eyes washed (as is sometimes assumed) but to see lifelike illusions, and, more than anything else, to be told dramatic stories. The film is not so much an art form as it is modern theatre. Whether a story is presented to us on a screen or on a stage, it is still a theatrical presentation. The movies are, in essence, popular theatre. When the mass audience goes to the movies rather than to a stage play, it is not only because tickets are cheaper or because the material is more easily comprehended, but because it is getting, in many ways, a better show.

This mass audience, from year to year, has come in for some extraordinary lambasting. The movie public is derided as being made up largely of adolescents, or of having a twelve-year-old mentality, of lacking taste and discrimination, of being fickle, capricious, ignorant, and vulgar. It is supposed to be an audience that punishes thought, that shies from the controversial, that laps up puerility, foolishness, the sensational, and the saccharine. Periodically on the stage will appear a play showing Hollywood to be a hotbed of asininity and cynicism, making products for the entertainment of morons. The movies, either out of courage or abject humility, will then buy the play and make a movie showing the same point.

On the other hand, the theatre audience is something else again. It is assumed to have taste, discrimination, a mature mentality, background, breeding, and, above all, a feeling for theatre.

Meanwhile, in spite of a passionate love for theatre on the part of a good many, the theatre continues its decline. There are now about seventy Broadway productions a year, in contrast to more than two hundred shows on the boards twenty-five years ago.

Luckily, the movies, more through accident than by design, are currently filling the gap, and providing us with theatre— good, bad, and indifferent, but theatre nevertheless. . . .

It took Laurence Olivier's *Henry V* to make a good many of us realize that a Shakespeare play could come on film to a stunning life never possible on the stage. Olivier's subsequent *Hamlet*, the Mankiewicz-Houseman *Julius Caesar*, Castellani's *Romeo and Juliet*, have made the realization clearer. All the cumbersome and obsolete stage trappings were thrown in the discard; the Elizabethan speech was able to shine amidst new, but quite proper settings. Interpretations may always be quarreled with; in staged Shakespeare as well as filmed Shakespeare. In the films there were cuts, excisions, even the elimination of a character here and there. When someone complains gloomily about the cuts in *Romeo and Juliet* it is considered only polite not to ask which of the speeches were most sorely missed, and to assume, instead, that every cultivated person reads the play at least once every two weeks. I, for one, will not look the gift horse in the mouth too closely. I would rather recognize the fact that Shakespeare now has a popular audience no one prior to 1930 could ever have dreamed of.

This isn't only because the movies can stage the Battle of Agincourt when the theatre cannot. In the cases I have mentioned above the lines came out clearer and more richly. They are, after all, spoken under optimum conditions; they can be heard as well by the pauper as by the rich man. In the Mankiewicz *Julius Caesar* millions have seen a magnificent— even fabulous—portrayal of Cassius, now also the possession of generations to come, as Booth's Hamlet was not. Part of the success of Cassius' interpretation by John Gielgud was made possible by the use of the close-up, a tool unavailable to the stage.

This notion that the theatre is one thing and the film quite another has been widespread for a long time. It has failed to take into account the continual development of the motion-picture form, from silence (and the eerie acting style the silence engendered) to the full use of modern screen and stage techniques. So astute a critic as the late James Agate put himself on record as follows:

I regard theatregoing as one thing, and filmgoing as quite another, and do not allow my films to impinge upon my plays. It is in the spectacular as opposed to the dramatic category that I place the films. The theatre, which talks about things rather than shows them, necessarily calls for a certain amount of imagination on the part of the playgoer, whereas the film, by showing everything, calls for no imagination at all.

I enjoy reading Agate, but on the above point I am afraid he was seeing through the mirror very darkly. It is axiomatic that, for dramatic effect, it is far more efficient to show some-

thing happening rather than to talk about it. Dialogue on the
stage, the screen, or in fiction has its best use when it advances
the action, and characterizes. That the movies were able to
eliminate that opening scene in which the maid and the butler
talked about how late the master came home last night has
been a relief to all of us. And when it is necessary to explain
why Aunt Sadie behaves so curiously it is sometimes better
not to have a friend of the family explain it, but instead to
backflash and show the significant moment that changed Aunt
Sadie. The movies in this respect have the freedom of the
novelist, a freedom playwrights have always envied. Talking
about things on the stage all too often brings on boredom,
instead of stimulating the imagination.

But good dialogue—talk that interests and that also advances the action—can occur in movies as in plays. Films
stimulate the imagination if the stories they tell are imaginatively stimulating. The limitation is not in the form, but in
the material.

Recently I had occasion to see some movies made from
Broadway plays of a few seasons ago. How much more satisfying, it struck me, to see *Summertime* (made from *The Time
of the Cuckoo* by Arthur Laurents) in its film version. Instead
of a stage Venice, we have a real Venice.

It is also astonishing how movies of mature content appear
more and more frequently. *The Country Girl* (enhanced considerably in its transition from stage to screen) catapults its
star to an Academy Award, and sets the producers to wondering which of its ingredients caused its success. Was it the
stars, Bing Crosby and Grace Kelly? Then *Marty*, without
name stars, comes along, a low-budget film that has become
one of the more successful of recent years. The writing is of
a high order in both these pictures; the characterizations are
sound and sensitive. It is no wonder that Hollywood currently
is bidding for plays, the best television scripts, novels, and
short stories. The audience, having grown increasingly more
selective in recent years, is showing a desire for the intelligent
motion picture. . . .

ALLARDYCE NICOLL

*Film and Theatre**

"If the theatre stands thus for mankind, the cinema stands
for the individual."

*In this comparison of drama and film, written not long after
the coming of sound, Allardyce Nicoll, then professor of the
history of drama at Yale, speaks up firmly for accepting the
conventions of the stage—its essential nature as a bold, imaginative, poetic, or spectacular illusion. Like Walter Kerr in our
own day, he declares that "the realistic theatre" has lost its
strength; we must reject naturalism, "the cheap and ugly
simian chatter of familiar conversation."*

*Evidently the film has more to do than take over this latter
function, for he suggests that realism in the film has unrestricted scope and therefore expands our imagination—in out-
door environment, in visual imagery, in Disney cartoon form.
Nicoll does not try to include in his theory the epic sense of
the crowd and of history found in documentary films from
Potemkin to The True Glory. The essential thing, he says, is
to become aware that in the dramatic realm, "absolutely
counter to what would have been our first answer," stage
characters are types, speaking lines that challenge mankind,
whereas we "impute greater power of individual life to the
figures we see on the screen."*

When we witness a film, do we anticipate something we should
not expect from a stage performance, and, if so, what effect
has this upon our appreciation of film acting? At first, we
might be tempted to dismiss such a query or to answer it
easily and glibly. There is no essential difference, we might

* Allardyce Nicoll, "Film Reality: The Cinema and the Theatre," from *Film and Theatre*. New York, Crowell, 1936. Pp. 164–
168, 171, 177–178, 182–186, 186–191.

say, save in so far as we expect greater variety and movement on the screen than we do on the stage; and for acting, that, we might reply, is obviously the same as stage acting although perhaps more stabilised in type form. Do we not see Charles Laughton, Cedric Hardwicke, Ernest Thesiger, Elizabeth Bergner now in the theatre, now in the cinema? To consider further, we might say, were simply to indulge in useless and uncalled-for speculation.

Nevertheless, the question does demand just a trifle more of investigation. Some few years ago a British producing company made a film of Bernard Shaw's *Arms and the Man*. This film, after a few exciting shots depicting the dark streets of a Balkan town, the frenzied flight of the miserable fugitives and the clambering of Bluntschli onto Raina's window terrace, settled down to provide what was fundamentally a screen-picture of the written drama. The dialogue was shortened, no doubt, but the shots proceeded more or less along the dramatic lines established by Shaw, and nothing was introduced which he had not originally conceived in preparing his material for the stage. The result was that no more dismal film has ever been shown to the public. On the stage *Arms and the Man* is witty, provocative, incisively stimulating; its characters have a breath of genuine theatrical life; it moves, it breathes, it has vital energy. In the screen version all that life has fled, and, strangest thing of all, those characters—Bluntschli, Raina, Sergius—who are so exciting on the boards, looked to the audience like a set of wooden dummies, hopelessly patterned. Performed by a third-rate amateur cast their life-blood does not so ebb from them, yet here, interpreted by a group of distinguished professionals, they wilted and died—died, too, in such forms that we could never have credited them with ever having had a spark of reality. Was there any basic reason for this failure?

THE CAMERA'S TRUTH

The basic reason seems to be simply this—that practically all effectively drawn stage characters are types and that in the cinema we demand individualisation, or else that we recognise stage figures as types and impute greater power of independent life to the figures we see on the screen. This judgment, running so absolutely counter to what would have been our first answer to the original question posited, may seem grossly distorted, but perhaps some further consideration will demonstrate its plausibility. When we go to the theatre, we expect theatre and nothing else. We know that the building we enter is a playhouse; that behind the lowered curtain actors are making ready, dressing themselves in strange garments and transforming their natural features; that the figures we later see on the boards are never living persons of king and bishop and clown, but merely men pretending for a brief space of time to be like these figures. Dramatic illusion is never (or so rarely as to be negligible) the illusion of reality: it is always imaginative illusion, the illusion of a period of make-believe. All the time we watch Hamlet's throes of agony we know that the character Hamlet is being impersonated by a man who presently will walk out of the stage-door in ordinary clothes and an autograph-signing smile on his face. True, volumes have been written on famous dramatic characters—Greek, Elizabethan English and modern Norwegian—and these volumes might well seem to give the lie to such assumptions. Have not Shakespeare's characters seemed so real to a few observers that we have on our shelves books specifically concerned with the girlhood of his heroines—a girlhood the dramas themselves denied us?

These studies, however, should not distract us from the essential truth that the greatest playwrights have always aimed at presenting human personality in bold theatric terms. Hamlet seizes on us, not because he is an individual, not because in him Shakespeare has delineated a particular prince of Denmark, but because in Hamlet there are bits of all men; he is a composite character whose lineaments are determined by dramatic necessity, and through that he lives. Fundamentally, the truly vital theatre deals in stock figures. Like a child's box of bricks, the stage's material is limited; it is the possibilities in arrangement that are well-nigh inexhaustible. Audiences thrill to see new situations born of fresh sociological conditions, but the figures set before them in significant plays are conventionally fixed and familiar. Of Romeos there are many, and of Othellos legion. Character on the stage is restricted and stereotyped and the persons who play upon the boards are governed, not by the strangely perplexing processes of life but by the established terms of stage practice. Bluntschli represents half a hundred similar rationalists; the idealism of thou-

sands is incorporated in Sergius; and Raina is an eternal stage
type of the perplexing feminine. The theatre is populated, not
by real individuals whose boyhood or girlhood may legitimately be traced, but by heroes and villains sprung full-bodied
from Jove's brain, by clowns and pantaloons whose youth is
unknown and whose future matters not after the curtain's fall.

In the cinema we demand something different. Probably
we carry into the picture-house prejudices deeply ingrained
in our beings. The statement that "the camera cannot lie" has
been disproved by millions of flattering portraits and by
dozens of spiritualistic pictures which purport to depict fairies
but which mostly turn out to be faintly disguised pictures of
ballet-dancers or replicas of figures in advertisements of night-
lights. Yet in our heart of hearts we credit the truth of that
statement. A picture, a piece of sculpture, a stage-play—
these we know were created by man; we have watched the
scenery being carried in back stage and we know we shall see
the actors, turned into themselves again, bowing at the conclusion of the performance. In every way the "falsity" of a
theatrical production is borne in upon us, so that we are prepared to demand nothing save a theatrical truth. For the
films, however, our orientation is vastly different. Several
periodicals, it is true, have endeavored to let us into the secrets
of the moving-picture industry and a few favored spectators
have been permitted to make the rounds of the studios; but
from ninety per cent of the audience the actual methods employed in the preparation of a film remain far off and dimly
realised. . . .

The strange paradox, then, results:—that, although the
cinema introduces improbabilities and things beyond nature at
which any theatrical director would blench and murmur soft
nothings to the air, the filmic material is treated by the audience with far greater respect (in its relation to life) than the
material of the stage. Our conceptions of life in Chicago gang-
sterdom and in distant China are all colored by films we have
seen. What we have witnessed on the screen becomes the
"real" for us. In moments of sanity, maybe, we confess that
of course we do not believe this or that, but, under the spell
again, we credit the truth of these pictures even as, for all our
professed superiority, we credit the truth of newspaper para-
graphs. . . .

That most of the films so far produced have not made use

of the peculiar methods inherent in the cinematic approach need not blind us to the fact that here is an instrument capable of expressing through combined visual and vocal means something of that analytical searching of the spirit which has formed the pursuit of modern poets and novelists. Not, of course, that in this analytic and realistic method are to be enclosed the entire boundaries of the cinema. The film has the power of giving an impression of actuality and it can thrill us by its penetrating truth to life: but it may, if we desire, call into existence the strangest of visionary worlds and make these too seem real. The enchanted forest of *A Midsummer Night's Dream* will always on the stage prove a thing of lath and canvas and paint; an enchanted forest in the film might truly seem haunted by a thousand fears and supernatural imaginings. This imaginary world, indeed, is one that our public has cried for and demanded, and our only regret may be that the producers, lacking vision, have compromised and in compromising have descended to banalities. Taking their sets of characters, they thrust these, willy-nilly, into scenes of ornate splendour, exercising their inventiveness, not to create the truly fanciful but to fashion the exaggeratedly and hyperbolically absurd. Hotels more sumptuous than the Waldorf-Astoria or the Ritz; liners outvying the pretentions of the *Normandie*; speed that sets Malcolm Campbell to shame; melodies inappropriately rich—these have crowded in on us again and yet again. Many spectators are becoming irritated and bored with scenes of this sort, for mere exaggeration of life's luxuries is not creative artistically. . . .

When the history of the stage since the beginning of the nineteenth century comes to be written with that impartiality which only the viewpoint of distant time can provide, it will most certainly be deemed that the characteristic development of these hundred-odd years is the growth of realism and the attempted substitution of naturalistic illusion in place of a conventional and imaginative illusion. In the course of this development stands forth Ibsen as the outstanding pioneer and master. At the same time, this impartial survey may also decide that within the realistic method lie the seeds of disruption. It may be recognised that, while Ibsen was a genius of profound significance, for the drama Ibsenism proved a curse upon the stage. The whole realistic movement which strove to impose the conditions of real life upon the theatre may have served a salutary purpose for a time, but its vitality was but shortlived and, after the first excitement which attended the witnessing on the stage of things no one had hitherto dreamt of putting there had waned, its force and inspiring power was dissipated. Even if we leave the cinema out of account, we must observe that the realistic theatre in our own days has lost its strength. No doubt, through familiarity and tradition, plays in this style still prove popular and, popular success being the first requirement demanded of dramatic art, we must be careful to avoid wholesale condemnation; *Tobacco Road* and *Dead End* are things worthy of our esteem, definite contributions to the theatre of our day. But the continued appearance and success of naturalistic plays should not confuse the main issue, which is the question whether such naturalistic plays are likely in the immediate future to maintain the stage in that position we should all wish it to occupy. Facing this question fairly, we observe immediately that plays written in these terms are less likely to hold the attention of audiences over a period of years than are others written in a different style; because bound to particular conditions in time and place, they seem inevitably destined to be forgotten, or, if not forgotten, to lose their only valuable connotations. Even the dramas of Ibsen, instinct with a greater imaginative power than many works by his contemporaries and successors, do not possess, after the brief passing of forty years, the same vital significance they held for audiences of the eighties and nineties. If we seek for and desire a theatre which shall possess qualities likely to live over generations, unquestionably we must decide that the naturalistic play, made popular towards the close of the nineteenth century and still remaining in our midst, is not calculated to fulfil our highest wishes.

Of much greater importance, even, is the question of the position this naturalistic play occupies in its relations to the cinema. At the moment it still retains its popularity, but, we may ask, because of cinematic competition, is it not likely to fail gradually in its immediate appeal? The film has such a hold over the world of reality, can achieve expression so vitally in terms of ordinary life, that the realistic play must surely come to seem trivial, false and inconsequential. The truth is, of course, that naturalism on the stage must always be limited and insincere. Thousands have gone to *The Children's Hour* and come away fondly believing that what they have seen is life; they have not realised that here too the familiar stock figures, the type characterisations, of the theatre have been presented before them in modified forms. From this the drama cannot escape; little possibility is there of its delving deeply into the recesses of the individual spirit. That is a realm reserved for cinematic exploitation, and, as the film more and more explores this territory, does it not seem probable that theatre audiences will become weary of watching shows which, although professing to be "lifelike," actually are inexorably bound by the restrictions of the stage? Pursuing this path, the theatre truly seems doomed to inevitable destruction. Whether in its attempt to reproduce reality and give the illusion of actual events or whether in its pretence towards depth and subtlety in character-drawing, the stage is aiming at things alien to its spirit, things which so much more easily may be accomplished in the film that their exploitation on the stage gives only an impression of vain effort.

Is, then, the theatre, as some have opined, truly dying? Must it succumb to the rivalry of the cinema? The answer to that question depends on what the theatre does within the next ten or twenty years. If it pursues naturalism further, unquestionably little hope will remain; but if it recognises to the full the conditions of its own being and utilises those qualities which it, and it alone, possesses, the very thought of rivalry may disappear. Quite clearly, the true hope of the theatre lies in a rediscovery of convention, in a deliberate throwing-over of all thoughts concerning naturalistic illusion and in an embracing of that universalising power which so closely belongs to the dramatic form when rightly exercised. By doing these things, the theatre has achieved greatness and distinction in the past. We admire the playhouses of Periclean Athens and Elizabethan England; in both a basis was found in frank acceptance of the stage spectacle as a thing of pretence, with no attempt made to reproduce the outer forms of everyday life. Conventionalism ruled in both, and consequently out of both could spring a vital expression, with manifestations capable of appealing not merely to the age in which they originated but to future generations also. Precisely because Æschylus and Shakespeare did not try to copy life, because they presented their themes in highly conventional forms, their works have the quality of being independent of time and place. Their characters were more than photographic copies of known originals; their plots took no account of the terms of actuality; and their language soared on poetic wings. To this again must we come if our theatre is to be a vitally arresting force. So long as the stage is bound by the fetters of realism, so long as we judge theatrical characters by reference to individuals with whom we are acquainted, there is no possibility of preparing dialogue which shall rise above the terms of common existence.

From our playwrights, therefore, we must seek for a new foundation. No doubt many journeymen will continue to pen for the day and the hour alone, but of these there have always been legion; what we may desire is that the dramatists of higher effort and broader ideal do not follow the journeyman's way. Boldly must they turn from efforts to delineate in subtle and intimate manner the psychological states of individual men and women, recognising that in the wider sphere the drama has its genuine home. The cheap and ugly simian chatter of familiar conversation must give way to the ringing tones of a poetic utterance, not removed far off from our comprehension, but bearing a manifest relationship to our current speech. . . .

Established on these terms native to its very existence, and consequently far removed from the ways of the film, the theatre need have no fear that its hold over men's minds will diminish and fail. It will maintain a position essentially its own to which other arts may not aspire.

THE WAY OF THE FILM

For the film are reserved things essentially distinct. Possibility of confusion between the two has entered in only because the playhouse has not been true to itself. To the cinema is given a sphere, where the subjective and objective approaches are combined, where individualisation takes the place of type characterisation, where reality may faithfully be imitated and where the utterly fantastic equally is granted a home, where Walt Disney's animated flowers and flames exist alongside the figures of men and women who may seem more real than the figures of the stage, where a visual imagery in moving forms may thrill and awaken an age whose ears, while still alert to listen to poetic speech based on or in tune with the common language of the day, has forgotten to be moved by the tones of an earlier dramatic verse. Within this field lies the possibility of an artistic expression equally powerful as that of the stage, though essentially distinct from that. The distinction is determined by the audience reactions to the one and to the other. In the theatre the spectators are confronted by characters which, if successfully delineated, always possess a quality which renders them greater than separate individuals. When Clifford Odets declares that by the time he came to write his first play, *Awake and Sing!* he understood clearly that his

interest was not in the presentation of an individual's problems, but in those of a whole class. In other words, the task was to find a theatrical form with which to express the mass as hero—

he is doing no more than indicate that he has the mind and approach of a dramatist. All the well-known figures created in tragedy and comedy since the days of Aristophanes and Æschylus have presented in this way the lineaments of universal humanity. If the theatre stands thus for mankind, the cinema, because of the willingness on the part of spectators to accept as the image of truth the moving forms cast on the screen, stands for the individual. It is related to the modern novel in the same respect that the older novel was related to the stage. Impressionistic and expressionistic settings may serve for the theatre—even may we occasionally fall back on plain curtains without completely losing the interest of our audiences; the cinema can take no such road, for, unless in frankly artificially created films (such as the Walt Disney cartoon), we cling to our preconceived beliefs and clamour for the three-dimensional, the exact and the authentic. In a stage play such as *Yellow Jack* we are prepared to accept a frankly formal background, because we know that the actors are actors merely; but for the treatment of similar material in *The Prisoner of Shark's Island* and *The Story of Pasteur* cinematic authenticity is demanded. At first glance, we might aver that, because of this, the film had fewer opportunities for artistic expression than the stage; but further consideration will demonstrate that the restrictions are amply compensated for by an added scope. Our illusion in the picture-house is certainly less "imaginative" than the illusion which attends us in the theatre, but it has the advantage of giving increased

appreciation of things which are outside nature. Through this
the purely visionary becomes almost tangible and the impossible assumes shapes easy of comprehension and belief. The
sense of reality lies at the foundation of the film, yet real time
and real space are banished; the world we move in may be far
removed from the world ordinarily about us; and symbols
may find a place alongside common objects of little or no
importance. If we apply the theory of "psychological distance"
to theatre and film we realise the force of each. For any kind
of aesthetic appreciation this distance is always demanded; before we can hope to feel the artistic qualities of any form we
must be able to set ourselves away from it, to experience the
stimulus its contemplation creates and at the same time have
no call to put the reactions to that stimulus into play. This
distance obviously may be of varying degrees; sometimes it is
reduced, sometimes it provides a vast gulf between the observer and the art object. Furthermore the variation may be
of two kinds—variation between one art and another, and
variation between forms within the sphere of a single art.
Music is further removed from reality than sculpture, but in
music there may be an approach towards commonly heard
sounds and in sculpture abstract shapes may take the place
of familiar forms realistically delineated. Determination of
the proper and legitimate approach will come from a consideration of the sense of distance between the observer and
the object; the masterpieces in any art will necessarily be
based on an adaptation to the particular requirements of their
own peculiar medium of expression.

Applying this principle to theatre and cinema, we will recognise that whereas there is a strong sense of reality in audience reactions to the film, yet always there is the fact that the
pictures on the screen are two-dimensional images and hence
removed a stage from actual contact with the spectators. What
may happen if successful three-dimensional projection is introduced we cannot tell; at present we are concerned with a
flat screen picture. This gulf between the audience and the
events presented to them will permit a much greater use of
realism than the stage may legitimately employ. The presence
of flesh-and-blood actors in the theatre means that it is comparatively easy to break the illusion proper to the theatre and
in doing so to shatter the mood at which any performance
ought to aim. This statement may appear to run counter to

others made above, but there is no essential contradiction involved. The fact remains that, when living person is set before living person—actor before spectator—a certain deliberate conventionalising is demanded of the former if the aesthetic impression is not to be lost, whereas in the film, in which immediately a measure of distance is imposed between image and spectator, greater approaches to real forms may be permitted, even although these have to exist alongside impossibilities and fantastic symbols far removed from the world around us. This is the paradox of cinematic art.

Herein lies the true filmic realm and to these things the cinema, if it also is to be true to itself, must tend, just as towards the universalising and towards conventionalism must tend the theatre if it is to find a secure place among us. Fortunately the signs of the age are propitious; experiments in poetic drama and production of films utilising at least a few of the significant methods basically associated with cinematic art give us authority for believing that within the next decade each will discover firmer and surer foothold and therefore more arresting control over their material. Both stage and cinema have their particular and peculiar functions; their houses may stand side by side, not in rivalling enmity, but in that friendly rivalry which is one of the compelling forces in the wider realm of artistic achievement.

RUDOLF ARNHEIM

Epic and Dramatic Film*

"The epic style . . . is not concerned with change and solution
but with the presentation of invariable existence."

In this provocative note on the difference between two general types of film, Rudolf Arnheim quotes from an essay by Goethe: "The epic poem preferably describes man as he acts outwardly: battles, travels, any kind of enterprise that requires some sensuous breadth; tragedy shows man led toward the inside." He suggests that the dramatic film undertakes the solution of a particular problem, which may succeed or fail, whereas "the epic style of narration has a preference for stringing episodes in sequences."

Like all dichotomies, this one probably cannot be made to cover all, or even most, cases, but film spectacles, documentaries, and biographies might deserve further study in the light of such a definition. Arnheim further urges that "there is no documentary theatre, but there are documentary films, and they are epic," and adds that biography is often in epic form. "Here the central figure does not journey through space, as does Ulysses, but through time." Professor Arnheim is a member of the psychology faculty at Sarah Lawrence College and is the author of Film as Art *and* Art and Visual Perception.

There are essentially three properties of film as an artistic medium that need to be considered when it comes to deciding which kinds of narrative subject matter are suitable and how they should be presented. First of all, film is a visual art, which tells its stories to the eyes—even when sound is also used. Second, the pictures that tell the story are obtained mechanically by photography, that is, they can portray reality

* Rudolf Arnheim, "Epic and Dramatic Film," *Film Culture*, Vol. 3, No. 1, 1957. Pp. 9–10.

with documentary faithfulness. Third, these pictures can be made to follow each other in an uninterrupted sequence even though they may show the most different settings and actions taken at different times. As an additional and more practical condition the film maker is expected to remember that on the average the telling of the story should not take longer than an hour and fifteen minutes.

Two concepts that have proved to be useful in literary criticism can be applied fruitfully also to the film. In an essay "On Epic and Dramatic Poetry," written in 1797, Goethe asserts: "The epic poem preferably describes man as he acts outwardly: battles, travels, any kind of enterprise that requires some sensuous breadth; tragedy shows man led toward the inside, therefore the plot of a genuine tragedy requires little space." For Goethe this distinction coincided with that between an action told in the form of a poem or novel (epic) and one performed on the stage (dramatic). Indeed, the broad descriptions of varying settings and extensive happenings, which are characteristically epic, hardly suit the theatre. The stage no more than alludes to the setting of the action; it is limited to narrow space and can move from one location to the other only by means of clumsy devices. We may say of the film that it has put the epos on the stage. In fact, this is one of the main characteristics of the film medium.

When the two concepts are applied to film, they no longer designate the difference between outwardly and inwardly directed action. What distinguishes the "dramatic" film is rather that it undertakes the solution of a particular problem: it ties the knot by presenting the problem, describes the conflict caused by it, then attempts to find a solution, and finally the catastrophe of the hero wrecked by his failure to solve the insoluble. Dramatic film, just as the dramatic stage play, is dynamic. It presents a plot that proceeds from step to step, and one of its most characteristic effects is "suspense." Also it rigorously limits the presentation to what is needed to explain the motives of the characters and to make the events progress. There is no time for broad description in dramatic film. As much as possible it cuts down on references to what happened before the beginning of the actual story, and it does not linger on the aftermath of the catastrophe. Also, secondary plots are kept in the background of the main conflict.

The epic film, on the other hand, neither deals with a prob-

lem nor offers a solution. True, it also can seize upon the great
discords of life, which create human suffering, but, unlike the
dramatic film, it limits itself to describing their manifestations. *Dr. Jekyll and Mr. Hyde*, a typically dramatic film,
poses a problem. A man gravely clashes with his environment because the good and the bad aspects of his nature have
produced two independent personalities. The film develops
the problem, creates suspense, and finally shows the protagonist killed by his environment, thus indicating that the conflict
was insoluble. Compare this kind of treatment with *Don
Quixote*, where again a man clashes with his world—this one
impelled by ideals of human perfection, nobility, and beauty.
But the problem is neither analyzed nor solved. The one permanent and unchanging conflict is shown in a sequence of
examples, which, however, do not represent steps toward a
solution. More or less accidentally, the story comes to an
end—or rather fails to continue—at some point. Epic film
is static.

Epic tasks may naturally be expressed through the film
because of its capacity to describe reality in all its detail and
to ignore the impediments of time and space. There is no
documentary theatre, but there are documentary films, and
they are epic. On the other hand, the film, just as the theatre,
can develop a plot in the dramatic manner and create suspense. Almost invariably, however, the dramatic film will be
found also to have epic, descriptive aspects. Even the kind
of intimate film play that limits itself strictly to a limited
space, a few characters, and a minimum of external action
will seem descriptive when compared to similar plays on the
stage because the camera inevitably captures with a single
sweep so many details of the setting that the stage looks bare
and abstract in comparison.

Film describes, but it describes swiftly. It leaps from one
place to the other, from small objects seen at close quarters
to the encompassing survey of the whole, and thus in a few
seconds records hundreds of things which the epic poet could
not enumerate in pages. It is for this reason that film can treat
an epic subject in little more than an hour.

The epic style of narration has a preference for stringing
episodes in sequences. Such chainlike composition stresses the
static character of the tale. Don Quixote passes through a

series of adventures; so does Ulysses. Sometimes the central figure is a mere pretext, which provides a common denominator for a series of descriptions, or he is a sharply drawn type whose conflicts with his surroundings are shown in ever new examples. The films of Chaplin and Buster Keaton are prototypes of the epic form. These films have been accused of lacking structure, of being episodes patched together. Of course, even an epic work needs unity and structure; but the basic shape of these films merely applies the ancient principle of epic narration. To some extent, the episodes that constitute them are mutually exchangeable, and even the famous endings (Chaplin walks away and disappears on the horizon without having married the pretty girl) are not only a personal expression of resignation but first of all a necessary feature of the epic style, which is not concerned with change and solution but with the presentation of invariable existence.

Occasionally three or four of Chaplin's short films have been combined to a full-sized "feature" film. The result seemed satisfactory because the epic film invites such enumeration whereas dramatic films that deserve the name would be expected to resist the same treatment.

Attempts have also been made to go beyond the narrow span of the movie theatre program and to create larger epic cycles. The films of Chaplin or those of Buster Keaton or Mickey Mouse form together a kind of continuing narrative, which can be presented in installments because each episode is self-contained. This is less true for the continuing adventures of some hero that used to keep the attention of the audiences from chapter to chapter over long stretches of time. The chase after a criminal, for instance, was presented, and the fans would wait for the next chapter as avidly as they were looking forward to the daily installment of a current novel in the newspaper.

A noteworthy variety of the epic film is the biography. Here the central figure does not journey through space as does Ulysses, but through time. We watch a man maintaining himself against afflictions that turn up through the years but remaining basically the same person in spite of the changes time imposes upon him. Externally, a man's entanglement with time appears as dynamic or dramatic because the passing of time suggests a progression; but basically it is static and epic. Therefore, biography suits the film medium well, and so does the historical presentation of several generations as in *Cavalcade*. Here not a single person but a central group of people serves as the nucleus around which a panorama of changing periods, mores, and fashions evolves. In such films the fundamental task of the epic style is clearly revealed: it insists on the unchangeable nature of man.

ROBERT NATHAN

*A Novelist Looks at Hollywood**

"A picture is not at all like a play . . . it is like a novel, but
a novel to be seen, instead of told."

*Robert Nathan says he was surprised to learn, when he
came to Hollywood, that his own "craft of the novelist" was
more valuable than that of dramatic writing. He further discovered that making use of "the elements of the picture itself
can create the same effect of style as in the most excellent
paragraph of prose. It may not sound like beauty; it will look
like it."*

This brief note by a master of the short novel (One More
Spring; The Enchanted Cottage) *offers much compact observation and some encouragement for the screenwriter. He
points out that in the novel there is likely to be, in any case,
"the counterparts of long shots and close-ups, trucking shots
and dissolves." History has caught up with one of his points:
"the quiet, contemplative flow of the novel" has found, after
all, a fairly close counterpart on the screen with the work of
Antonioni in Italy. Perhaps there are more "singular and
lonely" viewers today, or at least it is no longer necessary to
"appeal to the full congregation."*

*Mr. Nathan has requested this editor to point out to the
reader that his article was written twenty years ago and that
he would not necessarily make the same observations about
the film industry of today.*

When I first came to Hollywood, to work in pictures, I
thought that I should have to learn to be a dramatist, that
the craft of the novelist would be of no use to me. I was
mistaken.

* Robert Nathan, "A Novelist Looks at Hollywood," *Hollywood
Quarterly*, Vol. 1, No. 2, 1945. Pp. 146–147.

I do not pretend to be a very good screenwriter; one does not learn an entire art in a single thrust. But I have learned something about it—enough, for instance, to recognize the screen play or story as a valid form; and enough to feel a profound respect for those master screen writers whose work, never published, usually slighted by the critics, seems to me some of the best writing being done anywhere in the country.

I also learned, to my surprise, that a picture is not at all like a play; that on the contrary, it is like a novel, but a novel to be seen, instead of told.

Of course, seeing is simply another way of telling. But eye and ear are different organs, and to be treated each with courtesy. One of the most difficult lessons I had to learn was never to entice the ear too much, away from the eye. Eye and ear must march together, or else fly apart; the evocation of beauty or its opposite through words, is something to be delicately examined; it must never interfere with the eye which watches.

At the same time, the writer who uses his camera, who makes use of all the elements of the picture itself, can create the same effect of style as in the most excellent paragraph of prose. It may not sound like beauty; it will look like it.

The picture has other characteristics of the novel: it ranges where it pleases, it studies the reactions of single characters, it deals in description and mood, it follows, by means of the camera, the single, unique vision of the writer. You will find, in every novel, the counterparts of long shots and close-ups, trucking shots, and dissolves; but you will find them in words addressed to the ear, instead of in pictures meant for the eye.

It is true that so far, at least, the quiet, contemplative flow of the novel has no counterpart on the screen. Quiet and contemplation are for the singular and lonely reader; when people come together to be entertained, the pace and rhythm of entertainment must be set for them. It must be set to please them all, each singly, and all together, for all together they give back to the screen an emotional response which is as much a part of the picture as the writing or direction. That is why it is difficult to judge a picture in the projection room; and why we have previews. The audience adds its own element to a picture; what emerges is a give-and-take, an intangible (but very real) relationship between the two.

There is something in itself exciting about pace, whether

on the screen or the tennis court, the hockey rink, or the podium. It is a pattern of satisfaction; it stirs the pulse; the eye, the ear, the heart moves from suspense to suspense, from climax to climax; it is a kind of inner dance.

In writing for the films, the writer is not altogether master of his pace. For in the end, the rhythm of the picture depends less upon words than upon direction, and cutting. The written dialogue might be as lean as Hemingway's, and yet seem slow, if the director's pulse is slow—or if the cutter fails to use his shears at the right moment. What that right moment may be, no writer can ascertain from the written page; the proof is on the film itself.

There are other disadvantages. The written novel is all; it is the complete work of art. The script is only a part of the final whole; and even in the script, many accents are heard; voices of producer, director, and supervisor. In a sense, they are editors; their eye is on the audience, they imagine for themselves the finished picture, they warn, and advise. And once the picture goes into production, still other editors appear and take over; the camera, the composer, designers, architects, the many technicians, all superb masters of their crafts; and finally, of course, the actors. In the end, the picture belongs to all of them—but first, in the beginning, from the small idea to the finished script, it is the writer's; and with this much, if he wishes, he can do his best.

That disappointment often, discouragement, and even heartbreak await him in Hollywood, I do not deny. There are so many things he cannot write about, so much he cannot say. It is not altogether the fault of the industry; rather, it is the fault of a youthful art, which, like the first miracle plays, or the paintings of the early masters, must appeal to the full congregation.

So much for the cons, and for the pros. There is something to be said on either side; I have tried to suggest here what that may be. I do not believe that to the reading eye the script will ever displace or even seriously dispute the novel, for general satisfaction; or that the novelist will find it altogether a sufficient form. But it *is* a form, and one which I believe presents a challenge to the novelist on his own grounds.

GEORGE BLUESTONE

Novels Into Film*

"The history of the fitful relationship between novel and
    film: overtly compatible, secretly hostile."

*Rejecting the assumption that actual visual metaphors from
literary sources can ever be transcribed in screen language,
George Bluestone insists that the two forms are necessarily
distinct. "Between the percept of the visual image," he says,
"and the concept of the mental image lies the root difference
between the two media."*

*This young literary critic, now at the University of Wash-
ington, whose book is based upon his doctoral dissertation in
the aesthetics of literature at Johns Hopkins University, con-
cludes his introductory chapter with this statement: "The
filmed novel, in spite of certain resemblances, will inevitably
become a different artistic entity from the novel on which it is
based." This is because the newer art has limits which depend
on "a moving image, mass audience, and industrial production." Any adaptation is not concerned with the unique
aspects of the novel but only with the events in it, as raw
material.*

THE TWO WAYS OF SEEING

Summing up his major intentions in 1913, D. W. Griffith is
reported to have said, "The task I'm trying to achieve is above
all to make you see."[1] Whether by accident or design, the
statement coincides almost exactly with an excerpt from Conrad's preface to *Nigger of the Narcissus* published sixteen

* George Bluestone, "The Limits of the Novel and the Limits
of the Film," *Novels Into Film*. Baltimore, Johns Hopkins Press,
1957. Pp. 1–2, 5–6, 20–21, 24, 25–27, 61–64.

[1] Lewis Jacobs, *The Rise of the American Film*. New York,
1939, p. 119.

years earlier: "My task which I am trying to achieve is, by the power of the written word, to make you hear, to make you feel—it is, before all, to make you *see*."[2] Aside from the strong syntactical resemblance, the coincidence is remarkable in suggesting the points at which film and novel both join and part company. On the one hand, that phrase "to make you see" assumes an affective relationship between creative artist and receptive audience. Novelist and director meet here in a common intention. One may, on the other hand, see visually through the eye or imaginatively through the mind. And between the percept of the visual image and the concept of the mental image lies the root difference between the two media.

Because novel and film are both organic—in the sense that aesthetic judgments are based on total ensembles which include both formal and thematic conventions—we may expect to find that differences in form and theme are inseparable from differences in media. Not only are Conrad and Griffith referring to different ways of seeing, but the "you's" they refer to are different. Structures, symbols, myths, values which might be comprehensible to Conrad's relatively small middle-class reading public would, conceivably, be incomprehensible to Griffith's mass public. Conversely, stimuli which move the heirs of Griffith's audience to tears, will outrage or amuse the progeny of Conrad's "you." The seeming concurrence of Griffith and Conrad splits apart under analysis, and the two arts turn in opposite directions. That, in brief, has been the history of the fitful relationship between novel and film: overtly compatible, secretly hostile.

On the face of it, a close relationship has existed from the beginning. The reciprocity is clear from almost any point of view: the number of films based on novels; the search for filmic equivalents of literature; the effect of adaptations on reading; box-office receipts for filmed novels; merit awards by and for the Hollywood community.

The moment the film went from the animation of stills to telling a story, it was inevitable that fiction would become the ore to be minted by story departments. Before Griffith's first year as a director was over, he had adapted, among others, Jack London's *Just Meat (For Love of Gold)*, Tolstoy's

---

[2] Joseph Conrad, *A Conrad Argosy*. New York, 1942, p. 83.

Resurrection, and Charles Reade's *The Cloister and the Hearth.* Sergei Eisenstein's essay "Dickens, Griffith, and the Film Today"[3] demonstrates how Griffith found in Dickens hints for almost every one of his major innovations. Particular passages are cited to illustrate the dissolve, the superimposed shot, the close-up, the pan, indicating that Griffith's interest in literary forms and his roots in Victorian idealism[4] provided at least part of the impulse for technical and moral content. . . .

Such statements as: "The film is true to the spirit of the book"; "It's incredible how they butchered the novel"; "It cuts out key passages, but it's still a good film"; "Thank God they changed the ending"—these and similar statements are predicated on certain assumptions which blur the mutational process. These standard expletives and judgments assume, among other things, a separable content which may be detached and reproduced, as the snapshot reproduces the kitten; that incidents and characters in fiction are interchangeable with incidents and characters in the film; that the novel is a norm and the film deviates at its peril; that deviations are permissible for vaguely defined reasons—exigencies of length or of visualization, perhaps—but that the extent of the deviation will vary directly with the "respect" one has for the original; that taking liberties does not necessarily impair the quality of the film, whatever one may think of the novel, but that such liberties are somehow a trick which must be concealed from the public.

What is common to all these assumptions is the lack of awareness that mutations are probable the moment one goes from a given set of fluid, but relatively homogeneous, conventions to another; that changes are *inevitable* the moment one abandons the linguistic for the visual medium. Finally, it is insufficiently recognized that the end products of novel and film represent different aesthetic genera, as different from each other as ballet is from architecture.

The film becomes a different *thing* in the same sense that a historical painting becomes a different thing from the his-

[3] Sergei Eisenstein, *Film Form.* Translated by Jay Leyda. New York, 1949, pp. 195–255.
[4] Jacobs, pp. 98–99.

torical event which it illustrates. It is as fruitless to say that film A is better or worse than novel B as it is to pronounce Wright's Johnson's Wax Building better or worse than Tchaikovsky's *Swan Lake*. In the last analysis, each is autonomous, and each is characterized by unique and specific properties. . . .

Where the moving picture comes to us directly through perception, language must be filtered through the screen of conceptual apprehension. And the conceptual process, though allied to and often taking its point of departure from the percept, represents a different mode of experience, a different way of apprehending the universe.

The distinction is a crucial one, for it generates differences which run all the way down the line from the media's ability to handle tropes, affect beholders, render states of consciousness (including dreams, memories, feelings, and imagination), to their respective methods of handling conventions, time, and space.

The linguistic trope is the novel's special way of rendering the shock of resemblance. By juxtaposing similar qualities in violently dissimilar things, language gets its revenge on the apparent disorder of life. It binds together a world which seems atomized and therefore chaotic to the primitive mind. Modern theories of symbolic thinking demonstrate that we necessarily see resemblances in the most ordinary perceptions. Arnheim points out that an illusion, to be strong, does not have to be complete in every detail: "everyone knows that a clumsy childish scribble of a human face consisting of two dots, a comma, and a dash may be full of expression and depict anger, amusement, fear. . . ." A kind of basic tropism is involved in such a process: the mind sees resemblances in the disparate sources of scribbled drawing and angry face.

So similar are linguistic and cognitive processes in finding resemblances that critics like Cleanth Brooks build their analytical systems around the metaphor. The difference between the artist who coins metaphors and the ordinary mind which classifies objects derives largely from the fact that the artist casts his net much wider. Where the cognitive mind finds common traits in collies and boxers and calls them dogs, the maker of tropes finds common qualities in slings, arrows, and outrageous fortune. Literary tropes, however, are distin-

guished from cognitive classification, first, by their verbal
origins and, second, by a kind of connotative luxuriance. Not
only does the power of the trope inhere in its figurative
character but in its ability to compound itself without damage
to intended meanings. Virginia Woolf, contrasting the novel
and film, is especially sensitive to the unique power of the
figure of speech. The images of a poet, she tells us, are compact of a thousand suggestions, of which the visual is only the
most obvious:

Even the simplest image: "my love's like a red, red rose, that's
newly sprung in June," presents us with impressions of moisture
and warmth and the flow of crimson and the softness of petals
inextricably mixed and strung upon the lift of a rhythm which
is itself the voice of the passion and the hesitation of the love. All
this, which is accessible to words, and to words alone, the cinema
must avoid.[5]

EDITING: THE CINEMATIC TROPE

If the film is thus severely restricted in rendering linguistic
tropes (despite dialogue which will be discussed presently),
it has, through the process of editing, discovered a meta-
phoric quality all its own. . . .

Building his design out of individual strips, always thinking
plastically, the film-maker may use almost endless spatial
combinations. He may, for example, use contrast ironically.
When Alec Guinness, in *The Promoter,* achieves a social
triumph by dancing with the Countess of Chell, the film cuts
to a shot of greasy sausage frying in a skillet. It is the next
day and the "card's" mother is preparing his meal in their
dingy kitchen. Or the director may use what the Feldman
brothers call parallel editing.[6] A wife, to make her husband
jealous, is seen flirting with a willing lover. We cut to an
office where the husband is seen making advances to his
secretary. The director may use symbolism. In *Strike,* the

[5] Virginia Woolf, "The Movies and Reality," *New Republic,*
XLVII (August 4, 1926), 309.

[6] Joseph and Harry Feldman, *Dynamics of the Film.* New York,
1952, p. 86.

shooting down of workers is punctuated by shots of the slaughter of a steer in a stockyard. In *The Blue Angel,* birds are used with consummate artistry as a kind of leitmotif. In the opening scene, Professor Unrat coos at a caged canary. Later, having devoted himself to Lola, a music-hall singer, he watches pigeons flying up against a clock whose bronze figures ominously mark the passage of time. And at the height of his degradation, the Professor crows like a cock. The possibility for plastic comments like these, as distinct from verbal renditions of the same effects, is unprecedented in the arts.

A new kind of relationship between animate and inanimate objects springs up, a relationship which becomes the key to plastic thinking. Pudovkin points out quite cogently that relationships between human beings are, for the most part, illumined by conversation, by words. No one carries on conversation with objects, and that is why an actor's relationship to objects is of special interest to the film technician.

Within the composition of the frame, the juxtaposition of man and object becomes crucial. "The performance of an actor linked with an object and built upon it will always be one of the most powerful methods of filmic construction."[7] We have only to think of Chaplin to see the principle in operation. The dancing rolls in *The Gold Rush*, the supple cane, the globe dance in *The Great Dictator*, the feeding machine in *Modern Times*, the flowers and drinks in *Monsieur Verdoux*, the flea skit in *Limelight*—these are only isolated examples of Chaplin's endless facility for inventing new relationships with objects. He leans on a doorman as on a lamppost, and the animate becomes inanimate. The spring of the watch in *The Pawnshop* comes alive, and the inanimate becomes animate. The confusion dynamizes the relationship, and the distinction between man and object is obliterated. Man and object become interchangeable, and the inanimate joins the animate as an actor. Certainly this accounts for a good part of Chaplin's filmic genius.

Not only has the film discovered new ways to render meanings by finding relationships between animate and inanimate objects, but the human physiognomy itself has been

[7] V. I. Pudovkin, *On Film Technique.* Translated by Ivor Montagu. London, 1929, p. 115.

rediscovered. So pervasive has been the power of the close-up
to convey emotion that in "Der Sichtbare Mensch" Béla
Balázs places the film on a par with the invention of the
printing press. The method of conveying meaning by facial
expression, a method which according to Balázs fell into
desuetude with the advent of printing, has been revived by
the "microphysiognomy" of the screen image. The face
becomes another kind of object in space, a terrain on which
may be enacted dramas broad as battles, and sometimes more
intense. Physiognomy preëmpts the domain of nonverbal
experience: "The gestures of visual man are not intended
to convey concepts which can be expressed in words, but
such inner experiences, such nonrational emotions which
would still remain unexpressed when everything that can be
told has been told."[8]

Just as words are not merely images expressing our
thoughts and feelings, but in many cases their *a priori* limiting forms, the subtleties of the mobile face not only render
hitherto unrecorded experiences but also create the conditions
for new experiences to come into being. If, then, "the film
increases the possibilities for expression, it will also widen
the spirit it can express." If Balázs goes too far in calling for
an "encyclopedia of comparative gesturology," he at least
draws attention to the unprecedented possibilities of the
human face. These possibilities have given rise to a wholly
different kind of acting. The microdrama of the human
countenance permits the reading of the greatest conflicts in
the merest flicker of an eye. Understatement becomes the
key to film characterization. The subtleties of Mme. Falco-
netti's face in Dreyer's *The Passion of Joan of Arc*, or of
Giulietta Masina's in Fellini's *La Strada* would have been
incomprehensible to anyone in the dramatic arts before 1900.

In a real sense, then, Pudovkin is right when he says, "In
the discovered, deeply imbedded detail there lies an element
of perception, the creative element that gives the event shown
its final worth." By selecting and combining, by comparing
and contrasting, by linking disparate spatial entities, photographed images of "the deeply imbedded detail" allow the

---

[8] Béla Balázs, *Theory of the Film*. Translated by Edith Bone.
New York, 1953, p. 40.

film-maker, through editing, to achieve a uniquely cinematic equivalent of the literary trope.

What Griffith meant by "seeing," then, differs in quality from what Conrad meant. And effecting mutations from one kind of seeing to another is necessary not only because the materials differ but also because the origins, conventions, and audiences differ as well.

What happens, therefore, when the filmist undertakes the adaptation of a novel, given the inevitable mutation, is that he does not convert the novel at all. What he adapts is a kind of paraphrase of the novel—the novel viewed as raw material. He looks not to the organic novel, whose language is inseparable from its theme, but to characters and incidents which have somehow detached themselves from language and, like the heroes of folk legends, have achieved a mythic life of their own. Because this is possible, we often find that the film adapter has not even read the book, that he has depended instead on a paraphrase by his secretary or his screen writer. That is why there is no necessary correspondence between the excellence of a novel and the quality of the film in which the novel is recorded.

Under these circumstances, we should not be surprised to find a long list of discontented novelists whose works have been adapted to motion pictures. The novelist seems perpetually baffled at the exigencies of the new medium. In film criticism, it has always been easy to recognize how a poor film "destroys" a superior novel. What has not been sufficiently recognized is that such destruction is inevitable. In the fullest sense of the word, the filmist becomes not a translator for an established author, but a new author in his own right.

Balázs has, perhaps, formulated the relationship most clearly. Recognizing the legitimacy of converting the subject, story, and plot of a novel into cinematic form, Balázs grants the possibility of achieving successful results in each. Success is possible because, while "the subject, or story, of both works is identical, their content is nevertheless different. It is this different *content* that is adequately expressed in the changed form resulting from the adaptation." It follows that the raw material of reality can be fashioned in many different forms, but a *content* which determines the form is no longer such raw material. If I see a woman at a train station, her face sad, a little desperate, watching the approach of a hissing engine, and I begin to think of her as a character in a story, she has already, according to Balázs, become "semi-fashioned" artistic content. If I begin to think of how to render her thoughts in words, I have begun to evolve a character in a novel. But if, returning to my impression of that woman at the station, I begin to imagine Garbo in the role of Anna Karenina, I have again transformed her into a new artistic content.[9]

In these terms, says Balázs, the fully conscious film-maker who sets out to adapt a novel.

. . . may use the existing work of art merely as raw material, regard it from the specific angle of his own art form as if it were raw reality, and pay no attention to the form once already given to the material. The playwright, Shakespeare, reading a story by Bandello, saw in it not the artistic form of a masterpiece of story-telling but merely the naked event narrated in it.

Viewed in these terms, the complex relations between novel and film emerge in clearer outline. Like two intersecting lines, novel and film meet at a point, then diverge. At the intersection, the book and shooting-script are almost indistinguishable. But where the lines diverge, they not only resist conversion; they also lose all resemblance to each other. At the farthest remove, novel and film, like all exemplary art, have, within the conventions that make them comprehensible to a given audience, made maximum use of their materials. At this remove, what is peculiarly filmic and what is peculiarly novelistic cannot be converted without destroying an integral part of each. That is why Proust and Joyce would seem as absurd on film as Chaplin would in print. And that is why the great innovators of the twentieth century, in film and novel both, have had so little to do with each other, have gone their ways alone, always keeping a firm but respectful distance. . . .

[9] For an excellent analysis of contrasting ways in which a literary story, a filmed story, and human consciousness order reality, see Albert Laffay, "Le Récit, le Monde, et le Cinéma," *Les Temps Modernes*, No. 20 (May, 1947), pp. 1361–1375; No. 21 (June, 1947), pp. 1579–1600. See, too, Siegfried Kracauer, "The Found Story and the Episode," *Film Culture*, ii, No. 1 (1956), 1–5.

An art whose limits depend on a moving image, mass audience, and industrial production is bound to differ from an art whose limits depend on language, a limited audience, and individual creation. In short, the filmed novel, in spite of certain resemblances, will inevitably become a different artistic entity from the novel on which it is based.

INGMAR BERGMAN

Film Has Nothing To Do With Literature*

"I would say that there is no art form that has so much in
common with film as music."

*Ingmar Bergman, who retains his position as the leading
stage director in Sweden, has had the rare good fortune to be
substantially free to make films in his own way at Svenskfilm-
industri. Among the best-known titles are* The Seventh Seal,
Wild Strawberries, *and* The Magician. *His work, and his way
of working, have stirred both admiration and envy in directors
around the world, many of whom would be glad of the
chance to make films directly in the way an author writes a
book. Not all of them would be so firm as he is, however, in
saying that "we should avoid making films out of books. The
irrational dimension of a literary work, the germ of its existence, is often untranslatable into visual terms—and it, in turn,
destroys the special, irrational dimension of the film."*

*Even a script, for Bergman, is "an almost impossible task."
Once he has caught a glimpse of an idea, "a brightly colored
thread sticking out of the dark sack of the unconscious," he
tries to pursue the delicate task of materializing it, and this
continues throughout the direction and production process.
Montage is "the vital third dimension," the musical rhythm
and relationship of pictures, and this indescribable pulsation
is what makes the film breathe. His remarkable description
of the process of creation is followed by a statement about
the dangers of individualism in art—contrasting with his
practice, yet stirring in its challenge to a widely held ideal.*

* Ingmar Bergman, "Introduction," *Four Screenplays of Ingmar
Bergman.* New York, Simon and Schuster, 1960. Translated from
the Swedish by Lars Malmstrom and David Kushner. Pp. xv–
xviii, xxi–xxii.

A film for me begins with something very vague—a chance remark or a bit of conversation, a hazy but agreeable event unrelated to any particular situation. It can be a few bars of music, a shaft of light across the street. Sometimes in my work at the theatre I have envisioned actors made up for yet unplayed roles.

These are split-second impressions that disappear as quickly as they come, yet leave behind a mood—like pleasant dreams. It is a mental state, not an actual story, but one abounding in fertile associations and images. Most of all, it is a brightly colored thread sticking out of the dark sack of the unconscious. If I begin to wind up this thread, and do it carefully, a complete film will emerge.

This primitive nucleus strives to achieve definite form, moving in a way that may be lazy and half asleep at first. Its stirring is accompanied by vibrations and rhythms which are very special and unique to each film. The picture sequences then assume a pattern in accordance with these rhythms, obeying laws born out of and conditioned by my original stimulus.

If that embryonic substance seems to have enough strength to be made into a film, I decide to materialize it. Then comes something very complicated and difficult: the transformation of rhythms, moods, atmosphere, tensions, sequences, tones and scents into words and sentences, into an understandable screenplay.

This is an almost impossible task.

The only thing that can be satisfactorily transferred from that original complex of rhythms and moods is the dialogue, and even dialogue is a sensitive substance which may offer resistance. Written dialogue is like a musical score, almost incomprehensible to the average person. Its interpretation demands a technical knack plus a certain kind of imagination and feeling—qualities which are so often lacking, even among actors. One can write dialogue, but how it should be delivered, its rhythm and tempo, what is to take place between lines— all this must be omitted for practical reasons. Such a detailed script would be unreadable. I try to squeeze instructions as to location, characterization and atmosphere into my screenplays in understandable terms, but the success of this depends on my writing ability and the perceptiveness of the reader, which are not always predictable.

music → film
art form

Now we come to essentials, by which I mean montage, rhythm and the relation of one picture to another—the vital third dimension without which the film is merely a dead product from a factory. Here I cannot clearly give a key, as in a musical score, nor a specific idea of the tempo which determines the relationship of the elements involved. It is quite impossible for me to indicate the way in which the film "breathes" and pulsates.

I have often wished for a kind of notation which would enable me to put on paper all the shades and tones of my vision, to record distinctly the inner structure of a film. For when I stand in the artistically devastating atmosphere of the studio, my hands and head full of all the trivial and irritating details that go with motion-picture production, it often takes a tremendous effort to remember how I originally saw and thought out this or that sequence, or what was the relation between the scene of four weeks ago and that of today. If I could express myself clearly, in explicit symbols, then this problem would be almost eliminated and I could work with absolute confidence that whenever I liked I could prove the relationship between the part and the whole and put my finger on the rhythm, the continuity of the film.

Thus the script is a very imperfect *technical* basis for a film. And there is another important point in this connection which I should like to mention. Film has nothing to do with literature; the character and substance of the two art forms are usually in conflict. This probably has something to do with the receptive process of the mind. The written word is read and assimilated by a conscious act of the will in alliance with the intellect; little by little it affects the imagination and the emotions. The process is different with a motion picture. When we experience a film, we consciously prime ourselves for illusion. Putting aside will and intellect, we make way for it in our imagination. The sequence of pictures plays directly on our feelings.

Music works in the same fashion; I would say that there is no art form that has so much in common with film as music. Both affect our emotions directly, not via the intellect. And film is mainly rhythm; it is inhalation and exhalation in continuous sequence. Ever since childhood, music has been my great source of recreation and stimulation, and I often experience a film or play musically.

It is mainly because of this difference between film and literature that we should avoid making films out of books. The irrational dimension of a literary work, the germ of its existence, is often untranslatable into visual terms—and it, in turn, destroys the special, irrational dimension of the film. If, despite this, we wish to translate something literary into film terms, we must make an infinite number of complicated adjustments which often bear little or no fruit in proportion to the effort expended.

I myself have never had any ambition to be an author. I do not want to write novels, short stories, essays, biographies, or even plays for the theatre. I only want to make films— films about conditions, tensions, pictures, rhythms and characters which are in one way or another important to me. The motion picture, with its complicated process of birth, is my method of saying what I want to my fellow men. I am a film-maker, not an author.

People ask what are my intentions with my films—my aims. It is a difficult and dangerous question, and I usually give an evasive answer: I try to tell the truth about the human condition, the truth as I see it. This answer seems to satisfy everyone, but it is not quite correct. I prefer to describe what I *would like* my aim to be.

There is an old story of how the cathedral of Chartres was struck by lightning and burned to the ground. Then thousands of people came from all points of the compass, like a giant procession of ants, and together they began to rebuild the cathedral on its old site. They worked until the building was completed—master builders, artists, laborers, clowns, noblemen, priests, burghers. But they all remained anonymous, and no one knows to this day who built the cathedral of Chartres.

Regardless of my own beliefs and my own doubts, which are unimportant in this connection, it is my opinion that art lost its basic creative drive the moment it was separated from worship. It severed an umbilical cord and now lives its own sterile life, generating and degenerating itself. In former days the artist remained unknown and his work was to the glory of God. He lived and died without being more or less important than other artisans; "eternal values," "immortality" and "masterpiece" were terms not applicable in his case. The

ability to create was a gift. In such a world flourished invulnerable assurance and natural humility.

Today the individual has become the highest form and
the greatest bane of artistic creation. The smallest wound or
pain of the ego is examined under a microscope as if it were
of eternal importance. The artist considers his isolation, his
subjectivity, his individualism almost holy. Thus we finally
gather in one large pen, where we stand and bleat about our
loneliness without listening to each other and without realizing
that we are smothering each other to death. The individualists
stare into each other's eyes and yet deny the existence of each
other. We walk in circles, so limited by our own anxieties that
we can no longer distinguish between true and false, between
the gangster's whim and the purest ideal.

Thus if I am asked what I would like the general purpose
of my films to be, I would reply that I want to be one of the
artists in the cathedral on the great plain. I want to make a
dragon's head, an angel, a devil—or perhaps a saint—out of
stone. It does not matter which; it is the sense of satisfaction
that counts. Regardless of whether I believe or not, whether
I am a Christian or not, I would play my part in the collective building of the cathedral.

The Cinematic Essence

BELA BALÁZS

The Faces of Men*

"Man has again become visible."

The Hungarian critic Béla Balázs looked forward to a thoroughly revolutionary role for the art of the film. His vision was not so much political, however, as idealistic. His book, Theory of Film, *is sprinkled with dubious references to the "dialectic of history" and other Hegelian-Marxist assumptions, but it is basically a collection of insights and suggestions about ways to use camera, sound, and editing.*

Writing in 1923, when the silent film was at a peak of development in Germany, Balázs forecast his later interest in film in an eloquent article. Seldom has anyone so sweepingly declared the value of the visual—the many-leveled communication of action, gesture, facial expression, duration, and design. "The gestures of visual man are not intended," he explains, "to convey concepts which can be expressed in words, but such inner experiences, such non-rational emotions which would still remain unexpressed when everything that can be told has been told." It is for this reason he welcomed the silent film as a rediscovery of man himself, of the spirit which had become so fragmented, so word-conscious, since the age of printing.

The discovery of printing gradually rendered illegible the faces of men. So much could be read from paper that the method of conveying meaning by facial expression fell into desuetude.

Victor Hugo wrote once that the printed book took over the part played by the cathedral in the Middle Ages and became the carrier of the spirit of the people. But the thou-

* Béla Balázs, "Der Sichtbare Mensch," *Theory of Film.* London, Dobson, 1952. Pp. 39–43.

sands of books tore the *one spirit,* embodied in the cathedral, into thousands of opinions. The word broke the stone into a thousand fragments, tore the church into a thousand books.

The visual spirit was thus turned into a legible spirit and visual culture into a culture of concepts. This of course had its social and economic causes, which changed the general face of life. But we paid little attention to the fact that, in conformity with this, the face of individual men, their foreheads, their eyes, their mouths, had also of necessity and quite concretely to suffer a change.

At present a new discovery, a new machine is at work to turn the attention of men back to a visual culture and give them new faces. This machine is the cinematographic camera. Like the printing press, it is a technical device for the multiplication and distribution of products of the human spirit; its effect on human culture will not be less than that of the printing press.

For not to speak does not mean that one has nothing to say. Those who do not speak may be brimming over with emotions which can be expressed only in forms and pictures, in gesture and play of feature. The man of visual culture uses these not as substitutes for words, as a deaf-mute uses his fingers. He does not think in words, the syllables of which he sketches in the air like the dots and dashes of the Morse code. The gestures of visual man are not intended to convey concepts which can be expressed in words, but such inner experiences, such non-rational emotions which would still remain unexpressed when everything that can be told has been told. Such emotions lie in the deepest levels of the soul and cannot be approached by words that are mere reflexions of concepts; just as our musical experiences cannot be expressed in rationalized concepts. What appears on the face and in facial expression is a spiritual experience which is rendered immediately visible without the intermediary of words.

In the golden age of the old visual arts, the painter and sculptor did not merely fill empty space with abstract shapes and forms, and man was not merely a formal problem for the artist. Painters could paint the spirit and the soul without becoming "literary," for the soul and the spirit had not yet been confined in concepts capable of expression only by means of words; they could be incarnated without residue. That was the happy time when paintings could still have a "theme" and an "idea," for the idea had not yet been tied to the concept and to the word that named the concept. The artist could present in its primary form of manifestation the soul's bodily incarnation in gesture or feature. But since then the printing press has grown to be the main bridge over which the more remote interhuman spiritual exchanges take place and the soul has been concentrated and crystallized chiefly in the word. There was no longer any need for the subtler means of expression provided by the body. For this reason our bodies grew soulless and empty—what is not in use, deteriorates.

The expressive surface of our body was thus reduced to the face alone and this not merely because the rest of the body was hidden by clothes. For the poor remnants of bodily expression that remained to us the little surface of the face sufficed, sticking up like a clumsy semaphore of the soul and signalling as best it could. Sometimes a gesture of the hand was added, recalling the melancholy of a mutilated torso. In the epoch of word culture the soul learnt to speak but had grown almost invisible. Such was the effect of the printing press.

Now the film is about to inaugurate a new direction in our culture. Many million people sit in the picture houses every evening and purely through vision, experience happenings, characters, emotions, moods, even thoughts, without the need for many words. For words do not touch the spiritual content of the pictures and are merely passing instruments of as yet undeveloped forms of art. Humanity is already learning the rich and colourful language of gesture, movement and facial expression. This is not a language of signs as a substitute for words, like the sign-language of the deaf-and-dumb— it is the visual means of communication, without intermediary of souls clothed in flesh. Man has again become visible.

Linguistic research has found that the origins of language lie in expressive movement, that is, that man when he began to speak moved his tongue and lips to no greater extent than the other muscles of his face and body—just as an infant does to-day. Originally the purpose was not the making of sounds. The movement of tongue and lips was at first the same spontaneous gesturing as every other expressive movement of the body. That the former produced sounds was a secondary, adventitious phenomenon, which was only later used for practical purposes. The immediately visible message was thus turned into an immediately audible message. In the course of this process, as in every translation, a great deal was lost. It is the expressive movement, the gesture, that is the aboriginal mother-tongue of the human race.

Now we are beginning to remember and re-learn this tongue. It is still clumsy and primitive and very far removed as yet from the refinements of word art. But already it is beginning to be able sometimes to express things which escape the artists of the word. How much of human thought would remain unexpressed if we had no music! The now developing art of facial expression and gesture will bring just as many submerged contents to the surface. Although these human experiences are not rational, conceptual contents, they are nevertheless neither vague nor blurred, but as clear and unequivocal as is music. Thus the inner man, too, will become visible.

But the old visible man no longer exists to-day and the new visible man is not yet in existence. As I have said before, it is the law of nature that unused organs degenerate and disappear, leaving only rudiments behind. The animals that do not chew lose their teeth. In the epoch of word culture we made little use of the expressive powers of our body and have therefore partly lost that power. The gesturing of primitive peoples is frequently more varied and expressive than that of the educated European whose vocabulary is infinitely richer. A few more years of film art and our scholars will discover that cinematography enables them to compile encyclopedias of facial expression, movement and gesture, such as have long existed for words in the shape of dictionaries. The public, however, need not wait for the gesture encyclopædia and grammars of future academies: it can go to the pictures and learn it there.

We had, however, when we neglected the body as a means of expression, lost more than mere corporal power of expression. That which was to have been expressed was also narrowed down by this neglect. For it is not the same spirit, not the same soul that is expressed once in words and once in gestures. Music does not express the same thing as poetry in a different way—it expresses something quite different. When we dip the bucket of words in the depths, we bring up other things than when we do the same with gestures. But let no one think that I want to bring back the culture of movement and gesture in place of the culture of words, for neither can be a substitute for the other. Without a rational, conceptual culture and the scientific development that goes with it there can be no social and hence no human progress. The connecting tissue of modern society is the word spoken and written, without which all organization and planning would be impossible. On the other hand fascism has shown us where the tendency to reduce human culture to subconscious emotions in place of clear concepts would lead humanity.

What I am talking about is only art and even here there is no question of displacing the more rational art of the word. There is no reason why we should renounce one sort of human achievement in favour of another. Even the most highly developed musical culture need not crowd out some more rational aspect of culture.

But to return to the simile of the bucket: we know that the wells that dry up are the wells from which no water is dipped. Psychology and philology have shown that our thoughts and feelings are determined a priori by the possibility of expressing them. Philology is also aware that it is not only concepts and feelings that create words, but that it is also the other way round: words give rise to concepts and feelings. This is a form of economy practised by our mental constitution which desires to produce unusable things just as little as does our physical organism. Psychological and logical analysis has shown that words are not merely images expressing our thoughts and feelings but in most cases their a priori limiting forms. This is at the root of the danger of stereotyped banality which so often threatens the educated. Here again the evolution of the human spirit is a dialectical process. Its development increases its means of expression and the increase of means of expression in its turn facilitates and accelerates its development. Thus if then the film increases the possibilities of expression, it will also widen the spirit it can express.

RALPH BLOCK

Not Theatre, Not Literature, Not Painting*

"The movie is a primitive art, equally as the machine age is
a new primitive period in time."

*The moralists, on the one hand, and the aestheticians, on
the other, are incapable of measuring the meaning of the
movies, Ralph Block says. This is partly because films are
expected to be like painting or sculpture, arts which he says
"have completed their cycle." The movies exist—"a powerful
psychic magnet, an educing force which draws submerged
dreams from hidden places to the surface of the common life."
It will be some time before we can judge the movies by their
own laws. By that time, they "will have lost their excitement,
but at least they will be aesthetically correct."*

*Block suggests that literate, cultivated gentlemen don't
make good movie directors. Such men may think of movies
as a form of theatre or literature, but "it demands at best a
unique kind of imagination . . . a special kind of feeling
about the relationship between things and things, events and
events . . . The movie is in other words a new way in which
to see life."*

An art may have a large body of aesthetic tradition and be
moribund. It may have none to speak of and be very much
alive. The movies are this kind of art. It is not possible to
understand them, much less truthfully see them, within the
limitations, judgements, and discriminations of the aesthetic
viewpoint. The movies are implicit in modern life; they are in
their very exaggerations—as a living art often may be—an

* Ralph Block, "Not Theatre, Not Literature, Not Painting,"
The Dial, January 1927. Quoted in Lewis Jacobs (ed.), *Introduction to the Art of the Movies*. New York, Noonday, 1960. Pp.
101–106.

essentialization of that which they reflect. To accurately size them up, they should be seen functionally, phenomenalistically, in relation to their audience.

Like music, painting, and the drama in their primitive stages, the movies are manifestations in some kind of aesthetic form of a social will and even of a mass religion. They are in effect a powerful psychic magnet, an educing force which draws submerged dreams from hidden places to the surface of the common life. By releasing wishes which are on the margin of accepted behavior, they partake of the social function of art. In a transitional civilization the *mores* of the people no longer reflect their real social and tribal requirements, nor to any appreciable extent their individual and social hungers. The movies help to disintegrate that which is socially traditional, and to clear the field for that which, if not forbidden, has been at least close to the shade of the tabooed.

Primitive art is usually recognized as art only after it has become classical. In the manner of all primitive expression, the movies violate accepted contemporary canons of taste. Even as they arouse the sentinels of moral tradition, so they draw the attack of aestheticians, who are unconsciously measuring expressive works by the standards of those arts that have completed their cycle, especially painting and sculpture. But it is absurd to praise or blame the movies in their present state, or do any more than try to understand them. Whether the movies or what they reflect represent the Good Life depends on whose Good Life is being selected. They exist— massively, ubiquitous. It will be time enough to judge them as an art when they become a historical method of presenting selected truth, mellowed and tested by time, and captured by an audience saturated with tradition—acclimated by use to an understanding of the laws, intentions, and refinements of the medium. The movies by that time will have lost their excitement, but at least they will be aesthetically correct.

The movie is a primitive art, equally as the machine age is a new primitive period in time. But being a machine, the motion camera is not a simple instrument. Like the pianoforte, it is an evolved instrument, predicated on the existence and development of other forms. It is itself still in an evolving state. Indeed those who make use of it and those who appreciate it without empirical knowledge of its use, have failed to grasp, except in a loose intuitive sense, a full understanding of the complicated laws that govern it. Here and there in its past performance are startling bits of technical excellence, discoveries of how the instrument may be properly used in its own field. Bound together these form a rude body of technique, already complicated, but not yet pushed to any important limits by personal genius, nor classified significantly in use by any development of important schools.

It is fashionable to say that the camera is impersonal, but those who use the camera know this is untrue. Indeed, even abstractly, it is no more impersonal than a steel chisel, or a camel's-hair brush. The camera is on the one hand as intimate as the imagination of those who direct it; on the other hand it has a peculiar selective power of its own. Its mechanism is governed by an arbitrary set of rhythms—sixteen images to each foot of celluloid—and reality is seized by the camera according to a mathematical ratio, established between the tempo of what is in front of the lens and the tempo of the machine itself. The camera is also governed by another set of relations, which have to do with light and its refraction through lenses. These are no less arbitrary in a physical sense, but within their limits they are open to a large number of gradations and variations, according to the human will behind them. Far from being impersonal, the camera may be said to have pronounced prejudices of rhythm.

Most critical discussion of pantomime in the movies is vapor. Screen pantomime is not pantomime in the conventional Punch and Judy sense. In the theatre, pantomime is in the large, a matter of long curves of movement. On the screen the lens intervenes between the eye and its objective. The camera not only magnifies movement but it also analyzes action, showing its incompletions. It is indeed more prejudiced than the human eye itself, helping the eye to detect false rhythms in the utterance of action, or an absence of relationship between sequences of movement, where the eye alone might fail. The intervention of the camera necessitates not only a modification of what might be called the wave length of pantomime for the screen, but also a more closely knitted flow of movement. Traditional pantomime on the stage is a highly schematized and rigid organization of units of movement in which every motion has a definite traditional meaning. But for the camera, movement must be living, warm, vital, and flowing rather than set and defined in an alphabet of traditional interpretation. Like Bergsonian time, it must seem to renew and re-create itself out of the crest of each present moment. It is in this sense that it resembles music. It is also because of this necessity that the stage actor who essays the screen is often exposed at the outset in all the barrenness of habitual gesture and stock phrasing of movement.

Experience rather than theory has taught many actors on the screen the need of plasticity, composure, modulation of gesture, and an understanding of how to space movement—a sense of timing. The screen actor at his best—the Beerys, Menjous, and Negris—tries to give fluency to pantomime, so that action may melt out of repose into repose again, even in those moments when an illusion of arrested action is intended. He recognizes that against his own movement as a living organic action is the cross movement of the celluloid. It is only by long experience that the motion-picture actor discovers a timing which is properly related to the machine; but that experience has already produced screen pantomimists whose rhythmic freshness and vitality the modern stage can rarely match.

The actor is the living punctuation of reality. He is conscious and has the power to make his action valid in an imaginative sense. But Appearance—the face of Nature—is itself sprawling and only vaguely connotative. Words are packed with the reverberations of human history; Appearance on the other hand, must be selected, organized, and related to ideas that conform to the limitations and possibilities of the camera, before it can be robbed of inanity and made significant.

All this is the function of the director. The movies are full of mediocre directors. But, comparatively, there are not as many poor motion-picture directors as there are poor musicians, painters, and creative writers in the world; it is easier to go to school and become any of these than it is to direct a motion picture. In its present state of development, motion-picture direction demands not only logic, tact, sensibility, the ability to organize and control human beings and multifarious materials, and the power to tell a story dramatically, but it also requires a gift which cannot be learned in any school. This is a richness, even grossness, in the director's feeling for

Life, and abundance of perception, a copious emotional reflex to the ill-assorted procession of existence.

Good motion-picture direction has little to do with literacy or cultivation in its conventional sense. Several of the most cultivated and literate gentlemen in the movies are among the most prosaic directors. They have brought with them a knowledge of other arts, which has blinded them to the essential quality of the camera. They think of the movies as a form of the theatre, of literature, or of painting. It is none of these things. It demands at best a unique kind of imagination which parallels these arts but does not stem from them. It is true that the rigid economic organization of the modern studio demands the same kind of prevision and preparation on the part of the director as on the part of any other creator. Even aside from urgencies of this kind, the St. Clairs, Lubitschs, Duponts, Eisensteins, are under the same imaginative necessity to organize their material as a Cézanne or Beethoven. But there the similarity ceases. Directors of this kind know that their greatest need is the power to seize reality—in its widest sense—and make it significant in forms of motion. This power, this understanding, is a gift by itself. It requires a special kind of eye, a special kind of feeling about the relationship between things and things, events and events, and an intuitive as well as empirical knowledge of how to make the camera catch what that eye sees and that imagination feels. It has nothing to do with words, as such, nor with history or politics or any of the traditional matters which are politely assumed to represent cultivation, and which so often debase the metal of the imagination.

The movie is in other words a new way in which to see life. It is a way born to meet the needs of a new life. It is a way of using the machine to see what the machine has done to human beings. It is for this reason that the best motion-picture directors arise from strange backgrounds, with a secure grasp on techniques of living rather than on academic attitudes. They are not always preoccupied with proving that life is so small that it can be caught in the net of art. It is the pragmatic sanction hovering over them which offends academicians.

Here and there are indications that the movie is arising out of its phenomenalistic background into the level now occupied by the novel and the theatre, touched by the same spirit of light irony, and predicating the orientation of a special audience. But there are no signs at the moment that it can rise higher than this point. Pictures such as *The Cabinet of Dr. Caligari* are interesting laboratory results in experimental psychology, but they have as little to do with the direct succession of the motion picture as Madame Tussaud's has to do with Rodin. *The Last Laugh* and *The Battleship Potemkin* are technical explosions, important only in their power to destroy old procedures and light the path ahead.

American directors have always mistaken cruelty on the one hand and sentimental realism on the other, for irony. Satisfaction for the sadistic hunger of the crowd is present in almost all popular entertainment. Griffith early understood this crowd desire, and his technique in exploiting it has filtered through a thousand pictures since. De Mille, Von Stroheim, Brenon, and the many unnamed have all used it in one form or other. But none has reached irony empty of brutality—an unobstructed god-like view of the miscalculations of existence, yet touched by human compassion. There are no Hardys nor Chekhovs in the movies. *The Last Laugh* dribbled out into German sentimentality, although in substance it seemed familiarly like one of Constance Garnett's translations. The comedians—Keaton and Langdon as well as Chaplin—have touched near the edge of true irony, but only as children might. Chaplin rose to the intention in *A Woman of Paris*, but his forms were conventional and worn, cast in the clichés of irony of cheap fiction.

In the end, what remains wonderful about the movie is its instrument. Its ideas are still sentimental or bizarre, reflecting the easy hungers of life, and of today's shifting surface of life; it fails as yet to draw from the deep clear wells of human existence. Aside from its need of another kind of audience— even another world, a deep ironic point of view in the motion picture would require a great individual spirit equipped with a true knowledge of the medium. And none of this kind has arisen. He is rare in any art and any time.

MACK SENNETT

Cloud-Cuckoo Country*

"We made funny pictures as fast as we could for money."

Creator of slapstick, discoverer of the custard pie, promoter of "bathing beauties" and launcher of the Keystone Cops, Mack Sennett was the first and perhaps the greatest impresario of comedy. Presiding over his inner circle of directors and accountants from an enormous bathtub housed in a tower, he literally kept watch over the hard-pressed shenanigans of a horde of ill-paid jesters. Ruthless in the cutting room, as in the story conference, he showed the world what to do with fast action, wild characterization, and camera tricks. He took the commonplaces of daily life and carried them to hilarious extremes of absurdity. He used the resources of the screen to satisfy everyone's suppressed desire to see things blow up.

Recent wide-screen comedies of the chase—and even some of the more solemn spy pictures—are actually tributes to Sennett, fondly imitating (sometimes with embarrassing literalness) the fantastic mayhem he put on the screen. "We knew we were experimenting with something new," he says. But he is his old mischievous self when he notes that "it seems to be fashionable among educated writers to claim that we created a new art form in those morning-glory times." The critics and historians, he points out, taking us down a peg or two, always come after the event, with "all the philosophizing and the explaining and the phrases with lace on them."

We heard our first picture before we saw it, although sound didn't arrive in motion pictures until fifteen years later. A Shriners' parade, stepping to oom-pah and brass, was marching up Main Street.

* Mack Sennett, *King of Comedy* (as told to Cameron Shipp). Garden City, N.Y., Doubleday, 1954. Pp. 86–90.

"A gorgeous welcome to you it is indeed, O Maestro Mack Napoleon Sennett!" said Mabel.

"Now, hold your gorgeous, yapping mouth shut for just a minute," I said. "Maybe it is exactly that. Let's have a look and make a dollar."

The parade was a whopper and it would take a long time to pass a given point. A given point in my mind was a free lunch or wherever I could set up the camera and shoot unpaid actors.

"We got us a spectacle, kids," I said. "Bauman and Kessel are always hollering about costs. Look at that crowd scene— all free!"

Ford Sterling was hungry, Mabel wanted to go to the hotel. Fred Mace had seen a parade before. They held back. Pathé Lehrman got what I meant.

"What's the story, boss?" Pathé asked.

"Got no story. We'll make it up as we go along," I said. "Pathé, run over there to the department store and buy a baby doll. Here's a dollar and a half. Jim, you get the camera set up on the corner. Ford, you put on a tall overcoat and make like an actor."

Mabel Normand could throw herself into any part instantly, even into a part that didn't exist.

"Who am I?" was all she asked when she saw we were under way.

"A mother," I said.

"I would be the last to know," Mabel commented.

"Now take this doll," I ordered. "It's your baby. Get going. Run up and down the line of march and embarrass those Shriners. Make out that—"

"—I'm a poor lorn working girl, betrayed in the big city, searching for the father of my chee-iuld." Mabel finished the sentence. "This characterization requires a shawl. Who ever heard of a poor, forlorn little mother without a shawl over her poor little head?"

"Right," I said. "Get her a shawl, Pathé."

Mabel put on the comicalest act you ever clapped eyes on, pleading, stumbling, holding out her baby—and the reactions she got from those good and pious gentlemen in the parade were something you couldn't have caught on film after six days of D. W. Griffith rehearsals. Men were horrified, abashed, dismayed. One kind soul dropped out and tried to help Mabel.

"Move in, Ford," I told Sterling. Ford leaped in and started a screaming argument with the innocent Shriner, who didn't know he was being photographed to make a buck for Keystone.

The police moved in on Ford and Mabel. Ford fled, leaping, insulting the police, and they—God bless the police!—they chased him. I helped the cameraman and we got it all.

The Shriners were good, but the best scenes we nabbed were the running cops. I never got their names, but if there are any retired gentlemen of the Los Angeles Police Department who remember taking part in that incident, let them bask in fame: they were the original Keystone Cops.

We didn't even pause at the Alexandria Hotel. We went straight out to Edendale to our little studio, shot a few more scenes and close-ups to tie the picture together, and we had our first comedy. I wired Kessel and Bauman: "Got a spectacle first day and it's a whopper."

Kessel insisted for years later that the wire said, "Got pickled first day and it was a whopper."

Anything on film made money.

The only requirement was that it be reasonably new. Theatres, states'-rights franchise holders, distributors were starved for pictures. That is why some of the unlikeliest people in the world became parents of the new art. Some were sweatshop operators, bicycle repairmen, junk-heap scavengers, cloak-and-suit manufacturers, ex-bookmakers, and there was a prominent ex-boilermaker named Mack Sennett.

Well, pioneers are seldom from the nobility. There were no dukes on the *Mayflower*.

We hopped aboard the new thing and went to town. The town you think of in association with movies is Hollywood, but in the era when Woodrow Wilson was proving that a great scholar could be a great president, and tap-dancing with his daughters after supper in the White House, we were mainly concerned with the carryings-on in Edendale. Time does gallop on: the site of the first custard pie, Keystone Cops, and Bathing Beauty studio is now halfway between two newer landmarks, Aimee Semple McPherson's temple and Forest Lawn Cemetery.

Overnight our place was busting its seams with idiotics.

Anything went, and every fool thing you might think of under the influence of hashish or a hangover went big.

We were awash with pretty women, clowns, and story-tellers who couldn't write. We made a million dollars so fast my fingers ached from trying to count.

Let me catch my breath before leaping into that Cloud-Cuckoo land of *laissez faire* and turvy-topsy. Hear this:

Nowadays it seems to be fashionable among educated writers to claim that we created a new art form in those morning-glory times. They proclaim that our chase sequences and rhythms derived from classic ballet. Critics have come up with grand new phrases like "cineplastic art" and "unfailing precision of technique." A famous Frenchman wrote a book about us in which he claimed we were "poetic creators of myths and symbols who conceived the universe in its totality and translated it in terms of motion pictures."

My! . . .

Now, I won't contradict anybody, not right out in public, anyway, who wants to announce me as a wonderful fellow and the creator of a new kind of art. When you consider it and when you tell your false modesty to quit squirming, we *did* create a new kind of art. But while we were doing it we had no more notion of contributing to aesthetics than a doodlebug contributes to the *Atlantic Monthly*.

We did the best we could with what we had.

We made funny pictures as fast as we could for money. We knew we were experimenting with something new—but has there ever been a performer, or a creative person of any kind, from a talented potato peeler to Picasso, who didn't think he was original? But we didn't rear back and publish manifestoes like the modern poets and painters nobody can understand. All the philosophizing and the explaining and the phrases with lace on them, like "cineplastic art," came much later.

Of course comedy is a satire on the human race. It always has been. That is what clowns have been up to ever since kings kept fools. Our specialty was exasperated dignity and the dis-combombulation of Authority. We whaled the daylights out of everything in sight with our bed slats, and we had fun doing it. We cut our pictures sharply, having learned how from D. W. Griffith, and we did get "pace" into them. But if someone had pointed out that our sequences of leaping cops and fleeing comedians were an art form derived from the classic ballet, we'd have hooted like crazy and thrown a pie at him.

I never saw a ballet.

This brings me around to a contradiction. My people were artists, all right, and great ones. Chaplin—well, you can use all the learned words you want to about him and you'll probably be right. A genius. Mabel, and the Conklins, Mace, Buster Keaton, Ben Turpin, W. C. Fields, all those wonderful clowns were persons of enormous talent.

But not self-conscious. We merely went to work and tried to be funny, and there really was a wonder and a miracle then that no amount of expensive grammar can explain: I, Mack Sennett, the Canadian farm boy, the boilermaker, was the head man.

HERBERT READ

Towards a Film Aesthetic*

"Film is the art of space-time: it is a space-time continuum."

Sir Herbert Read, a philosopher and student of aesthetics, wrote these notes on the art of the film in 1932 and 1933, long before he was knighted for his contributions to the understanding of art. His interest in the film was that of a truly educated man, who feels the need to be curious and to analyze any important phenomenon.

When he lists the dimensions of movement on the screen, he misses one of the important ones—the movement brought about by the editing process itself. But he is aware of the importance of editing: "Montage is mechanized imagination. . . . It is the most important stage in the whole process of film-production, aesthetically considered." He says that painting is concerned with synthesis, whereas the cinema is "essentially analysis." He reminds us that the film "must be composed directly out of the lumbering material of the actual visible world." He also suggests that the film is so free it is "a runaway," that "its only unity is continuity."

The aesthetic of an art is always resented by the practitioner, and perhaps there is a particular reason why theory should not obtrude itself on the art of the film. That art is not yet formed, and to theorise about something which is not yet fully in being may seem the height of pedantic indiscretion. But one kind of aesthetics is essentially a priori: it is the discovery of universal laws of art, and if the film is to be an art, then these

* Herbert Read, "Towards a Film Aesthetic," *Cinema Quarterly*, Vol. 1, No. 1, Autumn 1932, pp. 7–10, 11. Also "The Poet and the Film," *Cinema Quarterly*, Vol. 1, No. 4, Summer 1933, p. 202.

theoretical considerations are as relevant to it as to any other art, and can guide its line of development.

If the film is an art—but what else can it be? A technical process? But so is etching, for example; so is every art that uses a tool. To determine whether a given process is an art or not, we need ask only one question—does it involve *selection*? For selection implies (*a*) a standard for which selection is made; (*b*) sensibility to distinguish according to this standard. The exercise of sensibility in the interests of a standard is an elementary definition of art. Selection, I think it can be shown, is the very first principle of the film; the film is therefore essentially an art.

The film is visual. That fact immediately links it—from the point of view of aesthetics—with the visual or, as they are more commonly but less accurately called, the plastic arts. "Moving pictures"—the Movies—that is the most descriptive title which has ever been given to the film. Picture and Movement: that is the definition of a film, and if we can introduce into the aesthetics of pictorial art the modifications required by this new factor, then we shall have an aesthetic of the film.

But it is not so simple as it sounds. To introduce this new factor into the picture involves conditions which almost entirely separate pictorial art (let us say painting) from the film. This is the essential distinction—even opposition—between the painting and the film: the painting is composed subjectively, the film objectively. However highly we rate the function of the scenario writer—in actual practice it is rated very low—we must recognise that the film is not composed directly and freely from the mind by means of a docile medium like paint, but must be composed directly out of the lumbering material of the actual visible world.

Painting is a synthesis (I ignore the crude notion that it is imitation); the film is essentially analysis. The painter composes within his mind (that is to say, makes a synthesis of) selected elements of his visual experience. (In the actual process of composition he goes beyond his experience, guided by imagination and sensibility.) The director of a film begins with the same visual experience, but he is anchored to his material. To make his material significant—significant of more than its actuality, its news value—he must break the continuity of his vision—jump from one stepping-stone of significance to another. He must analyse the scene for its significant aspects. (For example, in films like *Rain* or *Pierement* the camera's motto is "Say when." The producer goes about like a ferret for significance, crying "Now!")

The film purists insist on the mechanical nature of the process (as though a paintbrush, an engraving-tool, a piano, were not also pieces of mechanism). The true inspiration for the film, they say, is to be found in its technical possibilities. "Der Apparat ist die Muse" (Béla Balázs). But it is necessary to distinguish between the tool and the material (the medium), between the *Apparat* and that which is operated upon. The sculptor's muse is not his chisel, but the marble; perhaps more accurately it is the impact of these two factors, creative inspiration depending on a sensuous reaction to the feel of the chisel against the marble. There is the same sensuous factor in the application of a charged brush to canvas; and the same factor is obvious in music. The camera is the film-director's tool, his medium is light, or rather the impact of light on solid objects. It might be better still to regard the camera as a chisel of light, cutting into the reality of objects. In any case, light is the muse.

We might abandon the word "selection," because it is too static in its implications. We need to emphasise the mobility, the plasticity of the film. For this is the quality by virtue of which the film becomes an art. I have used these two words, "mobility" and "plasticity," as interchangeable. But note that in sculpture, for example, an object is moulded, made plastic, to arrive at an immobile, absolute, eternal object; in the film the immobility (even when moving!) of objects is, as it were, unmoulded, made plastic, to arrive at a mobile, relative, and transitory object. Sculpture is the art of space, as music is of time. The film is the art of space-time: it is a space-time continuum.

There are at least three directions (or dimensions) in which movement may take place: (1) movement of the camera, (2) movement of light, (3) movement of the object photographed. Combinations of such movements produce almost endless possibilities of plastic form.

The true plasticity of the film, the plasticity which gives the film its uniqueness, is a plasticity of light. An essential film would be an abstract film, a "pure" creation of light and darkness, just as an essential painting is an abstract painting. But such films are only for the purists.

The question of form is difficult. Even in painting we must distinguish between closed form (form determined by the frame and plane of the painted surface) and open form (form which ignores these limits and prolongs itself into the space about the painting, typified in Baroque form). We may select "stills" for their closed form—for their pictorial composition—but the film itself is essentially open form. It continually implies the space around the objects represented and beyond the limits of the screen; it endeavours to make the part represent the whole. It is an art of "cuts"—economy cuts.

Its freedom threatens the film; it is a runaway. The problem of the film as an art-form may be reduced to the invention of proper conventions. It must reject the unities proper to the drama (nothing is so feeble as the filmed play), but it must discover the unities proper to a space-time "continuum." Perhaps its only possible unity is the absence of any unity; the film is essentially alogical. In the film events can occur simultaneously; they can be represented in more than one unit of dimension; time itself can be controlled. Its only unity is continuity.

How easily this continuity may be destroyed is seen in the average talkie. The talk interrupts the continuity of the movement, or at least delays it. We begin to listen, instead of looking. But once we consciously listen in the cinema, we might as well be in the theatre.

It is difficult to see any art-form evolving out of the talkie. But we must distinguish between the talkie pure and simple, and the film with "effects." Even speech may be an effect, as we see most clearly in René Clair's films, where speech is used sparingly, and never interrupts the continuity of the film. Speech must keep time with the film, but the normal film annihilates time. Therefore it must annihilate speech.

The same observations may be made of musical accompaniment. It must keep time with the film. Therefore the film must either be a direct transcript of the music (as a film of a dancer dancing to music might be), or the music must be composed for the film (as Edmund Meisel's music for *Potemkin*).

This does not imply that the talkie has no future. But its laws will not be the laws of the pure film, and the sooner it works out its own salvation, the better. Rudolf Arnheim (*Film als Kunst*[1]) uses the following analogy. A piece of music may be composed as a solo for the piano. It may afterwards be transposed as a duet for piano and violin. It will remain essentially the same piece of music, but both the piano part and the violin part taken separately will not represent the original music; each has been modified to make a unity when played together. So both speech and film must be modified to make a perfect talkie.

Ignoring the plasticity of the filming process itself, we may still find a justification of the film as an art-form in the process of montage. Montage is mechanised imagination. The producer deliberately interferes with the anonymity, the impersonality of the camera. He takes its mechanical products (how little mechanical they need be we have already seen) and arranges them as freely as the painter arranges his forms and colours. It is the most important stage in the whole process of film-production, aesthetically considered. . . .

The more we insist on the plasticity of the film (that is to say, on its artistic possibilities), the more we require the imaginative artist in the process of production. This is quite against the present trend, which is to reduce the role of the scenario-writer to insignificance. But when the film has exhausted its technical élan, then it must inevitably return to the poets. For the quality of an art always depends finally on the quality of the mind directing it or producing it, and no art can survive on a purely mechanical inspiration. There will always be a place for the recording film, for the scientific film, the news film; but finally the public will demand the film of imagination, of vision. And then will come the day of the poet, the scenario-writer, or whatever we are to call him. For actually this artist will be a new type of artist—an artist with the visual sensibility of the painter, the vision of the poet, and the time-sense of the musician. Instead of doubting the artistic possibilities of the film as a medium, we should rather doubt the artistic capability of man to rise to the high opportunities of this new medium. It is a new Pandora's box that the movie-man carries about, from which he has already released all kinds of evils, but at the bottom of which hope still remains. . . .

[1] Ernst Rowohlt Verlag, Berlin.

The film of imagination—the film as a work of art ranking with great drama, great literature, and great painting, will not come until the poet enters the studio.

I know what is immediately advanced against that idea—the necessity of working in the strict terms of a new medium, exploiting a new technique: the camera is the film artist's muse: down with the literary film and so on.

About such a point of view I have only two things to say:—firstly, that in every art there is a good deal of cant spoken about technique. Most techniques can be learnt in a few days, at the most in a year or two. But no amount of technical efficiency will create a work of art in any medium if the creative or imaginative genius is lacking. Naturally the technique must appeal to the sensibility of the poet: he must love his medium and work in it with enthusiasm: but the vision necessary to create not merely the means, but the end—that is a gift of providence, and we call that gift poetic genius.

Secondly, those people who deny that there can be any connection between the scenario and literature seem to me to have a wrong conception, so much of the film as of literature. Literature they seem to regard as something polite and academic, in other words, as something god-forsaken and superannuated, compounded of correct grammar and high-sounding ciceronian phrases. Such a conception reveals the feebleness of their sensibility. If you ask me to give you the most distinctive quality of good writing, I would give it to you in this one word: VISUAL. Reduce the art of writing to its fundamentals and you come to this single aim: to convey images by means of words. But to *convey images*. To make the mind see. To project onto that inner screen of the brain a moving picture of objects and events, events and objects moving towards a balance and reconciliation of a more than usual state of emotion with more than usual order. That is a definition of good literature—of the achievement of every good poet—from Homer and Shakespeare to James Joyce or Ernest Hemingway. It is also a definition of the ideal film.

SLAVKO VORKAPICH

Toward True Cinema*

"It is not a question of artistically composed tableaux. It is a problem of composing visually, but in time."

Slavko Vorkapich has devoted a large part of his life to instilling in others an awareness of visual patterns of motion. Film students at the University of Southern California, and in Yugoslavia (where he grew up), and most recently in New York City have learned from him about "the phi effect," for example—the apparent movement of areas of light on the screen when shots follow each other rapidly. Such observations are not based on mere theory. As an expert on montage at M-G-M, he created the revolution sequence in Viva Villa!, *the famine and exodus in* The Good Earth, *and many others.*

Until transcripts are made available of his talks at the Museum of Modern Art in February 1965, this selection will remain one of the few written statements Vorkapich has given us. He is not one to emphasize the contribution of acting. Even the close-up, he says, is simply a telescopic view of a theatrical performance. "I am not opposed to the use of the film medium as an extension of the theatre," he explains. "I only object to calling such extension creative use of the unique characteristics inherent in cinematography."

1. TWO ASPECTS OF THE MOTION PICTURE: RECORDING AND CREATIVE

The name *motion picture* may stand merely for the technical process which consists in a rapid succession of pictures projected on a screen, or for any kind of popular entertainment

* Slavko Vorkapich, "Toward True Cinema," *Film Culture*, No. 19, March 1959, pp. 10–17. Reprinted in Lewis Jacobs, *Introduction to the Art of the Movies*. New York, Noonday, 1960, pp. 288–296.

produced and presented in such a way, or, among other things, for a truly creative use of a rapid succession of pictures projected on a screen. The name is a general one and a general name is expected to cover a variety of things. But a special meaning of a general name like *painting* becomes immediately apparent when it is placed in a simple context, for example, in "Teaching Painting at a University." Obviously here the sense of creative use of the tools of painting is intended, and not house- or furniture-painting and other similar uses of brush and paint. It may be worth noting that in the case of *painting* the general name is reserved for the creative use of the medium, while other uses have to be qualified.

Now, with the word *creative*, especially in connection with motion pictures, one can get into real semantic and philosophic difficulties if one tries to prove as true one's assumptions about it.

One of my claims is that most of the films made so far are examples not of creative use of motion-picture devices and techniques, but examples of their use as recording instruments and processes only. There are extremely few motion pictures that may be cited as instances of creative use of the medium, and from these only fragments and short passages may be compared to the best achievements in other arts.

Often, when a specific example, like the lunch-hour sequence in the documentary *The City*, is mentioned, a number of listeners would come up with some such question: "You mean a series of quick cuts?"—"Do you think it is possible to make a whole picture like that?" If I mention McLaren's *Fiddle-Dee-Dee*: "Oh, you mean abstract shapes dancing to music?"—If I describe passages from Cocteau's *Beauty and the Beast*, some jump at the conclusion that I mean fantasy and symbolism, and if, with some hesitation, I mention some of my own work I can almost hear a few of them thinking: "Now we know! You mean camera tricks! You mean montage: the Hollywood kind, not the Eisenstein kind! You mean flip-flops and wipes and zooms and the camera on the flying trapeze!"

Perhaps the right answer would be: Yes, all of these things and much more. But first let me try to explain what may *not* be considered as the creative use of the medium, what may be called the *recording* use only, or an *extension* of some other medium of communication or expression.

The technical nature of the film medium is such that it may very easily and profitably be utilized as such an extension. In this sense it may be compared to various uses of printing of words; to various uses of still photography: reporting, keeping records of events, people, things, etc.; to uses of drawing and painting for scientific exposition such as diagrams, charts, and illustrations in books on biology, botany, medicine, etc.; or it may be compared to various uses of the sound-recording devices for preserving speeches, lectures, memorable performances of music or for making transcriptions of radio shows. In fact, the film medium *is* used mostly as an extension of each of the various media mentioned. And it is natural that the chief value in such films should lie in that which is recorded: the event, the performance, the person, or the object photographed and the verbal and sound accompaniment that usually goes with it. Rarely is it required that the value consist in a unique filmic structure about the subject.

The fact that some of these recordings have been so effective and at times emotionally very moving may have led many people into believing that this efficient power came from the medium itself. Now, no one would call a *phonograph record* of a master conductor's interpretation of a great composer's composition—no one would call that record a musical masterpiece, no matter how technically perfect it was. But, quite often, technically polished *visual* and sound recordings of great performances in various fields have been hailed as great films. This applies, equally, to most dramatic or story films. Let me illustrate this with a hypothetical example.

Suppose we take a piece of creative writing, e.g., the famous soliloquy from *Hamlet*, and suppose we photograph with a motion-picture camera that passage just as it is printed on the page in a book. Or, for this particular shot, we may have had the monologue printed on parchment in some fancy type designed by a creative typographer, and we may, for extra embellishment, use some real "mood" lighting, like throwing a faint shadow of "a bare bodkin" upon the page. Now would this, in a "rapid succession of pictures projected on a screen," give us a motion picture? Technically, yes. But what creative contribution was achieved by the use of the motion-picture camera, apart from giving us another *record of Shakespeare's* creative work? Obviously, none.

Suppose we elaborate a little more on our shooting of the

174 SLAVKO VORKAPICH

monologue and we get a creative actor and we dress him in a costume designed by a creative designer and put him in a setting designed by a creative art director and we light him with lights full of mood and photograph him with a motion-picture camera and register on film all his expressive actions and gestures and movements of his lips and tongue and cheeks and record his voice on the best sound system available. What do we get this time? A performance really worth preserving and showing all over the world. *But what have we as makers of the picture created except making an embellished record of an actor's acting of a writer's writing?* Again the answer is: obviously nothing. No matter how "amazingly life-like" the picture may seem, strictly speaking, this is what was actually achieved: from a living creative performance a shadow was abstracted by mechanical means. This applies also to complete photoplays. *Photo plays*, how precisely descriptive that name is!

At this point the thought of the close-up as a real filmic contribution usually comes up. The close view is not something specifically filmic, if it is taken in the sense of something brought closer or magnified for closer scrutiny only. Long before the advent of the film, the close-up was to be found in all except stage arts and music. Portraits and still lives in painting, sculpture, and still photography; descriptive detail in literature.

There is a controversy about who "invented" the close-up. Probably the inventor got the idea from observing someone in the audience of a theatre—a *legitimate* theatre, of course—who was using a pair of binoculars to see an actor's or an actress's face at close range. And it is mainly in this telescopic sense that the close-up is still used. No doubt that it adds dramatic emphasis to a photoplay and thus makes up for some of the loss of the performers' living presence. Still we are talking in terms of the theater, and still we are using the medium to record bits of that other art, the actor's creative acting. Let me at this point make clear that I am not opposed to the use of the film medium as an extension of the theatre, I object only to calling such extension creative use of the unique characteristics inherent in cinematography.

Considered filmically or creatively, the close-up has two main functions: visual-dynamic and associative. "Close-up" here means close view of anything relatively small. We react bodily, kinesthetically to any visual change. As a rule the bigger the change, the stronger the reaction. For example, in a sudden cut from a long view of an object to a very close view of it there is, always, an inevitable optical and kinesthetic impact, an explosive magnification, a sudden leap forward. If the object is in motion, the close-up intensifies this motion; as a rule, the greater the area of the screen in motion, the greater the intensity. This seems obvious. And thinking in these terms, one should, obviously, be led into thinking of *degrees* of change, impact, and intensity, and how important—if one hopes to use film creatively—the relative organization of these factors must be. To use a visual medium artistically is to make the visual parts "go well together." Problems of duration, harmony, contrast, proportion, and rhythm, are involved in this sort of visual-dynamic organization, i.e., cutting, which is quite different from editing a sequence of long shots, medium shots, and close-ups according to literary-dramatic requirements only. And a little more thinking in this direction leads one to deeper fundamental differences, through proper shooting for that sort of cutting, down to the original conception, to the problem of how to express a theme filmically. And that is a long way from the stage.

In a close-up an object appears somehow dissociated from its context. It is thus more or less liberated and made available for new combinations, both in respect of its visual values and meaning connotations. The latter are called "association-fields" by Gyorgy Kepes in his remarkable book *Language of Vision*. (Although primarily a study of visual principles operative in static graphic arts, this book is full of fruitful suggestions applicable to motion pictures.) In certain combinations with other fields an object acquires a quality that may be compared to that of a poetic image, but this similarity should not be taken too literally. Each different aspect of the same object has a unique quality and thus it differs from a word, which is more readily variable in a different context. The possibilities of creative organization of filmic imagery are so little known and explored (to some extent by Cocteau) that it seems like an insolence to compare our crude gropings with masterpieces of other arts.

It is clear that the emphasis here is on visual values. But this means more than striking photography, unusual camera angles, and ingenious dolly and boom shots. It is not a question of artistically composed tableaux. It is a problem of composing visually, but in time. Individual shots may be incomplete, as individual musical tones are incomplete in themselves, but they must be "Just right and go well together" with other shots, as tones must with other tones, to make complete and esthetically satisfying units. Beautiful photography is only surface embellishment, while *cinematography* is the gathering of visual-dynamic-meaningful elements, which creative cutting combines into living entities.

The emphasis, then, is on the development of a visual dynamic language, independent of literature and theatrical traditions. The emphasis on the visual aspect does not exclude creative use of sound. It is, however, somewhat amusing to read a chapter on "counterpoint between sound and image" when no one can claim to have mastered the fundamental organization of the factors spoken of in connection with the close-up.

No doubt, the film medium is related, in some ways, to other arts. But relation does not imply imitation. It may learn from other media, but, if it is to be dignified with the name of art, it must not merely copy. In art "speaking likeness" is not a criterion of value.

2. A METHOD OF TEACHING THE CREATIVE USE OF THE MEDIUM

In essential ways the motion-picture medium is unique. And to the study of the possibilities inherent in the medium a method has to be worked out. I can give here only a rough idea of certain aspects of such a method, based on my own experiences teaching film at the Department of Cinema at the University of Southern California.

The teaching should be based on a literal interpretation of the name of the medium: *motion pictures*. *Pictures* should be taken in the sense of *images*. The goal is integration of motion, image, meaning, and sound, but at the beginning the emphasis should be laid on the first part of the name: *motion*.

An effort should be made to dissociate the meaning of the word from certain undesirable connotations. It does not stand merely for stage action, nor a certain type of agitation now so popular with film directors. This may be exemplified by the "movements" of a star, who, during the span of a brief dialogue moves from the couch to the fireplace and to the window, where with a toss she turns her back to her lover and comes to rest, staring out of the window. Nor does it stand merely for a perpetual agitation of the camera, also very popular with the movie directors, who treat the camera like an infant who is not satisfied until it is perambulated or dollied about. The students are asked to make a fresh mental start, if they can, by forgetting, for a while, the daily film fare they have seen. It is then explained that a whole new world is open to them for exploration: the world of motion.

The invention of the cinematic tools has not only given us the means to make "amazingly lifelike" recordings, it has also extended, immensely, the possibility of a heightened perceptual grasp of reality.

In static visual arts students are trained in a sensitive perception of the shape of things, while here they are directed toward a keener perception of the *shapes of the motions* that things generate. At first they are required to observe simple motions. An example of a simple motion would be a segment of space as it is cut out by a door opening or closing, a complex motion would be one traced by a newspaper dancing high in the wind. The emphasis is on object motion, because of the geometric simplicity of such motions. The students are requested to observe, analyze, compare, classify, and describe these motions.

The human perceptive mechanism is such that it may interpret as motion certain phenomena where no actual motion occurs. This was thoroughly investigated by Gestalt psychologists and is called phi-phenomenon or apparent movement. "Under appropriate conditions successive presentation of two lights at two points not too distant from each other results in an experience of movement from the first to the second" (Koehler). Our experiments show that there is a sensation of displacement or a visual leap in a cut between any two sufficiently different shots. This may be demonstrated very vividly if short strips of the shots, approximately ten frames each, are rapidly alternated. In certain cases a clear transformation of one shape into another may be experienced. By making their own selections of shots or designs and intercutting them in various ways students become aware of a new purely filmic force: more or less intense visual impact that occurs at each cut.

The project following these exercises consists in a thorough observation of a complete simple activity or occupation where a limited variety of motions is involved. Again the emphasis is on the motions of objects, for example in the wrapping of a package, preparing food, loading of a truck, etc. The complete action is broken down into as many simple motions as possible and each is shot from a great variety of angles. This kind of analysis, or overanalysis, is different from recording previously discussed. Here the motion-picture camera is in its natural element. This process is really a filmic liberation of bits of dynamic visual energies, extracted from a simple event in reality. Each angle is selected to take hold of a single clear visual note. None is intended for an individual display as a "best shot" in the picture, not any more than a note is intended to be the best in a melody. In the recreation of the event in cutting, each filmic facet acquires value only by its place in the total filmic structure. And the student's sense for structure grows out of these exercises in analysis.

Sometimes, in cutting, the movements are slightly overlapped, i.e., each new fragment begins a little back of the point already reached by the preceding fragment; in other words, in each new strip a small fraction of the preceding movement is repeated. Often surprisingly beautiful effects result. A sort of rhythmical time-stretching occurs. There are several striking instances of this effect in Eisenstein's earlier films.

Most students soon will become aware that very simple everyday actions may be made exciting by means of filmic analysis, and that there is a new kind of visual beauty to be found in the ordinary world around them. One can say that where there is physical action there is visual poetry.

The next stage in the student's work should consist in exploring the associative possibilities between images. Students should be asked to make simple statements entirely by visual means. Some may become capable of expressing truly poetic moods; those with vivid imaginations may bring in surprisingly effective free combinations of images, while others may succeed in making simple documentaries interesting and visually exciting.

The work done this way may be compared to the creation

of simple melodies. Once the student has mastered this elementary process, he should be prepared to orchestrate several movements within a shot and to achieve a more complex organization of images for themes of greater complexity, so that perhaps, some day, he may learn how to make, not *photoplays*, but dramatic *motion pictures*.

HANS RICHTER

The Film as an Original Art Form*

"The distortion and dissection of a movement, an object, or a
form, and its reconstruction in cinematic terms."

*Thus does Hans Richter attempt to describe one aspect of
the early experimental film. Yet neither "the orchestration
of motion in visual rhythms" nor "the use of the magic qualities of the film" does more than hint at the ways in which
motion-picture makers have sometimes left modern art, as
well as the traditional arts, behind. Avant-garde films are
almost impossible to describe, and they are "essentially cinematic," Richter says, because they are "not repeatable in any
other medium." They represent a "complete liberation from
the conventional story."*

*On the other hand, Richter—film teacher and experimental
director of 8×8 and* Dreams That Money Can Buy—*also
proposes that two of the most important "revolts" in film history revolved around the documentary style. In Russia, Eisenstein's* Potemkin *marked the beginning of a great period; even
for the outside world it was a shock and a stimulus. Similarly,
after World War II, Rosselini's* Paisan *began the neorealist
movement in Italy that affected directors as far away as India,
Korea, and Japan. In "the free use of nature, including man,
as raw material," the documentary approach goes back to a
form "not bound by theatrical or literary tradition."*

The main esthetic problem in the movies, which were invented
for reproduction (of movement), is, paradoxically, the overcoming of reproduction. In other words the question is: to
what degree is the camera (film, color, sound, etc.) developed
and used to reproduce (any object which appears before the

* Hans Richter, "The Film as an Original Art Form," *Film
Culture*, Vol. 1, No. 1, January 1955, pp. 19–23.

lens) or to produce (sensations not possible in any other art medium)?

This question is by no means a purely technical or mechanical one. The technical liberation of the camera is intimately inter-related with psychological, social, economic and esthetic problems. They all play a role in deciding to what use technique is put and how much it is liberated. Before this fundamental matter, with its manifold implications, is sufficiently cleared up it is impossible to speak of the film as an independent art form, even as an art form at all, whatever its promises might be. In the words of Pudovkin: "What is a work of art before it comes in front of the camera, such as acting, staging or the novel, is not a work of art on the screen."

Even to the sincere lover of the film in its present form it must seem that the film is overwhelmingly used for keeping records of creative achievements: of plays, actors, novels or just plain nature, and proportionately less for the creation of original filmic sensations. It is true that the commercial entertainment film uses many of the liberating elements, discovered since 1895 by Méliès, Griffith, Eisenstein and others, leading towards an original cinematic form. But the general tendency of the film industry, as an economic institution, is the distribution of each film to a maximum number of people. This institution has to avoid it to move away from the traditional forms of story-telling to which the maximum number of people are conditioned: the theatre, with the supremacy of the actor— and the novel or the play, with the writer. Both traditions weigh heavily upon the film and prevent it from coming into its own.

David Wark Griffith forced the stage actor, as early as 1909, into mosaic-acting, and broke up, in that way, the uninterrupted scene-acting of the stage actor into hundreds of separately acted scenes which assumed continuity only in the cutting room. His innovation of the close-up and the crosscutting of simultaneous events were revolutionary steps towards a filmic style. But when he broke with theater-acting he gave, involuntarily, an overwhelming influence back to the actor in the creation of the star. As Star the actor immortalized reproduction and dominated the film form once again.

The novel on the other hand has adapted itself in the last fifty years to the film. It has become increasingly image-minded. But its technique of psychological character-development, its style of story-telling, traditional property of literature, dominates the film and makes it also, from this side, reproduction (of literary works, which were original art before they were produced in Hollywood, London, Paris and Rome).

It does not concern us here that in spite of dependency upon other art forms, and in spite of the greater or smaller degree of reproduction, many films have shown exceptional qualities. It is known that the film industry has produced fascinating works, full of inventiveness, inspiration and human values. The problem with which we are dealing here is the film as an original art form. "Good" or "bad" has no meaning as long as it is not clear upon what esthetic fundamentals the film is supposed to be built.

The uncertainty of whether film as such (i.e., the entertainment film) is essentially theatrical, literary, or fine-art, ends with the doubt in the minds of many sincere film historians and critics as to whether the film is, or ever will be, an original art at all! There is also another school of thought which defies the present form of the film altogether, in spite of its overwhelming success and powerful influence, rejects its values as social compensator in offering paradises, complete with gods and goddesses, and sees in it a grandiose perversion of the medium.

Between the two schools I would prefer to say that the fictional film in its present form is a reproduction of several art forms mixed with original cinematographic elements. But the fact is that there are at least two film forms besides the fictional film, which, less spectacular than Hollywood, are more cinematographic in the proper sense of the word.

Several times in the history of the movies a revolt has temporarily broken the hold of the two traditional arts over the entertainment film. To state the two most important revolts: the post-revolutionary silent Russian film (*Potemkin*), and after the liberation of Italy from Fascism the post-war Italian film (*Paisan*). In both cases the fictional film has turned from fiction to history and from theatre style to documentary style in the use of natural setting, people not actors, and real events.

With the documentary approach the film gets back to its fundamentals. Here it has a solid esthetic basis: in the free use of nature, including man, as raw material. By selection, elimination and coordination of natural elements, a film form evolves which is original and not bound by theatrical or literary tradition. That goes of course, as much for the semidocumentary fictional film (*Potemkin, Paisan*), as for the documentary film itself. These elements might obtain a social, economic, political, general human meaning according to their selection and coordination. But this meaning does not exist a priori in the facts, nor is it a reproduction (as in an actor's performance). It is created in the camera and the cutting room. The documentary film is an original art form. It has come to grips with facts—on its own original level. It covers the rational side of our lives, from the scientific experiment to the poetic landscape-study, but never moves away from the factual. Its scope is wide. Nevertheless, it is an original art form only as far as it keeps strictly to the use of natural raw material in rational interpretation. The modern, more convenient technique of re-enacting factual scenes and events is sometimes not without setbacks, as it might easily introduce reproduction through the back door again: in reproducing enacted scenes.

The influence of the documentary film is growing, but its contribution to a filmic art is, by nature, limited. It is limited by the same token by which it has overcome the influence of the two old arts. Since its elements are facts, it can be original art only in the limits of this factuality. Any free use of the magic, poetic, irrational qualities to which the film medium might offer itself would have to be excluded a priori (as nonfactual). But just these qualities are essentially cinematographic, or characteristic of the film and are, esthetically, the ones which promise future development. That is where the second of the original film-forms has its place: the experimental film.

There is a short chapter in the history of the movies which dealt especially with this side of the film. It was made by individuals concerned essentially with the film medium. They were neither prejudiced by production clichés nor by necessity of rational interpretation nor by financial obligations. The story of these individual artists, at the beginning of the twenties, under the name of "avant-garde," can be properly read as a history of the conscious attempt to overcome reproduction and to arrive at the free use of the means of cinematographic expression. This movement spread over Europe and was sustained for the greatest part by modern painters who, in their own field had broken away from the conventional: Eggeling, Léger, Duchamp, Man Ray, Picabia, Ruttmann, Brugière, Len Lye, Cocteau, myself and others.

The fact that it was nearly exclusively modern artists who represented this movement gives a hint of the direction in which the liberation of the film was sought. Already, in the 1910's Canudo and Delluc in France spoke of "photogenic" as the new plastic quality of the film medium. René Clair went further and declared film as a visual medium per se: "A blind man in a regular theatre and a deaf mute in a movie theatre should still get the essentials from the performance." The spoken word for the stage, the silent image for the film— those are the elements!

These artists discovered that film as a visual medium fitted into the tradition of the art without violation of its funda- mentals. It was there that it could develop freely: "The film should positively avoid any connection with the historical, educational, romantic, moral, or immoral, geographic or doc- umentary subjects. The film should become, step by step, finally exclusively cinematography, that means that it should use exclusively photogenic elements" (Jean Epstein, 1923). Problems in modern art lead directly into the film. Organiza- tion and orchestration of form, color, the dynamics of motion, simultaneity, were problems with which Cézanne, the cubists, the futurists had to deal. Eggeling and I came directly out of the structural problems of abstract art, *nolens volens* into the film medium. The connection to theatre and literature was, completely severed. Cubism, expressionism, dadaism, abstract art, surrealism found not only their expression in films but a new fulfillment on a new level.

The tradition of modern art grew on a large front, logically, together with and into the film: the orchestration of motion in visual rhythms—the plastic expression of an object in mo- tion under varying light conditions, "to create the rhythm of common objects in space and time, to present them in their plastic beauty, this seemed to me worthwhile" (Léger)—the distortion and dissection of a movement, an object or a form and its reconstruction in cinematic terms (just as the cubists dissected and rebuilt in pictorial terms)—the denaturalization of the object in any form to re-create it cinematographically with light—light with its transparency and airiness as a poetic, dramatic, constructive material—the use of the magic qualities of the film to create original state of the dream—the complete liberation from the conventional story and its chronology in dadaist and surrealist developments in which the object is taken out of its conventional context and is put into new relationships, creating in that way a new content altogether. "The external object has broken away from its habitual environment. Its component parts had liberated themselves from the object in such a way that they could set up entirely new relationships with other elements"—André Breton (about Max Ernst).

The external object was used, as in the documentary film, as raw material, but instead of employing it for a rational theme of social, economic, scientific nature, it has broken away from its habitual environment and was used as material to express irrational visions. Films like *Ballet Mécanique*, *Entr'acte, Emak Bakia, Ghosts Before Breakfast, Andalusian Dog, Diagonal Symphony, Anaemic Cinema, Blood of a Poet, Dreams That Money Can Buy* and many others were not repeatable in any other medium and are essentially cinematic.

It is still too early to speak of a tradition, or of a style, comparable to those in older arts. The movement is still too young. There are, nevertheless, general traceable directions which cover a great deal of these efforts: abstract art and surrealism. Here in the United States is the work of the Whitney brothers and Francis Lee, the most characteristic of the one; the films of Curtis Harrington, Maya Deren, and Frank Stauffacher are examples of the other. There are many serious attempts but also many followers who use and abuse the sensations easily obtainable in this medium. Especially surrealism seems to offer a welcome excuse for the exhibition of a whole menu of inhibitions.

In England, France, Denmark, Holland, Belgium, experimental film groups of individual artists, mostly painters, have taken up the work begun by the avant-garde of the twenties. They are following the only realistic line which an artist can follow: artistic integrity. In that way a tradition, temporarily interrupted by the stormy political events in Europe, has been taken up by a young generation, here and abroad. It is obvious today that this tradition will not be eradicated again but will grow. As small or as big as this movement might become, it has opened a new road to film as an art-form and has, as such, more than mere historical significance.

The stronger and more independent the documentary and the experimental film become, and the more the general audience has occasion to see them, the more they will adapt themselves to a screen-style instead of a theater-style. Only after such a transformation of the general audience has taken place, the entertainment film can and will follow. At such golden times film entertainment and film-art might become identical.

ARNOLD HAUSER

Space and Time in the Film*

"The time experience of the present age consists above all in an awareness of the moment in which we find ourselves: in an awareness of the present."

In Arnold Hauser's two-volume study, The Social History of Art, *"The Film Age" is a brief but provocative finale. Included in it is an arresting analysis of the relation between the modern temper and the space-time aspects of cinema. The contemporary and the simultaneous are what preoccupy us, and this is part of the reason for the "abruptness" of modern art. In the film, space and time are interrelated. Close-ups and long shots are not merely matters of distance but also of timing and climax. Events in time are brought close to us or separated by flashbacks in much the same way that the camera goes in and out of separate rooms. Such potentialities separate the motion picture from theatre and from the plastic arts, which are restricted to certain limits in time and space.*

Dr. Hauser, who is a European author and professor of art history, goes on to say that writers who are aware of all this are "not finding their way to the film," and one reason is that motion-picture production is so dependent on the cooperation of many people. Alain Resnais and other "new wave" directors, who undoubtedly read some of Hauser's writings, have since shown us what can be done with time in film.

In another illuminating passage, Dr. Hauser compares the American and Russian fondness for machines, for motion pictures, and for the documentary reproduction of life. In fact, mechanical things—"running and racing, travelling and flying, escape and pursuit"—are basic for film: "the machine is its origin, its medium, and its most suitable subject."

* Arnold Hauser, *The Social History of Art* (2 vols.). New York, Knopf, 1951. Also Vintage Books, Vol. 4, pp. 239–249, 256–257.

187

The theatre is in many respects the artistic medium most
similar to the film; particularly in view of its combination of
spatial and temporal forms, it represents the only real analogy
to the film. But what happens on the stage is partly spatial,
partly temporal; as a rule spatial and temporal, but never a
mixture of the spatial and the temporal, as are the happenings
in a film. The most fundamental difference between the film
and the other arts is that, in its world-picture, the boundaries
of space and time are fluid—space has a quasi-temporal, time,
to some extent, a spatial character. In the plastic arts, as
also on the stage, space remains static, motionless, unchanging, without a goal and with a direction; we move about quite
freely in it, because it is homogeneous in all its parts and
because none of the parts presupposes the other temporally.
The phases of the movement are not stages, not steps in a
gradual development; their sequence is subject to no con-
straint. Time in literature—above all in the drama—on the
other hand, has a definite direction, a trend of development,
an objective goal, independent of the spectator's experience
of time; it is no mere reservoir, but an ordered succession.
Now, these dramaturgical categories of space and time have
their character and functions completely altered in the film.
Space loses its static quality, its serene passivity and now
becomes dynamic; it comes into being as it were before our
eyes. It is fluid, unlimited, unfinished, an element with its
own history, its own scheme and process of development.
Homogeneous physical space here assumes the characteristics
of heterogeneously composed historical time. In this medium
the individual stages are no longer of the same kind, the
individual parts of space no longer of equal value; it contains
specially qualified positions, some with a certain priority in
the development and others signifying the culmination of the
spatial experience. The use of the close-up, for example, not
only has spatial criteria, it also represents a phase to be
reached or to be surpassed in the temporal development of
the film. In a good film the close-ups are not distributed
arbitrarily and capriciously. They are not cut in independently
of the inner development of the scene, not at any time and
anywhere, but only where their potential energy can and
should make itself felt. For a close-up is not a cut-out picture
with a frame; it is always merely part of a picture, like,
for instance, the *repoussoir* figures in baroque painting which

introduce a dynamic quality into the picture similar to that created by the close-ups in the spatial structure of a film.

But as if space and time in the film were interrelated by being interchangeable, the temporal relationships acquire an almost spatial character, just as space acquires a topical interest and takes on temporal characteristics; in other words, a certain element of freedom is introduced into the succession of their moments. In the temporal medium of a film we move in a way that is otherwise peculiar to space, completely free to choose our direction, proceeding from one phase of time into another, just as one goes from one room to another, disconnecting the individual stages in the development of events and grouping them, generally speaking, according to the principles of spatial order. In brief, time here loses, on the one hand, its uninterrupted continuity, on the other, its irreversible direction. It can be brought to standstill: in close-ups; reversed: in flash-backs; repeated: in recollections; and skipped across: in visions of the future. Concurrent, simultaneous events can be shown successively, and temporally distinct events simultaneously—by double-exposure and alternation; the earlier can appear later, the later before its time. This cinematic conception of time has a thoroughly subjective and apparently irregular character compared with the empirical and the dramatic conception of the same medium. The time of empirical reality is a uniformly progressive, uninterruptedly continuous, absolutely irreversible order, in which events follow one another as if "on a conveyor belt." It is true that dramatic time is by no means identical with empirical time—the embarrassment caused by a clock showing the correct time on the stage comes from this discrepancy—and the unity of time prescribed by classicistic dramaturgy can even be interpreted as the fundamental elimination of ordinary time, and yet the temporal relationships in the drama have more points of contact with the chronological order of ordinary experience than the order of time in a film. Thus in the drama, or at least in one and the same act of a drama, the temporal continuity of empirical reality is preserved intact. Here too, as in real life, events follow each other according to the law of a progression which permits neither interruptions and jumps, nor repetitions and inversions, and conforms to a standard of time which is absolutely constant, that is, undergoes no acceleration, retardation or stoppages of any kind within the several sections (acts or scenes). In the film, on the other hand, not only the speed of successive events, but also the chronometric standard itself is often different from shot to shot, according as to whether slow or fast motion, short or long cutting, many or few close-ups, are used.

The dramatist is prohibited by the logic of scenic arrangement from repeating moments and phases of time, an expedient that is often the source of the most intensive aesthetic effects in the film. It is true that a part of the story is often treated retrospectively in the drama, and the antecedents followed backwards in time, but they are usually represented indirectly—either in the form of a coherent narrative or of one limited to scattered hints. The technique of the drama does not permit the playright to go back to past stages in the course of a progressively developing plot and to insert them *directly* into the sequence of events, into the dramatic present—that is, it is only recently that it has begun to permit it, perhaps under the immediate influence of the film, or under the influence of the new conception of time, familiar also from the modern novel. The technical possibility of interrupting any shot without further ado suggests the possibilities of a discontinuous treatment of time from the very outset and provides the film with the means of heightening the tension of a scene either by interpolating heterogeneous incidents or assigning the individual phases of the scene to different sections of the work. In this way the film often produces the effect of someone playing on a keyboard and striking the keys ad libitum, up and down, to right and left. In a film we often see the hero first at the beginning of his career as a young man, later, going back to the past, as a child; we then see him, in the further course of the plot, as a mature man and, having followed his career for a time, we, finally, may see him still living after his death, in the memory of one of his relations or friends. As a result of the discontinuity of time, the retrospective development of the plot is combined with the progressive in complete freedom, with no kind of chronological tie, and through the repeated twists and turns in the time-continuum, mobility, which is the very essence of the cinematic experience, is pushed to the uttermost limits. The real spatialization of time in the film does not take place, however, until the simultaneity of parallel plots is portrayed. It is the experience of the simultaneity of different, spatially separated happenings that puts the audience into that condition of suspense which moves between space and time and claims the categories of both orders for itself. It is the simultaneous nearness and remoteness of things—their nearness to one another in time and their distance from one another in space—that constitutes that spatio-temporal element, that two-dimensionality of time, which is the real medium of the film and the basic category of its world-picture.

It was discovered in a comparatively early stage in the history of the film that the representation of two simultaneous sequences of events is part of the original stock of cinematic forms. First this simultaneity was simply recorded and brought to the notice of the audience by clocks showing the same time or by similar direct indications; the artistic technique of the intermittent treatment of a double plot and the alternating montage of the single phases of such a plot only developed step by step. But later on we come across examples of this technique at every turn. And whether we stand between two rival parties, two competitors or two doubles, the structure of the film is dominated in any case by the crossing and intersecting of the two different lines, by the bilateral character of the development and the simultaneity of the opposing actions. The famous finish of the early, already classical Griffith films, in which the upshot of an exciting plot is made to depend on whether a train or a car, the intriguer or the "king's messenger on horseback," the murderer or the rescuer, reaches the goal first, using the then revolutionary technique of continuously changing pictures, flashing and vanishing like lightning, became the pattern of the denouement since followed by most films in similar situations.

The time experience of the present age consists above all in an awareness of the moment in which we find ourselves: in an awareness of the present. Everything topical, contemporary, bound together in the present moment is of special significance and value to the man of today, and, filled with this idea, the mere fact of simultaneity acquires new meaning in his eyes. His intellectual world is imbued with the atmosphere of the immediate present, just as that of the Middle Ages was characterized by an otherworldly atmosphere and

that of the enlightenment by a mood of forward-looking
expectancy. He experiences the greatness of his cities, the
miracles of his technics, the wealth of his ideas, the hidden
depths of his psychology in the contiguity, the interconnec-
tions and dovetailing of things and processes. The fascination
of "simultaneity," the discovery that, on the one hand, the
same man experiences so many different, unconnected and
irreconcilable things in one and the same moment, and that,
on the other, different men in different places often experience
the same things, that the same things are happening at the
same time in places completely isolated from each other,
this universalism, of which modern technics have made contemporary man conscious, is perhaps the real source of the
new conception of time and of the whole abruptness with
which modern art describes life. This rhapsodic quality, which
distinguishes the modern novel most sharply from the older
novel, is at the same time the characteristic accountable for
its most cinematic effects. The discontinuity of the plot and
the scenic development, the sudden emersion of the thoughts
and moods, the relativity and the inconsistency of the time-
standards, are what remind us in the works of Proust and
Joyce, Dos Passos, and Virginia Woolf of the cuttings, dissolves and interpolations of the film, and it is simply film
magic when Proust brings two incidents, which may lie thirty
years apart, as closely together as if there were only two hours
between them. The way in which, in Proust, past and present,
dreams and speculation join hands across the intervals of
space and time, the sensibility, always on the scent of new
tracks, roams about in space and time, and the boundaries
of space and time vanish in this endless and boundless stream
of interrelations: all this corresponds exactly to that mixture
of space and time in which the film moves. Proust never
mentions dates and ages; we never know exactly how old
the hero of his novel is, and even the chronological relationships of the events often remain rather vague. The experiences
and happenings do not cohere by reason of their proximity
in time, and the attempt to demarcate and arrange them
chronologically would be all the more nonsensical from his
point of view as, in his opinion, every man has his typical
experiences which recur periodically. The boy, the youth and
the man always experience fundamentally the same things;
the meaning of an incident often does not dawn on him until

years after he has experienced and endured it; but he can hardly ever distinguish the deposit of the years that are past from the experience of the present hour in which he is living. Is one not in every moment of one's life the same child or the same invalid or the same lonely stranger with the same wakeful, sensitive, unappeased nerves? Is one not in every situation of life the person capable of experiencing this and that, who possesses, in the recurring features of his experience, the one protection against the passage of time? Do not all our experiences take place as it were at the same time? And is this simultaneity not really the negation of time? And this negation, is it not a struggle for the recovery of that inwardness of which physical space and time deprive us?

Joyce fights for the same inwardness, the same directness of experience, when he, like Proust, breaks up and merges well-articulated, chronologically organized time. In his work, too, it is the interchangeability of the contents of consciousness which triumphs over the chronological arrangement of the experiences; for him, too, time is a road without direction, on which man moves to and fro. But he pushes the spatialization of time even further than Proust, and shows the inner happenings not only in longitudinal but also in cross-sections. The images, ideas, brain-waves and memories stand side by side with sudden and absolute abruptness; hardly any consideration is paid to their origins, all the emphasis is on their contiguity, their simultaneity. The spatialization of time goes so far in Joyce, that one can begin the reading of *Ulysses* where one likes, with only a rough knowledge of the context—not necessarily only after a first reading, as has been said, and almost in any sequence one cares to choose. The medium in which the reader finds himself is in fact wholly spatial, for the novel describes not only the picture of a great city, but also adopts its structure to some extent, the network of its streets and squares, in which people stroll about, walking in and out and stopping when and where they like. It is supremely characteristic of the cinematic quality of this technique that Joyce wrote his novel not in the final succession of the chapters, but—as is the custom in the production of films—made himself independent of the sequence of the plot and worked at several chapters at the same time.

We meet the Bergsonian conception of time, as used in

the film and the modern novel—though not always so unmistakably as here—in all the genres and trends of contemporary
art. The *"simultanéité des états d'âmes"* is, above all, the
basic experience connecting the various tendencies of modern
painting, the futurism of the Italians with the expressionism
of Chagall, and the cubism of Picasso with the surrealism
of Giorgio de Chirico or Salvador Dali. Bergson discovered
the counterpoint of spiritual processes and the musical structure of their interrelationships. Just as, when we listen
properly to a piece of music, we have in our ears the mutual
connection of each new note with all those that have already
sounded, so we always possess in our deepest and most vital
experiences everything that we have ever experienced and
made our own in life. If we understand ourselves, we read
our own souls as a musical score, we resolve the chaos of
the entangled sounds and transform them into a polyphony
of different parts.—All art is a game with and a fight against
chaos; it is always advancing more and more dangerously
towards chaos and rescuing more and more extensive provinces of the spirit from its clutch. If there is any progress
in the history of art, then it consists in the constant growth
of these provinces wrested from chaos. With its analysis of
time, the film stands in the direct line of this development:
it has made it possible to represent visually experiences that
have previously been expressed only in musical forms. The
artist capable of filling this new possibility, this still empty
form, with real life has not yet arrived, however.

The crisis of the film, which seems to be developing into
a chronic illness, is due above all to the fact that the film
is not finding its writers or, to put it more accurately, the
writers are not finding their way to the film. Accustomed to
doing as they like within their own four walls, they are now
required to take into account producers, directors, scriptwriters, cameramen, art-directors, and technicians of all kinds,
although they do not acknowledge the authority of this spirit
of co-operation, or indeed the idea of artistic co-operation at
all. Their feelings revolt against the idea of the production
of works of art being surrendered to a collective, to a "concern," and they feel that it is a disparagement of art that
an extraneous dictate, or at best a majority, should have the
last word in decisions of the motives of which they are often
unable to account for themselves. From the point of view

of the nineteenth century, the situation with which the writer is asked to come to terms is quite unusual and unnatural. The atomized and uncontrolled artistic endeavours of the present now meet for the first time with a principle opposed to their anarchy. For the mere fact of an artistic enterprise based on co-operation is evidence of an integrating tendency of which—if one disregards the theatre, where it is in any case more a matter of the reproduction than the production of works of art—there had really been no perfect example since the Middle Ages, and, in particular, since the mason's lodge. How far removed film production still is, however, from the generally accepted principle of an artistic co-operative group is shown not only by the inability of most writers to establish a connection with film, but also by such a phenomenon as Chaplin, who believes that he must do as much as possible in his films on his own: the acting of the main part, the direction, the script, the music. But even if it is only the beginning of a new method of organized art production, the, for the present, still empty framework of a new integration, nevertheless, here too, as in the whole economic, social and political life of the present age, what is being striven for is the comprehensive planning without which both our cultural and material world threaten to go to pieces. We are confronted here with the same tension as we find throughout our social life: democracy and dictatorship, specialization and integration, rationalism and irrationalism, colliding with each other. But if even in the field of economics and politics planning cannot always be solved by imposing rules of conduct, it is all the less possible in art, where all violation of spontaneity, all forcible levelling down of taste, all institutional regulation of personal initiative, are involved in great though certainly not such mortal dangers as is often imagined.

But how, in an age of the most extreme specialization and the most sophisticated individualism, are harmony and an integration of individual endeavours to be brought about? How, to speak on a practical level, is the situation to be brought to an end in which the most poverty-stricken literary inventions sometimes underlie the technically most successful films? It is not a question of competent directors against incompetent writers, but of two phenomena belonging to different periods of time—the lonely, isolated writer dependent on his own resources and the problems of the film which can only be solved collectively. The co-operative film-unit anticipates a social technique to which we are not yet equal, just as the newly invented camera anticipated an artistic technique of which no one at the time really knew the range and power. The reunion of the divided functions, first of all the personal union of the director and the author, which has been suggested as a way to surmount the crisis, would be more an evasion of the problem than its solution, for it would prevent but not abolish the specialization that has to be overcome, would not bring about but merely avoid the necessity of the planning which is needed. Incidentally, the monistic-individual principle in the discharge of the various functions, in place of a collectively organized division of labour, corresponds not merely externally and technically to an amateurish method of working, but it also involves a lack of inner tension which is reminiscent of the simplicity of the amateur film. Or may the whole effort to achieve a production of art based on planning only have been a temporary disturbance, a mere episode, which is now being swept away again by the torrent of individualism? May the film be perhaps not the beginning of a new artistic era, but merely the somewhat hesitant continuation of the old individualistic culture, still full of vitality, to which we owe the whole of post-medieval art?—Only if this were so, would it be possible to solve the film crisis by the personal union of certain functions, that is, by partly surrendering the principle of collective labour.

The film crisis is, however, also connected with a crisis in the public itself. The millions and millions who fill the many thousands of cinemas all over the world from Hollywood to Shanghai and from Stockholm to Cape Town daily and hourly, this unique world-embracing league of mankind, have a very confused social structure. The only link between these people is that they all stream into the cinemas, and stream out of them again as amorphously as they are pumped in; they remain a heterogeneous, inarticulate, shapeless mass with the only common feature of belonging to no uniform class or culture. This mass of cinema-goers can hardly be called a "public" proper, for only a more or less constant group of patrons can be described as such, one which is able to some extent to guarantee the continuity of production in a certain field of art. Public-like agglomerations are based on mutual understanding; even if opinions are divided, they diverge on one and the same plane. But with the masses who sit together in the cinemas and who had undergone no previous common intellectual formation of any kind, it would be futile to look for such a platform of mutual understanding. If they dislike a film there is such a small chance of agreement amongst them as to reasons for their rejection of the film that one must assume that even general approval is based on a misunderstanding. . . .

The film is the only art in which Soviet Russia has important achievements to its credit. The affinity between the young communist state and the new form of expression is obvious. Both are revolutionary phenomena moving along new paths, without a historical past, without binding and crippling traditions, without presuppositions of a cultural or routine nature of any kind. The film is an elastic, extremely malleable, unexhausted form which offers no inner resistance to the expression of the new ideas. It is an unsophisticated, popular means of communication, making a direct appeal to the broad masses, an ideal instrument of propaganda the value of which was immediately recognized by Lenin. Its attraction as an irreproachable, that is to say, historically uncompromised, entertainment was so great from the point of view of communist cultural policy from the very outset, its picture-book-like style so easy to grasp, the possibility of using it to propagate ideas to the uneducated so simple, that it seemed to have been specially created for the purposes of a revolutionary art. The film is, moreover, an art evolved from the spiritual foundations of technics and, therefore, all the more in accordance with the problems in store for it. The machine is its origin, its medium and its most suitable subject. Films are "fabricated" and they remain tied to an apparatus, to a machine in a narrower sense than the products of the other arts. The machine here stands both between the creative subject and his work and between the receptive subject and his enjoyment of art. The motory, the mechanical, the automatically moving, is the basic phenomenon of the film. Running and racing, travelling and flying, escape and pursuit, the overcoming of spatial obstacles is the cinematic theme par excellence. The film never feels so much in its element as when it has to describe movement, speed and pace. The wonders and mischievous tricks of instruments, automata, and vehicles are among its oldest and most effective subjects. The old film comedies expressed sometimes naïve admiration, at others arrogant contempt for technics, but they were in most cases the self-teasing of man caught in the wheels of a mechanized world. The film is above all a "photograph" and is already as such a technical art, with mechanical origins and aiming at mechanical repetition,[1] in other words, thanks to the cheapness of its reproduction, a popular and fundamentally "democratic" art. It is perfectly comprehensible that it suited bolshevism with its romanticism of the machine, its fetishism of technics, and its admiration for efficiency. Just as it is also comprehensible that the Russians and the Americans, as the two most technically-minded peoples, were partners and rivals in the development of this art. The film was, however, not only in accord with their technicism, but also with their interest in the documentary, the factual and the authentic. All the more important works of Russian film art are to some extent documentary films, historical documents of the building up of the new Russia, and the best we owe to the American film consists in the documentary reproduction of American life, of the everyday routine of the American economic and administrative machine, of the skyscraper cities and the Middle West farms, the American police and the gangster world. For a film is the more cinematic, the greater the share extrahuman, material facts have in its description of reality, in other words, the closer the connection in this description between man and the world, the personality and the milieu, the end and the means.

[1] Walter Benjamin, "L'Œuvre d'art à l'époque de sa reproduction mécanisée," *Zeitschrift fuer Sozialforschung*, 1936, Vol. 1, p. 45.

SUSANNE LANGER

A Note on the Film*

"Cinema is 'like' dream in the mode of its presentation; it creates a virtual present, an order of direct apparition."

In her book, Philosophy in a New Key, *Susanne Langer put forward the proposition that man differs from other creatures primarily because he uses symbolic means of communication. It is natural, therefore, that this Columbia University professor of philosophy would be interested in the film and would find it "not only a new technique, but a new poetic mode." This mode is not the mode of fiction, which is "like" memory, or of drama, which is "like" action. It is the mode of dream, with the dreamer "always at the center of it."*

Because of its unique character, this new art "seems to be omnivorous, able to assimilate the most diverse materials." She finds film more closely related to the epic and the novel than to the drama. The stage has a framework of fixed space; dream events are "often intensely concerned with space—intervals, endless roads, bottomless canyons, things too high, too near, too far—but they are not oriented in any total space." Film is free of temporal restrictions, too, because "the dream mode is an endless Now."

Here is a new art. For a few decades it seemed like nothing more than a new technical device in the sphere of drama, a new way of preserving and retailing dramatic performances. But today its development has already belied this assumption. The screen is not a stage, and what is created in the concep-

* Susanne Langer, "A Note on the Film," from *Feeling and Form.* New York, Scribner, 1953, pp. 411–415. Quoted in Daniel Talbot, *Film: An Anthology.* New York, Simon and Schuster, 1959, pp. 51–55.

tion and realization of a film is not a play. It is too early to systematize any theory of this new art, but even in its present pristine state it exhibits—quite beyond any doubt, I think—not only a new technique, but a new poetic mode. . . .

The moving camera divorced the screen from the stage. The straightforward photographing of stage action, formerly viewed as the only artistic possibility of the film, henceforth appeared as a special technique. The screen actor is not governed by the stage, nor by the conventions of the theatre, he has his own realm and conventions; indeed, there may be no "actor" at all. The documentary film is a pregnant invention. The cartoon does not even involve persons merely "behaving."

The fact that the moving picture could develop to a fairly high degree as a silent art, in which speech had to be reduced and concentrated into brief, well-spaced captions, was another indication that it was not simply drama. It used pantomime, and the first aestheticians of the film considered it as essentially pantomime. But it is not pantomime; it swallowed that ancient popular art as it swallowed the photograph.

One of the most striking characteristics of this new art is that it seems to be omnivorous, able to assimilate the most diverse materials and turn them into elements of its own. With every new invention—montage, the sound track, Technicolor—its devotees have raised a cry of fear that now its "art" must be lost. Since every such novelty is, of course, promptly exploited before it is even technically perfected, and flaunted in its rawest state, as a popular sensation, in the flood of meaningless compositions that steadily supplies the show business, there is usually a tidal wave of particularly bad rubbish in association with every important advance. But the art goes on. It swallows everything: dancing, skating, drama, panorama, cartooning, music (it almost always requires music).

Therewithal it remains a poetic art. But it is not any poetic art we have known before; it makes the primary illusion—virtual history—in its own mode.

This is essentially, *the dream mode*. I do not mean that it copies dream, or puts one into a daydream. Not at all; no more than literature invokes memory, or makes us believe that *we* are remembering. An art mode is *a mode of appearance*. Fiction is "like" memory in that it is projected to compose a finished experiential form, a "past"—not the reader's past, nor the writer's, though the latter may make a claim to it (that, as well as the use of actual memory as a model, is a literary device). Drama is "like" action in being causal, creating a total imminent experience, a personal "future" or Destiny. Cinema is "like" dream in the mode of its presentation; it creates a virtual present, an order of direct apparition. That is the mode of dream.

The most noteworthy formal characteristic of dream is that the dreamer is always at the center of it. Places shift, persons act and speak, or change or fade—facts emerge, situations grow, objects come into view with strange importance, ordinary things infinitely valuable or horrible, and they may be superseded by others that are related to them essentially by feeling, not by natural proximity. But the dreamer is always "there," his relation is, so to speak, equidistant from all events. Things may occur around him or unroll before his eyes; he may act or want to act, or suffer or contemplate; but the *immediacy* of everything in a dream is the same for him.

This aesthetic peculiarity, this relation to things perceived, characterizes the *dream mode:* it is this that the moving picture takes over, and thereby it creates a virtual present. In its relation to the images, actions, events that constitute the story, the camera is in the place of the dreamer.

But the camera *is* not a dreamer. We are usually agents in a dream. The camera (and its complement, the microphone) is not itself "in" the picture. It is the mind's eye and nothing more. Neither is the picture (if it is art) likely to be dreamlike in its structure. It is a poetic composition, coherent, organic, governed by a definitely conceived feeling, not dictated by actual emotional pressures.

The basic abstraction whereby virtual history is created in the dream mode is immediacy of experience, "givenness," or "authenticity." This is what the art of the film abstracts from actuality, from our actual dreaming.

The percipient of a moving picture sees with the camera; his standpoint moves with it, his mind is pervasively present. The camera is his eye (as the microphone is his ear—and there is no reason why a mind's eye and a mind's ear must always stay together). *He takes the place of the dreamer,* but in a perfectly objectified dream—that is, he is not in the story. The work is the appearance of a dream, a unified, continuously passing, significant *apparition*.

Conceived in this way, a good moving picture is a work of art by all the standards that apply to art as such. Sergei Eisenstein speaks of good and bad films as, respectively, "vital" and "lifeless";[1] speaks of photographic shots as "elements,"[2] which combine into "images," which are "objectively unpresentable" (I would call them poetic impressions), but are greater elements compounded of "representations," whether by montage or symbolic acting or any other means.[3] The whole is governed by the "initial general image which originally hovered before the creative artist"[4]—the matrix, the commanding form; and it is this (not, be it remarked, the artist's emotion) that is to be evoked in the mind of the spectator.

Yet Eisenstein believed that the beholder of a film was somewhat specially called on to use his imagination, to create his own experience of the story.[5] Here we have, I think, an indication of the powerful illusion the film makes not of things going on, but of the dimension in which they go on— a *virtual* creative imagination; for it *seems* one's own creation, direct visionary experience, a "dreamed reality." Like most artists, he took the virtual experience for the most obvious fact.[6]

[1] *The Film Sense*, p. 17.

[2] *Ibid.*, p. 4.

[3] *Ibid.*, p. 8.

[4] *Ibid.*, p. 31.

[5] *Ibid.*, p. 33: ". . . the spectator is drawn into a creative act in which his individuality is not subordinated to the author's individuality, but is opened up throughout the process of fusion with the author's intention, just as the individuality of a great actor is fused with the individuality of a great playwright in the creation of a classic scenic image. In fact, every spectator . . . creates an image in accordance with the representational guidance, suggested by the author, leading him to understanding and experience of the author's theme. This is the same image that was planned and created by the author, but this image is at the same time created also by the spectator himself."

[6] Compare the statement in Ernest Lindgren's *The Art of the Film*, p. 92, apropos of the moving camera: "It is the spectator's own mind that moves."

The fact that a motion picture is not a plastic work but a poetic presentation accounts for its power to assimilate the most diverse materials and transform them into nonpictorial elements. Like dream, it enthralls and commingles all senses; its basic abstraction—direct apparition—is made not only by visual means, though these are paramount, but by words, which punctuate vision, and music that supports the unity of its shifting "world." It needs many, often convergent, means to create the continuity of emotion which holds it together while its visions roam through space and time.

It is noteworthy that Eisenstein draws his materials for discussion from epic rather than dramatic poetry; from Pushkin rather than Chekhov, Milton rather than Shakespeare. That brings us back to the point that the novel lends itself more readily to screen dramatization than the drama. The fact is, I think, that a story narrated does not require as much "breaking down" to become screen apparition, because it has no framework itself of fixed *space,* as the stage has; and one of the aesthetic peculiarities of dream, which the moving picture takes over, is the nature of its space. Dream events are spatial, often intensely concerned with space—intervals, endless roads, bottomless canyons, things too high, too near, too far—but they are not oriented in any total space. The same is true of the moving picture and distinguishes it— despite its visual character—from plastic art; *its space comes and goes.* It is always a secondary illusion.

The fact that the film is somehow related to dream, and is in fact in a similar mode, has been remarked by several people, sometimes for reasons artistic, sometimes nonartistic. R. E. Jones noted its freedom not only from spatial restriction, but from temporal as well. "Motion pictures," he said, "are our thoughts made visible and audible. They flow in a swift succession of images, precisely as our thoughts do, and their speed, with their flashbacks—like sudden uprushes of memory—and their abrupt transition from one subject to another, approximates very closely the speed of our thinking. They have the rhythm of the thought-stream and the same uncanny ability to move forward or backward in space or time. . . . They project pure thought, pure dream, pure inner life."[7]

---

[7] *The Dramatic Imagination,* pp. 17–18.

The "dreamed reality" on the screen can move forward and backward because it is really an eternal and ubiquitous virtual present. The action of drama goes inexorably forward because it creates a future, a Destiny; the dream mode is an endless Now.

Dream and Reality

JOHN GRIERSON

*First Principles of Documentary**

"The little daily doings, however finely symphonized, are
not enough."

*John Grierson first used the word "documentary" in 1926
in a review in the New York* Sun *of Robert Flaherty's film*
Moana. *The game of trying to pin down a definition has
continued ever since. In this selection from his collected
writings, Grierson attempts to separate his work from the
naturalistic documentary of Flaherty on the one hand and
from contemporary "city" films on the other.*

*Young film makers who worked for him were expected
to "apply ends to their observation," and "this sense of social
responsibility makes our realist documentary a troubled and
difficult art." Beauty, if any, would not come from searching
for heroic subjects or from manipulating the medium, but as
"the by-product of a job of work done." That work, he
emphasizes, is to be done by observing life itself, using actual
locations and the real people who live and work in them.
"The young director cannot, in nature, go documentary and
go studio both."*

*Probably the most influential single figure in the history of
the nonfiction film, Grierson supervised hundreds of short
documentaries for government and private sponsors in England from 1929 to 1939. He helped write the law which set
up the Canadian National Film Board and was its first
Commissioner from 1939 to 1945.*

Documentary is a clumsy description, but let it stand. The
French who first used the term only meant travelogue. It
gave them a solid high-sounding excuse for the shimmying

* John Grierson, "First Principles of Documentary," from
Forsyth Hardy (ed.), *Grierson on Documentary*. New York,
Harcourt, Brace, 1947, pp. 99–106. First published in England in
three issues of *Cinema Quarterly*, 1932–1934.

(and otherwise discursive) exoticisms of the Vieux Colombier.
Meanwhile documentary has gone on its way. From shimmy-
ing exoticisms it has gone on to include dramatic films like
Moana, Earth and *Turksib*. And in time it will include other
kinds as different in form and intention from *Moana* as
Moana was from *Voyage au Congo*.

So far we have regarded all films made from natural
material as coming within the category. The use of natural
material has been regarded as the vital distinction. Where the
camera shot on the spot (whether it shot newsreel items or
magazine items or discursive "interests" or dramatized "interests" or educational films or scientific films proper or
Changs or *Rangos*) in that fact was documentary. This array
of species is, of course, quite unmanageable in criticism, and
we shall have to do something about it. They all represent
different qualities of observation, different intentions in observation, and, of course, very different powers and ambitions
at the stage of organizing material. I propose, therefore, after
a brief word on the lower categories, to use the documentary
description exclusively of the higher.

The peace-time newsreel is just a speedy snip-snap of
some utterly unimportant ceremony. Its skill is in the speed
with which the babblings of a politician (gazing sternly into
the camera) are transferred to fifty million relatively unwilling
ears in a couple of days or so. The magazine items (once a
week) have adopted the original *Tit-Bits* manner of observation. The skill they represent is a purely journalistic skill.
They describe novelties novelly. With their money-making eye
(their almost only eye) glued like the newsreels to vast and
speedy audiences, they avoid on the one hand the consideration of solid material, and escape, on the other, the solid
consideration of any material. Within these limits they are
often brilliantly done. But ten in a row would bore the
average human to death. Their reaching out for the flippant
or popular touch is so completely far-reaching that it dis-
locates something. Possibly taste; possibly common sense.
You may take your choice at those little theatres where you
are invited to gad around the world in fifty minutes. It takes
only that long—in these days of great invention—to see
almost everything.

"Interests" proper improve mightily with every week,
though heaven knows why. The market (particularly the

British market) is stacked against them. With two-feature programs the rule, there is neither space for the short *and* the Disney *and* the magazine, nor money left to pay for the short. But by good grace, some of the renters throw in the short with the feature. This considerable branch of cinematic illumination tends, therefore, to be the gift that goes with the pound of tea; and like all gestures of the grocery mind it is not very liable to cost much. Whence my wonder at improving qualities. Consider, however, the very frequent beauty and very great skill of exposition in such Ufa shorts as *Turbulent Timber,* in the sports shorts from Metro-Goldwyn-Mayer, in the *Secrets of Nature* shorts from Bruce Woolfe, and the Fitzpatrick travel talks. Together they have brought the popular lecture to a pitch undreamed of, and even impossible in the days of magic lanterns. In this little we progress.

These films, of course, would not like to be called lecture films, but this, for all their disguises, is what they are. They do not dramatize, they do not even dramatize an episode: they describe, and even expose, but in any aesthetic sense, only rarely reveal. Herein is their formal limit, and it is unlikely that they will make any considerable contribution to the fuller art of documentary. How indeed can they? Their silent form is cut to the commentary, and shots are arranged arbitrarily to point the gags or conclusions. This is not a matter of complaint, for the lecture film must have increasing value in entertainment, education and propaganda. But it is as well to establish the formal limits of the species.

This indeed is a particularly important limit to record, for beyond the newsmen and the magazine men and the lecturers (comic or interesting or exciting or only rhetorical) one begins to wander into the world of documentary proper, into the only world in which documentary can hope to achieve the ordinary virtues of an art. Here we pass from the plain (or fancy) descriptions of natural material, to arrangements, rearrangements, and creative shapings of it.

First principles. (1) We believe that the cinema's capacity for getting around, for observing and selecting from life itself, can be exploited in a new and vital art form. The studio films largely ignore this possibility of opening up the screen on the real world. They photograph acted stories against artificial backgrounds. Documentary would photograph the living scene and the living story. (2) We believe that the original (or native) actor, and the original (or native) scene, are better guides to a screen interpretation of the modern world. They give cinema a greater fund of material. They give it power over a million and one images. They give it power of interpretation over more complex and astonishing happenings in the real world than the studio mind can conjure up or the studio mechanician re-create. (3) We believe that the materials and the stories thus taken from the raw can be finer (more real in the philosophic sense) than the acted article. Spontaneous gesture has a special value on the screen. Cinema has a sensational capacity for enhancing the movement which tradition has formed or time worn smooth. Its arbitrary rectangle specially reveals movement; it gives it maximum pattern in space and time. Add to this that documentary can achieve an intimacy of knowledge and effect impossible to the shimsham mechanics of the studio, and the lily-fingered interpretations of the metropolitan actor.

I do not mean in this minor manifesto of beliefs to suggest that the studios cannot in their own manner produce works of art to astonish the world. There is nothing (except the Woolworth intentions of the people who run them) to prevent the studios going really high in the manner of theater or the manner of fairy-tale. My separate claim for documentary is simply that in its use of the living article, there is *also* an opportunity to perform creative work. I mean, too, that the choice of the documentary medium is as gravely distinct a choice as the choice of poetry instead of fiction. Dealing with different material, it is, or should be, dealing with it to different aesthetic issues from those of the studio. I make this distinction to the point of asserting that the young director cannot, in nature, go documentary and go studio both.

In an earlier reference to Flaherty I have indicated how one great exponent walked away from the studio: how he came to grips with the essential story of the Eskimo, then with the Samoans, then latterly with the people of Aran Islands: and at what point the documentary director in him diverged from the studio intention of Hollywood. The main point of the story was this. Hollywood wanted to impose a ready-made dramatic shape on the raw material. It wanted Flaherty, in complete injustice to the living drama on the spot, to build his Samoans into a rubber-stamp drama of sharks and bathing belles. It failed in the case of *Moana;*

it succeeded (through W. S. Van Dyke) in the case of *White Shadows of the South Seas,* and (through Murnau) in the case of *Tabu.* In the last examples it was at the expense of Flaherty, who severed his association with both.

With Flaherty it became an absolute principle that the story must be taken from the location, and that it should be (what he considers) the essential story of the location. His drama, therefore, is a drama of days and nights, of the round of the year's seasons, of the fundamental fights which give his people sustenance, or make their community life possible, or build up the dignity of the tribe.

Such an interpretation of subject matter reflects, of course, Flaherty's particular philosophy of things. A succeeding documentary exponent is in no way obliged to chase off to the end of the earth in search of old-time simplicity, and the ancient dignities of man against the sky. Indeed, if I may for the moment represent the opposition, I hope the Neo-Rousseauism implicit in Flaherty's work dies with his own exceptional self. Theory of naturals apart, it represents an escapism, a wan and distant eye, which tends in lesser hands to sentimentalism. However it be shot through with vigor of Lawrentian poetry, it must always fail to develop a form adequate to the more immediate material of the modern world. For it is not only the fool that has his eyes on the ends of the earth. It is sometimes the poet: sometimes even the great poet, as Cabell in his *Beyond Life* will brightly inform you. This, however, is the very poet who, on every classic theory of society from Plato to Trotsky, should be removed bodily from the Republic. Loving every Time but his own, and every Life but his own, he avoids coming to grips with the creative job in so far as it concerns society. In the business of ordering most present chaos, he does not use his powers.

Question of theory and practice apart, Flaherty illustrates better than anyone the first principles of documentary. (1) It must master its material on the spot, and come in intimacy to ordering it. Flaherty digs himself in for a year, or two maybe. He lives with his people till the story is told "out of himself." (2) It must follow him in his distinction between description and drama. I think we shall find that there are other forms of drama or, more accurately, other forms of film, than the one he chooses; but it is important to make the primary distinction between a method which describes only the surface values of a subject, and the method which more explosively reveals the reality of it. You photograph the natural life, but you also, by your juxtaposition of detail, create an interpretation of it.

This final creative intention established, several methods are possible. You may, like Flaherty, go for a story form, passing in the ancient manner from the individual to the environment, to the environment transcended or not transcended, to the consequent honors of heroism. Or you may not be so interested in the individual. You may think that the individual life is no longer capable of cross-sectioning reality. You may believe that its particular belly-aches are of no consequence in a world which complex and impersonal forces command, and conclude that the individual as a self-sufficient dramatic figure is outmoded. When Flaherty tells you that it is a devilish noble thing to fight for food in a wilderness, you may, with some justice, observe that you are more concerned with the problem of people fighting for food in the midst of plenty. When he draws your attention to the fact that Nanook's spear is grave in its upheld angle, and finely rigid in its down-pointing bravery, you may, with some justice, observe that no spear, held however bravely by the individual, will master the crazy walrus of international finance. Indeed you may feel that in individualism is a yahoo tradition largely responsible for our present anarchy, and deny at once both the hero of decent heroics (Flaherty) and the hero of indecent ones (studio). In this case, you will feel that you want your drama in terms of some cross-section of reality which will reveal the essentially co-operative or mass nature of society: leaving the individual to find his honors in the swoop of creative social forces. In other words, you are liable to abandon the story form, and seek, like the modern exponent of poetry and painting and prose, a matter and method more satisfactory to the mind and spirit of the time.

Berlin: The Symphony of a Great City initiated the more modern fashion of finding documentary material on one's doorstep: in events which have no novelty of the unknown, or romance of noble savage on exotic landscape, to recommend them. It represented, slimly, the return from romance to reality.

Berlin was variously reported as made by Ruttmann, or

begun by Ruttmann and finished by Freund: certainly it was begun by Ruttmann. In smooth and finely tempo'd visuals, a train swung through suburban mornings into Berlin. Wheels, rails, details of engines, telegraph wires, landscapes and other simple images flowed along in procession, with similar abstracts passing occasionally in and out of the general movement. There followed a sequence of such movements which, in their total effect, created very imposingly the story of a Berlin day. The day began with a processional of workers, the factories got under way, the streets filled: the city's forenoon became a hurly-burly of tangled pedestrians and street cars. There was respite for food: a various respite with contrast of rich and poor. The city started work again, and a shower of rain in the afternoon became a considerable event. The city stopped work and, in further more hectic processional of pubs and cabarets and dancing legs and illuminated sky-signs, finished its day.

In so far as the film was principally concerned with movements and the building of separate images into movements, Ruttmann was justified in calling it a symphony. It meant a break away from the story borrowed from literature, and from the play borrowed from the stage. In *Berlin* cinema swung along according to its own more natural powers: creating dramatic effect from the tempo'd accumulation of its single observations. Cavalcanti's *Rien que les Heures* and Léger's *Ballet Mécanique* came before *Berlin*, each with a similar attempt to combine images in an emotionally satisfactory sequence of movements. They were too scrappy and had not mastered the art of cutting sufficiently well to create the sense of "march" necessary to the genre. The symphony of Berlin City was both larger in its movements and larger in its vision.

There was one criticism of *Berlin* which, out of appreciation for a fine film and a new and arresting form, the critics failed to make; and time has not justified the omission. For all its ado of workmen and factories and swirl and swing of a great city, Berlin created nothing. Or rather if it created something, it was that shower of rain in the afternoon. The people of the city got up splendidly, they tumbled through their five million hoops impressively, they turned in; and no other issue of God or man emerged than that sudden besmattering spilling of wet on people and pavements.

I urge the criticism because *Berlin* still excites the mind of the young, and the symphony form is still their most popular persuasion. In fifty scenarios presented by the tyros, forty-five are symphonies of Edinburgh or of Ecclefechan or of Paris or of Prague. Day breaks—the people come to work—the factories start—the streetcars rattle—lunch hour and the streets again—sport if it is Saturday afternoon—certainly evening and the local dance hall. And so, nothing having happened and nothing positively said about anything, to bed; though Edinburgh is the capital of a country and Ecclefechan, by some power inside itself, was the birthplace of T. Carlyle, in some ways one of the greatest exponents of this documentary idea.

The little daily doings, however finely symphonized, are not enough. One must pile up beyond doing or process to creation itself, before one hits the higher reaches of art. In this distinction, creation indicates not the making of things but the making of virtues.

And there's the rub for tyros. Critical appreciation of movement they can build easily from their power to observe, and power to observe they can build from their own good taste, but the real job begins only as they apply ends to their observation and their movements. The artist need not posit the ends—for that is the work of the critic—but the ends must be there, informing his description and giving finality (beyond space and time) to the slice of life he has chosen. For that larger effect there must be power of poetry or of prophecy. Failing either or both in the highest degree, there must be at least the sociological sense implicit in poetry and prophecy.

The best of the tyros know this. They believe that beauty will come in good time to inhabit the statement which is honest and lucid and deeply felt and which fulfills the best ends of citizenship. They are sensible enough to conceive of art as the by-product of a job of work done. The opposite effort to capture the by-product first (the self-conscious pursuit of beauty, the pursuit of art for art's sake to the exclusion of jobs of work and other pedestrian beginnings), was always a reflection of selfish wealth, selfish leisure and aesthetic decadence.

This sense of social responsibility makes our realist documentary a troubled and difficult art, and particularly in a time like ours. The job of romantic documentary is easy in comparison: easy in the sense that the noble savage is already a figure of romance and the seasons of the year have already been articulated in poetry. Their essential virtues have been declared and can more easily be declared again, and no one will deny them. But realist documentary, with its streets and cities and slums and markets and exchanges and factories, has given itself the job of making poetry where no poet has gone before it, and where no ends, sufficient for the purposes of art, are easily observed. It requires not only taste but also inspiration, which is to say a very laborious, deep-seeing, deep-sympathizing creative effort indeed.

CESARE ZAVATTINI

Some Ideas on the Cinema*

"The true function of the cinema is not to tell fables."

In this ringing manifesto, Cesare Zavattini, who wrote such neorealist films as Shoeshine *and* Bicycle Thief *for the Italian director Vittorio de Sica, laid down a challenge to all film makers "to excavate reality, to give it a power, a communication, a series of reflexes, which until recently we had never thought it had." Like Kracauer, he declares that the camera has a "hunger for reality," that the invention of plots to make reality palatable or spectacular is a flight from the richness of real life. The problem, he says, "lies in being able to observe reality, not to extract fictions from it." Zavattini wants to "make things as they are, almost by themselves, create their own special significance," and to analyze fact so deeply that we see "things we have never noticed before." A woman buying a pair of shoes can become a drama if we dig deep enough into her life and the lives of those around her.*

Zavattini denies that we need to be bored by facts, or that we may get tired of poverty as a theme, or that there is anything beneath the notice of a film audience. In the manner of the postwar Marxists, he belabors bourgeois attitudes; declares himself against the "exceptional" man or hero; calls for a sense of solidarity, equality, and identification with the common man in the crowd. He wants the viewer to contribute an intensity of vision that will "give human life its historical importance at every minute." He wants the director to take both the dialogue and the actors from real life, from "the street." And in a momentary forecast of the work of Antonioni, he speaks of the film maker's need to "remain" in a scene, with all its "echoes and reverberations."

* Cesare Zavattini, "Some Ideas on the Cinema," *Sight and Sound*, October 1953, pp. 64–69. Edited from a recorded interview published in *La Revista del Cinema Italiano*, December 1952. Translated by Pier Luigi Lanza.

1

No doubt one's first and most superficial reaction to everyday reality is that it is tedious. Until we are able to overcome some moral and intellectual laziness, in fact, this reality will continue to appear uninteresting. One shouldn't be astonished that the cinema has always felt the natural, unavoidable necessity to insert a "story" in the reality to make it exciting and "spectacular." All the same, it is clear that such a method evades a direct approach to everyday reality, and suggests that it cannot be portrayed without the intervention of fantasy or artifice.

The most important characteristic, and the most important innovation, of what is called neorealism, it seems to me, is to have realised that the necessity of the "story" was only an unconscious way of disguising a human defeat, and that the kind of imagination it involved was simply a technique of superimposing dead formulas over living social facts. Now it has been perceived that reality is hugely rich, that to be able to look directly at it is enough; and that the artist's task is not to make people moved or indignant at metaphorical situations, but to make them reflect (and, if you like, to be moved and indignant too) on what they and others are doing, on the real things, exactly as they are.

For me this has been a great victory. I would like to have achieved it many years earlier. But I made the discovery only at the end of the war. It was a moral discovery, an appeal to order. I saw at last what lay in front of me, and I understood that to have evaded reality had been to betray it.

Example: Before this, if one was thinking over the idea of a film on, say, a strike, one was immediately forced to invent a plot. And the strike itself became only the background to the film. Today, our attitude would be one of "revelation": we would describe the strike itself, try to work out the largest possible number of human, moral, social, economic, poetic values from the bare documentary fact.

We have passed from an unconsciously rooted mistrust of reality, an illusory and equivocal evasion, to an unlimited trust in things, facts and people. Such a position requires us, in effect, to excavate reality, to give it a power, a communication, a series of reflexes, which until recently we had never thought it had. It requires, too, a true and real interest in what is happening, a search for the most deeply hidden human values; which is why we feel that the cinema must recruit not only intelligent people, but, above all, "living" souls, the morally richest people.

2

The cinema's overwhelming desire to see, to analyse, its hunger for reality, is an act of concrete homage towards other people, towards what is happening and existing in the world. And, incidentally, it is what distinguishes "neorealism" from the American cinema.

In fact, the American position is the antithesis of our own: while we are interested in the reality around us and want to know it directly, reality in American films is unnaturally filtered, "purified," and comes out at one or two removes. In America, lack of subjects for films causes a crisis, but with us such a crisis is impossible. One cannot be short of themes while there is still plenty of reality. Any hour of the day, any place, any person, is a subject for narrative if the narrator is capable of observing and illuminating all these collective elements by exploring their interior value.

So there is no question of a crisis of subjects, only of their interpretation. This substantial difference was nicely emphasised by a well-known American producer when he told me:

"This is how *we* would imagine a scene with an aeroplane. The 'plane passes by . . . a machine-gun fires . . . the 'plane crashes. . . . And this is how *you* would imagine it. The 'plane passes by. . . . The 'plane passes by again . . . the 'plane passes by once more. . . ."

He was right. But we have still not gone far enough. It is not enough to make the aeroplane pass by three times; we must make it pass by twenty times.

What effects on narrative, then, and on the portrayal of human character, has the neorealist style produced?

To begin with, while the cinema used to make one situation produce another situation, and another, and another, again and again, and each scene was thought out and immediately related to the next (the natural result of a mistrust of reality), today, when we have thought out a scene, we feel the need to "remain" in it, because the single scene itself can contain so many echoes and reverberations, can even contain all the situations we may need. Today, in fact, we can quietly say: give us whatever "fact" you like, and we will disembowel it, make it something worth watching.

While the cinema used to portray life in its most visible and external moments—and a film was usually only a series of situations selected and linked together with varying success— today the neorealist affirms that each one of these situations, rather than all the external moments, contains in itself enough material for a film.

Example: In most films, the adventures of two people looking for somewhere to live, for a house, would be shown externally in a few moments of action, but for us it could provide the scenario for a whole film, and we would explore all its echoes, all its implications.

Of course, we are still a long way from a true analysis of human situations, and one can speak of analysis only in comparison with the dull synthesis of most current production. We are, rather, still in an "attitude" of analysis; but in this attitude there is a strong purpose, a desire for understanding, for belonging, for participating—for living together, in fact.

3

Substantially, then, the question today is, instead of turning imaginary situations into "reality" and trying to make them look "true," to make things as they are, almost by themselves, create their own special significance. Life is not what is invented in "stories"; life is another matter. To understand it involves a minute, unrelenting, and patient search.

Here I must bring in another point of view. I believe that the world goes on getting worse because we are not truly aware of reality. The most authentic position anyone can take up today is to engage himself in tracing the roots of this problem. The keenest necessity of our time is "social attention."

Attention, though, to what is there, *directly*: not through an apologue, however well conceived. A starving man, a humiliated man, must be shown by name and surname; no fable for a starving man, because that is something else, less effective and less moral. The true function of the cinema is not to tell fables, and to a true function we must recall it.

Of course, reality can be analysed by ways of fiction. Fictions can be expressive and natural; but neorealism, if it wants to be worthwhile, must sustain the moral impulse that characterised its beginnings, in an analytical documentary way. No other medium of expression has the cinema's original and innate capacity for showing things, that we believe worth showing, as they happen day by day—in what we might call their "dailiness," their longest and truest duration. The cinema has everything in front of it, and no other medium has the same possibilities for getting it known quickly to the greatest number of people.

As the cinema's responsibility also comes from its enormous power, it should try to make every frame of film count, by which I mean that it should penetrate more and more into the manifestations and the essence of reality.

The cinema only affirms its moral responsibility when it approaches reality in this way.

The moral, like the artistic, problem lies in being able to observe reality, not to extract fictions from it.

4

Naturally, some film-makers, although they realise the problem, have still been compelled, for a variety of reasons (some valid, others not) to "invent" stories in the traditional manner, and to incorporate in these stories some fragments of their real intuition. This, effectively, has served as neorealism for some film-makers in Italy.

For this reason, the first endeavour was often to reduce the story to its most elementary, simple, and, I would rather say, banal form. It was the beginning of a speech that was later interrupted. *Bicycle Thieves* provides a typical example. The child follows his father along the street; at one moment, the child is nearly run over, but the father does not even notice. This episode was "invented," but with the intention of communicating an everyday fact about these people's lives, a little fact—so little that the protagonists don't even care about it—but full of life.

In fact *Paisà, Open City, Sciuscia, Bicycle Thieves, La Terra Trema*, all contain elements of an absolute significance —they reflect the idea that everything can be recounted; but their sense remains metaphorical, because there is still an invented story, not the documentary spirit. In other films, such as *Umberto D.*, reality as an analysed fact is much more evident, but the presentation is still traditional.

We have not yet reached the centre of neorealism. Neorealism today is an army ready to start; and there are the soldiers—behind Rossellini, de Sica, Visconti. The soldiers have to go into the attack and win the battle.

We must recognise that all of us are still only starting, some farther on, others farther behind. But it is still something. The great danger today is to abandon that position, the moral position implicit in the work of many of us during and immediately after the war.

5

A woman is going to buy a pair of shoes. Upon this elementary situation it is possible to build a film. All we have to do is to discover and then show all the elements that go to create this adventure, in all their banal "dailiness," and it will become worthy of attention, it will even become "spectacular." But it will become spectacular not through its exceptional, but through its *normal* qualities; it will astonish us by showing so many things that happen every day under our eyes, things we have never noticed before.

The result would not be easy to achieve. It would require an intensity of human vision both from the creator of the film and from the audience. The question is: how to give human life its historical importance at every minute.

6

In life, in reality today, there are no more empty spaces. Between things, facts, people, exists such an interdependence that a blow struck for the cinema in Rome could have repercussions all over the world. If this is true, it must be worthwhile to take any moment of a human life and show how "striking" that moment is: to excavate and identify it, to send its echo vibrating into other parts of the world.

This is as valid for poverty as for peace. For peace, too, the human moment should not be a great one, but an ordinary daily happening. Peace is usually the sum of small happenings, all having the same moral implications at their roots.

It is not only a question, however, of creating a film that makes its audience understand a social or collective situation. People understand themselves better than the social fabric; and to see themselves on the screen, performing their daily actions—remembering that to see oneself gives one the sense of being unlike oneself—like hearing one's own voice on the radio—can help them to fill up a void, a lack of knowledge of reality.

7

If this love for reality, for human nature directly observed, must still adapt itself to the necessities of the cinema as it is now organised, must yield, suffer and wait, it means that the cinema's capitalist structure still has a tremendous influence over its true function. One can see this in the growing opposition in many places to the fundamental motives of neorealism, the main results of which are a return to so-called "original" subjects, as in the past, and the consequent evasion of reality, and a number of bourgeois accusations against neorealist principles.

The main accusation is: *neorealism only describes poverty.* But neorealism can and must face poverty. We have begun with poverty for the simple reason that it is one of the most vital realities of our time, and I challenge anyone to prove the contrary. To believe, or to pretend to believe, that by making half a dozen films on poverty we have finished with the problem, would be a great mistake. As well believe that, if you have to plough up a whole country, you can sit down after the first acre.

The theme of poverty, of rich and poor, is something one can dedicate one's whole life to. We have just begun. We must have the courage to explore all the details. If the rich turn up their noses especially at *Miracolo a Milano,* we can only ask them to be a little patient. *Miracolo a Milano* is only a fable. There is still much more to say. I put myself among the rich, not only because I have some money (which is only the most apparent and immediate aspect of wealth), but because I am also in a position to create oppression and injustice. That is the moral (or immoral) position of the so-called rich man.

When anyone (he could be the audience, the director, the critic, the State, or the Church) says, "STOP the poverty," i.e. stop the films about poverty, he is committing a moral sin. He is refusing to understand, to learn. And when he refuses to learn, consciously, or not, he is evading reality. The evasion springs from lack of courage, from fear. (One should make a film on this subject, showing at what point we begin to evade reality in the face of disquieting facts, at what point we begin to sweeten it.)

If I were not afraid of being thought irreverent, I should say that Christ, had He a camera in His hand, would not shoot fables, however wonderful, but would show us the good one and the bad ones of this world—in actuality, giving us close-ups of those who make their neighbours' bread too bitter, and of their victims, if the censor allowed it.

To say that we have had "enough" films about poverty suggests that one can measure reality with a chronometer. In fact, it is not simply a question of choosing the theme of poverty, but of going on to explore and analyse the poverty. What one needs is more and more knowledge, precise and simple, of human needs and the motives governing them. Neorealism should ignore the chronometer and go forward for as long as is necessary.

Neorealism, it is also said, does not offer solutions. The end of a neorealist film is particularly inconclusive. I cannot accept this at all. With regard to my own work, the characters and situations in films for which I have written the scenario, they remain unresolved from a practical point of view simply because "this is reality." But every moment of the film is, in itself, a continuous answer to some question. It is not the concern of an artist to propound solutions. It is enough, and quite a lot, I should say, to make an audience feel the need, the urgency, for them.

In any case, what films *do* offer solutions? "Solutions" in this sense, if they are offered, are sentimental ones, resulting from the superficial way in which problems have been faced. At least, in my work I leave the solution to the audience.

The fundamental emotion of *Miracolo a Milano* is not one of escape (the flight at the end), but of indignation, a desire for solidarity with certain people, a refusal of it with others. The film's structure is intended to suggest that there is a great gathering of the humble ones against the others. But the humble ones have no tanks, or they would have been ready to defend their land and their huts.

8

The true neorealistic cinema is, of course, less expensive than the cinema at present. Its subjects can be expressed cheaply, and it can dispense with capitalist resources on the present scale. The cinema has not yet found its morality, its necessity, its quality, precisely because it costs too much; being so conditioned, it is much less an art than it could be.

9

The cinema should never turn back. It should accept, unconditionally, what is contemporary. *Today, today, today.*

It must tell reality as if it were a story; there must be no gap between life and what is on the screen. To give an example:

A woman goes to a shop to buy a pair of shoes. The shoes cost 7,000 lire. The woman tries to bargain. The scene lasts, perhaps, two minutes. I must make a two-hour film. What do I do?

I analyse the fact in all its constituent elements, in its "before," in its "after," in its contemporaneity. The fact creates its own fiction, in its own particular sense.

The woman is buying the shoes. What is her son doing at the same moment? What are people doing in India that could have some relation to this fact of the shoes? The shoes cost 7,000 lire. How did the woman happen to have 7,000 lire? How hard did she work for them, what do they represent for her?

And the bargaining shopkeeper, who is he? What relationship has developed between these two human beings? What do they mean, what interests are they defending, as they bargain? The shopkeeper also has two sons, who eat and speak: do you want to know what they are saying? Here they are, in front of you. . . .

The question is, to be able to fathom the real correspondences between facts and their process of birth, to discover what lies beneath them.

Thus to analyse "buying a pair of shoes" in such a way opens to us a vast and complex world, rich in importance and values, in its practical, social, economic, psychological motives. Banality disappears because each moment is really charged with responsibility. Every moment is infinitely rich. Banality never really existed.

Excavate, and every little fact is revealed as a mine. If the gold-diggers come at last to dig in the illimitable mine of reality, the cinema will become socially important.

This can also be done, evidently, with invented characters; but if I use living, real characters with which to sound reality, people in whose life I can directly participate, my emotion becomes more effective, morally stronger, more useful. Art must be expressed through a true name and surname, not a false one.

I am bored to death with heroes more or less imaginary. I want to meet the real protagonist of everyday life, I want to see how he is made, if he has a moustache or not, if he is tall or short, I want to see his eyes, and I want to speak to him.

We can look at him on the screen with the same anxiety, the same curiosity as when, in a square, seeing a crowd of people all hurrying up to the same place, we ask, What is happening? What is happening to a real person? Neorealism has perceived that the most irreplaceable experience comes from things happening under our own eyes from natural necessity.

I am against "exceptional" personages. The time has come to tell the audience that they are the true protagonists of life. The result will be a constant appeal to the responsibility and dignity of every human being. Otherwise the frequent habit of identifying oneself with fictional characters will become very dangerous. We must identify ourselves with what we are. The world is composed of millions of people thinking of myths.

10

The term neorealism—in a very latin sense—implies, too, elimination of technical-professional apparatus, screen-writer included. Handbooks, formulas, grammars, have no more application. There will be no more technical terms. Everybody has his personal shooting-script. Neorealism breaks all the rules, rejects all those canons which, in fact, exist only to codify limitations. Reality breaks all the rules, as can be discovered if you walk out with a camera to meet it.

The figure of a screen-writer today is, besides, very equivocal. He is usually considered part of the technical apparatus. I am a screen-writer trying to say certain things, and saying them in my own way. It is clear that certain moral and social ideas are at the foundation of my expressive activities, and I can't be satisfied to offer a simple technical contribution. In films which do not touch me directly, also, when I am called in to do a certain amount of work on them, I try to insert as much as possible of my own world, of the moral emergencies within myself.

On the other hand, I don't think the screenplay in itself contains any particular problems; only when subject, screenplay and direction become three distinct phases, as they so often do today, which is abnormal. The screen-writer as such should disappear, and we should arrive at the sole author of a film.

Everything becomes flexible when only one person is making a film, everything continually possible, not only during the shooting, but during the editing, the laying of tracks, the post-synchronisation, to the particular moment when we say, "Stop." And it is only then that we put an end to the film.

Of course, it is possible to make films in collaboration, as happens with novels and plays, because there are always numerous bonds of identity between people (for example, millions of men go to war, and are killed, for the same reasons), but no work of art exists on which someone has not set the seal of his own interests, of his own poetic world. There is always somebody to make the decisive creative act, there is always one prevailing intelligence, there is always someone who, at a certain moment, "chooses," and says, "This, yes," and "This, no," and then resolves it: reaction shot of the mother crying Help!

Technique and capitalist method however, have imposed collaboration on the cinema. It is one thing to adapt ourselves to the imposed exigencies of the cinema's present structure, another to imagine that they are indispensable and necessary. It is obvious that when films cost sixpence and everybody can have a camera, the cinema would become a creative medium as flexible and as free as any other.

11

It is evident that, with neorealism, the actor—as a person fictitiously lending his own flesh to another—has no more right to exist than the "story." In neorealism, as I intend it, everyone must be his own actor. To want one person to play another implies the calculated plot, the fable, and not "things happening." I attempted such a film with Caterina Rigoglioso; it was called "the lightning film." But unfortunately at the last moment everything broke down. Caterina did not seem to "take" to the cinema. But wasn't she "Caterina"?

Of course, it will be necessary to choose themes excluding actors. I want, for example, to make a report on children in the world. If I am not allowed to make it, I will limit it to Europe, or to Italy alone. But I will make it. Here is an example of the film not needing actors. I hope the actors' union will not protest.

12

Neorealism does not reject psychological exploration. Psychology is one of the many premises of reality. I face it as I face any other. If I want to write a scene of two men quarrelling, I will not do so at my desk. I must leave my den and find them. I take these men and make them talk in front of me for one hour or for twenty, depending on necessity. My creative method is first to call on them, then to listen to them, "choosing" what they say. But I do all this not with the intention of creating heroes, because I think that a hero is not "certain men" but "every man."

Wanting to give everyone a sense of equality is not levelling him down, but exalting his solidarity. Lack of solidarity is always born from presuming to be different, from a *But*: "Paul is suffering, it's true. I am suffering, too, *but* my suffering has something that . . . my nature has something that . . ." and so on. The *But* must disappear, and we must be able to say: "That man is bearing what I myself should bear in the same circumstances."

13

Others have observed that the best dialogue in films is always in dialect. Dialect is nearer to reality. In our literary and spoken language, the synthetic constructions and the words themselves are always a little false. When writing a dialogue, I always think of it in dialect, in that of Rome or my own village. Using dialect, I feel it to be more essential, truer. Then I translate it into Italian, thus maintaining the dialect's syntax. I don't, therefore, write dialogue in dialect, but I am interested in what dialects have in common: immediacy, freshness, verisimilitude.

But I take most of all from nature. I go out into the street, catch words, sentences, discussions. My great aids are memory and the shorthand writer.

Afterwards, I do with the words what I do with the images. I choose, I cut the material I have gathered to give it the right rhythm, to capture the essence, the truth. However great a faith I might have in imagination, in solitude, I have a greater one in reality, in people. I am interested in the drama of things we happen to encounter, not those we plan.

In short, to exercise our own poetic talents on location, we must leave our rooms and go, in body and mind, out to meet other people, to see and understand them. This is a genuine moral necessity for me and, if I lose faith in it, so much the worse for me.

I am quite aware that it is possible to make wonderful films, like Charlie Chaplin's, and they are not neorealistic. I am quite aware that there are Americans, Russians, Frenchmen and others who have made masterpieces that honour humanity, and, of course, they have not wasted film. I wonder, too, how many more great works they will again give us, according to their particular genius, with actors and studios and novels. But Italian film-makers, I think, if they are to sustain and deepen their cause and their style, after having courageously half-opened their doors to reality, must (in the sense I have mentioned) open them wide.

HUGO MAUERHOFER

Psychology of Film Experience*

"A voluntary escape from everyday reality is an essential
feature of the Cinema Situation."

*In the darkened theatre, the movie-goer is passive, uncriti-
cal, anonymous, private, eager for a limited degree of
imaginative release, unwilling to be told a story of everyday
life. Thus does Hugo Mauerhofer, a German psychologist,
estimate the needs of the film viewer. Freudian rather than
Marxist, his concern, in the end, is for the psychotherapeutical
function of cinema: "Day by day it makes life bearable for
millions of people." The film has become a modern necessity,
offering "compensation for lives which have lost a great deal
of their substance"—a comment which might apply with
redoubled force to the TV situation.*

*Thus, instead of an instrument for social communication,
a means of grappling with what Zavattini sees as the ordinary
facts of life, Mauerhofer finds film to be a healing opportunity
for withdrawal from everyday problems, a half-sleeping
acceptance of manufactured dreams. Because of the film's
unique capacity for intensified action, condensation of time,
and an unlimited sense of space, latent boredom can be
exorcised and the individual comforted.*

When modern man, particularly the city dweller, steps out of
the natural light of day or the artificial light of the night and
into a cinema, his consciousness undergoes a decisive psychological change. Subjectively he goes to the cinema in most
cases to find diversion and entertainment, or possibly instruc-
tion, for a couple of hours. He does not bother about the

* Hugo Mauerhofer, "Psychology of Film Experience," *Penguin
Film Review #8*, London, Penguin, 1949, pp. 103–109. Translated
by V. H. Adams.

technical, economic and sociological background of the industries which in the first instance enable him to see films; indeed, he feels no desire to bother about this. However, besides these subjective motives, certain objective factors come into play, namely, that psychological change of consciousness which automatically accompanies the everyday act of cinema-going, and which shall now be analysed.

One of the main symptoms of this everyday act, which we shall call the *Cinema Situation*, consists of the most complete possible isolation from the outside world, with its visual and aural causes of disturbance. The ideal theatre would be one where there are absolutely no sources of light (such as emergency and exit lighting, etc.), except the screen itself, and where not even the faintest sounds, other than the soundtrack of the film, could penetrate. This radical elimination of all visual and aural disturbances not connected with the film originate from the fact that only in complete darkness can the best results in film presentation be obtained. The perfect enjoyment of cinema-going is restricted by any visual or aural disturbance, for it reminds the spectator, against his will, that he has just been about to elicit a special experience by excluding the banal reality of everyday life. These disturbances remind him that there is an outside world, which is by no means in accord with the psychological reality of his cinema experience. The inevitable conclusion is that a voluntary escape from everyday reality is an essential feature of the *Cinema Situation*.

In order to assess accurately the psychological effects of the *Cinema Situation*, it is necessary, from the standpoint of experimental psychology, to recall the reactions produced by a person remaining for some time in a more or less darkened room. In such a situation, first of all the *Sense of Time* undergoes a change, in that the course of ordinary happenings appears to be retarded. The subjective impression is that time is passing more slowly than it does when we are kept at a distance from our experience of time by light, whether natural or artificial. The psychological effects of being in a darkened room can be gathered under the common denominator of experiencing *boredom*. This experience is characterised by the absence of "Something Happening," and simply expresses the hollowness of the bored person.

Another psychological result of visual seclusion in a darkened room is a change in one's *Sense of Space*. It is a known fact that inadequate lighting causes objects to lose something of their distinct shape, thereby giving greater scope to imagination in interpreting the world around us. The less clearly the human eye can recognise the real shape of objects, the greater is the part played by the imagination, which is extremely subjective in registering what still remains of visible reality. This change in the sense of space partly removes the barrier between consciousness and the unconscious. Consequently, the role of the unconscious in film experience cannot be overlooked.

Decisive parts in the *Cinema Situation* are played by the psychological effects of the changed sense of time and space, i.e., the incipient feeling of boredom and the intensified working of the imagination. The moment the cinema is plunged into darkness, these psychological changes take place. The film on the screen meets both the incipient boredom and the keyed-up imagination, relieving the spectator, who now steps into the different reality of the film.

Immediately there are two significant results: the roused imagination takes possession of the film, which records a specific action on the screen by visual means; at the same time, the changed sense of time creates a desire for *intensified action*. With certain exceptions it is simply intolerable to watch a story recorded on the screen at the same pace as events would occur in reality. The spectator is not satisfied with the action on the screen passing in the usual rhythm of real life. He feels a subjective desire for a concentrated form of film narrative. He expects the continuity of the action to be intensified. Unless this psychologically motivated desire is satisfied, his feeling of boredom, so far dormant, will inevitably reawaken. In other words, such a film is registered as boring. In this connection it is important to point out that this impression of a film being "dull" originates, not in the film as such, but in the changed state of the spectator's consciousness. Only for symbolic purposes or for the purpose of intensified dramatic effect may certain scenes from everyday life be presented in the real rhythm of everyday life. In these cases, the continual threat of boredom is temporarily removed by the inner tension and symbolic implication.

Simultaneously with the changed sense of time (i.e., the evoked latent boredom), the effects of the changed sense of

space (i.e., the unrestricted play of the imagination) become
apparent. Their readiness for action is stimulated by yet another essential element in the *Cinema Situation*, namely, the
passive state of the spectator. He arrives at this state of his
own accord. He sits comfortably and anonymously in a room
which is shut off from everyday reality, waiting for the film
in complete passivity and receptiveness. This condition causes
a psychological affinity between the *Cinema Situation* and the
state of sleep. Between these two there is a significant relationship. Both cases comprise a withdrawal from reality,
darkness as a prerequisite for sleeping or film viewing, and a
voluntary state of passivity. For this reason Ilya Ehrenburg
was right in calling the film a "factory of dreams." While in
sleep we ourselves produce our dreams, in the cinema they
are presented to us ready-made.

This *Cinema Situation*, with its results of continually imminent boredom, intensified power of imagination and voluntary passivity, causes the unconscious to begin to communicate
with the consciousness to a higher degree than in the normal
state. The whole arsenal of our repressions is set in motion.
As the experience of film-viewing takes shape, a decisive part
is played by our unfulfilled wishes and desires, our feelings of
incomplete resignation, the daydreams which we do not or
cannot realise, and which grow up on the edge of the *Cinema
Situation*, so to speak.

The spectator gives himself voluntarily and passively to the
action on the screen and to its uncritical interpretation supplied by his unconscious mind. There is no doubt that the
reason why film critics so often contradict one another is that
the difference between their unconscious minds play tricks on
them. For no two people experience a film in the same way.
The experience of Film is probably the most highly individual
of all experiences. Even the course of sexual experience, fundamentally speaking, seems more monotonous than the experience of Film in the half-light of imminent boredom,
unconsciously fomented imagination at work and passivity
in voluntary seclusion. It is just this radical switching off of
everyday reality and this voluntary renunciation of all dealings
with it which cause that strange phenomenon now under
investigation.

Recent psychology, in particular psychoanalysis, has frequently tackled the problem of daydreams as well as dreams

experienced while falling asleep; in other words, those border-line phenomena between full, wide-awake consciousness and the real deep dream. It is characteristic of these phenomena that, while the consciousness of reality is not yet completely cut off, it is largely deprived of its critical faculty, although at the same time the unconscious has not taken over full control of the psychic activity. The affinity between the *Cinema Situation* on the one hand and daydreams on the other cannot be ignored. Film experience supplies countless people with acceptable material for their daydreams and the dreams with which they fall asleep.

In this connection let us mention in passing the terrifying lack of imagination in modern man; the Press, Radio and Cinema are by no means suitable for bridging to any note-worthy degree this lack of imagination, which is an essential symptom of contemporary man. The position of the cinema is therefore that of an unreal reality, half-way between everyday reality and the purely personal dream. The experience of Film canalises the imagination, at the same time providing it with the material it urgently requires.

A tangible example of the above may be given. It is a fact that for quite a while after leaving a cinema the entire state of mind of the cinema-goer is changed: a change which is actually apparent to those with him. If for unconscious reasons he has identified himself with certain actors or situations, this mental co-ordination lasts until the film experience recedes before the claims of everyday reality and consequently fades away. In the case of sensitive people with a strong imagination and considerable repressions, the effect of film experience can even be observed in their attitude, gait and gestures.

Finally, let us indicate another psychological effect of the *Cinema Situation*, namely, the *Anonymity* of the spectator. Neither in the dimly lit concert hall nor in the darkened theatre are the spectators, in relation to one another, subjected to such anonymity as in the cinema. In the first place, neither of the former is darkened to such an extent as the cinema is for technical reasons. Secondly, the intervals serve to make at least visual contact with our neighbours as well as with the orchestra or theatre cast. For this reason, too, it is impossible for a "community," in the original sense of the word, to be formed in a cinema. This is prevented by the individualising effect of the experience of film, as well as by the almost complete anonymity of the spectator. We only sense the presence of our neighbour. He is usually already there when we arrive, and is gone by the time we leave. In the legitimate theatre and at concerts the individual spectators are frequently fused together in an emotional community of objective experience. In the cinema the private and personal participation of the individual is intensified. There is no more than a diffused mass formation. Apart from this, the individual is thrown back upon his most private associations. A factor which adds to this situation is that our feelings make no objective contact with the artists on the screen. To the individual film-goer they are not so much creative artists as representatives of his most secret wishful thoughts. He identifies himself with them un-critically.

These psychological elements—namely, the boredom lurking continually on the brink of the *Cinema Situation*, the increased readiness of the *imagination*, the uncritical, voluntary *passivity*, and lastly, the *anonymity* which guides the spectator into his most private sphere—these are the mainstays of the "Psychology of Film Experience" which we have sketched above. Its effects are manifold. The part played by the film in the life of modern man can hardly be over-estimated. It originates from its peculiar psychological conditions and the extraordinarily wide range of its influence, in many cases increased by the modest intellectual demands on the film-goer, who, indeed, has simply to follow his eyes and ears.

One of the decisive elements of the *Cinema Situation* may be called its *psychotherapeutical function*. Day by day it makes life bearable for millions of people. They salvage the shreds of the films they have seen and carry them into their sleep. The reaction produced by the film rids them of their belated longings and daydreams. The cinema offers compensation for lives which have lost a great deal of their substance. It is no less than a modern *necessity*, as yet unsung by any poet. The film makes us sad and it makes us gay. It urges us to reflect and delivers us from worries. It alleviates the burden of daily life and nourishes our impoverished imagination. It is a great reservoir for our boredom and an indestructible net for our dreams. Every day millions of people seek its seclusion, its warm anonymity, its noncommittal appeal to the *ego*, the concentrated stories it tells, the colourful interchange of emotion, force and love which passes across the screen. And then, changed for a short while, they step out into the daylight or into the night; each one his own film now, each possessed by the "bright reflection" of life—or at least the image of this reflection—until reality leads him relentlessly back to its characteristic harshness.

ELIZABETH BOWEN

*Why I Go to the Cinema**

"I have very little curiosity, and an inordinate wish to be
entertained."

*Speaking as a movie fan, not as a critic or even a writer,
Elizabeth Bowen assumes that her reasons for film-going are
not special or unique. She gets tired, like anybody else. She
visits a cinema in search of pleasure—"I slough off my preoccupations there"—particularly after a day with "such a
mess of detail that I am glad to see even the most arbitrary,
the most preposterous, pattern emerge." She is even willing
to be impressed somewhat by a film that she doesn't like
very much but those around her are responding to.*

*Miss Bowen, whose novels of British upper-class life
include* The Death of the Heart *and* The Heat of the Day,
*insists upon star personalities—glamour of some sort. She
recognizes the relaxed enjoyment of sitting opposite "dazzling,
exceptional beings" she does not have to interact with or
impress. She calls this "possession without the strain" or
"inoperative love." She often admires the extra documentaries
on the program, but that is not what she goes for—"I go for
what is untrue, to be excited by what is fantastic, to see what
has never happened happen." But then she adds, as an
honorable afterthought, "I could like my films better . . . I
should like to be changed by more films, as art can change
one."*

I go to the cinema for any number of different reasons—
these I ought to sort out and range in order of their importance. At random, here are a few of them: I go to be
distracted (or "taken out of myself"); I go when I don't

* Elizabeth Bowen, "Why I Go to the Cinema," from *Footnotes
to the Film*, Charles Davy (ed.). London, Lovat Dickson, 1937.
Pp. 205–210, 212–216, 218–220.

think; I go when I do want to think and need stimulus;
I go to see pretty people; I go when I want to see life ginned
up, charged with unlikely energy; I go to laugh; I go to be
harrowed; I go when a day has been such a mess of detail
that I am glad to see even the most arbitrary, the most
preposterous, pattern emerge; I go because I like bright light,
abrupt shadow, speed; I go to see America, France, Russia;
I go because I like wisecracks and slick behaviour; I go because the screen is an oblong opening into the world of
fantasy for me; I go because I like story, with its suspense;
I go because I like sitting in a packed crowd in the dark,
among hundreds riveted on the same thing; I go to have my
most general feelings played on.

These reasons, put down roughly, seem to fall under five
headings: wish to escape, lassitude, sense of lack in my nature
or my surroundings, loneliness (however passing) and natural
frivolity. As a writer, I am probably subject during working
hours to a slightly unnatural imaginative strain, which leaves
me flat and depleted by the end of a day. But though the
strain may be a little special in nature, I do not take it to
be in any way greater than the strain, the sense of depletion,
suffered by other people in most departments of life now.
When I take a day off and become a person of leisure, I
embark on a quite new method of exhausting myself; I
amuse myself through a day, but how arduous that is: by
the end of the day I am generally down on the transaction—
unless I have been in the country.

I take it that for the professional leisured person things,
in the long run, work out the same way. Writers, and other
inventive workers, are wrong, I think, in claiming a special
privilege, or in representing themselves as unfairly taxed by
life: what is taken out of them in some ways is saved them
in others; they work, for the most part, in solitude; they are
not worn by friction with other people (unless they choose
to seek this in their spare time); they have not to keep
coming to terms with other people in order to get what they
have to do done. They escape monotony; they are sustained
in working by a kind of excitement; they are shut off from
a good many demands. Their work *is* exhausting, and by
human standards unnatural, but it cannot be more exhausting
than routine work in office, shop or factory, teaching, running a family, hanging on to existence if one is in the

submerged class, or amusing oneself. I make this point in
order to be quite clear that my reasons for cinema-going are
not unique or special: they would not be worth discussing
if they were.

I am not at all certain, either, that the practice of one
art gives one a point of vantage in discussing another. Where
the cinema is concerned, I am a fan, not a critic. I have been
asked to write on "Why I Go to the Cinema" because I do
write, and should therefore do so with ease; I have not been
asked to write, and am not writing, *as* a writer. It is not as
a writer that I go to the cinema; like every one else, I slough
off my preoccupations there. The film I go to see is the
product of a kind of art, just as a bottle of wine is the
product of a kind of art. I judge the film as I judge the
bottle of wine, in its relation to myself, by what it does to
me. I sum up the pleasure it gives. This pleasure is, to an
extent, an affair of my own palate, or temperament, but all
palates and temperaments have something in common; hence
general "taste," an accepted, objective standard in judgment
of films or wine. Films, like wines, are differently good in
their different classes; some of us prefer to seek one kind,
some another, but always there is the same end—absolute
pleasure—in view.

Cinemas draw all sorts. In factory towns they are packed
with factory workers, in university cities with dons, at the
seaside with trippers (who take on a strong though temporary character), in the West End with more or less
moneyed people with time to kill, in country towns and
villages with small tradespeople and with workers scrubbed
and hard from the fields. Taste, with these different audiences,
differs widely, but the degree of pleasure sought is the same.
A film either hits or misses. So affectable are we that to sit
through a film that is not pleasing the house, however much
it may happen to please one personally, causes restless discomfort that detracts from one's pleasure. (Avoid, for instance, seeing the Marx Brothers in Cork city.) This works
both ways: the success of a film with its house communicates
a tingling physical pleasure—joining and heightening one's
private exhilaration—a pleasure only the most weathered
misanthrope could withstand—and your misanthrope is rarely
a cinema-goer. There is no mistaking that tension all round
in the dark, that almost agonised tension of a pleased house

—the electric hush, the rapt immobility. The triumphantly funny film, hitting its mark, makes even laughter break off again and again, and the truly tragic suspends the snuffle.

The happily constituted cinema-goer learns to see and savour a positive merit in films that may do nothing to him personally, films whose subjects, stars or settings may to him, even, be antipathetic. To reject as any kind of experience a film that is acting powerfully on people round seems to me to argue poverty in the nature. What falls short as aesthetic experience may do as human experience: the film rings no bell in oneself, but one hears a bell ring elsewhere. This has a sort of value, like being in company with a very popular person one does not oneself dislike but who does not attract one. Popularity ought to confer a sort of hall-mark, not have to be taken up as a challenge. I speak of the happily constituted cinema-goer—I mean, perhaps, the happily constituted, and therefore very rare, person. The generality of us, who hate jokes we cannot see and mysteries we are out of, may still hope to become sophisticates in at least this one pleasure by bringing with us, when we go to a cinema, something more active, more resourceful than tolerance. This is worth while: it doubles our chance of that fun for which we paid at the box-office. To my mind, any truly popular film is worth seeing —granted one happens to have the time and money to spare. I say, *truly* popular film, the film that after release has triumphantly stayed the course; not the *should-be* popular film, the film stuck with big names or inflated beforehand by misleading publicity. If nothing else, the popular film I don't like adds to my knowledge of what I don't like and don't want. One's own apathies are complex and interesting.

Films have—it is a truism of the trade—a predetermined destination. Every film made makes a bid for the favour of certain localities whose taste has been gauged in advance, correctly or not. Local appeal, at its strongest, is strongly delimited. If one is to go to a film for its popularity-interest, one should go to it in its own country—its areas may be social, not geographic, though largely they *are* geographic, for climate and occupation do condition an audience. For instance, my great respect for Miss Gracie Fields does not alter the fact that I would not willingly see, for its own sake, at my nearest London cinema, a film in which she appeared. But I should feel I had missed something if I missed seeing

a Gracie Fields film in the Gracie Fields country. There
she operates in full force, and I cannot fail to react—to the
audience, if not to her. I see a great girl in play. The
comedian's hold on his or her own public is hard to analyse:
in some cases (such as Miss Fields') it has a strong moral
element. Or it may have a healthily anti-moral element. The
determining factor must, I think, be social: hard-living
people like to have someone to admire; they like what is like
themselves. The sophisticated are attracted, titillated, by what
is foreign, outrageous, by what they may half deplore.

But it would be misleading, as well as precious, to over-
stress this rest-of-the-audience factor in my reaction to films.
I do really only like what *I* like, I go to please myself, and
when I sit opposite a film the audience is *me*. My faculties
are riveted, my pleasure can only be a little damped down
or my disappointment added to by the people cheek by jowl
with me in the dark. I expect a good deal, when I go to
the cinema: my expectations absorb me from the moment
I enter. I am giving myself a treat—or being given a treat.
I have little spare time or money, the cinema is my anodyne,
not my subject, and my objective interest in its emotional
mechanics is not really very great. Nine times out of ten, it
is alert, exacting expectations of pleasure that carry me to
the cinema. The tenth time I may go from abstract curiosity,
or at random—as when I have hours to pass in a strange
town where it is raining or there are no buildings to see.
This tenth time I will discount; it is seldom serious—though
it does sometimes turn out to have started up a new fancy,
or left a residue of interest behind. . . .

I hope never to go to the cinema in an entirely unpro-
pitious mood. If I do, and am not amused, that is my fault,
also my loss. As a rule, I go empty but hopeful, like some
one bringing a mug to a tap that may not turn on. The
approach tunes me up for pleasure. The enchantment that
hung over those pre-war façades of childhood—gorgeously
white stucco façades, with caryatids and garlands—has not
dissolved, though the façades have been changed. How they
used to beam down the street. Now concrete succeeds stucco
and chromium gilt; foyers once crimson and richly stuffy
are air-conditioned and dove-grey. But, like a chocolate-box
lid, the entrance is still voluptuously promising: sensation of
some sort seems to be guaranteed. . . .

I am one of the millions who follow Names from cinema to cinema. The star system may be all wrong—it has implications I hardly know of in the titanic world of Hollywood, also it is, clearly, a hold-up to proper art—but I cannot help break it down. I go to see So-and-So. I cannot fitly quarrel with this magnification of personalities, while I find I can do with almost unlimited doses of anybody exciting, anybody with beauty (in my terms), verve, wit, style, *toupet* and, of course glamour. What do I mean by glamour? A sort of sensuous gloss: I know it to be synthetic, but it affects me strongly. It is a trick knowingly practised on my most fuzzy desires; it steals a march on me on my silliest side. But all the same, in being subject to glamour I experience a sort of elevation. It brings, if not into life at least parallel to it, a sort of fairy-tale element. It is a sort of trumpet call, mobilising the sleepy fancy. If a film is to get across, glamour somewhere, in some form—moral, if you like, for it can be moral—cannot be done without. The Russians break with the bourgeois-romantic conception of personality; they have scrapped sex-appeal as an annex of singularising, anti-social love. But they still treat with glamour; they have transferred it to mass movement, to a heroicised pro-human emotion. I seek it, in any form.

To get back to my star: I enjoy sitting opposite him or her, the delights of intimacy without the onus, high points of possession without the strain. This could be called in-operative love. Relationships in real life are made arduous by their reciprocities; one can too seldom simply sit back. The necessity to please, to shine, to make the most of the moment, overshadows too many meetings. And apart from this—how seldom in real life (or so-called real life) does acquaintanceship, much less intimacy, with dazzling, exceptional beings come one's way. How very gladly, therefore, do I fill the gaps in my circle of ideal society with these black-and-white personalities, to whom absence of colour has added all the subtleties of tone. Directly I take my place I am on terms with these Olympians; I am close to them with nothing at all at stake. Rapture lets me suppose that for me alone they display the range of their temperaments, their hesitations, their serious depths. I find them not only dazzling but sympathetic. They live for my eye. Yes, and I not only perceive them but *am* them; their hopes and fears are my own; their

triumphs exalt me. I am proud for them and in them. Not
only do I enjoy them; I enjoy in them a vicarious life.

Nevertheless, I like my stars well supported. If a single
other character in the film beside them be unconvincing or
tin-shape, the important illusion weakens; something begins
to break down. I like to see my star played up to and played
around by a cast that is living, differentiated and definite.
The film must have background, depth, its own kind of
validity. Hollywood, lately, has met this demand: small parts
are being better and better played. Casts are smallish, characters clear-cut, action articulates. (Look at *It Happened
One Night, She Married Her Boss, My Man Godfrey.*) There
is family-feeling inside a good film—so that the world it
creates is valid, water-tight, *probable*.

What a gulf yawns between improbability—which is deso-
lating—and fantasy—which is dream-probability, likeliness
on an august, mad plane. Comedy films show this fantasy
element more strongly than tragedies, which attempt to approach life and fail too often through weakness and mis-
representation: comedies are thus, as a rule, better. A really
good comic (a Laurel and Hardy, for instance) is never
simply improbable: it suspends judgment on the workaday
plane. Comedy-drama needs some versimilitude.

When I say verisimilitude, I do not mean that I want the
film to be exactly *like* life: I should seldom go to the cinema
if it were. The effective film (other, of course, than the film
that is purely documentary) must have at least a touch of
the preposterous. But its distance from life, or from probability, should stay the same throughout: it must keep inside
its pitch. The film that keeps in its pitch makes, and imposes,
a temporary reality of its own.

Any cinema-goer, however anxious for peace and for his
own pleasure, may detect in a film a *gaffe* that he cannot
pass. I quarrel most, naturally, with misrepresentations of
anything that I happen to know about. For instance, I have,
being Irish, seen few films about Ireland, or set in Ireland,
that did not insult and bore me. (*The Informer* was one
remarkable exception.) But I could sit through a (no doubt)
equally misrepresenting film about Scotland, which I do not
know, without turning a hair. I know only a very small part
of America—and that superficially—so that American films
can take almost any licence with me. In fact, years of

cinema-going probably did condition my first view of America: I felt as though I were stepping into the screen. Dream-like familiarity in the streets and landscapes not only endeared the country but verified the cinema. But I cannot know how greatly Hollywood's representations, however idyllic, of New England small towns may offend New Englanders, or how cardboardy, to the Southerner, may seem the screen face of the Old Colonial Home. I cannot challenge falseness in setting, detail or manners past the point where my experience stops. As a woman, I am annoyed by improbability in clothes: English films offend rather badly in this way. Dressy at all costs, the English heroines hike, run down spies or reclaim lovers from storm-girt islands in their Kensington High Street Sunday bests. An equal unlikeliness blights the English film interior: I revolt from ancestral homes that are always Gothic, from Louis Seize bedrooms in poverty-stricken manors. . . .

I am discussing, throughout, the "story" (or "entertainment") film. That is the film I go to see; I go to the cinema for amusement only; my feeling for it may be exceptionally frivolous. I more than admire, I am often absorbed by, good "interest," or documentary films that may occur in a programme, but, as these are not the films I seek, I do not feel that I am qualified to discuss them. I go for what is untrue, to be excited by what is fantastic, to see what has never happened happen. I go for the fairy story. I state—I do not see why this should rank as a confession—that I would rather see a film in which a (probably doped) lion brings a tense plot to a close by eating a millionaire than the most excellent film about lions in their wild state, roving about and not furthering any plot. If I am to see a documentary film, I prefer what I can only describe with Lower-form vagueness as "films about foreign countries"—preferably, European countries. I like to get some idea how foreigners spend their day—and the incidental beauty of "interest" films is often very great, their rhythm admirable. But I have very little curiosity, and an inordinate wish to be entertained. If many more cinema-goers were as lazy-minded and fantasy-loving as I am what a pity it would be—but I take it that I am in a minority. I hope that the cinema may develop along all lines, while still giving me many more of the films I like—

grown-up comedies, taut thrillers, finished period pieces and dashing Westerns. I want no more American tragedies, Russian comedies or crepitating Teutonic analysis. I should like still more dramatic use of landscape and architecture. I like almost any French film—perhaps I have been lucky. I have rather dreaded beforehand, as one dreads drastic experience, any Russian film I have seen; have later wished, while it lasted, to protract every moment, and finally found it, when it was over, more powerful than a memory—besides everything else, there had been so much more fun than one foresaw.

I am shy of the serious aspect of my subject, and don't want to finish on an unnaturally high note. It is, of course, clear to me that a film, like any other attempt on art, or work of art—all being tentative—can have in it germs of perfection. Its pretension to an aesthetic need be no less serious than that of a poem, picture or piece of music. Its medium, which is unique to it, is important: fluid pattern, variation of light, speed. In time, the cinema has come last of all the arts; its appeal to the racial child in us is so immediate that it should have come first. Pictures came first in time, and bore a great weight of meaning: "the pictures" date right back in their command of emotion: they are inherently primitive. A film can put the experience of a race or a person on an almost dreadfully simplified epic plane.

We have promise of great art here, but so far few great artists. Films have not caught up with the possibilities of the cinema: we are lucky when we get films that keep these in sight. Mechanics, the immense technical knowledge needed, have kept the art, as an art, unnaturally esoteric; its technical progress (more and more discoveries: sound, now colour) moves counter to its spiritual progress. An issue keeps on being obscured, a problem added to. Yet we have here, almost within our grasp, a means to the most direct communication possible between man and man. What might be a giant instrument is still a giant toy.

How much I like films I like—but I could like my films better. I like being distracted, flattered, tickled, even rather upset—but I should not mind something more; I should like something serious. I should like to be changed by more films, as art can change one: I should like something to happen when I go to the cinema.

SIEGFRIED KRACAUER

Theory of Film*

"Film . . . is uniquely equipped to record and reveal physical
reality and, hence, gravitates toward it."

In his monumental study, Theory of Film, *Siegfried Kracauer
firmly establishes at the outset his own assumption that the
proper role of film is the presentation of physical reality. His
book is an attempt to prove by example and argument that
what he calls the formalism of the arranged plot is no more
suitable for cinematography than is careful staging proper in
a still photograph. Neither the novel nor the play fits the
cinema: anything literary is ultimately concerned with inner
ideas, not the moments of material life.*

*It is difficult to extract from his book an adequate brief
statement of Kracauer's position. In a chapter on "Basic
Concepts," he specifically defends his thesis and goes on to
deny that the film's inherent art is related to any of the
traditional arts: "it must always be kept in mind that the most
creative film maker is much less independent of nature in the
raw than the painter or poet; that his creativity manifests
itself in letting nature in and penetrating it." In his final
chapter, he returns to the aesthetic question, barring both
"average theatrical films and certain high-level avant-garde
films" from acceptance as cinematic. He agrees with Fellini
and Zavattini that a film should not be tidy, or even constructed according to the traditions of tragedy, but should
reflect the irregularities of life. The film artist is therefore
more like an explorer, always in danger of getting lost in
"the jungle of material phenomena." But if the inductive
process of film begins with things, it ultimately demands
thoughts. The material gropes toward the spiritual.*

* Siegfried Kracauer, "Basic Concepts" and "Film in Our Time,"
from *Theory of Film*. New York, Oxford, 1960. Pp. 12–13, 18–20,
38–40, 301–303, 308–309.

It may be assumed that the achievements within a particular medium are all the more satisfying aesthetically if they build from the specific properties of that medium. To express the same in negative terms, a product which, somehow, goes against the grain of its medium—say, by imitating effects more "natural" to another medium—will hardly prove acceptable; the old iron structures with their borrowings from Gothic stone architecture are as irritating as they are venerable. The pull of the properties of photography is, perhaps, responsible for the inconsistent attitudes and performances of some photographers with strong painterly inclinations. . . .

But if any medium has its legitimate place at the pole opposite that of painting, it is photography. The properties of photography . . . are fairly specific; and they have lost nothing of their impact in the course of history. Thus, it seems all the more justifiable to apply the basic aesthetic principle to this particular medium. . . .

Photographs in keeping with the photographic approach—where no misunderstanding is possible, they may just be called photographs—show certain affinities which can be assumed to be as constant as the properties of the medium to which they belong. Four of them call for special attention.

First, photography has an outspoken affinity for unstaged reality. Pictures which strike us as intrinsically photographic seem intended to render nature in the raw, nature as it exists independently of us. Now nature is particularly unstageable if it manifests itself in ephemeral configurations which only the camera is able to capture.[1] This explains the delight of early photographers in such subjects as "accumulation of dust in a hollow moulding,"[2] or a "casual gleam of sunshine."[3] . . . In the field of portraiture, it is true, photographers frequently interfere with the given conditions. But the boundaries between staged and unstaged reality are very fluid in this field; and a portraitist who provides a special setting or asks his model

[1] H. Mumford, *Technics and Civilization*, p. 340.
[2] B. Newhall, "Photography and the Development of Kinetic Visualization," *Journal of the Warburg and Courtauld Institutes*, 1944, Vol. 7, p. 40.
[3] Newhall, *The History of Photography . . .* , p. 40; quoted from H. Fox Talbot, *The Pencil of Nature* (London, 1844), p. 40.

to lower the head a bit may well be trying to bring out the typical features of the client before his lens. What counts is his desire to picture nature at its most characteristic so that his portraits look like casual self-revelations, "instinct with the illusion of life."[4] If, on the other hand, the expressive artist in him gets the better of the imaginative reader or curious explorer, his portraits inevitably turn into those ambiguous borderline cases dealt with above. They give you the impression of being overcomposed in terms of lighting and/or subject matter; they no longer catch reality in its flux, you feel, but arrange its elements into a pattern reminiscent of painting.

Second, through this concern with unstaged reality, photography tends to stress the fortuitous. Random events are the very meat of snapshots. "We want to seize, in passing, upon all that may present itself unexpectedly to our view and interest us in some respect," said a Frenchman about instantaneous photography nearly ten years before the first films appeared.[5] Hence the attractiveness of street crowds. By 1859, New York stereographs took a fancy to the kaleidoscopic mingling of vehicles and pedestrians,[6] and somewhat later Victorian snapshots reveled in the same inchoate agglomerates. Marville, Stieglitz, Atget—all of them, as has been remarked, acknowledge city life as a contemporary and photogenic major theme.[7] Dreams nurtured by the big cities thus materialized as pictorial records of chance meetings, strange overlappings, and fabulous coincidences. In portraiture, by the same token, even the most typical portraits must retain an accidental character—as if they were plucked en route and still quivered with crude existence. This affinity for the adventitious again implies that the medium does not favor pictures which seem to be forced into an "obvious composi-

[4] Quoted by Newhall, *ibid.*, p. 144, from John A. Tennant's 1921 review of a New York Stieglitz exhibition.

[5] Albert Londe, *La Photographie instantanée* (Paris, 1886), p. 139. I owe this reference to Mr. Beaumont Newhall, who kindly let me have some of his notes on instantaneous photography.

[6] Newhall, "Photography and the Development of Kinetic Visualization," *Journal of the Warburg and Courtauld Institutes*, 1944, Vol. 7, p. 41.

[7] McCausland, "Alfred Stieglitz," *The Complete Photographer*, 1943, Vol. 9, issue 51:3321.

tional pattern."[8] (Of course, photographs of the compositional inventions of nature or man-made reality are quite another thing.)

Third, photography tends to suggest endlessness. This follows from its emphasis on fortuitous complexes which represent fragments rather than wholes. A photograph, whether portrait or action picture, is in character only if it precludes the notion of completeness. Its frame marks a provisional limit; its content refers to other contents outside that frame; and its structure denotes something that cannot be encompassed—physical existence. Nineteenth-century writers called this something nature, or life; and they were convinced that photography would have to impress upon us its infinity. Leaves, which they counted among the favorite motifs of the camera, cannot be "staged," but occur in endless quantities. In this respect, there is an analogy between the photographic approach and scientific investigation: both probe into an inexhaustible universe whose entirety forever eludes them.

Fourth, and finally, the medium has an affinity for the indeterminate . . . for however selective photographs are, they cannot deny the tendency toward the unorganized and diffuse which marks them as records. It is therefore inevitable that they should be surrounded with a fringe of indistinct multiple meanings. . . .

In strict analogy to the term "photographic approach" the film maker's approach is called "cinematic" if it acknowledges the basic aesthetic principle. It is evident that the cinematic approach materializes in all films which followed the realistic tendency. This implies that even films almost devoid of creative aspirations, such as newsreels, scientific or educational films, artless documentaries, and so on, are tenable propositions from an aesthetic point of view—presumably more so than films which for all their artistry pay little attention to the given outer world. But as with photographic reportage, newsreels and the like meet only the minimum requirement.

What is of the essence in film no less than photography is the intervention of the film maker's formative energies in all the dimensions which the medium has come to cover. He

[8] Newhall, *The History of Photography* . . . , p. 126.

may feature his impressions of this or that segment of physical existence in documentary fashion, transfer hallucinations and mental images to the screen, indulge in the rendering of rhythmical patterns, narrate a human-interest story, and so on. All these creative efforts are in keeping with the cinematic approach as long as they benefit, in some way or other, the medium's substantive concern with our visible world. As in photography, everything depends on the "right" balance between the realistic tendency and the formative tendency; and the two tendencies are well balanced if the latter does not try to overwhelm the former but eventually follows its lead.

THE ISSUE OF ART

When calling the cinema an art medium, people usually think of films which resemble the traditional works of art in that they are free creations rather than explorations of nature. These films organize the raw material to which they resort into some self-sufficient composition instead of accepting it as an element in its own right. In other words, their underlying formative impulses are so strong that they defeat the cinematic approach with its concern for camera reality. Among the film types customarily considered art are, for instance, the above-mentioned German expressionist films of the years after World War I; conceived in a painterly spirit, they seem to implement the formula of Hermann Warm, one of the designers of *The Cabinet of Dr. Caligari* settings, who claimed that "films must be drawings brought to life." Here also belongs many an experimental film; all in all, films of this type are not only intended as autonomous wholes but frequently ignore physical reality or exploit it for purposes alien to photographic veracity. By the same token, there is an inclination to classify as works of art feature films which combine forceful artistic composition with devotion to significant subjects and values. This would apply to a number of adaptations of great stage plays and other literary works.

Yet such a usage of the term "art" in the traditional sense is misleading. It lends support to the belief that artistic qualities must be attributed precisely to films which neglect the medium's recording obligations in an attempt to rival

achievements in the fields of the fine arts, the theatre, or
literature. In consequence, this usage tends to obscure the
aesthetic value of films which are really true to the medium.
If the term "art" is reserved for productions like *Hamlet* or
Death of a Salesman, one will find it difficult indeed to appreciate properly the large amount of creativity that goes into
many a documentary capturing material phenomena for their
own sake. Take Ivens's *Rain* or Flaherty's *Nanook*, documentaries saturated with formative intentions: like any selective photographer, their creators have all the traits of the
imaginative reader and curious explorer; and their readings
and discoveries result from full absorption in the given material and significant choices. Add to this that some of the
crafts needed in the cinematic process—especially editing—
represent tasks with which the photographer is not confronted.
And they too lay claim to the film maker's creative powers.

This leads straight to a terminological dilemma. Owing to
its fixed meaning, the concept of art does not, and cannot,
cover truly "cinematic" films—films, that is, which incorporate
aspects of physical reality with a view to making us experience them. And yet it is they, not the films reminiscent of
traditional artworks, which are valid aesthetically. If film is
an art at all, it certainly should not be confused with the
established arts. There may be some justification in loosely
applying this fragile concept to such films as *Nanook* or
Paisan or *Potemkin* which are deeply steeped in camera life.
But in defining them as art, it must always be kept in mind
that even the most creative film maker is much less independent of nature in the raw than the painter or poet; that his
creativity manifests itself in letting nature in and penetrating
it.

The intrusion of Art into film thwarts the cinema's intrinsic
possibilities. If for reasons of aesthetic purity films influenced
by the traditional arts prefer to disregard actual physical
reality, they miss an opportunity reserved for the cinematic
medium. And if they do picture the given visible world, they
nevertheless fail to show it, for the shots of it then merely
serve to compose what can be passed off as a work of art;
accordingly, the real-life material in such films forfeits its
character as raw material. Here belong not only artistically

ambitious experimental films—e.g., Buñuel-Dali's *Un Chien Andalou*—but all the innumerable commercial films which, though completely devoid of art, nevertheless half-unintentionally pay tribute to it by following the ways of the theatre.

Nobody would think of minimizing the difference between *Un Chien Andalou*, a hybrid of great artistic interest, and ordinary screen entertainment along theatrical lines. And yet the routine product and the artist's work coincide in estranging the medium from pursuits which are peculiar to it. As compared with, say, *Umberto D.* or *Cabiria*, average theatrical films and certain high-level avant-garde films must be lumped together in spite of all that separates them. Films of this kind exploit, not explore, the material phenomena they insert; they insert them not in their own interest but for the purpose of establishing a significant whole; and in pointing up some such whole, they refer us from the material dimension back to that of ideology. Art in film is reactionary because it symbolizes wholeness and thus pretends to the continued existence of beliefs which "cover" physical reality in both senses of the word. The result is films which sustain the prevailing abstractness.

Their undeniable frequency should not lead one to underestimate the occurrence of films rejecting the "lie of 'art.' "[9] These range from plain films of fact—newsreels or purely factual documentaries—to full-grown feature films imbued with their authors' formative aspirations. The films of the first group, which are not even meant to be art, simply follow the realistic tendency, thereby at least meeting the minimum requirement of what has been called the "cinematic approach." As for the feature films, they are the arena of both the realistic tendency and the formative tendency; yet in these films the latter never tries to emancipate itself from, and overpower, the former, as it does in any theatrical movie. Think of *Potemkin*, silent film comedy, *Greed*, several Westerns and gangster films, *La Grande Illusion*, the major productions of Italian neorealism, *Los Olivdados*, *Mr. Hulot's Holiday*, *Pather Panchali*, etc.: all of them rely largely on the suggestive power of raw material brought in by the

[9] Quoted from Agel, "Du film en forme de chronicle," in Astre, ed., *Cinéma et roman*, p. 155.

cameras; and all of them more or less conform to Fellini's dictum that a "good picture" should not aim at the autonomy of a work of art but "have mistakes in it, like life, like people."[10]

Does the cinema gravitate toward films in this vein? In any case, their prominent features tend to assert themselves throughout the body of films and often in places where one would least expect them. It time and again happens that an otherwise theatrical film includes a scene whose images inadvertently tell a story of their own, which for a transient moment makes one completely forget the manifest story. One might say of such a film that it is badly composed; but its alleged shortcoming is actually its only merit. The trend toward semi-documentaries is, partly, a concession to the virtues of dramatic documentaries. The typical composition of the musical reflects the precarious, if not antinomic, relations that obtain in the depth of the medium between the realistic and formative tendencies. More recently, attempts are being made, or rather, resumed, to get away from literature and rigid story construction by having the actors extemporize their lines. (Whether these attempts are likely to introduce genuine incident is quite another question.)

All this does not imply that camera-realism and art exclude each other. But if films which really show what they picture are art, they are art with a difference. Indeed, along with photography, film is the only art which exhibits its raw material. Such art as goes into cinematic films must be traced to their creators' capacity for reading the book of nature. The film artist has traits of an imaginative reader or an explorer prodded by insatiable curiosity. To repeat a definition given in earlier contexts, he is "a man who sets out to tell a story but, in shooting it, is so overwhelmed by his innate desire to cover all of physical reality—and also by a feeling that he must cover it in order to tell the story, any story, in cinematic terms—that he ventures ever deeper into the jungle of material phenomena in which he risks becoming irretrievably lost if he does not, by virtue of great efforts, get back to the highways he left."

[10] Bachmann, "Federico Fellini: An Interview," in Hughes, ed., *Film: Book 1*, p. 103.

FROM BOTTOM TO TOP

All that has been said so far relates to elements or moments of physical reality, as displayed on the screen. Now much as the images of material moments are meaningful in their own right, we actually do not confine ourselves to absorbing them but feel stimulated to weave what they are telling us into contexts that bear on the whole of our existence. As Michel Dard puts it: "In lifting all things out of their chaos before replunging them into the chaos of the soul, the cinema stirs large waves in the latter, like those which a sinking stone produces on the surface of the water."[11]

The large waves roused in the soul bring ashore propositions regarding the significance of the things we fully experience. Films which satisfy our desire for such propositions may well reach into the dimension of ideology. But if they are true to the medium, they will certainly not move from a preconceived idea down to the material world in order to implement that idea; conversely, they set out to explore physical data and, taking their cue from them, work their way up to some problem or belief. The cinema is materialistically minded; it proceeds from "below" to "above." The importance of its natural bent for moving in this direction can hardly be overestimated. Indeed, Erwin Panofsky, the great art historian, traces to it the difference between film and the traditional arts: "The processes of all the earlier representational arts conform, in a higher or lesser degree, to an idealistic conception of the world. These arts operate from top to bottom, so to speak, and not from bottom to top; they start with an idea to be projected into shapeless matter and not with the objects that constitute the physical world. . . . It is the movies, and only the movies, that do justice to that materialistic interpretation of the universe which, whether we like it or not, pervades contemporary civilization."[12]

Guided by film, then, we approach, if at all, ideas no longer on highways leading through the void but on paths

[11] Dard, *Valeur humaine du cinéma*, p. 16.
[12] Panofsky, "Style and Medium in the Motion Pictures," *Critique*, Jan.–Feb. 1947, vol. 1, no. 3:27. See also Hauser, *The Social History of Art*, vol. II, p. 955.

that wind through the thicket of things. While the theatregoer watches a spectacle which affects primarily his mind and only through it his sensibility, the moviegoer finds himself in a situation in which he cannot ask questions and grope for answers unless he is saturated physiologically. "The cinema," says Lucien Sève, ". . . requires of the spectator a new form of activity: his penetrating eye moving from the corporeal to the spiritual."[13] Charles Dekeukeleire points to the same upward movement with an awareness of its implications: "If the senses exert an influence on our spiritual life, the cinema becomes a powerful ferment of spirituality by augmenting the number and quality of our sense perceptions."[14]

[13] Sève, "Cinéma et méthode," *Revue internationale de filmologie*, July–Aug. 1947, vol. I, no. 1:46.
[14] Dekeukeleire, *Le Cinéma et la pensée*, p. 15. Cf. also L'Herbier, "Théâtre et cinéma," in Ford, ed., *Bréviaire du cinéma*, p. 99.

MICHAEL ROEMER

The Surfaces of Reality*

"Film at its best uses the language of ordinary experience—
but uses it subtly and artfully."

*Simplicity, intimate detail, immediacy, ordinary situations,
concreteness—these are the concerns of film, according to
Michael Roemer. As an undergraduate at Harvard, he experimented with silent film fantasy. Later he wrote reviews for*
The Reporter *magazine. His first feature picture,* Nothing But
a Man, *was a study of Negro life; it was the only American
film invited to the Venice Film Festival in 1964.*

*Roemer's argument is pragmatic, penetrating, and full of
useful implications. The directness of his language may de-
ceive us into thinking it is a theory easily arrived at. Like
Kracauer, he accepts film as an image of physical appearances, using "the stuff of life itself," a medium closer than
any other to our own "random experience." Yet he differs
from Kracauer, and to some extent from the French new-wave
directors, in emphasizing that "a film, like a poem or painting,
is basically an artifact." Its concrete detail—very far, at its
best, from the conventional dialogue and action of play-acting
—is nevertheless meticulously planned to achieve the effect of
reality. Chaplin, Dreyer, Bresson, Fellini, Kurosawa succeed
in this (as Bergman, from the theatre, fails) because they use
the surfaces of reality to force us to draw our own conclusions, maintaining on the screen an unbroken artistic structure
of concrete detail, using "the commonplaces of life."*

As Siegfried Kracauer effectively demonstrates, the camera
photographs the skin; it cannot function like an X-ray machine and show us what is underneath. This does not mean,
however, that the film-maker has no control over the surfaces

* Michael Roemer, "The Surfaces of Reality," *Film Quarterly*,
Vol. XVIII, No. 1, Fall 1964, pp. 15–22.

rendered by his camera. On the contrary, he *chooses* his surfaces for their content, and through their careful selection and
juxtaposition builds a structure of feeling and meaning that
are the core of his work.

There are times in the history of the medium when story,
treatment and performance drift so far into a studio never-
never land that we cannot help but make a virtue of "pure"
reality, as free from interference on the part of the film-
maker as possible—even at the risk of creating something
shapeless. This should not, however, obscure the fact that a
film, like a poem or painting, is basically an artifact.

The assertion that film is nothing more than a documentary
recording of reality undoubtedly stems from the fact that the
medium must render all meaning in physical terms. This affinity for real surfaces, combined with great freedom of movement both in time and space, brings film closer than any
other medium to our own random experience of life. Even
the realistic playwright, who—until the advent of the camera
—came closest to rendering the appearance of reality, is
often forced in his structure to violate the very sense of life
he is trying to create. But the film-maker can use the flexible
resources at his command to approximate the actual fabric
of reality. Moreover, he need not heighten his effects in order
to communicate, for he can call on the same sensibilities in
his audience that we use in life itself.

All of us bring to every situation, whether it be a business
meeting or a love affair, a social and psychological awareness
which helps us understand complex motivations and relationships. This kind of perception, much of it nonverbal and
based on apparently insignificant clues, is not limited to the
educated or gifted. We all depend on it for our understanding
of other people and have become extremely proficient in
the interpretation of subtle signs—a shading in the voice,
an averted glance. This nuanced awareness, however, is not
easily called upon by the arts, for it is predicated upon a far
more immediate and total experience than can be provided by
literature and the theatre, with their dependence on the word,
or by the visual arts—with their dependence on the image.
Only film renders experience with enough immediacy and
totality to call into play the perceptual processes we employ
in life itself.

The fact that film exercises this sort of perceptual capacity is, I believe, one of its chief appeals to us. It gives us practice in the delicate and always somewhat uncertain skill of finding out what is going on. As an extreme example, take these lines from *Marty*. They are spoken in a dance hall during the first encounter between a lonely man and a lonely girl. She says: "I'm twenty-nine years old. How old are you? And he answers: "Thirty-six."

On the stage or the printed page these lines would fall ludicrously flat. But on the screen, when spoken by performers who can make every detail yield a wealth of meaning, they instantly convey—as they would in life itself—a complex web of feeling: the girl's fear that she might be too old for the man, her need to come right to the point, her relief when he turns out to be older, and finally a mutual delight that their relationship has crossed its first hurdle.

Film thrives on this kind of intimate detail, for the camera reports it so closely that nothing essential is lost to the eye or ear. The camera makes it possible to use the stuff of life itself, without amplification or overstatement and without any loss in dramatic value. What is achieved in a large action or an explicit moment on the stage can be rendered just as dramatically on the screen in small and *implicit* terms, for it is not the magnitude of a gesture that makes it dramatic but its meaning and intention.

This is *not* to say that the medium is most aptly used on the kind of everyday story told in *Marty*, or that low-key dialogue without conflict or strong feeling is always effective on the screen. I quote the scene merely as an example of the medium's capacity for finding meaning in the detail of everyday life and would like to suggest that out of such detail, out of the ordinary surfaces of life, the film-maker can structure *any* kind of situation and story—lyrical or dramatic, historical or contemporary.

Like so many films that deal with the past, Dreyer's *Passion de Jeanne d'Arc* might well have been filled with violent action and theatrical confrontations. Instead the story is told in terms of mundane detail. Thus Jeanne is betrayed at a critical moment by a priest who averts his eyes when she turns to him for help. There is no call for anything more explicit. The betrayal is what matters, and the camera renders it far more credibly and forcefully in a mundane detail than it would be in a highly dramatized gesture.

In *Rashomon* and *The Seven Samurai* Kurosawa deals with events of the thirteenth and sixteenth centuries in the most everyday terms. He knows that our basic daily experience of reality has not changed much over the centuries: a war between bandits and samurai in a feudal Japanese village was as full of mud and rain, as gritty and as grotesque as a twentieth-century skirmish. Film at its best uses the language of ordinary experience—but uses it subtly and artfully.

In a contemporary setting, Bresson's *A Man Escaped* chronicles the efforts of a French resistance fighter to break out of a German prison. Much of the film takes place within the confines of a cell, and the camera records how he painstakingly prepares his escape by fashioning tools out of spoons and rope out of blankets. It is all very ordinary and physical, but out of the grimy detail emerges a devout and heroic assertion of life and human freedom and of the need to preserve them in the face of all odds. In the hands of a sensitive filmmaker the ordinary moment becomes a channel for deep feeling and a sequence of apparently insignificant scenes is structured into a world of great complexity.

This use of ordinary surfaces requires great skill and discipline since the audience can sense every false move and movement, every false note in the dialogue, every unsubstantiated relationship. The very thing that works *for* the filmmaker if he can master it—reality—can quickly turn against him, so that the most ordinary moment becomes utterly unreal. Not surprisingly most directors avoid the challenge and set their stories in unfamiliar parts, among unusual people and in unusual circumstances.

Because most good films use the language of the commonplace, they tend to have an unassuming appearance, whereas films that make a large claim—that speak nobly and poetically about life, love and death—almost invariably prove to be hollow. A good film is concrete: it creates a sequence of objective situations, actual relationships between people, between people and their circumstances. Thus each moment becomes an objective correlative; that is, feeling (or meaning) rendered in actual, physical terms: objectified.

By contrast, most movies are a series of conventional communicative gestures, dialogues, and actions. Most moviemakers *play* on the feelings of their audience by setting up a sequence of incidents that have a proven effect. The events are not rendered; they are merely *cited*. The films do not use the vocabulary of actuality but rather a second-hand language that has proven effective in other films—a language that is changed only when the audience no longer responds.

This language of conventions gives most pictures the appearance of ludicrous unreality fifteen or twenty years after they have been acclaimed as masterpieces. The dramatic conventions of the 1940's are recognized as a system of hollow clichés by the sixties. When *The Best Years of Our Lives* was first shown, references to the war were enough to make an audience feel strongly about a situation or character without any substantiation whatever; there were feelings abroad which, when touched, produced the desired effect. By 1964 this is no longer true and the tissue of the film disintegrates.

Audiences can be "played" by a skillful movie-maker with a fair amount of predictability, so that even discriminating audiences are easily taken in. At the beginning of Bergman's *Wild Strawberries* Professor Borg dreams that he is on a deserted street with all its doors and windows shuttered tight. He looks up at a clock that has no hands and pulls out his own watch only to find that its hands are missing also. A man appears on the corner with his head averted; when he turns, he has no face and his body dissolves into a pool on the sidewalk. A glass hearse comes down the street and spills a coffin that opens. Borg approaches and discovers his own body in the coffin. The corpse comes to life and tries to pull him in.

The nightmare quality in this sequence is derivative. The deserted, shuttered street, the clock and watch without hands, the glass hearse, the faceless man are all conventions familiar to surrealist painting and literature. Bergman uses them skillfully and with conviction to produce an effect in the audience, but they are not true film images, derived from life and rendered in concrete, physical terms.

There is a similar nightmare in Dreyer's *Vampire*. A young man dreams that he has entered a room with an open coffin in it. He approaches and discovers that he himself is the corpse. The camera now assumes the point-of-view of the dead man: we look up at the ceiling. Voices approach and two carpenters appear in our field of vision. They close the coffin with a lid but we continue to look out through a small glass window. Talking indistinctly, they nail down the lid and plane the edges of the wood. The shavings fall onto the window. One of them has put a candle down on the glass and wax drips onto it. Then the coffin is lifted up and we pass close under the ceiling, through the doorway, beneath the sunlit roofs and the church steeple of a small town—out into the open sky.

Here the detail is concrete: an experience is rendered, not cited; the situation is objective and out of it emerges, very powerfully, the feeling that Dreyer is after: a farewell to life, a last confined look at the earth before the coffin is lowered into the grave. Once again we note that the unassuming detail can render a complex feeling (or meaning) which eludes the more obviously ambitious but abstract statement.

Good film dialogue, too, has this concrete quality. Like the speech of everyday life, it does not tell you *directly* what is felt or meant. One might call it symptomatic dialogue: symptomatic because it is a surface manifestation of what is going on inside the person. The dialogue in most films is, of course, the opposite: a direct statement of feeling or meaning: "I love you"; "I am so happy"; "You are this"; "I am that." But just as the action should be a physical or surface correlative that permits the audience to discover for itself the implicit meaning, so the dialogue should be a *surface* that renders its content by implication—not directly. The two lines quoted from *Marty* are good film dialogue. In contrast, here is an incident from Bergman's *The Seventh Seal*.

Shortly before his death the knight Antonius Block shares a meal with a young couple in front of their covered wagon. "I shall always remember this moment," he says. "The silence, the twilight, the bowls of strawberries and milk, your faces in the evening light. Mikhael sleeping, Jof with his lyre. I'll try to remember what we have talked about. I'll carry this moment between my hands as carefully as if it were a bowl filled to the brim with fresh milk. And it will be an adequate sign—it will be enough for me."

Without this lengthy and explicit verbalization, one would have little insight into the feelings of Antonius Block. The situation itself does not communicate them and Bergman uses dialogue as a way of getting us to understand and feel something the film itself does not render. In Kurosawa's *Ikiru*, a petty official who is dying of cancer and trying desperately to give meaning to his life by pushing a playground project through the sterile bureaucracy, stops on his way home from work to look at the evening sky. "It's beautiful," he says to his companion, "but I have no time." Here the dialogue is part of the objective situation. No direct statement is needed since the man and his feelings are clear.

What is true for dialogue is equally true for performance. A good film performance is a carefully integrated sequence of concrete actions and reactions that render the feelings and thoughts of a character. It is not a system of hollow gestures that, like bad dialogue, *tell* the audience what is going on. Most film performances are drawn from the vast repertory of acting conventions. Conversely, the good film actor— whether trained in the Method or not—tries to render feelings through the use of surface correlatives. He is not concerned with the demonstration of feeling but with the symptom of feeling.

Chaplin's best work is continuously physical and concrete. If his performance in *The Gold Rush* had been generalized (or conventionalized) the scene in which he boils and eats his shoe would have become preposterous. He executes it, however, in the most careful physical detail. While the shoe is cooking, he pours water over it as if he were basting a bird. He carves and serves it with meticulous care, separating the uppers from the sole as though boning a fish. Then he winds the limp laces around his fork like spaghetti and sucks each nail as if it were a delicate chicken bone. Thus a totally incongruous moment is given an absolute, detailed physicality; the extraordinary is made ordinary, credible—and therefore funny.

It must be noted again that while the screen exceeds all other media in verisimilitude, its reality is nevertheless a *mode*. We appear to be looking at reality but are actually looking at a representation of it that may be as carefully structured as a still-life by Cézanne. The film-maker uses the surfaces of life itself—literal photographic images and accurately reproduced sounds. But the arrangement of these images and sounds is totally controlled. Each moment, each detail is carefully co-ordinated into the structure of the whole—just like the details in a painting or poem. By artfully controlling his images, the film-maker presents an unbroken realistic surface; he preserves the appearance of reality.

This means that he should at no time interpose himself between audience and action. He must be absent from the scene. An example of this is the use of the camera. In the standard film the camera is often editorial; the director uses it to *point out* to the audience what he wants them to see. Imagine a scene between husband and wife: we see them in a medium-shot, talking; then we cut to a close-up of the woman's hand and discover that she is slipping her wedding ring off and on. The director has made his point: we now know that she is unhappily married. But by artificially lifting the detail out of context and bringing it to our attention, the autonomous reality of the scene is violated and the audience becomes aware of the film-maker. Of course a good director may also be said to use the camera editorially—to point out what he wants us to see. But he never seems to be doing so; he preserves the appearance of an autonomous reality on the screen. The moment with the ring would have been incidental to the scene—for the camera must follow the action, not lead it.

Since the process of editing is an obvious and continued intrusion by the film-maker on the material, an editor tries to make most of his cuts in such a way that the cut itself will be obscured. In order to cut from a medium-shot to a close-up of a man, he will probably use a moment when the man rises from a chair or turns rapidly. At such a time the audience is watching the action and is unaware of the jump; once again, the effort is to preserve an apparently autonomous reality.

At the end of *Notti di Cabiria* the girl and the man she has just married are sitting in a restaurant. We see her from the back, talking. Then Fellini cuts to a shot from the front and we see that she has taken out a large wad of bank notes—her savings. We immediately realize, with something of a shock, that the man is after her money. If Fellini had actually *shown* us Cabiria taking the money out of her pocketbook, the moment would have become self-conscious and overloaded with meaning; we would have had too much time to get the point. By jumping the moment and confronting us suddenly with the money, Fellini renders the meaning *and* preserves the apparent autonomy of the situation.

Spontaneity, the sense that what is happening on the screen

is happening for the first time and without plan or direction, is an essential factor in establishing a reality. It is also extremely difficult to achieve, since a huge industry has sprung up around the medium, putting enormous financial and technical pressure on the moment before the camera. Years of routine and a high degree of established skill in every department of film-making all conspire against it. From writing and casting to the angles of the camera a monstrous if unintended predictability crushes all life. Even a strong director is often helpless against the machinery; and even location shooting, which should be a liberating force, turns into a dead-end when a huge crew descends on the place, seals it off hermetically and effectively turns it into a studio. The channels have been set up too long and too well; all vision is trapped into standardized imagery and the living moment cannot survive.

For this reason an almost improvised film—like *Shadows* or *Breathless*, made without great skill or art by relatively inexperienced people—can carry far greater conviction than the standard theatrical product. In spite of obvious flaws there is a spontaneity to the action that endows it with life. Of course the experienced director, working in freedom and under good conditions, can achieve spontaneity without relying on improvisation. Kurosawa shot parts of *The Seven Samurai* with several cameras; this made it unnecessary for the actors to repeat, and so deaden, the action with every shift in camera position. Chaplin, on the other hand, used to rehearse and shoot endlessly to achieve a perfect but seemingly effortless result. Both men were after the same thing: spontaneity—and with it, reality.

Our sense of reality is so delicately attuned that certain moments are better left off the screen or the situation is destroyed. This is especially true for violence and death. When someone's head is cut off in a fiction film we know perfectly well that a trick is employed and unless a scene of this kind is handled with great care, it ends up being incredible or even funny. Similarly, when someone dies on the screen and remains in full view, many of us cannot resist watching for the slightest sign of life in the supposed corpse. We are pitting our own sense of reality against the movie-maker's; needless to say, *we* come out on top and the scene is destroyed.

In Dreyer's unproduced script on the life of Christ he describes the crucifixion by showing us the back of the cross, with the points of the nails splintering through the wood. On the screen these would be undeniably real nails going through real wood, and the authenticity of the moment would not be challenged. If, however, Dreyer had chosen to show us the cross from the front we would know absolutely that the nails going through the *flesh* are a deception—and the suffering figure would turn into a performer.

The nail splintering through the wood forces us to use our imagination—forces us to visualize what is happening on the other side of the cross. This involves us in a far deeper participation than could be achieved by the spurious horror of a nail going through the flesh of an actor.

There is something to be learned here about the entire process of perception in film. If we are explicitly told something, as we are in most pictures, we remain passive and essentially outsiders. If, however, we have to draw our *own* conclusions on the basis of evidence presented, as we do in life itself, we cannot help but participate. We become actively involved. When we are told something explicitly, we are in a sense deprived of the experience. It has been digested for us and we are merely informed of the results, or the meaning. But it is *experience* we are after, even if it remains vicarious experience.

This brings us to another characteristic of the medium— one that is profoundly related to our previous discussion. Although the experience of the motion-picture audience remains essentially vicarious, film comes closer than any other medium to giving us the illusion of a *primary* experience. This has been studied by psychologists who have found that the dark theatre, the bright hypnotic screen, the continuous flow of images and sounds, and the large anonymous audience in which we are submerged all contribute to a suspension of self-awareness and a total immersion in the events on the screen.

Beyond this, however, the medium itself encourages the illusion of a primary participation. The camera can induce an almost physical response—so that when Chaplin sits on a hypodermic needle in the lair of a dope fiend, or when Dreyer's Jeanne d'Arc has her head shaved and some of the hair falls onto her lip, the sensation produced in us is almost physical. Moreover, this physical participation is not limited to sharp sensory detail; it extends to the realm of movement.

Most directors think of the screen as of a *picture frame* within which each shot is carefully composed. They emphasize the *pictorial* quality of film. But while the medium is visual, it is not pictorial in the conventional sense. A sequence of beautifully composed shots tends to leave the audience outside the frame—spectators who are continually aware of the director's fine eye for composition. A good director tries to eliminate this distance between audience and action, to destroy the screen as a picture frame, and to drag the audience *through* it into the reality of the scene. That is the function of the running shots in *Rashomon* and of the extraordinarily emphatic camerawork of Fellini, who leans subtly into every movement and propels us into the action kinesthetically. By contrast, we have the autonomous camera motion and stiff pictorial composition of most films.

Images of movement rather than beautifully composed shots are at the heart of the medium, and significantly some of the most haunting moments in film derive their effect from motion. In Vigo's *L'Atalante,* a bride on her wedding night, still dressed in her white gown, walks along the deck of a moving barge. The barge moves forward, she is walking toward the stern, and the camera is set on the edge of the canal, so that there is a dark stationary line in the foreground. The combination of the silent forward gliding of the barge with the backward motion of the girl, whose gown and veil are streaming in the wind, has a profound emotional impact; it renders perfectly both her feelings and our own.

At the end of *Ikiru* the dying bureaucrat has succeeded in building the playground. It is a winter night; the camera moves slowly past a jungle-gym; beyond it we see the old man, swaying to and fro on a child's swing and singing to himself under the falling snow. The various components of this scene are hard to separate: the hoarse, cracked voice of the dying man; his happiness; the song itself. But the motion of the camera, the falling snow, and the slow movement of the swing certainly contribute to the extraordinary sense of peace and reconciliation that is communicated by the image.

A last example: in Dreyer's *Day of Wrath,* a witch is

burned in a seventeenth-century town. We see her bound to
the top rungs of a tall ladder. Then Dreyer cuts to a long-shot
and side view: on the left a huge pile of faggots is burning;
to the right soldiers are raising the ladder toward the fire by
means of long poles. When it stands perpendicular, they topple
it forward so that the woman falls screaming across the entire
frame toward the flames. The falling arc described by the
victim is rendered in coldly objective terms, from far away—
but it transmits her terror completely and draws us relentlessly
into the action.

Kurosawa has developed a way of staging that makes it
hard for an audience to remain detached. On the theory that
no one should be seen entirely from the back, many directors
stage their scenes in a three-quarter view. As a result, no
one is seen full-face: *we* look at the actors, but they look
away. In *Rashomon* and *The Seven Samurai,* however, the
actors either have their backs to camera or face us frontally.
When they face us, they are all but looking at us—with only
their eyes turned slightly left or right of lens to indicate that
they are addressing each other and not us. Of course, a face
seen frontally is much more exposed than a three-quarter
view, and far less likely to leave us detached.

Film can further strengthen the illusion of a primary
experience by using a subjective point-of-view. In the ancient
and Elizabethan theatres, while we remain in objective possession of the entire stage, the poetry and particularly the
soliloquy can focus our attention on one person and shift
it to his point-of-view. At any given moment the world can
be seen through his eyes, subjectively. In the realistic theatre,
with its fidelity to the surfaces of everyday life, this has
become difficult if not impossible. We *know* how Ibsen's
Nora sees the world but except for rare moments do not
experience it from her point-of-view. She cannot, as it were,
reach out and envelop us in her vision—as Hamlet and
Lear can.

On the screen it again becomes possible to shift from an
objective vision of a person to a vision of what *he* sees. This
is done continually, often with little understanding or control. We see a girl enter a room in an objective shot. Then
the camera renders what *she* sees: there is a party and her
husband is talking to another woman. The next moment might
be objective again, or it might be seen from the husband's

point-of-view. Montage makes it possible to shift from objective to subjective, or from one subjective point-of-view to another. Film can render a place, a person, or a situation not just as they are but in the context of the protagonist's experience—*as* his experience. A point-of-view can be so carefully articulated that we comprehend every object, every passing figure, every gesture and mood in terms of the protagonist. The medium thus extends the meaning of realistic surfaces beyond their objective value; it renders them in their subjective context as well.

This brings us to an apparent paradox, for we have insisted throughout that film is at its best when rendering an objective situation. It is true, of course, that a moment can be rendered subjectively on the screen and still retain its objective reality. When the girl sees her husband talking to another woman, we see them through her eyes and so become privy to a subjective state. But the husband and the other woman are *in themselves* rendered objectively: they look no different; they are not affected by the point-of-view. The basic language of the medium, the realistic surface, has not been violated. The same may be said of most flash-backs: a subjective recollection is rendered—but in objective, undistorted terms.

There are, however, moments on the screen in which the realistic surface is in fact destroyed and a purely subjective state is created. The processional at the end of Vigo's *Zero de Conduite* is shot in slow-motion, with the boys in their white gowns gliding through a snow of pillow feathers to the accompaniment of a totally distorted but oddly ecstatic song. In such scenes, and it must be noted that while they are often attempted they do not often succeed, the reality of the feeling is so compelling that an audience accepts and assimilates a totally subjective image. The participation is so intensive that instead of rejecting an image we know to be "unreal," we enter into it eagerly.

When successful, scenes of this kind are deeply moving for they are predicated on a rare and free flow of feeling between audience and material. But they are moments of grace and cannot be counted on—like those rare moments in a performance when pure feeling breaks out of the actor and is communicated directly, without the mediation of a physical correlative.

By and large the language of the medium remains the

surface of reality, and there seem to be few experiences that cannot be rendered in this language. Moreover, there is a great challenge in making the commonplaces of life, that have so long eluded art, yield up their meaning and take their rightful place in the larger patterns of existence. Film is indeed, as Kracauer put it, the redemption of physical reality. For we are finally able to use the much-despised and ephemeral detail of everyday life, the common physical dross, and work it into the gold of art.

Illustrations

John Ford (screenplay by Dudley Nichols): *The Informer*.
The shame of betrayal.

Carl Dreyer: *Day of Wrath*. The fear of witchcraft.

Vittorio de Sica (scenario by Cesare Zavattini): *Umberto D.*
The emptiness of old age.

Michelangelo Antonioni: *La Notte*. The languishing of love.

Orson Welles: *Citizen Kane*. Heroic biography as mystery.

Stanley Kubrick: *Dr. Strangelove.* Public dilemma as comedy.

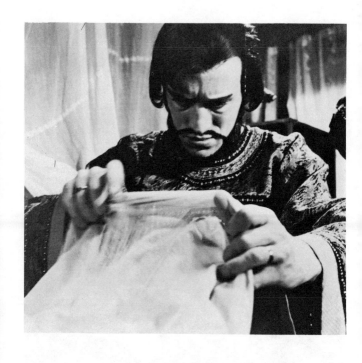

Ingmar Bergman: *The Magician*. Apotheosis of the
illusionist.

Federico Fellini: 8½. Dream-maker's dream and reality.

Alain Resnais: *Last Year at Marienbad*. The mirrored past.

Richard Lester: *The Knack*. The pellmell present.

Alfred Hitchcock: *The Trouble With Harry.* Mocking the macabre.

Philippe de Broca: *That Man From Rio*. Spoofing suspense.

Charles Eames: American National Exhibition in Moscow.
The nation in multiple images.

Francis Thompson: *N.Y.N.Y.* The city through shifting prisms.

François Truffaut: *The 400 Blows*. The challenge of spontaneity.

Michael Roemer: *Nothing But a Man*. The discipline of reality.

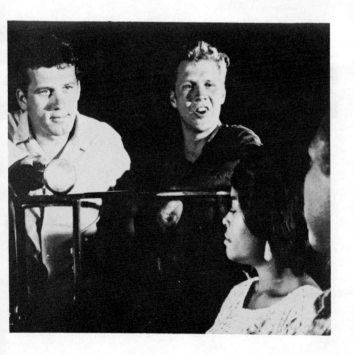

An Evolving Art

GIDEON BACHMANN, ROBERT DREW, RICHARD LEACOCK, D. A. PENNEBAKER

The Frontiers of Realist Cinema*

"Film should be in the first place something that you don't
doubt. You believe what you see."

*This statement by D. A. Pennebaker represents one of the
most important precepts of the new "direct cinema" movement. Often linked with the French cinéma vérité, these New
York cameramen have sharply influenced documentary work
in America since 1960. The source of the new impulse is new
technical equipment—lighter cameras and sound recording
that can be cheaply and easily synchronized. Two-man crews
are now able to shoot actuality programs for television, prob-
ing human life more realistically than the old silent films with
narration written in the projection room.*

*In this conversation with a journalist-producer (Robert
Drew) and two cameramen-directors (Richard Leacock and
D. A. Pennebaker), Gideon Bachmann raises old questions
of choice and of personal values. How can a film maker
always be there at just the right time to catch "the truth"?
Even if he is there, won't he select what seems most truthful
and significant to him? The answer seems to be that the cameraman with an open mind, like Leacock, is at least going
to catch some things he did not expect; he will find a reality
he did not know before. And it may well be that these things
will also seem new and significant to the audience and to
society in general.*

*Bachmann was for some years editor of a perceptive and
informative publication called* Cinemages, *and has interviewed many noted film people on the radio. He has been
working recently on an interview-style biography of Federico
Fellini.*

* Gideon Bachmann, "The Frontiers of Realist Cinema: The
Work of Ricky Leacock," condensed by Jonas Mekas from inter-
views by Bachmann on "The Film Art," Station WBAI, New
York. *Film Culture*, Nos. 22–23, Summer 1961, pp. 12–23.

GIDEON BACHMANN: I have sitting around the table with me three film-makers: Richard Leacock, Don Alan Pennebaker, and Robert Drew. All three are engaged in making films out of what there exists around us in a manner unusual and the same time conveying the complete feeling of reality. I think I put here in one sentence something that shouldn't be put in one sentence. But it is the purpose of this discussion to define their real aims and their esthetic principles. I'd like Mr. Drew to start by telling us in what the three of you are engaged at the moment.

ROBERT DREW: I am a reporter, and I had been working as photo-reporter for *Life* magazine before I got interested in motion pictures. I studied what other people were doing in film journalism, and I met Ricky Leacock. I found a man who was making films which were an extraordinary job of reporting, something that I hadn't seen before. His reporting not only showed what was going on, but also gave the feeling of being right on the scene. And I say this knowing quite well what's being done today in television or documentary film. What Ricky is doing is something really new, and, to me, as a reporter, incredibly exciting. I consider myself a reporter. And what we are really doing, all three of us, we are working full blast on developing a new kind of journalism.

BACHMANN: Completing the introduction, I should add that Mr. Drew is at this moment the producer at the Broadcast Division of Time, Inc. Richard Leacock doesn't need any introductions—we have admired his camera work many times since *Louisiana Story*. To Don Alan Pennebaker's films I was introduced recently at the Flaherty Film Seminar in Vermont, where one afternoon a young man showed up, and he did not say very much, in a pair of khaki trousers and a green shirt, and put on some films. The first thing he showed was one of the most exciting films I have ever seen about New York, with a jazz musical score by Duke Ellington— absolutely fascinating, beautiful movement, symphonic thing, far surpassing anything I have seen. Pennebaker—who is Pennebaker?—I asked myself. So I did some research and I found out that he is an engineer who used to manufacture electronic equipment and one day got a yen, and started making films. All three men plus Al Maysles, who is not here, are working now under their own independent company, Filmakers Inc. Among their most recent films are *Primary* and *Cuba Sí, Yankee No.*

Now, after this introduction, we can go into our proper subject.

RICKY LEACOCK: The problem of film journalism arose and became acute to me long ago. I started in film very young, as you know, in documentary film. Already when we were working on *Louisiana Story,* I saw that when we were using small cameras, we had tremendous flexibility, we could do anything we wanted, and get a wonderful sense of cinema. The moment we had to shoot dialogue, lip-sync—everything had to be locked down, the whole nature of the film changed. The whole thing seemed to stop. We had heavy disk recorders, and the camera that, instead of weighing six pounds, weighed two hundred pounds, a sort of monster. As a result of this, the whole nature of what we were doing changed. We could no longer watch things as they developed, we had to impose ourselves to such an extent upon everything that happened before us, that everything sort of died. And this problem kept coming up with me, sometimes making me absolutely furious. For one of the newsreels I was trying to chase Leonard Bernstein, and just record what happened. I was always delighted with what happened—but I also wanted to hear it. Especially, in this case, with a musician. You've got to hear it to make it meaningful. But it was just hopeless. Only recently, with all sorts of technical developments, we came to the verge of having equipment light and flexible enough to enable us to observe and record with a minimum of interference into what's going on. We are working now with equipment which is sufficiently light to make it possible for us to record both sound and image at the same time, and it is portable. And no lights, no tripods, no wires, no plugging in, you can film synchronous sound anywhere, any moment. It is this technical aspect that is the basis for a fundamentally different approach to filming.

If now, leaving the technical aspects, we come to esthetic approaches—to me, all filming until now has been essentially an extension of theatre, where you control what's happening. Only very few people—Flaherty always comes to mind—saw the cinema not as controlling, but as observing, watching, which in a way, ties up with journalism.

BACHMANN: Will I be correct if I say that your attitude towards film, then, is one where the personality of the film-maker himself interferes to a minimum?

DREW: I'd like to answer this. It's a key question. My feeling is that this question very often is misunderstood. It hasn't begun to be understood yet, in fact. And I'd say that on the scene, as things are happening, the film-maker's personality is in no way directly involved in directing the action. It is completely and totally absorbed in recording it in a certain way.

BACHMANN: You mean in your method of film making?

DREW: I'm speaking for the three of us. There is a tremendous effort that goes into being in the right place at the right time—understanding what's about to happen, understanding what we have to get as it happens, and being ready and sensitive to get it at the time of happening. The film-maker's personality has much more effect in this form of reporting on what's being shown and how, and has less obvious effect on the happening scene itself. His subjectivity is in recording, not in directing the scene. Hence comes much of his true authenticity.

LEACOCK: I'll use an example to illustrate this. In theatre, or in controlled filming, when you see it, as the end result, you can always question it. For instance, there was a film on racing. The driver bursts into tears. The audience was perfectly justified in questioning the development of this situation, in doubting the writer, the director, and the actor. Would this happen, or wouldn't it? they asked. The questions are bound to arise. But when we are filming—and this is the basic difference between our cinema and the controlled cinema —when we are filming an actual driver, and when he bursts into tears, the doubt never arises: he did it. The ultimate fact, that this did happen, is fundamentally different from anything that you can do in theatre or in controlled cinema. Many film-makers feel that the aim of the film-maker is to have complete control. Then the conception of what happens is limited by the conception of the film-maker. We don't want to put this limit on actuality. What's happening, the action, has no limitations, neither the significance of what's happening. The film-maker's problem is more a problem of how to convey it. Take, for instance, a storm, two films in which I remember a storm being depicted. In *Moby Dick,* where the storm was created in a studio, they were confronted with the problem of how big should the storm be, how rough should it be, will it be credible or not, etc. All these problems arose. When you saw the film, you accepted the fact that this is a storm, but, certainly, you learned nothing about storms. Then, I remember the storm in *Man of Aran,* where Flaherty waited for a year to get the right storm. The problem that arose in shooting the *Moby Dick* storm never arose for Flaherty. It was a totally different thing, and asked for a total involvement, how to convey the storm. Here is the storm, in actuality. Now the problem is how to convey this with the camera, how to observe it with the camera.

BACHMANN: You say "convey," you don't say "show"?

LEACOCK: No. You just can't show something to convey. You have to show it in a certain way. We have been in situations loaded with power, and come back without any power. That is the central problem: How to convey the feeling of being there. When you watch the action through the camera, you always see it as it never happened before, and it amazes you. Often it is as over-powering to you as it is to the audience. How to convey it, this is what always preoccupied a film-maker ever since Lumière, and the approaches are changing as the time does.

DREW: And it is here that the personality and the creativity of the film-maker make all the difference in the world. Shooting what happens as it happens is totally the film-maker's personality and sensitivity that enable him to do it.

We have been shooting in Latin America. And Ricky had a tremendously hard assignment. This tall blond Anglo-saxon man had to walk into a slum and spend most of the five days there, with very poor people—more or less living with them, recording life, recording slums. I was with him as a reporter and as assistant. And it was a fascinating thing to watch. Because Ricky was like an angler fishing a big fish with a very small line. This line could have snapped at any moment. By the line I mean his personal relationship to the situation. If he had made a wrong move in the beginning he would have been regarded as *a director*. And if he had ever become regarded as a director, people would have stopped being themselves, nothing would have occurred as it normally would occur as long as he stayed there. He had to insert himself into the situation, form relationships with people, and, somehow, subliminally, get across to them the idea that he was there to record a certain kind of truth about them and not to tell anybody what to do; not to direct anything but to observe. The fascinating thing to me was that everybody came to feel his frame of mind. The mobs and children who would cluster in front of the camera and shout the first day, on the second or third day began to disregard Ricky, as if he wouldn't be there.

PENNEBAKER: I think a perfect example was when Ricky was filming Jack Kennedy. Had Kennedy felt that Ricky was in any way an intruder, in a physical or a moral sense, if he'd felt differently, he wouldn't have allowed certain things to happen, or he wouldn't have acted himself in the natural way he did. What actually Ricky did put into the situation, was a sort of ease, so that people in the situation did not feel impelled to be directed by him, they forgot about him, in a sense. It was Ricky's moral attitude that affected their attitude to us during the shooting. They did not look at us as people who are making another newsreel. And that is essential in this kind of filming. It was, naturally, helped by the equipment, which was small and portable enough, which did not intrude into the situation by noise or by appearance. It would have been impossible, in the hotel where Kennedy was staying, to move in with a blimped Mitchell, and set the lights on, and all that.

DREW: I could add to this, to explain better what we are talking about, that Ricky spent an evening with Jack Kennedy during a crucial primary election, when returns were rolling in. No press was there, no photographer of any kind, no *Life* photographers . . . and yet, Ricky was there, with his camera, recording the sight and sound of what Kennedy did and said, and the atmosphere of the room throughout the evening.

BACHMANN: For the outsider, the description of your way of filming, basically, doesn't differ from usual documentary approaches: it still involves the selection, getting the feeling of the action taking place, of conveying rather than showing. And still I do feel that there is something else in what you are doing. Maybe it was facilitated by the equipment which you are using. I have seen some of your films, the Kennedy film, for instance (*Primary*), which is unique in television or any film making. Could you attempt to put in words some of the esthetic principles that differentiate you from other film-makers?

DREW: I have to say some things that Ricky can't say about his own work. You ask if there is a clear principle that separates Ricky's work from other documentary films. In my opinion, documentary films, in general, with very few exceptions, are fake. As a reporter, I don't believe them. I can see the people directing them, I can see the lights flashing, I can see the people looking for the cues. They aren't real, they are phony and hopeless. Like comic strips, or something. There is something puppet-like about them all, with very few great exceptions—many of them being Ricky's or Bob Flaherty's.

BACHMANN: I wouldn't call Flaherty a documentary film-maker.

DREW: All right . . . My general impression is that the documentary film—looking from my viewpoint, which is journalistic—is a direct outgrowth of U.S. press; it reports something that comes up in the press before it. TV reporting is working in the same guidance of the printed press. Basically, it is a word story illustrated with pictures. Illustrated well, sometimes, but usually not. Television reporting is reporting in words, taking its patterns from the press. It is impossible for the people doing TV reporting to escape the press, because they do not have any other concept of actuality. They follow their own official lines and sources, mainly the Washington perspective. What makes us different from other reporting, and from other documentary film-making, is that in each of the stories there is a time when man comes against moments of tension, and pressure, and revelation, and decision. It's these moments that interest us most. Where we differ from the TV and press is that we are predicated on being there when the things are happening to people that count. Maybe it is more a journalistic principle than a principle of film-making.

BACHMANN: You say that you are predicated on being there when the things are happening. Now, this requires an interminable vigil. How do you bridge this time-and-effort problem? It is known that certain things occur in certain situations or certain places. But it is impossible to be there when it occurs. For instance, an earthquake. So people are naturally used to re-creating situations in a dramatic way, trying to give them the feeling of believability, presence.

LEACOCK: It would seem that this eternal vigilance, this searching for the situations would impose a strain. I have come to realize that a great many ideas I have about the nature of the world I live in came just from being inundated in such situations, from this vigilance. For instance, I thought I had a very clear idea what it would be like if war would be declared. I saw troops marching down the street, just like in the movies, in steel helmets, and boarding a ship, and all that. And nothing of the sort happened, of course, it was utterly different. What I am saying is that wherever you go you are surrounded by new things happening with which you are not familiar enough. The problem is always of seeing it and conveying it in a believable manner.

PENNEBAKER: I was told, that in *Nanook* Flaherty chopped an igloo in half in order to get some pictures inside. But that doesn't bother me a bit. It's always *how* one does it.

BACHMANN: He built a half of an igloo.

PENNEBAKER: Even if he had brought some klieg lights, it wouldn't have mattered, because I believe what he is telling me, because he never tried to fake anything that was of importance. The human eye, after millions of years, has become an extremely sensitive instrument, and can spot, without any difficulty at all, what's real and what's not real. In any kind of film you see it right away, the earthquake is real or not real. And I think as soon as people doubt you on one level, they doubt you on all levels. There is one thing, at least to me, and it has nothing to do with equipment or style, but completely something else: It's like with people: some you believe, some you don't. Like with people in the bar. You watch how his eyebrow goes, his face moves, and you just believe him. A good film is one in which you can believe. How to make it believable, I am not entirely sure.

Ricky was talking about South America. All his life he wanted to take a picture of a child's funeral. And he imagined it as a procession, with father and mother weeping, you know, with children walking in front, with flowers. But what he found was so horrible to him that he could not film it. The people were laughing during the funeral, they got the thing into the graveyard, lots of confusion, children playing tag, they tried to take the hardware off the coffin, because they did not want to waste it—in other words, everything went wrong, from his viewpoint, and he was so shocked and was still looking for what he was expecting that he really could not shoot what was really happening. Later he cursed himself, because what he saw was life, and what he imagined was something else. He did not make a false film, though. There was a struggle, and since he couldn't make the true film, he didn't make any. His knowledge of film, what he believes in, told him that the only film is the one which is happening right there and then.

BACHMANN: What is your own approach to reality?

PENNEBAKER: I think my main feeling about film, I guess I got it from . . . Well, who knows where you get it—but it's the notion, the feeling that film should not lecture, and it's a terrible temptation to lecture. You have all that dark room before you, there is no other place where the eyes of the audience can go, so they have to keep watching. Film-makers always tend to take advantage of this situation of their own public and try to explain to them something that they do not know well enough themselves. For me, it is necessary to have a point of view, but at the same time it is necessary to be able—oh, let me give an example. In Moscow, for instance, I knew that there was only one synagogue in operation. There were two others, in the outskirts, but of little importance. And I have a section in the film which shows a young girl, an emotional girl, who goes to Russia. She is not looking at Russia objectively, and she is Jewish, and she is interested in the synagogue. So she goes to see it. Now, she did not know that this was the only synagogue in Moscow. So I didn't say it in the film. There was a terrible temptation to say: See, this is the only synagogue. If I'd said it, people would have accepted this information like from a newspaper, gratuitously. And I don't think films should provide information. Film should be in the first place something that you don't doubt. You believe what you see. And then, you can never tell all things. Every film tells only certain things.

BACHMANN: This leads us into a sort of dichotomy. On the one hand you want to show exactly what there is, without intruding with yourself between the thing shown and the person viewing it. But then, again, the most creative film-makers, and *Man of Aran* is a good example, create the thing that they want to show, it really doesn't exist before. It really never does. Not even Flaherty's storm, the way we see it in film. Even in your Kennedy film, where you have that fabulous shot of Kennedy coming out of the car, you follow him up the stairs, through all those crowds, and you end with the shot of Jacqueline Kennedy's hands, twisting her hands behind her back. That was all there, you see. But your perspective, and your choice, and your particular way of doing it, created a reality which was not there. Except that it was there by virtue of your having seen it.

DREW: No, it was there. Whether we saw it there that way or not, that doesn't mean it wasn't there. If you'd been six inches from Kennedy, as he pushed his way through that crowd, and had gone up the stairs, and on the stage—I mean, you'd have seen what we saw.

BACHMANN: Maybe I would have seen and shown her hat instead of her hands. If you'd be conveying the whole scene, in a long shot, maybe you wouldn't be creating. But you are conveying only a detail, and, therefore, you are being selective, and in that way you are artificially making something that wasn't there before. In film, even if you use reality, in a true sense, the film itself is still a contrived reality. Dorothy Lee, the anthropologist, in her lecture at Flaherty's Seminar, said that the world really doesn't exist, "man behaves it." Anything that you do or touch changes it.

LEACOCK: I want to clarify one thing: We are not simply filming what happens. We have a fairly good idea of what it is that we are after.

DREW: Even during the shooting of *Primary,* Ricky had to face Kennedy across a space of four feet and argue with him for a half hour in a very positive way to establish what his approach was.

LEACOCK: I am always aware of the fact that our conception of what's going to happen is wildly wrong. And we are always ready, as the situation unfolds, to adapt ourselves to what is happening rather than regretting that what we thought will happen is not happening. Because, usually, what's happening is more intriguing. But then, as something happens— I am thinking about a recent situation: I was hanging around in a house of a very, very poor family, in Venezuela. Not hanging around—we had been filming. But you know, after several days, and it was late, one evening, we were waiting for them to sit down for supper, and we had a fairly good idea that it was this that we wanted to film. But as we were waiting, and everyone was tired, two men started to talk.

Their children were playing on the floor, the wife was hovering around the stove, cooking—these men became involved in a conversation. We were standing around, we were tired, we were ready to leave, and suddenly we realized that the conversation that was in progress summed up everything that we had thought about these people. They were deeply involved in what they were talking about, upset, worried, the kids were around, they were unemployed. So we simply started to film. It was not a question of just recording the conversation. There were relationships that existed in this situation. I find, and this is totally new to me, that with a camera, which is able to watch and to hear, to go from the profoundly moving expressions of these men to the kids, what was happening to them during the conversation, and the wife's reaction, and all in one continuous scene, which literally floats from thing to thing, where editing is taking place as the thing is happening—I was tremendously moved by what was happening, it is not easy to describe.

DREW: It was one of the most extraordinary experiences that I have had in working in this type of reporting—filmmaking—or art—whatever you want to call it. It was a great moment of reporting, and, to me, it was also art. Two poor men talking about their poverty, one had tears in his eyes, he was out of work, he was living in the slums, in Caracas, Venezuela, his home was in the high Andes, far from there, he was living in a shack, with a dirty floor, and his children sitting under his feet, playing in the dirt, putting it on their heads, and inside their clothes, having a jolly time. But this was a moment when a man was revealing the core of his concern, and which was the core of our story. Ricky was filming, he was doing it, holding in his hands about twelve or fifteen pounds, that is, this camera, which was blimped, and he had a zoom-lens, and as the men talked, Ricky was playing the situation with the zoom-lens, selecting, first, the poor man who was depressed, then, his friend to whom he was talking, his reactions, then to interactions, and then, panning down the man's hand to the baby's head, and he saw that all the time this father was talking about his poverty his hand was fondling the baby's head, his round head. And the baby all this time was completely unconcerned with his father, but playing on the dirty floor. As this thing unfolds, Ricky had made a five-minute film in five minutes, which is edited in a way that no editor could have imagined, which has more real truth and impact than anybody could write, imagine, script, direct, cast. It was simply electrifying.

LEACOCK: This came as a surprise to both of us, I think. And we are only scratching the very surface of this kind of film-reporting. This is really to me a new aspect of film-making.

Another aspect has been very important to me. And this is that, essentially, we have been working as two people, not one: sound reporting, and camera reporting. The strange thing about the camera is that its vision is automatically limited. You see very little of what's going around. And it is terribly important to me that the person working with me is able to convey to me, by a slightest inflection, what's happening, to get a right rapport with the entire scene. By this communication, which is very delicate between two people working together, you sense it, at least. The decision, every camera movement is yours. If you get another cameraman, the decision is his. The camera is an instrument of seeing and recording, and of hearing; nobody can tell the cameraman what to do, the situation is fantastically delicate. I am photographing this situation, say. But if someone would ask me why at this instant it was important to photograph the man putting sugar in his coffee, which had nothing to do with anything that I can think of—I wouldn't be able to explain why I did it; yet, for some reason, it was important.

As soon as there are more cameramen involved in covering the same scene—the same people must be involved not just in photographing: they become involved in the whole process of film, they become involved in its editing, because all these conceptions, all these views of the process of seeing the scene, must be sort of glued together, where these different views become one single view. We don't just shoot it and show it. We edit it, to get across the feeling we want. It's essentially film editing, capitalizing on these new qualities and often we have more than one camera to enable us to do editing.

It should be also said that what we are working with here can have applications also in controlled filming. Jean Renoir is one who is very aware of this, for instance—the actors in his films become a sort of a poem; the whole huge technical machine, and the director, stand in the background, without intruding.

A. WILLIAM BLUEM

Television and the Documentary Quest*

"A part of a documentary's purpose is always social—somehow to let us discern more clearly, with greater compassion
and vision, the issues we must resolve."

*William Bluem suggests that the camera of "direct cinema"
is often so far from objectivity as to be a threat to clarity,
reason, and social justice. Approaching the subject not primarily from an artistic or technical standpoint but as a
historian of news and nonfiction on television, he rejects the
notion that "getting in close" on racial violence or any other
explosive issue is an adequate motivation for making a film.
He also explores the tendency in network documentary toward
"a situation that is carefully preselected to incorporate natural
dramatic crisis."*

Bluem is editor of Television Quarterly *and a professor at
the Newhouse Communications Center at Syracuse University.
In his final chapter, he further examines the social purpose
of the documentary in the light of a more affluent age. He
urges the possibility of going beyond Grierson's concern with
broad social action and also working against the "massness"
of the TV age by incorporating consciously the Flaherty way
—a concern with "the individuation of man."*

Because it can interfere with rationality (it is *designed* to do
so), the question fundamentally is whether *vérité* is legitimate
in News Documentary; and the answer lies in two Drew
productions: his *The Children Were Watching* (1960) and
Crisis: Behind a Presidential Commitment (1963). Both of
these programs involved presentation of an already emotion-

* A. William Bluem, *Documentary in American Television.*
New York, Hastings House, 1965. Pp. 128–133, 195–198, 200–
202, 204, 243–245.

laden issue in American life, civil rights for the Negro. If the *vérité* approach is to be regarded as a true journalistic method, here, above all, is where it was obliged to prove that capacity.

One of the many tragic chapters in the Negro's endless struggles for human rights was written at New Orleans in 1960, when the attempt to integrate the public schools there brought out a mass of angry racists who hovered near the schools and proclaimed their brutality and ignorance in deed and word. The violent outbursts of mob action were fully disclosed in all the communication media. On assignment from Drew, Richard Leacock went to New Orleans to record this raw, boiling-over hatred.

He chose to tell his story primarily through the actions of a Negro and a white family, both of whom sought to answer the call for integration. First we heard the soft voice of a narrator saying, "Some will learn to hate and some to love." Opening scenes of the Negro home placed emphasis upon the faces of the children as they observed adults in hushed discussions of the events of the day. Following upon his instincts to react spontaneously to a fluctuating situation, Leacock resolved to remain as unobtrusive as possible and record the story to the finish. His hand-held camera gave us a sequence of unsteady pictures, as the loose pan, the zoom in and out (and the momentary adjustment of focus), and every other kind of externally imposed movement was introduced. Projected thus into the milling crowds outside the school, we began to experience the restless energy of the crowd in close-ups of elbows, backs of heads, and twisted faces.

Now we hear the word "nigger" spoken in contempt, and the frame drops to show a small child, listening. There is a momentary pause on a man's unshaven face as he speaks of "gittin' a shotgun"—and above and behind all of this the ugly shouts and screams of the racist women fill our ears. We move back to the semi-peaceful Negro home, where nerves are taut, and overhear the parents talk of their plans for their daughter's future. The camera pans the family dog and to the father petting him.

Abruptly, with the briefest narrational transition, we are inside a car, riding along the trouble-ridden streets and listening to the words of the driver, a white segregationist leader. In a distorted blur his words crackle: ". . . Half of them are uninterested in bettering themselves. . . ." We cut away once more to the Negro

home for more discussion, then back to the car and a hazy sequence of visual impressions as the white segregationist speaks
of a "Communist plot—pushing the colored people to try and
destroy our nation." The pattern shifts, and we are in a car driven
by a Negro integration leader, introduced over a swirl of movement by the narrator's typical brief statement. We go intensely,
abruptly, to Leander Perez, to the car of the white leader (and
now the camera catches the blur of faces as they come rushing
to the car, collecting money for the "white cause," and we are
assaulted by the loud, tinny crash of a passing car radio). Next
to a PTA meeting, then to the bus arriving outside the school
where the shuffling, screaming crowd waits to take the white children home. More angry scenes, interspersed with curt statements
by the school superintendent, then a cut to the school exterior
and screaming "cheerleaders" hooting the white mother, Mrs.
Gabriel, who attempted to take her daughter to school and finally
retreated before the onslaught.

Now we go to the Gabriel home where the daughter, her face a
study in terror, watches from the window as the shouting mob
gathers outside. Inside the home there is confusion as the crowd
hammers at the door and windows. The police appear outside.
The tense action continues after a few words by the Police Chief
and we are in the mob again, where a frightened mother gathers
up her child and runs. Another face is suddenly seen, swearing,
"We gave those niggers all what they got," followed by a quick
pan to an infant sucking on a bottle as the words are still echoing
in our ears. At one point the screen goes black as a tumultuous
rush toward the cameraman makes us suspect that his camera has
been destroyed.

We return to the Gabriel home and hear the agonized comment,
"They are crucifying Him, just as surely as if He were right here."
The tension grows more and more ominous. A missing son arrives,
followed by the father who has quit his job under threat and pressure; his awkward admission of this with its intolerable despair, is
recorded. The home is quiet. The narrator comes in again over
the mob outside and asks, "What are the children learning?"
Among continuing scenes of horror we hear that these "were
some events of that week in New Orleans." And the credits fill
the screen.

Is this a valid recourse for the journalistic documentary in
a society groping to find answers to grave questions? Could

it, by any honest measure of journalism, be called a report, or even a record, of an event? These questions must be answered, for what we see in *The Children Were Watching* is a drama affected not only by the mere choice of a climactic moment in a crucial social situation (which may, after all, be what journalism is all about), but largely by cinematic techniques.

Leacock went to New Orleans seeking to witness the same ugly miscarriage of justice which all thinking men knew was occurring there. But, while others were trying to explain the meaning of these events in order to invoke the sobriety of reason, he was predisposed to show only hate and fear at its most tumultuous level, leaving us no room, no avenue, for thoughtful action.

What CBS Reports had done in its *Mississippi and the 15th Amendment* was not far distant, in some ways, from what the Drew unit recorded. We saw the hate there, too; we experienced the same sense of disgust with the machinations of the racists; and we felt the same sympathy with those being denied their basic liberties. But we saw it all in the framework of journalism to which drama was merely an additive. In *The Children Were Watching* we witnessed not only the drama, but were made participants in it. Emotional involvement in this Drew production was no longer a method by which to lead people to intellectual involvement, but an end in itself. When used in this way, *vérité* is a negation of that virtue which underlies the documentary idea.

Journalistic function aside, a part of a documentary's purpose is always social—somehow to let us discern more clearly, with greater compassion and vision, the issues we must resolve. *Vérité* revokes such purpose when it leaves us no time for clarity, when it exploits instinct alone, and when it makes technique an enemy of reason. If we add the responsibilities of journalism to documentary, we realize that only by undistorted appraisal of the crises in American life can rational men report the facts as they see them. They may introduce the scenes of anger and hate, but they must also help us to maintain detachment. In one sense, television journalism can truthfully say, "This is the way it was" or even "This is the way it is," but it is not the function of journalism to say "This is *it*." Certainly the news documentarist fails, as Fred Friendly has observed, if he cannot involve people. But the crux of this involvement—the whole art of the documentary-journalist—is in the skill with which he shows and tells us about human beings in conflict, *not* in the skill with which he can make us forget that we are witnessing a reconstruction.

If the rough and tumble "picture logic" of *The Children Were Watching* resulted in a disjointed and emotional treatment, there were rare moments, particularly in the Gabriel home, when we saw, overpoweringly, people who had lost consciousness of the presence of a camera. Drew's producers had attempted to establish what has been called "a gray area," in which the camera can operate at a level equal to people in such moments of crisis. Their hopes of neutralizing the effects of the camera's presence had been realized often enough to give them hope that they could enter into the reporting process at entirely different levels within our society.

In Gregory Shuker's 1963 production for Drew, *Crisis: Behind a Presidential Commitment,* the cameras were admitted into the offices of the President and the Attorney General of the United States throughout that period when Governor George Wallace of Alabama threatened to bar the entrance of Negro students to the University. The Drew production team pursued this legal combat between Wallace and the Kennedy administration in a program which purported to show us the decision-making process—the behind-the-scenes progress of a major national conflict.

Too much of this program followed the paths of formlessness of earlier Drew efforts, but the significant fact to emerge from the *Crisis* program may be offered as a simple law: the more responsibility men assume in democratic decision-making, the less they are willing, able, and liable to forget the presence of the camera. The promise that we would actually hear President Kennedy himself during this crisis never materialized, as he exercised his authority to delete his own comments throughout the conference. Obviously, no official would approve the recording of his full reactions at all times. What Wallace and the Kennedys allowed the nation to see were the official representations of their offices.

This in itself might destroy the validity of the "gray area" as journalistic material, for what was seen was always, in one way or another, either staged or irrelevant. So great was this program's departure from accepted standards that New York's educational TV station, WNDT, followed the national televising of the Drew program with a discussion titled "Presidency by Crisis," and invited several spokesmen for varying points of view to comment upon what they had seen. Whatever consensus could be drawn from their discussion focused entirely upon these matters of the danger of misuse of the technique in such sensitive social circumstances. Political sympathies notwithstanding, the participants were seemingly agreed on the point that the element of "play-acting" had entered the program on both sides of the controversy, and that the decision-making processes of our government had been brought too close to "show business." . . .

In the Living Camera series Drew's purpose became surer, the focus narrower, and the crises depicted more direct and specific in terms of a sharp either-or moment of resolution. This series treated human beings who, in terms of outward action, were heading for a crisis of greater magnitude. We saw a driver getting ready for a critical race, Jane Fonda preparing for an opening night, two football coaches just before a crucial game, and similar examinations of human beings who were undergoing inward stress because they faced an outward crisis which, in one way or another, would close the system. Of these, none carried a greater significance—a more definite finality—than *The Chair*.

In *The Chair* Drew's film-makers found all the eternal elements of the great courtroom drama clearly set in motion, with an inevitable crisis impending. The film detailed the case of Paul Crump, a Negro convicted of murder over a decade ago and sentenced to die. Through a series of legal moves his execution was delayed; and Drew's unit moved to Chicago to follow a young attorney who was fighting a major battle to have the sentence commuted. As the actual hearing neared, New York attorney Louis Nizer agreed to present the brief, which was, in effect, a strong argument for the possibility of rehabilitation.

The facts of this case happened also to be the precise conditions of drama. The hearing obviously would be held, and from this great crisis in Crump's life there had to come some resolution. This was, however, the only loose end, and in these terms it made little difference whether he won or lost. *The Chair*, then, was laid out in the form of the trial drama, and Drew's unit had to do no more than capture, with as much impact as possible, the total situation: the efforts of the protagonist (the young attorney), of the antagonist (the state's attorney), the crisis in the courtroom (where Nizer became assistant protagonist), and the final decision of the hearing board (a resolution to commute the sentence). The denouement was a traditional happy ending (if one chooses to regard a man's return to prison for life as an improvement upon electrocution), showing the buoyant young attorney off to the racetrack on a bus.

The difference between *The Chair* and a typical Perry Mason segment is dramaturgically small—and yet the severe distinction between them is that nothing seen in *The Chair* was not made from the raw material of life. In that difference lies still another testimony to *vérité*. On two occasions, for example, the attorney totally forgot the camera and sound equipment. At one point he learned, in a telephone conversation, that a highly placed community leader planned to make a public statement in behalf of Crump's commutation— a stroke of good fortune beyond his wildest hopes. The conversation ended and suddenly he was in tears, a reaction so intense and natural that it was a full minute before he recalled the camera's presence. And again, when he was informed that people in Steubenville, Ohio, were collecting pennies for his cause, there was an overpowering moment of choking back his emotions. Not since the early Philco Playhouse production of Mosel's character study of Howie in *The Haven* did one see a more naturally motivated analysis of a man so deeply moved that he wept before us—and only with great concentration can we remember that one was a drama and the other the revelation of a real man intensely involved in a real situation.

LIVING DRAMA

But the climactic moments in men's lives do not happen at the convenience of cameramen and sound men, however unobtrusively they may wait. A dramatic situation must not only exist; it must be approaching some definite climax when the producers arrive to record it. And if these elements are not present they must be manufactured. If they are manufactured, the documentarist runs the risk of destroying his very purpose.

This was the challenge which Irving Gitlin and his producers at NBC News Creative Projects faced in a series of Du Pont-sponsored productions in 1963 and 1964 which were called "living dramas." Several of their works over a two-year span are especially worth noting—William Jersey's *Prisoner-at-Large, Incident on Wilson Street* and *Manhattan Battleground,* Albert Wasserman's *High Wire: The Wallendas,* and Fred Freed's incomparable *Fire Rescue.*

One of Grierson's requirements for documentary was that a part of a society should see and comprehend the meaning of the lives of other parts of that society; if Grierson had seen *Fire Rescue* it is probable that he would have approved, at least in principle, its motive and achievement. The NBC camera crews followed the men of New York City Rescue Company One for a period of three months, recording them at work and in their moments of relaxation. Edited into a one-hour film, the story of these men held overwhelming power, carrying the Flaherty theme of man's indomitable spirit—expressed in ultimate terms of his capacity to exercise normality of function in the face of suffering, omnipresent danger, and death itself. . . .

In Jersey's *Manhattan Battleground* (1964) the drama of Paddy Chayefsky's "small crisis" and Benjamin's "man from the inside out" were once again reflected in the story of a young social worker's final weeks in a neighborhood where, with love and dedication, he had given new meaning to the lives of young people. We saw him as he walked the streets, counseling the weak, inspiring the indifferent, cheering the despairing. His indefatigable powers for good were chronicled for us by the camera which drifted with him, lingered as he lingered, and seemed almost a companion at his side. The boys prepared a little skit for his going-away party, and we shared their awkward expression of gratitude. Slowly, tenderly, we moved toward that moment when the van was finally loaded and there was no longer any reason for delay. And then we felt the reality of human experience: voices were breaking; out of the blur came faces, tearfully committed faces, to say a last farewell. A life of force and vigor and hope was being withdrawn from that small social situation. Something of a corner was turned; and this, in the final accounting, was crisis enough to sustain a moving human drama.

The high tragedy of *Fire Rescue* was lacking in *Prisoner-at-Large,* but the study of a Massachusetts parole officer who struggled to prevent a young man from destroying his life was made memorable by a treatment which involved intense examination of human beings in moments of emotional torment. Producer William Jersey also worked in that preselected structure which held its own inevitable climax, just as surely as had Drew in *The Chair.* Made with the cooperation of the Massachusetts Parole Board, this film was designed to acquaint the public with the work of a parole officer whose efforts were directed toward the rehabilitation of a young criminal. This natural line of action ended at a meeting of the Parole Board, at which time the young man's future was settled.

In this case the relationship with these two characters was established in a series of fine *vérité* scenes, and we became involved as we began to share the officer's conviction that the young man might reform. But the boy did not wait for the prestructured climax, and instead committed a criminal act while still on parole—an act which sealed his fate before the Parole Board even came to consider his case. The crisis spilled over, and finally was properly focused not in the Parole Board meeting, but in two scenes of intense emotional conflict between the officer and the criminal—the first when the officer confronted him after he had been arrested for housebreaking, and the second when the officer told him the Board had decided he must serve out his new sentence before being reviewed again for parole. In these scenes of raw hurt and anger the tensions were too high for the presence of any camera to hold them in check. We saw first the despair of the parole officer, whose faith and convictions had been ripped away by the boy's stupid and willful act, and later the desperation of the boy when he was told that he would have to serve out his new sentence.

Again, so intense was the feeling that playwright and actors would have been hard pressed to so effectively reconstruct it. Perhaps the only comparable scene in all of contemporary drama was that moment of confrontation in the taxi between Marlon Brando and Rod Steiger in the film *On the Waterfront,* a reference which leads us once more to appreciate the inevitable power of living drama in a situation that is carefully preselected to incorporate natural dramatic crisis. In *Prisoner-at-Large* we saw that power at work, and also learned that the unpredictable can add even greater impact to a preselected crisis. The events of reality shaped a different climax and theme, emphasizing not a battle won or lost for the boy, but a battle lost for the officer. . . .

From these experiments and departures in the documentary method of television some immediate conclusions may be offered. We are justified in saying that a true television aesthetic may exist, and that principles discovered in the golden age of the live television drama in the early 1950's strongly influenced the golden age of television Theme Documentary in the 1960's. For whatever method or style that documentarists have employed, as documentary began to record the life and the living which surround us in time, the form moved toward the *dramaturgical*—following Aristotle's division of ways in which we are told of men in action by pursuing the task of showing men living and moving before us. All that is missing is the full significance of Aristotle's *imitation*. Whether television's documentarists have served that method which emphasized plot building (as Benjamin and Eugene Jones have), or whether they have minimized narrative and become plot-finders (as Stuart, Drew, and Gitlin have), none of them is a plot-maker. None is free of the necessity to remain with the actual, and to structure it as his own conscience and honesty demand.

TELEVISION AND THE DOCUMENTARY QUEST

The lives and work of Robert Flaherty and John Grierson remind us again that there is little new under the sun; that all documentary efforts to help us "get on" in the world about us begin and end with their distinct ways of revealing life to us. In his own manner and style each expressed the ultimate needs of men and societies. Television's control of civilization's attention places a broader responsibility upon those who follow in the paths of these two giants. The documentarists of television must nurture two ideals: of men as social agents, and of each man as a *person*. . . .

The immediate decision, the innocent eye: these are the two great contradictory forces which underlie our confrontations with reality in all of its manifest forms. They succinctly characterize the work not only of Grierson and Flaherty, but of all who have since come to apply "creative treatment" to actuality. Of all those men of our century who must reflect a balance and wholeness between these two aspects of life, none may have more final effect upon our lives than the strange mixture of reporter and poet we call the documentarist. He, and the managers and editors who influence and control his work, may hopefully set the example by which all of us may not only survive, but prevail.

The possibilities are all but overwhelming. If we possess the technology by which to obliterate ourselves, we also have the capacities to harness technology in the responsible service of mankind—seeking not only an essential betterment and a new level of harmony among men and nations, but the individuation of man. Even the most skeptical detractors of the mass media will admit that television, in its greatest moments, has served both goals. For all can sense that the images on the TV screen help to create, for the first time in human history, *communicating man*—a creation which underlies both a social and an individual view of life. Through documentary, TV may show us that we are capable of identifying specific needs and issues of our world, and can adopt those intelligent plans of action which give us the positive security of a truly civilized social contract. And it can also apply its great force for individuation of the human spirit. This is what the American television documentary has attempted. If the function must be enlarged and made still more meaningful, the medium has at least engaged in the quest. And it is the *quest*, John Fitzgerald Kennedy once told us, that is the true adventure of this century.

CARL DREYER

Thoughts on My Craft*

"It is a waste of time to copy reality. We must use the camera
to create a new language of style."

The Danish director of Ordet *and* Day of Wrath, *believing
"in evolution, in the small step forward," declares himself on
the side of simplification and abstraction: "The artist must
describe inner, not outer life. The capacity to abstract is essential to all artistic creation." To this end—without losing the
world of reality, holding still to modes the audience can understand—he suggests, somewhat tentatively, some experiments
in simplified décor, in symbolic color, in flattened perspective.*

*Dreyer feels, unlike Kracauer and some other theorists, that
film is not a mere reflection of actuality but a construction.
He says that film is more like architecture than any of the
other arts, "because it is not an imitation of nature, but a
pure product of human imagination." It is not surprising, then,
that he emphasizes the director's responsibility for impressing
the stamp of his style on a film, and that his last word is a
tribute to the expressiveness of the actor's performance.*

I am not a film theorist. I am only a film director, and proud
of my craft. But a craftsman also gets his own ideas during
his work.

I have nothing revolutionary to say. I do not believe in
revolutions. They very often push development backwards.
I am more inclined to believe in *evolution*, in the small step
forward.

So I shall limit myself to saying that the film has possibilities
of artistic renewal from *inside*. Human beings dislike being

* Carl Dreyer, "Thoughts on My Craft," *Sight and Sound*,
Winter 1955–1956, pp. 128–129.

taken off the beaten track. They have got used by now to the correct photographic reproduction of reality, they enjoy recognising what they already know. When the camera appeared it won a quick victory, because in a mechanical objective way it could register the impressions of the human eye. So far this capacity has been the strength of the film, but for works of art it is becoming a weakness that must be fought.

We have got stuck with photography. We are now confronted with the necessity of freeing ourselves from it. We must use the camera to drive away the camera.

Photography as a means of reporting, of sightseeing, has compelled the film to remain with its feet on the ground. We have to wrench the film out of the embrace of naturalism. We have to tell ourselves it is a waste of time to copy reality. We must use the camera to create a new language of style, a new artistic form.

But first of all we have to understand what we mean by "art" and "style." The Danish writer Johannes V. Jensen defines art as a "spiritually interpreted form," a definition that seems to me perfect. Chesterfield considers style to be "the dress of thoughts," another simple and precise definition, provided that the dress is not too conspicuous. The characteristic of a good style, itself simple and precise too, must be that it enters into such intimate contact with the material that it forms a *synthesis*. If it is too pushing, if it tries to attract attention, it is no longer style but mannerism.

I would define style as the form in which artistic inspiration expresses itself. We recognise the style of an artist in certain features characteristic of him personally, which reflect his nature and his outlook.

The style of a film that is a work of art results from many different components, such as the effect of rhythm and composition, the mutual tension of colour surfaces, the interaction of light and shadow, the gliding rhythm of the camera. All these things, combined with the director's conception of his material as something that can be expressed in terms of creative film, decide his style. If he confines himself to the soulless impersonal photography of what his eyes can perceive, he has no style. If he uses his mind to transfer what his eyes can see into a vision, if he builds up his film in accordance with this vision, disregarding the reality that inspired it, then his work will bear the sacred stamp of inspiration. Then the film has a style.

The director is the man who must leave his hallmark on a film that is a work of art. This does not involve underestimating the poet's share; but even if the poet is Shakespeare, the literary idea in itself will not make the film a work of art. The director, creatively inspired by the poet's material, is necessary for this.

I do not underestimate, either, the team work of cameramen, colour technicians, designers and so on; but, within this collective, the director must remain the prime, inspiring power, the man behind the work, who makes us listen to the poet's words and who makes feelings and passions flare so that we are moved and touched.

This is my conception of the director's importance—and *responsibility*.

How can we define the film that is a work of art? First, let us ask what other art form is most closely related to films. In my opinion it must be architecture, which is the most perfect art form because it is not an imitation of nature, but a pure product of human imagination.

In all noble architecture the details are so finely balanced and harmonised as to fit in with the whole. No detail, however small, can be changed without giving the impression of a flaw in the harmony. (In a badly designed house, all measures and proportions are haphazard, variable.) Something similar applies to films. Only when *all* the artistic elements of a film have been welded together so firmly that no single unit can be left out or changed without damaging the whole, only then can the film be compared to a piece of architectural art. Films which do not satisfy this demand are like those conventional, uninspired houses that one passes by without even noticing.

In the architectural film the director takes over the role of architect.

Where is the possibility of artistic renewal in the cinema? I can answer only for myself, and I can see only one way: *abstraction*. In order not to be misunderstood, I must at once define abstraction as something that demands of the artist to abstract himself from reality in order to strengthen the spiritual content of his work.

More concisely: the artist must describe inner, not outer life. The capacity to abstract is essential to all artistic creation. Abstraction allows the director to get outside the fence with which naturalism has surrounded his medium. It allows his films to be not merely visual, but spiritual. The director must share his own artistic and spiritual experiences with the audience. Abstraction will give him a chance of doing it, of replacing objective reality with his own subjective interpretation.

This means that we must find some new creative principles. I would like to stress that I am thinking merely of the image. People think in images, and images are the primary factor of a film.

The closest road at hand is the road of simplification. Every creative artist is confronted by the same task. He must be inspired by reality, then move away from it in order to give his work the form provoked by his inspiration. The director must be free to transform reality so that it becomes consistent with the inspired, simplified image left in his mind. Reality must obey the director's aesthetic sense.

To make the form more evident, more striking, simplification must cleanse the director's inspiration of all elements that do not support his central idea. It must transform the idea into a symbol. With symbolism we are well on the way to abstraction, for symbolism works through suggestion.

This abstraction through simplification, so that a purified form emerges in a kind of timeless, psychological realism, can be practised by the director in a modest way in the actual rooms of his films. How many rooms without souls we have seen on the screen. . . . The director can give his rooms a soul through simplification, by removing all that is superfluous, by making a few significant articles and objects psychological witnesses of the inmate's personality.

Colour is a much more important means to obtain abstraction. Everything is possible with colour. But the colour film is still bound to the naturalistic chains of the black-and-white film. In the same way as French impressionists were inspired by classical Japanese woodcuts, so Western film directors can learn from the beautiful Japanese film *Gate of Hell*. Here the colours actually fulfil their purpose. I believe that the Japanese themselves consider this film naturalistic: a historical reconstruction, but still naturalistic. Through our eyes its style tends towards the abstract. Only in one scene does pure naturalism break through, the scene of the tournament on the open plain. The style is broken for a few minutes, though we quickly forget the feeling of uneasiness it gives us.

The colours in *Gate of Hell* have undoubtedly been chosen to a well-prepared plan. The film tells us a great deal about warm and cold colours, about the use of profound simplification. It should encourage Western directors to use colour more deliberately and with greater boldness and imagination.

At present we are moving on cats' paws. We can throw in some pastel shades, pink and light blue, to show we have taste. But, as far as the abstract film goes, taste will not be nearly enough. Artistic intuition and courage are necessary to select and compose contrasting colours, to support the dramatic and psychological contents of a film. Colour offers the greatest possibility of artistic renewal in the cinema, and it is a pity that after twenty years one can remember only three or four films with colour that produced an aesthetic experience. And the best one has come from Japan. We can learn something from the Japanese.

There is another factor worth mentioning. Photography, of course, presumes an atmospheric perspective; light and shadow fade towards the background. There may be an idea here to obtain interesting abstraction by deliberately eliminating atmospheric perspective, by giving up the much sought-after effects of depth and distance.

Instead, one should work towards an entirely new image-structure, one should plan one's colour surfaces so as to form one large, many-coloured surface. One should eliminate the conception of foreground, middle distance and background. It is possible that very remarkable aesthetic effects could be obtained in this way.

Abstraction may sound like a naughty word in the ears of film people. But I want only to point out that there is a world outside grey and boring naturalism: the world of imagination. Of course, the transformation must be made without the director losing grip on the world of reality. His remodelled reality must still be something the audience can recognise and believe in. It is very important for the first attempts at abstraction to be made with tact and discretion. People must not be shocked, they must be led along new roads slowly.

Should the attempt prove successful, enormous prospects open up. The film may never become three dimensional, but by means of abstraction it may be possible to introduce fourth and fifth dimensions.

A word about actors. Anyone who has seen my films—the good ones—will know how much importance I attach to performance. Nothing in the world can be compared to the human face. It is a land one can never tire of exploring. There is no greater experience in a studio than to witness the expression of a sensitive face under the mysterious power of inspiration. To see it animated from inside, and turning into poetry.

CHARLES BARR

CinemaScope: Before and After*

"A complex image organized in such a way that we are
induced to interpret it for ourselves."

*The wide screen has been hailed by some film makers as a
new challenge; most critics have deplored it. The argument is
theoretical and aesthetic: the close-up of face and of object,
the reaction of shot to shot, must be more contrived, more
lethargic, in CinemaScope, or else it will not work at all. The
argument may be practical, as put by George Stevens some
years ago: the wide screen is more suited to a boa constrictor
than a man.*

*Charles Barr, a young British critic of films, insists on a
wider, more tolerant look at the wide-screen systems. He
plunges in boldly, taking on the whole Eisenstein-Pudovkin
school of montage enthusiasts. He suggests that this new
stretching of the screen takes the film farther away from the
literary, in that "there is no literary equivalent for 'getting
things in the same shot.'" A writer must always describe successively, not totally; the film can wrap up more impressions
the wider it is. Furthermore, CinemaScope "increases the
involvement of the spectator and the physical integration of
the characters."*

*If 70mm and other similar processes do demand more of
the viewer and thus coincide with the thinking of some of the
more demanding directors of contemporary films, then Cinerama might logically present the most advanced involvement
of all. Mr. Barr has some reservations on that, and some tentative predictions about total immersion in visual perceptions
in the future which suggest a need for a crash program of
theoretical analysis.*

* Charles Barr, "CinemaScope: Before and After," *Film Quarterly*, Vol. XVI, No. 4, Summer 1963, Pp. 9–10, 11–17, 20–21,
23–24.

. . . . It is not only the horizontal line which is emphasized in CinemaScope (this was implied by critics who concentrated on the *shape* of the frame qua shape—as though it were the frame of a painting—and concluded that the format was suitable only for showing/framing horizontal things like crocodiles and processions). The more open the frame, the greater the impression of depth: the image is more vivid, and involves us more directly. The most striking effect in Cinerama is the roller-coaster shot, which gives us a very strong sensation of movement forward. Even though at the crucial moment we may be focussing only on the very center of the image, i.e., the area of track directly in front of the roller-coaster—an area, in fact, no larger than the standard frame—the rest of the image is not useless. We may not be conscious of what exactly is there, but we are marginally aware of the objects and the space on either side. It is this peripheral vision which orients us and makes the experience so vivid. . . .

Rudolf Arnheim, in *Film as Art*, claims that any such sensation of depth will be undesirable: compositional patterns which in the more abstract image would come across as being deliberate will, if the image is more vivid, seem natural, even accidental, so that the spectator may fail to note their symbolic force.[1]

From this point of view, an even more relevant Scope scene is this one from *River of No Return*, analyzed by V. F. Perkins in *Movie* 2. I think the narrative is clear enough from his description:

As Harry lifts Kay from the raft, she drops the bundle which contains most of her 'things' into the water. Kay's gradual loss of the physical tokens of her way of life has great symbolic significance. But Preminger is not overimpressed. The bundle simply floats away offscreen while Harry brings Kay ashore. It would be wrong to describe this as understatement. The symbolism is in the

[1] Arnheim also wrote, and I am not making it up: "Silent laughter is often more effective than if the sound is actually heard. The gaping of the open mouth gives a vivid, highly artistic interpretation of the phenomenon 'laughter.' If, however, the sound is also heard, the opening of the mouth appears obvious and its value as a means of expression is almost entirely lost." But I don't know that this argument against sound is any more unconvincing than that against Scope—the logic is identical.

event, not in the visual pattern, so the director presents the action clearly and leaves the interpretation to the spectator.

Arnheim would no doubt regard this as a *reductio ad absurdum*. His attitude, which is shared, deep down, by most critics, is based on his phobia of using the camera as a "recording machine" (reality is not art). It further reflects an unwillingness to leave the spectator any freedom to interpret action or behavior, or to make connections. This concept of "freedom" has been distorted as much as that of "reality." It's taken to be absurd that a director should allow a viewer any freedom of interpretation, for he may then notice things that he isn't meant to, or fail to notice things that he should; he may get the wrong point altogether. This is in line with the idea that the test of a good film is whether it "makes statements."

Now in this scene from *River of No Return*, the spectator is "free" to notice the bundle, and, when he does so, free to interpret it as significant. But there is nothing random about the shot. The detail is placed in the background of the shot, and integrated naturally, so that we have to make a positive act of interpreting, of "reading," the shot. The act of interpreting the visual field—and through that the action—is in itself valuable. The significance of the detail is not announced, it is allowed to speak for itself. An alert spectator will notice the bundle, and "follow" it as it floats offscreen.

The traditional method would be to make its significance unmistakable by cutting in close-ups. In this case we would gather that the bundle is meaningful *because* it is picked out for us. In Preminger's film, the process is reversed: we pick it out *because* it is meaningful. The emphasis arises organically out of the whole action; it is not imposed.

"The symbolism is in the event, not in the visual pattern." Before Scope, it was difficult to show the "event" lucidly, with each detail given its appropriate weight. It wasn't impossible: many Renoir films, as well as Mizoguchi's *Ugetsu Monogatari*, are superlative examples of the "opening-up" of the 1:1.33 frame to achieve this kind of fluidity. But on the whole the tendency was to split up the event into its component parts, and to impose, whether deliberately or not, a "visual pattern," a pattern of montage and/or of obtrusively "composed" images. And a *visual* pattern involves a pattern of motiva-

tion, a pattern of significance, which in certain films is appropriate, but is more often damagingly crude.

At this stage one can hardly avoid talking of "participation," which is another much-abused word. Everyone agrees,
in principle, that art should not so much state as reveal, and
that we should not just register its meaning but understand it.
Our experience of a work should involve active participation
more than passive assimilation.

The Russians, in their theoretical work, appropriated this
idea, and applied it in a somewhat outrageous way; but critics,
even intelligent ones, have continued to accept what they said.
The confusion rests on a misunderstanding of the relation between film and the other arts, notably literature. Eisenstein
said that "participation" took place in the association of successive images (as in the association of juxtaposed images in
poetry)—that it depended purely on montage. In *October* he
had intercut shots of Kerensky with ironic titles, and then with
shots of a peacock preening itself. These images in themselves
are fairly neutral, but the spectator fuses them together freely,
he "participates," and arrives at an "intellectual decision" at
the expense of Kerensky. In *Strike* we are shown, alternately,
shots of workmen being massacred and of bulls being slaugh-
tered: again, the two sets of images are independent of each
other and we have to make the imaginative link between the
two. Commenting recently on passages like these, an English
critic said, "Thus Eisenstein's 'intellectual cinema' proves itself
a superior means of communication by demanding the co-
operation of the spectator in consideration of the conflicting
ideologies that Eisenstein chose to convey."

This seems to me so much solemn nonsense. The whole is
more than the sum of its parts; but then the whole is *always*
more than the sum of its parts. The spectator "interprets" but
there is no genuine freedom of association. A montage link
of this kind reminds one of the children's puzzle which consists of a series of numbered dots: when they are joined together correctly, the outline of an animal appears. We participate in solving these, but only in a mechanical way, and
there is only one correct solution. The very last thing Eisenstein really wants us to do is to evaluate for ourselves, or even
experience for ourselves, what we are shown. He does not
show us heroic actions—which we can recognize or judge to
be heroic—he shows actions (not even that, but only *bits* of

actions) and tells us that they are heroic (or alternatively brutal). Vakoulintchouk, in *Potemkin*, is "defined" by the shots which are intercut with shots of his dead body: close-ups of weeping women, sympathetic titles. Similarly we are *told* how to react to Kerensky and to the killing of the workmen— told obliquely, it is true, by a form of visual code, but still told; nothing is in any useful sense communicated. It is revealing that the whole meaning of these films can be reversed, as happened apparently in places with *Potemkin*, by merely re-arranging certain shots and titles, just as one can reverse the meaning of a slogan by replacing one name with another. (This would be inconceivable with *Birth of a Nation*.)

What is in question is not Eisenstein's artistry, within his chosen field, but rather the way his technique has been rationalized, by him and by others, and a universal validity claimed for it. The style is appropriate to what he was aiming to do, namely, to make propaganda. He was not interested (in the silent films) in characterization or in shades of meaning, nor did he want to leave the spectator any freedom of response. The struggle of authority against revolution, and of Old against New, is one of Black and White. Andrew Sarris, in an excellent article on Rossellini in the *New York Film Bulletin*, contrasts this extreme montage style—"Eisenstein's conceptual editing extracts a truth from the collision of two mechanistic forces in history"—with "Rossellini's visual conception of a unified cosmos undivided by the conceptual detail of montage," and he implies one should accept each on its own terms. I think it's legitimate to say that, even if the style reflects the vision accurately, the vision is crude, and the style, although powerful, crude likewise. The words Eisenstein and his contemporaries use in describing it are significant: "impact," "collision," "clash," the juxtaposition of "concepts"; the approach is essentially a rhetorical one. What is obvious anyway from this is that Eisenstein is a special case, that few directors see things his way, and that few subjects are amenable to this treatment. Drama is not normally reducible to concepts, clashes and collisions. (This is quite apart from the implications of the change to the sound film, after which the technique becomes still less relevant.)

People complain sometimes that Eisenstein's methods of intellectual and ideological montage have been forgotten, as have the associative techniques of Pudovkin's *Mother*, and imply that directors today must be deficient in imagination:

but insofar as they reject these techniques they are more subtle. And a field where they do notably survive is that of the filmed commercial. The product may not in itself look very special (a "dead object") but it takes on associations when intercut with a smiling mother holding a smiling baby. The montage-unit style no doubt sells products, and puts over propaganda, more effectively than would a more fluid one, and there are other films too for which it is perfectly appropriate: educational work, certain documentaries, anything which aims to put over a message concisely. One would not advocate CinemaScope for these.

Jean Mitry in his interesting book *Eisenstein* criticizes him for at times indulging in arbitrary symbolism (the slaughterhouse in *Strike*), but he accepts Eisenstein's analogies between the interpretation of film and poetic images: the film-maker juxtaposing unrelated images by montage is like the poet juxtaposing words. But the reader genuinely "participates" in the associations he makes from the words, in building them up into a fused whole: words are allusive whereas the film image is concrete. Film images follow each other in rigid sequence, which we cannot vary; the interaction of words is much more flexible. The more one goes into the differences between word and shot, and between the literary and filmic sequences of description, the more shaky do all the analogies made by the Russians seem.

There is no literary equivalent for "getting things in the same shot." This seems never to have struck them. Both Eisenstein and Pudovkin made laborious comparisons between the word or ideogram and the individual shot, and between the sentence and the montage-sequence. This seems fantastically naïve. How else can you translate "the cat sat on the mat" into film except in a single shot? Disciples tend to admit that these theories went a bit far—after all, they never went quite so far in their films—but without realizing that the rest of their aesthetic, which sounds more plausible, is in fact equally shaky, and for similar reasons.

For instance: a writer has to describe details successively, even though they may exist together. In this case he will aim, by his description, to evoke a "total" simultaneous reality in the reader's mind. Because of the indirect, allusive quality of language this is not really a handicap. Thackeray, in his *Irish Sketchbook*, gives a description of a mountain scene, evoking it by a series of details and of comparisons; he adds,

"Printer's ink cannot give these wonderful hues, and *the reader will make his picture at his leisure*" (my italics). But the film image is direct, it *shows* things.

In *Lolita* (the book) there is a scene which, had it been presented without comment, might have seemed a perfect vindication of the rules laid down by Pudovkin in *Film Technique*, in that it consists of a series of details, which Nabokov describes successively, and which Pudovkin would have filmed successively ("showing them one by one, just as we would describe them in separate sequence in literary work"). It is the scene of the death of Humbert's wife: "I rushed out. The far side of our steep little street presented a peculiar sight. . . . *I have to put the impact of an instantaneous vision into a sequence of words; their physical accumulation on the page impairs the actual flash, the sharp unity of impression.* Rugheap, old-man doll, Miss O's nurse running with a rustle back to the screened porch . . ." (my italics).

It's naïve to suppose that even the most fragmented lines— "ships, towers, domes, theatres and temples lie/open unto the fields and to the sky"—can be given an exact cinematic equivalent by a montage of ships, towers, domes, and so on. Eisenstein makes much of the fragmentary narrative of Dickens; this is fair enough in that a change of scene would correspond to a cut in film, but it does not hold for the *texture* of a narrative. Thomas Hardy makes a useful reference here, and at the risk of seeming repetitive I'd like to consider some passages from his novels.

Often he will introduce a character by, as it were, discovering him within a landscape. Being a writer, he describes things one by one, but they all contribute to the creation of a broad, total environment. His protagonists emerge from this, and are in turn absorbed into it; they are never detached; we retain a mental picture of them as a part of it. The film equivalent is to *show* them as a part of it, to engulf them in it. Boetticher's *Ride Lonesome* and Ray's *The Savage Innocents* are two films which portray people dominated by, almost defined by, their natural environment, and this connection is perfectly conveyed in their first images. In *Ride Lonesome*, the camera is held on a shot of a vast plain, stretching away to mountains in the distance; then it tilts down slowly and we become aware of a rider coming toward us from deep among the rocks below. *The Savage Innocents* has a long, empty snowscape: the camera is still: a sledge enters frame left, deep within the shot, and is drawn gradually toward us. One can contrast this with the opening of *Scott of the Antarctic*: a montage of snow vistas, evocative music. We look *at* the scene instead of being involved in it, as we are in *The Savage Innocents*; and we accept, intellectually, for the purposes of the narrative, that the characters are there, instead of genuinely feeling it. Both Boetticher's and Ray's films are in Scope, and this helps enormously: it increases the involvement of the spectator and the physical integration of the characters.

It might be said that these are "landscape" films, that Scope is suitable for them but not for more confined drama. But the same principles hold; the dichotomy often expressed between interior and exterior drama is a false one.

Consider this passage from *Tess of the d'Urbervilles*. On her wedding night, Tess confesses to her husband about the child she had by Alec:

Her narrative had ended; even its reassertions and secondary explanations were done. Tess's voice throughout had hardly risen higher than its opening tone; there had been no exculpatory phrase of any kind, and she had not wept.

But the complexion even of external things seemed to suffer transmutation as her announcement proceeded. The fire in the grate looked impish—demoniacally funny, as if it did not care in the least about her strait. The fender grinned idly, as if it too did not care. The light from the water-bottle was merely engaged in a chromatic problem. All material objects around announced their irresponsibility with terrible iteration. And yet nothing had changed since the moments when he had been kissing her; or rather, nothing in the substance of things. But the essence of things had changed.

The Russians, again, might interpret this their own way: fragmentation, subjectivity, justifying a similar technique for film. But in film everything is concrete. Film shows the substance, it cannot *show* the essence, but it can *suggest* the essence by *showing* the substance. It suggests inner reality by showing outer reality with the greatest possible intensity. The writer has to build up a scene by description and allusion: images and metaphors, however fanciful, can help to strengthen our *objective* picture of the scene, whereas if transposed to film they would distract, and distort (imagine a close-up of the fender, grinning idly). For filming this passage from *Tess* I can't imagine a better method than to keep both of them in the frame the whole time, with the "material objects" around and between them, and to have her explanation, and then his silence, and reactions, in a single take, without any overt emphasis from the camera. Ideally, in CinemaScope, which makes the surroundings more palpable, and enables you to get close to one or both of the characters without shutting out the rest of the scene. The more precisely the camera charts the substance of things, the external movement of words, expressions, gestures, the more subtly can it express the internal movement: the essence of things. . . .

Writers like Manvell, Reisz, and Lindgren (all of whom base their aesthetic more or less closely on the Russians') advocate a method which gives us a *digest* of what we might see, in real life, if we were experiencing a given scene. Lindgren, in *The Art of the Film,* goes into this in most detail. He makes the usual comparisons with literary fragmentation, and then between what we see in life and in films. Sometimes we consciously see things as a whole, in their interrelationship (general shot). Sometimes we look round (pan) or walk (tracking shot). Normally we focus on one thing at a time (close-up or close-shot) and we look from one thing to another (cutting). Now it should be clear that the correspondence is by no means exact. In a film we sit facing the same direction all the time, looking at a screen which is set at a finite distance. In life we are oriented in our surroundings and our perception of them is continuous—continuous in time and space. But Lindgren claims that "in so far as the film is photographic and reproduces movement, it can give us a lifelike semblance of what we see; in so far as it employs editing, it can exactly [*sic*] reproduce the *manner* in which we see it."

At any time we see "central" things and "marginal" things; of the latter we may be aware, or half-aware, or they may serve merely to orient us. The traditional aesthetic separates out the central things: the marginal ones it either omits as inessential and distracting, or intercuts in close shot —in which case they are no longer marginal but central.

So an alternative method, a more strictly realistic one, which Lindgren and company pass over, is to present a complex image organized in such a way that we are induced to interpret it for ourselves. . . .

Cinerama does not project its image onto the squared-off

wall opposite the audience, as other wide-screen systems do (only in certain Todd-AO theatres is the screen significantly curved); instead, it wraps the image around in front of them. If one sits in a front seat and looks at the center of the image, one can't see anything but screen, and one can turn almost full left and full right and still be *facing* the screen. The bigger and more "realistic" screens get, the more will this be true, and it is confusing because it is too close to our perception of life: it demands an equivalent control over distances, which is impossible as yet. There is no problem, in principle or in practice, over giving the impression of a confined space in CinemaScope (think of *Les Amants, Bitter Victory, Les 400 Coups*); but to fill the curved Cinerama screen with a group of people does not give the impression of being hemmed in by people; the effect is rather of being surrounded by people at some distance away. The space within the scene automatically becomes expanded (again, if one sits close) to at least the dimensions of the front arc of the auditorium itself. The cameras, being at the center of an arc, instead of remaining outside the scene, can "interrupt" it. This means that a character can't look, or move, straight across from one side of the scene to the other, because this would entail going "across" the camera, and thus "across" the audience. Daniels explains that "an actor on the right or left cannot look directly at an actor at the center (if that's what the script calls for); if he does, he will look, on the screen, as if he is looking out front. This is because he is, of course, being photographed by a different camera at a different angle."

Cinerama is halfway between the traditional flat screen and an "all-around" cinema where the spectators are enclosed in a hemisphere of image. It is often assumed that this would be the ultimate in realism, but in fact there would still be this incongruous volume of space within the auditorium, a no-man's-land where the director and crew stood, surrounded by outward-looking cameras, and where, in turn, the audience now sit and look out from. I haven't any experience of this, not having been at the Brussels Fair, nor at the 1900 exhibition in Paris of Cinéorama, which surrounded the audience with views taken from a balloon, projected onto a circular screen of circumference 333 feet. But the problem would seem to be: how to show the balloon itself, and the people in it. It's like a planetarium, where you can reproduce perfectly the distant view, the night sky and the horizon all around, but could hardly put the audience *in* a house, or project close objects like over-hanging trees. The audience is too completely oriented to adjust to the distortion inherent in the means of projection.

No one could deny that planetaria, the various encircling 'Ramas, and Cinerama itself, achieve their spectacular effects admirably, but it seems doubtful whether even the relatively modest Cinerama is a good medium for storytelling. Todd-AO and the other 70mm. systems can be almost as stunning in physical impact, they eliminate distortions, are easier to control and more natural to look at. This seems the nearest we will get, under present technology, to a "total cinema."

It seems a pity to abandon the question here, and one can take it that theorists, and businessmen, will continue the quest for total cinema.

The problem is to devise some way of surrounding each individual in the audience with a *total* visual world, in the same way that it's possible to surround him with a total aural one. A radio play can give a satisfactory total representation of what we would hear in reality. Our visual perceptions are more complex than our aural ones, and are more closely bound up with the other factors in our experience. We can *imagine* a total visual reality, in reading a book or hearing a play, but even in a Circlorama-type cinema we are still at the center of our *own* reality—the people next to us, the ground beneath us, the space between us and the screen . . . so it's impossible to "submit" ourselves entirely to total cinema as we can to total radio.

This would need an entirely revolutionary technique, one which could engulf each spectator in a total new world substituted for his "real" one. A form of controlled, waking dream. It is what René Barjavel, in a fascinating book written in 1945, *Le Cinéma Total*, seems to envisage. He talks of a cinema transmitted by "waves" or "impulses." He gives no technical explanation, taking it for granted that They will invent it. More recently Arthur C. Clarke (in *Profiles of the Future*, pages 191–192) seems also to take into account the possibility of some such process. I have not the faintest idea whether, or when, or how, this would be feasible, but possibly the increasing power of mind over matter, and mind over mind, could culminate in this.

STAN VANDERBEEK

Compound Entendre*

"Motion pictures . . . are simply the most complete form imaginable for an artist to work in."

For the artist who wants to "change the whole scene," there are fascinating possibilities in multiple-image projection. Stan VanDerBeek proposes to do it side by side or by superimposition—and perhaps in your living room. The experience would be like looking at a painting, listening to a recording, and reading a poem all at once.

The origins of multiple projection are lost in the shadows of recency, but Charles Eames's seven-screen presentation of America at the Moscow fair was an early artistic landmark. The loop films at the Brussels fair were continuously repeating impressions of American life. The 1964–1965 New York fair offered a dizzy variety of 360-degree surround-films (like Disney's Circarama*), more Eames screens for IBM, a three-screen artistic achievement by Francis Thompson (*To Be Alive*), Cinerama projected on a dome, and environmental cinema (a ride through 130 screens and 15 minutes of American history).*

Stan VanDerBeek is a film maker who works mainly in animation techniques. This year he holds one of the $10,000 Awards To Assist in the Production of a Creative Non-Commercial Film from the Ford Foundation Program for Film Makers. He is an Associate in Dramatic Arts at Columbia University, where for several years he has taught a laboratory course in animation. Last Christmas he prepared an 8mm. Movie Mural *for the Museum of Contemporary Crafts' "Amusements" show: four short animated silent cart-*

* Reprinted in its entirety from *8: Newsletter of 8mm. Film in Education*, edited by Joan Rosengren Forsdale, and published by the Project in Educational Communication of the Horace Mann-Lincoln Institute of School Experimentation, Teachers College, Columbia University, New York 10027.

ridge loops of collage and optical-pattern material were con-
tinuously projected onto adjacent screens. Some of his films
which have been widely seen by the public are Ala Mode,
Breathdeath, Science Friction, Mankinda, *and* Skullduggery.
The following material, edited by Joan Rosengren Forsdale,
is drawn from an interview with Mr. VanDerBeek conducted
by John Swayze.

The loop intrigues me. There's a whole avenue of poetic and
cinematic and graphic ideas that can be evolved on the loop
form that just can't be reached in any other way. I would
shoot in any gauge of film, but the 8mm. loop happens to
be here, and it's the most economical thing I can find for
certain films I want to make.

I plan a kind of multifaceted presentation—maybe two,
and possibly three, projectors overlapped on one screen so
that you get a kind of visual sandwich. And because the
projectors are not running in sync or phase—you can stop
one and start another—the result will be a completely shifting
impression. It would be almost impossible to repeat any one
set of effects. I've done some experimental films that are
specifically designed for this; one is called *Night Eating*. It's
in two or three parts: one part consists of a series of line
drawings—black on white, and white on black; another part
is a poem written in a form of calligraphy.

When these two are projected together, the poem super-
imposes over the drawings and creates different variations of
poetic reference. The third cartridge in this visual sandwich
will be simply color images—maybe I'll use it as a pure color
overlay over the whole thing. I've shot the first two parts in
35mm. with the idea of reducing to "8"; the third part I'll
shoot in 8mm. original.

I've thought, too, about the natural presentation form for
these films, because it's important to figure out where these
things fit into your life. Maybe you would have projection
machines in your living room and you'd run the film whenever you felt like looking at it. Presumably it would have
sufficient variation to hold continuous interest. It would be
similar to our tradition of looking at a painting on the wall—
although not a background thing like a painting, but rather

something you would sit down and look at: like turning on the television set or like playing a record.

Of course, the fact that it's got words invites a literary response. That's one area where I think "8" has great possibilities, because it represents an inexpensive graphic format that movies can take. "16" is not very feasible for this kind of thing and "16" is expensive. I've borrowed the word "aniglyph" to describe this kind of film; I also like the term "illuminated poem": the idea of the illuminated manuscript, but shifted into everyday dress. It's a form of writing where you're dealing with time and space and you can make very compound images and words. In this case the page is the movie screen and you can just freeze the image or slip it by. The *double entendre* is more than possible; it's really compound at times: *compound entendre*. I have been doing this kind of literary graphic writing since about '56 or '57, before the loop machines were around, but now the cartridge form just seems to be the highly suitable thing to slip it right into.

So the two major ideas I have about using "8" are the loop form and multiprojection. A new film I'm working on now is basically cyclical: it's a series of continuous zoom dissolves, so you can pick up the last zoom dissolve at the beginning and splice the two ends together in a loop. The audience will never know where the thing has begun: it has no beginning and no end.

For my multiprojection I've built a 31-foot diameter dome which I am calling a "movie drome theater." (I use it as a studio as well as a theater.) In it I want to have a lot of projectors running at the same time, their images spaced all around the dome screen from various points of view but all run from some master control. That way I'm able to just push cartridges in and out to change the whole scene. I intend to fix them so that all the projectors can be phased in and out on cue so that I can ease images in and out and double and triple expose them.

One of the films I've planned for presentation in the "movie drome" is called *Panels for the Walls of the World*. In it I'll project 35mm. and 16mm., as well as "8," and also some stills—a mixture of "found" and specially prepared material.

The way I feel about motion pictures in general, quite without reference to "8" or "16" or "35," is that they are simply the most complete form imaginable for an artist to

work in. He can handle every conceivable medium and form
in it. It includes painting, poetry, music—everything. It's a
completely circumferential art form. It's only a question of
catching up to the times to realize that it is an artist's
medium.

JONAS MEKAS

Notes on the New American Cinema*

"As long as the 'lucidly minded' critics will stay out, with all
their 'form,' 'content,' 'art,' 'structure,' 'clarity,' 'importance,'
—everything will be all right."

*Center and publicity agent for the wide circle of ex-
perimental film makers in New York City, Jonas Mekas has
devoted himself to the task of encouraging an active "new
wave" of American directors, trained or untrained, to do the
work they feel like doing. He has written movie reviews for
the Greenwich* Village Voice *and directed* Guns of the Trees,
*which "attempted to break away from the last remnants of
the traditional manner of storytelling." But he will probably
be best remembered as editor of* Film Culture, *a magazine
for and about independent American film makers, which has
been appearing, more or less quarterly, since 1955.*

*It is not easy to choose a representative sample of Mekas's
writing: he is a fire-and-brimstone preacher and, like some
of his favorite films, he tends to ramble. Yet the flavor of
his passion comes through in this selection, even in his choice
of quotations from Stan Brakhage—his candid willingness to
accept all sorts of young artists as long as their work is
"new" or "free" or "deranged"—his particular pleasure in
techniques that are untutored—his Rousseauian conviction
that art must cut through the layers of culture to primitive
feelings.*

BRAKHAGE. BREER. MENKEN. THE PURE POETS OF CINEMA

Robert Breer, Stanley Brakhage and Marie Menken, the-
matically and formally, represent in the new American
cinema the best of the tradition of experimental and poetic

* Jonas Mekas, from "Notes on the New American Cinema,"
Film Culture, No. 24, Spring 1962, pp. 12–16.

cinema. Freely, beautifully they sing the physical world, its textures, its colors, its movements; or they speak in little bursts of memories, reflections, meditations. Unlike the early avant-garde films, these films are not burdened by Greek or Freudian mythology and symbolism, their meaning is more immediate, more visual, suggestive. Stylistically and formally their work represents the highest and purest creation achieved in the poetic cinema.

It was a short film by Stanley Brakhage, *Desistfilm* (1954) —still one of the most influential of all modern American films—that started the stylistic revolution which has now reached the documentary and is beginning to be noticeable in the commercial dramatic film. (Truffaut kicks and shakes his camera in *Jules et Jim* to destroy static, "professional," smooth pans and tilts.) Very few other film-makers have been as preoccupied with style and techniques as has been Brakhage. Ironically enough, it is Brakhage who is usually picked up by the old school critics when they need an example of bad style and bad techniques. They couldn't have chosen a more fallacious example, for Brakhage is truly one of the virtuosos of modern cinema.

Some of Brakhage's attitudes towards film style and techniques can best be illustrated through his own writings:

So the money vendors have begun it again. To the catacombs then, or rather plant this seed deeper in the underground beyond false nourishing of sewage waters. Let it draw nourishment from hidden uprising springs channeled by gods. . . . Forget ideology, for film unborn as it is has no language and speaks like an aborigine—monotonous rhetoric. . . . Abandon aesthetics. . . . Negate techniques, for film, like America, has not been discovered yet, and mechanization, in the deepest possible sense of the word, traps both beyond measuring even chances. . . . Let film be. It is something . . . becoming.

. . . somewhere, we have an eye capable of any imagining. And then we have the camera eye, its lenses grounded to achieve 19th century Western compositional perspective (as best exemplified by the 19th century architectural conglomeration of details of the "classic" ruin) in bending the light and limiting the frame of the image just so, its standard camera and projector speed for recording movement geared to the feeling of the ideal slow Viennese waltz, and even its tripod head, being the neck it swings on, balled with bearings to permit it that Les Sylphides motion (ideal to the contemplative romance) and virtually restricted to horizontal and vertical movements (pillars and horizon lines) a diagonal requiring a major adjustment, its lenses coated or provided with filters, its light meters balanced, and its color film manufactured to produce that picture post card effect (salon painting) exemplified by those oh so blue skies and peachy skins.

By deliberately spitting on the lens or wrecking its focal intention, one can achieve the early stages of impressionism. One can make this prima donna heavy in performance of image movement by speeding up the motor, or one can break up movement, in a way that approaches a more direct inspiration of contemporary human eye perceptibility of movement, by slowing the motion while recording the image. One may hand hold the camera and inherit worlds of space. One may over- or under-expose the film. One may use the filters of the world, fog, downpours, unbalanced lights, neons with neurotic color temperatures, glass which was never designed for a camera, or even glass which was, but which can be used against specifications, or one may photograph an hour after sunrise or an hour before sunset, those marvelous taboo hours when the film labs will guarantee nothing, or one may go into the night with a specific daylight film or vice versa. One may become vice versa, the supreme trickster, with hatfuls of all the rabbits listed above breeding madly. One may, out of incredible courage, become Méliès, that marvelous man who gave even the "art of film" its beginning in magic.

In his latest film, *Prelude* (1961), Brakhage achieves a synthesis of all his techniques. In this film of exquisite beauty the images become like words, they come back, in little bursts, and disappear, and come back again, like in sentences, creating visual and mental impressions, experiences. Within the abstract context, the flashes of memories of a more personal and temporal nature appear, always in a hinting, oblique, indirect manner—the images of foreboding clouds, memories of the atom bomb, endless cosmic spaces, dreams and fears that constitute the subconscious of modern man. If the contemporaneity of the other film-makers discussed here is very real, emotional, raw, still a part of our daily experience—in *Prelude* (as in the work of Robert Breer and

Marie Menken) this contemporaneity is abstracted, filtered, it becomes a thought, a meditation occurring in a world of its own, in the world of a work of art.

Brakhage, from a letter to a friend (1958), before beginning his work on *Prelude*:

I am now considering a second feature length film which will dwell cinematically upon the atomic bomb. But as *Anticipation of the Night* is a work of art rather than an indictment of contemporary civilization in terms of the child, so too my prospective film will dream upon the bomb, create it out of, as I envision it, an almost Spinozian world of mathematical theory, visualize the flowering of its form in relation to the beautiful growths as well as to those more intellectually parasitic, and in the wake of its smoke deal with the devastation it leaves in the human mind rather than material devastation, the nightmare and also the 'devoutly to be wished' which it engenders, ergo religion—the end, the resolve with death.

There are only one or two other film-makers working today who can transform reality into art as successfully as Brakhage, Breer, and Menken. A landscape, a face, a blotch of light—everything changes under their eye to become something else, an essence of itself, at the service of their personal vision. To watch, in Brakhage's *Whiteye*, a winter landscape transform itself, through the magic of motion, temperament and light into pure poetry of white, is an unforgettable experience. . . .

A SIDE NOTE ON THE MORALITY OF THE NEW

One may wonder, sometimes, why I am so obsessed with the new, why this hatred for the old.

I believe that true wisdom and knowledge are very old; but this wisdom and this knowledge have been covered with layers and layers of static culture.

If we know anything about man, it is this: he must be allowed to fulfill his own life, to live his life as fully as possible. The cul-de-sac of Western culture is stifling the spiritual life of man. His "culture" is misleading his thoughts and his intuitions. My position is this: Everything that keeps man in the molds of Western culture prevents him from living his own life. Surely, one of the functions of the artist is to listen to the true voice of man.

The new artist, by directing his ear inward, is beginning to catch bits of man's true vision. By simply being *new* (which means, by listening deeper than their other contemporaries)—Brakhage and Breer contribute to the liberation of man's spirit from the dead matter of culture, they open new vistas for life. In this sense, an old art is immoral —it keeps man's spirit in bondage to Culture. The very destructiveness of the modern artist, his anarchy, as in Happenings, or even action painting, is, therefore, a positive act, a confirmation of life and freedom.

> *Evil is that which is finite.*
> *Kabbala*

A NOTE ON IMPROVISATION

I have heard too often both American and foreign critics laugh at the words "spontaneity" and "improvisation." They say this is not creation, that no art can be created "off-the-cuff." Need I state here that such criticism is pure ignorance, that it represents only a snobbish, superficial understanding of the meaning of "improvisation"? The truth is that improvisation never excludes condensation, or selection. On the contrary, improvisation is the highest form of condensation, it points to the very essence of a thought, an emotion, a movement. It was not without reason that Adam Mickiewicz called his famous Konrad Walenrod soliloquy an Improvisation. Improvisation is, I repeat, the highest form of concentration, of awareness, of intuitive knowledge, when the imagination begins to dismiss the pre-arranged, the contrived mental structures, and goes directly to the depths of the matter. This is the true meaning of improvisation, and it is not a method at all, it is, rather, a state of being necessary for any inspired creation. It is an ability that every true artist develops by a constant and life-long inner vigilance, by the cultivation— yes!—of his senses.

A NOTE ON THE "SHAKY CAMERA"

I am sick and tired of the guardians of Cinema Art who accuse the new film-maker of shaky camera work and bad technique. In like manner, they accuse the modern composer, the modern sculptor, the modern painter of sloppiness and poor technique. I have pity for such critics. They are hopeless. I would rather spend my time in heralding the new. Mayakovski once said that there is an area in the human mind which can be reached only through poetry, and only through poetry which is awake, changing. One could also say that there is an area in the human mind (or heart) which can be reached only through cinema, through that cinema which is always awake, always changing. Only such cinema can reveal, describe, make us conscious, hint at what we really are or what we aren't, or sing the true & changing beauty of the world around us. Only this kind of cinema contains the proper vocabulary and syntax to express the true and the beautiful. If we study the modern film poetry, we find that even the mistakes, the out-of-focus shots, the shaky shots, the unsure steps, the hesitant movements, the over-exposed, the under-exposed bits, have become part of the new cinema vocabulary, being part of the psychological and visual reality of modern man.

THE SECOND NOTE ON IMPROVISATION

It was in his quest for inner freedom that the new artist came to improvisation. The young American film-maker, like the young painter, musician, actor, resists his society. He knows that everything he has learned from his society about life and death is false. He cannot, therefore, arrive at any true creation, creation as revelation of truth, by re-working and re-hashing ideas, images and feelings that are dead and inflated —he has to descend much deeper, below all that clutter, he has to escape the centrifugal force of everything he has learned from his society. His spontaneity, his anarchy, even his passivity are his acts of freedom.

ON ACTING

The fragile, searching acting style of the early Marlon Brando, a James Dean, a Ben Carruthers is only a reflection

of their unconscious moral attitudes, their anxiety to be—
and these are important words—honest, sincere, truthful.
Film truth needs no words. There is more truth and real
intelligence in their "mumbling" than in all the clearly pronounced words on Broadway in five seasons. Their incoherence is as expressive as one thousand words.

The young actor of today doesn't trust any other will than
his own, which, he knows, is still too frail and, thus, harmless
—it is no will at all, only the distant deep waves and motions
and voices and groans of a Marlon Brando, a James Dean,
a Ben Carruthers, waiting, listening (the same way Kerouac
is listening for the new American word & syntax & rhythm
in his improvisations; or Coltrane in his jazz; or De Kooning
in his paintings). As long as the "lucidly minded" critics will
stay out, with all their "form," "content, "art," "structure,"
"clarity," "importance,"—everything will be all right, just
keep them out. For the new soul is still a bud, still going
through its most dangerous, most sensitive stage.

CLOSING REMARKS

Several things should be clear by now:

The new American artist can not be blamed for the fact
that his art is in a mess: he was born into that mess. He is
doing everything to get out of that mess.

His rejection of "official" (Hollywood) cinema is not
always based on artistic objections. It is not a question of
films being bad or good artistically. It is a question of the
appearance of a new attitude towards life, a new understanding of man.

It is irrelevant to ask the young American artist to make
films like those made in Russia or France or Italy; their needs
are different, their anxieties are different. Content and form
in art cannot be transplanted from country to country like
beans.

To ask the American artist to make "positive" films, to
clean out—at this time—all the anarchic elements from his
work, means to ask him to accept the existing social, political
and ethical order of today.

The films being made by the new American artist, that is,
the independents, are by no means in the majority. But we
must remember that it is always the few, the most sensitive

ones who are the spokesmen of the true feelings, the truths of any generation.

And, finally, the films we are making are not the films we want to make forever, they are not our ideal of art: these are the films we *must* make if we don't want to betray our selves and our art, if we want to move forwards. These films represent only one specific period in the development of our lives and our work.

I can think of various arguments the critics or the readers of these notes may throw against me or against the young American artist of today as he is described here. Some may say that he is on a dangerous road, that he may never get out of his confusion in one piece; that he may succeed in destroying everything, that he will have nothing new to offer in its place, etc. etc.—the usual arguments that are thrown against anything young, budding, unknown.

I, however, I look at the new man with trust. I believe in the truth (victory) of the new.

Our world is too cluttered with bombs, newspapers, TV antennae—there is no place for a subtle feeling or a subtle truth to rest its head. But the artists are working. And with every word, every image, every new musical sound, the confidence in the old is shaken, the entrance to the heart is widened.

Natural processes are uncertain, *in spite of their lawfulness. Perfectionism and uncertainty are mutually exclusive.*

Research without mistakes is impossible. All natural research is, and was, from its very beginning, explorative, "unlawful," labile, externally reshaping, in flux, uncertain and unsure, yet still in contact with real *natural processes. For these objective natural processes are in all their basic lawfulness variable to the highest degree, free in the sense of irregular, incalculable, and unrepeatable.*

WILHELM REICH
"Orgonomic Functionalism"

PAULINE KAEL

Are Movies Going to Pieces?*

"The art-house audience accepts lack of clarity as complexity; clumsiness and confusion as style."

Pauline Kael is a critic who got her training as an exhibitor. Her art theatre in Berkeley, California, was famous for bringing to the attention of West Coast intellectuals the most provocative combinations of old and new American and foreign films. As critic, her language is cutting, but her position is not extreme. Her enemies appear to be those who would appropriate films for themselves alone—whether they be intellectuals, artists, academicians, or philistines. She thinks films should be enjoyed, and she does not feel upset when she finds that a mass audience with middle-class attitudes enjoys a film that she likes.

She is puzzled by "pure feeling," "pure form," and other concepts that make criticism superfluous. She is convinced that "words, unlike tones, refer to something, that movie images are rarely abstract or geometric designs, and that when they include people and places and actions, they have implications, associations." It does not seem to her that either Hollywood or the New American Cinema is advancing the art of the film by giving up the hard work of character development in favor of technical tricks with time, a development she calls "creeping Marienbadism."

Miss Kael has offered her film reviews to the readers of Partisan Review *and* Film Quarterly *and to the listeners of the Pacifica Foundation radio stations. These have been selectively included in her book* I Lost It at the Movies; *and the introduction to that book, which appeared in* The Atlantic Monthly *in somewhat shortened form, is reprinted here.*

* Pauline Kael, "Are Movies Going to Pieces?" *The Atlantic Monthly*, December 1964, pp. 61–66.

One evening not long ago, some academic friends came to my house, and as we talked and drank, we looked at a television showing of Tod Browning's 1931 version of *Dracula*. Dwight Frye's appearance on the screen had us suddenly squealing and shrieking, and it was obvious that old vampire movies were part of our common experience. We talked about the famous ones, Murnau's *Nosferatu* and Dreyer's *Vampyr*, and we began to get fairly involved in the lore of the genre—the strategy of the bite, the special earth for the coffins, the stake through the heart versus the rays of the sun as disposal methods, the cross as vampire repellent. We had begun to surprise each other by the affectionate, nostalgic tone of our mock erudition when the youngest person present, an instructor in English, said in a clear, firm tone, "*The Beast With Five Fingers* is the greatest horror picture I've ever seen." Stunned that so bright a young man could display such shocking taste in preferring a Warner Brothers mediocrity of the forties to the classics, I gasped, "But why?" and he answered, "Because it's completely irrational. It doesn't make any sense, and that's the true terror."

I was upset by his neat little declaration—existentialism in a nutshell—by the calm matter-of-factness of it, and by the way the others seemed to take it for granted. Yet this evaluation, which had never occurred to me, helped to explain some of my recent moviegoing experiences.

Last year I went to see a famous French film, Georges Franju's *Eyes Without a Face*, which had arrived in San Francisco in a dubbed version called *The Horror Chamber of Dr. Faustus* and was playing on a double-horror bill in a huge Market Street theatre. It was Saturday night, and the theatre, which holds 2,646, was so crowded that I had trouble finding a seat.

Even dubbed, *Eyes Without a Face*, which Franju called a poetic fantasy, is austere and elegant; the exquisite photography is by the great Shuftan, the music by Maurice Jarre, the superb gowns by Givenchy. It is a symbolist attack on science and the ethics of medicine, and though I thought this attack as simpleminded in its way as the young poet's usual denunciation of war or commerce, it is in some peculiar way a classic of horror.

Pierre Brasseur, as a doctor, experiments systematically, removing the faces of beautiful young kidnapped women and trying to graft them onto the ruined head of his daughter. He keeps failing, the girls are destroyed, and yet he persists— in some terrible parody of the scientific method. In the end, the daughter, still only eyes without a face, liberates the dogs on which he also experiments, and they tear off *his* head.

The movie is both bizarrely sophisticated and absurdly naïve. Franju's style is almost as purified as Robert Bresson's, and although I disliked the mixture of austerity and mysticism with blood and gore, it produced its effect: a vague, floating, almost lyric sense of horror, an almost abstract atmosphere, impersonal and humorless. It has none of the fun of a good old horror satire like *The Bride of Frankenstein*, with Elsa Lanchester's hair curling electrically instead of just frizzing as usual, and Ernest Thesiger toying with mandrake roots and tiny ladies and gentlemen in glass jars. It is a horror film that takes itself very seriously, and even though I thought its intellectual pretensions silly, I couldn't shake off the exquisite, dread images.

But the audience seemed to be reacting to a different movie. They were so noisy that the dialogue was inaudible; they talked until the screen gave promise of bloody ghastliness. Then the chatter subsided to rise again in noisy approval of the gory scenes. When a girl in the film seemed about to be mutilated, a young man behind me jumped up and down and shouted encouragement. "Somebody's going to get it," he sang out gleefully. The audience, which was, I'd judge, pre-dominantly between the ages of fifteen and twenty-five, and at least a third feminine, was pleased and excited by the most revolting, obsessive images. They had gotten what they came for; they had not been cheated. But nobody seemed to care what the movie was about or to be interested in the logic of the plot, the reasons for the gore.

And audiences have seemed indifferent to incomprehensible sections in big expensive pictures. For example, how is it that the immense audience for *The Bridge on the River Kwai*, after all those hours of watching a story unfold, failed to express discomfort or outrage or even plain curiosity about what exactly happened at the end—which through bad direc-tion or perhaps sloppy editing went by too fast to be sorted out and understood? Is it possible that audiences no longer care if a film is so untidily put together that information crucial to the plot or characterizations is obscured or omitted altogether? *What Ever Happened to Baby Jane?* was such a mess that *Time*, after calling it "the year's scariest, funniest and most sophisticated thriller," got the plot garbled.

In recent years, largely because of the uncertainty of producers about what will draw, films in production have shifted from one script to another, or have been finally cut in such a way that key sequences are omitted. And the oddity is that it doesn't seem to matter to the audience. I couldn't tell what was going on in parts of *55 Days at Peking.* I was flabbergasted when Cleopatra, in the movie of the same name, with no hint or preparation, suddenly demonstrated clairvoyant powers, only to dispense with them as quickly as she had acquired them. The audience for *The Cardinal* can have little way of knowing whose baby the priest's sister is having, or of understanding how she can be in labor for days, screaming in a rooming house, without anybody hearing her. They may also be puzzled about how the priest's argument against her marriage, which they have been told is the only Catholic position, can, after its leads to her downfall and death, be casually dismissed as an error.

It would be easy to conclude that people go to see a show and just don't worry if it all hangs together so long as they have something to look at. But I think it is more complicated than that. Audiences used to have an almost rational passion for getting the story straight: they might prefer bad movies to good ones (the *Variety* list of "all-time top grossers" such as *The Greatest Show on Earth* and *Going My Way* indicates that they did), but although the movies might be banal or vulgar, they were rarely incoherent. A movie had to tell some kind of story that held together: a plot had to parse. Some of the appreciation for the cleverness of, say, Hitchcock's early thrillers derived from their ability to conceal the loopholes, so that afterward one could enjoy thinking over how one had been tricked and teased. Perhaps now "stories" have become too sane, too explicable, too commonplace for the large audiences who want sensations and regard the explanatory connections as mere filler.

It is possible that television viewing, with all its breaks and cuts and the spinning of the dial to find some action, is partly responsible for destruction of the narrative sense—that delight in following a story through its complications to its conclusion, which is perhaps a child's first conscious artistic pleasure. The old staples of entertainment—inoffensive genres like the adventure story or the musical or the ghost story or the detective story—are no longer commercially safe for moviemakers, and it may be that audiences don't have much more than a television span of attention left. Something similar may be happening to reading tastes and habits: I find teen-agers who oftentimes have read Salinger, some Orwell, *Lord of the Flies*, some Joyce Cary, and sometimes even Dostoevsky, but they are not interested in the classic English novels of Scott or Dickens. What is more, they don't read the Sherlock Holmes stories or even the modern detective fiction that in the thirties and forties was an accepted part of the shared experiences of adolescents. Whatever the reasons— and they must have to do with modern life and the sense of urgency it produces—audiences can no longer be depended on to respond to conventional forms. They want something different. They are too restless and apathetic to pay attention to motivations and complications, cause and effect. They want less effort, more sensations.

A decade ago, *The Haunting*, an efficient, professional, and to all appearances commercial genre film, might have made money. By the end of 1963, its grosses in the United States and Canada, according to *Variety*, were $700,000. This may be compared with $9,250,000 for *Irma La Douce*, $4,600,000 for *The Birds*, $3,900,000 for *55 Days at Peking*—all three, I think, terrible movies and in varying degrees pointless and incomprehensible. A detective genre piece, *The List of Adrian Messenger*, also incomparably better than the three films cited, and with a tricky star-selling campaign, grossed only $1,500,000. It is easy to imagine that Robert Wise, after the excesses of *West Side Story*, turned to *The Haunting* for a safe, sane respite, and that John Huston, after wrestling with *Freud*, turned to an intriguing detective story like *Adrian Messenger* for a lucrative, old-fashioned holiday. But what used to be safe seems now to be folly. How can audiences preoccupied with identity problems of their own worry about a case of whodunit and why and how? Following clues may be too much of an effort for those who, in the current teen-age phrase, "couldn't care less." They want shock treatment, not diversion, and it takes more than ghosts to frighten them.

The Haunting is set in that pleasantly familiar "old dark

house" that is itself an evil presence and is usually inhabited by ghosts or evil people. In our childhood imaginings, the unknowable things that have happened in old houses, and the whispers that someone may have died in them, make them mysterious and "dirty"; only the new house that has known no life or death is safe and clean. But so many stories have used the sinister dark house-from-which-no-one-can-escape and its murky gardens for our ritual entertainment that we learn to experience the terrors as pleasurable excitations and reassuring reminders of how frightened we used to be before we learned our way around. In film, as in story, the ambience is fear; the film specialty is gathering a group who are trapped and helpless. The action is confined to the house and grounds (the maze); the town is usually far away, just far enough away so that "nobody will hear you if you scream."

In recent years film festivals and art houses have featured a peculiar variant of the trapped-in-the-old-dark-house genre (Buñuel's *The Exterminating Angel* is the classic new example), but the characters, or rather figures, are the undead or zombies of the vampire movies. "We live as in coffins frozen side by side in a garden"—*Last Year at Marienbad*. "I'm dead"—the heroine of *Il Mare*. "They're all dead in there"—the hostess describing the party of *La Notte*. Their vital juices have been sucked away, but they don't have the revealing marks on the throat. We get the message: alienation drains the soul without leaving any marks. Or, as Bergman says of his trilogy, "Most of the people in these three films are dead, completely dead. They don't know how to love or to feel any emotions. They are lost because they can't reach anyone outside of themselves." This "art" variant is a message movie about failure of communication and lack of love and spiritual emptiness and all the rest of that. It is the closest thing we've got to a new genre, but it has some peculiarities. The old dark house was simply there, but these symbolic decadent or sterile surroundings are supposed to reflect the walking death of those within the maze. The characters in the old dark house tried to solve the riddle of their imprisonment and tried to escape; even in *No Exit* the drama was in why the characters were there; but in the new hotel-in-hell movies the characters don't even want to get out of the maze —nor, one surmises, do the directors, despite their moralizing. And audiences apparently respond to these films as modern and relevant just because of this paralysis and inaction and minimal story line.

Although *The Haunting* is moderately elegant and literate and expensive, it is basically a traditional ghost story. There is the dedicated scientist, an anthropologist, who wants to contribute to science in some socially unacceptable or scientifically reproachable area—in this case, to prove the supernatural powers of the house. And in the expository style traditional for the genre, he explains the lore and jargon of psychic research, meticulously separating ghost from poltergeist, and so on. In the great tradition of Frankenstein, the scientist must have the abnormal or mad assistant; the role that would once have belonged to Dwight Frye is here modernized and becomes the Greenwich Village lesbian, Claire Bloom. And there is the scientist's distraught wife who fears that her husband's brilliant career will be ruined. The chaste heroine, Julie Harris (like an updated Helen Chandler, Dracula's anemic victim), is the movies' post-Freudian concept of the virgin: repressed, hysterical, insane, the source of evil.

It wasn't a great movie, but I certainly wouldn't have thought that it could offend anyone. Yet some of the audience at *The Haunting* were not merely bored, they were hostile—as if the movie, by assuming interests they didn't have, made them feel resentful and inferior. I have never felt this kind of audience hostility toward crude, bad movies. People are relaxed and tolerant about ghoulish quickies, grotesque dubbed shockers from Japan, and chopped-up Italian spectacles that scramble mythologies and pile on actions, one stupidity after another. Perhaps they prefer incoherent, meaningless movies because they are not required to remember or connect. I am afraid that the young instructor in English spoke for his times, that there is no terror for modern audiences if a story is carefully worked out and follows a tradition, even though the tradition was developed and perfected precisely to frighten entertainingly.

It is not only general audiences out for an evening's entertainment who seem to have lost the narrative sense or become indifferent to narrative. Processes of structural disintegration are at work in all types of movies, and though it is obvious that many of the old forms were dead and had to be discarded, it is rather scary to see what is happening, and not only at

the big picture palaces. Art-house films are even more confusing. Why at the end of Godard's *My Life to Live* is the
heroine, rather than the pimp that the rival gang is presumably
gunning for, shot? Is she just a victim of bad marksmanship?
If we express perplexity, we are likely to be told that we
are missing the existentialist point: it is simply fate; she had
to die. But a cross-eyed fate? And why is there so little
questioning of the organization of *My Name Is Ivan*, with its
lyric interludes and patriotic sections so ill-assembled that one
might think the projectionist had scrambled the reels?

The art-house audience accepts lack of clarity as complexity; clumsiness and confusion as style. Perhaps even
without the support of critics they would accept incoherence
just as the larger audience does; they may feel that movies
as incomprehensible as *Viridiana* are more relevant to their
experience, more true to their own feelings about life, and
more satisfying than works they can understand.

I trust I won't be mistaken for the sort of boob who attacks
ambiguity or complexity. I am interested in the change from
the period when the meaning of art and form in art was in
making complex experience simple and lucid—as is still the
case in *Knife in the Water* or *Bandits of Orgosolo*—to the
current acceptance of art as technique, the technique which,
in a movie like *This Sporting Life*, makes a simple, though
psychologically confused story look complex, and modern
because inexplicable.

It has become easy, especially for those who consider time
a problem and a great theme, to believe that fast editing, out
of normal sequence, is somehow more cinematic than a con-
secutively told story. For a half century movies have, when
necessary, shifted action in time and place, and the directors
generally didn't think it necessary to slap us in the face with
each cut or to call out, "Look what I can do!" Yet people
who should know better will tell you how cinematic *The
Loneliness of the Long Distance Runner* or *This Sporting Life*
is, as if fiddling with the time sequence were good in itself,
proof that the medium is really being used. Perhaps after a few
decades of indoctrination in high art they are convinced that a
movie is cinematic when they don't understand what's going
on. *This Sporting Life*, which Derek Hill, among others, has
called the best feature ever made in England, isn't gracefully
fragmented, it's smashed. The chunks are so heavy and humor-

less and, in an odd way, disturbing that we can tell the film is meant to be bold, powerful, tragic.

In one way or another, almost all the enthusiasts for a film like this one will tell you that however you interpret the film, you will be right. There is not much to be said for this theory except that it's mighty democratic. Rather pathetically, those who accept this Rorschach-blot approach to movies are hesitant and uneasy about offering reactions. They should be reassured by the belief that whatever they say is right, but since it refers not to the film but to them (turning criticism into autobiography), they are afraid of self-exposure. I don't think they really believe the theory; it's a sort of temporary public-convenience station. More and more people come out of a movie and can't tell you what they've seen or even whether they like it.

An author like David Storey may stun them with the information that *This Sporting Life* "works purely in terms of feeling. Only frivolous judgments can be made about it in conventional terms of style." Has Storey discovered a new method of conveying feeling without style? Or has he simply found the arrogance to frustrate normal responses? No one wants to have his capacity for feeling questioned, and if a viewer tries to play it cool and discuss *This Sporting Life* in terms of corrupt professional football, he still won't score on that muddy field: there are no goalposts. Lindsay Anderson, who directed, says, "*This Sporting Life* is not a film about sport. In fact, I wouldn't call it a story picture at all. . . . We have tried to make a tragedy . . . we were making a film about something unique." A tragedy without a story is unique all right: a disaster.

In movies, as in other art forms, whether you are interested only in technique or reject technique, the result is just about the same: if you have nothing to express, it is very much like thinking that you have so much to express that you don't know how to say it. Something related to absorption in technique is involved in the enthusiasm of young people for what is called the New American Cinema, though these films are often made by those who reject craftsmanship as well as meaning, who tend to equate technique with science and with the production of the Bomb. This approach, which is a little like the attack on scientific method in *Eyes Without a Face*, is used to explain why film-makers must make movies without taking time to learn how. They are in a hurry, and anyway, technique might corrupt them.

The spokesmen for this New American Cinema attack rationality as if it were the enemy of art. They have composed a rather strange amalgam in which reason equals lack of feeling and imagination equals hostility to art equals science equals the enemy equals Nazis and police equals the Bomb. Somewhere along the line, criticism is also turned into an enemy of art. The group produces a kind of euphoric publicity, which is published instead of criticism, but soon the group may have semi-intellectually respectable critics. In *The Nation* of April 13, 1964, Susan Sontag published an extraordinary essay on Jack Smith's *Flaming Creatures*, in which she enunciated a new critical principle: "Thus Smith's crude technique serves, beautifully, the sensibility embodied in *Flaming Creatures*—a sensibility based on indiscriminateness, without ideas, beyond negation." I think that in treating indiscriminateness as a value, Miss Sontag has become a real swinger. Of course, we can reply that if anything goes, nothing happens, nothing works. But this is becoming irrelevant. In Los Angeles, among the independent film-makers at their midnight screenings, I was told that I belonged to the older generation—that Agee-alcohol generation, they called it—who could not respond to the new films because they didn't take pot or LSD and so couldn't learn just to *accept* everything. This narcotic approach of torpid acceptance, which is much like the lethargy of the undead in the failure-of-communication movies, may explain why those films have seemed so "true" to some people, and why the directors' moralistic messages sound so false. The attitude of rejecting critical standards has the dubious advantage of accepting everyone who says he is an artist as an artist and conferring on all his "noncommercial" productions the status of art. Miss Sontag is on to something, and if she stays on and rides it like Slim Pickens, it's the end of criticism.

At the art-house level, critics and audiences haven't yet discovered the beauty of indiscriminateness, but there is a lot of talk about "purely visual content"—which might be called the principle of ineffability. *Time* calls Resnais's *Muriel* "another absorbing exercise in style." Dwight Macdonald calls *Marienbad* " 'pure' cinema, a succession of images en-

joyable in themselves." And Richard Roud, who was responsible (and thus guilty) for the film selection at the New York
film festivals, goes all the way: films like *La Notte*, he says,
provide an "experience in pure form."

Once matters reach this plane, it begins to seem almost
unclean to raise issues about meaning and content and character, or to question the relevance of a sequence, the quality
of a performance. Someone is sure to sneer, "Are you looking
for a paraphrasable content? A film, like a poem, *is*." Or
smile pityingly and remind you that Patroni Griffi had originally intended to call *Il Mare* "Landscape With Figures";
doesn't that tell you how you should look at it? It does
indeed, and it's not my idea of a good time. After a few dismal
experiences we discover that when we are told to admire a
film for its pure form or its structure, it is going to exhibit
irritating, confusing, and ostentatious technique, which will,
infuriatingly, be all we can discover in it. And if we should
mention that we *enjoy* the dramatic and narrative elements
in movies, we are almost certain to be subjected to the con-
temptuous remark, "Why does cinema have to *mean* something? Do you expect a work by Bach to *mean* something?"

The only way to answer this is by some embarrassingly basic
analysis, pointing out that words, unlike tones, refer to something, that movie images are rarely abstract or geometric
designs, and that when they include people and places and
actions, they have implications, associations. Robbe-Grillet,
the scenarist of *Marienbad*, may say that the film is a pure
construction, an object without reference to anything outside
itself, and that the existence of the two characters begins
when the film begins and ends ninety-three minutes later, but,
of course, we are not born when we go in to see a movie—
though we may want to die by the time we leave. And we
can't even leave *Marienbad* behind because, although it isn't
particularly memorable, a kind of creeping Marienbadism is
the new aesthetics of "poetic" cinema. What I am saying can
only sound like pedantry to those interested in "pure" art
who tend to consider analysis as an enemy.

Movies are going to pieces; they are disintegrating, and the
something called cinema is not movies raised to an art but
rather movies diminished, movies that look "artistic." Movies
are being stripped of all the "nonessentials"—that is to say,

faces, actions, details, stories, places, everything that makes
them entertaining and joyful. It is obvious that the most
talented film artists and the ones most responsive to our time
and the attitudes of Camus and Sartre are tending to go in
this direction. The others, who are trying to observe the older
conventions, are usually (though not always) banal, trivial,
ludicrously commercial, and somehow out of touch. It is the
highest talents, the most dedicated, who are driven to the
dead end of "pure" cinema, just as our painters are driven
to obliterate the image, and a dramatist like Beckett to reduce
words to sounds.

Cinema, I suspect, is going to become so rarefied, so
private in meaning, and so lacking in audience appeal that in
a few years the Foundations will be desperately and hopelessly trying to bring it back to life, as they are now doing
with theatre.

When movies, the only art form which everyone once felt
free to enjoy and have opinions about, lose their connection
with song and dance, drama, and the novel, when they become
cinema which people fear to criticize as much as they do a new
piece of music or a new poem or painting, they will become
another object of academic study and appreciation and an
object of excitement only to practitioners of the "art."
Although *L'Avventura* is a great film, had I been present at
Cannes in 1960, where Antonioni distributed his explanatory
statement beginning "There exists in the world today a very
serious break between science on the one hand," I might
easily have joined in the hisses, which he didn't really deserve
until the following year, when *La Notte* revealed that he
had begun to believe his own explanations, thus making liars
of us all.

When we see Dwight Macdonald's cultural solution applied
to film, when we see the prospect that movies will become a
product for "Masscult" consumption, while the "few who
care" will have their "High Culture" cinema, who wants to
take the high road? There is more energy, more originality,
more excitement, more art in American kitsch like *Gunga Din*,
Easy Living, in the Rogers and Astaire pictures like *Swingtime*
and *Top Hat*, in *Strangers on a Train*, *His Girl Friday*, *The
Crimson Pirate*, *Citizen Kane*, *The Lady Eve*, *To Have and
Have Not*, *The African Queen*, *Singin' in the Rain*, *Sweet
Smell of Success*, or more recently, *The Hustler*, *Lolita*, *The*

Manchurian Candidate, Hud, Charade, than in the presumed High Culture of *Hiroshima Mon Amour, Marienbad, La Notte, The Eclipse*, and the Torre Nilsson pictures. As Nabokov remarked, "Nothing is more exhilarating than philistine vulgarity."

Regrettably, one of the surest signs of the philistine is his reverence for the superior tastes of those who put him down. Macdonald believes that "a work of High Culture, however inept, is an expression of feelings, ideas, tastes, visions that are idiosyncratic and the audience similarly responds to them as individuals." No. The "pure" cinema enthusiast who doesn't react to a film but feels he should, and so goes back to it over and over, is not responding as an individual but as a compulsive good pupil determined to appreciate what his cultural superiors say is art. Movies are on their way into academia when they are turned into a matter of duty, and in this country respect for High Culture is becoming a ritual.

If debased art is kitsch, perhaps kitsch may be redeemed by honest vulgarity, may become art. Our best work transforms kitsch, makes art out of it; that is the peculiar greatness and strength of American movies, as Godard in *Breathless* and Truffaut in *Shoot the Piano Player* recognize. Huston's *The Maltese Falcon* is a classic example. Our first and greatest film artist, D. W. Griffith, was a master of kitsch.

I am not suggesting that we want to see new and bigger remakes of the tired old standbys of the film repertory: a new *Cimarron*, another *Quo Vadis*. And meanings don't have to be spread out for us like food on a free-lunch counter. There are movies that are great experiences like *Long Day's Journey Into Night*, and just a few years ago there were movies which told good stories such as *The Treasure of Sierra Madre, From Here to Eternity*, and *The Nun's Story*.

People go to the movies for the various ways in which movies express the experience of their lives, and as a means of avoiding and postponing the pressures they feel. This latter function of art, generally referred to disparagingly as escapism, may also be considered refreshment, and it may be a major factor in keeping the world sane.

In the last few years there has appeared a new kind of filmgoer: he isn't interested in movies but in cinema. In the West several of the academic people I know who have the least understanding of movies suddenly became interested in them by reading Laurence Alloway's piece called "Critics in the Dark" in *Encounter*. By suggesting that movie criticism had never gotten into the right hands—that is, into the hands of the academics—by indicating projects, and by publishing in the prestigious *Encounter*, Alloway focused on large vistas of respectability for future film critics. Perhaps, also, the academics were drawn to his condescending approach to movies as a pop art. Many of them have wondered why Agee cared so much about movies. Alloway, by taking the position that Agee's caring was a maladjustment, re-established their safe, serene world in which if a man gets excited about an idea or an issue, there must be something the matter with him. It's not much consolation, but I think the cinema the academics will be working over will be the cinema they deserve.

PENELOPE HOUSTON

Towards a New Cinema*

"The cinema moves a few steps closer to the minority arts."

*The young film artist makes his first film; he breaks tech-
nical rules; he shoots entirely on location; he experiments with
improvisation; he puts aside the audience expectation of logical
development of character; he leaves the meaning and purpose
of his film up in the air. Are experiment and ambiguity the
extent of the "new wave"? Penelope Houston, editor of* Sight
and Sound, *adds an important basic change: "A reaction has
set in against the cinema of straightforward social purpose . . .
We have a cinema of personal relationships, private worlds."
In a medium essentially objective, the film maker strives, like
the novelist, for "subjective landscapes"; he is more interested
"in the way things look and feel and sound than in what they
signify in general terms."*

In this last chapter of her book The Contemporary Cinema,
*Miss Houston approves the "necessary bravado" of new styles
in the cinema. But she is just nostalgic enough for the wonderful things that happened in the earlier days of studio production to wonder if a gap may be growing between the
majority audience and a kind of "snobbery of the specialized
cinemas." She has no wish for the cinema to go "out of
business as a mass entertainment."*

New cinema, new wave, new American cinema, Italian renaissance: the phrases crop up, forming a convenient kind of
critical shorthand, which like most shorthand can be effectively read back only by the writer. Of course nothing is
really new, so that antecedents can always be traced, ancestors

* Penelope Houston, "Towards a New Cinema," from *The Contemporary Cinema.* Harmondsworth, Middlesex, Penguin Books,
1963. Pp. 182–195.

run to earth; and of course new waves all too soon begin to look like tired conventions. One thing, however, seems certain. In the doldrums of the middle fifties, it would have been difficult to write a survey of this kind without casting sneaking glances over one's shoulder towards the supposed golden ages of film-making. Neorealism was dying with the whimper of an *Il Tetto,* British cinema somnolent, the French industry given over to a professionalism that masked an absence of original thought, Hollywood still narcissistically enchanted by the size of its own screens. Lethargy seemed to be creeping up, as though the cinema felt television closing up on it and had half-hearted ideas of conceding the race. Now, looking back, the period around 1956 seems a watershed: between the neorealists and the *nouvelle vague,* or (and this is not simply another way of saying the same thing) between a middle-aged cinema and a young one.

It was certainly time some of the rules were broken, technically as well as aesthetically. Raoul Coutard, the brilliant French cameraman, shoots straight into the light in *Lola*; the ubiquitous hand-held camera gets close in among the crowds; *Hiroshima mon Amour* obliterates the flashback; Antonioni takes over a golf club to shoot part of *La Notte*; Woodfall rents a house for *A Taste of Honey*; everyone, everywhere, discovers the advantage of making films outside studios, so avoiding that systematization which manages to impose the same kind of technical stamp on each and every subject. What the cinema of the middle fifties needed, to shake it up, was some artists prepared to have a go, to smash up a few conventions just to see what the pieces looked like. The fact that it found them, in France, spurred on other people. Everyone wanted a *nouvelle vague,* even if the French decided, as soon as they had it, that they were not entirely sure what they had got hold of. As a result, and to an extent unthinkable only a few years ago, we are living in the age of the first film. Godard, Truffaut, Varda, Demy, Pasolini, Olmi, Patroni Griffi, Polanski, Reisz, Schlesinger, Cassavetes: none of these have had to serve an apprenticeship in B-features, to await the moment of critical recognition. Festival entries tend to be divided between the films of the cinema's great and now ageing artists (Renoir, Buñuel, Ozu), of its post-war generation (Antonioni, Wajda, Torre Nilsson, Bergman) and of its established and unestablished newcomers. Missing on the whole, is the generation from the first decade of sound.

As always, the reaction is against the recent past. But although there is something just tangible enough to be called a new way of looking at the cinema, there certainly is no such thing as a collective spirit. Any generalization based on one group of films can be smartly cancelled out on the evidence of another. If there is no common ground between, say, Godard and Antonioni, there is not much more between Godard and Resnais, his fellow-countryman. But *some* movies, it can be said, are more spontaneous than they used to be, more inclined to snatch at the fleeting moment; they relish ambiguity, the kind of Pirandellian situations in which characters are always going in search of their own identities, are not even entirely sure where life ends and film begins; they are based on a knowledge of the cinema's past which enables them to use quotation and allusion, to work within a frame of reference necessary to the creators if sometimes perplexing to the audience; they look as though the people making them enjoyed what they were doing; and they admit their own imperfections.

Should one [to quote Truffaut] continue to pretend to be telling a story which is controlled and authoritative, weighted with the same meaning and interest for the film-maker and for the spectator? Or ought one rather to admit that one is throwing on the market a kind of rough draft of one's ideal film, hoping that it will help one advance in the practice of this terribly difficult art?

Any number of young artists are engaged in this exploration; and are assuming, as directors have not been able to do on this scale since the twenties, that they have a right of discovery, that the whole industrial framework of studios and big companies ought not to stand in their way. In America, inevitably, the problem comes most clearly into focus. From a round-table discussion published in the California magazine *Film Quarterly,* one extracts two quotations. According to the producer John Houseman:

Think how very few American films, even among the good ones, have a signature. This has something to do with the organization of the studios and the releasing companies, but it also has a lot to do with the audience. There is a very strong resistance to individual statements in American pictures, while among the worst European film-makers there is nearly always some kind of personal statement.

From Irvin Kershner, one of the younger American directors:

How do you make a film which is entertaining, which has ideas, which is let's say adult, which doesn't depend on violence for its shock, doesn't depend on sex for its excitement—how do you create this kind of drama for $200,000 when there's no time to play, to waste, to take a chance, to do all the things that an artist has to do to make a film?

The director is talking practically, in terms of the low-budget film made within the industrial system, and the producer theoretically. But both are preoccupied with this question of a "signature," of the stamp of personality as something which ought to be burnt into a film. A few years ago, in a Hollywood more easily confident of its own considerable assets, the distinction between one kind of movie and another might have been taken for granted, or at least accepted as a fact of cinema life. Now it has to be argued out, with the implication, which by no means all Europeans would subscribe to, that Europe has got the upper hand.

An answer, of a sort, is to work outside the studios; and within the last few years there has been a good deal of talk about a new American cinema, New York based, independent, radically minded. Some critics have resolutely battled to extract evidence of a "movement" from films made in half a dozen styles: from Lionel Rogosin's dramatized documentary of Skid Row, *On the Bowery*, to John Cassavetes's improvised actors' exercise, *Shadows*; from Shirley Clarke's *The Connection*, which wraps its study of junkies waiting for a fix within the elaborate protective cocoon of a film within a film, to Richard Leacock's television documentaries, where a remorseless camera moves close in on a football match or an election meeting; from the short-film work of numerous avant-garde experimentalists to the low-budget features with a toehold in the commercial market.

Jonas Mekas, a New York critic and one of the most energetic propagandists for this whole elusive idea of a new American cinema, sees it as

an ethical movement, a human act . . . It was in his quest for inner freedom that the new artist came to improvisation. The young American film-maker, like the young painter, musician, actor, resists his society. . . . He cannot arrive at any true creation by reworking and rehashing ideas, images and feelings that are dead and inflated—he has to descend much deeper, below all that clutter. His spontaneity, his anarchy, even his passivity, are his acts of freedom. [Further, argues Mekas] . . . If we study the modern film poetry, we find that even the mistakes, the out-of-focus shots, the shaky shots, the unsure steps, the hesitant movements, the over-exposed, the under-exposed bits, have become part of the new cinema vocabulary, *being part of the psychological and visual reality of modern man* [my italics].

Part of the vocabulary these things certainly are, though in employing resounding theory in defence of practical inadequacy, Jonas Mekas hardly makes the out-of-focus shots seem any less blurred. A shaky camera is much more likely to be evidence of financial stringency or practical inexperience than of sincerity. But it becomes very easy to get into a state of mind in which roughness is equated with honesty, in which the more raw and unfinished and obviously unprofessional a film looks, the more fervently it will be held to be asserting its independence. (Then, unfairly, Hollywood strikes back by trying to give some of its movies the fashionable grainy look of hard actuality.)

Resistance to Hollywood's pluperfact technique, precisely because it is Hollywood, and professional, and expensive, goes with the kind of unfocused protest against society and its works which turns a film such as Mekas's own *Guns of the Trees* into a tirade of outrage. Here the Americans part company with the markedly unpolitical French. But they come together again in their feelings about improvisation, the value of the film which evolves its own sense of direction as it goes along. In itself, improvisation can hold a different meaning for almost any film-maker who experiments with it. Jean Rouch, in a film such as *Chronique d'un Été*, uses the camera as a kind of psychiatric tool, allowing it to form a third in conversations in the belief that in its admonitory presence people are closer to revealing the truth about themselves. But he also shoots hours of footage, and it is in the editing of this that the film emerges. Truffaut and Godard improvise when it suits them. John Cassavetes, in *Shadows*, made a film which announced itself proudly as a work of total improvisation, in which the validity of any given moment depended on the degree of response the actor managed to bring to it. Improvisation may achieve that spontaneity many film-makers long for. But few directors, after all, arrive at their results through a single take, and what was spontaneous at the beginning of the day's shooting may by the end of it have become something quite different.

Advocates of improvisation, though, are much more concerned with the idea of release: the freeing of the actor to make contributions going beyond the range of his part, as the script records it, the freeing of the camera from any rigidly preconceived plan: the freedom, in fact, to invent at the moment of shooting, to send the film off at a tangent if it seems a good idea. Many of these semi-improvised films inevitably look embarrassingly naïve: a bad actor speaking good lines is probably a happier sight than a bad actor struggling to communicate some ill-defined, ineffable inner something or other. Even when the improvised film works, as *Shadows* mostly did, it seems to do so as a once-for-all experiment, a stage in a director's career which he could not revisit if he tried, and where others follow him at their own risk. The film-maker probably has to go through technique to emerge safely on the other side, needs to know exactly what effect he's after before he sets other people loose to achieve it for him. Directors of greater *naïveté* are liable to waste as much footage on pursuing their players aimlessly around, waiting for the elusive and significant truth to hit them like a thunderbolt, as Hollywood does on tracking its stars through romantic locations. And, of course, the conventions pile up: the dead-into-camera monologues, the shots of rubbish heaps, stretches of wasteland, all the well-worn symbols of city squalor which creep like so much ivy over experimental films.

Essentially, these improvised and semi-improvised works see their function not as a controlling and shaping of experience, the discovery of a pattern or logic in a series of events, but as a baring of immediate emotion, and the shattering of expected patterns through the intervention of the haphazard and the unplanned. Art itself is a word such film-makers might not care to accept too readily, because of its connotations of tradition and discipline. A moment of direct emotional truth can bite deep beneath the surface. *Shadows* pulls off such a moment, for instance, in the needling dialogue between the white boy who has come to take the coloured girl out for the evening, the girl resentful of his colour and her own, and her two brothers. And although such piercing insights may be few and far between, and the film-maker may not always be able to regulate their coming, or to sort out the absolutely genuine from the just-off-the-mark, they are the justification of his method. Film-making, like bird-watching, creeps up on the truth.

Improvisation is a technique and a tool, and one which many contemporary film-makers reject. It is an interesting exercise to compare the published texts of such films as *L'Année dernière à Marienbad* or *L'Avventura* with the pictures themselves, to see the extent to which two films very precise in their structure had a prior existence on paper, and also to note the points at which the director has moved away from the original text. Film-making is not an exact science: areas for improvisation always remain open. The creative process is continuous, from the thinking that goes on before the film actually goes into production, to the changes in the original conception effected at the shooting stage, to the final shaping of the picture during the editing.

"I go away by myself for half an hour or so before we begin shooting," says Antonioni, and "you might say I was inventing a little bit of film."

"I arrive in the morning knowing what I intend to do during the day, but not how I intend to do it," says Bresson.

"I have an idea at the back of my mind, and I develop it with my actors; although we work from a written text, the dialogue may be put down on paper only a few minutes before we start filming," says Godard.

Use of actual locations, for interior as well as exterior scenes, has also cut down on some of the elaborate preplanning customary where sets have to be constructed to order in the studio.

Another pointer for the new cinema, and one which links directors who otherwise have little in common, is the kind of relationship the film-maker assumes with his audience. Increasingly, he tells them as much as he cares to, and they take it from there. When one talks of the film as moving closer to the novel, this is to some extent what one means: that it addresses itself to each of us as an individual, that it deals in ambiguities of motivation and relationship which it is for us to elucidate, that it assumes our familiarity with the grammar of the screen. What does it mean? It means what you think it means. "Am I to sympathize with this character or not?"—"I've shown him to you as I see him, now it's for you to make up your mind." This is the sort of dialogue set up between spectator and director. Why does Anna disappear in *L'Avventura*, and what has happened to her? Have the man and the woman in *L'Année dernière* met last year, or this year, or never? Why does Patricia betray Michel in *À Bout de Souffle*, and what are we to make of her last enigmatic close-up? Why does Jeanne Moreau drive her car off the broken bridge in *Jules et Jim*? Are the various women we encounter in *Lola* meant to express aspects of Lola herself —Lola as she was, as she will be, as she might have been? Audiences may ask the questions, and critics speculate, at enormous length, about the answers. The directors concerned know that they have made the questions irrelevant, or have answered them to their own satisfaction.

It would not do to make too much of this: the cinema is in no danger of becoming as esoteric as all that. But it is, on a previously unprecedented scale, testing out some of its own powers, its ability to move freely in time as well as space, its ability to withhold as well as to deliver information, to surprise, and confuse. In Roger Leenhardt's *Rendezvous de Minuit* there is a café episode in which the conversation turns on the possibility that one of the new film-makers, from the shelter of a newspaper kiosk, is at that moment turning a hidden camera on the scene. A joke; a critic's conceit (Leenhardt is critic as well as film-maker); an affectation; and also a comment by the cinema on the cinema, on its determination that we should take it on its own terms, remember that we are sitting in a theatre watching a film, and adjust our conception of reality to admit that in the present-tense grammar of the movies there is only the reality of what is *now* on the screen.

Whether all this should be regarded as merely fashionable, or as symptomatic of the way art reacts to a disordered and confused society, a world in which areas of certainty contract, and judgements become relative, it certainly relates to another trend in contemporary film-making. A reaction has set in against the cinema of straightforward social purpose, and a *Grapes of Wrath* or a *Bicycle Thieves*, a *Stars Look Down* or a *Terra Trema*, is not very likely to be made today by any of the major film-makers in the West. Underlying many of the really significant films of the last few years is an unspoken sense that the public context, the social scene in all its complexity, is something too big to grasp and too unwieldly to be susceptible to change. We have a cinema of personal relationships, private worlds, with anti-heroes engaged in splicing together the broken and rough ends of personality, or in pursuing illusions half-recognized as such; an amoral cinema, or one endeavouring to construct its morality through a series of *ad hoc* judgements. *Hiroshima mon Amour* is not about peace or the Bomb, as much as it is about a woman trying to live with her past; *Shadows* is not about the colour question, as much as it is about a coloured family whose attitudes to each other are at least as relevant as their feelings about the way the world treats them; *À Bout de Souffle* is not about crime, but about Jean-Paul Belmondo and Jean Seberg; *La Notte* is not a tract on modern marriage. Within their context, these films are not uncommitted or disengaged works, but their commitments remain essentially to individuals. Any generalizations we care to make really become our own affair; and the films accept no responsibility (as did *The Grapes of Wrath* or *Bicycle Thieves*) to offer them on our behalf.

In an essay on the novel, Mary McCarthy has complained that what modern fiction lacks is the factual context: the calm, detailed, *interested* description of how factories are run, how a town is put together as a social organism, the accumulation of facts about freemasonry or whaling or the Chancery Courts, which characterized the nineteenth-century novel. Elsewhere she has written:

The writer must be first of all a listener and observer, who can pay attention to reality, like an obedient pupil, and who is willing, always, to be surprised by the messages reality is sending through to him. And if he gets the messages correctly he will not have to go back and put in the symbols; he will find that the symbols are there, staring at him significantly from the commonplace.

Such comments could be applied with almost equal relevance (which is hardly surprising) to the contemporary cinema. The artist's passion for putting in the symbols, like so many currants in a cake, and the critic's for pulling them out again, rapidly enough become a bore. And the film, as well as the novel, seems to be moving away from the period when information, the assembly of facts, engaged its major artists. If the cinema robbed the novel of much of its journalism and factual reporting, television has done the same thing to the cinema.

A cinema preoccupied with personal relationships and subjective landscapes may find itself losing contact with this hard, limiting, disciplinary, and necessary world of fact. But the cinema is also a more objective medium than the novel, in the most simple sense of the novelist being able to move so exclusively into areas of subjectivity that he no longer feels any need to tell us what his people and places look like, while the film must always, and by its nature, surround its characters with the clutter of their material existence. Even if we see events through the eyes of a central character, we also remain outside him, evaluating his actions as we watch them on the screen. Even a *L'Année dernière*, with its open invitation to a subjective response, is filmed objectively. The novelist may describe a scene, and forget it: the movie can hardly get away from its own scenery.

Insomuch as there is a new cinema worth talking about, it is because a number of directors are very consciously thinking in terms of how screen language can be made to work for them. They are more interested in the way things look and feel and sound than in what they signify in general terms; more interested in mood than in narrative; more concerned with how people behave and give themselves away in action than with how they might choose to see themselves. They are asking from their actors not the great neon-blazing star turns but performances which break through the hard professional surface: at the worst, an emotional strip-tease; at the best, a revelation. In players such as Jeanne Moreau and Monica Vitti, Jean-Paul Belmondo and Marcello Mastroianni, they have acquired willing accomplices. Above all, they give us the sense of the film itself as a risky and unique creative adventure.

Any amount of nonsense has been produced during the

last few years by directors whose main creative activity
consists in taking over other people's mannerisms. Entertainment-film clichés may afford restful and tranquillizing evidence that the conventions are still in working order.
New-wave clichés are deadly because they come from directors trying to pass them off as new currency. But all this
was to be expected. The cinema moves a few steps closer to
the minority arts: its passion for allusion and quotation, for
instance, is not really very far distant from the point reached
by poetry almost forty years ago; and its emphasis on the
immediate can not too implausibly be related to action
painting. And as it moves, so it acquires the affectations along
with the advantages. Antonioni occupies the painter's traditional position: far enough back from his subject to give us
our sense of dramatic distance. Some of the young French
directors keep our noses pressed up against it: we can distinguish a brilliant blob of colour here, some dashing brushwork there, but if we stand a few yards back all we can see
is a blurred image, with a signature scrawled boldly across
the corner.

Yet the exhibitionism and self-display and dandyish conceits have been symptoms of a necessary bravado. Whatever
comes out of all this restless activity of the late fifties and
early sixties, in the way of durable reputations and positive
advances, we are still in the middle of a whole series of
uncommonly difficult transitions, as the minority film-makers
move in to fill part of the gap left by the decline of the big
production empires. If iconoclasm and a certain optimistic
anarchy were necessary three or four years ago, a period of
consolidation and sorting out now looks equally important.
Can the new film-makers take enough of the audience with
them? Are we likely to have, by 1970 or so, a cinema split
between the mass-entertainment movies, made at huge cost
for huge audiences, and the small-scale films which have left
the majority audience lagging behind? It has happened in the
novel, in painting, in music, and it is not inconceivable that
it could happen in the cinema. Certainly one could no more
expect a mass public to go every step of the way with Antonioni or Resnais or Godard, or even Truffaut despite his
sensitivity to audience response, than one could have asked
them to go along with Proust or Henry James or Virginia
Woolf.

If the cinema had held itself down, at any given moment, to the kind of subtleties and complexities it assumed people would be able unquestioningly to follow, we would still be back with *The Great Train Robbery* and *Rescued by Rover*. But a creative cinema which leaves too much of its audience too far behind would be running a clear risk of widening the gap, already quite wide enough, between one kind of audience and another. A snobbery of the specialized cinemas can be much more debilitating and depressing than the free-for-all in which each film takes its chance with the rest. The artist who wants to put his own vision into his work is never likely to find the going entirely smooth: imagine even a Picasso who had to beg £100,000 or so before he could put paint to canvas. And the cinema enthusiasts will always be on the side of such an artist: they will look also to the takers of chances who help to keep this immensely difficult medium alive. But the showmen who found the sun shining in Los Angeles and settled down there half a century ago to make the movies were not thinking like this. They wanted the biggest audience in the world, and they got it; and along with the audience they built an art form not quite like any other.

The impulse which leads me to a Humphrey Bogart movie has little in common with the impulse which leads me to the novels of Henry James or the poetry of T. S. Eliot [wrote the American critic Robert Warshow]. That there is a connexion between the two impulses I do not doubt, but the connexion is not adequately summed up in the statement that the Bogart movie and the Eliot poem are both forms of art.

The new film-makers may be taking us that much closer to the James novel or the Eliot poem; but no one concerned about the future of the cinema, much less its past, would jettison the Bogart movie in the process. If the cinema ever goes out of business as a mass entertainment, then the fact that certain areas of experiment still remain open would be small consolation for anyone. We need the lot: films and movies, James and Bogart, minority art and mass medium. In spite of all the hazards of the last decade, which have produced so many dismal forecasts, so many pronouncements of commercial decline, it seems tolerably certain that the cinema will continue to give them to us. During the worst of its troubles, Hollywood adopted the defiant and appealing slogan "Movies are better than ever." Oddly enough, in the long run and on a world view, the publicists may have got it about right.

FRANÇOIS TRUFFAUT

We Must Continue Making Progress*

"I find myself longing to see a film with a well-told story."

When he was a reviewer for Arts *magazine, François Truffaut declared that it was no longer necessary for a film to have a story—"it is enough that they tell of a first love, that they take place on a beach, etc." In 1962, talking to an interviewer from* Cahiers du Cinéma, *the director of* The 400 Blows *and* Jules and Jim *points out that the films he called for have now become commonplace—that perhaps there is need again for a new look, if not a new wave.*

The restless paradoxes and the openness of thought reflected in this interview are also the qualities of Truffaut's films. But he seems far more aware of the public and of the audience than one would have guessed. "I honestly believe," he says, "that pleasing people is important." He goes so far as to propose that elements might be added to a script or a scene to please those who may be disturbed by the picture as a whole—"It is possible to keep from completely ruining anyone's evening." But more than anything, Truffaut feels that the director must now aim higher. The "new wave" has brought with it a greater sense of taste and beauty. The next step is to "try to make each of our films clear, interesting, intelligent, moving, and beautiful all at once"!

Now that you experience film-making from the "inside," don't you find your understanding of it different?

Certainly my judgment has changed. If I had to return now to criticism, I would definitely write differently, but for another reason. The kind of film-making that I believed in

* François Truffaut, "François Truffaut—an Interview," *Cahiers du Cinéma* No. 138, December 1962. Translated and condensed by Paul Ronder. Reprinted in *Film Quarterly*, Fall 1963, pp. 6–8, 10–13.

and advocated has arrived. And now I see its disadvantages—
there were bound to be some. This is why it is so annoying
to hear people still quoting some of my early writings. For
example, once just after seeing *And God Created Woman* at
a film festival, I wrote enthusiastically in *Arts*: "Films today
no longer need to tell a story—it is enough that they tell of
a first love, that they take place on a beach, etc." But today
films like these have become such commonplaces that I
wince to hear my words quoted now. In fact, in the films
made since then the scenarios have been so mistreated that
now I find myself longing to see a film with a well-told story.
At the same time, let's not assume we must return at all
costs to the kind of cinema that existed before the Nouvelle
Vague.

I made *Jules and Jim* somewhat in reaction against mistreated scenarios. For example, I was told that I would have
to modernize the period of the original book; and in sub-
stituting the Second World War for the First, the transposition
would have been simple. But since the film was to be about
a woman and love, I refused. I was anxious not to have my
film be like all the rest made today on these particular topics:
with a sports car (there would have had to be one in the
film, on the bridge), lots of scotch, and of course a high-
fidelity set, as compulsory equipment. Had I done this, I
would have been in complete conformity with the rules of
the "nouveau cinéma." However I chose to remain faithful
to the period of the book, and try and pattern *Jules and Jim*
after some of the small films made by M-G-M during the
forties, like *Mrs. Parkington* and *The Green Years*—films
whose only fault was being conventional, but films which succeeded marvelously in creating the mood of a huge 800-page
novel, of many years passing, of much white hair arriving.
You see, I didn't want to follow the fashion, even a fashion
that has produced so many films I love. . . .

Then if you had to return to being a critic?

I would be like everyone else: I would have lots of trouble.
And I would lack serenity. The critics I find I like best
today are those who are a bit outside the pale of film-
making. . . . One senses that they don't know any of the
directors and that they are simply pleased that there are more
interesting films than ever before. Therefore they try, with a
maximum of benevolence and a minimum of complaisance,

to convey the feelings a particular film gave them, objectively, as though they were writing about a film classic. That's the attitude one must have today. Perhaps I seem to contradict myself, since we used to be very heated critics. But at that time it was necessary; since we had to tear down certain ideas and build up certain others, we had to make lots of noise. Today, however, I think it necessary for a critic to be very calm.

Then it would be much harder to be a critic today?

Much. . . . It seems to be almost a general law among critics that they form into factions to defend unequivocally their own positions. Sometimes the animosity between factions results in articles which are unbelievably vicious, and which even the authors themselves seem to regret later on. But instead of indulging one's passions in one's criticism, one must at least try to be critical with some purpose. Today especially, taking sides is worthless. What is worthwhile, yet difficult, is analysis. . . . What is interesting is not pronouncing a film good or bad, but explaining why. . . .

Today I understand much better what makes a film interesting. Yet in making my own films, I readily admit the necessity of considering the public, for I believe that a film which is a popular failure cannot have been an artistic success. At the same time, I could never consider *Lola Montès* a bad film, or that Bresson was wrong because he had a popular failure. But then these are my personal theories, and I don't claim that they are valid for all people or for all films.

Then you would not make a film without thinking of the public?

No, I couldn't be enthusiastic enough about making films for myself. I wouldn't have the desire to make films if I knew that they weren't going to be seen. I need that knowledge: it gives me impetus. I must create a kind of "show for others." I know I wouldn't be able to write a novel: that kind of creativity would be too abstract for me. I would much rather be a singing coach, or better still, the director of a whole vaudeville show. It's necessary to me that my work, collective even in its origins, be seen by the public, and judged by it. . . .

Nor would I be able to make a film which I felt would automatically be a success. Each of my films has been a kind

of gamble. For me, shooting a film should be taking a chance
—and winning. . . .

I honestly believe that pleasing people is important, but
I also believe that every film must contain some degree of
"planned violence" upon its audience. In a good film, people
must be made to see something that they don't want to see:
they must be made to approve of someone of whom they had
disapproved, they must be forced to look where they had
refused to look. One could build a whole film around the
idea of making people understand what marriage, love, and
adultery would be in relation to some criminal act. . . .

Resnais would never say: I think of the public when making
a film. As a matter of fact, I don't think he does. But he *does*
think of his films as "spectacles." I am absolutely sure that
Marienbad is made with consideration given to such matters
as people's emotions, the sweep of the scenario, and the
equilibrium of the finished film. Otherwise, why not have
the film last eight hours? Resnais isn't Stroheim; his films
last an hour and a half, and they are constructed in a systematic and methodical fashion. Now, from the Resnais films
certain young film-makers draw a lesson of courage instead
of drawing a lesson of skill. Right after *Hiroshima*, they began
to say of Resnais: he's marvelous, he proves that everything
is possible. But that's not true. He proves that everything is
possible for Resnais. In the basic idea of *Hiroshima*, one finds
all the things that shouldn't be done: intermixing adultery and
the atomic bomb, that is, a very small problem with a very
large one, a very personal one with a very political one; and
attempting to equate the huge disgrace of the bomb with the
small scandals of the liberation. To attempt such a combination is really playing with explosives; to have made it
work is a phenomenal success. Nevertheless that doesn't mean
that everyone should try to do what Resnais, alone, knew how
to do.

Many films made today have been "inspired" by *Hiroshima*: films which no longer consider the plot or the public.
But Resnais considered them. He knew very well that by
having Riva do this or that in *Hiroshima*, he would create
this or that emotion in the spectator. Only a naïve film-maker
could have been encouraged, instead of being discouraged,
by *Hiroshima*. I don't say that *Hiroshima* necessarily must

be discouraging, but one must remember the great skill it demanded, and not simply think: "That fad's begun. All I have to do is follow." I think Resnais would render a great service to film-makers if he would stress the *difficulties* he has had, instead of letting them think they can do whatever comes into their heads. . . .

The success of certain unusual films can be attributed to their being so completely unusual, their being esteemed as such, and their being seen specially for their strangeness. Resnais, since he is considered a specialist in the offbeat, even as having something of a patent on it (for me this doesn't diminish his genius in the least, but rather increases it), has the right to be offbeat. But if he suddenly were to decide to make a normal film, that would have serious consequences for him. . . .

It has come to this: everybody wanted a change. Now the change has come, and they are irritated if the results are too special.

Even toward Antonioni (whom I don't like) there's a great ill-naturedness. People are delirious over his first two films, then turn on him with might and main. That was the case with Bergman, and also Losey. It begins in Paris, then spreads. It's specially sad for Bergman, since his last film is much better than his earlier ones.

The case of Godard is particularly interesting to me since he is an unconventional film-maker who could, if he wished, easily integrate himself. Yet his is a special case, since what interests him most is creating a complex mélange of styles: at the moment one of his films approaches the fictional, he quickly makes an about-face toward the documentary, once arrived there only to rush off again in still another direction. Nevertheless there is great logic in his career. Just look at his criticism in *Cahiers*: from the start one senses a disdain for complete fiction, coupled with an admiration for those films in which the plot is destroyed in the making. However his own personality is so strong that he never need question what he does: he does it, and it becomes right.

Do you think the conventional and unconventional film-makers could get together?

What is common to both is the desire to do good work. No one is happy doing a lousy job; actors, for example, are unhappy when they make bad films. It's something to remember, and something of a weapon for our side.

On the other hand, we mustn't be 100 percent daring. This remark could easily be misunderstood: what I mean is that we must think out our extravagances and measure out our audacity. We must have our trump card from the start, and try not to show all our tricks at once. . . .

As a director, what do you think of American cinema today?

In relation to the American film-makers, I think we French are all intellectuals, even me, and I am the least intellectual of my compatriots. But we mustn't cheat, we mustn't pretend to be rough or simple if basically we're reflective or analytical. We mustn't try to be what we're not. This is unquestionably where a film-maker like Melville makes his mistake: in trying to imitate American brutality and rusticity. But if we believe that the cinema is a popular art—and we all believe it, having grown up nourished by American films—we can arrive at another alternative: that of a discipline in our work sufficient to permit our films to be complete on several levels at once. And what better example of this than the films of Hitchcock?

He is one of those rare film-makers who is able to please everyone. I am convinced that his procedure is applicable to our films, or to be precise, to those which are made "coldly." Resnais works a great deal on his films, yet I don't believe that he created in *Marienbad* emotions or successful effects that can't also be found in *Vertigo*. Nor do I believe that *Vertigo* is made interesting to the general public through concession or compromise, but rather through supplementary discipline.

Are you suggesting that instead of working for a year and making Marienbad, *Resnais should have worked for a year and a half and ended up making a* Vertigo?

No, I maintain that Resnais was absolutely justified in making *Marienbad*. But if one isn't Resnais, if one doesn't have his extraordinary degree of control, I think it's better to be more modest. I'm not suggesting limiting one's ambitions, but simply being more modest in the way they are realized—that is, making films which are simple in appearance. Personally, I don't believe for a moment that the world needs either me or my films. I believe I must make the world accept me, and that only by hard work will I succeed.

I believe that today we must reverse our way of thinking about film-making. Formerly our object was to cut away everything considered extraneous to the underlying subject of a film in order to obtain a slender basic framework. But this slenderness is terribly annoying for all those who fail to understand the film's central idea (and there will always be those people). Therefore films should really contain two subjects: the genuine, plus another which everyone can understand. But today in France, this kind of cleverness is lacking. . . .

I like spectacle, music halls, variety shows, but I also have preoccupations which aren't interesting to the majority. The problem in *Jules and Jim*, for example, interests very few people. On top of that, out of every ten people who see the film, nine consider divorce scandalous. For me to ask these people to sympathize with two grotesques who do nothing all day, and live together with the same woman, is almost pure insolence. Therefore I must offer them something in exchange, like a moment of high emotion, a moment when the actors let loose—as they did in the crying scene (which was improvised) between Werner and Jeanne Moreau. I don't want people saying to themselves on the way out: "It was scandalous"; I'd be the first to suffer. Of course, it's impossible to satisfy everyone, but it *is* possible to keep from completely ruining anyone's evening. If people say on the way out: "Well, at least there was that song," or: "At least there were those lovely landscapes," or: "At least there were all those shots from the war,"—well, even that's better than nothing.

A director should know exactly what he wants to obtain in a film, and above all, he should not try to obtain more than *one thing at a time*. He must know how to create emotions: before each film, each scene, and each shot, he must stop and ask himself how he can create the particular emotion he desires. Everything in the film, the scene, or the shot which does not help to answer that question is parasitic and must be cut. We work in a domain which simultaneously is literary, musical, and spatial, and one in which we must always simplify to the uttermost. A film is like a boat: it's just asking to be sunk. And I swear that with both, it's a hundred times simpler to have a catastrophe than a success. If a film-maker doesn't understand this law, he's cooked. If he believes in luck and likes to take things as they come, he's irresponsible. The only film-maker I could admire would be one personally courageous enough to recite a poem by Rimbaud in the middle of two circus acts at Barnum and Bailey. . . .

Also, the massive arrival of the new French film directors created great competition here, and pushed the French system closer to the Hollywood system. It became much harder for directors to escape a sort of type-casting, and much harder for them to survive a failure. At present, it's better not to have done anything than to have made an unsuccessful film. . . .

It seems to me there is a balance to be found. The Hollywood system was in balance. And how awesome to witness the terrible fall of Hollywood when the old framework broke apart. All went well when the movies were mass-produced, when the directors weren't permitted to have opinions, when the scriptwriters were paid by the year, when films were edited by specialists without ever consulting the director, etc. But as soon as the screws began to loosen, everything fell apart. . . .

But the Americans had one inimitable quality: they knew, in each branch of their work, how to make what they did come alive. And often their scenarios were marvelous. Recently I received a scenario written by Philip Yordan, and everything's already there, even humor—it's ready to be shot without changing a thing. The American cinema was both the finest and the worst: it was most often brilliant with conventional films, but there the result was marvelous.

Finally, no one merits total freedom. Many new filmmakers here are immature and make terrible blunders. The majority of the films I see are really badly edited; through complacency, lack of critical sense, or mere laziness, their makers are reluctant to cut. Once I made fun of Jacques Becker who said: "Le cinéma, c'est très compliqué." I preferred personally those who said "c'est simple," but saying this is a luxury not everyone can afford. . . . In television they resort to lengthy shots and almost never achieve good *champs-contrechamps*. In films therefore, by reaction, it's good to cut a lot, to return to classical cutting. Five years ago, when I was still a critic, French films were ugly. That's why the first films of Vadim and Malle were so important: simply because they exhibited a minimum of good taste. Today, everyone has taste, and films, in general, are more handsome. Now we must begin to aim still higher. We must try to make each of our films clear, interesting, intelligent, moving, and beautiful all at once. We must try to shoot each, to quote Ingmar Bergman, "as though it were our last." In short, we must compel ourselves to continue making progress.

FEDERICO FELLINI

The Road Beyond Neorealism*

"A good picture has to have defects. It has to have mistakes
in it, like life, like people."

*In contrast with the perfectionism of Dreyer, Federico
Fellini thinks of making a picture as "like leaving for a trip.
And the most interesting part of a trip is what you discover
on the way." He feels that he is continuing the tradition of
neorealism established in part by Rossellini (for whom he was
a screenwriter), even though others accuse him of being "too
much of an individualist."*

Fellini—the director of La Strada, La Dolce Vita, *and*
8½—*is concerned especially with "the terrible difficulty people have in talking to each other—the old problem of communication." This is not necessarily a social problem in the
way Zavattini would describe it, but Fellini does hold to the
feeling of endlessness, the denial that there are any "solutions"
in life: "My pictures never end. They never have a simple
solution." He wants his camera to look at "any kind of reality:
not just social reality, but also spiritual reality, metaphysical
reality, anything man has inside him."*

BACHMANN: I do not want to talk to you about one or another
specific film, but rather more generally—about your attitudes
toward filmmaking, your reasons for making certain films,
and your philosophical and sociological approach to what you
use as film material. For example, many critics have said that
there is a deep symbolism in your work, that there are recurring motifs in all your films. Like the image of the piazza at

* Gideon Bachmann, "Federico Fellini: An Interview," *Film:
Book 1*, edited by Robert Hughes, New York, Grove Press, 1959.
Pp. 97–105. A transcript of a radio program. Copyright by Gideon
Bachmann.

night with a fountain, of the seashore, and others. Is there a conscious intention on your part in repeating these images?

FELLINI: It is not intentional. In choosing a location, I do not choose it for its symbolic content. Things happen. If they happen well, they convey my meaning. Concerning the specific examples you mention, I'd like to say that all my films to date are concerned with people looking for themselves. Night and the loneliness of empty streets, as shown in the shots of piazzas you mention, is perhaps the best atmosphere in which I see these people. Also, it is quite possible that the associations which make me choose these locations are based on autobiographical experiences, for I cannot remove myself from the content of my films. Possibly what is in my mind when I shoot these scenes is the memory of my first impression of Rome—when I had left my hometown of Rimini and was in Rome alone. I was sixteen; I had no job, no idea of what I wanted to do. Often I was out of work, often I didn't have the money to stay in a hotel or eat properly. Or I would work at night. In any case, it is quite possible that the image of the town at night, empty and lonely, has remained in my soul from those days.

BACHMANN: Did you intend to go into films when you first came to Rome?

FELLINI: No, I didn't really know what I wanted to do. Still, my coming to Rome did have something to do with films: I had seen so many American films in which newspapermen were glamorous figures—I don't remember the titles, that was twenty-five years ago—but I was so impressed with the lives of newspapermen, that I decided to become one too. I liked the coats they wore and the way they wore their hats on the back of their heads. Unfortunately, the job I found was very different from my dream—I became a cub reporter who was sent by the editor to hospitals and to the police to get the obvious news. Later I began to write for the radio—sketches, mostly. After that I was tempted by the stage; and I toured Italy with a small traveling musical show. That period was one of the richest in my life, and I still draw on many of my experiences from those days.

BACHMANN: Certainly touring musical shows are one of the recurring motifs in your films. By the way, how did you finally begin working in films?

FELLINI: First, I was a rewrite man—I used to add gags to

the scripts of dull comedies. My first original screenplay was called *Avanti c'è posto*, and it was the story of a bus conductor. Freely translated the title would be "Please Move to the Rear." It was directed by Bonnard, who had taken to directing pictures when his fame as a matinee idol had faded. That was 1940. After that, I wrote many scripts. Too many. All were produced. They were comedies, mostly, in a pathetic vein. After the war, I met Rossellini, and for him I worked on *Open City* and *Paisan*. That's when I began to understand —or at least to suspect—that one could express deep things too in films. So I continued for two or three years writing scripts for the postwar Italian directors. After that, though, I became . . . I don't want to say disappointed, but when one really loves films, one cannot stop at the written page. I decided to direct. My first film was called *Luci del varietà* (Footlights).

BACHMANN: You directed this yourself?

FELLINI: Yes, I wrote and directed it. It was the story of the small troupe with whom I had spent a year on the road.

BACHMANN: When did you write and appear in *The Miracle*?

FELLINI: When I worked for Rossellini. Before I began to direct.

BACHMANN: Your serious film career, then, began during the period of the flowering of Italian neorealism. The relation between your films and "classical" neorealism has been much debated by the critics. Do you feel that your work in any way derives from, or was influenced by the neorealist directors with whom you have worked, like de Sica, Rossellini, Lattuada, etc.?

FELLINI: Well, I was one of the first to write scripts for neorealist films. I think all my work is definitely in the neorealist style, even if in Italy today some people don't think so. But this is a long story. For me, neorealism is a way of seeing reality without prejudice, without the interference of conventions—just parking yourself in front of reality without any preconceived ideas.

BACHMANN: You don't mean simply to put the camera in front of "life" and photograph what's there?

FELLINI: No, it's a question of having the feeling for reality. Naturally, there is always the need for an interpretation. What has happened in Italy is that after the war everything for us

was completely new. Italy was in ruins; you could say everything you felt by just looking around. Later, the leftist press
capitalized on this inadvertent one-sidedness by saying that
the only valid thing to do in films is to show what happens
around you. But this has no value from an artistic point of
view, because always the important thing is to know *who* sees
the reality. Then it becomes a question of the power to con-
dense, to show the essence of things. After all, why are the
films we make so much better than newsreels?

BACHMANN: Though, of course, even newsreels are already
one step removed from reality, through the selectivity of the
cameraman who took them.

FELLINI: Right. . . . But why should people go to the
movies, if films show reality only through a very cold, objective eye? It would be much better just to walk around in the
street. For me, neorealism means looking at reality with an
honest eye—but any kind of reality: not just social reality, but
also spiritual reality, metaphysical reality, anything man has
inside him.

BACHMANN: You mean anything that has reality for the
director?

FELLINI: Yes.

BACHMANN: Then the completed film is really *two* steps removed from nature: first the personal *view* of it by the director, and then his *interpretation* of that personal view.

FELLINI: Yes, yes. For me, neorealism is not a question of
what you show—its real spirit is in *how* you show it. It's just
a way of looking around, without convention or prejudice.
Certain people still think neorealism is fit to show only certain
kinds of reality; and they insist that this is social reality. But
in this way, it becomes mere propaganda. It is a program; to
show only certain aspects of life. People have written that I
am a traitor to the cause of neorealism, that I am too much
of an individualist, too much of an individual. My own personal conviction, however, is that the films I have done so far
are in the same style as the first neorealist films, simply telling
the story of people. And always, in telling the story of some
people, I try to show some truth.

BACHMANN: Is there any underlying philosophy in your
films? I mean besides the depiction of what is truth for you.

FELLINI: Well, I could tell you what for me is one of the
most pressing problems, one which provides part of the

theme for all my films. It's the terrible difficulty people have in talking to each other—the old problem of communication, the desperate anguish to be *with*, the desire to have a real, authentic relationship with another person. You'll find this in *I Vitelloni*, in *La Strada*, in *Il Bidone*, and also in *Notti di Cabiria*. It may be that I'll change, but for now I'm completely absorbed in this problem—maybe because I have not yet solved it in my private life.

BACHMANN: Do you feel that the reason for this difficulty in interpersonal communication is that we have created a kind of society which makes it hard for people to have true relationships?

FELLINI: It is the fault of society only because society is made up of men. I believe that everyone has to find truth by himself. It is completely useless to prepare a statement for a crowd, or make a film with a message for everyone. I don't believe in talking to a crowd. Because what is a crowd? It is a collection of many individuals, each with his own reality. That is also the reason why my pictures never end. They never have a simple solution. I think it is immoral (in the true sense of the word) to tell a story that has a conclusion. Because you cut out your audience the moment you present a solution on the screen. Because there are no "solutions" in their lives. I think it is more moral—and more important—to show, let's say, the story of one man. Then everyone, with his own sensibility and on the basis of his own inner development, can try to find his own solution.

BACHMANN: You mean to say that by "ending" a problem, the filmmaker takes away from the audience the feeling that what they are seeing is the truth?

FELLINI: Yes, or even worse. For when you show a true problem and then resolve it, the spectator is beguiled into feeling that the problems in his own life, too, will solve themselves, and he can stop working on them for himself. By giving happy endings to films, you goad your audience into going on living in a trite, bland manner, because they are now sure that sometime, somewhere, something happy is going to happen to them, too, and without their having to do anything about it. Conversely, by not serving them the happy ending on a platter, you can make them think; you can remove some of that smug security. Then they'll *have* to find their own answers.

BACHMANN: This would seem to indicate that you're not

just making pictures to make pictures, but because there are certain things you want to say.

FELLINI: Well, I don't start that way. What usually starts me on a film idea is that something happens to me which I think has some bearing on other people's experiences. And the feeling is usually the same: to try, first of all, to tell something about myself; and in doing so, to try to find a salvation, to try to find a road toward some meaning, some truth, something that will be important to others, too. And when, as often happens, people who have seen my films come to visit me—not to discuss my films, but to talk to me about their personal problems—I feel I have achieved something. It is always a great satisfaction for me. Of course, I can't help them clarify their problems, but it means the picture has done some good.

BACHMANN: When you say you don't start that way, do you mean to say that the real "message" of your films develops out of the material?

FELLINI: Well, a picture is a mixture of things. It changes. That is one of the reasons why making films is such a wonderful thing.

BACHMANN: Could you tell me about the process in your film work? A kind of step-by-step description of your work on any given film?

FELLINI: First, I have to be moved by a feeling. I have to be interested in one character or one problem. Once I have that, I don't really need a very well-written story or a very detailed script. I need to begin without knowing that everything is in perfect order; otherwise I lose all the fun of it. If I knew everything from the start, I would no longer be interested in doing it. So that when I begin a picture, I am not yet sure of the location or the actors. Because for me, to make a picture is like leaving for a trip. And the most interesting part of a trip is what you discover on the way. I am very open to suggestions when I start a film. I am not rigid about what I do. I like the people with me on the film to share this new adventure. Certainly, I do remember that I am shooting, sometimes.

When the picture is finished, I would, if possible, like not to see it. I often say to my producer, joking: "Let's not cut this one; let's make a new one instead." But I cut all my own films. Cutting is one of the most emotional aspects of film-making. It is the most exciting thing to see the picture begin to breathe; it is like seeing your child grow up. The rhythm is not yet well identified, the sequence not established. But I never reshoot. I believe that a good picture has to have defects. It has to have mistakes in it, like life, like people. I don't believe that beauty, in the sense of perfection, exists—except maybe for the angels. A beautiful woman is attractive only if she is not perfect. The most important thing is to see to it that the picture is alive. This is the most rewarding moment in making films: when the picture begins to live. And I never go back to look at what I have already done—I edit the whole film right through. When it's finished, and I go into the projection room to see it for the first time, I like to be alone. I can express exactly what happens. I look at the picture; the picture looks at me. A lot of things happen. Some ideas are born; some die. Later I begin to "clean" the picture. In Italy we do not use the sound we shoot on location, but redo the whole track in the studio. But the first answer print still has the location sound on it. Once that is removed, something happens again. The answer print still has the flavor of the adventure of making the film—a train that passed, a baby that cried, a window that opened. I remember the people who were with me on location. I remember the trip. I would like to retain these memories. Once they put the clean, new track on it, it's like a father seeing his little girl wear lipstick for the first time. You have to get to know this new creature that is emerging; you have to try to like it. Then when you add the music, again something is added and something is lost. Every time you see it again, there is some new feeling. When it is completely finished, you have lost the objective point of view. Then, when others see it, I react personally—I feel they have no right to say anything about *my* picture. But I listen carefully, nevertheless—I am trying to find out whether for them the picture is alive.

BACHMANN: Do you feel that in all the films you have made you have always remained faithful to what you were trying to say when you started the picture?

FELLINI: Yes, I do.

BACHMANN: Do you feel there is a relation between your work and that of the current crop of Italian writers, like, for example, Carlo Levi and Ennio Flaiano?

FELLINI: Yes, I think this core of neorealism in films has influenced all the arts.

BACHMANN: Have you, yourself, done any writing except scripts?

FELLINI: No. Just some short stories when I worked for newspapers. But not since I've worked in films. It's a different medium. A writer can do everything by himself—but he needs discipline. He has to get up at seven in the morning, and be alone in a room with a white sheet of paper. I am too much of a *vitellone* to do that. I think I have chosen the best medium of expression for myself. I love the very precious combination of work and of living-together that film-making offers. I approach film-making in a very personal way. That's why I consider myself a neorealist. Any research that a man does about himself, about his relationships with others and with the mystery of life, is a spiritual and—in the true sense— religious search. I suppose that is the extent of my formal philosophy. I make movies in the same way that I talk to people—whether it's a friend, a girl, a priest, or anyone: to seek some clarification. That is what neorealism means to me, in the original, pure sense. A search into oneself, and into others. In any direction, any direction where there is life. All the formal philosophy you could possibly apply to my work is that there is no formal philosophy. In film-making, as in living, you must take the experiences that life presents, those which apply to yourself and to others. Except that in film-making only the absolute truth will work. In life I may be a swindler or a crook, but that wouldn't work in a film. A man's film is like a naked man—nothing can be hidden. I must be truthful in my films.

PLAY WITH FIRE

A KATE SHUGAK MYSTERY

DANA STABENOW

BERKLEY PRIME CRIME, NEW YORK

Grateful acknowledgment of permission is made to quote from *Archy and Mehitabel* by Don Marquis. Copyright © 1927 by Doubleday, a division of Bantam Doubleday Dell Publishing Group, Inc. Used by permission of Doubleday, a division of Bantam Doubleday Dell Publishing Group, Inc.

PLAY WITH FIRE

A Berkley Prime Crime Book / published by arrangement with the author

PRINTING HISTORY
Berkley Prime Crime hardcover edition / April 1995
Berkley Prime Crime mass-market edition / May 1996

The Putnam Berkley World Wide Web site address is http://www.berkley.com

ISBN: 0-425-15254-5

Berkley Prime Crime Books are published by The Berkley Publishing Group, 200 Madison Avenue, New York, NY 10016.
The name BERKLEY PRIME CRIME and the BERKLEY PRIME CRIME design are trademarks belonging to Berkley Publishing Corporation.

PRINTED IN THE UNITED STATES OF AMERICA

10   9   8   7

For Dixie and Brian and Sandy and Gary

and especially for Rhonda Lynn

here's to the Taylor Express
and the Malemute Saloon
and the motormouth in bunny boots
and the days we thought would never end

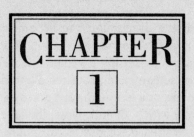

CHAPTER 1

The origin of mushrooms is the slime and souring juices of moist earth, or frequently the root of acorn-bearing trees; at first it is flimsier than froth, then it grows substantial like parchment, and then the mushroom is born.

—*Pliny*

"Kate. Look up."

Kate kept her head down, in part out of a natural obstinacy, in part because she lacked the energy to do otherwise.

The young woman with the blonde ponytail lowered her video camera and huffed out an impatient breath. "Kate, how am I supposed to make my Academy Award–winning documentary film on the Mad Mushroom Pickers of Musk Ox Mountain if you won't cooperate?" She slapped down a persistent mosquito. "Come on," she said in a coaxing voice and raised the camera again. "One teensy-weensy, insignificant little smile. What could it hurt?"

With the paring knife she held in her right hand,

1

Kate cut half a dozen more mushrooms and tossed them into the overflowing five-gallon plastic bucket next to her. Suppressing a groan, she straightened a back that screamed in protest and bared her teeth in the blonde's direction. Spread across a face covered equally with soot and sweat, the fake grin echoed the whitened, roped scar pulling at the otherwise smooth brown skin of the throat below. All in all, it was a fearsome sight.

"Great! Fantastic! Beautiful! You look like a woman who runs with the wolves!" The blonde's face scrunched into an expression of ferocious concentration behind the eyepiece. The camera lingered long enough for the grin to fade to a grimace as Kate stretched again, then panned down and left, to rest on the quizzical yellow stare of the gray wolf-husky hybrid sprawled on a rise of ground. "Get up, Mutt," the blonde pleaded. "Give me a little action. A grin, a snarl, anything! Look like the wolf Kate runs with!"

Mutt, chin resting on crossed paws, closed her eyes. It was too hot to do anything else.

The blonde grumbled. "You people are just not cooperating with me." The camera panned up and left, to linger on a sign nailed to a blackened tree trunk. The plywood base was painted white. Its message was lettered in neat block print, by hand, and was brief and to the point:

1 JOHN 2:22

The blonde lowered the camera and delved into the capacious left-hand pocket of her coat, a voluminous gray duster that swept behind her like a train, snapping twigs from blueberry bushes, trailing through narrow streams of peaty water, picking up the odd bear scat. It was wet to a foot above the hem. Her jeans were wet to the knee.

A paperback edition of The Holy Bible materialized from the duster pocket like the voice of God from the burning bush. A few seconds later she found it. " 'Who is a liar but he that denieth that Jesus is the Christ? He is antichrist, that denieth the Father and the Son.' " She looked up. "Only the third one today and we're almost to the end of the New Testament." She pondered a moment. "Let me pose you an existential question."

"Dinah."

"Oh quit, it'll be good for you." She didn't say why, only squared her shoulders, raised one arm in the obligatory oratorical stance and declaimed, "If scripture is posted in the forest and there's no one around to read it, does it make any sense?"

"Almost as much as if someone were," Kate couldn't resist replying.

"I was afraid of that," the blonde said gloomily, and slapped at another mosquito. "Damn these bugs! I feel like I'm running a blood blank for anything with three pairs of legs and two pairs of wings!" She slapped again. "Jesus! How do you stand it?"

Kate's jeans were wet to the thigh. Sweat was pooling at the base of her spine. It felt like eighty degrees on this Thursday afternoon in late June. The sun wasn't setting until it got good and ready— at this time of year not until midnight—and she'd had enough of existentialism two pages into *No Exit* and three weeks into English 211 at the University of Alaska in Fairbanks fourteen years before. She pushed back a strand of black hair, leaving another streak of soot on her cheek, and hoisted the bucket. Ten feet away sat a second white plastic bucket, similarly full, and she headed toward it with grim determination.

"You can't!" Dinah wailed. "Kate! Dammit, I've been waiting for this light all day! Ouch!" She smacked another mosquito.

Kate picked up the second bucket, balancing the load, and paused for a moment to wonder if, after all, she should have taken Billy Mike up on his crew share offer. Hands, arms and back, she now knew from bitter experience, ached just as badly after a week of picking fish out of a skiff as they did from a week of picking mushrooms off the forest floor. She hitched the buckets and followed Mutt up the hill.

Dinah scrambled after her. "Okay, okay, I'll get up with you tomorrow, we'll catch the morning light, it'll be all right."

"I'm so pleased for you," Kate said, plodding around a burned-out stump. "My whole life would be blighted if you missed your shot." Another trickle of sweat ran down her back. A mosquito whined past her ear, and behind her she heard another smack of flesh on flesh.

"Hah! Another victory of woman over *Aedes excrucians!*"

Kate didn't want to know, but there was a rustle of cloth as Dinah produced another book, a small paperback entitled *Some Notes on the Arthropod Insecta Diptera in the Alaskan Wilderness.* She dodged a blood-thirsty specimen, waved off another on final approach, slapped at a third and read, " '*Aedes excrucians* is the most abundant and annoying of Alaskan mosquitoes.' "

Kate remained silent, and goaded, the blonde turned up the volume. " 'It differs from other mosquitoes in that it remains active during warm sunny afternoons, especially aggravating to its victims. Its habitat is the marshlands attendant to rivers found from Wrangell to Fort Yukon, from Niniltna to Naknek, and from Kotzebue to Noatak.' " Dinah shut and pocketed the book. "I just hope you're happy, is all."

Kate hadn't called up this particular swarm of *Aedes excrucians,* or any other for that matter, but she held her peace. A buzzing specimen hovered near her right brow, sniffed the air, turned up its probiscus in disdain and whizzed past. From behind Kate a moment later there was a smack of flesh on flesh and a muttered curse.

·They kept climbing the slope before them, leaving the marsh behind and heading for higher ground, and eventually the bugs began to decrease in number, though they were never entirely absent, not at this time of year, not anywhere in Alaska. When at last the two women reached the top of the rise, Kate paused for breath.

They were hiking through what had once been a pristine primeval forest. The previous summer the worst fire in decades had swept through the area and torn a strip off the Alaskan interior in places as much as five miles wide. When the smokejumpers had at last battled it to a standstill, 125,000 square acres of interior Alaskan scrub spruce, white spruce, paper birch, quaking aspen and balsam poplar had been laid waste, not to mention—and what Kate grudged more—countless lowbush and highbush cranberry, raspberry, salmonberry, lingonberry and nagoonberry stands.

But nature, profligate and extravagant as always, had brought in the following spring wet and mild, and in the ashes of the devastating fire had sprung up a bumper crop of morel mushrooms that had produce buyers flying in en masse from Los Angeles to New York, cash in hand, and had Alaskans flying in en masse from all over the Interior, buckets in hand, in pursuit of that cash.

Kate stretched gingerly. Once upon a time she had liked mushrooms. Now she felt about them the way she did about salmon at the end of the fishing season: that if she never saw another she'd die happy. She raised a hand to scratch her scar, inhaled some soot and sneezed three times in rapid succession. Picking fish was looking better all the time.

At their feet the great loop of the Kanuyaq River gleamed a dull gold. Forty miles to the south of the rise, Mount Sanford rose sixteen thousand feet in the air, flanked by nine-thousand-foot Tanada and twelve-thousand-foot Drum, blue-white armor glinting in the late afternoon sun. If she squinted south-southeast, Kate made believe she could see Angqaq lording it arrogantly over the Quilaks. The peaks, sharped-edged and stern, looked normal and reassuring; it was the land between, a nightmare drawn in broad slashes of charcoal, that shocked and startled. The scar was a shadow on the land. Ash lay thick on the ground, showered from crisped branches. The trunks of trees had exploded in the heat of the fire and left acres of black splinters behind, looking for all the world like a game of pick-up-sticks frozen in an upright position.

It was a charred skeleton of a once-great forest. "What a waste," the blonde said, her voice subdued. "What started it, do you know?"

"Lightning."

"Lightning?" The blonde eyed the cumulus clouds gathering force on the southeastern horizon.

Kate nodded. "It's the main cause of forest fires."

"Oh." The blonde eyed the clouds again. "Even

Smokey the Bear might find it a little tough to fight lightning. What a waste," she repeated, raising the camera and surveying the scene through the eyepiece.

Kate heard the low whir of rolling film. "Not really."

The roll of film paused, the blonde raising a skeptical eyebrow.

"It's true. A forest fire is a way for the forest to renew itself and the wildlife in it. In the older forests the big trees get bigger and take over, and new growth doesn't have a chance. New growth is what moose eat. A couple of years after a fire and the moose start multiplying because there's more fodder. It happened on the Kenai after the 1969 fire there. It'll happen here, too."

"Uh-huh." Dinah didn't sound convinced. "It'll take a while, though, to regenerate."

Kate glanced around, and pointed. "What?" the blonde said suspiciously.

Kate stooped to brush at some ash. Something indisputably green peered back at them, an alder by the shape of the leaves.

"I'll be damned," Dinah said, impressed in spite of herself. Mutt sniffed at the shoot of green. Dinah focused on both and the camera whirred. "What a great shot. Death and resurrection. Destruction and regeneration! The green phoenix bursting from the black ashes of devastation!" Lowering the camera she delved once more in her left-hand pocket, producing the tattered Bible. Impatiently, she thumbed through the pages, muttering to herself. "Aha! And 'Death is swallowed up in victory!'" She slapped the book shut and shot Kate a triumphant look. "One Corinthians, 15:54. 'O death, where is thy sting?'" She slapped at a mosquito. "Damn. Did you know there are twenty-seven species of mosquito in the state of Alaska?" She looked back at Kate. "I can't believe there is something already growing here. I would have bet big bucks it'd be years."

Mutt raised a leg over the green shoot. Kate forbore to draw Dinah's attention to the act. "It doesn't take long." She dug a fist into the small of her back. "Of course, twenty-hour days and a good spring rain are a great head start." She picked up the buckets, took one step forward and halted abruptly.

Dinah bumped into her. "Sorry. What?" She followed Kate's gaze and the breath whooshed out of her. "Holy shit."

A brown bear stood to the right of the trail. He was about the biggest creature Dinah had ever seen in all her life outside a zoo, standing six feet at the shoulder and weighing literally half a ton. His brown fur was silver-tipped and his muzzle was sooty, as if he'd been nosing over burned logs.

For once, Dinah forgot she was holding a camera. She almost dropped it. "Holy *shit*," she said again. She knew it was an inadequate assessment of the situation but she didn't really know of anything to say that would be adequate.

"Relax," Kate said.

"What if it charges us?" Dinah hissed.

"Talk in your normal tone of voice," Kate said, and moved forward.

"Kate! What are you doing? You're walking right toward it! Kate!"

"Just follow me, Dinah," Kate said, still in that normal tone of voice.

Dinah swore helplessly and followed, hefting her camera to shoulder height, not sure if she were keeping it out of harm's way or preparing to use it for a weapon. Then she recollected her mission and rolled film. She could see it now. She Died Rolling. Death in the line of duty. The American Documentary Filmmakers Association'd probably name an award after her. She wondered if there was an American Documentary Filmmakers Association. She wondered if they had an award.

The bear looked even bigger through the lens, crowding the edges of the frame. It didn't help that her hands were shaking. She realized that the back of Kate's head was receding and quickened her step.

The bear watched them impassively for the longest minute of Dinah's life. When they had approached within ten yards he dropped his head and melted back into a pocket of alders at the edge of the burn area.

"Just relax," Kate repeated, steps even and unhurried. "There are two of us and we're talking. He wants to come down this way, though, and bears are kind of inflexible once they've made up their minds to do something. It's best we get out of his way. Lucky he wasn't a sow. They've usually just dropped a cub this time of year. A sow would have been cranky as hell."

She kept talking and kept walking. Dinah was so close behind her now that her toes caught Mutt's heels, and Mutt moved up to point, ears up but silent and unalarmed. The lens of the camera clipped Kate's head once, earning Dinah a hard look from hazel eyes. They passed the thicket into which the bear had retreated without incident and walked on up the hill unmolested.

Dinah was weak with relief, her legs wobbling, her knees barely able to hold her up. "Jesus, Kate. What if he had charged us?"

"You'd have been toast," Kate said serenely without pausing.

Dinah stared at the black braid hanging straight down a very straight spine. "Why me? Why me and not you?"

Kate grinned without turning. "Because I wouldn't have to outrun the bear. I'd only have to outrun you."

There was a moment while Dinah worked this out. When she did, she gave an unconvincing snort.

"Ha ha ha. Very funny." She plodded along in silence for a moment. "I didn't even know there were bears around here."

"You ain't in New York City anymore, Dorothy."

"That's why Bobby hangs everything from that tree every night."

"No bacon or sausage for breakfast, either."

"Bears like bacon?"

"Almost better than anything else." Kate could almost hear Dinah become a vegetarian for the duration in the sound of her footsteps. "Truthfully, bears will eat anything that'll sit still for it. They don't like to work for their food."

"We'd have been work?"

"Uh-huh. They'll eat anything or anyone that's within reach, whether it's been lying around for a day or a year, as long as it is just lying around." She added, "That's why you don't find any bodies near plane crashes."

Dinah swallowed audibly. "Bears eat them?"

"Uh-huh."

A breeze rose up, keeping the remaining mosquitoes off, and Dinah nosed into it gratefully. Over the top of the next rise the black ash stopped abruptly, as if a line had been drawn beyond which the fire was forbidden to cross. As they approached, an actual line appeared in the form of a six-foot ditch, a fire break dug by the smokejumpers the year before, one of many in an effort to direct the course of the fire away from the Glenn Highway, the main road between Anchorage and the Canadian border, and its sycophant settlements. On the other side of the ditch was a clearing, a small patch of new spring grass encircled by a stand of birch trees. Their white boles stood out against the rising ground of the blackened countryside, slender and strong.

In the center of the clearing was a rock-lined fire pit. Two tents faced each other across it. A square of bright blue plastic tarpaulin was spread to one side, a dozen full five-gallon buckets on it, the rest of the day's harvest. Kate let her two buckets thud down next to them and mopped her brow. Her palm came away smeared with soot.

"Oh Ward, I'm home!" The blonde hastened past her and into the ring of trees.

"In here, June!" replied a deep male voice.

The owner of the voice had installed fat, mountain bike tires on his wheelchair and it cornered around the rock fireplace like a '69 Corvette. The 350-horsepower engine slammed to a halt at the sight of the blonde. The driver threw back his head and, in a stentorian voice that caused the tops of the trees to sway, bellowed, "BAY-bee!"

"SWEET-heart!" In one movement Dinah shucked out of camera and duster. In a combined hop, skip and jump she leapt into Bobby's lap, flung her arms around his neck and smothered his face with kisses, all of which were returned with interest.

It was enough to make a grown woman vomit. "It's enough to make a grown woman vomit," Kate said, and had to repeat it a second time in a louder voice when the lovers ignored it the first time around.

"Why don't you run away and play, Kate," the blonde suggested around a mouthful of ear.

Bobby sent her a lascivious grin and said nothing at all. Biting the inside of her cheek to hold back an answering smile, Kate got her pack out of her tent and went past them and down the hill to the creek a quarter of a mile beyond.

The rush of spring runoff had carved a pool the size and depth of a tin washtub out of the side of the bank. Smooth, round stones slightly smaller than goose eggs shone up from the stream bed, fiddlehead ferns lined the bank, peat-colored water eddied around the edges of the little pool, and the whole scene looked like something out of Gerard Manley Hopkins. Mutt waded in as far as her ankles, buried her muzzle six inches deep and inhaled the better part of the volume of water. Exhausted from this gargantuan effort, she flopped down beneath a nearby tree and lapsed into a sated stupor. Mutt wasn't accustomed to and didn't approve of heat waves and had decided that the best way to endure this one was asleep.

Kate shucked out of her clothes and waded in. The water was clear and cold and she gasped from the shock of it against her overheated skin. The pool was just big enough to get all of her wet at the same time and she sank beneath the surface, shaking her head so that her hair swirled around her face. She exploded into the air with a tremendous splash and a laugh. On the bank Mutt opened one eye, saw that a rescue was not in her immediate future and relapsed into unconsciousness. Kate couldn't resist. She brought both palms down on the water, hard, and it fountained up over the bank and splashed down on and around Mutt. Mutt leapt to her feet and let out a yip like an outraged dowager pinched on the behind, shook herself vigorously, gave Kate a reproachful look and relocated behind a tree well out of range.

"You're no fun," Kate told her, and reached for the soap. It came in a plastic bottle, bought from REI in Anchorage during her stay with Jack that spring. She'd done a job for an oil company and they'd paid her obscenely well for it. She had done her best to spend every ill-gotten dime before she left town, and one of the places she'd done her best at was at REI. REI was going yuppie in its old age but it still had all kinds of fascinating and useless gadgets for the urban hiker. Kate had found the soap there and bought a bottle at once for the label, which announced that it contained "Dr. Bronner's Almond 18-in-1 Pure-Castile Soap, Always dilute for Shave-Shampoo-Massage-Dental-Soap Bath! . . . Use Almond Oil Soap for Dispensers-Uniforms-Baby-Beach! Dilute for good After Shave, Body

Rub, Foot Bath, Massage! Hot Towel Massage entire body, always toward heart! . . . Mildest soap Made! God-made Eggwhite pH9."

It was manufactured by All-One-God-Faith, Inc., and in the small space left over after instructions did its best to save sinners and convert the heathen. "Absolute cleanliness is Godliness! Teach the Moral ABC that unites all mankind free, instantly 6 billion strong & we're All-one." Kate noticed that rhyme was attempted more than once, as in "Our Brother's Teacher of the Moral ABC Hillel taught carpenter Jesus to unite all mankind free!"

Kate wondered who Hillel was. If they ever discovered who was nailing the biblical tracts to the trees, she might get an expert opinion. Uncapping the bottle, she sniffed cautiously. It was almonds, all right. Kate considered herself pretty much beyond redemption by now, but if cleanliness was next to godliness there might be hope for her yet. She washed her clothes first and then herself, soaping her hair twice and scrubbing her body three times, and only reluctantly waded out of the water when her feet began to lose all feeling.

She paused on the bank. The sun was warm on her eyelids, on her breasts and belly. Pine needles prickled the half-numb soles of her feet and she dug in her toes, balancing her weight on spread legs. A wisp of a breeze tiptoed into the little glade and stirred her hair so that the ends tickled her waist. She stood still, palms out, eyes closed, water running down the cleft of her buttocks, the insides of her legs, dripping from the tips of her fingers. Her breasts rose on a deep breath. The faint, acrid smell of charred wood mixed freely with the clean smell of soap, the sweet aroma of running pine sap and the fresh scent of new cottonwood leaves.

The rays of the afternoon sun slanted through leaf and branch to dapple the glade, her skin and the glimmering surface of the tiny pool and the murmuring creek. A bird sang, a clear, joyous, three-note descending scale. "Spring is here," Kate sang with it in a husky rasp, aggravated by the scar on her throat. "Here is spring."

Her arms lifted of their own volition, palms out to the sun, toes digging into grass. The earth's heart beat against her feet, her own kept time with it, and the power of their union seeped up through her soles, flowing into her blood and coursing through her body. Every sense was magnified; she could smell the slight, musty bitterness of the morels, taste the sweetness of the pine sap on her tongue. She heard the exultant scream of an eagle as she plummeted down, talons extended for the kill, the sense of it so vivid Kate felt the stretch of wings across her shoulders, the fan of tail feathers, the coppery taste of blood warm in her mouth. She opened her eyes and could see as far as the Quilaks and the Wrangells and beyond, to Prince William Sound and the rolling blue-green expanse of the mighty Gulf. Never had life seemed so rich with sensual promise. She felt ripe, ready to burst from her skin.

A blade of grass tickled her ankle. The breeze turned cool. She shivered and blinked. A deep, shuddering breath and she was back in her body, senses dazzled by all they had seen. A chuckle escaped her when she realized her nipples were erect. "Lover come back," she said, only half jesting. Mutt opened one eye to give her a quizzical look.

She dug in her pack for a bottle of Lubriderm (another result of the March shopping spree) and smoothed it on; hands, elbows, feet, luxuriating in the feel of it. One thing could be said for picking salmon out of a net: it was infinitely cleaner work than mushroom picking. She decided that in the future she'd take scales and gurry over soot and ash. "The next time Bobby gets a wild hair to go mushroom hunting," she told Mutt, "he can go by himself. Especially since he's so good at picking up casual labor."

Mutt, by way of agreement, closed her eye.

She strung a line between two trees, hung her wet clothes and put on clean ones. Sitting cross-legged, she brushed her hair dry, a straight, black, gleaming fall. By then she judged it was safe to go back to camp. Her stomach was growling, so it was too bad if it wasn't.

In the clearing the flap of Bobby's tent was zipped all the way down. Bobby was sitting on a blanket in cutoffs and no shirt, cleaning and sorting mushrooms.

"About time you did some work around here," Kate said.

He reached behind him and tossed her a package of Fig Newtons. "Not just a prince but a god," she said, ripping it open and shoving two in her mouth. He pursed his lips and blew her a kiss and went back to sorting as she rummaged in the cooler for a Diet 7-Up to wash the cookies down with. She popped the top and drank the whole can in one long swallow, submerged it in the melting ice until it refilled with water, and drank that, too. She eyed Bobby over the can, absorbed in his mushrooms.

He was worth watching. Thick through the shoulders like most wheelchair jockeys, his arms were roped with muscle that bunched and flexed beneath smooth skin the color of espresso. His chest was hairless, leaving every rib clearly defined and ridged with muscle. His cutoffs, an inch shorter than his stumps and frayed at the hems, hugged his behind, faithful to every tight, taut curve. The sight was enough to make a grown woman drool.

There was a rasp of a zipper, a rustle of fabric and the squeak of a rubber sole on pine needles. Bobby turned, torso straining, to reach for the bucket. "Yum," said a low voice behind Kate.

"Enough to make a grown woman drool," Kate agreed.

Dinah laughed and sprawled beside her. She was thin to the point of emaciation, had cheekbones to die for and wide, inquiring blue eyes that weren't as innocent as they seemed at first sight. The ponytail had been replaced by a mass of tangled strawberry blonde curls. She was glowing. Kate, years before having been taken up the same mountain and shown the view by the same guide, didn't blame her. She sternly repressed a pang of envy and bit into another Fig Newton. It didn't help much. Sublimation by any other name would taste as tame.

Dinah got a can of pop from the cooler and copped a handful of Fig Newtons and curled up next to Kate, who saw with dismay that she had produced yet another reference work, this one a grimy, dog-eared pamphlet titled *Fun With Fungi, A Mushroom Lover's Guide.* Dinah opened it. And with illustrations, no less. O joy.

"*Morchella elata,*" Dinah said, "also known as the black morel. Edible," she added in an aside to Kate.

Bobby threw one at her and she ducked. "The caps are yellowish-brown, spongelike, bell-shaped, and vary in color from cream to brown. They're found in April, May and sometimes June in Alaska. Morels are often particularly abundant in burned-over soil. Why, I wonder?" She turned a page. "Oh. It says here nobody really knows why, but the best guess is it doesn't like competition, from other vegetation, I guess. Hmm. You know why we're picking them?"

Kate took a wild stab. "Two dollars a pound?"

Dinah frowned at her. "Morels don't reproduce in captivity."

"Me, either," Bobby said.

Dinah paged forward and raised her voice. "Morels are perfect partners for sauces because of their ridged caps."

Bobby examined a specimen. "You mean because it grows like something Dr. Frankenstein would transplant inside an empty skull."

"I don't know why I waste my time on these people," Dinah told Mutt.

"Me, either," Bobby said again, and Kate laughed.

Dinah turned to the start of the book. "A Brief History of Fungi," she began the chapter, and had to duck again, this time from half a dozen incoming morels thrown from Bobby's direction, several of which scored direct hits. Deserting righteousness, she said, "Just listen, there's some neat stories in here about mushrooms. For instance"—she ducked again—"did you know that in ancient times the Greeks believed mushrooms were created by lightning bolts? In Scandinavia, though, it was thought that when Wotan ran from the demons, he foamed at the mouth and spit blood, and wherever it struck the ground a mushroom sprang up."

"Yuk. Wotan spit. Jesus." Bobby paused for a moment in his sorting, regarding the mushroom he was holding with knitted brow. "Did you ever stop to wonder who ate the first mushroom?"

"The first King crab?" Kate said, getting into the spirit of things.

"The first oyster?"

" 'He was a bold man that first eat an oyster,' " Kate agreed, with a gravity of which Jonathan Swift would have heartily approved.

"While the Chinese," Dinah said in a slightly louder voice, "considered mushrooms fit only for the poor, the Romans considered them fit only for the rich. They used special utensils to cook them and eat them with." She read further and gave a sudden shout of laughter. "Evidently the special pots for cooking mushrooms, they called them 'bol-etaria,' anyway, they weren't supposed to be used to cook anything else. But this one pot was, and nearly died of the disgrace. Listen to what Martial says the pot says: 'Although boleti have given me such a noble name, I am now used, I am ashamed to say, for brussels sprouts.' "

"Poor little pot," Bobby said sadly.

"How humiliating," Kate agreed, just as sadly.

Dinah, reading further, said, "And then there's a kind of fungus that kills grain, and the Romans had a festival each year on the twenty-fifth of April to propitiate the god Robigus, so he would intercede and keep the crops healthy. Everybody dressed up in their best bib and toga and marched out to a sacred grove and anointed the altar with wine and sacrificed a goat and 'buried the entrails of a rust-colored dog.' "

Mutt gave Dinah a wary look. "Oh, don't take everything so personally," Dinah told her, and returned to her book. "In Europe in the seventeen hundreds and eighteen hundreds mushrooms were so popular that kings had to pass laws against setting forest fires to grow more mushrooms." She looked up to quirk an eyebrow at Kate. "Maybe that's what happened here."

"No," Kate said. No one of her acquaintance had ever started a forest fire to grow mushrooms.

Bobby laughed without pausing in his sorting. Dinah gave him a curious look but he didn't explain, and she returned to her book.

"They didn't just eat mushrooms, either, they used them for medicine. Dioscorides prescribed them for colic and sores, bruises, broken bones, asthma, jaundice, dysentery, urinary tract infections, constipation, epilepsy, arthritis, hysteria and acne."

"Acne? You mean like zits?"

"That's what he says. Grind up a mushroom and mix it in with a little water and honey, and presto! B.C. Clearasil." Dinah paused. "Wow."

"What?" In spite of herself, Kate was getting interested.

"The Laplanders used it to cure aches and pains, too. They'd spread bits of dried mushrooms on whatever hurt and set them on fire. The water from the blisters supposedly carried away the pain."

"I think I'd rather have the aches and pains."

"Me, too," Bobby said. He finished sorting, ending with fourteen five-gallon buckets full of clean, dry mushrooms and a big aluminum bowl full of rejects, also clean and dry but deemed by the new mycological expert on the block as unsalable. He regarded the day's harvest with smug satisfaction, and looked over at the two of them, one cocky eyebrow raised. "You two gonna get these shrooms over to the buyer anytime today? I heard a rumor yesterday that the price might go up to three bucks a pound."

"From the same guy who told you the day before that a buyer was flying in from New York and would pay two-fifty?" Kate inquired sweetly.

"Git!" he said.

"A little Hitler, with littler charm," Dinah murmured.

"What was that?" Bobby said suspiciously, ears pricking up.

Dinah gave him a sweet smile. "Stephen Sondheim," she replied, and left him certain he'd been insulted but not quite sure how.

Dinah took a quick bath, finishing just in time to help Kate hump the last of the buckets down to Kate's truck, a red-and-white Isuzu diesel with a plywood tool chest riveted to the bed behind the cab. It was a half mile walk between campsite and the narrow turnaround on the gravel road, and on her last trip Kate said to Bobby, wheezing a little, "Next time you think of me to go mushroom hunting with?"

"Yeah?"

"Don't."

He hid a grin. "But Kate, I'm disabled." He looked down at his stumps with mournful eyes, and said wistfully, "Don't you think I'd help if I could?"

She just looked at him, and he could only hold the mournful expression for about three seconds before breaking into a roar of laughter Dinah could hear all the way down the hill. "What's so funny?" she said as Kate heaved the last two buckets up into the bed of the truck.

"Bobby thinks he is," Kate grunted, and leaned up against the side of the truck to catch her breath. Parked next to the truck was Dinah's 1967 Ford Econoline van; its pale blue color was barely visible beneath a thousand miles of AlCan Highway mud. Through the streaked windows Kate could see that all the seats except for the driver's had been removed, to be replaced with a camp stove, jugs of what she assumed was water, and boxes of supplies. She leaned forward, eyes narrowing. "Are those books?"

Dinah came over to peer in next to her. "Uh-huh."

"Reading books?"

Dinah shook her head. "Looking-up books."

Kate stared at her. "Such as?"

Dinah shrugged. "*The Riverside Shakespeare.* Edith Hamilton's *Mythology. Chamber's Etymological Dictionary. The World Almanac.* The King James Bible. Or no, I've got that here somewhere." She patted vaguely at one of the many pockets in her long, gray duster, which she had donned for the excursion into town. "And, oh, I don't know, an Alaskan atlas, an Alaskan almanac, an Alaskan bird book. The *Cambridge Encyclopedia of Astronomy.* The *Devil's Dictionary.*"

"The *Devil's Dictionary?*"

"Yeah. By Ambrose Bierce?" When Kate looked blank, Dinah said, "His definition of monkey is 'an arboreal animal which makes itself at home in genealogical trees.' " Kate laughed and Dinah said, "I'll dig it out on the way home."

"What have you got against fiction?"

"I don't know." Dinah thought it over, and said finally, "It's not real."

Kate looked at her, one brow raised. "I've always liked that about fiction, myself. Get in."

In first gear they bounced and jounced and bumped and thumped along the gravel road for the thirty minutes it took to navigate the two miles to another road. This one was gravel, too, but it was wide enough to take two cars at the same time, an Alaskan interstate, and Dinah said, "Slow traffic keep right."

Kate turned right, shifted into second and the

truck purred along the road, the occasional frost heave and runoff ditch nothing to compare with the game trail they'd left behind. A quarter of a mile from the turnoff the forest of scrub spruce, alder and birch changed abruptly from the exuberantly lush, leafy green of a normal Alaskan spring to blasted heath black, the trees no more than splintered stumps, branches charred and unbudded. Dinah's breath drew in sharply, and when Kate looked at her she said sheepishly, "I know, I've seen it every day for a week now. It just gets to me. Every time, it gets to me."

Two more miles of this and the road widened briefly. A sprawling building with a U.S. flag flying out front and a sign that read U.S. POST OFFICE, CHISTONA, ALASKA hung next to another sign that read CHISTONA MERCANTILE, which hung above a third sign that read, AMMUNITION, BAIT AND GROCERIES. The road narrowed again and then widened to accommodate the turnoff for a white clapboard church with a small spire. Past it, the road narrowed yet again and stayed that way for another ten miles, until they came to the gravel road's junction with the Glenn Highway. Tanada consisted of a sprawling log cabin set well back from the road. Poppies, daisies and forget-me-nots grew from the roof and a Miller sign blinked from the window. A gas pump occupied center stage of the large parking lot, which was otherwise filled with a dozen trucks and cars parked in haphazard fashion around a flatbed truck. The flatbed bore license plates from Washington State. Kate pulled in between a dusty gray International pickup with the right front fender missing and Wyoming plates and a blue Bronco with Minnesota plates packed so high with cardboard boxes and wadded-up clothes that she couldn't see through the windows.

"Look at that," Dinah said, pointing. A Subaru Brat with the gate down and boxes stacked in the bed was parked to one side of the lot with a sign advertising Avon's Skin-So-Soft for sale. Dinah looked at Kate. "Avon's Skin-So-Soft?"

Kate shrugged. "It's the best mosquito repellent around, according to some people. You get in line, I'll pack the buckets over."

"Okay." Dinah headed for the flatbed, camera in hand, and when Kate came up with two buckets there were already three people behind her. There were six in front of her. There was a scale on the back of the flatbed and a man standing next to it; behind him, a steadily rising pile of boxes attested that they had arrived just in time. Tall and thin with tired eyes, the man had a pencil behind one ear, a notepad in one hand and a wad of cash big enough to choke an elephant in the other. He was explaining, in a patient tone that told Kate that it was for the twenty-third time that day, that he was paying two dollars and two dollars only, a pound; that if he paid any more he wouldn't see any profit himself; that he'd been buying mushrooms in Tok for the last two days and didn't know who had started the three-dollar-a-pound rumor, and that the nearest ladies' room was in the Tanada Tavern but they weren't letting the pickers use it and he had a roll of toilet paper in the cab of the flatbed if the ladies wanted to use the bushes.

The door to the Tanada Tavern slammed back against the wall and two men staggered out in a drunken embrace that turned out to be a fight, although neither one was sober enough to connect a blow. Grunting and swearing, they stumbled into the line waiting in back of the flatbed, nearly trampling Kate and causing her to spill half of one of her buckets. She set the buckets down out of the way before she spilled any more. In the meantime the two pugilists had reeled off in a new direction. They didn't see the little boy standing in their way, staring at them with his mouth half open.

"Hey!" Kate took six giant steps, reaching the site of the collision at impact. The little boy went down and the two drunks went down on top of him. Kate grabbed one of them by the hair and yanked his head back and he howled and rolled off the pile. She put an ungentle foot in the other's belly and he rolled in the other direction. She picked the boy up and stood him on his feet. He swayed a little. "Are you okay?" she said. She ran her hands over him. He was covered with dust but everything felt intact and she didn't see any blood. "Kid? Are you all right? Say something."

His blue eyes were enormous and she expected them to fill with tears at any moment. His face was soft and round and she judged him to be seven or eight and tall for his age.

He didn't cry, although his indrawn breath was shaky and his voice thin. "I—no. I'm okay."

"Kate!" Dinah's voice was loud and alarmed. "Look out!"

Kate looked around in time to see one of the drunks make a clumsy rush for her, arms outspread and fists clenched. She shoved the boy backward and took a step back herself and, unable to either change his trajectory or abort his launch the drunk rushed right between them, or he would have if Kate hadn't tripped him. He sprawled in the dirt, cursing, and when he tried to get back to his feet she kicked him in the ass hard enough to send him sprawling again. He kept trying to get to his feet and she kept kicking him, all the way over to a Chevy pickup parked in front of the bar, half orange, half rust, University of Alaska plates. Ah. A scholar. She let him open the door. When he fumbled his keys out she took them away from him, assisted him into the cab of his truck with her foot and closed the door behind him. He toppled over on his right side and very wisely passed out.

She looked around for his friend, who had been terrified by the ungentle manner in which she assisted the first drunk into his truck and who was headed back to the bar for a little liquid courage.

Kate was right behind him. Inside the door, he scuttled out of her way and she walked up to the bar, behind which a big burly man stood mixing drinks. She tossed the keys on the bar and the buzz of conversation died. "It's illegal in this state to serve a drunk," she said into the silence, eyes and voice equally hard.

Somebody laughed. The bartender regarded Kate without expression for a moment, and then added a maraschino cherry to one drink and straws to all. He uncapped a bottle of beer, loaded everything on a tray and carried it away. The conversation came back up.

Kate closed her eyes, shook her head and went back outside. To her credit, Dinah had held on to their place in line. A few people gave Kate curious looks. Most were studiously examining the sky, the trees, the ground, their fingernails. The boy was gone. Kate went back to the truck for the next two buckets.

She had the truck half unloaded when the sound of her name halted her. "Katya."

She looked around. A massive figure, square-shouldered and big-bellied, clad in a dark blue house dress Kate would have sworn she'd seen her wearing when Kate was in kindergarten, stood planted in front of her as if she'd grown there. "Emaa." She hadn't seen her grandmother since April. She smiled. It was less of an effort than it used to be.

Ekaterina Moonin Shugak regarded her out of calm brown eyes, her brown face seamed with wrinkles, her black hair pulled back into a neat bun at the nape of her neck. "You are picking the mushrooms."

"Yes." Kate nodded toward the road. "I'm here with Bobby. We're camped a couple miles past Chistona. Just above the Kanuyaq."

"The fourth turnoff?"

"The fifth."

Ekaterina nodded. "Cat's Creek."

Kate, surprised, said, "I didn't know it had a name."

Not by so much as the lifting of an eyebrow did Ekaterina betray that she lived to show up her grandchildren, but Kate knew, and with difficulty repressed a smile. If it hadn't been named Cat's Creek before, it was now.

Kate nodded at the mushroom buyer standing on the back of the flatbed. "You cut a deal with him?"

Ekaterina said nothing.

"How much are we getting off the top of every pound? A dime?"

Ekaterina still said nothing, and Kate said, "More?"

Her grandmother said, in a knowledgeable manner that reminded Kate irresistibly of Bobby in all his newfound mycological expertise, "It is known that the mushrooms sell for twenty-five dollars a pound or more in stores and restaurants Outside, and up to forty dollars a pound in Europe and Japan."

"We're getting a piece of the *retail*?" Ekaterina permitted a slight smile to cross her face, equal parts satisfaction and triumph, and Kate said respectfully, "Not bad, Emaa. The last buyer was saying before he left for Tok that he figured he'd shipped thirty thousand pounds in twelve days. Not bad at all."

Ekaterina gave a faint shrug. "They are tribal lands."

"And tribal mushrooms," Kate agreed gravely, and laughed. So that was why Ekaterina was here. She would be on the scene, watching over the tribal investment, ensuring full payment in cash on the barrelhead. It was no more than Kate expected. Ekaterina never did anything for only one reason, especially when it benefited the bank account of the Niniltna Native Association, of which Ekaterina had at one time been chairman of the board, and the direction of which she still guided with an unseen but very firm hand.

Dinah was waving violently to catch Kate's eye, and when she did, she waved just as violently to beckon Kate closer. To her surprise Ekaterina accompanied her, and to her even greater surprise allowed Kate to introduce her. The fleeting thought occurred that they were both feeling their way through this new relationship, and that Ekaterina was trying as hard as she was to lay the ghost of the years of antagonism that lay between them.

"Wow," Dinah said, interrupting Kate's words without apology, swinging the omnipresent video camera to her shoulder, "Kate's granny. I could tell from fifty feet away; there's a strong family resemblance. You have the most fabulous face, Mrs. Shugak. Do you mind if I shoot a few feet? Turn your head a little to your right, that's it, we want the light to fill up those wrinkles. Has anyone ever told you you've got the greatest wrinkles?"

Ekaterina, formal words of welcome on her lips, was stopped in her tracks with her mouth open, and in spite of their new understanding Kate had to struggle against a certain inner glee. "Nope," she said out loud, "I don't think anyone's ever told Emaa that before. This is Dinah Cookman, Emaa. Dinah's a photojournalist," she explained to her grandmother in a kind voice. "She ran out of gas and stopped to pick mushrooms so she could buy enough to get her to Anchorage. Dinah, this is my grandmother, Ekaterina Shugak."

Ekaterina regarded the wide lens of the camera, about all she could see of Dinah except for the mass of strawberry blonde curls billowing out behind it, with a fascination bordering on horror that nearly upset Kate's gravity for the second time.

"It's great to meet you, Mrs. Shugak. Is that right, Mrs. Shugak?"

"Yes, it is," Ekaterina replied with a readiness that surprised Kate.

"Were you born in Alaska?"

"Yes."

"In Chistona?"

"No, Atka."

"Is that another village nearby?"

"No, it is an island in the Aleutian Chain."

"Wow," Dinah said in hushed tones. "The Aleutians. How come you still don't live there?"

"My family moved here when the Japanese invaded Attu and Kiska."

"Wow!" Dinah said. "You mean you were expatriated! I read about that!" She struggled, one-handed, with her duster, eventually producing a book Kate saw was a paperback copy of Brian Garfield's *The Thousand-Mile War*. Someday when Dinah's back was turned Kate was going to inventory the pockets of that duster, just to reassure herself there wasn't an aperture to the fourth dimension secreted in one seam.

"Ah yes," Ekaterina said, nodding, "Mr. Garfield's book. Yes, we were among those people."

"It must have been an awful experience," Dinah said soberly, focusing the lens on Ekaterina's face, "forced out of your homes, moved hundreds of miles away from everything you knew."

"I was only a child," Ekaterina said (she had probably been close to Kate's present age, Kate thought), "and it was war."

"Why didn't you go back, after?"

Ekaterina shook her head. "There was nothing to go back to. Our village had been bombed, either by

the Japanese or by the Americans so the Japanese
could not use it for shelter. And we had relatives in
Cordova and in Chenega. So we stayed."

Kate hadn't heard this many words come out of
Ekaterina's mouth all at once in years. "Enough,
Dinah," she said. "People are going to think that
thing is permanently attached."

"Okay." Dinah lowered the camera. "This tape
is almost full, anyway." Her eyes were bright and
excited. "There's stories all over this place just
walking around on two legs. See that girl over
there? She quit her job waitressing to pick mushrooms. Said she could make more money. And that
guy? He builds log homes. He says the rain made
them stop, so he's picking mushrooms instead. That
guy cuts and sells firewood, but he said he can always cut wood. He says it's been two good years
for Chistona, the first year they made money fighting the fire for the BLM, and now they're picking
mushrooms for two bucks a pound."

She hesitated, shooting Kate a doubtful glance,
and said hesitantly, as if suggesting something she
knew to be in dubious taste, "Kate, nobody around
here sets fires on purpose, do they?"

"Good heavens, no," Kate said. "Who's that
guy?" She nodded at a tall, spare man with a high,
smooth forehead and a full head of pure white hair.

Diverted, as Kate had meant her to be, Dinah
said, "The guy who looks like an Old Testament
prophet? I don't know. Kid next to him looks like

a choirboy, though, doesn't he? Say, that's the same kid, isn't it?"

It was. The boy was back, standing at the old man's elbow, his fair, soft curls clustering around rosy cheeks and blue eyes. He looked positively cherubic, and at the same time the family resemblance between the two was evident in the broad brows, in the firm chin, in the expressive blue eyes that in the boy's face were wide and curious and in the man's, stern and curiously grim. Kate wondered how long it would be before the boy's eyes became like the man's.

The boy looked up suddenly and their eyes met. He didn't blush or duck his head or grab his grandfather's leg or do any of the things children do when confronted with the interest of strangers, and Kate revised her estimate of his age upward, to ten, maybe even eleven.

Fortunately the transformation of the boy's eyes from curious to grim was no concern of hers. "Look, it's our turn. Help me lift the buckets up on the flatbed. Emaa? Are you staying with Auntie Joy?" Ekaterina nodded, and Kate said, "Tell her I'll come visit on my way home. Come on, Dinah, tote that barge, lift that bale."

Bobby cooked lavishly that evening, roasting caribou in a Dutch oven over hot coals, stirring up a raspberry vinegar–white wine sauce in the interim out of the two crates of supplies he had insisted

were essential to civilized life as we know it, at
home or in the bush. The smell made Kate's mouth
water, and was almost enough to make her forgive
him for coercing her into hauling the crates up the
hill to the campsite. The roast was served with a
morel garnish, or rather, as Bobby explained, "We
like a little meat with our mushrooms."

Dinah, her mouth full, said indistinctly, "It tastes
so good I don't want to swallow. Bobby? Marry
me."

"You only want me for my cooking."

"Damn straight. And there's no 'only' about it."

Kate didn't say anything at all. Afterward, the
three of them lay around the fire in the setting sun,
too stuffed to move, listening to thunder rumble at
them from the edge of the horizon. They could see
the rain come down from where they were, thin
gray sheets of it hanging between the campsite and
the Quilaks, turned to silver gilt by the slanting rays
of the sun. "Well," Dinah said, burping without excuse, "that beats anything I ever bought out of the
produce section at Safeway. *Agaricus bisporus* has
nothing on *Morchella elata*." Nobody asked but she
told them anyway. "*Agaricus bisporus* is the cultivated mushroom. The one you get at your local grocery store for two-ninety-eight a pound."

Kate stirred herself enough to say, "Did you bring
that desk encyclopedia you said you had in the
van?"

Dinah waved a hand in the general direction of

her backpack. With a burst of energy that left her exhausted, Kate snagged the pack by one strap and dragged it to her. The *Concise Columbia Encyclopedia* was on top of the pile inside. "Oh God," Bobby moaned, hiding his eyes, "not you, too."

"What you looking up?" Dinah said.

"Hillel," Kate replied absently. "Here he is. Hillel, flourished—I love that word, who knows now if he flourished or he withered on the vine?—from thirty B.C. to ten A.D. Born in Babylonia, he was a Jewish scholar and president of the Sanhedrin, which fostered a systematic, liberal—I wonder what liberal was in thirty B.C.?"

"Probably advocated crucifixion over burning," Bobby said lazily.

"—liberal interpretation of Hebrew Scripture, and was the spiritual and ethical leader of his generation. Shammai opposed his teachings."

"Who the hell was Shammai?"

Kate, taking that as an invitation, turned to the S's. "Shammai was a leader of the Sanhedrin who adopted a style of interpretation of Halakah that opposed the teachings of Hillel."

"So Hillel flourished in spite of Shammai," Dinah suggested.

Unheeding, Kate said, "And what, you ask, was the Halakah? It just so happens—" she turned back to the H's. "Aha. Halakah, or halacha"—she spelled it for their edification—"refers to that part of the Talmud concerned with personal, communal and international activities, as well as with religious observance. Also known as the oral Law, as codified in the Mishna." Kate turned to the M's. "Mishna, Mishna, sounds like a Hari Krishna chant. Here we go. The Mishna's the basic textbook of Jewish life and thought, covers agriculture, marriage and divorce, and all civil and criminal matters."

Dinah said, "So if you wanted to know when to plant your corn, sing a psalm, party hearty, get hitched or hang a thief, you consulted the Mishna and it told you."

"I guess."

"Sort of like the Marine Bible," Bobby said admiringly, and at Dinah's questioning look added, *The Marine Battle Skills Training Handbook.* You're issued one in boot camp. Covers everything from digging latrines to kissing brass ass. Where'd you hear about this guy Hillel?" he asked Kate.

"I was reading about him on my soap bottle," Kate replied blandly, and Bobby, after one incredulous stare, flopped back with a theatrical groan, but not without grabbing Dinah on his way down.

"May I ask you a personal question, Kate?" Dinah said, snuggling into Bobby's embrace with what Kate considered a disgustingly content expression on her face.

"No," Kate said.

"Where'd you get that scar on your throat?"

There was a brief silence. "A knife fight," Kate said finally. "Three years ago. Almost four, now."

"Tell me about it?"

Another silence. "I caught a child molester in the act. He had a knife."

Dinah winced. "Ouch."

Kate's mouth curled up at one corner, and Bobby, watching curiously, was surprised. "I'll say."

"What happened to him?"

"I took the knife away from him."

"He in jail?"

Kate shook her head. "Dead."

Dinah didn't ask how; she didn't have to.

Kate stared at the fire for a moment, and then raised her eyes, meeting the blonde's with growing awareness. "You're good."

"You sure as hell are," Bobby agreed. He'd heard that story once, the first time he'd seen the scar. Then it had been new and swollen and red and angry, especially angry, but it had paled by comparison to Kate's barely restrained, all-consuming rage. By virtue of their long friendship he had been owed an explanation. She had given one, in short, terse sentences, every word of which cost her more than she could afford to pay, and Bobby had a strong enough sense of self-preservation and a high enough value of Kate's continuing friendship never to raise the subject again.

And now this blonde, from Outside no less, the rawest of cheechakos, the most innocent of Alaskan naifs, a literal babe in the woods, had asked a few simple questions and gotten the whole story, all of it, simply and succinctly and more, gotten it without attitude or resentment. "*Real* good," he said.

She nodded, taking the compliment as simple fact, without a trace of false modesty. "I know. It's what I do." She looked beyond Kate and her face lit up. "Oh! Look!"

Kate turned and beheld a full rainbow, a slender arch of primary colors stretching from the Canadian border to Tonsina. It was a delicate, perfect thing, and the three of them were held captive by the sight. Bobby had a slight smile on his dark face, Dinah looked dazed with delight, and Kate, after a moment, recognized a feeling of proprietary pride.

The sun, taking its own sweet time, finally intersected the horizon and the rainbow began to dim. Dinah let out a sigh of pure rapture. "A full rainbow at twenty minutes past eleven in the evening. Only in Alaska."

Later, drifting off to sleep in her tent, Kate heard Bobby say in a cranky voice, "Just what the hell was the Sanhedrin, anyway?"

The next day was a repeat of the previous six at slightly lower temperatures. Mutt roused from her state of heat-induced stupor and nipped Kate's behind as she bent over a patch of morels. Kate abandoned a bucket not half full and gave chase. For fifteen minutes they played tag, moving deeper into the blackened forest and becoming totally covered in black soot, until Kate tripped over a branch and went sprawling on her face. Spitting out ash, she raised her head to see Mutt staring down at her with an expression of gathering delight. Kate could just imagine what she looked like, and told the half-breed, "You should talk! You look like you've been hit with a bucket of creosote."

Then she noticed the mushrooms. Morels, hundreds of them, thousands of them, a virtual carpet of them. She jumped to her feet. "Dinah! Bring the buckets! There be fungi here!"

One clump of mushrooms perched on an elongated mound and seemed to grow thicker there than anywhere else. Kate waded toward it and began to pick.

"Kate! Kate, where are you? I found another sign! Amos 5:24!"

"Right here! I—" Kate paused, her hands full of mushrooms. Next to her, the wolf-husky hybrid froze, head lowering between her shoulders, hackles rising, ears flattening, as a low, continuous growl issued from deep in her throat.

"Kate?" Dinah stumbled into the clearing, three empty buckets dangling from each hand. "Wow! Shroom heaven! I found another sign, Kate, Amos 5:24. Kate? What is it? What's wrong?"

"Stay there." Kate rose to her feet, and at the other woman's involuntary step forward repeated sharply, "Stay there."

"What is it?" Dinah said.

"Someone's body."

CHAPTER 2

As a safeguard, all should be eaten with a draught of olive oil and soda or lye ashes, for even the edible sorts are difficult of digestion and generally pass whole with the excrement.

—Dioscorides

"Dinah," Kate said. "Dinah?"

The blonde's face was white and pinched. Kate had to say her name a third time before she looked up from the body to meet Kate's eyes. "Go get your camera."

The blue eyes widened. "What?"

"Go get your camera," Kate repeated.

"You want me to photograph—it?" Dinah swallowed.

"Yes. Go get it."

Dinah swallowed again, opened her mouth to protest, met Kate's hard stare, closed her mouth and went to get her camera. Kate turned back to the body. Mutt, nose wrinkled, lips drawn back from her teeth, growled again. "Easy, girl."

She was squatting at what would have been the hips. Now that she knew what she was looking at, she could see the legs, the left one drawn up, a horsetail sprouting from just behind the bend of his knee. Her eyes traveled back up his torso. Both arms were outflung, as if he'd tripped and tried at the last moment to catch himself as he fell forward. The little mounds that would be his hands cradled between them half a dozen shoots of fireweed the color of lime sherbet. He was covered with black ash turning silver, dissolving into the forest floor, becoming one flesh with the earth, fertilizing the fireweed, fodder for *Morchella esculenta*.

There was something about his pose, the raised knee, the outflung arms, a sense of vulnerability. Dead, almost literally ashes to ashes, he seemed still to be moving, still to be in flight. Flight from what? Had he been chased by a bear? Running in front of the fire?

She frowned. When had it become a he?

A moment later Dinah came crashing back. Breathing hard, she skidded to a halt next to Kate and raised the camera. "What do you want me to shoot?"

"Can you get me and the body in the same shot?"

Dinah backed up a step, another, focusing the lens. "Yes."

Kate raised her voice. "I'm Kate Shugak, it's June sixteenth, the location is just under two miles east of Cat's Creek." She pointed. "That's north. Chis-

tona is about a mile that way cross-country. It's—"
she looked at her watch "—nine forty-five A.M.
Dinah Cookman and I were picking mushrooms
when I stumbled across the body." She looked over
her shoulder. "Is the mike picking up my voice?"

Dinah, her voice steadier now that she was viewing things through a lens, said, "Yes."

"Can you get a shot of the whole clearing?"

"Yeah." Dinah panned slowly around, coming to
rest again on Kate and the body.

"From the width of the shoulders and hips I'd
guess male. Can't tell race or age. He doesn't appear
to be much burned, the fire must have jumped a
spot here. There's plenty of ash, though, and from
the ash and the mushrooms growing in the ash I'd
say he's been here since last summer. Something's
been chewing on his ass, probably after death, probably before freeze-up." She took a breath, held it,
and leaned closer to pluck a few mushrooms free.
Ash came up with them, leaving a gash of putrefy-
ing human flesh behind. There was no mistaking
that smell, ever. Even with her breath held against
it Kate felt it invading her nostrils, her lungs. Mutt,
with olfactory senses ten times more evolved than
her own, gave a distressed whine and backed up to
stand beside Dinah.

"Decay is advanced," Kate said tightly. Pulling
her sleeve down over her hand, she held her breath
and reached out to lift up an arm. There was a
sickening, sucking sound. For one horrible moment

Kate feared that the arm had separated from the body at the shoulder. "There doesn't appear to be any ash beneath the body, so my best guess is it was here before last year's fire. Probably caught out in the fire. Dumb bastard."

Something tickled at the back of her brain, some unanswered question that jumped up and down and demanded her attention, but the smell was increasing and increasingly bad and she was afraid if she didn't back off she would vomit. She rose, brushing ash from her knees, and looked at Dinah. "You can quit."

Dinah lowered the camera, relief on her face. "You're not going to look closer?"

"He'll fall apart if I roll him over."

"Kate?"

"What?"

"Why didn't the bears get him?"

"What?"

"You said they'd eat anything that would sit still for it." She jerked her chin at the body. "Why not him?"

"Good question," Kate said, wishing one had. "They would have, if they'd stumbled across him first."

"Instead of which, we did."

"Just lucky, I guess," Kate agreed. "It may be he just this week thawed out. It stayed cold late this year, and the dirt and the ash forms a pretty good layer of insulation. Not to mention the mushrooms.

Even Mutt didn't smell it until we were right on it. During the winter—" She shrugged. "Bears sleep through the winter, body's frozen and snowed over. He'd sit until spring."

"And last fall?"

"Last fall there was a forest fire. Wasn't much in the way of any kind of life, wild or otherwise, around after that. What was did some chewing on his butt." She pointed. Dinah didn't look. "Give me the tape."

Dinah ejected the tape and handed it over. Kate took it and headed for camp, leaving the half-filled bucket behind. She wasn't sure she would ever be able to pick another mushroom again as long as she lived.

Bobby took one look at her face and said one word. "What?"

Kate jerked her head. "We found a body."

He stared. "You kidding me."

She shook her head. His gaze slid past her to Dinah, regarded her pale face for a frowning moment, and came back to Kate, examining the tense hold she had on her wide mouth, the tight look around her eyes. She'd picked up her pack and was slipping the tape inside. "You going for Chopper Jim?"

She nodded, zipping the pack closed.

"You okay?" She nodded again, and he shook his head, a disgusted expression crossing his face. "Sorry. Stupid question." He caught her hand and gave it a brief squeeze. "But you will be." He was rewarded with a small smile. "And we were having such a good time," he said, adding bitterly, "It's positively disgraceful, Shugak, the way bodies follow you around."

The smile was more genuine this time. She slung the pack. "The nearest phone's at the junction. I'll be back as soon as I can." She looked at Dinah.

Young as she was, the blonde was quick. She swallowed hard. "You want me to go back and see that nothing disturbs the body."

Kate gave a small shrug. "It's been out there going on a year already."

"But still," Dinah said.

"But still," Kate agreed.

Dinah swallowed again. "Okay."

"Can my chair make it out there?" Bobby said.

Dinah's face lightened. "We can try."

"Then let us do so."

"I'll be back as soon as I can," Kate said again, and headed out.

Tanada was sleepy in the hot noon sun. The mushroom wholesaler's flatbed stood alone in the parking lot. The only living thing in sight was a bald eagle roosting in the top of a scrub spruce.

The tavern was equally deserted. It was a different bartender than the one of the previous afternoon, a sad-looking man of forty with two wisps of lank, dark hair descending from his upper lip that were trying hard to look like a mustache. He polished a glass and rode along with Dwight Yoakum, sitting in the back of a long, white Cadillac. He raised eyes to Kate that looked as sorrowful as his singing voice sounded. "Phone?" she said. Without missing a beat his head nodded toward a corner.

She dialed the operator and asked for the trooper office in Tok. When they answered she asked for Jim Chopin and they put her on hold. Next to her Mutt flopped down with less than her usual grace, the heat starting to get to her again. While they were waiting a couple came in the door. They were middle-aged and wide-eyed and had the air of something indefinably foreign about them. Maybe it was the way the woman wore her clothes, casual yet too elegant to be American. Maybe it was the way the man carried his chin, up and ever so slightly arrogant. Maybe it was the tiny, exquisitely manicured poodle, his topknot caught up in a red sateen bow, cradled in the woman's arms and staring about him with beady little eyes.

"Bonjour," the man said to the bartender.

The bartender looked blank.

"Hello?" a voice said in Kate's ear.

She straightened and turned her face toward the wall. "Jim?"

The voice was deep, slow and calm. "Kate? Is that you?"

"Yes."

"Hey, lady. Where you at?"

"Tanada."

A thread of amusement crept into the deep voice. "You picking mushrooms?"

"I was."

There was a brief silence. Like Bobby, Jim knew Kate rather well. "What's up?"

"I found a body."

The voice sharpened. "Where?"

"Cat's Creek."

A pause. "Where's Cat's Creek?"

"Fifth turnoff south of Chistona."

"Oh." There was another pause, while Kate imagined him looking at a map. His next words confirmed it. "Okay, I got it."

"How soon can you be here?"

"If I fly straight to Tanada, an hour. You wait for me, give me a ride in?"

"Yeah. Jim?"

"What?"

"Body's been there a while."

"How long?"

"It's covered with ash."

He was silent for a moment. "So you think it was somebody caught out in the fire last year?"

"Looks that way."

"Okay, I'll see you in a bit."

"Bring a mask. Bring two." She hung up. On the tape deck, Dwight Yoakum had moved from the Cadillac to the honky-tonk, and two glasses of white wine had materialized on the bar. The woman reached for hers and took a small sip. An involuntary sound escaped her and she looked distressed. "Monsieur," her husband said to the bartender, "you tell moi, uh, where me find un traineau à chiens? For picture?" The bartender looked blank, and the man looked thwarted.

Eons before, back in the Stone Age, Kate had fulfilled the foreign language requirement for her B.A. with four semesters of French. Somewhat to her own surprise she discovered an ambition to try it out, thought up what might be a recognizable sentence and walked up to the man and tapped him on the shoulder. "Pardonnez-moi, monsieur? Peut-être je vous aiderai?"

They turned to her in surprise, and she repeated herself. Mutt stood next to her, panting slightly. The poodle, regarding them both with disfavor, let out a sharp yip pitched so high it hurt Kate's eardrums. Mutt returned no reply, merely fixed a considering yellow gaze on the other dog, still panting, maybe showing a centimeter more canine than was absolutely necessary but otherwise remaining calm.

The woman, intercepting that considering yellow stare, clutched the poodle closer to her breast. "Pauvre petit chien. C'est bien, petit, c'est bien." She gave Mutt a hostile glance, and seemed ready to include Kate in it until Kate repeated herself, this time speaking more slowly, taking more care with her pronunciation. Surprise gave way to comprehension. For a moment the notorious French disdain for their mother tongue spoken atrociously warred with the desire for rational communication. Communication won. Speaking slowly and carefully, enunciating every syllable with care in a manner that left Kate in little doubt that the intervening years had not been kind to whatever accent she might once have possessed, Monsieur gave a little bow and said, "Bonjour, mademoiselle. Vous parlez français?"

"Un peu seulement," she said, the only phrase she remembered word-perfect twelve years after her last class, "et pas pour un long, long fois."

He winced a little but covered it up immediately. Everyone shook hands, the poodle taking a surreptitious nip at Kate's when Kate let go of Madame's. He missed Kate but he didn't miss Monsieur. Monsieur snatched his hand back and dog and man exchanged a malevolent glance. Madame's stare was suspicious, and Monsieur quickly smoothed his own expression into an acceptable blandness.

From the other red marks on the back of Monsieur's hand Kate deduced that this wasn't the first time Pauvre Petit Chien had taken his best shot. From Monsieur's evident willingness to put up with the attacks, she further deduced Madame and Monsieur's relationship to be in its earlier stages. Not for nothing had Kate once been the star of the Anchorage D.A.'s investigator's office.

It looked like a case of love her, love her dog. Or aimez elle, aimez sa chien. Pleased with herself, Kate said, "Qu'est-ce que vous voulez? What do you want?"

They brightened a little. Monsieur held up a camera. "Pour prendre un picture d'un traineau à chiens."

To take a picture of something, but what? Chien meant dog, but traineau? A train? "Oh." Kate's brow cleared. "A dog sled? You want to take a picture of a dog sled? Like the Iditarod?" Their faces broke into smiles and they nodded vigorously and Kate was sorry she had to disappoint them. "Je regrette, monsieur, il n'y a pas de dogsleds running during, uh—" What was the word? Madame Buss-Stowell would be disgusted with her, not that Kate, whose tongue was better suited for Aleut gutturals than French nasals, had ever been one of Madame's star pupils "—le summer. I mean, l'été." She shook her head from side to side. "Pas de dogsleds de chien pendant l'été. No dogsleds during the summer."

Their faces fell. "Pourquoi?"

"No snow in the summer," she said.

After a puzzled moment he got it. "Ah. Pas de neige."

"Neige," Kate said, nodding. "No neige during the summer. Not at this altitude, anyway."

"Ah." They thought for a moment, exchanged a phrase or two, and turned back to her. "Eh bien. Y-a-t'il un maison d'Esquimau ici, peut-être?"

A picture of a little Japanese man, waddling like Charlie Chaplin and shouting, "Bangoon! Bangoon!" in the Prudhoe Bay airport terminal three months before flashed through her mind, and she gave a sudden laugh. Well, maison was house. House of Eskimo. "Igloo?" Kate hazarded, and when they nodded again, smiled back, she said, even more apologetically, "Je regrette, pas de igloos, either. Only Eskimos build igloos, and there aren't any around here. Eskimos, I mean. Although there aren't any igloos, either." She tugged at the front of her sooty T-shirt, the neckline of which seemed to have gotten a little tighter.

Madame was starting to get a little indignant. "Pas de traineau à chiens?" Kate shook her head. "Pas de igloo?" Kate shook her head, and the woman snorted and tossed off a paragraph that Kate had no trouble interpreting as, "Then what the hell are we doing here?"

Monsieur, displaying a touching anxiety to please that confirmed Kate's belief that their relationship was in its infancy, turned back to Kate. By now she was almost as anxious as he was to find something intrinsically Alaskan for him to photograph. "Aha!"

"Yes?" Kate said eagerly. "Qu'est-ce que c'est?"

"Ici, here, c'est la terre de le soleil de minuit." He beamed at her, and with a sinking heart Kate realized what was coming. "Me photographie, ah, le couchant du soleil de minuit. Ou, um, where le meilleur view he is?" He looked at her expectantly.

Alaska was the land of the midnight sun all right, but it was the middle of June. Why hadn't she minded her own business and gone outside to wait for Chopper Jim? "Monsieur, sorry, but the sun doesn't set right now, uh, il ne couche pas maintenant."

He was incredulous. "Le soleil ne couche pas *jamais?*"

"No, no, not *never,* the sun will set, just not this month. Or not much, or not enough to take a picture of . . ." Her voice trailed away when she looked at them. Monsieur was crushed, Madame piqued, the poodle still assessing the distance between his teeth and Kate's ankle. "Je regrette mille fois," Kate said, and escaped.

Outside, she collapsed on a bench on the porch and mopped a heated brow. "That's the last time I try my hand at interpretation," she told Mutt.

Mutt flopped down next to the bench, mouth open, panting. She looked pitiful.

"I couldn't agree more," Kate told her.

It was hot, too hot, so hot even the dust lay unresisting when a car trundled down the road. She squinted around for a thermometer. There was a big white round one with large numbers that told her it was a sizzling seventy-nine degrees Fahrenheit. Funny, it hadn't felt that hot until she saw proof positive, but now the sweat trickled down her back in an unending stream, pooling at the base of her spine. "Give me twenty below anytime," she muttered.

She leaned back, looking in vain for even the wisp of a cloud. The eagle was still roosting in his treetop, and he looked pissed, but that was an eagle's natural expression and so Kate couldn't put it down wholly to the weather. There was a rustle of undergrowth and she turned to see a cow moose browsing in the alder thicket at the edge of the gravel lot. Two soft-nosed calves stood next to her on wobbly legs, nuzzling at mama's belly. Kate wondered how anybody could be hungry at this temperature.

The tavern door opened and Monsieur, Madame and Pauvre Petit Chien came out and saw mother and children at the same moment. There was a loud exclamation and a torrent of excited language, not one word in ten of which did Kate catch or need to. Mama moose looked around in mild bemusement, a strip of leaves hanging out of one side of her mouth. Neither calf, having reached Nirvana, paused in their busy suckling.

"Oooohhh!" Madame cooed, which meant the same thing in any language. She dropped the poodle and trotted off across the parking lot. The poodle yipped and tore after her.

Mutt's ears went straight up. The dangers of heat exhaustion forgotten, Kate surged to her feet. "Hey! Wait! Don't do that! DON'T!"

Monsieur gaped at the scene, Madame never turned around and the poodle, yipping hysterically, bounced in the rear on tiny legs, trying frantically to catch up. Kate and Mutt took off in hot pursuit but neither of them had gotten up enough speed to intercept by the time Madame reached the moose and stretched out a hand to pet one of the calves.

Madame stood five feet five inches tall in her two-inch heels and at best guess weighed in at 115 pounds wringing wet. *Alces alces* stands on average five and a half feet high at the shoulder, measures nine feet stem to stern and weighs in anywhere from 800 to 1,400 pounds on the hoof. Bull moose have big racks they use to bang on each other with in rut that can weigh as much as 85 pounds all by themselves; because she lacks this rack the cow is not to be considered less dangerous, especially if she has two newborn calves fastened to the faucets. In Kate's experience, no female of any species was to be trifled with fresh out of the delivery room. "For God's sake, madame, HOLD IT!"

Mama moose watched that human hand reach out for baby, waited until the range was just right and let fly with her left rear hoof. It caught Madame squarely in the solar plexus. She flew backward, in what Kate was pleased to identify (from a different class lo those many years ago), as an arc, or any part of a curve that does not intersect itself. This arc intersected all right, with the ground, hard. Kate, reaching Madame, stooped and without cer-

emony grabbed one of her arms and hauled her to
her feet. She hooked the arm around her waist and
started moving as fast as she could toward the
porch. Behind her she heard Mutt give one short,
sharp warning bark. Monsieur, recovering from the
shock that had kept him immobile with his mouth
open, rushed forward and supported Madame on
the other side. Together they got back to the porch
and safely behind the railing. Kate dumped Madame, who had yet to inhale, on the bench and
turned to look. Mama was back at the alder and
baby was back at the faucet.

Kate blew out a breath and turned, relief giving
way to anger. "Don't you EVER do anything that
stupid again! Have you no sense? You're lucky she
didn't charge you! She could have knocked you on
your ass and tap danced on your breastbone until
there wasn't enough left to scrape up with a
spoon!"

She came to herself enough to realize that she was
yelling, which never got anybody anywhere, and
that she was yelling in English, which in this case
would get her nowhere faster than that. She took a
deep breath and gathered her composure. "Never,"
she said carefully, "never, never, never pet the
moose. Comprenez-moi, madame? Jamais, jamais,
jamais pet le moose."

At that moment Madame got her breath back in
one enormous "WHOOOSH!" gulping in air like a
bellows, breast heaving.

There was another "WHOOOSH" and for a moment Kate thought it also had come from Madame, but something was off in the direction the sound came from, which was behind her. She heard a high-pitched, terror-stricken yip and turned to see the eagle, launching itself from the top of the scrub spruce, glide down and snatch up the poodle in its talons. "Yip, yip, yip," went the poodle, flap, flap, flap went the eagle's wings, and the last anyone ever saw of Pauvre Petit Chien, except for maybe Mama Eagle's hungry offspring, was him dangling below the great flapping wings as he disappeared over the tops of the trees to the south.

Madame started screaming, first at Kate, then at Monsieur, then at Kate again. It didn't take an advanced degree in French to figure out the content, not when you took the hand gestures in context. Monsieur kept his head bent against the storm and his eyes fixed on the ground; Kate felt sorry for him but Mutt felt sorrier and uttered one deep, brief "WOOF."

It was remarkable the attention one woof got when it came from a half-husky, half-wolf hybrid with a set of healthy white teeth, most of which were displayed to advantage in a wide, panting grin. Madame stopped screaming in mid-invective, glaring from Mutt to Kate to Monsieur, who was still regarding the ground with fascination. Ten long, slow seconds ticked by. With an angry sob Madame whirled and stumbled to the car.

Monsieur stirred. Kate touched his arm. "Je regrette, monsieur, je regrette mille fois, but—" He looked up and the words caught in her throat. Monsieur was working hard to look subdued but there was a definite twinkle lurking at the back of his eyes. "Monsieur?" she said uncertainly.

He gave another bow, caught her hand in his, the one covered with red tokens of Pauvre Petit Chien's affection, and raised it to his lips. It was the first time Kate had ever had her hand kissed and after she got over the shock she kind of enjoyed it, which was a good thing, because he kissed it again. "Bonjour, mademoiselle," he said warmly. "Merci mille fois pour un visite très agréable." He pressed her hand between both of his and smiled. "Très, *très* agréable."

He released her hand, marched to the car with a stride like William the Conqueror, opened the driver's side door, told Madame to move over to the passenger seat, got in, started the car and drove off, pulling onto the road with a definite flourish. A moment later there was nothing but a thin, ephemeral haze of dust hanging a foot above the ground to show where they had been.

Kate tried to fight it and lost. Her head fell back and she started to laugh, large, loud whoops that echoed off the parking lot and mildly alarmed Mama Moose. Her eyes streamed, her belly hurt, she gasped for breath and off she went again. And that was how Chopper Jim found her when the Bell Jet Ranger settled down in front of the gas pump.

"Phew."

"Yeah, I know," Kate said, voice muffled behind the mask.

Chopper Jim, immaculate in dark blue pants with a gold stripe down the outside seams, dark blue tie knotted meticulously over pale blue shirt, tie clipped with a gold seal of the State of Alaska, flat brim of his round-crowned hat adjusted at precisely the right angle, stood with his hands riding his gun belt, pistol grip gleaming in the afternoon sun. He looked trim and calm and authoritative. He wasn't even sweating. Kate resented it.

They stood in the little clearing, the acrid scent of the morels losing to the rising stench of fleshy decay.

His calm, level gaze matched his voice. "You clear away some of the mushrooms?"

"Enough to be sure of what I was looking at. Dinah got it all on the tape. Dinah Cookman, Jim Chopin. He's the state trooper assigned to the Park."

He looked past her at the blonde. "How do."

She met his eyes, pale but composed. "Sir."

His smile had too much charm and far too many teeth in it for any woman in her right mind to trust. It was also guaranteed of effect. Kate, who con-

gratulated herself on her own immunity to that
smile every chance she got, watched with something
between exasperation and amusement as a pink
flush began somewhere below Dinah's collar and
rose to her cheeks. "Call me Jim," he said in his
deep voice.

"Jim," she said obediently, a stunned look in her
dazed blue eyes. Kate cleared her throat and Dinah
blinked. "Right. Yes. Uh, Bobby says overnight
temperatures have dropped below forty every night
until last Wednesday."

Jim dropped his gaze back to the body. "Which
is why it's only just starting to smell." He produced
a pair of white rubber gloves and pulled them on.
Walking around to the head of the body, he squat-
ted and reached out to pluck more mushrooms out
of the way. "I didn't know mushrooms would grow
on flesh."

Behind them Dinah cleared her throat. "Sapro-
bic." Chopper Jim looked at her and she blushed
again but retained enough composure to produce
from the bottomless pocket of her gray duster a
book Kate recognized as *Fun with Fungi*. "Means
mushrooms that live on decayed vegetable or animal matter. A lot of them do."

Chopper Jim gave her an approving smile, and
her blush deepened. "Although these aren't necessarily growing off the, er, body."

"Why not?"

"Mushrooms propagate themselves through

spores. The spores germinate into threads called mycelia. Some mycologists believe that the mycelia are always present, and that it only takes the requisite conditions to bring the fruiting bodies, that is, the mushrooms, forth."

Jim's warm gaze rested on Dinah's face. "And what are the requisite conditions?"

"Well." Dinah paged through the book. "It says here that when the temperature gets up to between forty degrees and sixty degrees Fahrenheit and there has been a lot of rain, but not too much, the strings begin to generate the caps and stems, or the fruiting bodies of the mushroom."

The trooper looked back at the body, a meditative expression on his face.

"These are morels," Dinah volunteered. "They're not exactly predictable, but they do tend to show up the year following a forest fire, if the fire was in the spring or the fall, and if the rain comes along at exactly the right moment and in exactly the right amounts."

"Temperamental little buggers, aren't they," Jim murmured.

"Yes. They can't be grown domestically."

He reached out one hand and brushed at what might have been a shoulder. Dinah flinched. His brows snapped together, and he plucked some more, clearing the area that might have been the remains of someone's back. He pulled, carefully, at the burned, decaying flesh, until it separated into what might have been a torso and an arm. He moved to the feet and brushed them free of fungi and ash, and stood looking, a frown drawing his eyebrows together in a straight line.

Kate moved to stand next to him, staring. "Dammit, that was what was tickling my funny bone. I knew there was something strange."

"What?" Dinah said, coming a step closer.

"He doesn't have any clothes on."

Kate helped Chopper Jim roll the body into a body bag and tote it back to the truck. She drove him back to Tanada and helped load it into the chopper. He paused, one hand on the door. "Where'd you pick up the blonde?"

"We didn't," Kate said, and when he raised one eyebrow said reluctantly—but after all, Bobby was a grown man and Dinah was a grown woman and it wasn't like it was love ever after now, was it— "She picked us up, at our first delivery. She drove up the AlCan this spring and ran out of money paying Canada prices for gas. She stopped to pick mushrooms to earn enough to get her to Anchorage."

"What's she do?"

"I think she just got out of school."

"Looking for adventure in whatever comes her way?"

Reluctantly, Kate had to laugh. "I don't think she waits for it to come to her."

"My kind of woman." He hoisted himself up into the pilot's seat and spoke again, one hand on the open door. "I'm flying direct to Anchorage."

She nodded. "I'll call tomorrow."

"I'll push it, but you know Metzger."

She almost smiled.

"Something else," he said.

"What?"

He readjusted his hat to throw a more perfectly aligned shadow over his face. Beneath the flat brim, his eyes were keen and direct. "I checked before I left. There are no missing person reports from Chistona. Not this year. Not last year. Not the year before. The closest I've got is a report of a missing wife from Tok, and I know where she is, and she doesn't want to be found."

"No one else?"

He shook his head. "No one. Everybody for a hundred miles around is present and accounted for."

Her brow creased. "What about smokejumpers? Were any lost during the fire last year?"

"Nope." He smiled faintly at her expression. "I know. Why isn't anything ever easy?"

She stood back and listened to the whine of the engine, felt the breeze generated by the increasing spin of the rotors, watched as the craft rose up vertically and lifted out over the trees, bound south-southwest.

CHAPTER 3

Fungi which grow in the meadows are best; it is not well to trust others.

—Horace

B obby looked offended. "Excuse me. Are you trying to con me into believing this guy was shroomed to death?"

Kate smiled involuntarily. "No, Bobby. Just that he's been there a while."

He cocked an intelligent eyebrow in her direction and stopped fooling around. "You think he got caught in the fire."

She frowned at the can of pop in her hand. "That's what I thought at first."

"What made you change your mind?"

"There was no ash beneath his body. And he doesn't have any clothes on."

He stared at her. "What?"

"He doesn't have any clothes on," Kate repeated.

"Shoes, shorts, nothing. He's naked."

He thought this over, frowning in his turn. "Maybe he was swimming in the creek," he said, jerking a thumb over his shoulder. "Maybe he underestimated the speed of the fire and it caught up with him and he made a run for it and didn't make it."

"Maybe."

"You don't sound convinced."

Kate swallowed some Diet 7-Up. It went down cold and clean and not too sweet. "Aside from the fact that that kind of behavior is almost too dumb to believe—"

"Almost but not quite," he interrupted, "as you well know from thirty-three years of personal experience in the Alaskan bush."

"Aside from that fact," she repeated, "Chopper Jim says there are no reports of missing persons within a hundred miles of Chistona."

And Bobby, of course, said immediately, "How about smokejumpers? There were over a hundred of them fighting that fire last fall."

"He's checking. He doesn't think so."

"What do you think happened?"

"I don't know," she said firmly, "and what's more, I don't care." She grinned at him. "I'm more interested in what's for dinner. What is for dinner?"

"Yeah," Dinah said, "I'm starved."

So Bobby whipped up a moose pot roast with potatoes and onions and carrots and celery and no mushrooms. They emptied the pot and sat back, watching the fire burn down to red coals and the sun travel around the horizon, which reminded Kate of her close encounter of the third kind with the French aliens.

"Nature red in tooth and claw," Dinah said, a little awed, but not as awed as she would have been before their own close encounter with the bear.

When Bobby stopped laughing he said, his natural bellow restored, "Good for the moose! And good for that goddam eagle, too! Fuck the French every chance we get is what I say!"

"What have you got against the French?" Dinah wanted to know.

"Everything!" Bobby bellowed. "Dien Bien Phu! Ho Chi Minh! They stuck us with Ngo Dinh Diem and never looked back!"

"Who?" Dinah said.

He was arrested in mid-roar and stared at her. It was one of the few times Kate had ever seen Bobby Clark lose his cool. "How old did you say you were?"

She smiled at him, half urchin, half siren. "Old enough."

"I oughtta demand to see some ID," he mumbled and leaned back against a tree, conveying the impression that he was no longer young enough to sit upright, and as an afterthought snagged Dinah on his way back. He tucked in his chin to peer at her. "You know who Jerry Lewis is?"

Dinah said, a little stiffly, "Of course I know who Jerry Lewis is."

"Well," Bobby said with relish, "the French *like* Jerry Lewis. They think he's a *genius*."

"So do I," Dinah said, even more stiffly.

"Good God!"

Kate wondered if the happy couple was going to survive the night. A movement at the edge of the clearing caught her eye and she looked up.

Standing just inside the ring of trees, face gleaming whitely in the half-twilight, a young boy stared gravely back at her.

It was the choirboy from Chistona.

The three of them gaped at him.

Kate opened her mouth but the boy beat her to it. "Are you Kate Shugak?"

Startled, Kate said, "Yes."

His blue eyes looked past her, at Bobby, lingering on the black skin and the thigh stumps, and at Dinah, at her white skin and the way she snuggled into the crook of Bobby's arm, before returning to Kate. "*The* Kate Shugak?"

Amused, Kate said gravely, "I believe so."

"The one who got the bootlegger in Niniltna that time?"

Kate's eyes narrowed. "Yes."

The boy gave a single, crisp nod, and Dinah sat up and unobtrusively reached for the camera. "My grandfather says you were an agent of God." He paused and added, sounding for the first time like his age, "Everybody else says you're the best." He met her eyes squarely. "I should have thanked you yesterday."

"No need."

He shook his head and said sternly, "Thank you."

"You're welcome," Kate murmured, since it was obviously expected.

"Who the hell are you," Bobby demanded, "and what are you doing out alone at this time of night?"

Dinah rolled film. Kate was struck again at how poised the boy was. In her experience few adults reached that level of self-possession. He looked eight, acted twelve or older and was probably ten. She wondered what had caused the early onset of maturation. She wondered if she wanted to know.

"Well?" Bobby said. "What's your name? Where's your folks?"

The boy ignored him, fixing Kate again with that unnerving blue stare. "My name is Matthew Seabolt. I want you to find my father."

For a moment the campsite was still but for the hum of Dinah's camera.

All trace of amusement gone, Kate eyed the boy, who stood unflinching, meeting her look for look. "Your father is missing?"

He nodded.

"For how long?"

"Since last August."

The camera never paused. Bobby stirred and shot

Kate a look. She gave him a slight shake of her head and he subsided. "Who is your father?"

"His name is Daniel. Daniel Seabolt."

"And he's been missing ten months, almost a year?"

The boy nodded, and Kate stared at him, a frown creasing her brow. Chopper Jim had said there were no missing person reports from anywhere in the area. "Does your father live in Chistona?"

"Yes."

Again Bobby stirred and again Kate shot him a quelling look. "And your mother?"

His voice was flat. "She's dead."

"I'm sorry," Kate said automatically. She thought. "So if your father's missing and your mother's dead, who do you live with?"

"My grandfather. Simon Seabolt."

This time Bobby would not be silenced. "That preacher guy from the Chistona Little Chapel?"

The boy nodded, and Dinah stopped rolling and said, "Was he the man you were with yesterday afternoon at the Tanada Tavern?"

The boy nodded again, and Dinah shot Kate a triumphant look. "Told you he looked like an Old Testament prophet."

Not so sotto voce Bobby muttered, "A Bible-thumper. Just what we need. Jesus Christ."

The boy looked disapproving.

Kate said, "Does your grandfather know where your father went?"

He shook his head. "Nobody does. They woke up one morning and he was gone."

"You haven't heard anything from him?"

The boy shook his head again. "No one has."

"He didn't leave a note?"

Another shake.

"He hasn't written you or your grandfather?"

A third shake.

It sounded to Kate like the usual case of drop-out syndrome, but for the body in the mushrooms. *The Body in the Mushrooms;* it sounded like the title of an Agatha Christie novel. She wondered what Miss Marple would have thought of this case. Not that this was a case, or anything remotely resembling one, she reminded herself, and contradicted that thought with her next question. "Matthew," she said carefully, keeping her ruined voice as gentle as she could, "your father has been missing for over a year. I'm sure your grandfather has talked to the state troopers, and if they can't—" She stopped. The boy was shaking his head, a very definite shake, back and forth, one time only, but for all that, a gesture that held absolute certainty. "He didn't talk to the troopers?"

Matthew didn't reply, just shook his head.

"If he didn't talk to the troopers, Matthew," she said as gently as she knew how, "chances are he knows where your father is. If he didn't file a missing person's report, it might mean that your father doesn't want to be found."

He shook his head some more.

Kate, unadmiring of the rigid set of his spine, said, "Then what does your grandfather think happened to your father?"

The blue eyes didn't waver and the young voice had lost none of its moral certainty. "He doesn't know."

Not only was the spine rigid, the jaw was outthrust and pugnacious. Kate regarded both for a long, thoughtful moment. If the kid got any more tense he might break. "How did you get here?"

"On my bike."

"Your grandfather know where you are?"

He shook his head and she sighed.

"We'd better get you home before he finds out you're gone and starts to worry." She rose to her feet and dusted off the seat of her pants.

"I can ride home."

She gave him an affable smile. "Sure you can. With me, in my truck. We'll put your bike in the back."

He hesitated a moment before giving in. "Okay." She got the impression he had more to say, but a sidelong glance at Dinah, face hidden behind her camera, and a glowering, hostile Bobby restrained him. "God bless you both, brother and sister."

"I'm not your brother," Bobby snapped.

"We are all brothers and sisters in the eyes of the Lord."

Kate got the boy down the hill before Bobby

melted his ears. As she lifted the fat-tired mountain bike into the back of the pickup the boy said, "*I'm hiring you.*"

The bike settled into the bed of the pickup with ease. She looked up and met the steady blue gaze. "You mean your grandfather isn't."

"No." He said it firmly, without equivocation.

She looked at him in silence for a moment. He stood there like Peter at the gates, inflexible, unyielding, unswerving in his devotion to duty. Only the righteous and the godly got by.

"All right," she said at last. "Get in."

In the half-dawn, half-dusk twilight that passes for night in Alaska in the summer, it took Kate that much longer to negotiate the distance between the turnaround and Chistona. The store and the church were deserted. "No, don't," the boy said sharply when Kate would have pulled into the parking lot next to the church. "Drive a little down the road."

"That your grandfather's house?" Kate nodded at the log cabin sitting in back of the simple white frame church. He said it was, and she said, "Then here we stop and I don't move until I see you inside the front door."

His lips tightened. "Okay, but you can't come in."

"I don't want to," she said, opening the door and getting out. She pulled the bike out of the back and stood it up.

He took it from her and looked up at her, hesitating. "Will you find my father for me?"

Kate didn't have the heart to tell him she was fairly certain she already had. Time enough for that when she was sure. "Yes."

Leaning the bike against his hip, he dug in the pocket of his jeans and produced a fistful of crumpled bills. "Here," he said. "I can pay."

"Good," she said, and accepted the money. When she counted it later it came to thirty-four dollars, all in dollar bills, all covered with the grime that is standard issue in ten-year-old pockets.

"It's my money," he said, anxious for the first time. "I earned it myself, picking mushrooms."

"Good for you. Kid," she said when he would have turned away.

"What?"

"You know who your father's dentist was?"

He looked surprised. "Sure. Dr. White."

"Where's he at?"

"Fairbanks. We drive up for checkups, once a year." He paused, and said, "Was that part of the investigation?"

She never lied to a client. "Yes." She prayed he wouldn't ask why.

All he said was, "So you're hired."

"Looks like," Kate agreed, relieved, and watched as he leaned his bike against the cabin wall and went inside.

• • •

Back at camp Dinah said meditatively, "He's kind of like the Blues Brothers, isn't he."

Bobby and Kate both swiveled to look at her, identical expressions of incredulity on their faces. "He's on a mission from God," the blonde explained.

"I don't know about that," Kate said. "I do know he's scared to death about something."

"He's a sanctimonious little shit," Bobby said shortly.

"He's a client," Kate said.

"So? Doesn't make him any less sanctimonious." And with that Bobby crawled into his tent. Dinah looked at Kate, gave an uncomprehending shrug, and crawled after him.

"Like we thought. No shirt, no pants, no shoes, nothing," Chopper Jim said. "Guy didn't have a stitch on him."

"What was he doing out in a forest fire with no clothes on?" Kate said.

Dinah smacked a mosquito. "What was he doing out without any clothes on, period? These damn bugs would have eaten him alive."

Chopper Jim rewarded her with a wide smile. She wilted visibly, which was what Kate was pretty sure he'd flown up for this Sunday morning and buzzed the camp, setting the chopper down in a burned-out clearing a quarter of a mile away, instead of letting her phone in for the information on Monday. Bobby, predictably, bristled. Kate said, "Cause of death?" confidently expecting a reply of, "Smoke inhalation."

She didn't get it. Chopper Jim allowed the smile to linger on Dinah just long enough before turning it on Kate. A sensible woman, she distrusted it on sight, and her distrust was fully justified by his next two words. "Anaphylactic shock."

"What?"

"What?" Bobby said, startled.

"What's anaphylactic shock?" Dinah said, and turned immediately to search in vain for *The Concise Columbia Encyclopedia*. Thwarted, she reached for her camera.

Chopper Jim made a pretense of scanning his notebook but Kate knew that steel-trap mind had it all memorized, indexed and filed, on tap for instant recall. "Anaphylaxis is a physical reaction certain people have to certain substances, among them certain drugs, maybe penicillin, insulin, even aspirin, or certain foods, maybe shellfish, maybe strawberries, or certain insect bites. Bee stings, mostly."

"Bee stings?"

"Mostly. Upon exposure, the onset of anaphylaxis is sudden and severe, beginning with a constriction of the airways and the blood vessels. Other symptoms parallel allergic reactions, itching eyes, plugged-up nose, hives, swollen lips and tongue, impaired breathing, increased pulse rate.

Untreated, it gets worse, including nausea, vomiting, abdominal cramps, loss of consciousness, cardiorespiratory failure, and death. All within minutes of exposure." He closed his notebook. "Treatment must be immediate. Recommended therapy is an injection of epinephrine or adrenaline."

"So this guy didn't get caught in the fire?" Kate said, readjusting her ideas.

"I didn't say that," Chopper Jim said.

Her look was pointed and said, *Don't be coy,* and there was that grin again. She hated that grin.

"Could be the fire caught up with him."

"After he died," she guessed, and he nodded. "So. Anaphylaxis."

There was another, briefer silence, broken only when Dinah put down her camera and made a beeline for the bottle of Skin-So-Soft she'd bought off the back of the Subaru. She started at her ankles and worked her way up. Chopper Jim watched her. Bobby watched Chopper Jim.

"So this guy," Kate said, "this guy strips down to his birthday suit, goes jogging, gets bitten on the ass by a bee and falls down dead in front of a forest fire. That pretty much cover things so far?"

Chopper Jim gave a judicious nod.

"And nobody notices."

Chopper Jim shook his head.

Kate thought it over and came to a well-reasoned conclusion. "Bullshit."

"Couldn't have put it better myself," Jim said.

"Metzger did notice something a little strange."

Kate looked at him.

"Okay, stranger. Body had some deep cuts on his upper right arm. Metzger said the deltoid muscle was almost severed."

"What caused the cuts?"

"Metzger says it looks like glass."

"Glass? As in drinking?"

"As in window."

"As in windshield? As in maybe he got hit by a car?"

He shook his head. "As in window. It wasn't safety glass."

Kate was silent for a moment. "You want a name to go with what's left of the face?" She was pleased when the trooper sat up and took notice. "I think he was a guy by the name of Daniel Seabolt, lived in Chistona."

"Seabolt. Related to the minister at the chapel there?"

"His son."

"He missing?"

"According to his son, since last August."

"Since the fire, then."

"Yeah."

The four of them thought about it for a while. "I don't get this," Chopper Jim said finally. "I haven't heard a word about anybody missing from this area, not a peep."

"Yeah," Kate said, "like I said. Bullshit." She

added, "His kid says they went to the dentist in Fairbanks regular once a year. Dentist's name is Dr. White."

He nodded. "Okay."

"Good." Kate stood up. To Bobby she said, "I'll be late getting back."

"Why? Where you going?"

"It's Sunday. I think I'll go to church."

The singing sounded good from the steps outside and Kate was sorry she'd missed the whole hymn. The Chistona Little Chapel was a small church, six rows of two pews each. All twelve were packed solid this morning and she had to stand in the back. There was an empty space against the wall next to a plump brunette with three toddlers clustered around her and a fourth on her hip. Kate folded her arms and prepared to listen.

Contrary to what his appearance suggested, Pastor Seabolt did not roar or thump the pulpit. He did not even raise his voice; on the contrary, he was calm, reasoned, articulate, and convincing. He began with a story about the two angels who visited Lot in Sodom and drew the obvious (to his congregation, anyway, judging from the emphatic nods punctuating each of his statements) connection to the current condition of the United States of America. With a serious expression and a doleful shake of the head, Pastor Seabolt said it was not too late to bring America back to God, and he urged his parishioners to become champions for Christ. How, specifically? Kate wondered, and Pastor Seabolt told her. Protest. By lifting the ban on the gays in the military, the current administration, Congress and the courts had endorsed what God had condemned. America was becoming a modern-day Sodom and Gomorrah, for which Hollywood and Washington, D.C., were equally at fault. He was pleased to quote the Reverend Jerry Falwell on the subject, in that Hollywood, Washington, D.C., and Hell were three localities with much in common.

At that Kate laughed out loud and was immediately the cynosure of many pairs of shocked eyes, including those of the blue-eyed choirboy standing between two other blue-eyed choirboys on the opposite side of the pulpit from the preacher. She turned the laugh into a cough.

Pastor Seabolt urged his champions for Christ to marry and beget more champions and to raise them up in the moral and traditional family values. He declared that it was right and natural to marry, and unnatural and against the law of God to remain single. He digressed a moment to attack the women's movement (he spat the word "feminist" like it was a curse), proclaiming any true Christian woman would not, could not participate in such a movement. He named names so that the female members of the congregation would be perfectly clear on this: the proscribed organizations included the National Organization for Women, Emily's List, the Alaska Women's Political Caucus and Planned Parenthood. Mention of Planned Parenthood naturally led to a comprehensive condemnation of abortion, the Freedom of Choice Act and RU-486.

He closed neatly with a return to Lot and the destruction of Sodom and in case they'd missed it the first time, pointed out the similarities between Sodom and Gomorrah and present-day America, and warned of the disastrous future facing them if they did not become champions of Christ and fight to rescue their country from the vast and morally perverted swamp into which it was currently sinking. "Let us pray," he said, and they bowed their heads forthwith. He'd given them plenty to pray about, Kate would grant him that much. She, a practicing heathen, was feeling a little unsettled herself.

The service ended with another hymn, "Onward Christian Soldiers," and the highest and sweetest voice in the choir came from the ten-year-old standing in the middle.

Outside the church the mother of four said to Kate, "I haven't seen you in church before, have I?"

"No, I've been picking mushrooms."

She laughed. "Haven't we all. I'm Sally Gillespie." The baby on her hip started to fuss and the other three to become restless.

"Kate Shugak."

"Where are you from?" Two of the boys started playing tag.

"I've got a homestead outside Niniltna."

"In the Park?" Kate nodded, and Sally said, "At least you're not as far from home as some of the pickers are."

The older boy growled and pretended to be a monster, and the other two boys got into the act. Kate felt surrounded by whirling dervishes. Sally said something else and Kate had to ask her to repeat herself.

"I said, would you like to come to Sunday dinner? My husband's the postmaster, we live in back of the post office, you could come about five—"

"I'm T. Rex and I'm going to chomp you up! Grrrr!" Standing up on his tiptoes, arching his arms into claws, the older boy chased the smaller boys behind Kate. The two smaller boys shrieked with delighted terror and ran for their lives.

Sally's face went white and for a moment Kate thought she might faint. "Brandon!" She grabbed the biggest boy by the back of his shirt as he dashed past her.

Startled, he overbalanced and would have fallen if she hadn't been holding him up. "What, Mom? What's the matter?"

"Don't you ever let me hear you say that again! We don't talk about those kinds of things and you know it!" She swatted him ineffectively, hampered by the baby, and cast an apprehensive look behind her at the church. In the doorway stood Pastor Seabolt, regarding her impassively, and if possible her face went even whiter. She gathered her children up and with the barest of farewells marched her family homeward.

Seabolt's gaze shifted to Kate. His eyes were the coldest blue she'd ever seen, cold and clear and assessing, and without thinking she laid a hand on Mutt's head, a real and reassuring presence at her side. She stood a little straighter, pulled her shoulders a little squarer, lifted her chin a little higher beneath that coldly speculative gaze. She would not scuttle away in fear from the challenge issued by those eyes, although later she wondered why fear, and later still, why the challenge. A challenge that was almost a dare. As if he were invulnerable, and knew it.

Someone touched him on the shoulder and he broke off the staring match to talk to a parishioner. Kate felt what amounted to a physical release that actually had her rocking back on her heels, just a little, just enough to make itself felt. She turned and made for the truck, shaken and determined not to show it.

She had her hand on the door when she heard her name, and turned to see Matthew Seabolt. He looked over his shoulder to reassure himself that his grandfather was no longer standing in the doorway of the church. He wasn't, and Matthew turned back to Kate. "Have you found my father?"

She busied herself, opening the door, sitting on the footboard, retying one shoelace that had gone limp beneath the Right Reverend Seabolt's fiery rhetoric. "Tell me again when he went missing. Everything you can remember."

"I wasn't here, I was at Bible camp."

She looked up. "So he was here when you left?" He nodded. "And gone when you came back." He nodded again. "Do you remember the dates?"

He frowned, blond brows knitting in concentration. "Bible camp always starts the first Monday in August."

"How long does it last?"

"Two weeks."

Kate looked at him, blond hair gleaming in the sun like a helmet, blue eyes sharp as the point of a sword, a little champion for Christ in the making. "Matthew, is this the first time you've told anyone that your father is missing?"

"Yes."

"And you haven't seen your father since last August?" He nodded. "Why did you wait so long? Why hasn't someone else said something? This is a small community. I presume everyone knows everyone else."

For the first time she saw a trace of vulnerability in those steady blue eyes. "Grandfather says Dad abandoned me, and that I shouldn't talk about him."

"Does he know where your father went?"

He shook his head.

She tried again. "Does he have any ideas where he might be?"

"I told you," he said, lips tightening. "We don't talk about him."

The light morning breeze had dissipated beneath the hot sun and a stray mosquito wandered by, to settle almost desultorily on Matthew Seabolt's arm. He felt the sting and pinched it off between thumb and forefinger. A smear of blood stained his skin.

"Do you think your father abandoned you?"

The answer was firm and direct. "No. Dad wouldn't do that. He wouldn't leave me without a word."

Another mosquito took the first one's place. The boy smacked it and it fell to the ground. The place where the first one had bitten was already red and swelling. Kate nodded at it. "They like you."

He looked down at the bite and rubbed it with one finger. He looked up again, more animated than Kate had yet seen him. "That's nothing. You should see Dad. When he gets bit first thing in the spring his eyes and his hands swell shut. One time when we were picking salmonberries, the mosquitoes bit him so bad his ankles swelled over his shoes and we thought we were going to have to cut them off him. We used to order Cutter's by the case."

"Used to?"

His gaze slid away. "Well. Dad wasn't home this year, so . . ." He watched a third mosquito buzz around Kate, give an almost visible shrug and zero in on the back of his neck. He swiped at it and missed. "They don't bother you much."

She shook her head. "No. Not much."

"You're lucky." They stood in silence for a moment. "You know what happened to him, don't you."

She met his eyes. "I think so."

He looked back down at his arm, rubbing the bite. When next he spoke his voice was almost inaudible. "He's dead, isn't he."

"I don't know for sure, Matthew," she said, "and I don't want to say anything until I am absolutely sure."

"Matthew." His grandfather's voice carried clearly, effortlessly to them across the expanse of parking lot.

It was like watching special effects in a movie, one person usurping the face and body of another in a seamless meld of shifting flesh. The vulnerable little boy stiffened into a champion for Christ, a soldier for God. His spine stiffened, his chin came up, even his voice deepened. "I've got to go."

On a mission from God, no doubt. "All right," Kate said. "I might know something more in a couple of days. I'll come and tell you if I do."

"God bless you." He hesitated, looking from her to the tall, spare man with the shock of white hair standing in the doorway to the little church, the tiny steeple stretching overhead like an extension of his backbone. "If he's dead, it's God's will, and I must learn to accept it." He saw her expression and repeated stubbornly, "It's God's will." He turned and walked back to the church, steps firm, chin up, spine straight. The door closed behind him.

So it was God's will, was it? Kate thought.

Maybe.

Then again, maybe not.

CHAPTER 4

Gold and silver and dresses may be trusted to a messenger, but not boleti.

—Martial

T he post office was closed but the general store it cohabited with was open and doing a rousing trade that Sunday afternoon, or as rousing a business as a one-room store does in the Alaskan bush when the salmon are running. The building was a structure typical of the bush, beginning with a double-wide trailer, a lean-to built on to the double-wide, a log room added to the lean-to, and a prefab with slick metal siding going up into a dizzying second story added on to the log room. The four different roof levels were crowned with five chimneys and a satellite dish, and the various eaves were hung with—Kate counted—seventeen sets of wind chimes that tinkled monotonously in the light breeze. There was a weather vane in the shape of a rooster; that afternoon its beak pointed into the southeast.

Except for the chimes, it all reminded her a little of her grandmother's house in Niniltna. The eaves of her grandmother's house were festooned with racks and skulls, the first kills of anyone related to Ekaterina by blood within the last fifty years. The antlers from Kate's own first deer, a gracefully balanced four-pointer, neat but not gaudy, were positioned near the ridgepole. Kate could still taste the steaks. Best meat she'd ever eaten.

The store occupied the log cabin part of this preposterous structure, and it was packed so solid with shelves so crammed with goods there was barely room enough for customers, but they managed to wedge themselves inside, fill their arms with purchases and wait in a line that grew steadily longer in front of a counter with one register and one man working that register. He was short and stocky, with straight dark hair, big brown eyes, and a taciturn expression alleviated by a sudden and infrequent grin that relaxed his whole face and turned him from wood into flesh. "Russell, how much for these spinners?" somebody called from the back, holding up a box of silver lures.

"Price on the box," Russell said, ringing up a carton of Kools and a case of Rainier.

"No, it's not."

"Look on the shelf underneath."

A housewife dueled with two toddlers over a box

of Captain Crunch. She won, only to refight the same battle over a bag of Doritos. Kate and Mutt stood to one side, out of the line of fire.

A plane sounded overhead. Without looking up Russell said, "There's Slim with that new 185."

The thin man with the ponytail and the intense look who was next in line paused in counting out money. "Didn't I hear tell where he stole it off some poor guy for only sixty-five grand?" Russell nodded and the hippie shook his head in admiration. "With less than six hundred hours on the engine. Damn. He could turn the sucker around for eighty-five tomorrow. Like money in the bank."

"Don't think he wants to, he says it always starts." Another plane approached and the store-keeper cocked his head a little, listening. After a moment his brow smoothed out. "Butch in the Tripacer. Been a while since he's been up."

"Wonder if he brought his wife," the hippie said.

"We can only hope."

The hippie gathered up his dried apricots, gorp and stone cut oatmeal and headed for the door, pausing on his way for a long, appreciative look at Kate. The housewife wrestled her kids two throws out of three for a bag of butterscotch drops, won, and arrived at the counter flushed with triumph. Behind her back, the four-year-old swiped a Snickers bar and hid it in his pocket. Something in the air triggered the suspicious instinct alert in every mother when her back is turned and her head

snapped around and she stared down at him sternly.
He stood it for maybe ten seconds before caving,
pulled the candy bar out of his pocket and put it
back on the shelf, red-faced. She nodded once,
sternly, and then spoiled the effect by getting two
fruit wraps from the top shelf and handing them
over, one each. Their faces lit up. It wasn't chocolate but it wasn't a bad second best. They grabbed
for the goodies and streaked out the door quick before she changed her mind.

Russell rang up her order and ducked around the
counter to hold the door open for her as she staggered through, arms full of bags. He let it swing
shut and looked at Kate, standing patiently next to
the counter. "Something I can help you with?"

"I'm Kate Shugak," she said. "I met your wife at
church this morning."

"Kate Shugak?" She nodded. "Any relation to
Ekaterina Shugak?" She nodded again. He took in
the color of her skin and the epicanthic folds of her
eyes, she the slant of his cheekbones and the thick,
straight black hair. He didn't say, "Aleut?" and she
didn't say, "Athabaskan?" but they both relaxed a
little, the way people of color always do when the
door closes after the last white person has left the
room.

Her eyes traveled past him to the wall in back of
the counter. "Is that a hunter's tunic?"

He turned to look. "Yeah."

They looked at it some more, silent, taking their

time. It was worth it, a testament to hundreds of hours of painstaking, eye-straining, finger-cramping labor. It was made of caribou hide, tanned to ivory. Red, white and blue beads were worked around the collar in a pattern that sort of resembled the Russian Orthodox cross, or maybe those were birds; Kate wasn't sure. The seams at shoulders, armholes and underarms were heavily fringed and hung with dyed porcupine quills. Dentalium shells gleamed from a sort of a breastplate, and something in the order in which they were sewn to the hide hinted at the shape of a fish. You could see the fish better if you didn't look straight at the design.

"Your grandfather's?" she said after a while. He nodded. "I saw Chief William in one of those last year. He had leggings, dancing slippers, even a nosepin. The work on it reminds me of this one."

"Maybe by the same hand," he said.

"Maybe. It's looks about the same age. A lot of this stuff around?"

"Some. What there is, people don't bring out much."

"Why do you?"

"I like to look at it."

"You ever wear it?"

He shook his head. "It's too small for me. I'm always afraid I'll split the seams." He turned to face the counter and her. "You need something?"

"Got any Diet 7-Up?"

"In the cooler."

She got a can, paid for it and popped the top. "Like I was saying, I met your wife in church this morning."

His face closed up. "Oh?"

Kate ignored the uncompromising syllable. "Yeah, she invited me to dinner but she took off before I could tell her I can't make it today." She gave him one of her very best smiles. "I just stopped by to see if maybe I could weasel a rain check out of her."

He wilted visibly in the presence of that smile, a force of nature Jack Morgan could have told him was lethal and always effective. It was much like Chopper Jim's grin, but Kate would never have admitted that, even if Jack had had the guts to draw a comparison between the two. "She's in the house, I can go get her."

"Nah, I've got to get back or my picking partners will think I'm slacking off on them." She drank some pop. From outside the door came a low, impatient "Woof."

Kate looked for beef jerky and had to settle for a package of teriyaki pepperoni. She stripped off the shrink wrap and opened the door. Mutt caught the stick of meat neatly in her teeth.

She felt Russell Gillespie come up behind her. "Nice dog. Got some wolf in him."

"Her. Half."

"You breed her?"

"Not intentionally."

Russell smiled, that sudden, transforming expression that seemed momentarily to change him into a different person. "Come around back. Got something to show you."

"Okay."

He locked up the store and took her around back and of course there were about a hundred dogs staked out over an acre of ground cleared between tree stumps, and of course Mutt had to exchange greetings with each and every one of them, reminding Kate yet again of Ekaterina Moonin Shugak working the room at the Alaska Federation of Natives' annual convention. No nose went unsniffed, and no tail, either, and Kate was thankful they were well past Mutt's estrus. One old lop-eared male did give an exploratory growl, which Mutt dealt with summarily. The male yipped and jumped away from the nipping teeth, and Mutt moved on.

Russell Gillespie watched, standing next to Kate. "She'd make one hell of a lead dog. You do any mushing?"

"No. You?" A disingenuous question, since she'd seen the sled and the harnesses hung on the wall, as well as the dog pot fashioned from a fifty-five-gallon drum.

"Some."

"Race?"

"Some." As with most mushers she had known and loved, the urge to show off his dogs was irresistible, and it was twenty minutes of dog talk before Kate judged it safe to raise the topic again. "I didn't see you at church. Did I miss you?"

"I don't go," he said flatly. "I leave that to the wife."

"Oh?"

"Yeah." He hesitated, then went on. "She got the call and was born again and then she tried to convert me. It didn't take." The grin turned thin and sour, like good wine gone bad. "So now she prays for me."

Kate shrugged. "Every little bit helps." He almost smiled, but not quite, and she trod warily. "Quite a sermon the pastor preaches."

"Yeah," he said, and there was no trace of humor left. "Old Seabolt damns and blasts with the best of them."

"I haven't been up this way in a while, but I don't remember the church being here before."

"It wasn't here until seven years ago," he said shortly, red creeping up the back of his neck. "Seabolt led a crusade or some damn thing up from Outside. About ten families altogether, they drove up the AlCan, bought Ralph Satrie's homestead and divided up the one hundred and thirty acres eleven ways."

"Eleven?"

"One part for the church."

"Oh. Where they from, originally?"

He shrugged, but there was a wariness in him that sparked her curiosity. She would have pursued it but in the distance came the sound of a plane and he cocked his head, listening intently.

"Somebody you know?" Kate said, watching him.

"Don't think so," he said, "it's a Super Cub, but it doesn't sound familiar."

The three of them, man, woman and dog, waited, looking into the western sky until the white plane with the faded red trim came into view over the tops of the trees. "Seven Four Kilo," he said, squinting at the tail letters. "Nope, never saw it before." The engine throttled back and the flaps came down. "Better open up the store, they might buy something."

It was a hint, and Kate, realizing confidences were at an end for the day, took it.

As they came around the corner of the store, they surprised a woman in the act of picking up a garden hoe propped against the open door of the greenhouse. Not seeing them, she turned to walk away. "Hey," Russell said.

She paused and looked over her shoulder. "Oh. Hi." She was in her late sixties, gray hair cropped short and permed in tight little curls, face weathered and brown from ten years of retirement. Her jeans were loose and faded. Her faded pink T-shirt commemorated the Alaska Highway's Fiftieth Anniversary.

"Where do you think you're going with my hoe?" Russell said.

The woman looked at the hoe as if she'd never seen it before. "This is your hoe?"

"Yes."

She said accusingly, "I thought this was a ghost town."

"You thought wrong," Russell said, and retrieved his hoe.

She wasn't embarrassed, watching him lean the hoe back up against the greenhouse with a speculative expression. "You're Indian, aren't you?" She looked over at Kate. "Both of you? Could you wait a second while I get my camera so I can take your picture?"

Russell looked at Kate. Kate looked at Russell. They both looked back at the woman.

"Ugh," Kate said.

"How," Russell said.

Mutt, having completed her social obligations, chose this moment to trot up, pausing next to Kate and examining the woman with a long, curious yellow stare. The woman paled. Mutt yawned widely. The woman turned and trotted around the building. Mutt gave Kate an inquiring glance. "Good girl," Kate said.

Russell went back inside, and Kate arrived in the parking lot in time to see a Winnebago with Georgia plates kick gravel as it pulled out onto the road, going the wrong way if they wanted to get back to the main road, but it wasn't Kate's RV and it wasn't her problem. She just hoped she wouldn't have to help pull them out of a ditch on the way home.

She turned and saw the hippie loitering with intent. "Hi."

She paused. "Hi."

"You're Kate Shugak."

She was surprised. "You know who I am?"

He shrugged, straddling a tree stump. "Everybody knows who you are." He looked her over, his eyes frankly assessing the possibilities and as frankly approving of them. "You the one who found the body?"

She barely repressed a jump. "What?"

"Rumor going around that a body was found. Heard some pickers out the road found it. Heard the trooper flew into Tanada and got picked up by a woman who looked like you. Heard the woman drove him back, accompanied by a body bag."

"Heard a lot, didn't you?"

He nodded. "I'm Brad Burns, by the way." He extended a hand. "Why don't you come out to my cabin, have a beer?"

The Alaska bush equivalent of "What's your sign?" He was small and wiry, fined down to muscle and bone without being skinny. She noted again the ponytail, the plaid flannel shirt nearly worn through at the elbows, the jeans the same at the knee. His eyes were dark and shrewd, with the same intensity she'd noticed only in passing in the store, and he didn't smell. "I don't drink."

His gaze was knowing. "I heard."

"Then why ask?"

He shrugged again. "Can't hurt to try. Well, then. Coffee? Tea? Me?" He grinned this time, confidently, cockily. "My cabin's a mile upriver from the second turnoff."

Amused, Kate started to say, "Maybe some other time," and then caught the words back. He lived here, and although something told her he wasn't a member in good standing of the congregation of the Chistona Little Chapel, maybe he'd heard something over the mukluk telegraph. The same way he'd heard of her. "Okay," she said, "I'd like to see your cabin."

He jerked a thumb at her truck. "Catch a ride?"

She had to laugh.

The three of them bumped down the road to the second turnoff, parked and walked down what was little more than a game trail. There was no sign of fire here.

His cabin was small, just one room, perched precariously on the edge of a ten-foot bank, the wide, gray expanse of the Kanuyaq River, still swollen with spring runoff, rushing past below. The door had a sign on it:

ERIC CLAPTON IS GOD

Nope. Brad Burns probably didn't belong to the Chistona Little Chapel.

Inside, the cabin was neat and clean, if somewhat spartan. The single bunk was built into the wall and made up beneath an olive green Army blanket, the corners of the pillowcase squared just so. "You were in the service," Kate said.

He slipped a tape into the battery-operated boom box resting on a rough wood shelf above the bed and the sounds of the waltz version of "Layla" filled the room. "Yeah. How'd you know?"

She pointed at the bunk. "I've been around vets before. Can you bounce a quarter off that thing?"

"I could if I had a quarter, but Russell took my last one this afternoon."

"Russell Gillespie?"

He nodded without looking around.

"I met his wife. She invited me to dinner."

He paused in lighting a camp stove. "You religious?"

She shook her head.

"Then don't go."

"Why?"

"She's got a map of Chistona and suburbs. Red flags for sinners, blue flags for the saved. Sally rotates Sunday dinner invitations around the red flags, serving up scripture with the roast and biscuits, doing her bit to convert the ungodly into the path of righteousness." She heard the smile in his voice. "I rate the biggest flag on the map."

"Glad I came here instead," Kate said.

He gave her a once-over that was as blatant as it

was suggestive. "Me, too." He waggled his eyebrows like Groucho Marx, his eyes twinkling, and she grinned involuntarily, unable to take offense. He filled a kettle from a jerry can and put it on to boil. "She's a terrific cook, though," he added as an afterthought. "Sally. In case you get hungry. There are times when a sermon is a small price to pay for a full stomach."

Kate smiled. "I'll keep it in mind."

He spooned loose tea into a teapot. A rich, orangey aroma drifted through the room. "Mmm, that smells good. What is that?"

"Samovar tea. The Kobuk Coffee Company mails me some from Anchorage every month."

Over the door was a gun rack, holding a twelve-gauge and a .30-06. A holster with a .22 in it hung next to the door. On the opposite wall was a bear-skin, a nice one, soft and rich to the touch. "You do your own tanning?"

He nodded. A beaver's skin hung on another wall, a wolf's from a third. Mutt curled her lip and turned her back pointedly.

A wood stove had been fashioned from a fifty-five-gallon drum, matching the design of the honey bucket in the outhouse, the fish smoker on the riverbank and, its barrel sliced diagonally and mounted on a nose wheel, the wheelbarrow in the garden. A workbench with a disassembled trap sitting on it leaned up against the wall beneath the wolf pelt. An Olympia beer box spilled over with cassette tapes, another with paperback books. A gas lamp hung from the center of the ceiling, unlit, probably since May, maybe since April. Kate herself started turning her lamps off in March. Couldn't get a jump on spring too soon in Alaska. Groceries were stacked neatly in open shelves on the fourth wall, above and below the counter, which held a sink with a drain but no faucet. A bucket, half full of water, sat in the sink. "You have a well?"

He nodded.

"Good water?"

"Fair." He grinned at her over his shoulder. "Gives the tea an interesting flavor."

Kate took one of the two chairs next to the tiny table, all three handmade from spruce and sanded as smooth as a baby's behind. "You come here after you got out?"

"By way of APD."

She sat up. "You were a cop?" He nodded. "How long?"

He turned, leaning against the counter, arms folded, and grinned at her again. "Long enough to hear all about Kate Shugak and her dog Mutt."

Mutt, sitting just inside the door, put her ears up at mention of her name. Kate looked at Brad Burns. He was younger than she was, late twenties, she figured. She didn't remember him from her time with the D.A. so he must have come on board after she left. But she'd only been gone four years. She wondered why he'd left the force for the bush, but didn't want to talk about why she had, so she didn't ask.

The kettle whistled and he strained the tea into two mugs. He held up a bottle of Grand Marnier. "Sure you don't want a shot?"

She shook her head, and he shrugged and put the bottle back in its place on the shelf without adding any to his own mug, either, and brought both to the table and sat down. Kate sipped. Oranges and cloves, strong and sweet. "Mmm. Good stuff."

He nodded. "What were you doing up here when you stumbled across the body? You live around Niniltna, don't you?"

She ignored the second half of his question. "Picking mushrooms."

"You and half the state and two-thirds of the rest of the country."

"You, too?"

He nodded. "Good for a little of the long green. Who was it? Daniel Seabolt?"

Her head came up at that. "How did you know?"

His bright brown eyes studied her for a moment. "I knew him."

"You were friends?"

"More or less." He shrugged. "He came down here a few times. Was interested in the subsistence lifestyle. Really interested. I figured him for a stayer." He nodded at the bearskin. "Helped me tan that. Didn't try to save my soul, either, which is more than I can say for the rest of that churchy bunch." He shook his head and drank tea. "The best thing about winter is that it snows me in and them out."

She asked the question Russell Gillespie had not answered. "Where were they from originally? The Seabolts?"

"I don't know, Idaho, Oklahoma, Iowa. One of those redneck states with vowels on both ends."

"You mean like Alaska?" she said dryly, and he laughed.

"I met Seabolt's grandson."

"Yeah? Now there's a knockoff of the old man."

"What about his father?"

"Daniel?" She nodded, and he shook his head firmly. "Daniel was a human being. The fanatic skipped a generation in that family. He loved his father, but I didn't blame him when he went down the river."

"Why?"

He jerked his chin up the road. "He was teaching at the school—"

"They've got a school?"

"Yeah, a Molly Hootch, new three years ago. Chistona petitioned for eligibility when the population in the area started growing and the state came in and built it."

"I didn't see it."

"It's off the road, about halfway to Tanada. They wanted it as central to the population as possible, there's homesteads scattered all over the place, you know how it is. Anyway, there was some hoorah about what Daniel was teaching, and his father took exception, and got the whole congregation into it with him, and Daniel split."

"Just left?"

"Yeah."

"Without even telling his son?"

His eyes met hers. "That's what everybody said, Pastor Seabolt and all the churchy people." He paused, letting her think about that for a while. "They say he left in August, just before the school year started. I figure he thought he'd better get out on his own before they ran him out on a rail, tarred and feathered."

Startled, Kate said, "What the hell was he teaching? Devil worship?"

"Close enough. Dinosaurs, evolution, radical stuff like that."

Kate remembered Sally Gillespie's white face, and her T. Rex son, and the cold, vigilant presence of Pastor Seabolt in the doorway of the church.

Brad Burns added, "Dan told me once he was going up to Fairbanks, to arrange a tour of the museum there, or maybe get one of their fossilologists or whatever they call them to come down and give a talk. I think the Jesus freaks put a stop to it." He drank tea. "There was something about reading assignments, too, some of the parents wanted to ban some books from the school library."

"Which ones?"

He shrugged. "I don't remember exactly. I don't have kids myself, so I didn't pay much attention. Probably the usual suspects, works by those well-known American subversives Mark Twain and J. D. Salinger." He eyed her over the rim of his mug. "Wouldn't mind a couple rugrats around the place, though. How about you?"

She smiled and shook her head, waving a hand at Mutt, who had her chin on her paws and looked bored. "Got a roommate." She finished her tea and rose to her feet. "Thanks. I'd better be getting back, my friends will be wondering where I am." He tried to get her to stay for dinner, but she refused, as kindly as she could in the face of his disappointment. Company was hard to come by in the bush, and only reluctantly surrendered.

"Come back anytime," he called after her, and she turned to wave. He stood, silhouetted in the door of his tiny cabin, the Kanuyaq, gray with glacial silt, flowing behind him.

"Well?" Dinah said when Kate reappeared in camp.

"Bill and Hilary Clinton are New Age heretics, America is a modern-day Sodom and Gomorrah, and you were right, Matthew Seabolt is a choirboy." She held out a hand. "Got your Bible?"

"Sure." Dinah pulled it out and handed it over, and watched Kate thumb through the pages. "What are you looking for?"

"There's a story about Lot the pastor quoted

from. I wanted to look it up. You know where it is?"

"What, the one about his wife turning into a pillar of salt? Everybody knows that story, even devout pagans. Maybe especially devout pagans." Dinah's brow puckered. "What was her name, anyway? You ever notice how a lot of biblical women never have their own names?"

"No, not that story, the one where Lot lived in Sodom where all the men were homosexuals and when two angels showed up for dinner the men of Sodom gathered outside Lot's house and demanded they be turned over for a gang-bang."

Dinah blinked. "What?"

"That's what Seabolt told us."

"Whew. No, I don't know where that is. I must have missed that story in Sunday school."

"Me, too," Kate said, still searching for the passage without success.

"You never went to Sunday school in your life," Bobby growled, and plucked the book from Kate's hands. He turned to the front of the book and found the page without hesitation. "Genesis, Chapter 19." He handed it to her. "Go ahead. Read it." He didn't add, "I dare you," but it was there in his voice.

Giving him a curious look, Kate took the Bible and started reading Genesis, chapter 19, verse 1.

By the time she came to verse 38 and the end of the chapter, all the hair on the back of her head was standing straight up. She closed the book and looked at Bobby. "Jesus Christ," she said.

"Not for another thirty-eight books and six hundred and fifty pages," Bobby said. "That's the problem, or part of it."

"He offered up his two virgin daughters to the angry mob so they wouldn't tear him and his visitors up?"

"What a guy."

"And then after he escapes the destruction of Sodom and Gomorrah and all the other men are dead, his daughters get him drunk so he'll sleep with them and make them pregnant?"

"What a guy," Bobby repeated. "Did you notice how it calls him 'righteous'?"

"I noticed."

He examined her expression, not without satisfaction. "You look a little pale around the gills, Shugak."

"I feel a little pale around the gills. Twelve pages into one of the most influential books ever written and you've got the advocation of gang rape and incest. No wonder those people are screwed up."

"Screwed up doesn't even come close," Bobby said.

She looked at him thoughtfully. His lips were drawn into a thin line and his eyes were angry. "What's with you and the holy rollers? You've been on the prod since Matthew Seabolt showed up here."

His jaw clenched. Moving on instinct with quick, quiet moves Dinah set up her camera on a tripod to roll on a close-up of Bobby's face. He didn't seem to notice. The sun poured a clear golden light into the clearing, a breeze whispered through the trees, leaves rustled, a bird sang. Another golden-crowned sparrow, Kate noted; *spring is here, here is spring.* The sweet, three-note call was *the* sign of Alaskan spring, the precursor of summer, the call to renewal and reproduction and rebirth, the signal for the sun to come up and stay up, the signal that the long winter was over for another year and the next far enough away to forget, at least for a little while.

"There was a girl," Bobby finally said into the stillness. "In high school. She got pregnant."

He paused. This wasn't easy for him and it showed. They waited in silence.

"This was southwestern Tennessee, you understand," he said, looking first at Kate, then at Dinah, "Tina Turner country. There was a church on every corner and a Bible next to every bed and a tent revival down to the fair grounds at least once every month during the summer." His mouth quirked in what was almost a smile. "Those were fun. Always some old guy up at the front of the tent, sweating and praying and praising the Lord. The singing was the best part, it practically took the roof off. I figure I was saved once a year every year until I was thirteen." He paused.

"What happened?" The question was softly spoken and from Dinah.

"I grew up, and grew away from it." He shook his head. "It all seemed so—I don't know, so goddam unlikely, I guess. That God would give us sex and forbid us to enjoy it. That God would make us smart enough to figure out ways to prevent conception and forbid us to use them. That the world was really only five thousand years old when I'd found fossils in an abandoned quarry older than that. Little inconsistencies like those. And then I started reading history, and it seemed like everywhere blood was spilled, there was religion, causing it, and the more religion, the more blood. I'd ask why, and the answer was always the same. It was God's will. It was just never a good enough reason for me."

"So," Dinah said, "you don't believe in God."

He looked irritated. "Of course I believe." He waved a hand, encompassing the Kanuyaq River valley and the distant Quilak Mountains. "Who could look at that and not believe?" He paused, and tried for a laugh. "It's just that nowadays I put my faith in rock and roll. I mean, let's face it, the lyrics to *Imagine* make more spiritual sense than any ten sermons Jerry Falwell ever gave."

Dinah, unsmiling, adjusted the lens of her camera. Kate sat silent.

He sighed. "Anyway, when I was sixteen there was this girl, and of course nobody bothered to tell

us how not to, so she got pregnant. Her father was
the minister of our church. She was scared to death
he was going to find out, and I was scared to death
my father was." He looked down at his clenched
hands. "That was back in the days when it wasn't
legal. I talked around, got a phone number, made
an appointment. I borrowed a car and drove us to
Memphis, and we met this guy who looked like
Count Dracula in a motel on Interstate Fifty-five. I
was ready to call it off right then, I even told her
we could get married, but she said no. We both had
plans, you know? We were getting out, going away
to school, she was going to be a doctor and join the
Peace Corps, I was—well, that don't matter. She
insisted on going through with it."

He looked up and caught their expressions. "No,
she didn't die. Something did go wrong, though,
and she wound up in the hospital and our parents
found out everything, and her father came after me.
Mine did, too, for that matter. They beat on me,
taking turns. My momma watched."

He stretched his shoulders, as if remembering the
blows. "I guess I deserved it. Anyway, I didn't fight
it. I thought—hell, I don't know what I thought, I
guess I thought if I took my punishment, that'd be
an end to it."

"It wasn't," Dinah said. It wasn't a question.

"No." His hands opened, rubbed his stubs as if
they ached. "In church the next Sunday, they called
me a fornicator. From the pulpit." His smile was

twisted. "In front of the whole congregation, in front of our families, in front of all our friends, in front of all the people we'd grown up next to, had known all our lives."

The smile faded. His face tightened. "They called her a whore. And a murderer."

Kate closed her eyes, opened them again.

"That night she got in the bathtub and slit her wrists."

Dinah's breath drew in audibly.

Bobby stared out, unseeing, across the valley, at the Kanuyaq gleaming blue-white in the sun, at the white clouds massed against the horizon, interrupted by the occasional mountain peak. "I lit out."

"Where'd you go?" Again, the question came from Dinah.

"Memphis. Lied about my age and joined the Marines. Got shipped way down yonder to Vietnam. I didn't care." Kate flinched at his smile. "I'll tell you, the Nam seemed like an oasis of sanity, compared to what I'd left behind."

"And when you got out you came to Alaska."

He nodded. "When I got out of rehab, anyway." He rubbed his stumps again. "It took a long time to heal these suckers up." He looked up at Kate and saw her watching him, and he glared at her, daring to see pity in her eyes.

She lowered them before he could. His parents' religion had gotten its claws into Bobby at an early age and sunk them in deep, so that pain and sacrifice were concepts he subconsciously understood and accepted, maybe even embraced. He'd traded his legs in Vietnam for that girl's life back in Nutbush, Tennessee, whether he knew it or not. No wonder there had never been any bitterness over their loss, no anger over what the lack of them prevented him from doing. Somewhere in the back of Bobby's mind, his legs had been offered up on a sacrificial altar, attached to a bill made out to him and stamped "Paid in Full." He wouldn't have called it a fair price, either. He might even feel he still owed.

Kate hoped not.

In fourteen years, this was the most she'd ever heard about his past. Oh, she knew about his military service, the missing legs had to be explained, and the Tet Anniversary Party he held every year for the Park's vets would have been a slight clue anyway. Alaska was funny that way. When Outsiders came into the country, it was as if their previous life had never existed. Alaska was a place to start over, to begin anew, to carve a new identity out of the wilderness, or what was left of it. Bobby Clark and Simon Seabolt had both come to Alaska for the same reason, for the anonymity and the open-ended opportunity afforded the immigrant by a last frontier.

"I had a friend once," Dinah said, her voice thoughtful. "She got the call along about our sophomore year. I've never seen anything like it. She was as normal as you or me, could carry on a rational conversation without dragging God into every other sentence, and then all of a sudden she was this raving maniac, preaching the Ten Commandments like she'd written them herself. She tried to convert me, but fortunately I never have been very convertible."

"More of a hardtop," Bobby couldn't resist saying, and the three of them relaxed enough to laugh. It was a brief laugh but it went a long way toward easing the tension in the little glade. The golden-crowned sparrow trilled his three-note message of hope and at the clear, pure sound they relaxed even more. "What happened to her? Your friend?"

"She transferred to Liberty College. I think it's the one Jerry Falwell runs. But she never gave up hope on me, no sir. She still writes, sends me little tracts with biblical quotations on them. She tells me she prays for me, every day, long and hard, in hopes I'll see the light in time."

Kate thought of Russell Gillespie, prayed over by his wife. "In time for what?"

"Before I die. So I won't go to hell. Only thirty thousand people are actually going to heaven, didn't you know? There's going to be this thing called the Rapture, according to her, and only thirty thousand of the choicest spirits are going to be accepted into heaven. She's worried I won't be one of them."

Words rose unbidden to Kate's mind, words like "elite" and "fascist."

Echoing her thoughts, Dinah said, "You know, I asked her once about all the people who haven't had a chance at this great enlightenment, all the heathens living in the African bush, and the Muslims in Afghanistan, and the Hindus in India and the Taoists in China and the Buddhists in Japan. Just because Oral Roberts or Jimmy Swaggert or Jim Bakker didn't get to them first, they're all going to hell?"

"What'd she say?"

"She said they were." Dinah shook her head. "The hell with that. If everybody doesn't get to go, I'm not going either."

"Why do they make believing so goddam hard?" Bobby said, staring across the valley at the mountains. "God is or isn't. You either believe or you don't. The rest is just dress up and make believe from words somebody else wrote."

"Maybe partly because not believing isn't any easier," Kate said.

"What do you mean?"

"Well, for one thing, not believing is lonely. It must be nice to know some great, all-knowing, all-seeing, omnipotent power exists who sees even the little sparrow fall. Because if it sees even the little sparrow fall, then it's always there for you to talk to, always listening. To go it alone takes guts."

"You think it's easy being a Catholic?" Dinah demanded. "It requires sacrifice and devotion. It requires a willing suspension of disbelief, a true leap of faith. I believe in the sacrament. I believe at communion that I am eating and drinking of the body and the blood of Christ. I didn't stop going to church because I stopped believing."

This was the first Kate and Bobby had heard that Dinah had ceased being a Catholic, or that she had ever been one, for that matter. Bobby said mildly, "Why did you stop going?"

"Because I got tired of being told how to vote from the pulpit. Every Sunday before an election, the priest would get up there and identify the pro-choice candidates by name, and call them murderers." She snorted. "The real kicker was when my mother got a letter from the church, saying that since we had the house we did and lived in the neighborhood we did that we must be making this much of an income and therefore we could and should write the Catholic Church a check in the amount of three thousand dollars, thank you very much."

"Jaysus," Bobby said, impressed. "And I suppose if you didn't you were going straight to hell to burn in eternal damnation. That's one hell of an incentive to make a campaign contribution. Wonder if the Republicans have thought of that?"

"Isn't there a story about Jesus whipping the money-lenders from the Temple?" Kate said.

"Why, yes, I believe there is," he said, sober as she. "Matthew, 21:12."

"Is there a single reference from the Bible you

don't know chapter and verse?" Kate demanded.

"I don't believe so," he said, still sober. "I was dragged through it, cover to cover, about once a year every year until I left home."

"Poor kid."

"You have no idea," he said with feeling. "Try reading Leviticus some time."

"So I don't go to church anymore," Dinah said. "And I'm still mad about it, because I still believe in the sacrament, and it pisses me off that the church got in the way of me and God."

"Scary."

"Yeah." Bobby nodded. "More than you'll ever know. I saw it, all the time, growing up. When that kind of fanaticism gets hold of you, it's like dope or booze. The more you have, the more you want, and the more you want the more you have to have. It never lets up, and it never lets go."

It was a chilling pronouncement. Kate wondered if it had held true for Daniel Seabolt. "Brad Burns said Daniel Seabolt had been teaching evolution at the Chistona school."

"Oh, well, then." Bobby spread his hands, as if to say, What can you expect? "That's grounds for murder right there."

Kate looked at him. He was quite serious.

It was the first time any of them had said the word "murder" out loud in connection with Daniel Seabolt. Nobody liked the sound of it.

"You ever notice," Dinah said into the uneasy silence, "how Bible-thumpers don't read? Anything except the Bible, I mean. No books, half the time they don't even read the newspapers."

"Of course not," Bobby said, still in that "What can you expect?" tone. "God forbid they should introduce themselves to a new and probably heretical idea from a writer who is probably a tool of Satan anyway."

Kate looked at him and said, "Don't you think you're being a little harsh?"

"No."

"Why would you think so?" Dinah demanded.

"I don't mean to leap to their defense," Kate said, "but a lot they do is good, too."

Bobby bristled. "Like what?"

"Like when a lot of people get religion they stop drinking," she shot back.

Bobby threw up his hands. "Should have known you'd drag that into it sooner or later."

Kate felt heat creep up the back of her neck. "Yes," she said as mildly as she could, "you should have."

Dinah said, "What was it that kid said about a bootlegger?"

Bobby looked at Kate, who said nothing. "Niniltna's a damp town," he told Dinah, "you can have booze and drink it but you can't sell it within tribal boundaries. Someone was. Kate made him stop."

Dinah got the distinct impression that there was a lot more to the story, along with another distinct impression that she wasn't going to hear it. She was right.

CHAPTER 5

Some people say that the bark of the white and black poplar cut into small pieces and scattered over dunged earth will produce edible fungi at all seasons.

—*Dioscorides*

A t ten A.M. the following morning, an hour after Daniel Seabolt's dental records arrived in the coroner's office in Anchorage, the body in the mushrooms was positively identified as Daniel Dale Seabolt, white male aged thirty-six, teacher, Chistona Public School, born April 4, 1959 in Enid, Oklahoma, graduated from Oklahoma State University in 1980, certified to teach secondary education by the Oklahoma State Board of Education, last known address P.O. Box 963, Chistona, Alaska, survived by his father, Simon John Seabolt, aged fifty-seven, and one son, Matthew Simon Seabolt, aged ten. Kate heard the news when she drove up to Tanada at noon and called Chopper Jim from the bar.

She was silent for so long he thought she'd hung up. "Kate?"

The same bartender from her last visit was polishing the same glass behind the same bar and not answering a request for directions to Skinny Dick's Halfway Inn. The tourist, a plump gentleman in his sixties, finally gave up and went back outside.

"Kate?" Jim said again.

She stirred. "You want to tell his family?"

"Not particularly."

"Good. I do."

That didn't sound like the Kate Shugak Jim Chopin knew. "All right," he said slowly.

"I have to report the results of my investigation to my client, anyway."

He remembered that handful of crumpled dollar bills. "Right. What's going on, Kate?"

She settled herself more comfortably against the wall. The same guy was passed out with his head on the bar. Billy Ray Cyrus had taken Dwight Yoakum's place on the radio. The bartender polished his glass. The air, cooler inside than out, smelled of stale cigarettes and the sour tang of spilled beer. Another man, red-faced and perspiring, came in and asked, "Am I on the Denali Highway?" The bartender pointed the glass at the map on the wall. The man walked over to look at it. From his expression, it didn't help much. He left, too.

"I talked to some folks yesterday, after church,"

Kate said. "Do you know what went on up here last year?"

"You mean that stuff at the school?"

"You know then. Tell me about it."

"I don't know much. One of the teachers—was it Seabolt?—was practicing evolution without a license or some such, and a bunch of the parents who go to that born-again Baptist church got up in arms to give creationism equal time. That's really about all I know, Kate. Nobody took any shots at anybody over it, so I didn't pay much attention."

"Daniel Seabolt *was* the teacher," Kate said.

"And you think that had something to do with his death?"

"I don't know," Kate admitted. "But I have to start somewhere."

"Why?"

Silence.

"Look, Kate, the guy got caught out without his clothes on. Maybe he was enjoying the delights of nature alfresco. Maybe he was enjoying them a deux. Maybe—"

Kate could almost hear one wicked eyebrow go up and interrupted before Jim got seriously creative. "Why is his kid the only one to notice he's missing? Why didn't his father the pastor report his son's disappearance? Why didn't anyone else in Chistona? The population there is only about one hundred and eighty, everyone knows everyone else, somebody must have noticed he was missing."

"We don't know anything about him. Maybe he made a habit of splitting like this. Some people do, you know."

True, some people did. Kate was related to more than a few of them. "Jim, who would know what went on at the school there last year?"

"Hell, I'd guess just about anyone in the area."

"They're not doing much talking."

"You interviewed everyone in the borough?" he said dryly.

"Not yet. There has to be some kind of superintendent for the school district. Do you know who it is, and where they're located?"

"Hang on a minute."

There was a click and someone started playing Muzak at her and she nearly hung up. Why didn't anyone ever play Jimmy Buffet or Cindy Lauper on hold? But no, it was always 101 Silver Strings playing Your Favorite Broadway Tunes. There were few things worse in life than listening to thirteen violins playing "Too Darn Hot" from *Kiss Me, Kate*. She wondered if anyone had ever been driven to murder under the influence of Muzak.

The thought perked her up a little. An original defense, ranking right down there with Roger McAniff's, who had claimed to have massacred nine people under the influence of too much sugar ingested in the form of Hostess Twinkies, which to the jury had sounded like the standard diet of any six-year-old American child. It had taken them the sum total of thirty-seven minutes to bring in a guilty verdict on all nine counts of first degree murder. The judge had sentenced him to life plus ninety-nine years for each offense, and Mr. McAniff was presently enjoying the hospitality of the state at the Spring Creek Correctional Facility in Seward.

"Too Darn Hot" ended. Almost without pause the orchestra swung into "There Is Nothing Like a Dame." McAniff really should have tried the Muzak defense instead. "No jury in the land would convict," she said out loud.

"Of what?" Chopper Jim said.

"Oh, you're back."

"You talking to yourself again?"

"I hear it's only when you start answering yourself that you're in trouble," she said. "What you got for me?"

"The district superintendent's name is Frances Sleighter. She's got an office in Fairbanks." He gave her the address. "You going up there?"

"Tomorrow," she said, deciding on the spot.

"It's June, Shugak," he reminded her.

"Damn, that's right, tourist season. There won't be an empty hotel room within a hundred miles."

"You know anybody there?"

"Not anymore." She thought. "Wait a minute, I think I paid my alumni dues this year." She pulled out her wallet and fumbled through the plastic cards. "Yeah, I did, I'm current."

"So?"

"So that means I can stay in the dorm for forty-five bucks a night. Do me a favor?"

"What?"

"Call the English department, see if Tom Winkle-bleck is on campus this summer. If he is, tell him I'm coming, and ask him to make a reservation for me at the dorm."

"Spell it." She did, and he said, "It's done. What if he's not there?"

"I'll wing it. If I have to, I can always sleep in the truck."

"Kate?"

"What?"

"Why?"

Good question, one it took her a while to answer. "The kid hired me to find out what happened to his father."

"You found out what happened to his father."

"No, I just found the body. I want to know how he died, and this business at the school might have had something to do with it." There was silence on the other end of the line. "Jim?"

"What?"

"How are the troopers calling it?"

"Kate, there is no evidence of foul play."

She was silent.

"Kate," he said, and she gritted her teeth at the saintly patience she heard in his voice. "If you want to walk around the Kanuyaq River delta in your

birthday suit, that's pretty much your privilege."
His voice deepened. "In fact, I'd pay real money to
see it." He stopped there, but then Jim Chopin had
always had an uncanny instinct for pushing things
just as far as they would go and no farther. "In the
meantime, I've got two traffic accidents involving
three fatalities to investigate, one in Tok, the other
in Slana. I've got what looks like a murder-suicide
in Skolai. I've got a hiker missing in the Mentastas,
I've got a shooting in Northway and another in Na-
besna, I've got an eighty-four-year-old woman who
fell into the Chistochina while she was whitewater
rafting and has yet to be found, and I've got the
Chitina villagers threatening the lives of the construction crew trying to finish that friggin' road to
Cordova. I've got no time to waste on Daniel Seabolt."

"Something else you could do, you could call
Oklahoma and see if they have any record of the
Seabolt family."

"What do I get for it if I do?"

"Trooper Chopin, are you attempting to trade
sexual favors for services rendered?"

"Did I mention I've also got the Free the Earth
League demanding unlimited, permitless entry into
the Park, and who at last report were waving signs
out in front of the Niniltna access road? Dan
O'Brian'll have my ass if one of his precious rangers
so much as sprains a toe."

"You do have fun in your job," Kate observed.

"You're going to Fairbanks, aren't you?"

"Yes."

He sighed. "Good-bye and keep cold."

"All this encouragement and Robert Frost, too, how'd I get so lucky," she said, and hung up quick before he thought she was flirting with him.

Outside in the parking lot she was stunned into immobility by the sight of a fire-engine-red Porsche with a lot more people inside it than provided for by the designer. It skidded to a halt and the driver's door popped like the cork on a bottle. The contents spilled out and resolved into two men and three women. Kate could smell the booze coming off them from twenty feet away.

The driver spotted her. "Just what we need, folks, a native guide!" He weaved across the gravel on unsteady feet to where she stood. Mutt looked askance up at her and back toward the approaching horde, uncertain of how to deal with either.

The driver pronounced. "I am Dr. Higgins." He drew himself more or less upright. "My card."

Kate took it automatically. He was a dentist, it said, specializing in smile care. It really said that on the card: Specializing in Smile Care.

"This is my colleague, Dr. Sarton." Dr. Sarton bowed over Kate's hand, almost losing his balance, flinging out one arm to catch it again and making a near miss of Kate's left breast. She straightened him up with more haste than grace. Unheeding, Dr.

Higgins said, "And this—" he drew the women forward "—is Pat, this is Lynn and this is Alison. Or maybe this is Alison and that is Lynn. They're all so beautiful I forget." He leered. Alison, or maybe Lynn, yawned.

The two men wore tuxedos, although they'd lost their ties and cummerbunds. The three women wore dresses constructed of less material than a dishcloth although more than a napkin, sprinkled liberally with sequins, and heels so high Kate's calves ached just looking at them. Dr. Higgins leaned down to look soulfully into Kate's eyes. She backed up a step to stay out of range of his breath. "The thing is," he said confidingly, "is we're looking for the Iditarod."

After her abortive attempt to aid the French couple Kate had sworn off the tourist industry but this was a gambit even she could not refuse. "The Iditarod?"

"Yes. You know. The dogsled race?"

"I know," Kate agreed.

"Well." He waved a hand. "The girls wanted to see it. So we took a little drive up, and here we are!" He beamed at her, all innocent expectance.

Kate looked at him. She looked at his friends. She looked at the Porsche, which had California plates. She looked back at him and said gravely, "I'm terribly sorry, Dr. Higgins, you just missed it." By over three months. With great restraint, she managed to refrain from pointing out that the start was approximately two hundred miles farther down the road, as well.

"Nonsense," he replied, weaving a little on his feet. He waved a hand again, a regal, all-encompassing gesture, his best. "The girls want to see it."

Never argue with a drunk. "Well," she replied solemnly, "if you're set on it, I suppose you could always stick around for the next one."

"Marvelous!" For a moment Kate was afraid he was going to kiss her. "Absolutively splendid! Didja hear that, girls? Didja hear that, Howard?"

Howard and the girls heard. Howard looked at her adoringly. Kate murmured modestly that she was pleased to be of service.

Dr. Higgins leaned forward to looked deeply into her eyes. "I think you're wonderful. Isn't she wonderful, Howard?"

Howard said she was. The girls were looking less bored now, possibly due to the fact that the mosquitoes had discovered their state of dress, or in this case, undress, and had assembled en masse for brunch and Bloody Marys. The three of them together looked like a cross between a windmill in a gale and both rotor blades of a helicopter.

Dr. Higgins, still gazing soulfully at Kate, was recalled to his duties as host. "Maybe just a beer while we wait then." He rocked back on his heels, recovered his balance, rocked forward on his toes, leaned in the direction of the tavern's front door and let gravity and inertia do the rest. Howard and the girls followed him in a stumbling mass.

Kate went over to the Porsche, turned off the engine and closed the door.

Simon Seabolt took the news of his only son's death without perceptible reaction, and Kate knew, because she was watching him very carefully indeed. He was watching her just as carefully, although it was some time before she realized it.

They sat across from each other, silent, in the room tucked into one corner of the log cabin that served as the pastor's study. One wall had a tiny window cut into the logs through which a minuscule amount of sunshine stretched tentatively inside, not enough to warm the monastic little cell and barely enough to illuminate the other three walls, which were bare. There was a desk and two chairs. The desk had a Bible on it, the King James version, and a copy of Cruden's *Complete Concordance*. That was all. The desk and chairs were army surplus, painted battleship gray and as uncomfortable as they were unattractive. The floor, like the rest of the house she had seen, was made of wooden planks, roughly planed, and Kate pitied the person who walked on it barefoot. Maybe Pastor Seabolt considered it a modern version of the hair shirt.

Splinters in the souls of your feet brought you closer to God, that kind of thing. Herself, she'd stick with her Nikes.

He had yet to say anything. She knew the trick; keep silent long enough, the other person felt compelled to fill that silence. Pastor Seabolt did not know with whom he was in competition, however. Alaska Native children learn by watching and listening. Direct questions are not often asked, and when words finally are used, they are honored and remembered and so not wasted in trivia. The lack of verbal communication could frustrate and bewilder an Anglo dealing with a Native for the first time, as witness the three classes Kate had dropped her first year in college because the teachers kept asking her questions.

It could also lead to the Anglo underestimating the Native, and it made Seabolt underestimate Kate. "My dear, what is it I can do for you? I know you must have sustained a severe shock, finding the body that way. A dreadful thing." He shook his head. "I would not for the world have had it happen to you."

"It was a bit upsetting," Kate agreed, trying her best to look upset. It was more of an effort than he made.

"Of course," he said.

She pasted a look of sympathetic inquiry on her face and leaned forward, all concern. "But Pastor

Seabolt, how came your son to be up there in the first place?"

He looked sad. "I don't know. Perhaps he was walking in the woods and simply got caught out in the fire."

"With no clothes on?"

He looked at her sharply and she met his gaze with limpid innocence. He relaxed back into melancholy. "Had he no clothes on?"

She shook her head, as sad as he. "I'm afraid not."

He thought. "Then perhaps they caught fire and he stripped them off as he ran."

"Perhaps," Kate agreed. She hesitated, and caused a puzzled frown to crease her brow. "It was a very dry summer, last summer."

He nodded his head regally, as if he himself had been responsible for it. "It was."

"And the Park Service had the area on fire alert."

"They had."

She gave a tiny sigh. "Then, Pastor Seabolt, I'm afraid I simply cannot make any sense of this." She looked up and met his eyes with every evidence of frank bewilderment, and repeated, "What *was* your son doing out there in the first place? During a fire alert? With no clothes on?"

They both pondered this knotty problem for a few moments. She watched him, and finally he spread his hands, reminding Kate of nothing so much as a picture she had once seen of Christ ascending to heaven, hands spread benignly in just that same fashion. "Who can say, Sister Shugak?" He dropped his voice to a confidential tone. "You knew my son was a widower."

"I did," she said, equally grave.

He shook his head again, and looked so sad that for a moment Kate thought he might burst into tears. "I'm afraid he never recovered from her loss."

She said, too bluntly, "Are you saying he was mentally imbalanced over her death, and that was why he was out wandering around naked in front of a forest fire?"

He withdrew a little. "Those matters are for God and God alone to judge," he said austerely. He thawed again, and leaned forward to place an avuncular hand on her knee. "Have you been born again, Sister Shugak?"

"No."

"Oh, my dear, my dear." He shook his head. "Let Jesus knock at the door of your heart, and accept the joy of walking with God for yourself, before it is too late."

She slid her knee from beneath that avuncular, suddenly very heavy hand. "Jesus Christ will come knocking at the door of my heart in his own good time, not yours," she said, and was immediately annoyed that she had allowed him to goad her into the retort.

He knew it. There was a flash of triumph in his eyes, immediately repressed and replaced by the carefully cultivated appearance of dignified grief.

Kate wanted to say something to wipe out the smirk lurking behind the very affecting sorrow he had on display. No. Best to hold her hand until she knew more. She rose to her feet and offered a formal apology for being the bearer of such sad tidings. With a saintly expression that made her want to bite him, he forgave her.

His voice stopped her at the door. "Sister Shugak?"

She turned her head. "Yes?"

"I would, if I may, direct you to a verse in the Bible." She waited as he opened the Bible on his desk and thumbed the pages at the back of the book. "Ah yes, here it is. Romans. Chapter 12, Verse 19." He closed the book and sat with it between his hands, looking, in the scant shaft of sunlight, very upright and patriarchal.

"I'm afraid I'm not familiar with that verse, Pastor Seabolt."

He gave her a forgiving smile and did not reply.

"I'll look it up," she promised.

He inclined his head in acknowledgment and dismissal.

Outside the cabin, she heard a low voice call out. "Hey."

She looked around and beheld her client. She

pulled the door shut behind her and walked toward him, halting when he held up one hand like a traffic cop. "Hi."

He was very much the champion for Christ today and went straight to the point. "I hired you to find my father. You found him. You don't have to do any more."

"I see." She studied him. His spine was straight, his chin was up, his blue eyes steady and unswerving. Even righteous. In spite of the redness left by the tears. "Matthew, I—"

"It's done," he said, and produced another fistful of crumpled dollar bills. "You did your job. You can go home now."

She looked from him to the fistful of bills and back to him. "Matthew. Don't you want to know what happened?"

He thrust the bills at her. "You want more? I can get more."

"Matthew, don't you want to know what your father was doing out there? Don't you want to know how he died?"

His voice rose. "You *found* him. That's all I wanted. You can stop now. He's dead. Nothing is going to bring him back to life."

"I assume your grandfather has spoken," Kate said.

It was the wrong thing to say. Humor did not dare raise its ugly head in the presence of the Almighty. His chest rose and fell. "You're fired. Do you hear me? You're *fired*. You're not working for me anymore. I want you to *stop*."

"No, Matthew," she said. "I won't stop."

He thrust the wad of bills back in his pocket and stiffened into a miniature replica of the man inside the house. "God will punish you for your willfulness and your pride." He turned to march off.

Sanctimonious little shit, she thought, watching him go. Bobby was right.

But a sanctimonious little shit who'd had a very hard time and was in a lot of pain. She wished she could like him.

She didn't have to, to help him.

It would be easier, though.

She drove back down the road to Chistona and hung out arounnd the store. Russell Gillespie did not look pleased to see her and did his best to ignore her. She stood in a corner and watched his customers shop and him ring up tabs. The hunting tunic hung on the wall above his head and glowed like a gem in the half-light.

Russell's attitude was one his customers shared. Kate hadn't felt this frozen out since she chased Toni Hartzler down in a raging blizzard on the North Slope. When she said hello to someone, they moved past her. When she tried to introduce herself, they looked through her. When she asked a question, they pretended they had not heard.

She moved to a spot outside and tried to engage

people in friendly conversation as they emerged, but the mukluk telegraph had done its usual thorough job and the most she got was from an older woman with defeated eyes who said, edging toward her Subaru, "Really, I don't know anything about it."

"About what?" Kate said.

"About whatever it is you want to talk about," the woman said, and climbed into her car and drove off.   Kate gave up finally and went around back to see if Sally were home. She was. She even answered the door. She stood on the threshold, one hand on the knob, looking at Kate with an expression that was easy to identify. Fear. She asked one question of her own. "Is it true you found Daniel Seabolt's body?"

"Yes."

The other woman's eyes filled with tears and a hand came up to cover her mouth. "Oh my dear lord."

Kate waited. Sally got herself under control and started to close the door. Kate put one hand against it, holding it open. "Wait. Please. I'd just like to ask you a few questions."

Sally shook her head blindly. "I can't. I'm sorry. Please go away and leave me alone." One of her children was standing directly behind her, clutching his mother's waist and peering around her hips with a scared face. "And please, don't ever come back here again. Please."

Kate was not in the habit of frightening women

and children. She removed her hand and the door swung shut in her face.

"Damn it." Huffing out an exasperated sigh she stood, hands on hips, thinking. She could talk to Brad Burns again, see if he had anything to add. She doubted it; he would have advertised, held it out as bait for her return.

She thought of driving up the road to Gakona and visiting Auntie Joy to see if she or Emaa had heard anything useful. If there was anything to be heard, those two would have heard every syllable, every nuance.

She looked at her watch. It was getting on for six o'clock, and she was tired and hungry and so she decided to return to camp instead.

Negotiating the lumps and bumps and washouts of the road to the turnoff, Kate realized that not one of the local residents she had told of Daniel Seabolt's death had asked how he had died.

Not even his father.

The attack came in the early hours of the morning, when the sun had dropped below the horizon for a few hours, leaving a pale smudge of burnt umber on the horizon to mark its departure and promise its speedy return. They swooped down on the two tents in a quick, silent rush. Kate was summoned from sleep by a sudden scramble of Mutt's feet outside the tent and a warning bark. "What?" she said groggily. "What is it, girl?"

The roof of the tent seemed to cave in over her head. Something blunt came down hard on her left shoulder. "Ouch!" Her right thigh caught a smart, stinging rap and she rolled instinctively into a ball, arms protecting her head.

"What the fuck!" she heard Bobby roar, a cry of pain came from Dinah, and blows rained down on Kate's forearms. "Mutt!" she yelled, her voice muffled in the tangling folds of tent and sleeping bag. "Take! Take, Mutt!"

There was an answering snarl and a man's cry of pain.

"Ouch!"

"Get that goddam dog away from me!"

"Shit!"

A yelp from Mutt, another snarl and snap, a shriek of real pain and fear this time, and a third voice yelled, "Come on, we've given her enough to think about, let's get outta here!"

The blows ceased abruptly and the crunch of heavy, rapidly moving footsteps receded down the hill, Mutt's rumbling growl following close behind.

"Mutt!" Kate yelled, still muffled in the folds of bag and tent. "Come!"

A few moments later came the roar of an engine. One of them must have stayed in their truck with the engine running. Kate lay for a moment, panting, and listened to the truck's engine shift into gear and recede into the night. She recovered enough to move her limbs cautiously, one at a time, checking by feel to see if anything had been broken. Nothing had, but she hurt all over, especially her forearms and her right thigh. It took a while longer to fight her way out of the smothering folds of her sleeping bag and find the zipper to the flap of the tent, which had rolled with her when she rolled to protect her head.

She emerged to see Bobby's head poke through the folds of his collapsed tent on the other side of the clearing. He turned immediately to assist Dinah and Kate hurried to help. The blonde hissed with pain when Kate gripped her arm, moaned when Kate shifted her hold to the elbow, and whimpered when Kate tried to grasp her shoulder.

Bobby batted her hands out of the way, rocked forward on his stumps and had Dinah free in three quick moves. She could walk, barely, and limped over to collapse next to the fire. The rocks of the fireplace had been scattered across the clearing, the grill knocked off its legs and a coal was trying to ignite a patch of grass before Kate grabbed the up-ended cooler and poured what was left of the melted ice over it. She reassembled the fire ring, scooped up some kindling and blew on the remaining coals until one of them caught. She fed it, one stick at a time, until the fire was crackling with energy and giving off a solid amount of heat. She retrieved a few pieces of scattered firewood and piled it on. Dinah, shivering, scooted nearer.

Kate rose to her feet, her joints creaking with the

effort. "Where's Mutt?" she said suddenly. She felt her first real flare of panic. "Mutt? Mutt, where are you? Mutt!"

There was one terrifying moment of silence that for Kate lasted at least a year, and then Mutt limped into the circle of light. "Are you hurt, girl? Come here, let me see." Kate dropped to her knees to run exploring hands over her. When they encountered her right foreleg, Mutt gave a quick, distressed yelp, of which she immediately looked ashamed.

Kate went over her one more time, to be sure. The bruised foreleg was all she found. Relief that nothing was broken was quickly followed by rage and she shot to her feet, hands clenched at her sides. "Those sanctimonious, self-righteous, Jesus-freaking sons of *bitches*."

"Not now," Bobby said tersely, puzzling out the framework of his tent. "Better keep moving. You won't be able to later."

She knew he was right and after a tense, inner struggle packed the rage away for a later time. A later time that would come, she vowed fiercely to herself. She went to her tent to see what she could make of the mess. Dinah, moving painfully, went to collect the scattered heap of supplies.

An hour later, when most of the camp had been more or less returned to its previous condition, Bobby made a pot of coffee and the three of them sat down stiffly around the campfire, heavily sugared mugs in hand. Mutt leaned up against Kate, who knotted one hand in her ruff, taking as much comfort from the warm, solid presence as she gave with her own. The sweet, scalding coffee blazed down her throat and burned into her gut. Her stomach lurched once and then steadied beneath the assault. "I'm sorry, guys," she said, the apology coming out in a husky rasp. "This was my fault."

"Cut it out," Bobby growled.

"Oh," Dinah inquired, "is that what you were doing in Chistona all day? Hiring those men to come out here and beat us up?"

"No, but I was doing something just as bad."

"What?"

"Asking questions. I know better. You don't go poking your nose into other people's business out here. It's not smart. And it sure as hell isn't safe."

"More to the point," Bobby said, "what is it they are so all-fired afraid of, that they come up here and try to scare you off?"

"I wish I knew," she said, nursing her mug, staring into the fire. "They won't talk. And this little demonstration proves how determined they are not to."

"Think it has something to do with your finding Seabolt's body?"

"Yes."

"Gonna give up trying to find out what happened to him?"

Kate's answer was immediate and unequivocal. "No."

Bobby's white teeth flashed in the firelight. "Didn't think so."

Finishing her coffee, she rose to return to her interrupted sleep and paused. "Dinah?"

The blonde, caught in the act of a slow and careful rising, sank back down gratefully on the ground. "What?"

"You still have that Bible with you?"

Dinah gestured with her chin. "In the left pocket of my duster. In the tent. Or it was."

Kate searched until she found it, and brought the book back to read it by the light of the fire, although by now she was almost able to read it in the light of the dawn.

"What are you looking for?" Dinah said, watching her.

"Seabolt quoted a verse at me this afternoon. I forgot until now."

"Which one?"

"Romans. Chapter 12, Verse 19." She lost her place. "Rats, I can't find it."

"You don't have to," Bobby said. " 'Vengeance is mine; I will repay, saith the Lord.' "

Her head snapped up and she stared at him, Bible forgotten in her hands, and he nodded once, grimly. "Yes. It was a warning."

Kate put the Bible back and crawled into her tent without a word. Mutt lay in the open flap, body a solid presence against Kate's feet. Neither of them moved a muscle for what remained of the night.

CHAPTER
6

Now whether this imperfection of the earth, for it cannot be said to be anything else, grows, or whether it has at once assumed its full globular size, whether it lives or not, are matters which I think cannot be easily understood.

—Pliny

K ate left for Fairbanks the next morning at eight A.M. Dinah had a shiner turning an attractive shade of purple, the entire left side of Bobby's face was swollen and all three of them were stiff and careful in motion. At least no bones had been broken and they *were* in motion, as Dinah helpfully pointed out. Kate suggested the two of them pack up and head back to the Park. "Hell with that," Bobby roared. "We came to pick shrooms, let's goddam pick shrooms!" He shifted from defense to offense. "Why the hell you going to Fairbanks, anyway? Is there some Aleut proverb that says if you find a body you have to find out how it got there?"

There followed a brisk discussion during which

the defects of certain personalities were identified
and examined. Dinah, mercifully, did not record
any of it for posterity. Kate finally shouldered her
pack and stamped out of camp, Mutt limping at her
heels. She had tried to get her to stay behind but
Mutt wasn't having any that morning, either.

They arrived at their destination at four-thirty
that afternoon. A smoky haze from the three separa-
rate forest fires burning in the Interior hung over
the city like a pall. Ice fog in winter, smoke in summer, Kate couldn't remember very many days in
Fairbanks when the sky obtained its normal shade
of blue. Of the two, ice fog or smoke, she preferred
ice fog. Ice fog meant the temperature would be
something decent and endurable, like twenty below.
Thirty below was more the norm and forty below
not rare, but, she remembered, you could always
tell when it got up to twenty below because the guys
went from the dorm to the commons in their T-
shirts. At thirty below, they put on their jackets. At
forty below, they might even wear gloves.

As she turned onto University Avenue her sinuses
suddenly seized up like a muscle with a charley
horse. She'd forgotten about the lack of moisture in
Fairbanks's air, but they hadn't. You promised, they
wailed all the way up University Avenue and left on
Taku Drive, you promised you'd never do this to us
again. They moaned and sobbed and cried as she
turned right on Tanana Loop and left on Yukon
Drive, until she parked in front of the upper campus

dorms and they shut up and made her breathe through her mouth instead, just to show her. She hoped her nose wouldn't start bleeding.

The desk was presided over by a polite girl with the longest, straightest, most colorless hair Kate had ever seen. It swept behind her like a train and there was enough of it to weigh more than she did. In the act of handing over the key to Bartlett 713, she saw Mutt. "Uh, no animals allowed in the dorm."

"Okay," Kate said equably. She jerked a thumb at Mutt. "You explain to her how she's going to have to sleep in the truck."

She went to the elevator, Mutt padding at her side.

Emerging on the seventh floor, the first sound to greet her was the insistent ring of the telephone. As easily and as instantly as that, she was transported back in time.

There was one phone for every floor of every dorm on campus. Since it is a demonstrably true fact of life that most people in their late teens and early twenties live on the phone, it follows that an entire floor of them generate a lot of phone calls. Answering the phone was a job purportedly shared by everyone on the floor but in reality defaulted to those whose rooms were closest to the booth. Having answered the phone, it was then the resident's responsibility to locate the person the caller wished to speak to. About a month into the semester, the phone rang unanswered. Her first year, Kate's room

had been one door down from the phone booth.
Her second, third and fourth years, she had requested the room farthest from it.

The phone was still ringing and still no one was
answering it when Kate found 713 and unlocked
the door. Inside was just as depressing as it had ever
been, a single bed, a row of closets, a sort of a desk
with shelves, not enough plug-ins, cement walls
painted a hideous electric blue, linoleum squares
laid down over a cement floor, stained acoustical
tiles overhead, exposed pipes and conduit. Any
freshman in his or her right mind would have run
screaming at first sight.

There was a tall, narrow window, the bottom of
which opened in and had a handle, all the better
for use as a beer cooler in winter. Kate remembered
one Inupiat girl from Point Hope who had received
care packages of maqtaq from home and would
hang it outside from that handle. Truth be told,
most of the dorms during the winter had various
bags hanging outside their windows, giving the
buildings the look of an itinerant tinker, laden with
wares.

There was a tap at the door. Kate opened it and
there stood Jack Morgan.

He looked needy, quite a feat for a man six feet
two inches tall and weighing 220 pounds, all of it
muscle. "Hi." He sounded needy, too.

"Hello."

"Jim Chopin called me, told me you'd be here."
He made a vague gesture toward an unseen airport.
"I flew up this morning."

"So I see."

The blue eyes were wary beneath the thatch of
untidy brown hair. "I hope you don't mind?"

It was a legitimate question, given the way they
had parted two months before. He had told her he
loved her, and she had run like a thief.

"How'd you know which room?"

"I showed the clerk my ID."

"Oh."

"Kate?"

"What?"

"I've missed you."

The hell with it. Life was too short to pick fights
in which everyone lost. She stretched out a hand
and pulled him inside. "Show me how much."

The door opened a second later and Mutt was
assisted into the hall. She curled up on the thin
brown carpeting, stuck her nose under her tail and
prepared to enjoy a better night's sleep than the two
people on the other side of the door.

It was a single bed. They didn't notice. They
missed dinner. They didn't care. The phone in the
hall rang every ten minutes. They never heard it.
They went at each other like pirates after plunder.
It was loot, pillage and burn all night long, and as
Jack said ruefully the following morning, surveying

in the mirror the marks she'd left on his back, "There's nothing like that little touch of frenzy to spice up your sex life."

Her answer was to move behind him and run her tongue down one of the red lines scoring his skin, and it was another hour before they got up the second time and managed to keep their hands off each other long enough to dress and go in search of breakfast. They found it at Sourdough Sam's Cafe, a restaurant where the waitresses still wore their hair in beehives and the menus promised the short stacks really would be sour. A table next to the window was free and they slid into it just ahead of a family of four from Des Moines and ordered pancake sandwiches. When they came, the sausage was patty and the cakes lived up to their reputation. "As good as Emaa's," Kate said thickly, and applied herself to her meal. She was hungry.

So was he. He finished before she did and watched her sop up the rest of the syrup with the last bite of pancake. The view was superb. Her hazel eyes were sleepy, a little secretive, and her brown skin glowed as if lit from behind. She looked like she had just spent the night doing exactly what she had been doing. He wondered what he looked like. The same, probably.

She glanced up and flushed beneath his regard. "What?"

He reached across the table and filched the last

of her sausage. "You know very well what."

His voice was deep and a little husky and Kate thought it best to change the subject before they wound up back in her room for the rest of the day. "How's Johnny?"

He knew exactly what she was doing and the gravity of his tone was belied by the amusement in his eyes. "Fine."

"He living with you now?"

"Yeah, Judge Finn gave me temporary custody, pending final disposition."

"And Jane?"

One eyebrow quirked. "She's on her third attorney. They keep dumping her."

"Who've you got?"

"Dorothy Ganepole."

Kate nodded. "She's good. She's even halfway human. For an attorney."

"Yeah, Johnny likes her, too. She's the only other person besides me who reads the same science fiction authors he does."

"And me."

"And you."

"Who'd you leave him with?"

"Jane." Her face changed, and he said, "She has visitation rights. She is his mother, Kate."

"Not so's you'd notice," she muttered, but he wisely refused to be drawn into a discussion of Jane's shortcomings. Kate had never lived with the woman; she didn't know the half of it. He shied away from the thought of what might happen if she did.

She pushed her chair back. "Where we going?" he said.

"Up to the museum."

She parked again in front of Bartlett and they walked the rest of the way. Between the upper campus dorms and the museum, a new science building had been constructed with federal funds; Kate thought what a pity it was some of those funds had not been earmarked for new dorms. Adequate housing—hell, even just enough housing—had always been a problem on the Fairbanks campus. She remembered first-year students sleeping on the floor of the student union building. Didn't look like much had changed.

The haze had thinned enough to see the river valley and the rolling hills that surrounded the campus, although the smell of burning timber was still a tangy and tangible presence. "What are you doing here anyway?" Jack said, as if he'd just thought of it.

"Didn't Jim say?"

He shook his head. He didn't tell her, but when he'd heard she would be in a place with a functioning airstrip he'd been in such a hurry to arrange for the days off and get out to his tiedown at Merrill Field that he hadn't bothered to ask. He said now, with elaborate unconcern, "I presume it has something to do with the bruises I saw last night."

His even, indifferent tone invited her to admire how well he was behaving. She stopped dead in her tracks and gave him that patented Shugak glare. He sighed. "Well, I could hardly help noticing. You've got defensive marks all up and down the underside of your forearms, and one real beauty of a bruise on your right thigh turning an interesting shade of yellow." He gave her a wicked grin, and she would never know the effort it cost him to maintain it. "Kind of hard for me to miss that one. Who jumped you, and how come, and does he or she look worse than you do?"

She started walking again. Evidently Jack had his protective instincts well in hand, for a change. "I doubt it. They were in and out of camp pretty fast."

"Who is 'they'?"

"I don't know."

They arrived at the museum before she could say more. Mutt flopped down in a patch of shade and Kate and Jack paid their entry fees and walked inside.

The first thing they saw was the woolly mammoth. "I'll be damned, I didn't know they had one of these here," Jack said. "Our official Alaska state fossil."

"He's the woolly mammoth, big and hairy," Kate said.

"He's the woolly mammoth, ooh, he's scary," Jack came back in a high falsetto, and they both laughed.

"And how is Mr. Whitekeys and the Fly-By-Nite Club?"

"Still packing in the Houseguests from Hell. Have you seen 'The Duct Tape Song' yet?" She shook her head and he said, grinning, "It's worth the drive into Anchorage all by itself. The tourists don't know quite what to make of it, but the locals love it."

The mammoth's tusks spiraled up from the display, graceful in spite of their mass, nearly full curls of fossil ivory. "You kind of wonder how they held their heads up under all that weight."

"Make you feel kind of insignificant, don't they?" Kate said. "That something that big, that indestructible was stamping and snorting around here twelve thousand years ago? And now they're gone. Extinct. Like that." She snapped her fingers.

He considered the skull mounted over the tusks. "They make me horny."

She turned her head so he wouldn't see her grin. "Everything makes you horny."

"No, really," he said, and she looked back and found he was serious. "They make me want to procreate, as fast and as often and as much as I possibly can."

She looked at the fossil, the huge, bony skull, the long curving tusks, and understood. "You don't think anyone's going to preserve your skeleton after you die and stick it up on a museum wall?"

"Nope. There's even a poem about it."

"About preserving your skeleton?"

"No, idiot, about them." He nodded at the tusks. "Something about how all they are now is billiard balls."

The tusks gleamed beneath small, carefully directed spotlights. " 'Look on my works, ye mighty, and despair'?" He nodded. "And that bugs you?"

He shrugged. "Sure. Gotta leave a mark."

She looked from the tusks to him, his relaxed stance, his meditative expression. He didn't look as if he were frantically in search of immortality to her, but then he had Johnny. She looked back at the tusks. "Funny you should feel that way."

"Funny ha-ha?"

"Funny strange. I've been running up against immortality and/or the possibility of it a lot lately."

"Tell me."

Behind them a busload of tourists flooded through the doors, all the women in pastels, all the men in plaid, everyone in polyester and no one under sixty-five. They drifted over to Blue Babe and paused.

"You know what we were doing in Chistona?" Kate asked.

"No," he said gravely, "somehow we never got around to discussing that last night. Must have been distracted. Who's we?"

"Bobby and me."

"And?"

"And we drove up to Chistona to pick mush-rooms."

"And?"

"And I found a body when I was out picking Saturday morning. Chopper Jim flew up and took it to town that afternoon."

"The Body in the Mushrooms," Jack said. "Sounds like a Jane Marple murder mystery."

It made her nervous that his first thought would be the same as hers. "Jim flew in and took the body back," she said, sticking firmly to the story. "It was a guy named Daniel Seabolt." She told him the rest of it, omitting nothing. "And then last night, somebody jumped us. Just jumped us, out of the blue, in our tents. Dinah got one hell of a shiner, Bobby—"

"Dinah?"

"Dinah Cookman, she was driving up the AlCan and ran out of gas money about the same time the mushrooms popped up."

"Fortuitous."

Kate said demurely, "Bobby would agree."

"Aha."

She grinned. "At any rate, all I know is there was some fuss at the school over what Seabolt was teaching. You ever know a cop at APD by the name of Brad Burns?"

"Brad Burns?" He looked down at her, an arrested expression in his eyes.

"Yeah, he knew Daniel Seabolt. He's the one who told me about the business at the school."

"He's in Chistona?"

"Yes. Well, in a cabin on the Kanuyaq near Chistona."

Jack gazed off into the distance, a frown pulling his eyebrows together. "So that's where he went after."

Kate looked at him. When he didn't speak, she said impatiently, "After what?"

His gaze focused on her face with a considering expression. "How much did he tell you?"

"Nothing," she said promptly, "except that he'd been a cop with APD." She waited, expectant. "Jack. What?"

He sighed and looked down at her. "He was new on the force, about four years ago. They used him undercover on a narcotics sting. It went bad and he shot a kid."

Kate closed her eyes briefly.

"Yeah. It was a clean shoot, the kid was armed, but he was only thirteen. Burns couldn't handle it. I think they gave him a partial disability for psychological reasons. So he's on the Kanuyaq, is he? How is he?"

"I only met him the one time." She rolled her hand once, side to side. "He didn't volunteer any information, I didn't ask. He seemed okay. He wanted to get laid, but then I've never met a guy in the bush who didn't."

His grin was involuntary. "So, Burns tells you there was a fuss at the school, and Seabolt disappears. Until you stumble over him, planted amongst the mushrooms."

"Right."

"I'll probably never be able to eat another mushroom again. You think it's cause and effect?" Unaware, she rubbed one bruised forearm. His hands clenched in his pockets. He realized it and forced them to relax, hoping she hadn't noticed.

"Yes," she said. "No. Oh, hell. I don't know."

"That doesn't have your usual ring of moral certainty," he said. "Try again."

She looked down her nose at him, difficult since he was over a foot taller than she was, and marched off to find a museum aide, who in turn directed her to the museum's director, a trim, blonde woman with a vivacious manner, who summoned a third person from the depths of the museum's artifact collection. For a moment, Kate thought the director had called forth one of the artifacts in person.

He was a fussy little man, and in spite of pink cheeks with nary a wrinkle and wide brown eyes and quantities of light brown hair contrived to seem as dry and desiccated as one of his fossils. He looked at the world over the tops of a pair of spectacles perched low on his nose, reserving the more exclusive view through the lens for his precious specimens, although Jack was sure they were just for show, like the affected shoulder stoop and the calipers protruding from one breast pocket. He couldn't have been more than thirty years old, and he was annoyed at having his work interrupted and he told them so. Kate apologized, several times, but he remained annoyed. "Mr. Campbell—" she began, only to be immediately interrupted.

"Dr. Campbell, if you please."

The shine on his doctorate must not have worn off yet. "I beg your pardon, Dr. Campbell." She made her glance admiring. A doctor. And are you faster than a speeding bullet, too? "Doctor, do you happen to remember talking to a Daniel Seabolt?"

"Seabolt?" he said brusquely. "Seabolt? Certainly not. Now if you'll excuse me—"

"He was a teacher," she said quickly. "No, not here, at the public school in Chistona. He contacted you last year for help in conducting a course study in dinosaurs."

"Seabolt," Dr. Campbell said.

"Daniel," Kate said.

"Daniel Seabolt. Of course I remember. A teacher at Chistona Public School. He contacted me last year for help in conducting a course study in dinosaurs."

"Yes, sir," Kate said. Jack's face was carefully blank, and she turned slightly so she wouldn't have to look at it.

"I was unable to help him, of course," Dr. Campbell sniffed.

"Why?"

He sniffed again, more reflectively than offensively this time. "Really, we have no adequate specimens of dinosaurs in the collection. We have as yet no adequate specimens of dinosaurs in the state of Alaska."

Jack hooked a thumb over his shoulder. "What about the woolly mammoth?"

He was promptly withered by a look of intense scorn. "That is not a dinosaur, that is a Pleistocene mammal. A warm-blooded, milk-producing vegetarian."

"Oh," Jack said weakly, and subsided into the background. Campbell lifted one weary eyebrow in Kate's direction, as if to mutually deplore these amateurs who plague us from time to time. Kate did not know what had elevated her from their ranks but she took the promotion and the accompanying rise in patronizing respect with appropriate gratitude. Which is to say she hung on Campbell's every word with wide-eyed, enraptured attention.

Campbell preened himself beneath that regard and proceeded to tell them everything he knew about the Pleistocene Era, which was considerable, and all of it in words of not less than four syllables. He began two million years in the past and in forty-five minutes had worked himself all the way up to the last Neanderthals and early Paleolithic art when

Kate managed to insert a breathless comment. "Then there were Homo sapiens on earth when the woolly mammoth was alive?"

"My dear girl!" Though he could never get her to admit it later, Jack distinctly saw her flutter her eyelashes at Campbell. "My dear girl," Campbell repeated, placing a less than professorial hand in the small of her back and urging her toward the mammoth exhibit. Jack trailed along behind, a forgotten third, keeping an eye on Campbell's hand. He understood perfectly Kate's promotion from the rank of novice to that of confidante. Dry and desiccated as he might affect to be, Campbell wasn't dead.

The two hunched over the display case in front of the tusks, Jack peering over their shoulders. " 'These tusks of an infant mammoth,' " Kate read aloud, " 'were found with this stone projectile point near Ester. This discovery suggests that people occupied the Fairbanks area during the Pleistocene period and hunted mammoths.' "

Campbell beamed at her. "You see?" He dropped his voice and said in a deferential tone, "I hope you don't mind my asking, but would you be an Alaska Native?"

"I would," she said, dropping her own voice an octave, a difficult feat since the scarring on her larynx brought her voice out in a throaty rasp perilously close to a bass anyway.

"I thought so," he said smugly, and flung out one

hand. "Then you should take considerable pride in the strength and the skill and the sheer daring of your ancestors. They faced down one of the largest mammals in their coevolutionary time frame and served him up for Sunday dinner."

She frowned up at the skull and tusks displayed above the case. "Why does the display say mastodon on one side and mammoth on the other?"

He guided her around to the front of the exhibit, the better to stare head-on into the mammoth skull's empty eyes. "They were both proboscideans, my dear. The American mastodon, or *Mammut americanus,* and the woolly mammoth, or *Mammuthus primigenius.*"

"Proboscideans?" Jack said involuntarily. "What the hell is a proboscidean when it's at home?"

Campbell disdained even a single glance over his shoulder at the amateur. "The first elephants, Mr., er—"

"Morgan," Jack supplied.

"Yes, of course, Mr. Gorman."

Kate ignored them both and ran her fingers over the samples of teeth displayed at the front of the exhibit below a sign saying, PLEASE TOUCH. She closed her eyes and ran her tongue over her own teeth. She had molars that felt like the mastodon's teeth, canines that felt like the mammoth's. She opened her eyes and gave Campbell one of her best smiles. Before it wore off, she tucked one hand in his arm and said confidingly, "So when Daniel Seabolt asked for help with a class on dinosaurs, of course you couldn't help him."

"Certainly not," Campbell said, mesmerized, reminding Jack irresistibly of Mowgli falling deeper under Kaa's spell.

She fussed a little with the front of his shirt, straightening a collar, smoothing a lapel. "What subject did you suggest he cover instead? The woolly mammoth?"

"It was what he was interested in, at first, after I told him I couldn't help with the dinosaur project."

"No," she murmured encouragingly.

"And of course I have made a special study of taphonomy."

"Of course." Again with the admiring glance. And do you leap tall buildings with a single bound?

Jack wondered what taphonomy was but he wasn't fool enough to ask.

"So I suggested he have his class conduct a study of mammals of the Pleistocene instead. These would include the woolly mammoth, the saber-toothed tiger and the steppe bison, of which we have a very fine specimen." He guided her carefully around the mammoth exhibit to the mounted figure of Blue Babe, a steppe bison discovered on a mining claim near Fairbanks. They regarded the figure. The museum was between busloads for the moment, and silent. Babe was prone, legs folded beneath him, and he looked a little annoyed, in Jack's opinion, as if he hadn't taken kindly to having his eternal rest disturbed for the satisfaction of a lot of gawking tourists. "I pointed out that some of the mammals that existed during the Pleistocene still exist today— the caribou, the musk ox, the wolf—and that these were creatures with whom his students were undoubtedly familiar, and so would present a link, past to present."

"Very neat," Kate said approvingly. Campbell beamed. "What happened?"

The beam dimmed. "I'm sure I don't know. We had it all arranged, including a field trip over which I myself would have presided, not that I really have the time for such extraneous nonsense. He didn't contact me again, of course." His superior smile was world-weary. "They never do, these dilettantes. No scholarship, no perseverance, no intellectual curiosity whatever. Simply any little thing to keep the kiddies amused and off the streets, and then not even that."

"Dreadful," Kate said sympathetically.

Enough was enough. Jack excused himself and went to wait outside in the smoke-filtered sun with one of the survivors of the Pleistocene era. Kate found him a few moments later, playing tag on the brown lawn with Mutt. "So," Jack said, panting to a halt in front of her, "you make a date for later, or what?"

"No, I've already got a date for later, with someone else." Mutt bounced over and demanded attention, and it was a while before Kate slid to a halt next to Jack and added blandly, "One of my old teachers."

"Good," he said, recovering his composure, "there's a guy I want to drop in on at the Center for Justice. Meet you in an hour in front of the fountain?"

"Make it an hour and a half."

"Okay."

They parted and Kate cut through Wood Center, the student union building. The stairway that went nowhere was still there, as was the sunken lounge, although with a lot less chairs in it than she remembered. The pizza parlor on the second floor was new and smelled of garlic even though it was closed, promising well of the cuisine.

She remembered the building as full of students, all in a hurry, all with the same look of urgency on their faces. Today it was deserted. She saw one person wiping tables in the second-floor cafeteria, another behind the information counter downstairs. A strip bulletin board ran around the wall and Kate paused to read a few of the notices.

NEED TO RENT HOUSE
3 PEOPLE: MOM & 2 DAUGHTERS
(AGES 9 & 12)
PLUS: CAT; SMALL, WELL-BEHAVED
HOUSE DOG, & 7 SLED DOGS
(PREFER RUNNING H20)

Kate liked the placement of the seven sled dogs. Almost an afterthought. Made the cat, the well-behaved house dog and the two daughters seem insignificant by comparison.

Written in Marksalot on a sheet of typing paper, another notice read:

AIRPLANE TICKET
ONE WAY UNITED AIRLINES
ANCHORAGE-CHICAGO-WASHINGTON, D.C.
AUGUST 20
$450

Transportation to Anchorage was evidently your option. Well, there was always the train. She wondered if college students still hitched. Probably. They all thought they were immortal. So had she, once.

SEMINAR
THE INTERHEMISPHERIC
BERING STRAIT
TUNNEL AND RAILROAD

Now, there was a seminar Kate would like to attend. Nonstop, Nome to Anadyr, Anchorage to Vladivostok, Washington, D.C., to Moscow without ever leaving the wheel of your car. She wondered how one bought gas in Russia. She wondered if Russian teachers were allowed to teach their students that gas was refined from petroleum, which was a fossil fuel formed over millions of years from decayed plant and animal remains, such as dinosaurs. She wondered how long it would be before the same people who protested Daniel Seabolt's teachings in Chistona stormed the ivied halls of the University of Alaska.

The prospect depressed her, and she left Wood Center through the front door, crossed between Gruening and Rasmuson, circled the fountain and found the engineers' stone right where she'd left it the day she graduated. The pyramidal shape was painted a color something between nauseous lavender and bilious pink but no one had stolen it lately and the bronze plaque affixed to the front was still firmly affixed. "Fundatori Mundi," Kate said in greeting, and read the inscription through from beginning to end, and laughed like she always did. Her first year up, it was about the only laugh she got.

She walked back to Gruening and her feet took her the rest of the way on their own, up to the third floor and down the hall. The door opened inward, she saw Tom Winklebleck look up from behind his desk and smile, and the memories rolled back as if it were yesterday, as if it were 1981 again and Kate that silent, miserable eighteen-year-old in the back row of the classroom.

Short of height, spare of frame, dressed in worn twill trousers and plaid shirt and shoepaks, long hair combed back from his face in soft gray waves, gray beard and mustache neatly trimmed to chin length, at first sight Tom Winklebleck had given the impression of barely contained energy perilously close to achieving critical mass. Her first day in his class, he had swept the room with one piercing, all-encompassing glance that had left Kate feeling a little singed around the edges. He had perched one hip on the corner of the desk at the front of the room, and produced three books. One was a thin, tattered paperback; the other two were thick and hardbound and equally old.

The class, most of them freshmen and sopho-mores whose natural youthful optimism had been burned out after four years of Sophocles, Dante and Shakespeare droned at them with as much indiffer-ence as ineptitude, eyed him with wariness and in some cases downright hostility. He waited out war-iness and hostility with equal calm, without speak-ing, and something in the intensity of his dark eyes and the patient quality of his silence got to them. The whispers and the rustling died away, the signal for him to open the larger of the three books and begin to read aloud.

He had the most beautiful reading voice Kate had ever heard in her life and ever would hear again. A flowing, mellow tenor without stammer, stutter or mispronunciation, sensitive to feeling, rich with power, it rolled out full-throated and deep, deep as the sound of the biggest bell on the steeple. It reverberated throughout the room, and it reverberated through each and every instant convert sitting before him.

> Our legions are brimful, our cause is ripe:
> The enemy increaseth every day;
> We, at the height, are ready to decline.

With that reading of those three lines he brought them up, erect in their chairs, tense and expectant. If the cause was ripe and the enemy increasing every day, then the time to strike was obvious; it was now, this very moment. They waited but for him to tell them how and when before arming themselves and setting out forthwith.

> There is a tide in the affairs of men,
> Which taken at the flood, leads on to fortune;
> Omitted, all the voyage of their life
> Is bound in shallows and in miseries.

He looked at the class over the top of the page, accenting the last syllables with a drawling scorn that expected little more of them. It stung their pride, as he had meant it to, and they stared back at him almost angrily.

> On such a full sea are we now afloat,
> And we must take the current when it serves,
> Or lose our ventures.

He closed the book. "This is poetry," he said.

They stared at him, dazed and dumb, more than one with their hearts thudding in their breasts as they traveled back two thousand years from the plains of Philippi to arrive with a thump in the drab, humdrum twentieth-century classroom.

They were his from that moment and he knew it.

He picked up the paperback, opened it and read again into the deepening silence.

> expression is the need of my soul
> i was once a vers libre bard
> but i died and my soul went into the body of a
>   cockroach
> it has given me a new outlook on life

From the summons of far-off trumpets to the hesitant clacking of typewriter keys was a great distance, but Winklebleck bridged it effortlessly with his voice. There were a few promising snorts and at least one definite giggle and he smiled to himself and continued.

> there is a rat here . . .
> he is jealous of my poetry
> he used to make fun of it when we were both
>   human
> he was a punk poet himself
> and after he has read it he sneers
> and then he eats it

They were all laughing by then. He closed the book and said, "And so is this poetry."

"But that was *funny*," an incredulous voice protested.

He ignored it and picked up the third book, a fat anthology, and thumbed through the pages. "And so is this poetry:

It little profits that an idle king . . ."

To sail beyond the sunset, Kate thought dreamily afterward, to touch the Happy Isles, to strive, to seek, to find, and not to yield, no, never to yield. She strode into Mr. Hauptmann's bonehead science class with pennons snapping in the breeze. Mr. Hauptmann, disillusioned from years of teaching science to incoming freshmen who lay false claim to having a high school education, began with the atom. Atoms, thought Kate scornfully, atoms when she had just set sail on the Aegean Sea in company with Ulysses. She had no patience with atoms.

But then something caught her attention. Atoms, Mr. Hauptmann told them without much hope of being heard, much less understood, were the smallest part of the elements and the building blocks of molecules. Kate examined her palm, as if she could look close enough to see the individual protons and neutrons of the nuclei and the electrons buzzing around them. Her bones, her skin, her hair, the very blood in her veins, all were made of these energetic individual parts, all in constant motion. The idea dizzied her, and for a moment she felt as if every atom in her body was taking off in a different direction.

And then she thought, but I am an atom, too, my whole self is an atom. I am an atom of the earth, and the earth is an atom of the solar system, and the solar system is an atom of the Milky Way, and the Milky Way is an atom of the universe. A line from the Tennyson poem flashed through her mind and she thought with amazement, I *am* a part of all that I have met.

The astounding discovery that poetry could make sense of science and science of poetry was Kate's intellectual awakening. Until then most of her education had taken place outdoors; she could track a moose, bring it down with one shot, gut it, butcher it, pack it out and cut and wrap it with the best of them. In the bush, she had to eat to live. She didn't have to read to live, and indoors had been an indifferent scholar at best.

All this changed her sophomore year in college. In reading she found her escape from the lonely days away from home and family and everything familiar to her. She read everything, in bulk and indiscriminately, too shy to ask her teachers for guidance. The process was not all joy. The sugary excesses of Rupert Brooke and Gerald Manley Hopkins put her into a mild diabetic coma, Yeats and Eliot made her feel miserably ignorant, but when

Mr. Winklebleck by accident learned of her determination to read through the Rasmuson Library from A to Z and managed tactfully to steer her toward the practical acerbity of Wallace Stevens and the sly forked tongue of Robert Frost, she fell instantly and forever in love.

She smiled now, thinking of that semester of discovery, and Tom Winklebleck saw the smile and knew instantly what she was thinking. "How the hell did you wind up in my poetry class anyway, Kate?" he said. "I've always wondered."

"I needed three more credits in English and I couldn't bear the thought of another composition course. I petitioned the English department and they let me substitute."

"You weren't that bad a writer, as I recall." He motioned her to a seat. "What was wrong with composition?"

"I don't know." She sat down and tilted the chair up on its back two legs, hands linked across her stomach, considering. "It was too—I don't know—too personal."

He knew immediately what she meant, but then he'd always been better than average bright. "You couldn't write without revealing more about yourself than you wanted to expose."

Still uncomfortable with it, a dozen years later, she shrugged dismissively. "I guess."

He saw her discomfort and changed the subject. "So how have you been, Kate? Railroaded any innocent victims into the hoosegow lately? Violated anyone's First through Fifth Amendment rights?"

"I'm not with the D.A.'s office anymore."

His eyes dropped for a moment to the scar on her throat. "I know."

She was surprised. "How? They managed to keep most of it out of the papers."

He shrugged. "I've lived in Alaska a long time. You get to know people. They tell you things you probably have no business knowing."

"The mukluk telegraph," she suggested.

He chuckled. "Told you you should have switched your major to English."

Her answering smile was wry. "Yes, you did, didn't you."

"Well," he said. " 'Let us not burden our remembrances with a heaviness that's gone.' "

"Let's not," she agreed. "How's the pedagogical prestidigitation going? Still brainwashing students too young and too inexperienced to resist?"

"I try like hell."

"Good."

A corner of his mouth pulled down. "Summer semesters aren't bad, we get a lot of continuing ed students then, and they're mostly adults who know what they want and are working toward a goal. It's when the high school kids arrive in the fall that it gets really depressing. You get entire classes filled with students glorying in their own ignorance."

" 'With foreheads villainous low,' " she said,

pleased and proud to have remembered the right quotation at just the right time, instead of at two A.M. the following morning.

He laughed, but shook his head. "Sometimes I'd kill for just one student sitting in the back row, upright and awake."

"You'd kill anybody who tried to take the job away from you," she said shrewdly, and he laughed again and admitted it.

"What's up with you? To what do we owe the honor?" He made a pretense of dusting the front of his shirt.

"I was in the area, didn't want to pass through without saying hello." She hesitated. He was a teacher, and the best of a dying breed. "You ever hear of a village named Chistona?"

He laced his fingers behind his head and leaned back in his chair, his gaze on her face speculative. "Yeah. They're picking mushrooms somewhere around down there, I hear."

"So was I, until Friday."

"Oh?"

She told him.

"Ah yes," he said meditatively, "I remember now, I heard something about that. Via mukluk telegraph, with maybe a little assist from Denise Gallagher over at the education department. More of it coming, too, I imagine, the more active the Bible Belt gets. The creationists. Interesting if implausible theory, God creating the world and four and a half billion years of evolution and history in the snap of his—or her—fingers. Amazing what people can talk themselves into believing."

He was silent for a moment, a pensive expression on his face. "Have you ever heard of the Paluxy Creek discovery?"

She shook her head.

"Ah. Well, Paluxy Creek is in Glen Rose, Texas. It hosts the site of an archaeological dig in which a dinosaur's footprint and a human footprint were said to have been found in the same bed of limestone." He smiled at her expression. "Yes, it was a, shall we say, God-given sign for the fundamentalists. A graven in stone, so to speak, affirmation of the book of Genesis. They could point to Paluxy Creek and say, 'See! God did make man and all the animals in one week!' "

"And?" Kate said, skepticism writ large upon her countenance.

He gave a faint smile. "You're quite right, of course. Some nasty, suspicious little paleontologist got wind of the discovery and went down to Glen Rose to take a look. It turns out that the Paluxy 'man' prints were as much as twenty inches long. Subsequent tests proved the prints to be those of a tridactyl, a three-toed dinosaur walking through soft mud. Of course, some nasty, suspicious little journalist got wind of the nasty, suspicious little paleontologist's doings and wrote them up. Got a lot of publicity, as you may well imagine. The upshot was that the evidence against was so substantive and so convincing that a self-proclaimed creation scientist subsequently rejected his authentication of the Paluxy Man and caused his publisher to recall the book he'd written about it."

He paused, looking at her expectantly, and she caved. "Okay. What's the punchline?"

"The punchline, Kate, is that the true believers have never lost faith in the Paluxy Man. They say the prints were made by a biblical giant, a man thirteen feet tall, a man weighing six hundred pounds." He clicked his tongue disapprovingly. "Don't look so surprised. What's a little concrete evidence in the face of divine revelation? Remember the Red Queen."

"Why the Red Queen?" Kate said, mystified.

"What, don't tell me I've never exposed you to the Red Queen Theory of Religion?" he asked in mock reproach, and wagged his head sorrowfully at her reply. "How remiss of me. I should probably be defrocked. It reads as follows: Believe six impossible things before breakfast. It'll get you in practice for the Virgin Birth and the Second Coming."

Kate admitted, "I never have understood the concept of saving up good behavior in this life as payment for passage into the next."

"You're Aleut, right?" She nodded, and he said, "What do you believe?"

"Me, personally? Or the entire Aleut race?"

"Both," he said, unabashed.

She shrugged. "Me, personally, wasn't raised religious. Abel, my foster father, believed in capitalism." Winklebleck chuckled. "My grandmother was raised Russian Orthodox and she pays it lip service for political purposes, but that's about as far as it goes. I've never read the Bible, although I regret that sometimes when I don't get the references made to it in the books I read." She looked at him and smiled. "And in the poems. John Donne gets to be something of a mystery."

He smiled back. "And the Aleuts?"

"The Aleuts believed that everything, animate and inanimate, had its own soul, its own spirit, its own anua." She reached into her pocket and pulled out a tiny velveteen bag. Untying the drawstring, she produced a tiny otter, no more than three inches tall, standing erect on its hind legs, thick tail curved in a broad swath, front paws held just so, head cocked to one side, black eyes regarding him with a bright and inquisitive gaze.

The front legs of his chair came down with a thump. One stubby forefinger touched the back of the otter's head, caressed the sleek fur down the back to the tail. "Look at him, he looks like he might drop down on all fours and scamper off to the nearest creek any second now."

She smiled, pleased that the otter had struck Winklebleck the same way he had her that first moment in the art gallery. He hadn't been out of her pocket since. "A couple of hundred years ago, a hunter might have worn a carving like this to hunt sea otters."

"To honor the otter's sacrifice to the hunter's greater need," he said.

"Yes. They believed that everything in life was connected with everything else, depended on everything else. For example, in the Aleut view of life, the salmon knew it was food and accepted the fact that it would die so that the People would live."

"Practical."

"That's why when a hunter went hunting, he did so in new clothes, with his harpoon and his kayak decorated with walrus whiskers and ivory charms and beads." She thought of the hunter's tunic on Russell Gillespie's wall. "It was to show respect for the salmon's sacrifice—"

"Or the otter's," Winklebleck said, nodding at the carving.

"—or the otter's, or the walrus's, or whatever he was hunting that day. You don't find a lot of that in the fundamentalist concept of Christianity," she added.

"A lot of what? Sacrifice?"

"Respect. The Christian God doesn't respect his followers enough to allow them to make their own choices, and they don't respect Him enough to look out for them enough to stop their everlasting petitioning for help."

Curious, he said, "Have you ever felt the call? Ever felt the spirit move you?"

Kate looked past him, out the window and into the hazy afternoon. There had been those moments next to the stream in the forest, the kiss of the wind on her skin, the strong and joyous pulse of the earth beating up through the soles of her feet. And she would never forget the animate, vindictive menace of the sea on board the *Avilda* during the ice storm. Or the enchanted dance with the aurorae on top of Angqaq. "I've felt what I thought was a presence from time to time," she said cautiously. "It was real to me." Suddenly self-conscious, she said, "Talking out loud about that kind of stuff always sounds so idiotic."

"No," he said after a moment, somewhat heavily. "If anything, I'm envious. I've never had that leap of faith, myself."

She laughed at him and he looked at her, startled. She pointed at the books, lined up on shelves, floor to ceiling, on all four walls. "You don't need religion; you have literature."

"True," he said, brightening. "Did you know that the King James version of the Bible has a vocabulary of only eight thousand words? In contrast to Shakespeare, who has more than thirty-two thousand?"

Amused, Kate said gravely, "I believe Shakespeare made up quite a few on his own."

"True again," he said, inclining his head, and they passed an hour talking of old times and mutual friends.

As they rose to their feet, Kate having invited him to lunch, she said suddenly, "Why do people cling so strongly to faith in God, do you think? Is it only the comfort of a belief in what happens after? In that something comes after at all?"

He paused, thinking it over. "No," he said finally. "They cling so strongly to it because it's easy."

She was startled. "Easy?"

"Sure. Well, easier, anyway."

"Easier than what?"

"Easier than doing it yourself. Easier to know you can sin and be forgiven than to keep yourself from sinning in the first place."

Kate was silent for a moment. "I never thought of it that way."

"Plus," he added, "any form of organized belief in God is an excuse for one person to say to another, 'Believe as I do or you'll go to hell, or I'll burn you at the stake, or I'll kill you and the horse you rode in on *and* everyone else who thinks like you.'"

Deep down, Kate felt it had been worth driving 269 miles just to hear those words. "So it's about power?"

"The most powerful and destructive of all the aphrodisiacs. There was a bishop during the Albigension Crusade in southern France, the one against the Cathars. Riding into battle, he gave the order to take no prisoners, to kill anything and everything that moved. One of his subordinates said, 'Even the children, monseigneur?' His reply was, 'Kill! Kill! God will know his own!' " He paused, fiddling with a pencil. "Kate," he said without looking up, "if you decide to go up against these people . . ."

"Yes?"

He looked up then, at the direct eyes, the firm chin, the stubborn line of jaw, and sighed inwardly. "Just remember one thing."

"What?"

" 'There are no tricks in plain and simple faith.' "

He watched the intent look come into her eyes as she traced the quotation to its source, the triumphant smile that curled the corners of her mouth. "*Julius Caesar.*"

He inclined his head in approval. "Shakespeare always gets the last word."

She picked the otter up and put him back in his bag and put the bag back in her pocket. Tom held the door for her. "Where are you staying?"

"Bartlett."

"Oh my poor dear."

"Are they ever going to replace those dorms? Or at least redo them?"

"The lower campus dorms are older and they're still in service. I believe," he added blandly, "there is a movement afoot to generate private funds to give the college president a new and bigger house."

"He's already got one."

"Ah, but he has to entertain."

And, joined by Jack, they spent their lunch talking of the venality and perfidy of university administrations everywhere, and other pleasant subjects. Jack and Winklebleck got on like a house on fire. That, too, made Kate nervous.

CHAPTER 7

Noxious kinds must be entirely condemned; for if there be near them a hob-nail, or a bit of rusty iron, or a piece of rotten cloth, forthwith the plant, as it grows, elaborates, the foreign juice and flavor into poison; who could discern the different kinds, except country-folk and those who gather them?
—Pliny

T he drive to the borough school administration offices took Kate through the abomination of south Fairbanks, an echoing expanse of pavement divided into four lanes and two frontage roads. One strip mall was succeeded by another and one parking lot rolled into the next with occasional fast food restaurant interruptions, Kentucky Fried Chicken, McDonald's, Denny's. There was even a Super 8 Motel next to Denny's. Progress. It looked like Dimond Boulevard in Anchorage, except Dimond had the single saving grace of the Chugach Mountains in the background.

Why do people allow this to happen in the places they live? she wondered, idling at a stop light. Why is there no testimony before the planning commissions that perpetrate these horrors? Are all the tree huggers and posy sniffers too busy saving the whales to join hands and lie down in front of even one cement truck?

Maybe it was that the locals didn't live here, they just visited when they had to shop and so they didn't care what it looked like. Afterward, they hurried back to their homes in the suburbs, where trees grew and children played and traffic wasn't roaring by at forty-five miles an hour. Or it wasn't until they woke up one morning and found the encroaching wave of tarmac lapping at their doorstep and a belly-dumper burying the lot next door in a mound of gravel, preparatory to the erection of the next Costco.

Maybe, Kate thought, warming to her topic, maybe the Fairbanks city planners thought the only way to control ugliness like this was to pick up the town by the northern border, shake it fiercely and confine all the junk that fell into the southern half behind chain link, the better to guard against it ever spilling over into the real world. She hoped they guarded well, and was glad when her way took her through the old town. Nordstrom's was gone, so was the Chena Bar, and it was with real horror she discovered the North Star Bakery was closed. No more Lady Lou sandwiches, no more roast beef and cheddar cheese and tomatoes grilled between a slice of rye and a slice of white. She nearly wept.

Otherwise the town remained much as it had been eleven years before, narrow of street, a trifle seedy, but a real town that lived and breathed and had sidewalks with people walking down them. None of Fairbanks's founding fathers had gone in for much in the way of landscaping here, either, and there wasn't any room for it now, but the sight of all those squatty little unprepackaged buildings was insensibly reassuring. When Fred Meyer's megastore had crumbled to bits at the corner of University and Airport Way, Kate had a feeling that Tommy's Elbow Room would still be presiding over the banks of the Chena River.

She parked in front of the borough school district building and went inside to ask her way to the right office.

Frances Sleighter's grip was as firm as her eyes were keen. She was a thin, spare woman in her midfifties, dressed in a well-worn tweed suit with a string of pearls and well-polished penny loafers with dimes in the slots instead of pennies. Her short, white hair was perfectly cut. Her manner was brisk. Kate felt that Ms. Sleighter had not a minute to waste, but she wasted one anyway. "Is that Sleighter, like the glacier?"

"Why, yes. My grandfather came up with Dall." Her eyes narrowed. "Shugak. Are you any relation to Ekaterina Shugak?"

"She's my grandmother."

"Ah." Frances Sleighter adjusted a paper on her desk with precision. "Well, naturally, anything I can do."

Naturally, Kate thought, and proceeded to exploit her relationship to Ekaterina Moonin Shugak without delay. "I wanted some information on Daniel Seabolt."

Not a muscle in Ms. Sleighter's face moved but something in the atmosphere of the room changed. Kate stiffened imperceptibly in her chair, hands resting lightly on the armrests, every cell alert though she couldn't have said precisely why.

All Ms. Sleighter said was, "Really?"

Something about that cool, clipped syllable annoyed Kate and she decided to go in with the shock troops. "Did you see the *News-Miner* this morning, Ms. Sleighter?"

"I'm afraid not." Ms. Sleighter looked politely inquiring.

"There was a story on the front page about a body being found in the vicinity of Chistona."

Ms. Sleighter looked slightly less smug. "Oh?"

"The body was identified as that of Daniel Seabolt."

Ms. Sleighter permitted her spine to rest for just a moment against the back of her chair, the first chink Kate had seen in the bureaucratic armor.

"I found him," Kate added.

Ms. Sleighter's eyes were wide and fixed on

Kate's face. "How—how awful. How simply awful for you."

"It wasn't very pleasant," Kate admitted. "I was picking mushrooms at the time."

"Picking mushrooms?"

Kate had the pleasure of seeing Ms. Sleighter at a loss twice in the same day. "Yes, there is a bumper crop of morel mushrooms springing up in that area. The forest fire last year, you know. Morel mushrooms," Kate said, mindful of Dinah's extensive tutoring, "in particular, seem to flourish the spring following a forest fire."

"The fire? Oh, yes, I remember now, of course. The big one. It spread all the way up through Mentasta Pass, didn't it?" Kate detected a distinct note of relief in the carefully modulated voice. "Well, there's your answer, then. It's obvious. He was caught out in last summer's fire."

"Yes," Kate said, looking at her thoughtfully, "it is obvious, isn't it." She paused. "Daniel Seabolt was an employee of yours, I believe."

Ms. Sleighter's eyebrows came together a fraction of an inch, the picture of perfectly groomed perplexity. "Daniel Seabolt. Oh. Ah. Yes. Of course." Ms. Sleighter's brow smoothed out and she met Kate's eyes with an expression of complete frankness that Kate immediately distrusted. "Yes, I believe he did teach at Chistona Public School."

"When did he leave?"

"Why, I don't believe I know. I'd have to look it up in his employee file." Kate waited. A minute passed, slowly. Ms. Sleighter permitted herself a thin smile and produced a manila folder from the teak IN basket on her desk and leafed through it. "Seabolt, Daniel. Yes, of course, I remember now. He had been teaching at Chistona for two years before he left."

"When did he leave?"

Ms. Sleighter looked thoughtful. "I assumed sometime over the summer. He finished the spring semester and failed to appear in the fall. We had to bustle about to fill his place, believe me."

Kate couldn't believe she'd used "bustle about" in a sentence and made it work. "Did he give notice?"

"No, he didn't. I must say, I was surprised at that."

"Why?"

Ms. Sleighter gave a slight shrug, not forgetting the correct set of her shoulders and the proper hang of the tweed jacket from them. "He was up to date with every report, his material requests were always on time, his student grades were always filed by the deadline, he never failed to answer any query the main office had by return of post. I would have expected him to follow the correct protocols, to submit a letter of resignation before he left."

"Oh." Kate thought for a moment. "What weren't you surprised at?"

The eyebrows went up again. "I beg your pardon?"

"You said you *were* surprised that Seabolt didn't give notice. What in the situation *weren't* you surprised at?"

Ms. Sleighter gave a little laugh and a dismissing motion of one graceful hand. Kate wondered if she rehearsed the gesture in front of the mirror. "You must have misheard me."

"I see," Kate said. "Why do you think he left?"

"I couldn't say." Ms. Sleighter caused her expression to exude exasperated indulgence. "As you may well be aware, Kate, may I call you Kate?"

"Of course," Kate said agreeably. "Fran."

Ms. Sleighter's smooth brow creased almost imperceptibly. "Frances."

It might only have been wishful thinking on her part but Kate thought she heard an edge in that controlled voice, and rejoiced inwardly. "Frances it is."

Frances smiled, showing all her teeth and some to spare. "As I was saying, Kate, as you may already be aware and so I apologize in advance if I sound patronizing, it is not the easiest task to find qualified teachers for remote schools. In some of the very remotest locations, we frequently—and I may say, unfortunately—experience a very rapid turnover."

"Because of the lack of access to the area," Kate suggested, "and the subsequent high cost of transportation."

Ms. Sleighter sent her an approving smile. "Yes. It's difficult to find qualified applicants willing to live nine months of the year completely cut off from most of the amenities of civilization."

"And perhaps," Kate suggested smoothly, "it is also difficult because of community criticism? Say, criticism of the method of teaching employed?" She paused. "Or, perhaps, of the content of the course work?"

The smile vanished. "I'm happy to say, that kind of thing has only very rarely occurred during my administration."

"But it does occur."

"Very rarely," Ms. Sleighter said firmly.

"Did it occur in Chistona?"

A blunt enough question, easily answerable with a "yes" or a "no," but there were no easy answers forthcoming from Ms. Sleighter, who gave a small, indulgent laugh and repeated the dismissing wave of the hand. "You know these little Alaskan communities, Kate. Each one has its own eccentricities. As long as the teachers are qualified, we are satisfied. Thus, we were very glad to find such an experienced teacher in Daniel Seabolt, one, I may add, with impeccable references from the Oklahoma public school system, who also had strong ties to the community in which he would be teaching."

"His father."

"Yes."

"Pastor of the local church."

"Yes."

"A fundamentalist church," Kate said, "with a strong bias against teaching the theory of evolution."

"And of course," Ms. Sleighter said, "since the Molly Hootch settlement, we have more schools than ever with positions to fill, all over the Alaskan bush." Ms. Sleighter looked at Kate again, assessingly. "You would be about the right age. Were you one of the complainants?"

"Yes." Kate extended a hand. "May I see Mr. Seabolt's file?"

Ms. Sleighter closed the folder and gave her thin smile. "I'm afraid not. All personnel files are confidential."

Of course they were. Just to see what she'd say, Kate said, "What do you think might have happened to him?" Ms. Sleighter raised her eyebrows. "If he weren't caught in the fire, that is."

Ms. Sleighter spread her hands in a helpless gesture that was greatly at odds with her brisk, take-no-prisoners demeanor. "I know no more than the troopers, and they seem to think it was death by misadventure."

"I thought you said you didn't read the paper this morning," Kate said.

Ms. Sleighter had the grace to flush slightly. The next words came out with just the suggestion of gritted teeth behind them. "I'm sorry, of course, for the loss to the community of such a promising young man, and naturally my heart goes out to his family."

And that was that. Kate left Frances Sleighter's office with two more questions than she went in with.

Why was Ms. Sleighter so eager for Daniel Seabolt to have died in the forest fire?

And how was it she could barely remember his name when she had his personnel file in her IN basket?

"So you think she's lying?" Jack said.

The woman in line in front of Kate was short and blocky with hair like gray steel wool. She wore a black T-shirt with a picture of the American flag on it. Below the flag was the message, "Try to burn this one, asshole." The man in front of her at the Safeway check-out counter was tall and thin and had mousy blond hair pulled back into a ponytail that hung down his back to his belt, longer than Brad Burns's. His T-shirt was blue. It had a picture of Planet Earth on it, with the message "Good planets are hard to find" lettered beneath.

Looked like a fairly representational cross-section of the Alaskan population to Kate. "Not lying, Jack," she said. "She's a bureaucrat. If, by some cosmic error, bureaucrats are not at birth exposed on a hillside with their ankles pierced"—the woman in the flag T-shirt turned to give her an approving, gap-toothed grin—"they mature into government employees adept in the disclosure of just so much of the pertinent data as reflects nonpejoratively upon themselves."

"Say what?"

The man in the Planet Earth T-shirt refused paper or plastic and loaded bean sprouts, a bag of chickpeas and a quart of Ben and Jerry's Cherry Garcia into a canvas bag. The woman in the flag T-shirt snorted audibly and turned to say in a voice reduced to a coarse husk of sound from three packs of unfiltered Camels a day, "They lie like snakes."

"Thank you," Kate told her. "They lie like snakes," she told Jack.

"Thank you for clearing that up," Jack told the woman in the flag T-shirt.

"Any time." She opted for plastic and the checker loaded two cartons of Camels, three packages of Ding Dongs and half a dozen roast beef TV dinners inside. She paid in very used fives and ones, winked at Jack and left.

They paid for their groceries and drove back up University Avenue to park at the Chena River wayside. The smoke haze had cleared to reveal wisps of high cloud, the sky was a very pale blue and the temperature had dropped all the way down to seventy-five degrees, too hot. "I knew there was a reason we went to school in the winter," Kate grumbled. She took the rubber band that held the butcher paper around her deli special and used it to fasten her hair up off her neck. She tore the paper off a beef bone and gave it to Mutt, who took it and retired beneath the table.

Jack unwrapped his meatball sandwich, opened the bag of Olympic Deep Ridge Dippers, placed bags of green grapes, red grapes and Rainier cherries at strategic intervals, set the package of Pepperidge Farm Soft Baked Chocolate Chocolate Walnut cookies within reach, and sat back to survey the scene through critical eyes. For a moment Kate feared they were going to have to return to the store, and then he raised one finger upright in inspiration and went to the truck, returning with a six-pack of Heineken, for him, and one can of Diet 7-Up, for her. He settled on the bench across the picnic table with a long, satisfied sigh and set to, reminding Kate of nothing so much as a vacuum cleaner in overdrive, but she knew better than to get between him and food and concentrated on her own meal. It wasn't the handiwork of the North Star Bakery, but in either Jack or Kate's case it was a simple matter of putting the hay down where the goats could get at it and staying out of the way.

"This is nice," Jack decided when he came up for air. "Peaceful. Pretty."

It was. Kate closed her eyes and took it in through her ears. The river gurgled placidly by. At the next table a toddler took her first shaky steps, to the great delight of her proud parents. A slight breeze, just enough to keep off the mosquitoes, rustled the leaves of the birches and alders that over-hung the water. A couple floated downriver in a canoe. Miracle of miracles, no one roared up on a Jet-Ski, and no one else turned Janet Jackson up to nine on a boom box. The most noise came from the traffic on University Avenue, and at eight o'clock there was little of that. Like Toledo, Ohio, Fair-banks, Alaska rolled up the sidewalks precisely at ten.

"You haven't been here in a while, have you?"

Kate came back into her body and opened her eyes. She looked across the table at him, wiping mustard from his mouth. It was a good mouth, firm-lipped, crooked up a little in one corner, ready to break into an easy grin. He had shaved his full, luxuriant mustache and beard the year before. "Felt like a change," he'd said vaguely when she'd asked why, but something in the way he said it told her that wasn't it. At least he hadn't been hiding any-thing. He had a chin, his teeth were straight, his skin was clear. And then she thought how super-ficial that sounded, and tried to feel ashamed of her-self.

"Have you?" he repeated.

Recalling the question with an effort, she shook her head. "No. This is the first time I've been back to Fairbanks since I graduated."

"Why?"

Her eyes returned to the river. The canoers had stopped in mid-paddle to nuzzle. Nuzzling isn't an activity best undertaken in a canoe and they disentangled to head downstream again at a more rapid pace. "Not much worth remembering in those four years."

He ignored the hands-off sign. "Why? What's wrong with Fairbanks?"

She shrugged. "No mountains, and the only water around was that filthy river." She nodded at the Chena. "I came from Prince William Sound and the Quilaks to this. I hated it."

He waited, patient. It was his best quality, and one that served him well with Kate.

It worked this time, too. "It was Abel's idea, college." It was the first time in a long time Jack had heard Kate speak of her dead foster parent without pain. "Emaa, too, she thought it was a good idea. She didn't think it was so great when I didn't come back to the village after I graduated, but that was after, and she couldn't do anything about it then." She took another bite of sandwich, and Jack watched her and waited.

"So, the two of them pretty much decided I would go, and I went fishing with my Uncle Kenty that summer and made enough for resident tuition and books, and one day in late August in 1979 we got in the truck and drove to the railroad. Abel waved down the Fairbanks train and put me on board. When we got to Fairbanks, they slowed down enough for me to jump off across from the university."

She looked up and he was jolted by the look in her eyes. "I was terrified. I'd never been out of the Park before in my life, never had to meet new people all on my own. I'd never talked on the phone, I'd never watched television, I'd never seen a movie, I'd never driven down a paved road or in traffic." She gave a short, unamused laugh. "I'd never even seen traffic. There was a two-lane highway between the railroad tracks and the campus. There were three cars on it, one going west, the other two east. I was almost hit by all three of them. One of the drivers yelled out the window at me, called me a stupid fucking Native."

A warm pressure settled on her foot. She looked under the table and saw Mutt's chin resting on her instep, yellow eyes gazing up at her. "They'd sent a map with the rest of the registration paperwork, and I figured out where Lathrop Dorm was, where I'd been assigned a room. A double room. On top of everything else, we couldn't afford a single room for me, and I had to share a room with a total stranger. I was terrified," she repeated, and shook her head. "Terror. It's just a word. I can't explain, you can't possibly understand what it felt like."

"No."

His slow, deep voice affected her as it always did, steadied her, calmed her. She took a deep breath and let it out slowly. "I checked in with the resident advisor and they took me up to the fourth floor and let me into a room. My room. Mine and some stranger's. She'd be in the next day, they explained, and then they left me alone."

She examined her can of Diet 7-Up as if she'd never seen one before. "All evening, all night, I could hear voices outside my door, in the hall, going in and out of the bathroom, the showers, answering the phone. It rang all the time, nonstop. The voices were strangers' voices. Mostly women's voices. Sometimes men's. People I'd never met, people I didn't know, people I was going to have to learn to live with."

She paused, and the struggle to get the words out was almost too painful for him to watch. "I was so scared I couldn't even go across the hall to the bathroom."

She raised her head and it was all there, as if the intervening fifteen years had never happened, the paralyzing fear, the bitter, enduring shame.

"I peed in the wastebasket."

On the river a duck quacked. The couple with the baby got into their car and drove off. A mosquito hummed past Jack's ear. He ignored it. He would have ignored a thousand of them. With every ounce of self-control he possessed, he kept his eyes down, kept himself from offering sympathy, or worse, pity. Kate Shugak might forgive a display of sympathy; pity, never.

When he said nothing, she went on, more easily now, Mutt's head warm and heavy on her foot. "The food was weird, no moose, no caribou, no

seal, no fish, just a brown lettuce salad bar and mystery meat in gloppy sauces and too much grease. It
took all semester for my stomach to settle down."
She shook her head, mouth twisting. "Once I got
brave enough to go to meals. I dropped twenty
pounds that semester; Emaa called me a skeleton at
Christmas and wanted to force-feed me fried bread
morning, noon and night."

He found what might pass for a voice in certain
circles. "It's what's she's best at."

She gave an abstracted nod. "I was so lonely,"
she said with a sigh. "My roommate was okay, but
she was white and her father was a colonel or a
general or something in the Air Force and she'd
never been in the bush in her life. I couldn't talk to
her. I didn't talk much at all, that first year, and
never in class." She met his eyes and almost smiled.
"It upset some of the teachers."

"What if they called on you?"

"The first time? I wouldn't answer. The second
time, I'd drop the class."

"Why didn't you just drop out completely, if you
were that miserable?"

Her eyes slid past his, to the river, brown water
chuckling serenely past, indifferent, uncaring.
"Quitter just wasn't in Abel's vocabulary. And
Emaa—" She gave another of those short laughs.
"My dropping out would have been a disgrace to
her personally and to the family as a whole, not
to mention our entire tribe. If I wanted to be able

to go home again, I had to finish."

He thought of that frightened, lonely eighteen-year-old, sacrificed to the ambition of her elders, and felt anger knot into a hard, hot lump at the pit of his stomach.

She shifted on the bench. "Sleighter asked me if I was one of the Molly Hootch plaintiffs. I was."

"Were you?" Jack said in surprise. "You never told me."

She shrugged. "Subject never came up."

"How'd that happen?"

A corner of her mouth quirked. "Mostly because Emaa said that nothing but drunks and mothers came back from Mount Edgecumbe and that none of her grandchildren were going there if she had anything to say about it."

"And of course she did."

"Of course. So I was. One of the plaintiffs, and one of the beneficiaries. Because of Molly Hootch, Niniltna got its own public school, grades one through twelve, and I didn't have to go away for my high school diploma like my mother did."

"Your father didn't?"

"He was twenty years older than her. They weren't doing that to bush kids, or maybe they didn't have the enforcement capability, when he was in school. He never finished. I don't think he ever started." She drained her pop. "Mom did. They sent her to Chemawa, in Oregon. She said it got so hot she nearly died. She'd spent most of her life on the Kanuyaq and Prince William Sound. Seventy degrees and she started to whine."

"Like you."

Her face lightened a little. "Like me."

"But you didn't have to go."

"No, I didn't have to go. At least not for four more years."

He uncapped another bottle of Heineken. He felt he deserved it, and a dozen more after it. "Almost would have been better if you had gone Outside for high school. Wouldn't have put you into so much culture shock when you went to college."

She shook her head. "No. I made it through, barely, at eighteen. At fourteen, I wouldn't have stood a chance. Most of the kids they sent away to school did quit. The drop-out rate in the Alaska bush has fallen to about twelve percent since the kids started being able to stay home for school."

A seagull flew downstream, gliding low on outspread wings, until its beak was nearly skimming the water. They both watched it until it was out of sight. "You know how parents in the bush make their kids mind?" He smiled. She didn't. "In the village, even today, parents tell a child who misbehaves that they'll give him away to white people if he doesn't shape up."

He stared at her, all humor gone. "You're kidding."

She shook her head. "No. And they believe it, too, the kids, because it wasn't that long ago that their parents did get sent away. They remember, in the villages."

"Poor little shits," he muttered, thinking of Kate's experience in Fairbanks and multiplying it by thousands. "No wonder they dropped out." He finished his third Heineken and pitched the bottle into the garbage can. "Things ever get any easier? For you, I mean? Here?"

She shrugged. "You tough anything out long enough, it has to get better."

"Been down so long, it looks like up to me?"

She nodded. "By my sophomore year, I'd made a few friends. I met Winklebleck and took his class. That helped. I learned to read, and after that I was never lonely. Well. Not very."

A swallow of beer went down the wrong way and he choked and wheezed and gasped for air. "You didn't know how to read when you went to college?"

She shook her head. "It's a long story. Anyway, after a while maybe the newness wore off, or maybe my calluses got thicker. Maybe both."

They fell silent, Jack finished the last of the cookies. He chewed stolidly, masticating without taste. No wonder you don't need me, he thought. You're determined not to need anyone ever again as bad as you did that first year away from home.

When he judged that enough time had passed to make the question tolerable, he said, "What made you decide on justice? That's what your degree is in, isn't it? I don't remember exactly."

"Bachelor of Arts in Social Sciences, with a major in justice." She smiled, a real smile this time. "My sophomore year, the same semester I found Winkleback, I took a police administration course, a three-hour-a-week class that met on Thursday nights, so at least one night a week I wouldn't have to spend in the dorm. It was a two hundred level course, Introduction to Criminal Justice. It was all about the Constitution, and the Bill of Rights, and civil and criminal law, and the difference between felonies and misdemeanors."

"Bonehead cop," he said, and she laughed, and it was a real laugh, too.

"I guess. This guy taught it who'd been a cop in Chicago's Cook County—" Jack whistled "—yeah, I know, for sixteen years, and he had a few stories to tell, and he told us all of them. He was funny, and he was smart. The first class—the *first* class, mind you—he told us he thought all drugs should be legalized and taxed, that fighting against a victimless crime was a waste of the policeman's time and the taxpayer's money." Jack grinned and Kate saw it. "Yeah, I know, I was the only non–law enforcement person in the class, it was filled with cops and corrections officers going for their degrees, and I thought for a minute they were going to lynch him. But he ended up making us see his point, even me."

"Even you?"

"Even me. Abel raised me to believe that smoking marijuana led straight to mainlining heroin and mugging little old ladies for their social security checks, but this guy wound up convincing me he was right. The second class he told us stories about his favorite wienie wagger, and taught us how to deal with them."

Jack raised his eyebrows.

"Laugh. That was all. Just laugh at them, he said, and this is what happens." She demonstrated, forefinger at first erect, then slowly drooping forward, and grinned when he laughed. "The next semester I took Criminal Investigation from the same guy. I was hooked."

He caught her hand in his own. "I'm glad."

She smiled at him. "Me, too."

They sat like that for a while, holding hands like a couple of college kids, watching the river flow by on its unhurried journey to confluence with the Tanana. "School shouldn't be like that," she said suddenly.

He agreed, wholeheartedly, only to discover she wasn't talking of her own experience. "No, I mean in Chistona. No one ought to be able to ban books, or color the learning process with their religious beliefs. Can you imagine what those kids in Chistona are going to have to unlearn when they go away to college? They already know enough not to question or they'll go straight to hell." She shook her head. "Winklebleck wouldn't give a bucket of warm spit for a class full of students who agreed with every word he said. He'd listen to any theory you had about what a poem meant, no matter how bizarre, as long as you could support it from the text. School is supposed to be like that, questions, challenges, discoveries. You don't just push the edge of the envelope, you push it to the red shift limit. Maybe I wasn't happy here, but I learned that much."

He studied her. "Is that why you're pursuing this thing with Seabolt? Because he was a teacher?"

Her wide mouth compressed, relaxed again. She shook her head. "I don't know. All I know is I have to find out what happened to him." She met his eyes with determination hardening in her own. "I have to, Jack."

That night he made love to her as if she were made of the finest porcelain, one rough touch and she would shatter. It was the only solace she would allow.

CHAPTER 8

During thunderstorms, flame comes from soft vapors. Deafening noises come from soft clouds. Why then, if two such violent forces could issue from softness, should not violent lightning, striking the ground, cause soft truffles?

—Plutarch

On her way north to Fairbanks Kate had taken the long way around through Tok, partly because it was about the same distance as if she took the Richardson Highway but mostly because it had been a long time since she had driven that section of the AlCan. The preponderance of recreational vehicles with Georgia, Florida and New Jersey plates also driving that section of the road convinced her to take the Richardson home. She started early the next morning, the enticement of a warm bed filled with Jack Morgan notwithstanding. "You are a cold and heartless woman," he said, snagging her for one last, long, eminently seductive kiss.

"Get thee behind me, Satan," she said, wriggling

free the moment his grip loosened to go in search of further inducements.

"Hey."

She stopped at the door and looked back, keeping one hand on the doorknob.

"There's a line from a Don Henley song."

"Oh?" She smiled slightly.

He didn't return her smile. "Some guy has a vision and sees Jesus. Or, he decides, maybe it might be Elvis." Jack paused, and looked at her, sober, even stern. "He can't tell the difference."

The professorial effect was somewhat diminished by the fact that the teacher was lying naked in a rumpled bed, but Kate thought it over. "So the people who see Elvis are the same kind of people who see Jesus."

He cocked his finger and fired. "And they're just as nuts."

"Thanks for the tip," she said, and swung the door open. Mutt padded past her into the hallway.

He leaned out of the bed to call after her, "I'm taking ten days around the Labor Day weekend."

She blew him a kiss. "See you then." The door swung almost closed and then opened again when she poked her head back in. "Bring the kid, if you want."

Fortunately for him, she was gone before the wide, pleased grin spread all the way across his face.

She stopped at Carr's for a cafe mocha, a sugar doughnut, and five pounds of green grapes, road food for herself and an apology to Bobby and Dinah for her short temper the morning she left. She found a truck stop with a diesel pump and filled up the Isuzu, which cost the grand sum of $14.37. Fourteen dollars for five hundred miles. "I heart Japan," she told Mutt, reholstering the diesel nozzle in the pump. "Or I heart their automobile designers."

She went inside to pay. "Little drizzly this morning," the man behind the counter observed.

"Yeah, but it sure feels good on the nasal passages," she replied.

The register ka-chunged and the drawer slid out. "Yeah, oughta lay a little of this smoke. That your dog?"

Kate looked up at Mutt, trotting back to the truck from a close encounter with the thicket at the edge of the parking lot. The limp was almost gone. Lucky for whoever had inflicted it. "Yeah."

"Female?"

"Yeah."

"Nice. Got some wolf in her."

"Half."

"Ever give you any trouble?"

"Trouble?" Kate looked at him, honestly bewildered.

"Guess not," he said, handing her the change. "Some of those half-breeds do. Always reading about it in the papers. People take them and try to make pets out of them." He shook his head. "Ever want to breed her, I've got a Shepherd mix I'd be interested to see crossed with her."

"That's kind of up to her." She smiled and took her leave.

It was raining, hard enough to put the wipers on hesitation but not enough to interfere with vision or traction. After the Eielson Air Force Base turnoff the traffic was negligible and Kate kept the truck at a steady sixty-five miles per hour straight through to Delta Junction. She thought about stopping for breakfast there, but the only restaurant she saw was on the wrong side of the road and there were plenty of Bobby and Dinah's grapes so she took the Richardson Highway turnoff and kept on going. The Richardson was a narrow, two-lane blacktop with even less traffic than the AlCan and Kate put her foot down and left it there. On one curve a sign told her to slow down to thirty-five; she slowed from seventy to fifty, what any Alaskan driver would have considered a reasonable compromise between the letter and the spirit of the law.

The sky stayed overcast, the rain kept drizzling down, and having left the Tanana behind at Delta Junction it was just one creek after another: Ruby, Darling, Ann, Suzy Q, Gunnysack. Gunnysack? It was easy for her mind to wander back to the discovery of Daniel Seabolt's body six days before.

Why did it haunt her so? Why was she so determined on an explanation? She'd heard stories all her life about cheechakos being caught out in the bush without proper clothing and going mad from the mosquitoes. She'd heard stories all her life about sourdoughs going out into the bush with all the equipment in the world and still going mad from the mosquitoes, for that matter.

A yearling moose hesitated next to the guardrail in the oncoming lane. Kate took her foot off the gas in case he decided he really did want to get to the other side, but when the truck came abreast of him he leapt the rail in a panic and crashed off through the brush. She put her foot down again.

The idea of murder in the case of Daniel Seabolt was ludicrous. There was no evidence, and there were no suspects.

But what the hell was Seabolt doing out there in the bush, a mile or more from the nearest cabin, without any clothing at all, proper or otherwise? She imagined the day: hot, the sun shining down, sweat trickling down his back as he bushwhacked his way from swamp to swamp, in search of— what? It had been too late for fiddlehead ferns and too early for hunting season. Not that it meant anything in the bush, and if Brad Burns was to be believed Seabolt might have had a subsistence permit. She imagined him taking off his shirt, his T-shirt, and then she imagined him putting them both back on again immediately when he realized what he'd let himself in for in the way of aerial bombardment. The pants and the boots he would have left on regardless, the sharp brush taking too great a toll on exposed flesh, as Kate well knew from painful personal experience.

But he had had no clothes on, none. She wondered what his last moments had been like. She imagined him stripped to the skin, running frantically, crashing headlong over rock and stump, into bush and tree. She imagined the whine of a thousand pairs of wings, the sting of a thousand bites, the frantic slap of hands in futile defense, the running, running, running, with nowhere to run to. She imagined him maddened beyond the point of following a slope down to a cooling stream, or perhaps the shadowing fire sweeping down on him in one such stream and chasing him out into the woods again. She imagined him exhausted, tripping, falling, facedown, the collapse, the settling swarm of insects hungry for blood.

A shiver began at the base of her spine and worked its way up under her skin. Mutt looked at her, cocking a concerned ear. "No one should die like that," she said, consciously loosening the grip she had on the steering wheel. "No one."

The rain had let up and she pulled over onto the nonexistent shoulder. Buds barely open, a great drift of wild roses spilled over the slight rise on their right to pool in the hollow beneath. Kate reached across and opened the door. Mutt leapt out and plunged into the undergrowth. Yes, the limp was almost gone. She rubbed the bruise on her thigh. It was still sore.

She got out of the truck and stretched, taking deep breaths of moist air. Her unforgiving sinuses had finally begun to relax, and it was the first breath she had taken in two weeks without a trace of burn in it. Lush greenery clustered thickly at the edges of the pavement, just waiting for an opportunity to slip over the edge and take the road back. No fires here for a while. She hoped it would be a while longer before there were.

Suppose he had been a serious jogger? A cross-country runner? Maybe even an orienteer? Burns had said he was interested in the subsistence life-style; maybe he'd gone on a cross-country hike and gotten lost. It happened all the time; now that she remembered it, it had happened just this past week, that hiker lost in the Mentastas that Chopper Jim had cited as part of his case load.

The hood of the car was wet and the seat of her jeans became damp as she leaned up against it. She had a good imagination, all right, but even Kate could not imagine Daniel Seabolt stripping off his clothes for a jog through the Alaskan bush. Nothing of the admittedly little she had learned of him thus far led her to believe he was that stupid. And he'd been taking sourdough lessons from Brad Burns to boot. He would have known that wild roses had thorns, and there were nettles, and Devil's club, and pushki, which could raise blisters if you got the juice on you and didn't wash it off fast enough. Not to mention no-see-ums and biting flies. And Dinah's twenty-seven known species of mosquitoes. She remembered again the instant swelling of Matthew Seabolt's arm after the mosquito bit him.

And Jim's amorous inclinations notwithstanding, she didn't think even he would strip to the buff deep in the heart of the interior Alaskan bush in summertime, not even to scratch what appeared to be a ceaseless itch of a different kind. And even if Seabolt had been experiencing love au naturel, where was his girlfriend? Why hadn't she reported him missing? Or, if she had perished in the fire, too, where was *her* body? And why hadn't someone reported *her* missing?

From somewhere off to the right side of the road came a cluck and a hoot and a cackle and an explosion of wings. A caribou cow, looking harried, emerged from the leaves at the edge of the road and paused, one hoof on the pavement, looking at Kate. Deciding the human was no threat, she stepped out into the lane, followed by two more cows and four calves. They looked good, all seven of them, new racks growing velvet, coats thick and glossy, bodies well filled out. Looked like Thanksgiving dinner to Kate, but it wasn't hunting season, and she made no move for the rifle behind her seat. They tippetty-tapped across the road and vanished unmolested into the undergrowth on the other side.

Kate doubted that Seabolt had been sunbathing, either. Or swimming, since he was two-plus bush-whacking miles from the nearest creek. There was plenty of swamp nearby, but no running water to speak of. If he'd been taking a leak, only his zipper would have been open. If he'd been taking a dump, his pants might have been down around his ankles. In either case, he still would have had most of his clothes on.

A rainy gust of wind tore over the rise, swooped across the road and tossed up the leaves of a stand of birches, exposing their lighter undersides. A lusty laugh and the gust was gone and with a scandalized rustle the birches shook their skirts back down over their white boles, and all was still again, except for the patter of returning rain. Kate turned her face up and closed her eyes. The drops were cool on her skin.

She was left with only one solution. Daniel Seabolt didn't have his clothes off by choice.

Unless he was out of his mind.

Of course, with that father and that son, she wouldn't blame him if he was, and certainly that assumption was the easiest way out for her. Who can explain a nut's behavior? As his father had more or less said. Which generated an entirely irrational impulse on her part to doubt it at once.

The only alternative to madness was that he'd been killed, stripped and dumped where she had found him. But there was no evidence of murder, why would his killer strip him anyway, and why on earth go to all the trouble of dragging him out there if they weren't going to bury him? Even supposing

last year's fire had been breathing down their necks?
The area had been flooded with smokejumpers;
odds were at least even that one of them would have
stumbled over the body. Or the following year by
a ranger assessing the damage.

Or her. Picking mushrooms.

Full circle, and still no answers. Giving a frustrated shake of her head, she called, "Mutt!" and
climbed back behind the wheel. After a moment
Mutt crashed out of the bushes and leapt up beside
her, smelling exotically of roses. A ptarmigan
feather hung from one side of her mouth. Kate
started the truck and drove on.

An hour later the Isuzu topped a rise, the sun
burst out of the clouds and Summit Lake appeared
on the right. She stopped at the lodge to use the
bathroom and get a cup of coffee. When she came
out Mutt was lapping up some of the lake. She
walked down to stand next to the dog and gaze out
at the expanse of water, a pool of iridescent gray
brimming over the sides of an elongated bowl of
emerald green, behind which the Amphitheater
Mountains leapt up and crashed down again in
great waves of rock and ice.

Turning, she looked across the valley at the silver
snake of the TransAlaska Pipeline, which had been
with them most of the way south from Fairbanks,
slithering up out of the ground here, outlined
against the sky on the crest of a ridge there, outwardly stolid and serene, inside filled with the daily

rush of a million barrels of Prudhoe Bay crude, from Pump Station One at the edge of the Arctic Ocean to the Oil Control Center in Valdez. Eight hundred miles of it, crossing three mountain ranges, two earthquake faults, with a river or a creek for every mile of pipe. It was a triumph of engineering over terrain, in situ testimony to the human ability to manage the environment, and it meant a one-eighth share of Prudhoe Bay proceeds, measured in billions of dollars per year, for the state of Alaska.

Kate had no objection to that; the oil was there and because of it the state could afford big budget items like Molly Hootch without requiring her to pay state income taxes. She just wished the pipeline ran all the way south through Canada, as one of the original designs had called for, instead of terminating in Valdez. It was a route the Cordova Aquatic Marketing Association, the Cordova District Fishermen's United and the Lower Cook Inlet Fishermen's League, among others, had lobbied for and lobbied hard, on their own time and with their own money. No one had listened to them, of course; they were only the people out on those waters every day, who knew them better than anyone else living, who fed their families on the bounty nurtured therein.

Instead, the line went to Valdez and the oil was shipped out by tanker, and twelve years after oil in to the Operations Control Center the *RPetCo Anchorage* went hard aground on Bligh Reef, and

spilled nearly eleven million gallons of Prudhoe Bay
crude across Prince William Sound and the Gulf of
Alaska, in the process proving the fishermen's fears
all too true. Kate never saw the pipeline without
thinking of them and the damage done to their
homes and livelihoods. For the coastal dwellers of
the south-central part of the state, the Gulf of
Alaska was one and the same.

But her last job had put a face on the monster,
and now she looked at the pipeline and wondered
how the people at the other end of the line were
doing, the people living and working at the RPetCo
Base Camp at Prudhoe Bay. She wondered if Dale
and Sue had gang-beeped anyone lately. She wondered how the archaeological dig was progressing
at Heald Point. She wondered how Cindy Sovalik
was getting back and forth to work now that the
snow was gone. Four-wheeler, probably. She hoped
Cindy would take it slow and easy over the thirty
miles of tundra between her home in Ichelik, east
of Prudhoe, and her job at the Prudhoe Hilton in
Prudhoe Bay. Remembering the time Cindy, in a
snow machine, had bluffed the fifty-six-passenger
bus Kate was driving out of its right-of-way, she
doubted it.

Mutt nudged Kate's hand with her head. "Okay,
okay," Kate told her, and together they walked
around the lodge and back to the truck. The parking lot was overflowing with a bicycle touring
group, men and women in their thirties and forties

wearing Spandex and helmets. One woman was loading her panniers as Kate approached. "Hi," Kate said.

"Hi," the woman said, looking up briefly.

"Where'd you come from?"

The woman secured the last strap and straightened, one fist rubbing the small of her back. "We came eighty-seven miles yesterday. We're doing sixty-nine today."

Kate had noticed this phenomenon in bicyclers before. Killer hills, dead man's curves, stubborn headwinds, flat stretches, record times, all these received intense attention and merited close and involved discussion, but "Where did you come from?" never got a direct answer. Bicyclers didn't care where they had come from, or where they were going, or anything that happened in between, except as how it related to their miles per day. They probably had not even noticed the frozen, striated flood of ice that was Gakona Glacier, spilling down from Mount Gakona east of the road, one peak in a queenly procession of peaks that formed the Alaska Range, a sight that, as many times as Kate had seen it, never failed to take her breath away.

She tested the theory. "Gakona sure looks pretty today."

"Yeah," the woman grunted, "with the sun up there'll probably be a hell of a headwind coming down off Rainbow Ridge, really cut into our time."

Mutt took a leak near her rear tire, but the

woman was so involved with the quick release hub on the front tire that she didn't notice, and Kate would never tell. They climbed back into the truck.

Twenty miles past Paxson the clouds parted enough for Kate to catch a distant glimpse of the Quilaks, and she felt an easing of the close-held tension that always accumulated in direct proportion to the amount of time she'd been gone and the amount of distance between her and home. The Kanuyaq River valley lay broad and deep, an immense gulf of forest and river that hardly went unnoticed, but the eyes tended to skip over it for the more striking profile of the Quilak Mountains, and maybe even a hint of the blue-white peak of Angqaq.

At any rate, Kate's eyes did.

At that moment of well-being, at just the point when the surface of the road deteriorated into one series of patches after another and its course began to twist and turn worse than one of the Kanuyaq's tributaries, they came upon a line of slow-moving vehicles. Closest to Kate was a Volkswagen bus with Washington State plates. The curtains were closed across the back window so she couldn't see who was driving it. Next car up was a white Ford four-door, a rental, through the back window of which she could see four white-haired heads, men in the front, women in the back. Ahead of them was an old black, rusty Ranchero with Alaska Veteran plates and no chrome left on it anywhere Kate could see. In front of the Ranchero was a brave new Bronco with the sticker still on the rear window, and in front of the Bronco were three RVs from— Kate squinted—it couldn't be Alabama. She goosed the gas a little to close up on the Volkswagen's bumper.

It was, by God, Alabama, yet another redneck state with vowels on both ends. I wish I was in Dixie, hooray, hooray. And they drove like it, too, thirty-five miles an hour, except when they hit a straight stretch, when they reached speeds considerably in excess of the speed limit on German autobahns. Kate wished they were in Dixie, too. It didn't help matters when it began to rain again. She dropped back three car lengths and occupied herself by counting pull-offs the RVs could have taken to let the rest of the traffic pass.

She'd reached five when she looked in the rearview mirror and beheld a sight fit to strike terror into the heart of the most intrepid driver: a Toyota truck from Tennessee with two teenage boys in it closing rapidly on her rear bumper. They tailgated her for five minutes, waiting for a blind curve. When one came they pulled out into the left lane to pass. A pickup with a camper on the back lumbered around the curve and the Toyota truck from Tennessee slid back behind Kate with inches to spare. As he came abreast of Kate the white-faced pickup driver was saying something that was undoubtedly educational for all concerned and flipped off the

driver of the truck from Tennessee. The truck from
Tennessee responded on the next curve, which
turned out to be blind, deaf and dumb, by pulling
into the oncoming lane again, flooring the acceler-
ator and roaring past Kate, the Volkswagen bus
from Washington State, the rented Ford sedan, the
rusty Ranchero, the brand-new Bronco with the
sticker in the window and was just fixing to take
on the first RV from Alabama when a police cruiser
driven by an Alaska State Trooper materialized on
his front bumper.

Everyone slammed on the brakes.

Kate was in better shape than the rest of them
because she liked living, had years of experience in
driving Alaska highways and had been braking
since the Toyota truck from Tennessee passed her.
Even so, Mutt landed with her front paws on the
dashboard and Kate was glad she was wearing her
seat belt when her brakes locked up. The Isuzu
bucked and stalled and the rear wheels skidded over
the wet pavement and hit the grass and gravel of
the very narrow shoulder and mercifully came to a
halt just short of the mess rapidly accumulating
inches in front of the passenger side door.

The cruiser hit lights, siren and the ditch simultaneously. The Toyota truck from Tennessee swerved
to avoid going into the ditch on top of the cruiser
and whizzed between the second and third RVs to
run head-on into a tree. Due to the latitude and the
thin layer of topsoil overlaying the permafrost, trees

in interior Alaska never get very thick through the trunk, and this one snapped like a matchstick. So did the next three. Scrub spruces, Kate noticed, gripping the wheel with both hands so tightly it felt like her arm muscles were going to burst out of their skin. A thicket of diamond willow proved tougher and the Toyota truck from Tennessee came to a stop buried in the middle of it.

The Volkswagen bus from Washington State rear-ended the rented Ford, which rear-ended the Alaska Ranchero, which rear-ended the brand-new Bronco with the sticker in the window. The brand-new Bronco was hurled forward toward the last Alabama RV and the driver hauled on the wheel to avoid a collision and that and the high center of gravity on the vehicle rolled it over on its right side. It slid twelve feet down the yellow line and stopped.

The three RVs screeched to a halt, unharmed except for the fifteen feet of rubber they left behind them on the road.

For one frozen moment nobody moved.

Then everybody did, doors springing open, people leaping out onto the pavement, lots of yelling.

"Are you hurt?"

"Are y'all okay?"

"Yes! You?"

"We're all right!"

"The Bronco!"

"Yeah, check the Bronco!"

They reached the Bronco in a body. The engine

was still running, the wheels spinning against air. Kate was the smallest and they hoisted her up on the side. She brushed ineffectually at the water streaming down the driver's window and knocked on the glass. "Hey! Hey in there, are you okay?" She tried opening the door, which of course was locked. "Hey, in the Bronco! You alive?" She thought she heard a reply and looked over the side. "You guys shut up!" She looked back in the window and saw movement, an arm maybe, reaching toward her. "Can you unlock the door? The door, can you unlock the door so we can get you out?"

The arm moved lower. There was a low hum and the window descended. The Bronco had electric windows, and they still worked. The first thing Kate did was reach down and turn off the ignition. The engine sputtered and died and the rear wheels rolled to a stop. A man, blood trickling down his forehead, was crouched on the passenger side door, unfastening the seat belt of a woman in the passenger seat. "It's my wife. She's unconscious."

Kate yelled over the side, "Anybody got a first aid kit?" Half a dozen people scrambled for their vehicles. The white-haired driver of the rented Ford sedan said, "Miss? I'm a doctor."

Relief washed over her. "Good." Her eyes fell on the woman standing next to him, the driver of the Volkswagen. "He's going to need help getting her out."

The woman, fiftyish and clad in jeans and a Pendleton shirt, swung up next to Kate. The Bronco rocked a little. The driver's side door opened, but it wouldn't stay open, so they left it closed and together with the unconscious woman's husband, maneuvered her through the window. "Put her in my rig," the driver of the Volkswagen bus said, and ran ahead to slide open the side door and pull down the bed in back.

They got her inside and on the bed and the doctor squeezed in next to her, his black bag fetched by one of the white-haired ladies who had been sitting in the backseat of the rented Ford. The Bronco driver wedged in between the refrigerator and the table, anxious eyes on his wife. The rest of them clustered around the open door, watching the doctor run competent hands down the woman's body. "Doesn't feel like anything's broken. She's got a lump on her right temple; she probably whacked her head on the window when you went over. What's her name?" he said, one hand on her wrist, eyes on his watch.

"Elaine."

"Elaine?" The doctor leaned over and looked into her face, one hand on her wrist, counting her pulse. "Elaine? Can you hear me?"

Her eyelids fluttered. "Elaine? Elaine, this is Dr. Westfall. Open your eyes." Still holding her wrist, he moved her arm across her breast, counting respirations.

The tension in the group eased when they heard

the small groan and saw the woman's eyes open.
One hand came up and the doctor caught it before
it could feel her head. "Elaine?" He smiled down
at her. "I'm Dr. Westfall. That's right, you've hurt
your head. Don't move." He held up one hand in
front of her face, two fingers raised. "How many
fingers do you see?" She muttered something and
he said insistently, "How many fingers do you see,
Elaine?"

"Two."

"Good. How many this time? Elaine?"

"Three."

"Good." He held both her hands. "Will you
squeeze my hands, please?"

She blinked, and spoke again, her voice rising.
"Where's Steve? Where's my husband?"

"He's right here, Elaine."

"I'm right here, honey," Steve said, crowding up
behind the doctor, relief flooding his voice. "I'm
right here, and I'm okay."

"Steve." She tried to reach for him and Dr. Westfall said firmly, "In a minute, Elaine. First squeeze
my hands. Squeeze. That's good." He moved the
palms of his hands to the soles of her feet. "Press
your feet down for me. Press harder. Good girl."
He got a penlight out of his bag and shone it in her
eyes, one at a time. "Good." He put the penlight
back in his bag. "I think you're going to be fine,
Elaine. You took a bump on the side of your head,
but your pupils aren't dilated and they're respond-

ing, so it doesn't look like there's anything wrong internally. I'd recommend an X ray to be sure, maybe a night in the hospital for observation."

He turned to Steve. "How about you?"

Steve, oblivious to the blood running down the side of his face, said, "Huh?"

It was just a scratch from a piece of the shattered window and the doctor cleaned it up and sat back. "They could both use something hot to drink."

The driver of the Volkswagen bus said, "Hot tea, maybe? With honey?"

"Perfect."

In back of the crowd someone cleared his throat. They turned as one and beheld First Sergeant James M. Chopin, trooper in residence at Tok and the pride of the Alaska Department of Public Safety.

He'd been busy, Kate realized, looking beyond him. There were flares burning brightly at both ends of the curve. The cruiser was up out of the ditch and parked by the side of the road. There was a clipboard beneath his arm with a drawing of the accident and the relative positions of the vehicles already sketched on an accident report.

"What are you doing here?" Kate demanded, but so only he could hear her. "I thought they didn't let you out without your helicopter."

He touched one finger to the brim of his hat in reply, calm, dignified, even stately. "Kate. Ladies and gentlemen, if you'll identify your vehicles for me, I'll need to see your licenses and registrations.

You can get them after you move your vehicles to the side of the road."

"It was his fault!" a big, beefy man in an Alyeska cap growled. "He was passing on a curve." He was the driver of the Ranchero with the vet plates, and he was pointing at the driver of the Toyota truck from Tennessee, who gulped and looked young and scared. His companion was edging to one side, looking as if he wished he'd hit his dad up for that plane ticket to the cannery job with Peter Pan Seafoods in Dillingham after all.

Now that there was time, now that nobody had died, they got mad, and there was a concerted move toward the driver of the Toyota truck from Tennessee, with son of a bitch the nicest epithet hurled at him and shooting the least painful method of execution suggested. Chopper Jim quelled the incipient riot without effort and went about the business of taking statements, patient, imperturbable, his absolute calm infectious, his innate authority unquestioned. From the front seat of the Isuzu, Kate watched him move from one group of people to the next, doing more listening than talking, taking notes, letting each of the drivers walk him through their version of the accident.

She dug out a piece of beef jerky from the glove compartment and split it with Mutt. Gnawing on her share, she watched Chopper Jim do the trooper thing and thought of the first time she'd ever seen an Alaska state trooper in action. Back before the

DampAct, when there were still two bars in Niniltna, a gold miner had made the mistake of pulling
a knife on one of the Moonin boys in front of three
of his brothers. The miner had died shortly
thereafter. The death had been messy and public
and the miner was white so somebody radioed for
the trooper from Tok. Back then the trooper had
made his rounds in a Piper Cub and a group of
curious kids, Kate among them, had been waiting
at the airstrip when he landed.

The Cub rolled out to a stop. The door opened
and a man climbed out. He was too tall to stand
up straight beneath the wing, Kate remembered; he
had to stoop a little until he cleared it. Before the
days of EEO, there had been a height requirement
for the Alaska State Troopers and this officer ex-
ceeded it handily. Or so it seemed to the little eight-
year-old girl goggling from the end of the runway,
and a little nearer to the end of it than she had been
before the door to the plane opened.

He was immaculately dressed in blue and gold,
the colors of the state flag, the colors of the University of Alaska Fairbanks, now that she thought
of it. His pistol rode obviously on his hip, but the
closest it ever got to being drawn was the casual
hitching motion he made with his belt, a habitual,
even professional gesture echoed by every state
trooper Kate ever saw walk into in a dicey situation,
and one that never failed in its effect. In motion, he
walked slow, he talked slower, and he never, ever

raised his voice, not even when Henry Moonin threatened to open him up the way he had the miner.

Kate had been spending the weekend with Ekaterina and she had seen her cousin knifed in front of the bar, and the fight and all the blood that followed had shaken her badly. She never remembered that trooper's name but she knew, with a bone-deep, unshakable conviction that never left her, that he had brought all the might and authority of the law with him to Niniltna, Alaska, and the ground had felt that much steadier beneath her feet.

It was years since she'd thought of that day. For the first time, she realized it wasn't only the ex-cop from Cook County who had influenced her to take up a career in law enforcement.

The Ranchero had a come-along and they had the Bronco right side up in ten minutes. The passenger door window was broken and the door wouldn't open. It started; it even went into drive, but the doctor ruled out Steve behind the wheel this soon, so the woman in the Volkswagen volunteered to drive him and Elaine to the clinic in Glennallen. The driver of the Alaska Ranchero flatly refused to pull the Toyota truck from Tennessee out of the willow thicket. Jim insisted. The Ranchero driver growled and gave in. It ran, too. It also didn't have a scratch on it. The rest of the vehicles had dinged front and back ends and a couple of the doors were hard to open and close, but on the whole were serviceable.

Jim ticketed the driver of the Toyota truck from Tennessee for speeding, reckless driving and driving uninsured. He warned him to stop at the trooper's office in Glennallen, speculated out loud on the possibility of charging him with attempted vehicular homicide if he did not, and dwelled for a few graphic moments on the delights awaiting young and nubile hard-timers at the Spring Creek Correctional Facility in Seward. This sounded like a fine idea to everyone else and they said so. The drivers of the three RVs from Alabama were especially vociferous in their support, until Jim ticketed them for not pulling off the road when they had five vehicles behind them. They were even less happy when he held them up long enough for everyone else to take to the road in front of them. Of course, he'd cited everyone else for tailgating, so it was with a united air of general disenchantment that the convoy finally hit the road.

" 'Attempted vehicular homicide'?" she said when Jim came up to her.

He grinned.

"What are you doing on the road? And behind the wheel of a car, no less?" Kate added.

"You make it sound like a penance."

"For you it is."

He resettled the hat on his head. "I flew into Glennallen and borrowed one of their cruisers. Jack called; I knew you were on your way down, and I wanted to talk to you."

"Why didn't you just wait at the junction?"

"And miss this opportunity to help balance the state budget?"

Chopper Jim loved writing tickets, and there wasn't much opportunity for that a thousand feet up, his usual milieu. "What's going on?"

The rain was coming down harder now. "Let's get in the cruiser."

"Okay." She climbed in next to him.

He moved the shotgun out of her way and then had to get out and open the back door for Mutt when she gave an imperious yip outside the driver's window. He got back in again and shut the door. He sniffed. "What is that smell?"

Kate looked innocent.

"Is that roses?"

Mutt looked coy.

"Don't ask," Kate said.

Jim shook his head. He didn't say, "Women!" but only because he knew it'd probably get him killed. "Jack marched into Frances Sleighter's office at 8:01 A.M. today."

Kate paused in the act of slicking rain off her braid. A smile spread slowly across her face. "Oh he did, did he?"

"He told me to tell you he intimidated her with his male superiority. I told him even I wasn't dumb enough to say that to Kate Shugak. So then he told me to tell you he showed her his ID and said he was investigating a murder."

"Since when are you calling it murder?"

"*We* aren't."

"Oh. And?"

"And she caved and let him see Seabolt's file."

"Hmm." Even an entrenched bureaucrat could be cowed by a threatened charge of obstructing justice, it seemed. Good old Jack. Morgan's Second Law was "Evidence first, admissibility second, and don't be too lavish with the truth when you're interviewing potential witnesses, either." Jack Morgan always took ruthless advantage of the fact that the D.A.'s investigators were not cops. He could always, and always did, bat his eyes and say innocently, "What do I know? I just work the cases APD is too understaffed to handle, clean up the messes they leave behind." It endeared him neither to the D.A. nor to the cops but it got the job done. Morgan's First Law was "The nearest and the dearest got the motive with the mostest," but that was a different case and another story. "What was in the file?" Kate said.

"To begin with, there was one almighty stink in Chistona over Seabolt's teaching practices."

"Ah. Specifically?"

"Specifically, he was teaching the theory of evolution."

She'd heard that before, but this time Kate also heard an audible click, as if the last tumbler had fallen into place and the safe door was about to swing wide. "As in we come from monkeys?"

"Yup."

"As in the earth is about four million four hundred and ninety-five thousand years older than his father preaches?"

"Yup."

"I bet his father loved that. How do we know all this?"

"Jack says the first half of Seabolt's file is filled with letters of testimonial from Simon Seabolt and all of his parishioners, recommending him for the position of teacher at Chistona, pointing out his family ties in the community, citing chapter and verse from his last employment in Oklahoma."

"When did the tone of the file change?"

"Seabolt taught at Chistona for two years. The school district got the first letter of complaint just before school let out the first year, May something, 1992."

"What'd it say?"

"It wasn't a letter of complaint, really. It was very polite, and very politely pointed out that since Chistona Public School was a public school and supported by taxpayer dollars, that all of the relevant theories of the creation of the universe should be taught there, and not just the one that held current political favor in Washington, D.C."

"The significant word in that sentence being 'creation.' "

"Uh-huh. She wanted the district to understand that she wasn't protesting the teaching of the theory of evolution, and Jack says she underlined the word *theory*. She was merely pointing out that it was only a theory, and that other theories should be given equal time."

He flipped the page in his notebook. "That was it for that year. School lets out, summer vacation, school starts again. October 10, another letter from Mrs. Gillespie."

"Gillespie?"

"Yeah," he frowned at his notes, "Mrs. Sally Gillespie." He looked over at her. "Why?"

"We've met."

"She the one who stiffed you when you were asking questions?"

"One of them. Go on, what else?"

He looked back down at his notes. "Now she's complaining about a time line Seabolt is having his students draw, one that runs from prehistory to the present." His eyes narrowed, trying to make out a word. "Jack said something about the Pest—the Pless—"

"The Pleistocene."

"Right, the Pleistocene. And something about Babe the Blue Ox?"

"Blue Babe, the steppe bison on display in the UAF museum."

"Um," he said dubiously, regarding his notes. "Maybe that was it. Again, Mrs. Gillespie was very polite. Again, she suggested equal time for alternative points of view. But this time, she wasn't alone."

Kate smiled. It wasn't a nice smile. "The rest of the Chistona Little Chapel weighs in."

"In spades. Jack and I looked on the calendar. There were twenty-one letters, all saying the same thing as Mrs. Gillespie, and all dated on the same Monday or the day after."

"Following the Sunday sermon."

"I don't care what people say about you, Shugak, you are smarter than the average bear."

"You're too kind. What else did Jack say?"

"He said there were a few letters supporting Daniel Seabolt, too. One of them came from a Philippa Cotton. She was a member of the school board, and she was a lot less polite. She said she didn't believe that God had brought down the Holocaust on the Jews because the Jews were responsible for killing Christ, and she didn't want her children being taught that in a school supported by her tax dollars."

Kate swiveled to stare at him incredulously, and he said, "Uh-huh. Ms. Cotton further stated that if the school district continued to allow 'those churchy people,' quote end quote, to run the Chistona school that she was going to yank her kids out and, furthermore, she'd call the *Anchorage Daily News* and tell them why."

"Oho."

"Uh-huh. There were a couple of other letters, one from a Gabrielle Jordan, one from a Smitty Taylor, who said pretty much the same thing." Jim refolded his notebook and stowed it away.

Kate sat still, thinking. "Pastor Seabolt must have brought in a ringer."

"Yeah," he said, "that's what we figured."

"One of the elders of the church, maybe."

"Or a guest speaker, air-freighted in from Glennallen or Anchorage."

"Did Jack ask Ms. Sleighter if she knew about the ringer?"

He shook his head. Mutt stuck her muzzle over the back of the seat and he reached up to scratch her behind the ears. Her eyes half-closed; if she'd been a cat she would have been purring. Disgusting. "We only figured it out on the phone. He was going to go back to see her this afternoon. He's going to call me in Glennallen tonight. But we figure she had to know."

"Just won't say until forced to it."

"The Cover-Your-Ass Principle of good government," Jim agreed cheerfully. "You learn it your first year of public service or you're out on said ass the second. If there's trouble, you run. There was a lot of trouble at Chistona Public School last year. From what Jack said, Sleighter must be getting close to retirement." He grinned. "And I'm here to tell you, a retirement pension from the state of Alaska is a pension you can live on. You don't jeopardize one of those with the truth, especially if the truth makes you look bad."

Kate sat in silence for a moment longer. "I'd like

to talk to one of those letter-writers. Not one of the churchy people. One of the disloyal opposition."

He raised his eyebrows in well-simulated surprise. "Would you indeed? Philippa Cotton, perhaps?"

She eyed him suspiciously. "Perhaps."

He started the engine and pulled the cruiser level with her truck. "Zen vollow me to zee casbah, pretty lady. She's living in Glennallen now, and I just happen to know where."

"It was one hell of a mess," Philippa said. She was a bouncy, apple-cheeked woman with short, shiny brown hair. Her brown eyes had laugh lines around them and a merry grin to match, neither in evidence at the moment. "They had the school district superintendent down from Fairbanks, the president of the State Board of Education, a lawyer from the ACLU, hell, there was even a guy here from the Anti-Defamation League of B'nai B'rith in Seattle. Oh my yes, we had a fine time there for a while. The ACLU guy told us that giving equal time to the creation theory was unconstitutional. Some school in Louisiana tried it and the parents sued and in, oh, in 1986 I think he said, the courts ruled that teaching creationism in the public schools promoted a certain religious belief in which all the students might not share and therefore violated the First Amendment's guarantee of freedom of religion." She paused. "He said the case went all the way to the Supreme Court."

"The Supreme Court of Louisiana?"

She shook her head. "The Supreme Court of the United States of America."

"In Washington, D.C.?"

Philippa gave a single, firm nod. "The same."

"Were Pastor Seabolt and the rest of them made aware of this?"

"Of course."

"And they still brought in a ringer."

"Yes, one of the church elders, a guy by the name of Bill Prue. He didn't have a teaching certificate, but the district superintendent said he could come in anyway."

"Frances Sleighter?"

The nod again. "She came down in January, I think it was, on an inspection tour or something, and gave this speech about the Molly Hootch law, and how the most important thing about it was that it won for the people in the Alaskan villages who chose to have high schools built in their communities the right to have a say in what their children were taught."

Kate sat up straight in her chair. "The intent of the Molly Hootch law was not to promote the teaching of any community's pet religious theories."

"No? Doesn't matter. Ms. Sleighter said she was happy to see the community of Chistona taking such an interest in the curriculum. She said she wished more citizens got involved in their children's education." Phil's words were bitten off and bitter.

"She didn't say anything about obeying the Constitution of the United States of America. She didn't say anything about the oath teachers have to sign, swearing they will uphold both the constitution of the state of Alaska *and* the Constitution of the United States of America."

"Then what happened?"

"Then she left. And the very next week, the Chistona Little Chapel wasn't letting the grass grow under its feet, Bill Prue came in and told my daughter and her ten classmates that it didn't do to take everything scientists said too literally or too seriously."

Kate and Jim laughed.

Phil wasn't laughing. "Then he moved from science on over into history, biblical history, and explained that the Old Testament was one long account of how God kept smiting the Jews for their collective sin of egregious pride. The gist of it was He visited Hitler on them because they were too proud."

Kate closed her eyes and shook her head.

"Yeah. So, you'd think Pastor Seabolt and the rest of them would be satisfied. They got their licks in, the kids had been exposed to an alternative look at the beginning, middle and ending of the world. But noooooooo. Then they had to start banning books."

"Which ones?"

Phil fortified herself with coffee. "First it was only

books out of the library, books we could have at home if we wanted to let the kids read them. When we didn't make too big a fuss over that, they started in on the textbooks." She saw their expressions and nodded again, that single, decisive gesture that seemed to be characteristic of her. "They went after the science books first, the ones with the E word in them. Evolution," she added, in case they didn't know.

They did, and they didn't like it. "Then what?" Jim said.

"The history books were next. Seabolt and company didn't care for the chapter on ancient history, or the one on World War II." She gave a thin smile. "And then one of the kids brought home a poem. I will never forget the title of it as long as I live. 'Church Going,' by Philip Larkin."

"What's it about?" Jim said.

"A guy who goes to church and finds nobody home," Kate said. "What happened next?"

"As if that wasn't bad enough," Phil said grimly, "next the teacher plays them a song, another title I will never forget, 'Something to Believe In,' by a rock group named Poison."

"What's *it* about?" Jim said. "Or do I have to ask?"

"Pretty much the same thing," Kate said, "and no, you didn't."

"Smart ass," Jim said, but so only she could hear him.

"What happened?" Kate asked Phil.

Phil's usually merry mouth was stretched into a tense line. The time had obviously been a bad one and she wasn't enjoying reliving it. "The English teacher, she quit the following spring, before they could fire her, you know what she told me? She told me if she'd wanted to participate in a religious war she'd have moved to Jerusalem where she'd heard tell there was one already in progress. All she wanted was to try to draw some parallels, make the kids realize poetry could be as everyday as rock and roll. I mean, it's hard enough trying to get a generation raised on MTV to pay attention in class—I *hate* satellite dishes—but when you're trying to get adolescents with five-second attention spans to read literature and understand it . . ." She shook her head and drank coffee.

"So, she sent them home with an assignment to compare and contrast the poem with the song lyrics. One of Seabolt's congregation got hold of the textbook with the poem in it, and so then they started purging the English books."

" 'Purging?' " Jim said.

"Purging," Phil said with that single nod of her head. "I don't know what else you'd call reading through them and blacking out with Marksalots whatever you found objectionable."

Kate didn't either.

"That wasn't the worst of it, though."

Kate didn't see how it could get much worse, but she didn't say so.

"You know how it is with the smaller schools in the bush; one teacher winds up teaching three subjects to six different grades." Kate nodded. "It's the same in Chistona, one school, kindergarten through the twelfth grade, forty students, two full-time teachers, two part-time. Dan taught history and science, and his second year it was his turn to teach P.E., and of course that meant he got stuck with the health class, too."

"AIDS," Jim said immediately. "I knew that was coming."

"AIDS?" Kate said, momentarily confused by this jump from the lyric to the epidemic.

"Sex education," Phil explained. "The churchy people wanted the school to teach abstinence, period. Actually, they didn't want the school to teach anything at all on the subject, but if the state insisted, a lecture on abstinence was in order." She added, voice acid, "Essentially what they said was that they'd rather bury their kids than teach them how to protect themselves from what's out there."

Kate thought of Bobby, and the girl in the bathtub.

Phil ran a hand through her hair and made a face. "Sorry. I don't mean to sound so bitter. Anyway, Daniel didn't agree. He told the ninth through twelfth grades where babies came from, and about sexually transmitted diseases and AIDS."

"I knew it," Jim said.

"My daughter, Meta, was in that class. He told them the only sure way not to catch any or all of the above was, in fact, abstinence. He even told them that joke about the pill, you know the one how the pill is one hundred percent effective only if you hold it between your knees? Meta said he got a big laugh out of that. And then he told them that sometimes abstinence wasn't the first thing you thought of in situations where abstinence might be required, and the smart thing was to be prepared, and he suggested a couple of methods. He even showed them one."

"Condoms," Jim said.

"Uh-huh," Phil said.

"Horrors," Jim said, "the C word."

"Uh-huh," Phil said.

"He wasn't preaching sexual permissiveness," Kate said. "What were they so afraid of?"

"You mean other than the twentieth century?"

Phil got up and refilled everyone's coffee cups and passed around a plate of doughnuts, still hot to the touch. They ate them in silence around the table, in a kitchen filled with the not unpleasant smell of deep fried fat. The linoleum floor was scrubbed down to its fading pattern, the top of the oil stove gleamed blackly, the refrigerator was festooned with clippings from the newspaper, coupons and a history quiz graded with a big, red C on it and Meta

Cotton's name written in pencil in the upper right corner.

"I would have toughed it out," Phil said, dabbing her mouth with a napkin. "If Dan had been willing, I would have fought it with him, through the school district administration, through the legislature, through the courts. Those people were subverting the learning process, not to mention contravening the Constitution." Unknowingly she echoed Kate's words to Jack. "I want my kids to go to college. Can you imagine what life would be like for them, going away to school with crap like that stuffed into their heads?"

Kate could imagine.

"When he left—" Phil said, and stopped. "After he was gone," she resumed, "they hired another teacher, this time a teacher personally approved by Pastor Seabolt and every member of the Chistona Little Chapel. I knew what that meant. And there was so much bad feeling in the town. I mean, there are less than two hundred people in Chistona, it's not like you can get away from what's going on. I couldn't buy my groceries anymore at Russell's because Sally was always there. Gordon—my husband—was getting harassed because I was his wife. So I resigned my position on the school board, and Gordon and I packed up the kids and moved here."

Yes, Kate thought, that was the way these things happened. The people of good conscience were made so uncomfortable they were forced out of their homes and communities, leaving the petty dictators and the fanatics behind to run things in their own image.

"You know what the worst thing is?" Phil said. "Meta liked Dan. She really liked him. She might even have had a bit of a crush on him, but I didn't mind that. He encouraged her to think for herself. She read more because of him. She was going to do a comparison study of AIDS and the black plague in Europe in the Middle Ages. She found this huge book, must have been six hundred pages long, and she read the whole thing, cover to cover, that's got to be the first time in her life she's read a book that long all the way through, on her own. She got an A in history Dan's first year. First time that happened, too.

"And now he's dead." Her eyes filled with unexpected tears. "Dammit. God *damn* it." She sniffled and wiped one eye. "Sorry. I don't usually do this."

They sat in awkward silence while she mopped up her tears and blew her nose. Regaining control, she looked at Kate, her expression strained. "You want to hear something funny? Dan loved his father. He really did. He'd loved his wife, you could see how much he missed her every time you looked at him. He'd followed his father up here after she died because his father was the only family he had left. He wanted to be close to him, wanted Matthew to know him. He didn't want to go up against him."

"What made him do it then?" Kate said. "He had a home, he had family, a job. A friend of his told me he was getting into the subsistence lifestyle, so he might even have been a stayer. Why didn't he just let it ride?"

"My best guess?"

Kate raised her shoulders and spread her hands. "Serve it up."

"Matthew." Phil nodded once. "Simon got to Matthew right away. Dan wasn't going for the word according to Simon Seabolt, and Simon settled for Matthew instead." She paused, frowning. "I think Matthew was looking for his mother, and Simon saw that need and moved right in. A mother resurrected and looking down on him from heaven was one way to fill the hole she left behind when she died. And Dan saw it happen, and this was his way of fighting back. Matthew might want to go to church, but he had to go to school, too. It was Dan's only way of reaching out to him. His only hope of retaining contact."

The struggle for Matthew's soul, Kate thought. It looked as if Simon Seabolt had won that fight. At any rate, with Matthew's father dead, the field was left to Matthew's grandfather by default.

Then again, maybe not. She remembered those thirty-four crumpled dollar bills. Thirty-four dollars was a fortune to a ten-year-old. And he had searched her out on his bike, two miles late at night down a lonely dirt road, a quarter of a mile up a forest path almost in the dark, to ask her to find his father.

Pastor Seabolt might not have it all his own way, after all. Kate hoped not.

The kitchen door slammed. "Hi, Mom."

"Hi, Mom, what's for dinner? Oh."

The two teenagers were close in age and appearance, both bouncy and brunette like their mother. Their smiles faded as they saw the expression on their mother's face. Two pairs of bright brown eyes looked at Kate, and slid past her to settle on Chopper Jim's uniform. There was a short silence. "What's wrong?" one said.

The other one, taller and a little older, probably Meta, said, "Is Dad okay?"

Phil managed a smile. "He's fine. There's nothing wrong, or nothing we have to talk about now. Go on, up to your rooms, do your homework." They hesitated. "Go on now. It's spaghetti for dinner."

They brightened at once. "All *right*," the younger girl said. She grabbed a doughnut and charged up the stairs.

Meta lingered in the doorway, looking back at her mother, looking longer at Kate this time, lingering a little longer than necessary on Chopper Jim, but she was female and that was only to be expected. "Is it Mr. Seabolt?"

Phil's head snapped around. "What?"

The girl was solemn, but her mouth wobbled a

little around the edges. "They're saying at the school that somebody found his body. Is it true?"

The mukluk telegraph was still on the job. There was a short, heavy silence. Phil held out a hand. After a moment Meta took a step forward and took it. "Yes, honey," Phil said gently, "I'm afraid it is." She nodded at Kate. "This is Kate Shugak. She found him."

Meta looked at her. "I'm sorry," Kate said.

Meta swallowed hard. "So am I," she said, with a valiant attempt at control. She fumbled for the right words, but at sixteen years of age the right words are never close at hand. "Mr. Seabolt . . . I . . . he was okay." She was silent for a moment, then nodded once, firmly, her mother's characteristic gesture. "He was okay."

Kate thought of Tom Winklebleck. A younger Kate might have described him exactly the same way.

CHAPTER 9

Moreover, they imbibe other noxious qualities besides; if, for instance, the hole of a venomous serpent be near, and the serpent breathes upon them, as they open, from their natural affinity with poisonous substances, they are readily disposed to imbibe this poison. Therefore, it will be well to exercise care in gathering them until the serpents retire, into their holes.

—Pliny

"I regard," Chopper Jim said judiciously, "all forms of organized religion as a blight, an abomination and a public nuisance. It is the fifth horseman of the Apocalypse. I'm not talking about the guy who takes a vow of silence, or poverty, or celibacy"—he shivered—"and goes and sits on top of a mountain to meditate for the rest of his life." He fixed Kate with a stern look. "It's the people who follow him up that mountain, and then come back down and beat His word into their fellow man who annoy me."

She didn't reply, and he forked up a french fry. Mutt, well aware of who was the soft touch at this table, sat pressed against his side, looking yearningly up into his face. He forked up another french fry and she took it delicately between her teeth, casting him a look of adoration in the process. "Most of those people—not all, I admit—but most of the people who subscribe to organized religion are too lazy and or too frightened to answer the hard questions themselves, and so hand their souls over for safe-keeping to a bunch of thieves and charlatans who know more about separating fools from their money than they do about God. Any God." He took a bite of cheeseburger. "Religion is a crutch. You lean on it long enough, you forget how to walk on your own two feet."

Bobby had called it an addiction, Kate remembered.

They were sitting in a booth by a window of the Caribou Restaurant and Motel, a faux cedar chalet fifty feet off the Glenn Highway in beautiful downtown Glennallen, a wide spot in the road 180 miles north of Anchorage. It was a lot prettier when it wasn't raining.

Kate was trying to eat her own meal but she didn't have much of an appetite. Outside in the gravel parking lot, a line of recreational vehicles pulled up single file. Drivers emerged, stretching, rubbing their butts. Their vehicles were covered with mud; there must be some construction going on up the road. The mud made it hard to read the plates. Illinois? Only one vowel on one end. Must not be a redneck state.

"Furthermore," Jim stated, "organized religion

legitimizes genocide. It authorizes it, encourages it, sanctifies it, and then forgives you for anything you had to do with it. As a practicing policeman, I object to jihads, crusades, murder on a large scale of any kind. It backlogs the morgues, it absorbs too much of the coroner's time, and it's a mess to clean up." He stabbed his last french fry with his fork and pointed it at Kate. "W. H. Auden was right. He said in revelation is the end of reason."

Illinois was looking pretty good right then, redneck or not. "Some people might say, only in revelation is salvation."

"About one hundred and eighty people sixty miles right up that road might say that," Jim agreed, relieved that she could still talk but smart enough not to say so. "Auden hit the nail on the head. Have you ever seen a born-again Christian? Right out of the baptismal font? He's like a reformed drunk who won't be happy until everyone else is reformed, too. Scary. Jekyll and Hyde."

Kate remembered Dinah's friend.

"Religion is dangerous," Jim said thickly around another bite of cheeseburger, chewed, swallowed, and added, "And the most seductive thing about it is you don't have to think for yourself. Nice never having to grow up and take responsibility for your own actions."

"God made me do it," Kate said.

"Exactly. Like the guy who killed the doctor who worked at the women's health clinic, where was that, Florida? Shot him in the back four times. Said it was God's will." He shook his head. "Guys like him, they been listening too long to guys like Jerry Prevo in Anchorage and Jerry Falwell Outside. Man in the pulpit says abortion is murder, doesn't take long for the people in the congregation to figure out that the women who have abortions and the doctors who perform them are murderers." He turned one hand palm up and raised an eyebrow. Mutt, always alert, swiped the french fry he was holding. "The law says abortion isn't murder, God—by way of the man in the pulpit—says it is. The law therefore must be wrong, so the man in the congregation convinces himself it's his spiritual duty to step in to redress the situation." He shook his head. "Yeah. Prevo and Falwell and Robertson and the rest of them, they should wash the blood off their own hands before they start telling everybody else how to wash theirs."

Which naturally made Kate think of Pontius Pilate. She hadn't stopped with Genesis in her perusal of Dinah's Bible. An amazing book, with an example of and an answer for everything, if you only knew where to look. And maybe knew how to read it in the original Greek. " 'I am innocent of the blood of this just person: see ye to it.' "

"I beg your pardon?"

"Pontius Pilate. When he was washing his hands of the responsibility of Christ's crucifixion. He did take responsibility, though; when he got done washing his hands he said, 'His blood be on us, and on our children.' "

"I'm sure that was a real comfort to Christ, on his way out to the cross," Jim said.

She looked out the window again, brow creased. "You ever think about crucifixion as a way of dying? All your body weight pulling at those nails through your palms. Probably the flesh tore up to the bones, and the bones were what lodged against the nail and kept your palms from ripping apart and you from falling. Sometimes maybe you'd push with your feet against the single nail through them, no matter how much it hurt, just to give your hands a rest. The strain on your arms, the deltoid muscles." She looked back at Jim, expression sober. "I'd rather be caught in a forest fire. At least the smoke inhalation'd probably knock you out before the fire ever got to you." Not that she thought Daniel Seabolt had been that lucky.

Jim, fork halfway to his mouth, gave Kate a long, assessing look. Mutt, not one to miss an opportunity, lipped the fry off the fork. "You been alone in that cabin too long, Shugak."

"You sound like my grandmother," she muttered under her breath. Out loud she said, "Why is it suddenly everyone I know is an expert on religion?" Except Jack, she remembered with a spurt of gratitude. At least she didn't have to go all the way to Vietnam to find her oasis of sanity.

He filched a handful of fries from her plate, and

was surprised and a little alarmed when she didn't take his hand off at the elbow. "It isn't sudden, Kate. It takes years of indoctrination. Like the song says, you've got to be carefully taught."

She looked across at him with pardonable irritation. "For crying out loud, you, too? Isn't anyone in this country allowed to grow up and learn to think for themselves?"

He recognized the question as being rhetorical and swiped another french fry in reply. "You forgot to ask me something."

"What?"

He finished the fry, reached for a napkin and began a meticulous cleaning of his hands. When he was through he examined the result with a critical eye, used the tine of a fork to clean his left ring fingernail, and settled back to look at Kate.

The penny dropped. "You called Oklahoma," she said.

He bestowed an approving smile on her. "No."

"Then who did?"

"You know Kenny Ellis?"

"Trooper assigned to Glennallen?"

Another approving smile. "He used to be from there, was a cop in Tulsa, came up to work security on the Pipeline in the seventies, joined the troopers after. He still knows people, has family down there, so I asked him if he'd call for me."

Kate eyed him narrowly. Jim Chopin looked as if

he might lick his chops at any moment. "So. Give."

"The Right Reverend Pastor Simon Seabolt is well known in certain law enforcement circles in Oklahoma, and maybe in other states as well. He started out as some kind of traveling tent preacher, all over the Midwest and the South."

Kate remembered Bobby's revival meetings. Seabolt was old enough. Maybe Bobby'd been saved by him a time or two.

"He sold out a lot of tents and made a lot of money and started looking around for a place to set a spell. That's how they talk in Oklahoma, 'set a spell.' " He shook his head. "And then a bunch of people with a church in Moore, which is like semi-attached to Tinker Air Force Base, which is like semi-attached to Oklahoma City, paid him a visit and invited him to take their pulpit and preach against the godless Communists, which were almost but not quite as bad as Democrats."

"And?"

Jim patted his lips and put the napkin aside. "Nothing can be proved, you understand."

"Can it ever?"

He ignored that with superb indifference. "They started out picketing schools teaching sex education, and escalated their activities from there."

"To what?"

"Lying down in front of teachers' cars. Taking license plate numbers at PTA meetings and follow-

ing school board members home and harassing
them. The school finally had to take a restraining
order out against them."

"Seabolt was involved in this?"

He raised his eyebrows and looked bland. "Heavens to Murgatroyd, listen to the woman. Certainly
not. Pastor Seabolt maintained his proper place,
which was the pulpit, every Sunday at ten."

Of course. He still did. "What next?"

"Next, four of his parishioners were arrested for
a gay-bashing in Omaha. There'd been other attacks on gays, but they couldn't make Seabolt's
parishioners for them." He looked bland again.
"Pastor Seabolt just naturally had an ironclad alibi
for the night in question. In fact, for every night in
question."

"Naturally. They get off?"

"Who's telling this story?"

"Sorry. Did they get off?"

He grinned that shark's grin, tight, white and
wide. "All the members of Pastor Seabolt's church
swore on a stack of Bibles the accused were at a
church social or Bible study or something the night
those two unfortunate and misguided young men
were attacked. And the physical evidence didn't
hold up, so they walked." He paused. "One of the
victims was blinded in one eye."

"What next?"

"That's what I like about you, Shugak, you're
never satisfied."

She ignored that, but her indifference was not quite as convincing as his. "What else?"

"The Oklahoma state police are pretty sure that Seabolt's bunch was behind the bombing of a women's health clinic in Oklahoma City in 1987. Two people died."

Kate sat up straight. "The year before he came up here."

"Yeah. Interesting timing, isn't it?"

"Very."

"Not as interesting as one of the victims, though."

"Oh."

"Nope." He raised his eyes from contemplation of the remains of his coffee. "She was the daughter of a state senator."

Kate gave a short, unamused laugh and shook her head. "But they couldn't prove anything, of course."

He shrugged. "He's here. He'd made Oklahoma too hot to hold him, but that didn't mean he couldn't move somewhere else and start over."

Lucky us, Kate thought. Maybe someone had taken hold of the United States by the southern coast and had given one good shake and everything nobody Outside wanted to live with had fallen into Alaska.

"So?" Jim said, draining his coffee. "What now?"

The line of RVs was taking turns at the gas pump

at the station next door. "I think I'll go see Auntie Joy."

"That Joy Shugak, in Gakona?" She nodded. "How come?"

She pushed her plate back and slid out of the booth. "Because nobody sneezes within a hundred miles of here without Auntie Joy hearing about it. And because Emaa's staying with her, and nobody sneezes within a *thousand* miles of here without *her* hearing about it."

"Good enough," he decided, and slid out to tower over her. "Mind if I tag along?"

"Sure. Fine. Has this become an official investigation?"

He smoothed the crown of his hat and put it on his head, centering it just so, the brim absolutely straight, the tie of the gold cord directly over his eyes. "Shall we say, I'm satisfying a personal curiosity." He gave that shark's grin again. "Means I get to spend some more time with you, babe."

She smiled back at him. "Jim?"

"Yes?"

"The next time you call me babe?" She dropped her voice so he had to lean closer to hear. "I'll rip your tongue out."

Auntie Joy's house was an old one, originally built of logs but added on to every ten years or so for the last century. It looked a lot like Emaa's house in Niniltna, and the Gillespies' store in Chistona, with a roof that lurched from one level to another like a sailor on leave, exterior walls made variously of log festooned with moss, clapboards chipping white paint, blue aluminum siding and tar paper shingles. Inside it was crowded with bodies, noisy with laughter and smelled of baking bread. Kate followed her nose to the kitchen, Jim bringing up the rear.

"Kate!"

"Hi, Kate!"

"Kate, long time no see!"

"Kate, where have you been?"

A black-haired, thickset man Jim didn't know but who reminded him of Cal Worthington planted himself in Kate's path and put a confiding hand on her shoulder. "Kate, you think you could get your grandmother to get behind a logging operation down the Kanuyaq? A guy I met—"

She smiled, mumbled something, shrugged off the hand and edged around him.

"Hey, Kate," a thin man sitting in one corner of the living room said, not unenthusiastically, but not with any great pleasure, either.

She paused. "Hey, Martin. How you been?"

"Okay."

"I missed you in Anchorage last March."

"I made it home all right, as you can see." He patted the hip of the girl sitting in his lap. "You know Suzy?"

"Sure, Suzy—Kompkoff, isn't it?"

The girl shook her head. "Not anymore."

"Oh."

"Or it won't be, once the divorce comes through."

Kate nodded. The last time she'd seen her, Suzy had been pregnant. She wondered who had the baby, and hoped with all her heart Suzy hadn't left it with Mickey.

"We're both straight now, Kate," Martin said.

"I didn't ask, Martin," Kate said in a level voice.

"You didn't have to," he replied, words and tone edgy, and Kate shook her head, produced a smile that had a lot of work in it and passed on into the kitchen. Jim nodded at Martin, with whom he'd had extensive professional dealings over the years, touched the brim of his hat to Suzy and followed. He was beginning to understand why Kate spent so much time alone on her homestead.

Half a dozen old women sat at the kitchen table playing cards. Each shuffled through a deck, built black on red on black on the cards in front of them and by suit on the aces pooled in the center of the table. The play was fast and furious, there was heard more than one cheerful curse when a player beat another to the center pile, and the backs of two or three hands sported long, red scratches that were almost but not quite bleeding arterially. "Snerts!" somebody yelled and there was a loud, collective groan.

"Joy, you cheated!"

"Auntie, not again!"

"Darn it, that was *my* three of spades, Joy."

"That's *it*, Auntie, there's no point in playing with you, you *always* win, I *quit*."

"You always say that, Helen," a broad-faced, merry-eyed woman said, "but you always come back for more."

"I'm out of my mind is all," the other woman replied, and spotted Kate. "Kate!"

Kate grinned. "Hi, Helen. Hi, Gladys. Hi, Tanya."

This time the welcome was warm and genuine, and Jim stood back and watched the other women swarm around Kate, hugging her, kissing her, taking her face in both hands and examining it closely for the passage of time. It was a noisy, rambunctious scene, and over the hubbub his eyes met those of Ekaterina Moonin Shugak. She nodded once, coolly, and he walked around the crowd to pay his respects. "Mrs. Shugak," he said, making almost a bow over her hand.

"Sergeant Chopin," she replied, inclining her head regally. Ekaterina was always very formal with Chopper Jim, possibly because she harbored the suspicion, correctly, that more than one of her grandchildren had been fathered by him, possibly because he had been the proximate cause of so many of her children's close encounters with the law. The latter might have been simply because she'd had so many of them; if in certain circles

Chopper Jim was known as the Father of the Park, Ekaterina was as surely known as the Mother. And Grandmother, and the Great-Grandmother, and if she lived long enough, and she had every intention of doing so, the Great-Great-Grandmother.

Kate, arm around Auntie Joy, watched them. Jim said something and a smile forced its way across Ekaterina's face, softening her wintry expression. Kate shook her head. Even Emaa. The man was a menace.

The room cleared and Joy busied herself at the stove. "Coffee? Tea?"

"Coffee'd be great, thanks, Joy," Jim said.

"How about some cocoa, Auntie?" Kate said hopefully, and a grin split Joy's brown, seamed face.

"Nestle's Quik?"

"What else?"

"Lumpy?"

"How else?"

An enormous kettle steamed on the back of Auntie Joy's stove. She turned the burner beneath it to high and went about assembling two plates of homemade cookies four inches in diameter and glazed with sugar. Kate sat down across from Ekaterina. Jim hung his jacket and hat on a peg by the kitchen door and sat next to Kate, the leather of his holster creaking. With all that hardware, badges and guns and cuffs and radios and nightsticks, he must have felt like he was in armor. But then, Jim

Chopin looked as if he could swim a moat in a coat of heavy iron mail.

The idea tickled Kate. A knight of the Last Frontier, jousting the length of Alaska's highways, challenging champions from foreign climes to duels of high speed and reckless endangerment. Sir Winnebago of Wisconsin. Baron Jayco of Virginia. Count Coachman of Connecticut.

"What?" he said suspiciously, eyeing her smile.

She shook her head. "Nothing." Sir James of Tok Junction. The Duke of the Department of Public Safety.

"So how was your trip to Fairbanks, Katya?"

Kate regarded her grandmother with a wry smile. "So you heard about that, did you?"

Emaa shrugged, a superbly nonchalant gesture. Of course, the gesture said, of course I heard, I hear everything.

And she does, too, Kate thought, which is why I'm here. "It went well. I found out some things I need to know. Jack came up."

"Ah," Ekaterina said. "And how is Jack?"

"Healthy," Kate said, "very healthy," and next to her Jim Chopin turned a sudden laugh into a cough.

Joy saved him by bringing him a cup of coffee and he buried his nose in it. She set one of the plates of cookies down on the table and took the other one into the living room, returning to put three cups of cocoa on the table and take a seat next to Ekaterina. She looked at Kate with bright eyes. "So, Kate, what's this I hear about a teacher being murdered up in Chistona?"

Jim's coffee went down the wrong pipe and came back up out his nose. Kate thumped him on the back and Joy got him a Kleenex. "Thanks," he said, mopping his watering eyes. "What makes you think he was murdered?"

Joy gave him a look of impatient scorn. "Oh for heaven's sake, Jim, everyone knows Daniel Seabolt has been missing since last year, and everyone knows Kate found the body in suspicious circumstances." She liked the sound of that; it was a phrase she'd heard many times on television, direct from Chicago through the satellite dish mounted on her roof, whenever somebody found a body in Lake Michigan. "In suspicious circumstances," she repeated, and leaned forward. "How suspicious were they?"

Kate looked at Jim, who shook his head and threw up his hands and took a cookie. It was smooth and buttery and a little crispy around the edges. Perfect. Well worth the price of a little inside information.

Kate looked at Ekaterina. "At first I thought he'd been caught in the fire last year, but he didn't have any clothes on. And the coroner says he didn't burn to death or die of smoke inhalation."

"What did he die of?"

"Anaphylactic shock. It's an allergic reaction, where your mucous membranes swell up and you can't breathe. If you're not treated immediately, you can go into cardiac arrest. Some people get it from bee stings."

Ekaterina, listening intently, said, "And this is what happened to Daniel Seabolt?" Kate nodded, and Ekaterina sat back in her chair, frowning. "He could have been swimming in Cat's Creek."

Kate shook her head. "This was two or so miles from the creek."

"How far from Chistona?"

Kate looked at Jim. "A little over four miles by road. Maybe one, one and a half, cross-country?"

The trooper nodded. "About that."

Ekaterina looked at him. "I hear no one reported him missing."

He looked at her, a slight smile on his face. "No."

"So you didn't even know he was."

"Not until Kate told me she found him."

Ekaterina turned to Kate. "How did you know who he was?"

"His son hired me to find him."

"Oh." Ekaterina frowned. "The little boy?"

Kate nodded.

"Not his father, Daniel's father, I mean?" Joy exclaimed.

"No, the boy. Said his father had been gone since last year. Said he'd heard how I used to do this kind of work, and he wanted me to find his father for

him." Kate chased a lump of cocoa around the rim
of her mug with a spoon, captured it and mashed
it between her tongue and the roof of her mouth.
She swallowed the burst of chocolatey flavor reluctantly. "One morning, Dinah and I are out picking
mushrooms and we stumble across the body. That
night, this kid comes into camp and wants me to
find his father."

"That was easy," Jim observed.

"I thought so," Kate said, a trifle grimly.

"Daniel Seabolt was the son of the church pastor,
Simon Seabolt," Ekaterina said.

"Yeah."

"And was the father of the boy, Matthew," Ekaterina, who liked to have things made perfectly
clear, said.

"Yes."

"He taught at the school," Joy said.

"We know. I've just been talking to his boss in
Fairbanks."

"There was a big fuss up there year before last
about what he was teaching in the school," Joy
said.

"We know that, too. Jim and I have just been
talking to Philippa Cotton, who used to be on the
school board up there, before they moved down
here."

Joy nodded. "That old man caused a bunch of
trouble for those folks. Good folks, too, most of
them."

"What do you know of him, Auntie?" Kate said. "You live right down the road from Chistona. You must get up there sometimes."

"We went up for services right after they got the church built," she said.

"Really?" Kate raised her eyebrows. "You attended a sermon?"

Joy nodded. "The first one he gave. It was the first church to open in the area in a long time. We were all very excited about it. The whole family"— that would make twenty-three people altogether, if Kate remembered correctly—"we all dressed up in our best clothes and piled into four cars and drove up Sunday morning." She stopped, pressing her lips together.

Watching her, Kate said gently, "What happened, Auntie?"

Ekaterina put a restraining hand on Joy's arm.

Joy shook her head. "No, it's all right." She looked back at Kate. "He said we had to destroy our totems, our clan hats, our button blankets. We had to burn them all."

"What? Why?"

"Because they were idols. 'Thou shalt have no other gods before me,' he said." She looked at Ekaterina and shrugged. "I wanted to get up and walk out, but you don't do that. You just don't do that to a man of God."

"So you stayed."

"Yes."

"What happened next?"

Joy was speaking more to Ekaterina now, twisting to face her. Ekaterina kept her steady gaze on Joy's face, her hand on Joy's arm. One of the kids wandered in from the hubbub in the next room and gave the sober group at the table a curious look. Kate jerked her head at him and he made a face and went out again.

"What happened next, Joy?" Ekaterina repeated.

"Next? Next, he told us we couldn't dance anymore."

Ekaterina's mouth tightened into a thin line. She shifted and her chair creaked. "Why not?"

"He said we were worshipping Satan when we danced."

Kate thought back to the potlatch in Niniltna the year before, the one Ekaterina had called in honor of Roger McAniff's victims. There had been dancing, and she had joined it. The drums had called to her and she had answered their beat with joy in motion, sharing the dance with her friends and family and tribe, comforting the sorrowful, paying respect to loved ones now gone, saying good-bye. And later the dance on top of the mountain, her head touching the sky, the world at her feet.

The knowledge that Pastor Simon Seabolt would have disapproved lent extra zest to a memory she already cherished.

"When the service was over," Joy said, "I stayed behind to talk to him, to try to make him understand. I told him the designs on the button blankets and tunics and the dance robes weren't objects of worship, they identified the wearer's clan. I told him totems identified the clan of the home they were put up in front of. Sometimes they told stories, sometimes they marked a special day in the family's or the tribe's history, but they were never graven images of idols, and they had more to do with our culture than with our religion."

"What did he say?"

Joy sighed. "He had an answer for everything, and always with scripture to back him up. He said cultural pride was a sin against God. He quoted Revelations, and how we wouldn't be dancing in heaven in a button blanket. Everyone laughed."

Hearing the pain in her voice, Kate could barely look at her aunt.

"Everyone laughed," Joy repeated, her voice soft and sad. "I've never been so hurt." Ekaterina's hand moved down Joy's arm to close over her hand. Joy held on tight. "I've never felt so humiliated. It was like he was ignoring all the Anglos and preaching directly at us, the Natives, the only sinners in the room. And our only sin, so far as I could tell, was in being born and raised Native."

She drained her mug and set it back down on the table gently. "I never went back. Not ever."

"When was that, Auntie?"

Joy blinked at her. "When?" She came back to the present. "Oh, let me see, I think he was here a year before the church went up. I suppose, 1989? It was winter. I remember, the road was icy. We almost went into the ditch a half a dozen times. One of the cars did, and we had to stop and push it out."

Ekaterina looked at Kate. "You think Pastor Seabolt had something to do with his son's death." Kate nodded. "What?"

Kate shrugged. "I have no proof of anything, Emaa. It's just a hunch."

"You know?" Joy said suddenly. "When the pastor stood up there and said, 'Thou shalt not worship any other god before me?' " She looked at Kate. "It was like he meant himself. We should not worship any other god before *him*, personally."

And his son refused to worship at the shrine, Kate thought.

Outside, Jim paused with one hand on the door of the cruiser. "What now?"

"Now nothing," she said. "Like I told Emaa, there's no proof of anything, Jim. Do you want to go up to Chistona and charge Seabolt with not reporting a missing person? It's not exactly a Class A felony, is it? Seabolt says his son was distraught over the death of his wife. He says he thought he ran away because he couldn't live with it anymore. Okay, he didn't pass this information on to his grandson, but that's not exactly a crime, either. And," she added, "I forgot to tell you. I was fired."

"What?"

"Yeah, three days ago. Matthew Seabolt said he'd hired me to find his father. I'd found him, he said, so I could stop looking. I said didn't he want to know how his father died, and he said no. I said I wouldn't stop, and he condemned me for the sin of pride and fired me."

He frowned. "You think his grandfather put him up to it?"

"At this point, I think we can assume that anything Matthew does, he's been put up to by his grandfather."

"Except hire you in the first place," he pointed out. He adjusted the brim of his hat. Beneath it, his eyes were direct and a little stern. "You need to remember, Kate, he's lost his mother and his father. Maybe he's just hanging on with both hands to the only person he's got left."

And it was that thought that kept at her all during the drive up the road to the Chistona turnoff, as the clouds dissipated and the sky acquired that soft clarity it always got after a hard rain. Through it the mountains looked higher and more sharply edged, the valleys and passes between as if they went on forever, to Shangri La and beyond. A wisp of mist threaded through a stand of spruce and settled into a green hollow for the night. A ray of sun filtered through the broken overcast, another, and soon the clouds were on the run. The sky was a neutral shade of blue, with little color and less substance, a sky without stars, a sky in waiting.

Oblivious to it all, Kate drove and thought and drove some more.

Matthew Seabolt had hired her to find his father. She had. She had exhausted all possible avenues on the question of how he got there in the first place, followed up every lead, questioned all the usual suspects. She might have another go at Sally Gillespie, whom she was convinced knew more than she was telling, but the woman was frightened, terrified, really, and a creature of Seabolt's to boot. She held out no serious hopes of Sally Gillespie.

Morgan's Third Law came unbidden and unwelcome to mind. "In every murder some questions always go unanswered, usually the ones that are the most interesting."

Kate disliked unanswered questions. That dislike had helped make her the star of the D.A.'s office during her tenure as an investigator there. It had also led to her departure: A question concerning the stability of a father had sent her looking for the answer over the blade of his knife.

It was settled. Jim was right. Best to let the boy resume some semblance of a normal life. He was fed, housed, cared for, not abused in any way.

Unless you counted the gray matter between his ears.

"*No.*" She hit the steering wheel with the palm of her hand. Mutt looked over at her, ears up, eyes wide. "Sorry, girl," Kate said, stretching to ruffle the thick fur. She faced forward, both hands back on the wheel, jaw set.

No. Pursuing the circumstances of Seabolt's death would at this point be nothing more than an exercise in self-indulgence. She would not cater to her own curiosity in this matter.

She would let it go.

Kate walked into the clearing as the sun played a lazy game of tag with the horizon. Bobby took one look at her face and said, "So how's Jack?"

CHAPTER 10

This is the picture of the Cat that walked by himself walking by his wild lone through the Wet Wild Woods and waving his wild tail. There is nothing else in the picture except some toadstools. They had to grow there because the woods were so wet.

—Rudyard Kipling

"S o, what do you think," Bobby said the next morning. "One more day's picking?"

Dinah groaned. Her shiner had faded. Now it just looked as if someone had tattooed an iris around her eye.

"Come on," Bobby cajoled. He produced a fistful of cash and waved it beneath her nose. His face had returned to normal, and Kate was glad to see them both moving easier.

"No," Bobby had told her the night before, "no more trouble. They didn't know you'd left and taken Mutt with you, of course. And they probably knew they could only take us by surprise like that once." He had patted his shotgun significantly.

"One more day," Bobby said imploringly now.

"Another couple hundred or so."

"Mushrooms?"

"Dollars. Just enough to lay in a few supplies on the way home. Then we'll head into the Park. I promise. I swear. I vow. I attest. I take my oath. I give testimony."

"I'll only do it if you *won't* give testimony," Dinah growled. Until that moment Kate wasn't aware that the wraithlike blonde knew how to growl. It was obvious she'd been spending entirely too much time with Bobby.

"Picking's about over anyhow," Bobby said. "Masterson says we've flooded the market, and he's about to pack up and go home."

"How'd you do while I was gone?"

"Fair. We got my chair far enough back in the woods where I could get down and outpick her." He winked at Kate. "Closer to the ground, you know."

"Yes," Dinah told Kate, "he took a perverse thrill out of filling up buckets which I then had to haul down the hill to the van."

"Hey." Bobby spread his hands and did his best to look wounded. "I can't help it if I'm a helpless cripple."

"You're not a cripple, you're an opportunist," Kate told him.

That was about as serious as the conversation got the rest of the day. By unspoken consent they picked away from the site where the body had been. It was another hot one, the temperature rising to eighty degrees by two o'clock, according to the zipper thermometer on Bobby's jacket. All the buckets were full by then and they knocked off and bathed in the creek and drank cans and cans of beer and Diet 7-Up and generally lazed away the rest of the afternoon.

At five-thirty they were ready to go sell mushrooms. Dinah stood at the edge of the clearing, staring down across the broad expanse of the Kanuyaq River valley and at the mountains rising in blue-white splendor beyond. She looked unnatural, standing there without her camera, taking it all in with both her own eyes instead of one of Japanese manufacture, but her awed expression was just right.

"God in heaven," she said, and it was more of a prayer than a curse, "I have never seen anything so beautiful in all of my life." She gave a long, drawn-out sigh and turned to look at them. Her smile dazzled. "Thanks," she said simply.

"Thank *you*," Bobby said.

It was meant to have been pure sexual innuendo, a Bobby Clark specialty, and instead it came out with a funny little twist on the end that turned it into something else. Dinah met his eyes and there was something in the way they looked at each other that made Kate simultaneously be happy for them both and wish she was somewhere else.

It was almost enough to make her forget Daniel
Seabolt.

Almost.

She cleared her throat and said briskly, "We'd
better get these shrooms up to the tavern before the
buyer bugs out on us."

Dinah followed her down the hill, buckets in both
hands. Bobby put on his racing gloves, balanced a
bucket behind and before and slipped and slid and
crashed through the brush down the hill to a halt
next to the driver's side door. He grinned up at Kate
cockily, and she had to laugh.

They squeezed the buckets and Mutt and Bobby's
chair into the back of the truck and the three of
them into the cab and set out. They were agreeably
surprised when they saw the flatbed in the parking
lot in front of the Gillespies' store in Chistona.
"Hey, great," Dinah said, "we don't have to drive
all the way to Tanada."

There were fewer cars than there had been in
front of the tavern and the line to sell was much
shorter. The man on the back of the truck confirmed Bobby's words: the mushroom picking season was about over. "Yeah," he said, "after tonight,
I'll have as much as I can handle alone, and so far
as I know, I'm the last one buying."

"How much?" Bobby said.

"Buck and a quarter."

"What!"

The man shrugged. "Take it or leave it. I'm the last one buying, and I'm too tired to argue."

He looked it, and nobody wanted to drive all the way to Tanada to see if he was lying about being the last buyer.

They unloaded the buckets and got into line. Kate heard a door slam shut and turned to see Sally Gillespie and her children come out of the store and walk in their direction.

She had thought that she'd handled it. She'd thought she was under control. She'd thought she was going to leave it alone. She waited until Sally looked up and saw her. "Hello, Sally."

The other woman jumped, halted, changed color, took another step, halted again. She didn't want to look at Kate but her eyes slid in that direction anyway. "Hello." She hitched her baby up on her hip. "I thought you left."

"I did."

"Oh."

"Don't you want to know where I went?"

"Why should I care?" But she did, eyes fixed almost painfully on Kate's face.

"I went to Fairbanks to see Frances Sleighter." She watched Sally's expression change with satisfaction. "And then I went to Glennallen. To talk to Philippa Cotton. I know a lot more about what went on here last year than I did before."

One of her children tugged at her skirt and she dropped a hand to his head. She looked back at

Kate with beseeching eyes. "Why won't you let it go? There's nothing you can do about it now. Just let it go."

"I was hired to do a job," Kate said, and even to her own ears it sounded priggish.

"The problem is over now," Sally said earnestly. "It was never much more than a personality conflict to begin with, and all those people are gone."

"And one of them is dead," Kate said. "How convenient for anyone whose personality he conflicted with."

Sally flushed beet red. "If you'll excuse me, we have to get to Bible study," she said with a poor assumption of dignity. She hitched up the baby again and grabbed somebody's hand and whisked past Kate, marching down the road toward the beckoning spire. Onward Christian soldier.

"Why don't you pick on somebody your own size," Bobby said.

Kate's instantaneous rage surprised them all, not least herself. She rounded on him. "Daniel Seabolt is *dead*." Her voice was rising. Heads turned and she lowered it to a raspy whisper and pointed a finger at Sally's retreating back. "*She* knows what happened to him. For all I know she could be an accessory. At the very least, she's concealing evidence. I will *pick* until the scab comes off this goddam town if I want; if I want I will pick until it fucking well *bleeds*." She paused for breath, glaring down at him.

He looked at her without expression for a long moment. "Okay," he said finally, and patted the air with his palms. "I give."

She straightened, furious with herself for losing her temper. "I'm sorry."

"Me, too. I was out of line."

"No. I was." The anger drained out of her and she put both hands on the arms of his chair and leaned down to rest her forehead against his. "I'm sorry. Please forgive me."

"Never." He kissed her, a big, smacking kiss that made her feel better, but not much.

Dinah raised an eyebrow, and Kate, embarrassingly near to tears, said, "Relax. He'll only run around on you when you're not looking."

"I resemble that remark," Bobby said, and they all laughed, if a bit hysterically.

The line was short but everyone had had the same idea, to load up for the final day, and it was over an hour before Kate handed the last bucket up to be weighed.

"Hey," she heard someone say, "what's that?"

She turned her head. A black column of smoke billowed up, parallel to the white spire of the church.

"Oh my God, it's a fire!"

"A fire!"

"The church!"

"Somebody sound the alarm!"

"Somebody get on the radio!"

Kate ran for the truck, buckets forgotten. Bobby hoisted himself into the cab while Dinah tossed his chair in the back. Mutt leapt in beside it, Kate jammed the truck in gear and spit gravel pulling out.

The church was a quarter of a mile down the road and they were there in less than a minute. Kate slammed on the brakes and the Isuzu slid to a halt on the loose gravel. The three of them stared at the scene in front of them. Bobby broke the silence. "What the hell's going on here?"

There was a fire, and it was a burner, but it had been deliberately set, a pile of wood doused with gas they could smell from inside the cab. Kate opened the door and got out. "Mutt," she said, and Mutt jumped down to stand next to her. "Stay close, girl."

Mutt gave an uneasy woof. Little fires she could tolerate. Big ones made her ruff stand up. Dinah lifted Bobby's chair out of the bed and set it down next to the open door. He walked his knuckles down into it and the three of them moved toward the fire as other vehicles arrived.

A group of people formed a ring around the fire, the tallest of whom was the Right Reverend Pastor Simon Seabolt. Matthew stood next to him. There were twenty children and twice as many adults, and all of them were feeding the flames of the fire.

Kate looked closer. Feeding the flames with books and albums of music. She recognized a Mi-

chael Jackson CD, a book with a picture of Albert
Einstein on the cover. One woman tossed in what
looked like a small totem. A bottle of vodka was
thrown in and shattered and flames roared up, just
in time to be recorded for posterity by Dinah's camera. It recorded everything faithfully, so faithfully
that Kate couldn't bear to watch it, even long afterward, even with the filter of the medium between
her and the event.

The images were burned forever into her memory: the light of the fire turning the faces of the
crowd into gilded masks, the fixed look in their
wide, staring eyes, lips half-open in the ecstasy of
ritual sacrifice. Seabolt's voice, too, was recorded
clearly, deep, demanding, a call to arms. "Show
your children the devil must be cast out and committed to the everlasting fire of damnation!" he
shouted above the crackle and roar of the flames.
"The dangers of failing to instruct them in God's
holy laws are great! If we don't take advantage of
this opportunity, Satan will!"

There was a chorus of amens. A flame jumped up
and someone screamed. "Satan! I see the serpent!"
A woman fell to her knees, her head buried in her
hands.

The red light of the fire reflected back on Seabolt's face, casting it in exaggerated shadows so that
his eyebrows and the lines that bracketed his mouth
looked carved and deep.

A gilt album Kate recognized as "Elvis' Greatest

Hits" went into the flames. Elvis and Jesus, she thought, remembering the line from the Henley song Jack had quoted, they kind of look the same. She just hadn't been aware until now that she was required to make a choice.

A Nirvana T-shirt went in, followed by half a dozen cassette tapes. Kate saw one woman about to throw in a book she recognized from her own library, a copy of *The Riverside Shakespeare*. She started forward with an inarticulate protest and Bobby grabbed her arm. "No, Kate," he said, his voice low, his gaze as fierce as Seabolt's.

"But—"

"*No.*" His deep voice was inflexible. "You try to stop this and you'll be the next thing they toss on that fire."

Unexpectedly Mutt erupted, barking ferociously. She lunged forward and Kate was only just in time to catch her ruff, one arm knotted in the fur at the back of Mutt's neck, the other still caught in Bobby's hard grasp.

"What the hell!" A big, beefy man who had just tossed a half dozen paperbacks into the fire jumped back. "You better watch that dog, lady!"

Mutt barked wildly, straining, pulling so strongly that Kate grabbed her with both hands, Bobby still gripping one arm. "Quiet, girl," she said urgently. But Mutt would not quiet, and suddenly Kate knew. She stared at the man, at Mutt, at the man again. "You son of a bitch," she said softly.

"What?" Dinah said. "What's wrong?"

Wary, the man looked at Mutt, backing up a step. "You mind that dog, you hear!"

Kate almost let Mutt go. The temptation was so great to just open her hands, loosen her grip, turn Mutt loose. It could always take a while to get her under control. A big strong animal like that, as tiny and frail as Kate could look when she put her mind to it, no one could blame her.

She almost did it. She came so close. She saw the fear the big, beefy man tried to cover with bluster, and she knew Mutt wouldn't stop with him. Mutt's nose worked far too well for that. Four men had attacked the camp that night, and not for one moment did she doubt that the other three were present here, too.

Sally Gillespie burst into the ring of people surrounding the fire, a bundle wadded at her breast. She hurled it up and in the air it unfolded enough to reveal itself as the hunter's tunic that had once graced the wall of Russell's store.

Kate screamed, the involuntary sound torn out of her ruined throat. "No!" Mutt barked again. "Sally, no, *don't,* DON'T!"

"No, Kate," Bobby said again, hanging on with a grip like grim death. "It's too late."

She knew he was right and stopped fighting him, swaying on her feet, watching with anguished eyes. The flames licked at the dentalium shells, the beads melted, the porcupine quills flared up and were consumed. The caustic smell of burnt hide mingled with the wood smoke and spread across the parking lot.

She raised a hand and discovered her cheek was wet.

They watched until the last book was thrown, until the last cassette tape melted, until the last T-shirt burst into flame. They watched until the flames began to die down, until the wood beneath had collapsed into a pile of smoldering embers. Only then did people began to drift away in ones, twos, families. Many stopped to shake Seabolt's hand, to receive his blessing.

Bobby's grip had loosened and before he could stop her Kate pulled free and went around the dying fire to confront Matthew Seabolt. "You wanted to know what happened to your father," she said, traces of tears still on her face. She pointed at his grandfather. "This man killed him."

"No," the boy said in a small voice.

"Yes," Kate said relentlessly. "Yes, he did, and you know it. You told me how he did it. You know it, and I know it, and everyone in this town knows it. Your father loved you, and your grandfather killed him." She grabbed Matthew by his shoulders and shook him once, hard. "Don't forget," she said fiercely. Bobby's hands pulled at her. "And don't forgive!"

The last sight she had of Matthew Seabolt was of him standing next to his grandfather, blue eyes wide and wild, as Bobby and Dinah dragged her away. "Don't forget, Matthew!"

Bobby muscled her into the truck. "Jesus, Kate! Let it alone!" He pulled himself up and slammed the door and grabbed her again before she went out the other side. He shook her once, hard. "What the hell do you think you're doing! The kid's barely ten! You think he needs to hear somebody say something like that about his grandfather, the only family he's got left, the guy he's got to live with? Jesus!"

Dinah drove.

When they came to the Gillespies' store Kate said suddenly, "Stop."

"What?"

"Stop the goddam truck!"

They slid to a halt and Kate was out and running before Dinah and Bobby knew what happened. She went around to the back and slammed through the door without knocking.

The Gillespies were all sitting in their living room and looked up at her, at first startled, and then not. Sally's eyes were the first to fall. Kate looked at Russell. "I want to know what happened to Daniel Seabolt."

"I don't—" he began.

Her voice cracked like a whip. "I want to know what happened to Daniel Seabolt!"

The words hung in the air, written in the fire and smoke of burnt offerings.

She glared at him and he glared back. His shoulders were rigid, his jaw taut, and then in the next moment all the fight seemed to drain out of him. He slumped back in his chair, shaking his head so that it was almost a nervous twitch.

"Russell," Sally said, her voice pleading.

He shook his head again, this time a slow movement that spoke of a bone-deep weariness. "She knows most of it. She might as well know the rest."

"Russell, no."

He raised his head and Sally flushed beneath the contempt in his eyes. There was a fresh bruise on her left cheek. Kate wondered dispassionately if she'd received it during the theft of the hunter's tunic or after she'd returned home without it. Either way, she could not find it in her heart to care.

There was a map on the wall opposite, a map of Chistona and the surrounding area, the map Brad Burns had spoken of, the map with red flags for the sinners, blue flags for the saved. She wondered if the flag for Daniel Seabolt was still up. She wondered how many other unsatisfactory residents of Chistona had been flagged for disposal. They could get away with it, at least for a while, as isolated as they were. They could do it. There was no one to stop them.

No one had stopped them last time.

"Tell her," Russell said.

Sally said, "At least let me put the kids to bed."

"Let them stay," he said, his voice heavy.

"Russell, no, they're too young—"

"Let them stay." The three words were flat and final, and she was silenced.

Dinah and Bobby came up behind Kate to stand in the doorway. Happy, even eager for the interruption, Sally said, smile stretched into a travesty of hospitality, "Would you like to sit down? I could get you some coffee and—"

Kate almost choked on the disgust she felt. *"No."*

Sally flinched beneath the single syllable, and looked imploringly again at her husband.

"Tell her," he said again. "Tell her what you did, all for the love of God. Show your children what their mother is."

Sally broke down then. It was hard to make out the words between the sobs but Kate understood enough to wish she couldn't understand any of it. She'd asked for it, though, and she stood there and took it, all of it, all there was to take.

"He sent Matthew away," Sally said between sobs. "Along with all the rest of the children, to Bible camp. And then we waited until the first fishing period was called and everyone else was gone. We waited a day, and then we went down to the little trailer Daniel and Matthew were living in. He was surprised to see us, but he invited us inside. He even offered us coffee."

She broke down again, and they waited. When it was obvious nobody was leaving until the story was finished, she resumed. "We warned him of the consequences of his actions. We gave him one last chance to stop teaching those lies about the creation and all that other filth." She sobbed again. "He refused. He was very nice about it, but he said no."

She swallowed. "So we stripped him of his clothes."

One of the children made a noise. Russell held out an arm and the little boy rushed into it. Sally watched the boy with hungry eyes. "He fought us. He was young and strong, and he fought." She rubbed one shoulder with an absent hand, as if an old bruise suddenly pained her. "It took four of us to hold him while we locked the door. He kept trying to get in the car with us. Then he started running next to us and we had to floor it to get back to our houses and lock the doors."

She folded her arms across her chest and bent over them. Her voice dropped. "He was outside here for a while. I heard him. He banged on the door and yelled. Then he screamed and begged me to let him in. He tried breaking a window but it was too small for him to fit in and all it did was cut his arm. I cleaned up the blood the next morning."

The cuts on Seabolt's upper right arm, Kate thought.

She looked around, her eyes haunted. "It wasn't supposed to take so long. He was allergic to mosquitoes, his father told us so. He should have died right away. But he didn't. When he screamed, I'll never forget when he screamed—" Her voice caught on the word and she wept silently, hands pressed against her ears.

Why hadn't he tried to break in somewhere else? Kate wondered. The answer was as simple and as terrible as the Alaskan bush itself. It was a long way between cabins in Chistona. There was the church, and the store, and then there were acres of trees and swamp and miles of river and gravel road before the next outpost of civilization. Seabolt's best chance would have been to return to the church and the pastor's cabin and try to get in there, but in a very short time the allergic reaction would have set in, and it is never easy to think clearly when you can't breathe. Kate had had first-hand experience of that not long ago, inside a crab pot ten fathoms below and dropping fast.

It was amazing Daniel Seabolt had made it as far as he did, naked and ill, a mile and more cross-country from the church and the store. And by the time he had followed Sally and her lynch mob down the rough gravel road, his bare feet would have been torn and bloody, and that wouldn't have helped either.

Sally rocked a little, back and forth. "After a while, he went away, and I didn't hear him any-more."

Kate felt sick, suffocated. From the expressions of revulsion on the other faces in the room, she wasn't alone. A second boy crawled into his father's lap.

"Who reserved the privilege of shoving him out the door?" Kate said thinly. "His father?"

"Oh, no," Sally said, shocked out of her misery. "Pastor Seabolt wasn't there. He wasn't with us that evening. He was in Glennallen, lecturing at the Bible college."

They stared at her, dumbfounded, and she said, turning peevish, "I don't know why you're all looking at me like that. We were serving God. Daniel was a blasphemer and a corrupting influence on our children. He was a tool of Satan. He had to be destroyed."

She was like a child reciting scripture by rote.

Bobby stirred. "You ever hear of a little verse that goes, 'Vengeance is mine; I will repay, saith the Lord'?"

"We are but instruments *of* the Lord," Sally said, and again her voice was the voice of a child, obedient and well disciplined. Kate looked at Russell and then as swiftly away, unwilling to witness what she saw there.

Sally sat back against the couch, looking around the room with wide eyes, as if awakening from a bad dream. With a sigh she said, "Gosh, I feel better." She stretched and yawned. "I feel like I could get some sleep now."

Kate wasn't sure she was ever going to be able to sleep again. She looked at Russell, all pity gone, lips pressed together against a rising gorge. He was waiting for it; he flung up one hand, warding her off. "I wasn't here."

The whip was back in Kate's voice. "Where were you?"

"I was dip-netting for silvers in the Kanuyaq that day. I didn't know anything about it until I got home the next morning, and right after that the storm came, and the lightning, and we had the fire to fight."

"Why didn't you tell someone what happened?"

He became angry in his turn, angry and defensive. He pointed at Sally. "That is my wife, God help me. These are my kids." He waved a hand. "This is my home. That's my store. Those people are my neighbors. I have to live here. Besides—" He fell silent.

"Besides what?"

He sat back a little, squaring his shoulders, and raised his eyes. There was a quality of patient endurance there that she had not seen before, a quiet, stubborn determination in the thrust of his jaw, a sort of immovability in the set of the stocky shoulders. With a small shock she realized that in this moment he resembled Ekaterina. "They won't last."

"Who won't last?"

"The Jesus freakers. The born-agains. The Bible-thumpers. Remember the Russian Orthodox priests when they came and told us we didn't have to pay taxes to the Czar if we went to their church? Remember the missionaries when they came and forbade us to dance? Where are they now?" He answered his own question. "They're gone, all of them, and we still dance at the potlatches. We still carve our totems and bead our shirts. We outlasted the priests. We outlasted the missionaries. They're all gone and we're still here. We'll outlast these bastards, too."

"Oh Russell, Russell," Sally whispered. "I will pray for you, that God will forgive you that blasphemy."

He stood up and for a moment Kate thought he was going to strike his wife. And then she thought he might take a swing at her. An angry red ran up under his skin, his eyes narrowed and his right hand curled into a fist and rose a foot or so in the air. He trembled with the desire to hit, to strike out blindly, she could see it in his eyes, and she stiffened. Next to her Bobby gripped his wheels, as if to roll between them. Dinah put one hand on his shoulder, and he stilled.

They stared at each other.

The fist unclenched and fell to his side. "We'll outlast them," Russell said, tired now. "They'll be gone, and we'll still be here."

Kate's shoulders slumped, the anger draining out of her in her turn. "Maybe you're right," she said, her voice the barest thread of sound.

"But it doesn't make Daniel Seabolt any less dead."

They were back at camp before anyone spoke. "What are we going to do?" Dinah said in a subdued voice, standing next to the firepit and looking around at the campsite as if she'd never seen it before.

"Nothing," Kate said.

Dinah stared at her. "Nothing? They killed him, Kate. They killed him, as sure as if they'd held a gun to his head and pulled the trigger. We have to do something."

"What?" Bobby said.

"Call the trooper," she said hotly. "Have him arrest them. Try them for murder."

"Just because they told us about it don't mean they'll tell the trooper. Russell won't. You heard him. His wife. His kids. His neighbors. His home."

"Bobby's right," Kate said softly. She felt tired and old. "Nothing for us to do now but pack up and go home."

"The sooner the better," Bobby agreed grimly, "before those yahoos get ideas in their heads about coming up here and finishing us off for good."

"But—" Dinah said.

"But nothing," Bobby said, his voice still grim. "Welcome to Alaska. You said it yourself. Nature red in tooth and claw."

"I meant animals," Dinah said in a small voice.

"What do you call us?" He looked at Kate. "You knew, didn't you."

"I saw a mosquito bite the kid on the arm. He swelled up like a poisoned pup. He told me his dad was even worse."

"And something like that would be known in the family."

"Yes."

"He would have known. Daniel. When they did it to him."

"Yes."

There was silence. Dinah said, the words wrenched out of her, "Can you imagine what it was like, his last moments—"

"Yes," Kate said shortly, "we can imagine."

Moving together in unspoken accord they broke camp, washing the mushroom buckets out in the cold, clear water of the creek, sacking up the last of the garbage and stowing it in the back of Kate's truck, rolling the sleeping bags, taking down the tents.

Dinah found her paperback copy of the Bible and stood frowning down at the fine print. "Here it is."

"What?"

She read, " 'But let judgement run down as waters, and righteousness as a mighty stream.' " She closed the book.

"Amos," Bobby said. "Chapter 5, verse 24."

Kate stared at Dinah, who looked solemnly back,

and then she remembered. "So somebody did come looking for him."

Dinah gave a somber nod. "And they even put up a tombstone, of sorts."

"What?" Bobby said. Dinah told him of the sign they had found, tacked to a nearby tree, the day they had stumbled across Daniel Seabolt's body. To their surprise, Bobby's face turned dark red. The muscles in his neck bulged. He looked as if he were about to explode.

Kate looked at Dinah, who spread her hands and looked confused and a little frightened. "Bobby. What is it? What's wrong?"

"Those bastards." His jaw muscles worked. "It's a verse Martin Luther King used a lot," he said tightly. "I think he said it at the Lincoln Memorial that day in August. 'Let judgement run down as waters, and righteousness as a mighty stream.' It's even on the Civil Rights Monument in Montgomery."

Fury got the better of him again and he hit the arm of his chair with enough force to make him bounce up off the seat. That felt good so he did it again. He looked up in time to see them exchange a wary glance and made a visible effort to tone it down. He was only partially successful. "I'm sorry, I . . ." He tried to shrug off the tension in his shoulders. "I don't know, in this context, that particular verse just seems so—"

"Blasphemous?" Dinah suggested.

"Sacrilegious?" Kate suggested.

"Fanatical?"

"Egotistical?"

"Profane?"

"Insane?"

There was a brief, tense silence. "Yeah." Bobby inhaled and blew out a big breath. "Yeah. All of the above."

Dinah said, voice somber, "Even the devil can quote scripture for his purpose."

Winklebleck was right. Will always had the last word.

Dinah pocketed the Bible and they worked together to collapse and pack Bobby's tent. The last aluminum rod went into the stuff sack. Kate sat back on her heels and pulled the drawstring tight, and suddenly, uninvited, unwelcome, Daniel Seabolt's last moments came back to her, running, running, running, every man's hand against him, every door closed to him, feeling the sting of a thousand thousand bites, running, running, running, breath short and labored, skin scraped and torn, and then, mercifully, darkness and death.

She found she had to hold herself upright with one hand on the trunk of a tree. "I hate this," she said violently, "I feel so helpless, so *impotent*. I *hate* this."

Bobby, having regained his poise, tucked the remnants of the package of Fig Newtons into the cooler. When he was done, he gave Kate an appraising look. "Your problem is you're a little in love with him."

"Who?" Dinah said.

"Daniel Seabolt."

Kate opened her mouth to deny it, met Bobby's hard brown gaze, and closed it again. It was true. Daniel Seabolt had loved his wife and his son. He'd been a born teacher, a profession Kate revered. He'd even loved his father enough to stay when his father had stolen his son's allegiance. He'd had enough family loyalty not to involve anyone else in their personal, private fight, and had fought back on his own terms, with his own tools. Loving, loyal, intelligent, he'd been an admirable man, and now he was gone.

She didn't even know what he looked like. She'd never seen so much as a wallet photo of him. Matthew had never offered, and there had been none in sight when she visited Seabolt.

Maybe love wasn't the right word. Maybe it was only that she mourned the passing of a good man.

Somebody had to.

"There are twenty-seven known species of mosquitoes in Alaska, did I tell you that?" Dinah said, looking out across the valley. "They've been known to kill dogs, they even go for bears, for the eyes and the nose because the bear's pelt is so thick, and the mucous membranes swell up and the bear dies of asphyxiation."

"That's an apocryphal story," Bobby said.

"Then why is it in my book?" Dinah demanded.

"The better to suck you in with, my dear."

"I bet the Native Americans who live out here wouldn't say that," she said, determined to defend her illusions to the death. "I bet it has, too, happened."

They both looked at Kate, hands clenched on the straps of her pack, eyes staring at nothing.

"You know, Kate," Bobby said, locking the lid of the cooler down, "it's like the song says."

She blinked, shook her head and looked at him, confused. "What?"

"Sometimes you're the windshield." He reached for his jacket. "Sometimes you're the bug."

The wry smile on his face clearly invited a similar response. She didn't have one left in her, but there was really nothing more here for them to do, and she knew it. Dinah had picked up the last two crates of Bobby's essential back-country supplies and was already starting down the hill. Bobby lifted the cooler into his lap and paused, watching her. Mutt stood at the edge of the clearing, yellow eyes expectant, straining for home.

She rose to her feet, shouldered her pack and picked up the tent bag. The little glade, stripped of their belongings, looked empty and a little forlorn. The sun was teasing the horizon, just brushing the tops of the trees with pale fingers, gilding the surface of the Kanuyaq and its thousand tributaries, outlining only the very tips of violet peaks. As heart-stopping as the view was, she knew a sudden, intense longing for her own roof, her own trees, her own creek, her own mountains, her own sky.

"All right then," she said.

"Scrape me off and take me home."

Here's a special excerpt from the next
Kate Shugak Mystery by
Dana Stabenow . . .

Blood Will Tell

. . . available in hardcover from
G. P. Putnam's Sons

T he bad news was the blood in her hair.

The good news was that it wasn't hers.

The day before, the bull moose had walked
into the homestead clearing, the same day hunting season opened on the first year in six Kate had drawn a
permit, on the first year in ten the feds had declared a
hunting season in her game management unit. On a
potty break from digging potatoes, she was buttoning
her jeans in front of the outhouse when the sound
drew her attention. She looked up to find him head
and shoulders into a stand of alders whose dark green
leaves had just started to turn. For a moment she stood
where she was, transfixed, mouth and fly open, unable
to believe her luck. One limb stripped of bark, the
moose nosed over to a second, ignoring her presence
with what could have been regal indifference but given
the time of year was probably absolute disdain for any
creature not a female of his own species.

He'll run when I move, she thought.

But I have to move; the rifle's in the cabin.

But if I move, he'll head out, and then I'll have to
bushwack after him and pack him home in pieces.

But he can't outrun a bullet.

If I don't move soon, she thought, Mutt will get back from breakfast and then he will run and this argument you're having with yourself will be academic.

The bull was a fine, healthy specimen, three, maybe four years old by the spread of his rack, his coat thick and shiny, his flanks full and firm-fleshed. She figured four hundred pounds minimum, dressed out. Her mouth watered. She took a cautious, single step. The ground was hard from the October frost, and her footstep made no sound. Encouraged, she took another, then another.

The .30-06 was racked below the twelve-gauge over the door. She checked to see if there was a round in the chamber. There always was, but she checked anyway. Reassured, she raised the rifle, pulled the stock into her shoulder and sighted down the barrel, her feet planted wide in the open doorway, the left a little in advance of the right, knees slightly bent. She blew out a breath and held it. Blood thudded steadily against her eardrums. The tiny bead at the end of the barrel came to rest on the back of the bull's head, directly between his ears. Lots of bone between her bullet and his brain. Moose have notoriously hard heads. She thought about that for a moment. Well, what was luck for if it was never to be chanced? "Hey," she said.

He took no notice, calmly stripping the bark from another tree limb. "You must lower the average moose IQ by ten points," she said in a louder voice. "I'm doing your entire species a favor by taking you out of the gene pool." He turned his head at that, a strip of bark hanging from one side of his mouth. She exhaled again and the bead at the end of the rifle barrel centered directly on one big brown eye. Gently, firmly, she squeezed the trigger. The butt kicked solidly into her shoulder and the report of the single shot rang in her ear.

He stopped chewing and appeared to think the matter over. Kate waited. He started to lean. He leaned over to his left and he kept on leaning, picked up speed, leaned some more and crashed into the alder, bringing most of it down with him. The carcass settled with a sort of slow dignity, branches popping, twigs snapping, leaves crackling.

As silence returned to the clearing, Kate, not quite ready yet to believe her eyes, walked to the moose and knelt to put a head on his neck. His hair was rough against her skin, his flesh warm and firm in the palm of her hand, his mighty heart still. She closed her eyes, letting his warmth and strength flow out of him and into her.

A raven croaked nearby, mischievous, mocking, and she opened her eyes and a wide grin split her face.

"All *right!*" She tossed her head back and saw Mutt standing at the edge of the clearing, a quizzical look in her yellow eyes. Kate dropped the rifle, let out a yell and took the gray half-wolf, half-Husky in a long, diving tackle. Mutt gave a startled yip and went down beneath the assault. They rough-housed all over the clearing in a free-for-all that ended only when they rolled up against the side of the garage with a solid thump that robbed them both of breath.

Kate rolled to her back. The sky was a clear and guileless blue, the air crisp on an indrawn breath. It was her favorite time of the year—October—in her favorite place in the world, the homestead she'd inherited from her parents, in the middle of twenty million acres of national park in Alaska, and with one bullet fired from her front doorstep she had just harvested enough meat to last her the winter, with enough

left over to share with Mandy and Chick and Bobby
and Dinah and maybe even Jack, if he behaved. She
laughed up at the sky. Mutt lay panting next to her,
jaw grinning wide, long pink tongue lolling out, and
seemed to laugh with her, loud whoops of jubilant
laughter that rollicked across the clearing to where the
old woman stood.

The sound of a low cough cut the laughter like a
knife. Mutt lunged to her feet, hackles raised. Kate
jerked upright and stared across the clearing.

Her grandmother stood at the edge of the clearing,
rooted in place with the trees, a short, solid trunk of
a woman dressed in worn Levis and a dark blue down
jacket over a plaid flannel shirt, hair only now beginning to go gray, pulled back in a severe bun, her
brown face seamed with lines in which could be read
the last eighty years of Alaskan history. She looked
solemn and dignified as always.

Kate was suddenly aware of the dirt under her fingernails and the birch leaves in her hair. "How nice
to see you, emaa," she said insincerely, and stood up,
only to discover her half-fastened fly when her jeans
started to slide down her hips. Ekaterina waited impassively while Kate did up her buttons and tried ineffectually to beat off the dirt caked on the knees and
seat of her jeans. Mutt gave herself a vigorous shake,
spraying Kate with leaves and twigs and dirt, and sat,
panting, her jaw open in a faint grin. Kate gave her a
look that promised retribution and looked back at her
grandmother.

It might have been her imagination but she thought
she saw the corners of Ekaterina's lips quiver once before that seamed face was brought back under stern
control. The old woman nodded at the moose. "There
is work to do."

Harold Pinter

Complete Works: Three

The Homecoming, Tea Party,
The Basement, Landscape, Silence,
That's Your Trouble, That's All, Applicant, Interview,
Dialogue for Three, Night

Harold Pinter is the most original writer to have emerged from the 'new wave' of dramatists who gave fresh life to the British theatre in the late fifties and early sixties. He is now firmly established as 'our best living playwright' (*The Times*).

This book is Volume Three of the Complete Works of Harold Pinter. It contains the full-length play, *The Homecoming* (staged in 1965), as well as four shorter plays written during the same period, *Tea Party*, *The Basement*, *Landscape* and *Silence*. Also included is the short story version of *Tea Party* and six revue sketches. Introducing the volume is his memoir of the actor-manager, Anew McMaster, which, incidentally, casts some light on Pinter's early days as an actor.

Harold Pinter was born in London in 1930. He wrote his first plays, The Room, The Dumb Waiter *and* The Birthday Party *in 1957 and achieved his first great success with* The Caretaker *in 1960. Since then he has written three more full-length plays,* The Homecoming *(1964),* Old Times *(1970) and* No Man's Land *(1974), as well as a number of shorter plays for the stage, radio and television. For the cinema his screenplays include* The Servant, Accident, The Go-Between, The Last Tycoon *and* A la Recherche du Temps Perdu, *published as* The Proust Screenplay.

HAROLD PINTER
Complete Works: Three

The Homecoming
Tea Party
The Basement
Landscape
Silence
Revue Sketches:
Night
That's Your Trouble
That's All
Applicant
Interview
Dialogue for Three

With the memoir, 'Mac', and the short story, 'Tea Party'

GROVE PRESS, INC.
NEW YORK

This collection first published in 1978 by Eyre Methuen Ltd.,
11 New Fetter Lane, London EC4P 4EE, England.

The Homecoming first published by Methuen & Co. in 1965
Tea Party and *The Basement* first published by Methuen & Co. in 1967
Landscape, Silence and *Night* first published by Methuen & Co. in 1969
Applicant first published by Methuen & Co. in 1961
Dialogue for Three first published in *Stand* Vol. 6, no. 3, 1963
That's Your Trouble, That's All, Interview first published in *The Dwarfs
and eight Review Sketches,* Dramatists Play Service, New York, 1966
/"Mac" first published by Emanuel Wax for Pendragon Press, 1968
"Tea Party" (short story) first published in *Playboy,* January 1965

First Edition 1978
First Printing 1978
ISBN: 0-394-17051-2
Grove Press ISBN: 0-8021-4183-8
Library of Congress Catalog Card Number: 77-002449

Library of Congress Cataloging in Publication Data   (Revised)

Pinter, Harold, 1930-
  Complete works : with an introduction "Writing for the
theatre."

  CONTENTS: v. 1. The birthday party. — The room. — The
dumb waiter. — A slight ache. — A night out. — The black and
white. [etc.]
PR6066.I53A19   1975   822'.9'14   77-2449
ISBN 0-394-17051-2

Manufactured in the United States of America

Distributed by Random House, Inc., New York

GROVE PRESS, INC., 196 West Houston Street, New York, N.Y. 10014

Contents

Harold Pinter: A Chronology

Year of writing		First performance
1954–5	The Black and White	(short story)
1955	The Examination	(short story)
1957	The Room	15 May 1957
1957	The Birthday Party	28 April 1958
1957	The Dumb Waiter	21 January 1960
1958	A Slight Ache	29 July 1959
1959	Revue sketches—	
	Trouble in the Works; The Black and White	15 July 1959
	Request Stop; Last to Go; Special Offer	23 September 1959
	That's Your Trouble; That's All; Applicant; Interview; Dialogue for Three	February–March 1964
1959	A Night Out	1 March 1960
1959	The Caretaker	27 April 1960
1960	Night School	21 July 1960
1960	The Dwarfs	2 December 1960
1961	The Collection	11 May 1961
1962	The Lover	28 March 1963
1963	Tea Party	(short story)
1964	Tea Party	25 March 1965
1964	The Homecoming	3 June 1965
1966	The Basement	28 February 1967
1967	Landscape	25 April 1968
1968	Silence	2 July 1969
1969	Night	9 April 1969
1970	Old Times	1 June 1971
1972	Monologue	10 April 1973
1974	No Man's Land	23 April 1975

Mac

BIOGRAPHICAL NOTE

ANEW MCMASTER was born in County Monaghan on Christmas Eve 1894 and was 16 when he made his first stage appearance as 'The Aristocrat' in 'The Scarlet Pimpernel' with Fred Terry at the New Theatre, London. He died in Dublin on August 25th, 1962, a few days after appearing in the 'dream scene' from 'The Bells' at an Equity concert. His acting career had spanned half a century and his death was the end of an era. He was the last of the great actor-managers, unconnected with films and television.

From 1925 onwards he and his company played a repertoire of Shakespeare's plays across the world and the roles which made his reputation were Hamlet, Macbeth, Coriolanus, Petruchio, Richard III, Shylock and, above all, Othello. He occasionally played outside his company as when he took over from Fredric March to tour America in the Broadway production of O'Neill's 'Long Day's Journey into Night', but he was never long away from Shakespeare or Ireland. When asked why, he replied 'I suppose I'm a wanderer and I like playing in the theatre. It makes no difference to me if I'm on Broadway or in the smallest village hall in Ireland. The only thing that matters is that I am playing.'

I've been the toast of twelve continents and eight hemispheres! Mac said from his hotel bed. I'll see none of my admirers before noon. Marjorie, where are my teeth? His teeth were brought to him. None before noon, he said, and looked out of the window. If the clergy call say I am studying King Lear and am not to be disturbed. How long have you been studying King Lear, Mac? Since I was a boy. I can play the part. It's the lines I can't learn. That's the problem. The part I can do. I think. What do you think? Do you think I can do it? I wonder if I'm wise to want to do it, or unwise? But I will do it. I'll do it next season. Don't forget I was acclaimed for my performance in Paddy The Next Best Thing. Never forget that. Should I take Othello to the Embassy, Swiss Cottage? Did you know Godfrey Tearle left out the fit? He didn't do the fit. I'm older than Godfrey Tearle. But I do the fit. Don't I? At least I don't leave it out. What's your advice? Should I take Othello to the Embassy, Swiss Cottage? Look out the window at this town. What a stinking diseased abandoned Godforgotten bog. What am I playing tonight, Marjorie? The Taming of the Shrew? But you see one thing the Irish peasantry really appreciate is style, grace and wit. You have a lovely company, someone said to me the other day, a lovely company, all the boys is like girls. Joe, are the posters up? Will we pack out? I was just driving into this town and I had to brake at a dung heap. A cow looked in through the window. No autographs today, I said. Let's have a drop of whiskey, for Jesus' sake.

Pat Magee phoned me from Ireland to tell me Mac was dead. I decided to go to the funeral. At London Airport the plane was very late leaving. I hadn't been in Ireland for ten years. The taxi

raced through Dublin. We passed the Sinn Fein Hall, where we
used to rehearse five plays in two weeks. But I knew I was too late
for the funeral. The cemetery was empty. I saw no one I knew. I
didn't know Mrs. Mac's address. I knew no one any more in
Dublin. I couldn't find Mac's grave.

I toured Ireland with Mac for about two years in the early 1950's.
He advertised in 'The Stage' for actors for a Shakespearian tour of
the country. I sent him a photograph and went to see him in a
flat near Willesden Junction. At the time Willesden Junction
seemed to me as likely a place as any to meet a manager from
whom you might get work. But after I knew Mac our first meeting
place became more difficult to accept or understand. I still wonder
what he was doing interviewing actors at Willesden Junction. But
I never asked him. He offered me six pounds a week, said I could
get digs for twenty-five shillings at the most, told me how cheap
cigarettes were and that I could play Horatio, Bassanio and
Cassio. It was my first job proper on the stage.

Those two? It must be like two skeletons copulating on a bed of
corrugated iron. (The actor and actress Mac was talking about
were very thin.) He undercuts me, he said, he keeps coming in
under me. I'm the one who should come under. I'm playing
Hamlet. But how can I play Hamlet if he keeps coming under me
all the time? The more under I go the more under he goes. Nobody in the audience can hear a word. The bugger wants to play
Hamlet himself, that's what it is. But he bloodywell won't while
I'm alive. When I die I hope I die quickly. I couldn't face months
of bedpans. Sheer hell. Days and months of bedpans. Do you
think we'll go to heaven? I mean me. Do you think I'll go to
heaven? You never saw me play the Cardinal. My cloak was
superb, the length of the stage, crimson. I had six boys from the
village to carry it. They used to kiss my ring every night before
we made our entrance. When I made my tour of Australia and the
southern hemisphere we were the guests of honour at a city

banquet. The Mayor stood up. He said: We are honoured today to welcome to our city one of the most famous actors in the world, an actor who has given tremendous pleasure to people all over the world, to worldwide acclaim. It is my great privilege to introduce to you – Andrew MacPherson!

Joe Nolan, the business manager, came in one day and said: Mac, all the cinemas in Limerick are on strike. What shall I do? Book Limerick! Mac said. At once! We'll open on Monday. There was no theatre in the town. We opened on the Monday in a two thousand seater cinema, with Othello. There was no stage and no wingspace. It was St Patrick's night. The curtain was supposed to rise at nine o'clock. But the house wasn't full until eleven thirty, so the play didn't begin until then. It was well past two in the morning before the curtain came down. Everyone of the two thousand people in the audience was drunk. Apart from that, they weren't accustomed to Shakespeare. For the first half of the play, up to 'I am your own for ever', we could not hear ourselves speak, could not hear our cues. The cast was alarmed. We expected the audience on stage at any moment. We kept our hands on our swords. I was playing Iago at the time. I came offstage with Mac at the interval and gasped. Don't worry, Mac said, don't worry. After the interval he began to move. When he walked onto the stage for the 'Naked in bed, Iago, and not mean harm' scene (his great body hunched, his voice low with grit), they silenced. He tore into the fit. He made the play his and the place his. By the time he had reached 'It is the very error of the moon; She comes more near the earth than she was wont, And makes men mad.', (the word 'mad' suddenly cauterized, ugly, shocking) the audience was quite still. And sober. I congratulated Mac. Not bad, he said, was it? Not bad. Godfrey Tearle never did the fit, you know.

Mac gave about half a dozen magnificent performances of Othello while I was with him. Even when, on the other occasions, he conserved his energies in the role, he always gave the patrons their moneysworth. At his best his was the finest Othello I have seen. His age was always a mystery, but I would think he was in his sixties at the time. Sometimes, late at night, after the show, he looked very old. But on stage in Othello he stood, well over six foot, naked to the waist, his gestures complete, final, nothing jagged, his movement of the utmost fluidity and yet of the utmost precision: stood there, dead in the centre of the role, and the great sweeping symphonic playing would begin, the rare tension and release within him, the arrest, the swoop, the savagery, the majesty and repose. His voice was unique: in my experience of an unequalled range. A bass of extraordinary echo, resonance and gut, and remarkable sweep up into tenor, when the note would hit the back of the gallery and come straight back, a brilliant, stunning sound. I remember his delivery of this line: 'Methinks (bass) it should be now a huge (bass) eclipse (tenor) Of sun and moon (baritone) and that th'affrighted globe (bass) Should yawn (very deep, the abyss) at alteration.' We all watched him from the wings.

He was capable, of course, of many indifferent and offhand performances. On these occasions an edgy depression and fatigue hung over him. He would gabble his way through the part, his movement fussed, his voice acting outside him, the man himself detached from its acrobatics. At such times his eyes would fix upon the other actors, appraising them coldly, emanating a grim dissatisfaction with himself and his company. Afterwards, over a drink, he would confide: I was bad tonight, wasn't I, really awful, but the damn cast was even worse. What a lot.

He was never a good Hamlet and for some reason or other rarely bothered to play Macbeth. He was obsessed with the lighting in Macbeth and more often than not spent half his time on stage glaring at the spot bar. Yet there was plenty of Macbeth in him. I believe his dislike of the play was so intense he couldn't bring himself to play it.

It was consistent with him that after many months of coasting through Shylock he suddenly lashed fullfired into the role at an obscure matinee in a onehorse village; a frightening performance. Afterwards he said to me: What did I do? Did you notice? I did something different. What did you think of it? What was it I did? He never did it again. Not quite like that. Who saw it?

In the trial scene in The Merchant of Venice one night I said to him (as Bassanio) instead of 'For thy three thousand ducats here is six', quite involuntarily, 'For thy three thousand *buckets* here is six'. He replied quietly and with emphasis: 'If every *bucket* in six thousand *buckets* were in six parts, and every part a *bucket* I would not draw them – I would have my bond'. I could not continue. The other members of the court scene and I turned upstage. Some walked into the wings. But Mac stood, remorseless, grave, like an eagle, waiting for my reply.

Sometimes after a matinee of Macbeth and an evening of Othello we all stayed on stage, he'd get someone to put on a record of Faust, disappear behind a curtain, reappear in a long golden wig, without his teeth, mime Marguerite weaving, mime Faust and Mephistopheles, deliver at full tilt the aria from Verdi's Othello 'Era La Notte e Cassio Dormia', while the caretaker swept the dust up, and then in a bar talk for hours of Sarah and Mrs. Pat Campbell, with relish, malice and devotion. I think he would still be talking about them now, if he wasn't dead, because they did something he knew about.

In order to present Oedipus the company had to recruit extras from the town or village we were in. One night in Dundalk Mac was building up to his blind climax when one of the extras had an epileptic fit on stage and collapsed. He was dragged to the wings where various women attended to him. The sounds of their ministrations seeped onto the stage. Mac stopped, turned to the wings and shouted: 'For God's sake, can't you see I'm trying to act!'

His concentration was always complete in Oedipus. He was at his best in the part. He acted with acute 'underness' and tenacity. And he never used his vocal powers to better or truer effect. He acted along the spine of the role and never deviated from it. As in his two other great roles, Othello and Lear, he understood and expressed totally the final tender clarity which is under the storm, the blindness, the anguish. For me his acting at these times embodied the idea of Yeats' line: 'They know that Hamlet and Lear are gay, Gaiety transfiguring all that dread'. Mac entered into this tragic gaiety naturally and inevitably.

He did Lear eventually. First performance somewhere in County Clare, Ennis, I think. Knew most of the lines. *Was* the old man, tetchy, appalled, feverish. Wanted the storm louder. All of us banged the thundersheets. No, they can still hear me. Hit it, hit it. He got above the noise. I played Edgar in Lear only a few times with him before I left the company. At the centre of his performance was a terrible loss, desolation, silence. He didn't think about doing it, he just got there. He did it and got there.

His wife, Marjorie, was his structure and support. She organised the tours, supervised all business arrangements, sat in the box office, kept the cast in order, ran the wardrobe, sewed, looked after Mac, was his dresser, gave him his whiskey. She was tough, critical, cultivated, devoted. Her spirit and belief constituted the backbone of the company. There would have been no company without her.

Ireland wasn't golden always, but it was golden sometimes and in 1950 it was, all in all, a golden age for me and for others.

The people came down to see him. Mac travelled by car, and sometimes some of us did too. But other times we went on the lorry with the flats and props, and going into Bandon or Clough-jordan would find the town empty, asleep, men sitting upright in dark bars, cowpads, mud, smell of peat, wood, old clothes. We'd find digs; wash basin and jug, tea, black pudding, and off to the hall, set up a stage on trestle tables, a few rostra, a few drapes, costumes out of the hampers, set up shop, and at night play, not always but mostly, to a packed house (where had they come from?); people who listened, and who waited to see him, having seen him before, and been brought up on him.

Mac wasn't any kind of dreamer. He was remote from the Celtic Twilight. He kept a close eye on the box office receipts. He was sharp about money, was as depressed as anyone else when business was bad. Where there was any kind of company disagreement he proved elusive. He distanced himself easily from unwelcome problems. Mrs Mac dealt with those. Mac was never 'a darling actor of the old school'. He was a working man. He respected his occupation and never stopped learning about it, from himself and from others.

For those who cared for him and admired him there must remain one great regret; that for reasons I do not understand, he last played in England, at Stratford, in 1933. The loser was the English theatre.

Mac wasn't 'childlike' in temperament, as some have said. He was evasive, proud, affectionate, mischievous, shrewd, merry, cynical, sad, and could be callous. But he was never sour or self-pitying. His life was the stage. Life with a big L came a bad second. He had no patience with what he considered a world of petty sufferings, however important they might seem to the bearer. He was completely unsentimental. Gossip delighted him, and particularly sexual gossip. He moved with great flexibility and amusement through Catholic Ireland, greatly attracted by the ritual of the Church. He loved to speak of the mummy of the Blessed Oliver Plunkett in Drogheda 'with a lovely amber spot on its face'. He mixed freely with priests and nuns, went to Mass, sometimes, but despised the religious atrophy, rigidity and complacency with which he was confronted. He mixed with the priests partly because he enjoyed their company, partly because his livelihood depended upon them. He was a realist. But he possessed a true liberality of spirit. He was humble. He was a devout anti-puritan. He was a very great piss-taker. He was a great actor and we who worked with him were the luckiest people in the world and loved him.

The Homecoming

THE HOMECOMING was first presented by the Royal Shakespeare Company at the Aldwych Theatre on 3 June, 1965, with the following cast:

MAX, *a man of seventy*	Paul Rogers
LENNY, *a man in his early thirties*	Ian Holm
SAM, *a man of sixty-three*	John Normington
JOEY, *a man in his middle twenties*	Terence Rigby
TEDDY, *a man in his middle thirties*	Michael Bryant
RUTH, *a woman in her early thirties*	Vivien Merchant

Directed by Peter Hall

The play was presented by the Royal Shakespeare Company and Alexander H. Cohen at the Music Box Theatre, New York, on 5 January, 1967 with one change in the cast: the part of Teddy was played by Michael Craig.

SUMMER

An old house in North London.

A large room, extending the width of the stage.

The back wall, which contained the door, has been removed. A square arch shape remains. Beyond it, the hall. In the hall a staircase, ascending up left, well in view. The front door up right. A coatstand, hooks, etc.

In the room a window, right. Odd tables, chairs. Two large armchairs. A large sofa, left. Against the right wall a large sideboard, the upper half of which contains a mirror. Up left, a radiogram.

Act One

Evening.

LENNY *is sitting on the sofa with a newspaper, a pencil in his hand. He wears a dark suit. He makes occasional marks on the back page.*

MAX *comes in, from the direction of the kitchen. He goes to sideboard, opens top drawer, rummages in it, closes it.*

He wears an old cardigan and a cap, and carries a stick.

He walks downstage, stands, looks about the room.

MAX. What have you done with the scissors?

Pause.

I said I'm looking for the scissors. What have you done with them?

Pause.

Did you hear me? I want to cut something out of the paper.

LENNY. I'm reading the paper.

MAX. Not that paper. I haven't even read that paper. I'm talking about last Sunday's paper. I was just having a look at it in the kitchen.

Pause.

Do you hear what I'm saying? I'm talking to you! Where's the scissors?

LENNY (*looking up, quietly*). Why don't you shut up, you daft prat?

MAX *lifts his stick and points it at him.*

MAX. Don't you talk to me like that. I'm warning you.

He sits in large armchair.

There's an advertisement in the paper about flannel vests. Cut price. Navy surplus. I could do with a few of them.

Pause.

I think I'll have a fag. Give me a fag.

Pause.

I just asked you to give me a cigarette.

Pause.

Look what I'm lumbered with.

He takes a crumpled cigarette from his pocket.

I'm getting old, my word of honour.

He lights it.

You think I wasn't a tearaway? I could have taken care of you, twice over. I'm still strong. You ask your Uncle Sam what I was. But at the same time I always had a kind heart. Always.

Pause.

I used to knock about with a man called MacGregor. I called him Mac. You remember Mac? Eh?

Pause.

Huhh! We were two of the worst hated men in the West End of London. I tell you, I still got the scars. We'd walk into a place, the whole room'd stand up, they'd make way to let us pass. You never heard such silence. Mind you, he was a big man, he was over six foot tall. His family were all MacGregors, they came all the way from Aberdeen, but he was the only one they called Mac.

Pause.

He was very fond of your mother, Mac was. Very fond. He always had a good word for her.

Pause.

Mind you, she wasn't such a bad woman. Even though it made me sick just to look at her rotten stinking face, she wasn't such a bad bitch. I gave her the best bleeding years of my life, anyway.

LENNY. Plug it, will you, you stupid sod, I'm trying to read the paper.

MAX. Listen! I'll chop your spine off, you talk to me like that! You understand? Talking to your lousy filthy father like that!

LENNY. You know what, you're getting demented.

Pause.

What do you think of Second Wind for the three-thirty?

MAX. Where?

LENNY. Sandown Park.

MAX. Don't stand a chance.

LENNY. Sure he does.

MAX. Not a chance.

LENNY. He's the winner.

LENNY *ticks the paper.*

MAX. He talks to me about horses.

Pause.

I used to live on the course. One of the loves of my life. Epsom? I knew it like the back of my hand. I was one of the best-known faces down at the paddock. What a marvellous open-air life.

Pause.

He talks to me about horses. You only read their names in the papers. But I've stroked their manes, I've held them, I've calmed them down before a big race. I was the one they used to call for. Max, they'd say, there's a horse here, he's highly strung, you're the only man on the course who can calm him. It was true. I had a . . . I had an instinctive understanding of animals. I should have been a trainer. Many times I was offered the job – you know, a proper post, by the Duke of . . . I forget his name . . . one of the Dukes. But I had family obligations, my family needed me at home.

Pause.

The times I've watched those animals thundering past the post. What an experience. Mind you, I didn't lose, I made a few bob out of it, and you know why? Because I always had the smell of a good horse. I could smell him. And not only the colts but the fillies. Because the fillies are more highly strung than the colts, they're more unreliable, did you know that? No, what do you know? Nothing. But I was always able to tell a good filly by one particular trick. I'd look her in the eye. You see? I'd stand in front of her and look her straight in the eye, it was a kind of hypnotism, and by the look deep down in her eye I could tell whether she was a stayer or not. It was a gift. I had a gift.

Pause.

And he talks to me about horses.

LENNY. Dad, do you mind if I change the subject?

Pause.

I want to ask you something. The dinner we had before, what was the name of it? What do you call it?

Pause.

Why don't you buy a dog? You're a dog cook. Honest. You think you're cooking for a lot of dogs.

MAX. If you don't like it get out.

LENNY. I am going out. I'm going out to buy myself a proper dinner.

MAX. Well, get out! What are you waiting for?

LENNY *looks at him.*

LENNY. What did you say?

MAX. I said shove off out of it, that's what I said.

LENNY. You'll go before me, Dad, if you talk to me in that tone of voice.

MAX. Will I, you bitch?

MAX *grips his stick.*

LENNY. Oh, Daddy, you're not going to use your stick on me, are you? Eh? Don't use your stick on me Daddy. No, please. It wasn't my fault, it was one of the others. I haven't done anything wrong, Dad, honest. Don't clout me with that stick, Dad.

Silence.
MAX *sits hunched.* LENNY *reads the paper.*
SAM *comes in the front door. He wears a chauffeur's uniform. He hangs his hat on a hook in the hall and comes into the room. He goes to a chair, sits in it and sighs.*

Hullo, Uncle Sam.

SAM. Hullo.

LENNY. How are you, Uncle?

SAM. Not bad. A bit tired.

LENNY. Tired? I bet you're tired. Where you been?

SAM. I've been to London Airport.

LENNY. All the way up to London Airport? What, right up the M4?

SAM. Yes, all the way up there.

LENNY. Tch, tch, tch. Well, I think you're entitled to be tired, Uncle.

SAM. Well, it's the drivers.

LENNY. I know. That's what I'm talking about. I'm talking about the drivers.

SAM. Knocks you out.

Pause.

MAX. I'm here, too, you know.

SAM *looks at him.*

I said I'm here, too. I'm sitting here.

SAM. I know you're here.

Pause.

SAM. I took a Yankee out there today . . . to the Airport.

LENNY. Oh, a Yankee, was it?

SAM. Yes, I been with him all day. Picked him up at the Savoy at half past twelve, took him to the Caprice for his lunch. After lunch I picked him up again, took him down to a house in Eaton Square – he had to pay a visit to a friend there – and then round about tea-time I took him right the way out to the Airport.

LENNY. Had to catch a plane there, did he?

SAM. Yes. Look what he gave me. He gave me a box of cigars.

SAM *takes a box of cigars from his pocket.*

MAX. Come here. Let's have a look at them.

SAM *shows* MAX *the cigars.* MAX *takes one from the box, pinches it and sniffs it.*

It's a fair cigar.

SAM. Want to try one?

MAX *and* SAM *light cigars.*

You know what he said to me? He told me I was the best
chauffeur he'd ever had. The best one.

MAX. From what point of view?

SAM. Eh?

MAX. From what point of view?

LENNY. From the point of view of his driving, Dad, and his
general sense of courtesy, I should say.

MAX. Thought you were a good driver, did he, Sam? Well,
he gave you a first-class cigar.

SAM. Yes, he thought I was the best he'd ever had. They all
say that, you know. They won't have anyone else, they only
ask for me. They say I'm the best chauffeur in the firm.

LENNY. I bet the other drivers tend to get jealous, don't they,
Uncle?

SAM. They do get jealous. They get very jealous.

MAX. Why?

Pause.

SAM. I just told you.

MAX. No, I just can't get it clear, Sam. Why do the other
drivers get jealous?

SAM. Because (a) I'm the best driver, and because . . . (b)
I don't take liberties.

Pause.

I don't press myself on people, you see. These big businessmen, men of affairs, they don't want the driver jawing all
the time, they like to sit in the back, have a bit of peace and
quiet. After all, they're sitting in a Humber Super Snipe,
they can afford to relax. At the same time, though, this is
what really makes me special . . . I do know how to pass
the time of day when required.

Pause.

For instance, I told this man today I was in the second world war. Not the first. I told him I was too young for the first. But I told him I fought in the second.

Pause.

So did he, it turned out.

LENNY *stands, goes to the mirror and straightens his tie.*

LENNY. He was probably a colonel, or something, in the American Air Force.

SAM. Yes.

LENNY. Probably a navigator, or something like that, in a Flying Fortress. Now he's most likely a high executive in a worldwide group of aeronautical engineers.

SAM. Yes.

LENNY. Yes, I know the kind of man you're talking about.

LENNY *goes out, turning to his right.*

SAM. After all, I'm experienced. I was driving a dust cart at the age of nineteen. Then I was in long-distance haulage. I had ten years as a taxi-driver and I've had five as a private chauffeur.

MAX. It's funny you never got married, isn't it? A man with all your gifts.

Pause.

Isn't it? A man like you?

SAM. There's still time.

MAX. Is there?

Pause.

SAM. You'd be surprised.

MAX. What you been doing, banging away at your lady customers, have you?

SAM. Not me.

MAX. In the back of the Snipe? Been having a few crafty reefs in a layby, have you?

SAM. Not me.

MAX. On the back seat? What about the armrest, was it up or down?

SAM. I've never done that kind of thing in my car.

MAX. Above all that kind of thing, are you, Sam?

SAM. Too true.

MAX. Above having a good bang on the back seat, are you?

SAM. Yes, I leave that to others.

MAX. You leave it to others? What others? You paralysed prat!

SAM. I don't mess up my car! Or my . . . my boss's car! Like other people.

MAX. Other people? What other people?

Pause.

What other people?

Pause.

SAM. Other people.

Pause.

MAX. When you find the right girl, Sam, let your family know, don't forget, we'll give you a number one send-off, I promise you. You can bring her to live here, she can keep us all happy. We'd take it in turns to give her a walk round the park.

SAM. I wouldn't bring her here.

MAX. Sam, it's your decision. You're welcome to bring your bride here, to the place where you live, or on the other hand you can take a suite at the Dorchester. It's entirely up to you.

SAM. I haven't got a bride.

> SAM *stands, goes to the sideboard, takes an apple from the bowl, bites into it.*

Getting a bit peckish.

He looks out of the window.

Never get a bride like you had, anyway. Nothing like your bride . . . going about these days. Like Jessie.

Pause.

After all, I escorted her once or twice, didn't I? Drove her round once or twice in my cab. She was a charming woman.

Pause.

All the same, she was your wife. But still . . . they were some of the most delightful evenings I've ever had. Used to just drive her about. It was my pleasure.

MAX (*softly, closing his eyes*). Christ.

SAM. I used to pull up at a stall and buy her a cup of coffee. She was a very nice companion to be with.

Silence.
JOEY *comes in the front door. He walks into the room, takes his jacket off, throws it on a chair and stands.*
Silence.

JOEY. Feel a bit hungry.

SAM. Me, too.

MAX. Who do you think I am, your mother? Eh? Honest. They walk in here every time of the day and night like bloody animals. Go and find yourself a mother.

LENNY *walks into the room, stands.*

JOEY. I've been training down at the gym.

SAM. Yes, the boy's been working all day and training all night.

MAX. What do you want, you bitch? You spend all the day sitting on your arse at London Airport, buy yourself a jamroll. You expect me to sit here waiting to rush into the kitchen the moment you step in the door? You've been living sixty-three years, why don't you learn to cook?

SAM. I can cook.

MAX. Well, go and cook!

Pause.

LENNY. What the boys want, Dad, is your own special brand of cooking, Dad. That's what the boys look forward to. The special understanding of food, you know, that you've got.

MAX. Stop calling me Dad. Just stop all that calling me Dad, do you understand?

LENNY. But I'm your son. You used to tuck me up in bed every night. He tucked you up, too, didn't he, Joey?

Pause.

He used to like tucking up his sons.

LENNY *turns and goes towards the front door.*

MAX. Lenny.

LENNY (*turning*). What?

MAX. I'll give you a proper tuck up one of these nights, son You mark my word.

They look at each other.
LENNY *opens the front door and goes out.*
Silence.

JOEY. I've been training with Bobby Dodd.

Pause.

And I had a good go at the bag as well.

Pause.

I wasn't in bad trim.

MAX. Boxing's a gentleman's game.

Pause.

I'll tell you what you've got to do. What you've got to do is you've got to learn how to defend yourself, and you've got to learn how to attack. That's your only trouble as a boxer. You don't know how to defend yourself, and you don't know how to attack.

Pause.

Once you've mastered those arts you can go straight to the top.

Pause.

JOEY. I've got a pretty good idea . . . of how to do that.

> JOEY *looks round for his jacket, picks it up, goes out of the room and up the stairs.*
> *Pause.*

MAX. Sam . . . why don't you go, too, eh? Why don't you just go upstairs? Leave me quiet. Leave me alone.

SAM. I want to make something clear about Jessie, Max. I want to. I do. When I took her out in the cab, round the town, I was taking care of her, for you. I was looking after her for you, when you were busy, wasn't I? I was showing her the West End.

Pause.

You wouldn't have trusted any of your other brothers. You wouldn't have trusted Mac, would you? But you trusted me. I want to remind you.

Pause.

Old Mac died a few years ago, didn't he? Isn't he dead?

Pause.

He was a lousy stinking rotten loudmouth. A bastard uncouth sodding runt. Mind you, he was a good friend of yours.

Pause.

MAX. Eh, Sam . . .

SAM. What?

MAX. Why do I keep you here? You're just an old grub.

SAM. Am I?

MAX. You're a maggot.

SAM. Oh yes?

MAX. As soon as you stop paying your way here, I mean when you're too old to pay your way, you know what I'm going to do? I'm going to give you the boot.

SAM. You are, eh?

MAX. Sure. I mean, bring in the money and I'll put up with you. But when the firm gets rid of you – you can flake off.

SAM. This is my house as well, you know. This was our mother's house.

MAX. One lot after the other. One mess after the other.

SAM. Our father's house.

MAX. Look what I'm lumbered with. One cast-iron bunch of crap after another. One flow of stinking pus after another.

Pause.

Our father! I remember him. Don't worry. You kid your-self. He used to come over to me and look down at me. My old man did. He'd bend right over me, then he'd pick me up. I was only that big. Then he'd dandle me. Give me the bottle. Wipe me clean. Give me a smile. Pat me on the bum. Pass me around, pass me from hand to hand. Toss me up in the air. Catch me coming down. I remember my father.

BLACKOUT.
LIGHTS UP.
Night.
TEDDY *and* RUTH *stand at the threshold of the room.*
They are both well dressed in light summer suits and light raincoats.
Two suitcases are by their side.
They look at the room. TEDDY *tosses the key in his hand, smiles.*

TEDDY. Well, the key worked.

Pause.

They haven't changed the lock.

Pause.

RUTH. No one's here.
TEDDY (*looking up*). They're asleep.

Pause.

RUTH. Can I sit down?
TEDDY. Of course.
RUTH. I'm tired.

Pause.

TEDDY. Then sit down.

She does not move.

That's my father's chair.
RUTH. That one?
TEDDY (*smiling*). Yes, that's it. Shall I go up and see if my room's still there?
RUTH. It can't have moved.
TEDDY. No, I mean if my bed's still there.
RUTH. Someone might be in it.
TEDDY. No. They've got their own beds.

Pause.

RUTH. Shouldn't you wake someone up? Tell them you're here?
TEDDY. Not at this time of night. It's too late.

Pause.

Shall I go up?

He goes into the hall, looks up the stairs, comes back.

Why don't you sit down?

Pause.

I'll just go up . . . have a look.

He goes up the stairs, stealthily.
RUTH *stands, then slowly walks across the room.*
TEDDY *returns.*

It's still there. My room. Empty. The bed's there. What are you doing?

She looks at him.

Blankets, no sheets. I'll find some sheets. I could hear snores. Really. They're all still here, I think. They're all snoring up there. Are you cold?

RUTH. No.

TEDDY. I'll make something to drink, if you like. Something hot.

RUTH. No, I don't want anything.

TEDDY *walks about.*

TEDDY. What do you think of the room? Big, isn't it? It's a big house. I mean, it's a fine room, don't you think? Actually there was a wall, across there . . . with a door. We knocked it down . . . years ago . . . to make an open living area. The structure wasn't affected, you see. My mother was dead.

RUTH *sits.*

Tired?

RUTH. Just a little.

TEDDY. We can go to bed if you like. No point in waking anyone up now. Just go to bed. See them all in the morning . . . see my father in the morning. . . .

Pause.

RUTH. Do you want to stay?

TEDDY. Stay?

Pause.

We've come to stay. We're bound to stay . . . for a few days.

RUTH. I think . . . the children . . . might be missing us.

TEDDY. Don't be silly.

RUTH. They might.

TEDDY. Look, we'll be back in a few days, won't we?

He walks about the room.

Nothing's changed. Still the same.

Pause.

Still, he'll get a surprise in the morning, won't he? The old man. I think you'll like him very much. Honestly. He's a . . . well, he's old, of course. Getting on.

Pause.

I was born here, do you realize that?

RUTH. I know.

Pause.

TEDDY. Why don't you go to bed? I'll find some sheets. I feel . . . wide awake, isn't it odd? I think I'll stay up for a bit. Are you tired?

RUTH. No.

TEDDY. Go to bed. I'll show you the room.

RUTH. No, I don't want to.

TEDDY. You'll be perfectly all right up there without me. Really you will. I mean, I won't be long. Look, it's just up there. It's the first door on the landing. The bathroom's right next door. You . . . need some rest, you know.

Pause.

I just want to . . . walk about for a few minutes. Do you mind?

RUTH. Of course I don't.

TEDDY. Well . . . Shall I show you the room?

RUTH. No, I'm happy at the moment.

TEDDY. You don't have to go to bed. I'm not saying you have to. I mean, you can stay up with me. Perhaps I'll make a cup of tea or something. The only thing is we don't want to make too much noise, we don't want to wake anyone up.

RUTH. I'm not making any noise.

TEDDY. I know you're not.

He goes to her.

(*Gently.*) Look, it's all right, really. I'm here. I mean . . . I'm with you. There's no need to be nervous. Are you nervous?

RUTH. No.

TEDDY. There's no need to be.

Pause.

They're very warm people, really. Very warm. They're my family. They're not ogres.

Pause.

Well, perhaps we should go to bed. After all, we have to be up early, see Dad. Wouldn't be quite right if he found us in bed, I think. (*He chuckles.*) Have to be up before six, come down, say hullo.

Pause.

RUTH. I think I'll have a breath of air.

TEDDY. Air?

Pause.

What do you mean?

RUTH (*standing*), Just a stroll.

TEDDY. At this time of night? But we've . . . only just got here. We've got to go to bed.

RUTH. I just feel like some air.

TEDDY. But I'm going to bed.

RUTH. That's all right.

TEDDY. But what am I going to do?

Pause.

The last thing I want is a breath of air. Why do you want a breath of air?

RUTH. I just do.

TEDDY. But it's late.

RUTH. I won't go far. I'll come back.

Pause.

TEDDY. I'll wait up for you.

RUTH. Why?

TEDDY. I'm not going to bed without you.

RUTH. Can I have the key?

He gives it to her.

Why don't you go to bed?

He puts his arms on her shoulders and kisses her.
They look at each other, briefly. She smiles.

I won't be long.

She goes out of the front door.
TEDDY goes to the window, peers out after her, half turns from the window, stands, suddenly chews his knuckles.
LENNY walks into the room from U.L. He stands. He wears pyjamas and dressing-gown. He watches TEDDY.
TEDDY turns and sees him.
Silence.

TEDDY. Hullo, Lenny.

LENNY. Hullo, Teddy.

Pause.

TEDDY. I didn't hear you come down the stairs.

LENNY. I didn't.

Pause.

I sleep down here now. Next door. I've got a kind of study,
workroom cum bedroom next door now, you see.

TEDDY. Oh. Did I . . . wake you up?

LENNY. No. I just had an early night tonight. You know how
it is. Can't sleep. Keep waking up.

Pause

TEDDY. How are you?

LENNY. Well, just sleeping a bit restlessly, that's all. Tonight,
anyway.

TEDDY. Bad dreams?

LENNY. No, I wouldn't say I was dreaming. It's not exactly
a dream. It's just that something keeps waking me up. Some
kind of tick.

TEDDY. A tick?

LENNY. Yes.

TEDDY. Well, what is it?

LENNY. I don't know.

Pause.

TEDDY. Have you got a clock in your room?

LENNY. Yes.

TEDDY. Well, maybe it's the clock.

LENNY. Yes, could be, I suppose.

Pause.

Well, if it's the clock I'd better do something about it, Stifle
it in some way, or something.

Pause.

TEDDY. I've . . . just come back for a few days
LENNY. Oh yes? Have you?

Pause.

TEDDY. How's the old man?
LENNY. He's in the pink.

Pause.

TEDDY. I've been keeping well.
LENNY. Oh, have you?

Pause.

Staying the night then, are you?
TEDDY. Yes.
LENNY. Well, you can sleep in your old room.
TEDDY. Yes, I've been up.
LENNY. Yes, you can sleep there.

LENNY *yawns.*

Oh well.
TEDDY. I'm going to bed.
LENNY. Are you?
TEDDY. Yes, I'll get some sleep.
LENNY. Yes I'm going to bed, too.

TEDDY *picks up the cases.*

I'll give you a hand.
TEDDY. No, they're not heavy.

TEDDY *goes into the hall with the cases.*
LENNY *turns out the light in the room.*
The light in the hall remains on.
LENNY *follows into the hall.*

LENNY. Nothing you want?

TEDDY. Mmmm?

LENNY. Nothing you might want, for the night? Glass of water, anything like that?

TEDDY. Any sheets anywhere?

LENNY. In the sideboard in your room.

TEDDY. Oh, good.

LENNY. Friends of mine occasionally stay there, you know, in your room, when they're passing through this part of the world.

> LENNY *turns out the hall light and turns on the first landing light.*
>
> TEDDY *begins to walk up the stairs.*

TEDDY. Well, I'll see you at breakfast, then.

LENNY. Yes, that's it. Ta-ta.

> TEDDY *goes upstairs.*
> LENNY *goes off* L.
> *Silence.*
> *The landing light goes out.*
> *Slight night light in the hall and room.*
> LENNY *comes back into the room, goes to the window and looks out.*
> *He leaves the window and turns on a lamp.*
> *He is holding a small clock.*
> *He sits, places the clock in front of him, lights a cigarette and sits.*
> RUTH *comes in the front door.*
> *She stands still.* LENNY *turns his head, smiles. She walks slowly into the room.*

LENNY. Good evening.

RUTH. Morning, I think.

LENNY. You're right there.

> *Pause.*

My name's Lenny. What's yours?

RUTH. Ruth.

She sits, puts her coat collar around her.

LENNY. Cold?

RUTH. No.

LENNY. It's been a wonderful summer, hasn't it? Remarkable.

Pause.

Would you like something? Refreshment of some kind? An aperitif, anything like that?

RUTH. No, thanks.

LENNY. I'm glad you said that. We haven't got a drink in the house. Mind you, I'd soon get some in, if we had a party or something like that. Some kind of celebration . . . you know.

Pause.

You must be connected with my brother in some way. The one who's been abroad.

RUTH. I'm his wife.

LENNY. Eh listen, I wonder if you can advise me. I've been having a bit of a rough time with this clock. The tick's been keeping me up. The trouble is I'm not all that convinced it was the clock. I mean there are lots of things which tick in the night, don't you find that? All sorts of objects, which, in the day, you wouldn't call anything else but commonplace. They give you no trouble. But in the night any given one of a number of them is liable to start letting out a bit of a tick. Whereas you look at these objects in the day and they're just commonplace. They're as quiet as mice during the daytime. So . . . all things being equal . . . this question of me saying it was the clock that woke me up, well, that could very easily prove something of a false hypothesis.

He goes to the sideboard, pours from a jug into a glass, takes the glass to RUTH.

Here you are. I bet you could do with this.

RUTH. What is it?

LENNY. Water.

She takes it, sips, places the glass on a small table by her chair.

LENNY *watches her.*

Isn't it funny? I've got my pyjamas on and you're fully dressed.

He goes to the sideboard and pours another glass of water.

Mind if I have one? Yes, it's funny seeing my old brother again after all these years. It's just the sort of tonic my Dad needs, you know. He'll be chuffed to his bollocks in the morning, when he sees his eldest son. I was surprised myself when I saw Teddy, you know. Old Ted. I thought he was in America.

RUTH. We're on a visit to Europe.

LENNY. What, both of you?

RUTH. Yes.

LENNY. What, you sort of live with him over there, do you?

RUTH. We're married.

LENNY. On a visit to Europe, eh? Seen much of it?

RUTH. We've just come from Italy.

LENNY. Oh, you went to Italy first, did you? And then he brought you over here to meet the family, did he? Well, the old man'll be pleased to see you, I can tell you.

RUTH. Good.

LENNY. What did you say?

RUTH. Good.

Pause.

LENNY. Where'd you go to in Italy?

RUTH. Venice.

LENNY. Not dear old Venice? Eh? That's funny. You know,
I've always had a feeling that if I'd been a soldier in the last
war – say in the Italian campaign – I'd probably have found
myself in Venice. I've always had that feeling. The trouble
was I was too young to serve, you see. I was only a child, I
was too small, otherwise I've got a pretty shrewd idea I'd
probably have gone through Venice. Yes, I'd almost certainly have gone through it with my battalion. Do you mind
if I hold your hand?

RUTH. Why?

LENNY. Just a touch.

He stands and goes to her.

Just a tickle.

RUTH. Why?

He looks down at her.

LENNY. I'll tell you why.

Slight pause.

One night, not too long ago, one night down by the docks,
I was standing alone under an arch, watching all the men
jibbing the boom, out in the harbour, and playing about
with a yardarm, when a certain lady came up to me and
made me a certain proposal. This lady had been searching
for me for days. She'd lost tracks of my whereabouts. However, the fact was she eventually caught up with me, and
when she caught up with me she made me this certain
proposal. Well, this proposal wasn't entirely out of order
and normally I would have subscribed to it. I mean I would
have subscribed to it in the normal course of events. The
only trouble was she was falling apart with the pox. So I
turned it down. Well, this lady was very insistent and started
taking liberties with me down under this arch, liberties

which by any criterion I couldn't be expected to tolerate, the facts being what they were, so I clumped her one. It was on my mind at the time to do away with her, you know, to kill her, and the fact is, that as killings go, it would have been a simple matter, nothing to it. Her chauffeur, who had located me for her, he'd popped round the corner to have a drink, which just left this lady and myself, you see, alone, standing underneath this arch, watching all the steamers steaming up, no one about, all quiet on the Western Front, and there she was up against this wall – well, just sliding down the wall, following the blow I'd given her. Well, to sum up, everything was in my favour, for a killing. Don't worry about the chauffeur. The chauffeur would never have spoken. He was an old friend of the family. But . . . in the end I thought . . . Aaah, why go to all the bother . . . you know, getting rid of the corpse and all that, getting yourself into a state of tension. So I just gave her another belt in the nose and a couple of turns of the boot and sort of left it at that.

RUTH. How did you know she was diseased?
LENNY. How did I know?

Pause.

I decided she was.

Silence.

You and my brother are newly-weds, are you?
RUTH. We've been married six years.
LENNY. He's always been my favourite brother, old Teddy. Do you know that? And my goodness we are proud of him here, I can tell you. Doctor of Philosophy and all that . . . leaves quite an impression. Of course, he's a very sensitive man, isn't he? Ted. Very. I've often wished I was as sensitive as he is.
RUTH. Have you?

LENNY. Oh yes. Oh yes, very much so. I mean, I'm not saying I'm not sensitive. I am. I could just be a bit more so, that's all.

RUTH. Could you?

LENNY. Yes, just a bit more so, that's all.

Pause.

I mean, I am very sensitive to atmosphere, but I tend to get desensitized, if you know what I mean, when people make unreasonable demands on me. For instance, last Christmas I decided to do a bit of snow-clearing for the Borough Council, because we had a heavy snow over here that year in Europe. I didn't have to do this snow-clearing – I mean I wasn't financially embarrassed in any way – it just appealed to me, it appealed to something inside me. What I antici-pated with a good deal of pleasure was the brisk cold bite in the air in the early morning. And I was right. I had to get my snowboots on and I had to stand on a corner, at about five-thirty in the morning, to wait for the lorry to pick me up, to take me to the allotted area. Bloody freezing. Well, the lorry came, I jumped on the tailboard, headlights on, dipped, and off we went. Got there, shovels up, fags on, and off we went, deep into the December snow, hours before cockcrow. Well, that morning, while I was having my mid-morning cup of tea in a neighbouring cafe, the shovel standing by my chair, an old lady approached me and asked me if I would give her a hand with her iron mangle. Her brother-in-law, she said, had left it for her, but he'd left it in the wrong room, he'd left it in the front room. Well, naturally, she wanted it in the back room. It was a present he'd given her, you see, a mangle, to iron out the washing. But he'd left it in the wrong room, he'd left it in the front room, well that was a silly place to leave it, it couldn't stay there. So I took time off to give her a hand. She only lived up the road. Well, the only trouble was when I got there I couldn't move this mangle. It must have weighed about half a ton. How this brother-in-law got it up there in the first place I can't even begin to envisage. So there I was, doing a bit of shoulders on with the mangle, risking a rupture, and this old lady just standing there, waving me on, not even lifting a little finger to give me a helping hand. So after a few minutes I said to her, now look here, why don't you stuff this iron mangle up your arse? Anyway, I said, they're out of date, you want to get a spin drier. I had a good mind to give her a workover there and then, but as I was feeling jubilant with the snow-clearing I just gave her a short-arm jab to the belly and jumped on a bus outside. Excuse me, shall I take this ashtray out of your way?

RUTH. It's not in my way.

LENNY. It seems to be in the way of your glass. The glass was about to fall. Or the ashtray. I'm rather worried about the carpet. It's not me, it's my father. He's obsessed with order and clarity. He doesn't like mess. So, as I don't believe you're smoking at the moment, I'm sure you won't object if I move the ashtray.

   He does so.

And now perhaps I'll relieve you of your glass.

RUTH. I haven't quite finished.

LENNY. You've consumed quite enough, in my opinion.

RUTH. No, I haven't.

LENNY. Quite sufficient, in my own opinion.

RUTH. Not in mine, Leonard.

   Pause.

LENNY. Don't call me that, please.

RUTH. Why not?

LENNY. That's the name my mother gave me.

   Pause.

Just give me the glass.

RUTH. No.

Pause.

LENNY. I'll take it, then.

RUTH. If you take the glass . . . I'll take you.

Pause.

LENNY. How about me taking the glass without you taking me?

RUTH. Why don't I just take you?

Pause.

LENNY. You're joking.

Pause.

You're in love, anyway, with another man. You've had a secret liaison with another man. His family didn't even know. Then you come here without a word of warning and start to make trouble.

She picks up the glass and lifts it towards him.

RUTH. Have a sip. Go on. Have a sip from my glass.

He is still.

Sit on my lap. Take a long cool sip.

She pats her lap. Pause.
She stands, moves to him with the glass.

Put your head back and open your mouth.

LENNY. Take that glass away from me.

RUTH. Lie on the floor. Go on. I'll pour it down your throat.

LENNY. What are you doing, making me some kind of proposal?

She laughs shortly, drains the glass.

RUTH. Oh, I was thirsty.

She smiles at him, puts the glass down, goes into the hall and up the stairs.
He follows into the hall and shouts up the stairs.

LENNY. What was that supposed to be? Some kind of proposal?

Silence.
He comes back into the room, goes to his own glass, drains it.
A door slams upstairs.
The landing light goes on.
MAX *comes down the stairs, in pyjamas and cap. He comes into the room.*

MAX. What's going on here? You drunk?

He stares at LENNY.

What are you shouting about? You gone mad?

LENNY *pours another glass of water.*

Prancing about in the middle of the night shouting your head off. What are you, a raving lunatic?
LENNY. I was thinking aloud.
MAX. Is Joey down here? You been shouting at Joey?
LENNY. Didn't you hear what I said, Dad? I said I was thinking aloud.
MAX. You were thinking so loud you got me out of bed.
LENNY. Look, why don't you just . . . pop off, eh?
MAX. Pop off? He wakes me up in the middle of the night, I think we got burglars here, I think he's got a knife stuck in him, I come down here, he tells me to pop off.

LENNY *sits down.*

He was talking to someone. Who could he have been talking to? They're all asleep. He was having a conversation with

someone. He won't tell me who it was. He pretends he was
thinking aloud. What are you doing, hiding someone here?

LENNY. I was sleepwalking. Get out of it, leave me alone, will
you?

MAX. I want an explanation, you understand? I asked you
who you got hiding here.

Pause.

LENNY. I'll tell you what, Dad, since you're in the mood for a
bit of a . . . chat, I'll ask you a question. It's a question
I've been meaning to ask you for some time. That night
. . . you know . . . the night you got me . . . that night
with Mum, what was it like? Eh? When I was just a glint
in your eye. What was it like? What was the background to
it? I mean, I want to know the real facts about my background. I mean, for instance, is it a fact that you had me in
mind all the time, or is it a fact that I was the last thing you
had in mind?

Pause.

I'm only asking this in a spirit of inquiry, you understand
that, don't you? I'm curious. And there's lots of people of
my age share that curiosity, you know that, Dad? They
often ruminate, sometimes singly, sometimes in groups,
about the true facts of that particular night – the night they
were made in the image of those two people *at it*. It's a
question long overdue, from my point of view, but as we
happen to be passing the time of day here tonight I thought
I'd pop it to you.

Pause.

MAX. You'll drown in your own blood.

LENNY. If you prefer to answer the question in writing I've
got no objection.

MAX *stands.*

I should have asked my dear mother. Why didn't I ask my dear mother? Now it's too late. She's passed over to the other side.

> MAX *spits at him.*
> LENNY *looks down at the carpet.*

Now look what you've done. I'll have to Hoover that in the morning, you know.

> MAX *turns and walks up the stairs.*
> LENNY *sits still.*
> BLACKOUT.
> LIGHTS UP.

> *Morning.*
> JOEY *in front of the mirror. He is doing some slow limbering-up exercises. He stops, combs his hair, carefully. He then shadowboxes, heavily, watching himself in the mirror.*
> MAX *comes in from* U.L.
> *Both* MAX *and* JOEY *are dressed.* MAX *watches* JOEY *in silence.* JOEY *stops shadowboxing, picks up a newspaper and sits.*
> *Silence.*

MAX. I hate this room.

> *Pause.*

It's the kitchen I like. It's nice in there. It's cosy.

> *Pause.*

But I can't stay in there. You know why? Because he's always washing up in there, scraping the plates, driving me out of the kitchen, that's why.

JOEY. Why don't you bring your tea in here?

MAX. I don't want to bring my tea in here. I hate it here. I want to drink my tea in there.

He goes into the hall and looks towards the kitchen.

What's he doing in there?

He returns.

What's the time?
JOEY. Half past six.
MAX. Half past six.

> *Pause.*

I'm going to see a game of football this afternoon. You want to come?

> *Pause.*

I'm talking to you.
JOEY. I'm training this afternoon. I'm doing six rounds with Blackie.
MAX. That's not till five o'clock. You've got time to see a game of football before five o'clock. It's the first game of the season.
JOEY. No, I'm not going.
MAX. Why not?

> *Pause.*
> MAX *goes into the hall.*

Sam! Come here!

> MAX *comes back into the room.*
> SAM *enters with a cloth.*

SAM. What?
MAX. What are you doing in there?
SAM. Washing up.
MAX. What else?
SAM. Getting rid of your leavings.
MAX. Putting them in the bin, eh?

SAM. Right in.

MAX. What point you trying to prove?

SAM. No point.

MAX. Oh yes, you are. You resent making my breakfast, that's
what it is, isn't it? That's why you bang round the kitchen
like that, scraping the frying-pan, scraping all the leavings
into the bin, scraping all the plates, scraping all the tea out of
the teapot . . . that's why you do that, every single stinking
morning. I know. Listen, Sam. I want to say something to
you. From my heart.

He moves closer.

I want you to get rid of these feelings of resentment you've
got towards me. I wish I could understand them. Honestly,
have I ever given you cause? Never. When Dad died he
said to me, Max, look after your brothers. That's exactly
what he said to me.

SAM. How could he say that when he was dead?

MAX. What?

SAM. How could he speak if he was dead?

Pause.

MAX. Before he died, Sam. Just before. They were his last
words. His last sacred words, Sammy. You think I'm
joking? You think when my father spoke – on his death-
bed – I wouldn't obey his words to the last letter? You
hear that, Joey? He'll stop at nothing. He's even prepared to spit on the memory of our Dad. What kind of a
son were you, you wet wick? You spent half your time doing
crossword puzzles! We took you into the butcher's shop,
you couldn't even sweep the dust off the floor. We took
MacGregor into the shop, he could run the place by the
end of a week. Well, I'll tell you one thing. I respected my
father not only as a man but as a number one butcher! And

to prove it I followed him into the shop. I learned to carve a carcass at his knee. I commemorated his name in blood. I gave birth to three grown men! All on my own bat. What have you done?

Pause.

What have you done? You tit!

SAM. Do you want to finish the washing up? Look, here's the cloth.

MAX. So try to get rid of these feelings of resentment, Sam. After all, we are brothers.

SAM. Do you want the cloth? Here you are. Take it.

> TEDDY *and* RUTH *come down the stairs. They walk across the hall and stop just inside the room.*
> *The others turn and look at them.* JOEY *stands.*
> TEDDY *and* RUTH *are wearing dressing-gowns.*
> *Silence.*
> TEDDY *smiles.*

TEDDY. Hullo . . . Dad . . . We overslept.

Pause.

What's for breakfast?

> *Silence.*
> TEDDY *chuckles.*

Huh. We overslept.

> MAX *turns to* SAM.

MAX. Did you know he was here?

SAM. No.

> MAX *turns to* JOEY.

MAX. Did you know he was here?

Pause.

I asked you if you knew he was here.

JOEY. No.

MAX. Then who knew?

Pause.

Who knew?

Pause.

I didn't know.

TEDDY. I was going to come down, Dad, I was going to . . be here, when you came down.

Pause.

How are you?

Pause.

Uh . . . look, I'd . . . like you to meet . . .

MAX. How long you been in this house?

TEDDY. All night.

MAX. All night? I'm a laughing-stock. How did you get in?

TEDDY. I had my key.

MAX *whistles and laughs.*

MAX. Who's this?

TEDDY. I was just going to introduce you.

MAX. Who asked you to bring tarts in here?

TEDDY. Tarts?

MAX. Who asked you to bring dirty tarts into this house?

TEDDY. Listen, don't be silly –

MAX. You been here all night?

TEDDY. Yes, we arrived from Venice –

MAX. We've had a smelly scrubber in my house all night. We've had a stinking pox-ridden slut in my house all night.

TEDDY. Stop it! What are you talking about?

MAX. I haven't seen the bitch for six years, he comes home without a word, he brings a filthy scrubber off the street, he shacks up in my house!

TEDDY. She's my wife! We're married!

Pause.

MAX. I've never had a whore under this roof before. Ever since your mother died. My word of honour. (*To* JOEY.) Have you ever had a whore here? Has Lenny ever had a whore here? They come back from America, they bring the slopbucket with them. They bring the bedpan with them. (*To* TEDDY.) Take that disease away from me. Get her away from me.

TEDDY. She's my wife.

MAX (*to* JOEY). Chuck them out.

Pause.

A Doctor of Philosophy, Sam, you want to meet a Doctor of Philosophy? (*To* JOEY.) I said chuck them out.

Pause.

What's the matter? You deaf?

JOEY. You're an old man. (*To* TEDDY.) He's an old man.

> LENNY *walks into the room, in a dressing-gown.*
> *He stops.*
> *They all look round.*
> MAX *turns back, hits* JOEY *in the stomach with all his might.*
> JOEY *contorts, staggers across the stage.* MAX, *with the exertion of the blow, begins to collapse. His knees buckle. He clutches his stick.*
> SAM *moves forward to help him.*
> MAX *hits him across the head with his stick,* SAM *sits, head in hands.*

JOEY, *hands pressed to his stomach, sinks down at the feet of*
RUTH
She looks down at him.
LENNY *and* TEDDY *are still.*
JOEY *slowly stands. He is close to* RUTH. *He turns from*
RUTH, *looks round at* MAX.
SAM *clutches his head.*
MAX *breathes heavily, very slowly gets to his feet.*
JOEY *moves to him.*
They look at each other.
Silence.
MAX *moves past* JOEY, *walks towards* RUTH. *He gestures*
with his stick.

MAX. Miss.

RUTH *walks towards him.*

RUTH. Yes?

He looks at her.

MAX. You a mother?
RUTH. Yes.
MAX. How many you got?
RUTH. Three.

He turns to TEDDY.

MAX. All yours, Ted?

Pause.

Teddy, why don't we have a nice cuddle and kiss, eh? Like
the old days? What about a nice cuddle and kiss, eh?
TEDDY. Come on, then.

Pause.

MAX. You want to kiss your old father? Want a cuddle with
your old father?

TEDDY. Come on, then.

   TEDDY moves a step towards him.

Come on.

   Pause.

MAX. You still love your old Dad, eh?

   They face each other.

TEDDY. Come on, Dad. I'm ready for the cuddle.

   MAX begins to chuckle, gurgling.
   He turns to the family and addresses them.

MAX. He still loves his father!

Curtain

Act Two

Afternoon.

MAX, TEDDY, LENNY *and* SAM *are about the stage, lighting cigars.*

JOEY *comes in from* U.L. *with a coffee tray, followed by* RUTH. *He puts the tray down.* RUTH *hands coffee to all the men. She sits with her cup.* MAX *smiles at her.*

RUTH. That was a very good lunch.

MAX. I'm glad you liked it. (*To the others.*) Did you hear that? (*To* RUTH.) Well, I put my heart and soul into it, I can tell you. (*He sips.*) And this is a lovely cup of coffee.

RUTH. I'm glad.

   Pause.

MAX. I've got the feeling you're a first-rate cook.

RUTH. I'm not bad.

MAX. No, I've got the feeling you're a number one cook. Am I right, Teddy?

TEDDY. Yes, she's a very good cook.

   Pause.

MAX. Well, it's a long time since the whole family was together, eh? If only your mother was alive. Eh, what do you say, Sam? What would Jessie say if she was alive? Sitting here with her three sons. Three fine grown-up lads. And a lovely daughter-in-law. The only shame is her grandchildren aren't here. She'd have petted them and cooed over them, wouldn't she, Sam? She'd have fussed over them and played with them, told them stories, tickled them – I tell you she'd have been hysterical. (*To* RUTH.) Mind you, she taught those boys everything they know. She taught them all the morality they know. I'm telling you. Every single bit of the moral code they live by – was taught to them by their mother. And she had a heart to go with it. What a heart. Eh, Sam? Listen, what's the use of beating round the bush? That woman was the backbone to this family. I mean, I was busy working twenty-four hours a day in the shop, I was going all over the country to find meat, I was making my way in the world, but I left a woman at home with a will of iron, a heart of gold and a mind. Right, Sam?

Pause.

What a mind.

Pause.

Mind you, I was a generous man to her. I never left her short of a few bob. I remember one year I entered into negotiations with a top-class group of butchers with continental connections. I was going into association with them. I remember the night I came home, I kept quiet. First of all I gave Lenny a bath, then Teddy a bath, then Joey a bath. What fun we used to have in the bath, eh, boys? Then I came downstairs and I made Jessie put her feet up on a pouffe – what happened to that pouffe, I haven't seen it for years – she put her feet up on the pouffe and I said to her, Jessie, I think our ship is going to come home, I'm going to treat you to a couple of items, I'm going to buy you a dress in pale corded blue silk, heavily encrusted in pearls, and for casual wear, a pair of pantaloons in lilac flowered taffeta. Then I gave her a drop of cherry brandy. I remember the boys came down, in their pyjamas, all their hair shining, their faces pink, it was before they started shaving, and they knelt down at our feet, Jessie's and mine. I tell you, it was like Christmas.

Pause.

RUTH. What happened to the group of butchers?

MAX. The group? They turned out to be a bunch of criminals like everyone else.

Pause.

This is a lousy cigar.

He stubs it out.
He turns to SAM.

What time you going to work?

SAM. Soon.

MAX. You've got a job on this afternoon, haven't you?

SAM. Yes, I know.

MAX. What do you mean, you know? You'll be late. You'll lose your job. What are you trying to do, humiliate me?

SAM. Don't worry about me.

MAX. It makes the bile come up in my mouth. The bile – you understand? (*To* RUTH.) I worked as a butcher all my life, using the chopper and the slab, the slab, you know what I mean, the chopper and the slab! To keep my family in luxury. Two families! My mother was bedridden, my brothers were all invalids. I had to earn the money for the leading psychiatrists. I had to read books! I had to study the disease, so that I could cope with an emergency at every stage. A crippled family, three bastard sons, a slutbitch of a wife – don't talk to me about the pain of childbirth – I suffered the pain, I've still got the pangs – when I give a little cough my back collapses – and here I've got a lazy idle bugger of a brother won't even get to work on time. The best chauffeur in the world. All his life he's sat in the front seat giving lovely hand signals. You call that work? This man doesn't know his gearbox from his arse!

SAM. You go and ask my customers! I'm the only one they ever ask for.

MAX. What do the other drivers do, sleep all day?

SAM. I can only drive one car. They can't all have me at the same time.

MAX. Anyone could have you at the same time. You'd bend over for half a dollar on Blackfriars Bridge.

SAM. Me!

MAX. For two bob and a toffee apple.

SAM. He's insulting me. He's insulting his brother. I'm driving a man to Hampton Court at four forty-five.

MAX. Do you want to know who could drive? MacGregor! MacGregor was a driver.

SAM. Don't you believe it.

> MAX *points his stick at* SAM.

MAX. He didn't even fight in the war. This man didn't even fight in the bloody war!

SAM. I did!

MAX. Who did you kill?

> *Silence.*
> SAM *gets up, goes to* RUTH, *shakes her hand and goes out of the front door.*
> MAX *turns to* TEDDY.

Well, how you been keeping, son?

TEDDY. I've been keeping very well, Dad.

MAX. It's nice to have you with us, son.

TEDDY. It's nice to be back, Dad.

> *Pause.*

MAX. You should have told me you were married, Teddy. I'd have sent you a present. Where was the wedding, in America?

TEDDY. No, Here. The day before we left.

MAX. Did you have a big function?

TEDDY. No, there was no one there.

MAX. You're mad. I'd have given you a white wedding. We'd

have had the cream of the cream here. I'd have been only
too glad to bear the expense, my word of honour.

Pause.

TEDDY. You were busy at the time. I didn't want to bother
you.

MAX. But you're my own flesh and blood. You're my first born.
I'd have dropped everything. Sam would have driven you
to the reception in the Snipe, Lenny would have been your
best man, and then we'd have all seen you off on the boat. I
mean, you don't think I disapprove of marriage, do you?
Don't be daft. (*To* RUTH.) I've been begging my two
youngsters for years to find a nice feminine girl with proper
credentials – it makes life worth living. (*To* TEDDY.) Anyway, what's the difference, you did it, you made a wonderful
choice, you've got a wonderful family, a marvellous career
. . . so why don't we let bygones by bygones?

Pause.

You know what I'm saying? I want you both to know that
you have my blessing.

TEDDY. Thank you.

MAX. Don't mention it. How many other houses in the district
have got a Doctor of Philosophy sitting down drinking a cup
of coffee?

Pause.

RUTH. I'm sure Teddy's very happy . . . to know that you're
pleased with me.

Pause.

I think he wondered whether you would be pleased with me.

MAX. But you're a charming woman.

Pause.

RUTH. I was . . .
MAX. What?

Pause.

What she say?

They all look at her.

RUTH. I was . . . different . . . when I met Teddy . . . first.
TEDDY. No you weren't. You were the same.
RUTH. I wasn't.
MAX. Who cares? Listen, live in the present, what are you worrying about? I mean, don't forget the earth's about five thousand million years old, at least. Who can afford to live in the past?

Pause.

TEDDY. She's a great help to me over there. She's a wonderful wife and mother. She's a very popular woman. She's got lots of friends. It's a great life, at the University . . . you know . . . it's a very good life. We've got a lovely house . . . we've got all . . . we've got everything we want. It's a very stimulating environment.

Pause.

My department . . . is highly successful.

Pause.

We've got three boys, you know.
MAX. All boys? Isn't that funny, eh? You've got three, I've got three. You've got three nephews, Joey. Joey! You're an uncle, do you hear? You could teach them how to box.

Pause.

JOEY (*to* RUTH). I'm a boxer. In the evenings, after work. I'm in demolition in the daytime.

RUTH. Oh?

JOEY. Yes. I hope to be full time, when I get more bouts.

MAX (*to* LENNY). He speaks so easily to his sister-in-law, do you notice? That's because she's an intelligent and sympathetic woman.

He leans to her.

Eh, tell me, do you think the children are missing their mother?

She looks at him.

TEDDY. Of course they are. They love her. We'll be seeing them soon.

Pause.

LENNY (*to* TEDDY). Your cigar's gone out.

TEDDY. Oh, yes.

LENNY. Want a light?

TEDDY. No. No.

Pause.

So has yours.

LENNY. Oh, yes.

Pause.

Eh, Teddy, you haven't told us much about your Doctorship of Philosophy. What do you teach?

TEDDY. Philosophy.

LENNY. Well, I want to ask you something. Do you detect a certain logical incoherence in the central affirmations of Christian theism?

TEDDY. That question doesn't fall within my province.

LENNY. Well, look at it this way . . . you don't mind my asking you some questions, do you?

TEDDY. If they're within my province.

LENNY. Well, look at it this way. How can the unknown merit reverence? In other words, how can you revere that of which you're ignorant? At the same time, it would be ridiculous to propose that what we *know* merits reverence. What we know merits any one of a number of things, but it stands to reason reverence isn't one of them. In other words, apart from the known and the unknown, what else is there?

Pause.

TEDDY. I'm afraid I'm the wrong person to ask.

LENNY. But you're a philosopher. Come on, be frank. What do you make of all this business of being and not-being?

TEDDY. What do you make of it?

LENNY. Well, for instance, take a table. Philosophically speaking. What is it?

TEDDY. A table.

LENNY. Ah. You mean it's nothing else but a table. Well, some people would envy your certainty, wouldn't they, Joey? For instance, I've got a couple of friends of mine, we often sit round the Ritz Bar having a few liqueurs, and they're always saying things like that, you know, things like: Take a table, take it. All right, I say, *take* it, *take* a table, but once you've taken it, what you going to do with it? Once you've got hold of it, where you going to take it?

MAX. You'd probably sell it.

LENNY. You wouldn't get much for it.

JOEY. Chop it up for firewood.

LENNY *looks at him and laughs.*

RUTH. Don't be too sure though. You've forgotten something. Look at me. I . . . move my leg. That's all it is. But I wear . . . underwear . . . which moves with me . . . it . . . captures your attention. Perhaps you misinterpret. The action is simple. It's a leg . . . moving. My lips move. Why don't you restrict . . . your observations to that? Perhaps the fact that they move is more significant . . . than the words which come through them. You must bear that . . . possibility . . . in mind.

Silence
TEDDY stands.

I was born quite near here.

Pause.

Then . . . six years ago, I went to America.

Pause.

It's all rock. And sand. It stretches . . . so far . . . everywhere you look. And there's lots of insects there.

Pause.

And there's lots of insects there.

Silence.
She is still.
MAX stands.

MAX. Well, it's time to go to the gym. Time for your workout, Joey.

LENNY (*standing*). I'll come with you.

JOEY sits looking at RUTH.

MAX. Joe.

JOEY stands. The three go out.
TEDDY sits by RUTH, holds her hand.
She smiles at him.
Pause.

TEDDY. I think we'll go back. Mmnn?

Pause.

Shall we go home?

RUTH. Why?

TEDDY. Well, we were only here for a few days, weren't we? We might as well . . . cut it short, I think.

RUTH. Why? Don't you like it here?

TEDDY. Of course I do. But I'd like to go back and see the boys now.

Pause.

RUTH. Don't you like your family?

TEDDY. Which family?

RUTH. Your family here.

TEDDY. Of course I like them. What are you talking about?

Pause.

RUTH. You don't like them as much as you thought you did?

TEDDY. Of course I do. Of course I . . . like them. I don't know what you're talking about.

Pause.

Listen. You know what time of the day it is there now, do you?

RUTH. What?

TEDDY. It's morning. It's about eleven o'clock.

RUTH. Is it?

TEDDY. Yes, they're about six hours behind us . . . I mean . . . behind the time here. The boys'll be at the pool . . . now . . . swimming. Think of it. Morning over there. Sun. We'll go anyway, mmnn? It's so clean there.

RUTH. Clean.

TEDDY. Yes.

RUTH. Is it dirty here?

TEDDY. No, of course not. But it's cleaner there.

Pause.

Look, I just brought you back to meet the family, didn't I?
You've met them, we can go. The fall semester will be
starting soon.

RUTH. You find it dirty here?

TEDDY. I didn't say I found it dirty here.

Pause.

I didn't say that.

Pause.

Look. I'll go and pack. You rest for a while. Will you?
They won't be back for at least an hour. You can sleep.
Rest. Please.

She looks at him.

You can help me with my lectures when we get back. I'd
love that. I'd be so grateful for it, really. We can bathe till
October. You know that. Here, there's nowhere to bathe,
except the swimming bath down the road. You know what
it's like? It's like a urinal. A filthy urinal!

Pause.

You liked Venice, didn't you? It was lovely, wasn't it? You
had a good week. I mean . . . I took you there. I can speak
Italian.

RUTH. But if I'd been a nurse in the Italian campaign I would
have been there before.

Pause.

TEDDY. You just rest. I'll go and pack.

TEDDY *goes out and up the stairs.*

She closes her eyes.
LENNY appears from U.L.
He walks into the room and sits near her.
She opens her eyes.
Silence.

LENNY. Well, the evenings are drawing in.
RUTH. Yes, it's getting dark.

Pause.

LENNY. Winter'll soon be upon us. Time to renew one's wardrobe.

Pause.

RUTH. That's a good thing to do.
LENNY. What?

Pause.

RUTH. I always . . .

Pause.

Do you like clothes?
LENNY. Oh, yes. Very fond of clothes.

Pause.

RUTH. I'm fond . . .

Pause.

What do you think of my shoes?
LENNY. They're very nice.
RUTH. No, I can't get the ones I want over there.
LENNY. Can't get them over there, eh?
RUTH. No . . . you don't get them there.

Pause.

I was a model before I went away.

LENNY. Hats?

Pause.

I bought a girl a hat once. We saw it in a glass case, in a shop. I tell you what it had. It had a bunch of daffodils on it, tied with a black satin bow, and then it was covered with a cloche of black veiling. A cloche. I'm telling you. She was made for it.

RUTH. No . . . I was a model for the body. A photographic model for the body.

LENNY. Indoor work?

RUTH. That was before I had . . . all my children.

Pause.

No, not always indoors.

Pause.

Once or twice we went to a place in the country, by train. Oh, six or seven times. We used to pass a . . . a large white water tower. This place . . . this house . . . was very big . . . the trees . . . there was a lake, you see . . . we used to change and walk down towards the lake . . . we went down a path . . . on stones . . . there were . . . on this path. Oh, just . . . wait . . . yes . . . when we changed in the house we had a drink. There was a cold buffet.

Pause.

Sometimes we stayed in the house but . . . most often . . . we walked down to the lake . . . and did our modelling there.

Pause.

Just before we went to America I went down there. I walked

from the station to the gate and then I walked up the drive.
There were lights on . . . I stood in the drive . . . the
house was very light.

> TEDDY *comes down the stairs with the cases. He puts them
> down, looks at* LENNY.

TEDDY. What have you been saying to her?

> *He goes to* RUTH.

Here's your coat.

> LENNY *goes to the radiogram and puts on a record of slow
> jazz.*

Ruth. Come on. Put it on.

LENNY (*to* RUTH). What about one dance before you go?

TEDDY. We're going.

LENNY. Just one.

TEDDY. No. We're going.

LENNY. Just one dance, with her brother-in-law, before she
goes.

> LENNY *bends to her.*

Madam?

> RUTH *stands. They dance, slowly.*
> TEDDY *stands, with* RUTH'S *coat.*
> MAX *and* JOEY *come in the front door and into the room.
> They stand.*
> LENNY *kisses* RUTH. *They stand, kissing.*

JOEY. Christ, she's wide open.

> *Pause.*

She's a tart.

> *Pause.*

Old Lenny's got a tart in here.

> JOEY *goes to them. He takes* RUTH'S *arm. He smiles at* LENNY. *He sits with* RUTH *on the sofa, embraces and kisses her.*
> *He looks up at* LENNY.

Just up my street.

> *He leans her back until she lies beneath him. He kisses her. He looks up at* TEDDY *and* MAX.

It's better than a rubdown, this.

> LENNY *sits on the arm of the sofa. He caresses* RUTH'S *hair as* JOEY *embraces her.*
> MAX *comes forward, looks at the cases.*

MAX. You going. Teddy? Already?

> *Pause.*

Well, when you coming over again, eh? Look, next time you come over, don't forget to let us know beforehand whether you're married or not. I'll always be glad to meet the wife. Honest. I'm telling you.

> JOEY *lies heavily on* RUTH.
> *They are almost still.*
> LENNY *caresses her hair.*

Listen, you think I don't know why you didn't tell me you were married? I know why. You were ashamed. You thought I'd be annoyed because you married a woman beneath you. You should have known me better. I'm broadminded. I'm a broadminded man.

> *He peers to see* RUTH'S *face under* JOEY, *turns back to* TEDDY.

Mind you, she's a lovely girl. A beautiful woman. And a

mother too. A mother of three. You've made a happy woman out of her. It's something to be proud of. I mean, we're talking about a woman of quality. We're talking about a woman of feeling.

> JOEY *and* RUTH *roll off the sofa on to the floor.*
> JOEY *clasps her.* LENNY *moves to stand above them. He looks down on them. He touches* RUTH *gently with his foot.*
> RUTH *suddenly pushes* JOEY *away.*
> *She stands up.*
> JOEY *gets to his feet, stares at her.*

RUTH. I'd like something to eat. (*To* LENNY.) I'd like a drink. Did you get any drink?

LENNY. We've got drink.

RUTH. I'd like one, please.

LENNY. What drink?

RUTH. Whisky.

LENNY. I've got it.

> *Pause.*

RUTH. Well, get it.

> LENNY *goes to the sideboard, takes out bottle and glasses.*
> JOEY *moves towards her.*

Put the record off.

> *He looks at her, turns, puts the record off.*

I want something to eat.

> *Pause.*

JOEY. I can't cook. (*Pointing to* MAX.) He's the cook.

> LENNY *brings her a glass of whisky.*

LENNY. Soda on the side?

RUTH. What's this glass? I can't drink out of this. Haven't you got a tumbler?

LENNY. Yes.

RUTH. Well, put it in a tumbler.

He takes the glass back, pours whisky into a tumbler, brings it to her.

LENNY. On the rocks? Or as it comes?

RUTH. Rocks? What do you know about rocks?

LENNY. We've got rocks. But they're frozen stiff in the fridge.

RUTH *drinks.*

LENNY *looks round at the others.*

Drinks all round?

He goes to the sideboard and pours drinks.

JOEY *moves closer to RUTH.*

OEY. What food do you want?

RUTH *walks round the room.*

RUTH (*to* TEDDY). Has your family read your critical works?

MAX. That's one thing I've never done. I've never read one of his critical works.

TEDDY. You wouldn't understand them.

LENNY *hands drinks all round.*

JOEY. What sort of food do you want? I'm not the cook, anyway.

LENNY. Soda, Ted? Or as it comes?

TEDDY. You wouldn't understand my works. You wouldn't have the faintest idea of what they were about. You wouldn't appreciate the points of reference. You're way behind. All of you. There's no point in my sending you my works. You'd be lost. It's nothing to do with the question of intelligence. It's a way of being able to look at the world. It's a question of how far you can operate on things and not in things. I mean it's a question of your capacity to ally the two, to relate the two, to balance the two. To see, to be able to *see*! I'm the one who can see. That's why I can write my critical works. Might do you good . . . have a look at them . . . see how certain people can view . . . things . . . how certain people can maintain . . . intellectual equilibrium. Intellectual equilibrium. You're just objects. You just . . . move about. I can observe it. I can see what you do. It's the same as I do. But you're lost in it. You won't get me being . . . I won't be lost in it.

BLACKOUT.
LIGHTS UP.
Evening.
TEDDY *sitting, in his coat, the cases by him.* SAM.
Pause.

SAM. Do you remember MacGregor, Teddy?
TEDDY. Mac?
SAM. Yes.
TEDDY. Of course I do.
SAM. What did you think of him? Did you take to him?
TEDDY. Yes. I liked him. Why?

Pause.

SAM. You know, you were always my favourite, of the lads. Always.

Pause.

When you wrote to me from America I was very touched, you know. I mean you'd written to your father a few times but you'd never written to me. But then, when I got that letter from you . . . well, I was very touched. I never told him. I never told him I'd heard from you.

Pause.

(*Whispering.*) Teddy, shall I tell you something? You were always your mother's favourite. She told me. It's true. You were always the . . . you were always the main object of her love.

Pause.

Why don't you stay for a couple more weeks, eh? We could have a few laughs.

LENNY *comes in the front door and into the room.*

LENNY. Still here, Ted? You'll be late for your first seminar.

He goes to the sideboard, opens it, peers in it, to the right and the left, stands.

Where's my cheese-roll?

Pause.

Someone's taken my cheese-roll. I left it there. (*To* SAM.) You been thieving?

TEDDY. I took your cheese-roll, Lenny.

Silence.
SAM *looks at them, picks up his hat and goes out of the front door.*
Silence.

LENNY. You took my cheese roll?
TEDDY. Yes.
LENNY. I made that roll myself. I cut it and put the butter on. I sliced a piece of cheese and put it in between. I put it on a plate and I put it in the sideboard. I did all that before I went out. Now I come back and you've eaten it.
TEDDY. Well, what are you going to do about it?
LENNY. I'm waiting for you to apologize.
TEDDY. But I took it deliberately, Lenny.

LENNY. You mean you didn't stumble on it by mistake?

TEDDY. No, I saw you put it there. I was hungry, so I ate it.

Pause.

LENNY. Barefaced audacity.

Pause.

What led you to be so . . . vindictive against your own brother? I'm bowled over.

Pause.

Well, Ted, I would say this is something approaching the naked truth, isn't it? It's a real cards on the table stunt. I mean, we're in the land of no holds barred now. Well, how else can you interpret it? To pinch your younger brother's specially made cheese roll when he's out doing a spot of work, that's not equivocal, it's unequivocal.

Pause.

Mind you, I will say you do seem to have grown a bit sulky during the last six years. A bit sulky. A bit inner. A bit less forthcoming. It's funny, because I'd have thought that in the United States of America, I mean with the sun and all that, the open spaces, on the old campus, in your position, lecturing, in the centre of all the intellectual life out there, on the old campus, all the social whirl, all the stimulation of it all, all your kids and all that, to have fun with, down by the pool, the Greyhound buses and all that, tons of iced water, all the comfort of those Bermuda shorts and all that, on the old campus, no time of the day or night you can't get a cup of coffee or a Dutch gin, I'd have thought you'd have grown more forthcoming, not less. Because I want you to know that you set a standard for us, Teddy. Your family looks up to you, boy, and you know what it does? It does its best to follow the example you set. Because you're a great source of pride to us. That's why we were so glad to see you come back, to welcome you back to your birthplace. That's why.

Pause.

No, listen, Ted, there's no question that we live a less rich life here than you do over there. We live a closer life. We're busy, of course. Joey's busy with his boxing, I'm busy with my occupation, Dad still plays a good game of poker, and he does the cooking as well, well up to his old standard, and Uncle Sam's the best chauffeur in the firm. But nevertheless we do make up a unit, Teddy, and you're an integral part of it. When we all sit round the backyard having a quiet gander at the night sky, there's always an empty chair standing in the circle, which is in fact yours. And so when you at length return to us, we do expect a bit of grace, a bit of je ne sais quoi, a bit of generosity of mind, a bit of liberality of spirit, to reassure us. We do expect that. But do we get it? Have we got it? Is that what you've given us?

Pause.

TEDDY. Yes.

JOEY *comes down the stairs and into the room, with a newspaper.*

LENNY (*to* JOEY). How'd you get on?
JOEY. Er . . . not bad.
LENNY. What do you mean?

Pause.

What do you mean?
JOEY. Not bad.
LENNY. I want to know what you *mean* – by not bad.
JOEY. What's it got to do with you?
LENNY. Joey, you tell your brother everything.

Pause.

JOEY. I didn't get all the way.
LENNY. You didn't get all the way?

Pause.

(*With emphasis.*) You didn't get all the way?
But you've had her up there for two hours.
JOEY. Well?
LENNY. You didn't get all the way and you've had her up there
for two hours!
JOEY. What about it?

LENNY *moves closer to him.*

LENNY. What are you telling me?
JOEY. What do you mean?
LENNY. Are you telling me she's a tease?

Pause.

She's a tease!

Pause.

What do you think of that, Ted? Your wife turns out to be
a tease. He's had her up there for two hours and he didn't
go the whole hog.
JOEY. I didn't say she was a tease.
LENNY. Are you joking? It sounds like a tease to me, don't it
to you, Ted?
TEDDY. Perhaps he hasn't got the right touch.
LENNY. Joey? Not the right touch? Don't be ridiculous. He's
had more dolly than you've had cream cakes. He's irresistible.
He's one of the few and far between. Tell him about the
last bird you had, Joey.

Pause.

JOEY. What bird?

LENNY. The last bird! When we stopped the car . . .

JOEY. Oh, that . . . yes . . . well, we were in Lenny's car one night last week . . .

LENNY. The Alfa.

JOEY. And er . . . bowling down the road . . .

LENNY. Up near the Scrubs.

JOEY. Yes, up over by the Scrubs . . .

LENNY. We were doing a little survey of North Paddington.

JOEY. And er . . . it was pretty late, wasn't it?

LENNY. Yes, it was late. Well?

Pause.

JOEY. And then we . . . well, by the kerb, we saw this parked car . . . with a couple of girls in it.

LENNY. And their escorts.

JOEY. Yes, there were two geezers in it. Anyway . . . we got out . . . and we told the . . . two escorts . . . to go away . . . which they did . . . and then we . . . got the girls out of the car . . .

LENNY. We didn't take them over the Scrubs.

JOEY. Oh, no. Not over the Scrubs. Well, the police would have noticed us there . . . you see. We took them over a bombed site.

LENNY. Rubble. In the rubble.

JOEY. Yes, plenty of rubble.

Pause.

Well . . . you know . . . then we had them.

LENNY. You've missed out the best bit. He's missed out the best bit!

JOEY. What bit?

LENNY (*to* TEDDY). His bird says to him, I don't mind, she says, but I've got to have some protection. I've got to have some contraceptive protection. I haven't got any contraceptive protection, old Joey says to her. In that case I won't do it, she says. Yes you will, says Joey, never mind about the contraceptive protection.

LENNY *laughs.*

Even my bird laughed when she heard that. Yes, even she gave out a bit of a laugh. So you can't say old Joey isn't a bit of a knockout when he gets going, can you? And here he is upstairs with your wife for two hours and he hasn't even been the whole hog. Well, your wife sounds like a bit of a tease to me, Ted. What do you make of it, Joey? You satisfied? Don't tell me you're satisfied without going the whole hog?

Pause.

JOEY. I've been the whole hog plenty of times. Sometimes . . . you can be happy . . . and not go the whole hog. Now and again . . . you can be happy . . . without going any hog.

LENNY *stares at him.*
MAX *and* SAM *come in the front door and into the room.*

MAX. Where's the whore? Still in bed? She'll make us all animals.
LENNY. The girl's a tease.
MAX. What?
LENNY. She's had Joey on a string.
MAX. What do you mean?
TEDDY. He had her up there for two hours and he didn't go the whole hog.

Pause.

MAX. My Joey? She did that to my boy?

Pause.

To my youngest son? Tch, tch, tch, tch. How you feeling, son? Are you all right?

JOEY. Sure I'm all right.

MAX (*to* TEDDY). Does she do that to you, too?

TEDDY. No.

LENNY. He gets the gravy.

MAX. You think so?

JOEY. No he don't.

Pause.

SAM. He's her lawful husband. She's his lawful wife.

JOEY. No he don't! He don't get no gravy! I'm telling you.
I'm telling all of you. I'll kill the next man who says he gets
the gravy.

MAX. Joey . . . what are you getting so excited about? (*To*
LENNY.) It's because he's frustrated. You see what happens?

JOEY. Who is?

MAX. Joey. No one's saying you're wrong. In fact everyone's
saying you're right.

Pause.

MAX *turns to the others.*

You know something? Perhaps it's not a bad idea to have
a woman in the house. Perhaps it's a good thing. Who knows?
Maybe we should keep her.

Pause.

Maybe we'll ask her if she wants to stay.

Pause.

TEDDY. I'm afraid not, Dad. She's not well, and we've got to
get home to the children.

MAX. Not well? I told you, I'm used to looking after people
who are not so well. Don't worry about that. Perhaps we'll
keep her here.

Pause.

SAM. Don't be silly.

MAX. What's silly?

SAM. You're talking rubbish.

MAX. Me?

SAM. She's got three children.

MAX. She can have more! Here. If she's so keen.

TEDDY. She doesn't want any more.

MAX. What do you know about what she wants, eh, Ted?

TEDDY (*smiling*). The best thing for her is to come home with me, Dad. Really. We're married, you know.

MAX *walks about the room, clicks his fingers.*

MAX. We'd have to pay her, of course. You realize that? We can't leave her walking about without any pocket money. She'll have to have a little allowance.

JOEY. Of course we'll pay her. She's got to have some money in her pocket.

MAX. That's what I'm saying. You can't expect a woman to walk about without a few bob to spend on a pair of stockings.

Pause.

LENNY. Where's the money going to come from?

MAX. Well, how much is she worth? What we talking about, three figures?

LENNY. I asked you where the money's going to come from. It'll be an extra mouth to feed. It'll be an extra body to clothe. You realize that?

JOEY. I'll buy her clothes.

LENNY. What with?

JOEY. I'll put in a certain amount out of my wages.

MAX. That's it. We'll pass the hat round. We'll make a donation. We're all grown-up people, we've got a sense of responsibility. We'll all put a little in the hat. It's democratic.

LENNY. It'll come to a few quid, Dad.

Pause.

I mean, she's not a woman who likes walking around in
second-hand goods. She's up to the latest fashion. You
wouldn't want her walking about in clothes which don't
show her off at her best, would you?

MAX. Lenny, do you mind if I make a little comment? It's
not meant to be critical. But I think you're concentrating
too much on the economic considerations. There are other
considerations. There are the human considerations. You
understand what I mean? There are the human considerations. Don't forget them.

LENNY. I won't.

MAX. Well don't.

Pause.

Listen, we're bound to treat her in something approximating,
at least, to the manner in which she's accustomed. After
all, she's not someone off the street, she's my daughter-in-
law!

JOEY. That's right.

MAX. There you are, you see. Joey'll donate, Sam'll donate.
. . .

   SAM *looks at him.*

I'll put a few bob out of my pension, Lenny'll cough up.
We're laughing. What about you, Ted? How much you
going to put in the kitty?

TEDDY. I'm not putting anything in the kitty.

MAX. What? You won't even help to support your own
wife? You lousy stinkpig. Your mother would drop dead if
she heard you take that attitude.

LENNY. Eh, Dad.

   LENNY *walks forward.*

I've got a better idea.

MAX. What?

LENNY. There's no need for us to go to all this expense. I know these women. Once they get started they ruin your budget. I've got a better idea. Why don't I take her up with me to Greek Street?

Pause.

MAX. You mean put her on the game?

Pause.

We'll put her on the game. That's a stroke of genius, that's a marvellous idea. You mean she can earn the money herself – on her back?

LENNY. Yes.

MAX. Wonderful. The only thing is, it'll have to be short hours. We don't want her out of the house all night.

LENNY. I can limit the hours.

MAX. How many?

LENNY. Four hours a night.

MAX (*dubiously*). Is that enough?

LENNY. She'll bring in a good sum for four hours a night.

MAX. Well, you should know. After all, it's true, the last thing we want to do is wear the girl out. She's going to have her obligations this end as well. Where you going to put her in Greek Street?

LENNY. It doesn't have to be right in Greek Street, Dad. I've got a number of flats all around that area.

MAX. You have? Well, what about me? Why don't you give me one?

LENNY. You're sexless.

JOEY. Eh, wait a minute, what's all this?

MAX. I know what Lenny's saying. Lenny's saying she can pay her own way. What do you think, Teddy? That'll solve all our problems.

JOEY. Eh, wait a minute. I don't want to share her.

MAX. What did you say?

JOEY. I don't want to share her with a lot of yobs!

MAX. Yobs! You arrogant git! What arrogance. (*To* LENNY.) Will you be supplying her with yobs?

LENNY. I've got a very distinguished clientele, Joey. They're more distinguished than you'll ever be.

MAX. So you can count yourself lucky we're including you in.

JOEY. I didn't think I was going to have to share her!

MAX. Well, you *are* going to have to share her! Otherwise she goes straight back to America. You understand?

Pause.

It's tricky enough as it is, without you shoving your oar in. But there's something worrying me. Perhaps she's not so up to the mark. Eh? Teddy, you're the best judge. Do you think she'd be up to the mark?

Pause.

I mean what about all this teasing? Is she going to make a habit of it? That'll get us nowhere.

Pause.

TEDDY. It was just love play . . . I suppose . . . that's all I suppose it was.

MAX. Love play? Two bleeding hours? That's a bloody long time for love play!

LENNY. I don't think we've got anything to worry about on that score, Dad.

MAX. How do you know?

LENNY. I'm giving you a professional opinion.

LENNY *goes to* TEDDY.

LENNY. Listen, Teddy, you could help us, actually. If I were to send you some cards, over to America . . . you know, very nice ones, with a name on, and a telephone number, very discreet, well, you could distribute them . . . to various parties, who might be making a trip over here. Of course, you'd get a little percentage out of it.

MAX. I mean, you needn't tell them she's your wife.

LENNY. No, we'd call her something else. Dolores, or something.

MAX. Or Spanish Jacky.

LENNY. No, you've got to be reserved about it, Dad. We could call her something nice . . . like Cynthia . . . or Gillian.

Pause.

JOEY. Gillian.

Pause.

LENNY. No, what I mean, Teddy, you must know lots of professors, heads of departments, men like that. They pop over here for a week at the Savoy, they need somewhere they can go to have a nice quiet poke. And of course you'd be in a position to give them inside information.

MAX. Sure. You can give them proper data. I bet you before two months we'd have a waiting list.

LENNY. You could be our representative in the States.

MAX. Of course. We're talking in international terms! By the time we've finished Pan-American'll give us a discount.

Pause.

TEDDY. She'd get old . . . very quickly.

MAX. No . . . not in this day and age! With the health service? Old! How could she get old? She'll have the time of her life.

RUTH *comes down the stairs, dressed.*
She comes into the room.
She smiles at the gathering, and sits.
Silence.

TEDDY. Ruth . . . the family have invited you to stay, for a little while longer. As a . . . as a kind of guest. If you like the idea I don't mind. We can manage very easily at home . . . until you come back.

RUTH. How very nice of them.

Pause.

MAX. It's an offer from our heart.

RUTH. It's very sweet of you.

MAX. Listen . . . it would be our pleasure.

Pause.

RUTH. I think I'd be too much trouble.

MAX. Trouble? What are you talking about? What trouble? Listen, I'll tell you something. Since poor Jessie died, eh, Sam? we haven't had a woman in the house. Not one. Inside this house. And I'll tell you why. Because their mother's image was so dear any other woman would have . . . tarnished it. But you . . . Ruth . . . you're not only lovely and beautiful, but you're kin. You're kith. You belong here.

Pause.

RUTH. I'm very touched.

MAX. Of course you're touched. I'm touched.

Pause.

TEDDY. But Ruth, I should tell you . . . that you'll have to pull your weight a little, if you stay. Financially. My father isn't very well off.

RUTH (*to* MAX). Oh, I'm sorry.

MAX. No, you'd just have to bring in a little, that's all. A few pennies. Nothing much. It's just that we're waiting for Joey to hit the top as a boxer. When Joey hits the top . . . well . . .

Pause.

TEDDY. Or you can come home with me.
LENNY. We'd get you a flat.

Pause.

RUTH. A flat?
LENNY. Yes.
RUTH. Where?
LENNY. In town.

Pause.

But you'd live here, with us.
MAX. Of course you would. This would be your home. In the bosom of the family.
LENNY. You'd just pop up to the flat a couple of hours a night, that's all.
MAX. Just a couple of hours, that's all. That's all.
LENNY. And you make enough money to keep you going here.

Pause.

RUTH. How many rooms would this flat have?
LENNY. Not many.
RUTH. I would want at least three rooms and a bathroom.
LENNY. You wouldn't need three rooms and a bathroom.
MAX. She'd need a bathroom.
LENNY. But not three rooms.

Pause.

RUTH. Oh, I would. Really.
LENNY. Two would do.
RUTH. No. Two wouldn't be enough.

Pause.

I'd want a dressing-room, a rest-room, and a bedroom.

Pause.

LENNY. All right, we'll get you a flat with three rooms and a bathroom.

RUTH. With what kind of conveniences?

LENNY. All conveniences.

RUTH. A personal maid?

LENNY. Of course.

Pause.

We'd finance you, to begin with, and then, when you were established, you could pay us back, in instalments.

RUTH. Oh, no, I wouldn't agree to that.

LENNY. Oh, why not?

RUTH. You would have to regard your original outlay simply as a capital investment.

Pause.

LENNY. I see. All right.

RUTH. You'd supply my wardrobe, of course?

LENNY. We'd supply everything. Everything you need.

RUTH. I'd need an awful lot. Otherwise I wouldn't be content.

LENNY. You'd have everything.

RUTH. I would naturally want to draw up an inventory of everything I would need, which would require your signatures in the presence of witnesses.

LENNY. Naturally.

RUTH. All aspects of the agreement and conditions of employment would have to be clarified to our mutual satisfaction before we finalized the contract.

LENNY. Of course.

Pause.

RUTH. Well, it might prove a workable arrangement.

LENNY. I think so.

MAX. And you'd have the whole of your daytime free, of course. You could do a bit of cooking here if you wanted to.

LENNY. Make the beds.

MAX. Scrub the place out a bit.

TEDDY. Keep everyone company.

> SAM *comes forward.*

SAM (*in one breath*). MacGregor had Jessie in the back of my cab as I drove them along.

> *He croaks and collapses.*
> *He lies still.*
> *They look at him.*

MAX. What's he done? Dropped dead?

LENNY. Yes.

MAX. A corpse? A corpse on my floor? Get him out of here! Clear him out of here!

> JOEY *bends over* SAM.

JOEY. He's not dead.

LENNY. He probably was dead, for about thirty seconds.

MAX. He's not even dead!

> LENNY *looks down at* SAM.

LENNY. Yes, there's still some breath there.

MAX (*pointing at* SAM). You know what that man had?

LENNY. Has.

MAX. Has! A diseased imagination.

> *Pause.*

RUTH. Yes, it sounds a very attractive idea.

MAX. Do you want to shake on it now, or do you want to leave it till later?

RUTH. Oh, we'll leave it till later.

> TEDDY *stands.*
> *He looks down at* SAM.

TEDDY. I was going to ask him to drive me to London Airport.

He goes to the cases, picks one up.

Well, I'll leave your case, Ruth. I'll just go up the road to the Underground.

MAX. Listen, if you go the other way, first left, first right, you remember, you might find a cab passing there.

TEDDY. Yes, I might do that.

MAX. Or you can take the tube to Piccadilly Circus, won't take you ten minutes, and pick up a cab from there out to the Airport.

TEDDY. Yes, I'll probably do that.

MAX. Mind you, they'll charge you double fare. They'll charge you for the return trip. It's over the six-mile limit.

TEDDY. Yes. Well, bye-bye, Dad. Look after yourself.

They shake hands.

MAX. Thanks, son. Listen. I want to tell you something. It's been wonderful to see you.

Pause.

TEDDY. It's been wonderful to see you.

MAX. Do your boys know about me? Eh? Would they like to see a photo, do you think, of their grandfather?

TEDDY. I know they would.

MAX brings out his wallet.

MAX. I've got one on me. I've got one here. Just a minute. Here you are. Will they like that one?

TEDDY (*taking it*). They'll be thrilled.

He turns to LENNY.

Good-bye, Lenny.

They shake hands.

LENNY. Ta-ta, Ted. Good to see you. Have a good trip.
TEDDY. Bye-bye, Joey.

> JOEY *does not move.*

JOEY. Ta-ta.

> TEDDY *goes to the front door.*

RUTH. Eddie.

> TEDDY *turns.*
> *Pause.*

Don't become a stranger.

> TEDDY *goes, shuts the front door.*
> *Silence.*
> *The three men stand.*
> RUTH *sits relaxed on her chair.*
> SAM *lies still.*
> JOEY *walks slowly across the room.*
> *He kneels at her chair.*
> *She touches his head, lightly.*
> *He puts his head in her lap.*
> MAX *begins to move above them, backwards and forwards.*
> LENNY *stands still.*
> MAX *turns to* LENNY.

MAX. I'm too old, I suppose. She thinks I'm an old man.

> *Pause.*

I'm not such an old man.

> *Pause.*

(*To* RUTH.) You think I'm too old for you?

> *Pause.*

Listen. You think you're just going to get that big slag all

the time? You think you're just going to have him . . .
you're going to just have him all the time? You're going to
have to work! You'll have to take them on, you understand?

Pause.

Does she realize that?

Pause.

Lenny, do you think she understands . . .

He begins to stammer.

What . . . what . . . what . . . we're getting at? What
. . . we've got in mind? Do you think she's got it clear?

Pause.

I don't think she's got it clear.

Pause.

You understand what I mean? Listen, I've got a funny idea
she'll do the dirty on us, you want to bet? She'll use us,
she'll make use of us, I can tell you! I can smell it! You
want to bet?

Pause.

She won't . . . be adaptable!

*He begins to groan, clutches his stick, falls on to his knees by the
side of her chair. His body sags. The groaning stops. His body
straightens. He looks at her, still kneeling.*

I'm not an old man.

Pause.

Do you hear me?

He raises his face to her.

Kiss me.

She continues to touch JOEY'S *head, lightly.*
LENNY *stands, watching.*

Curtain

Tea Party

TEA PARTY was commissioned by sixteen member countries of the European Broadcasting Union, to be transmitted by all of them under the title, *The Largest Theatre in the World*. It was first presented by B.B.C. Television on 25 March 1965 with the following cast:

DISSON	Leo McKern
WENDY	Vivien Merchant
DIANA	Jennifer Wright
WILLY	Charles Gray
DISLEY	John Le Mesurier
LOIS	Margaret Denyer
FATHER	Frederick Piper
MOTHER	Hilda Barry
TOM	Peter Bartlett
JOHN	Robert Bartlett

Directed by Charles Jarrott

A stage version of TEA PARTY, in double-bill with THE BASEMENT, opened at the Duchess Theatre, London, on 17 September 1970, directed by James Hammerstein and produced by Eddie Kulukundis for Knightsbridge Theatrical Productions Ltd, with the following cast:

DISSON	Donald Pleasence
WENDY	Vivien Merchant
DIANA	Gabrielle Drake
WILLY	Barry Foster
TOM	Robin Angell
JOHN	Kevin Chippendale
DISLEY	Derek Aylward
LOIS	Jill Johnson
FATHER	Arthur Hewlett
MOTHER	Hilda Barry

An electric lift rising to the top floor of an office block. WENDY *stands in it.*

Corridor.
The lift comes to rest in a broad carpeted corridor, the interior of an office suite. It is well appointed, silent. The walls are papered with Japanese silk. Along the walls in alcoves are set, at various intervals, a selection of individually designed wash basins, water closets and bidets, all lit by hooded spotlights.
WENDY *steps out of the lift and walks down the corridor towards a door. She knocks. It opens.*

Disson's office. Morning.
DISSON *rising from a large desk. He goes round the desk to meet* WENDY *and shakes her hand.*
DISSON. How do you do, Miss Dodd? Nice of you to come. Please sit down.
    DISSON *goes back to his seat behind the desk.* WENDY *sits in a chair at the corner of the desk.*
That's right.
    He refers to papers on the desk.
Well now, I've had a look at your references. They seem to be excellent. You've had quite a bit of experience.
WENDY. Yes, sir.
DISSON. Not in my line, of course. We manufacture sanitary ware . . . but I suppose you know that?
WENDY. Yes, of course I do, Mr Disson.
DISSON. You've heard of us, have you?
WENDY. Oh yes.
    WENDY *crosses her left leg over her right.*

DISSON. Well, do you think you'd be interested in . . . in this area of work?

WENDY. Oh, certainly, sir, yes, I think I would.

DISSON. We're the most advanced sanitary engineers in the country. I think I can say that quite confidently.

WENDY. Yes, I believe so.

DISSON. Oh yes. We manufacture more bidets than anyone else in England. (*He laughs.*) It's almost by way of being a mission. Cantilever units, hidden cisterns, footpedals, you know, things like that.

WENDY. Footpedals?

DISSON. Instead of a chain or plug. A footpedal.

WENDY. Oh. How marvellous.

DISSON. They're growing more popular every day and rightly so.

WENDY *crosses her right leg over her left.*

Well now, this . . . post is, in fact, that of my personal assistant. Did you understand that? A very private secretary, in fact. And a good deal of responsibility would undoubtedly devolve upon you. Would you . . . feel yourself capable of discharging it?

WENDY. Once I'd correlated all the fundamental features of the work, sir, I think so, yes.

DISSON. All the fundamental features, yes. Good.

WENDY *crosses her left leg over her right.*

I see you left your last job quite suddenly.

Pause.

May I ask the reason?

WENDY. Well, it's . . . a little embarrassing, sir.

DISSON. Really?

Pause.

Well, I think I should know, don't you? Come on, you can tell me. What was it?

WENDY *straightens her skirt over her knees.*

WENDY. Well, it is rather personal, Mr Disson.

DISSON. Yes, but I think I should know, don't you?

Pause.

WENDY. Well, it's simply that I couldn't persuade my chief . . . to call a halt to his attentions.

DISSON. *What?* (*He consults the papers on the desk.*) A firm of this repute? It's unbelievable.

WENDY. I'm afraid it's true, sir.

Pause.

DISSON. What sort of attentions?

WENDY. Oh, I don't . . .

DISSON. What sort?

Pause.

WENDY. He never stopped touching me, Mr Disson, that's all.

DISSON. Touching you?

WENDY. Yes.

DISSON. Where? (*Quickly.*) That must have been very disturbing for you.

WENDY. Well, quite frankly, it is disturbing, to be touched all the time.

DISSON. Do you mean at every opportunity?

WENDY. Yes, sir.

Slight pause.

DISSON. Did you cry?

WENDY. Cry?

DISSON. Did he make you cry?

WENDY. Oh just a little, occasionally, sir.

DISSON. What a monster.

Slight pause.

Well, I do sympathize.

WENDY. Thank you, sir.

DISSON. One would have thought this . . . tampering, this . . . interfering . . . with secretaries was something of the past, a myth, in fact, something that only took place in paperback books. Tch. Tch.

WENDY *crosses her right leg over her left.*

Anyway, be that as it may, your credentials are excellent and I would say you possessed an active and inquiring intelligence and a pleasing demeanour, two attributes I consider necessary for this post. I'd like you to start immediately.

WENDY. Oh, that's wonderful. Thank you so much, Mr Disson.

DISSON. Not at all.

They stand. He walks across the room to another desk.

This'll be your desk.

WENDY. Ah.

DISSON. There are certain personal arrangements I'd like you to check after lunch. I'm . . . getting married tomorrow.

WENDY. Oh, congratulations.

DISSON. Thanks. Yes, this is quite a good week for me, what with one thing and another.

The telephone rings on his desk.

He crosses and picks it up.

Hullo, Disley. How are you? . . . What? Oh my goodness, don't say that.

Disson's house. Sitting-room. Evening.

DIANA. This is my brother Willy.

DISSON. I'm very glad to meet you.

WILLY. And I you. Congratulations.

DISSON. Thank you.

DIANA (*giving him a drink*). Here you are, Robert.

DISSON. Thanks. Cheers.

DIANA. Cheers.

WILLY. To tomorrow.

DISSON. Yes.

They drink.

I'm afraid we've run into a bit of trouble.

DIANA. Why?

DISSON. I've lost my best man.

DIANA. Oh no.

DISSON (*to* WILLY). My oldest friend. Man called Disley.
Gastric flu. Can't make it tomorrow.

WILLY. Oh dear.

DISSON. He was going to make a speech at the reception – in
my honour. A superb speech. I read it. Now he can't make it.
Pause.

WILLY. Isn't there anyone else you know?

DISSON. Yes, of course. But not like him . . . you see. I
mean, he was the natural choice.

DIANA. How infuriating.
Pause.

WILLY. Well, look, I can be your best man, if you like.

DIANA. How can you, Willy? You're giving me away.

WILLY. Oh yes.

DISSON. Oh, the best man's not important; you can always get
a best man – all he's got to do is stand there; it's the speech
that's important, the speech in honour of the groom. Who's
going to make the speech?
Pause.

WILLY. Well, I can make the speech, if you like.

DISSON. But how can you make a speech in honour of the
groom when you're making one in honour of the bride?

WILLY. Does that matter?

DIANA. No. Why does it?

DISSON. Yes, but look . . . I mean, thanks very much . . .
but the fact is . . . that you don't know me, do you? I
mean we've only just met. Disley knows me well, that's the
thing, you see. His speech centred around our long-standing
friendship. I mean, what he knew of my character . . .

WILLY. Yes, of course, of course. No, look, all I'm saying is
that I'm willing to have a crack at it if there's no other solution. Willing to come to the aid of the party, as it were.

DIANA. He *is* a wonderful speaker, Robert.

Wedding reception. Private room. Exclusive restaurant.

DISSON, DIANA, WILLY, DISSON'S PARENTS, DISSON'S
SONS. WILLY *is speaking.*

WILLY. I remember the days my sister and I used to swim
together in the lake at Sunderley. The grace of her crawl,
even then, as a young girl. I can remember those long
summer evenings at Sunderley, my mother and I crossing
the lawn towards the terrace and through the great windows
hearing my sister play Brahms. The delicacy of her touch.
My mother and I would, upon entering the music room,
gaze in silence at Diana's long fingers moving in exquisite
motion on the keys. As for our father, our father knew no
pleasure keener than watching his daughter at her needle-
work. A man whose business was the State's, a man eternally
active, his one great solace from the busy world would be to
sit for hours on end at a time watching his beloved daughter
ply her needle. Diana – my sister – was the dear grace of
our household, the flower, the blossom, and the bloom. One
can only say to the groom: Groom, your fortune is im-
measurable.

Applause. DIANA *kisses him.*

DISSON *shakes his hand warmly.*

TOASTMASTER. My lords, reverend gentlemen, ladies and
gentlemen, pray silence for Mr William Pierrepoint Torrance, who will propose the toast in honour of the groom.

WILLY *turns. Applause.*

WILLY. I have not known Robert for a long time, in fact I have
known him only for a very short time. But in that short time
I have found him to be a man of integrity, honesty and
humility. After a modest beginning, he has built his business
up into one of the proudest and most vigorous in the land.
And this – almost alone. Now he has married a girl who
equals, if not surpasses, his own austere standards of
integrity. He has married my sister, who possesses within
her that rare and uncommon attribute known as inner beauty,

not to mention the loveliness of her exterior. Par excellence
as a woman with a needle, beyond excellence as a woman of
taste, discernment, sensibility and imagination. An excellent
swimmer who, in all probability, has the beating of her
husband in the two hundred metres breast stroke.

Laughter and applause.

WILLY *waits for silence.*

It is to our parents that she owes her candour, her elegance
of mind, her *sensibilité*. Our parents, who, though gone, have
not passed from us, but who are here now on this majestic
day, and offer you their welcome, the bride their love, and
the groom their congratulations.

Applause. DIANA *kisses him.*

DISSON *shakes his hand warmly.*

DISSON. Marvellous.

WILLY. Diana, I want to tell you something.

DIANA. What?

WILLY. You have married a good man. He will make you
happy.

DIANA. I know.

DISSON. Wonderful speeches. Wonderful. Listen. What are
you doing these days?

WILLY. Nothing much.

TOASTMASTER. My lords . . .

DISSON (*whispering*). How would you like to come in with me
for a bit? See how you like it, how you get on. Be my second
in command. Office of your own. Plenty of room for initiative.

TOASTMASTER. My lords, reverend gentlemen, ladies and
gentlemen –

WILLY. Marvellous idea. I'll say yes at once.

DISSON. Good.

DIANA *kisses* DISSON.

DIANA. Darling.

TOASTMASTER. Pray silence for the groom.

DISSON *moves forward.*

Applause. Silence.

DISSON. This is the happiest day of my life.

Sumptuous hotel room. Italy.
The light is on. The camera rests at the foot of the bed. The characters are not seen. Their voices heard only.

DISSON. Are you happy?

DIANA. Yes.

DISSON. Very happy?

DIANA. Yes.

DISSON. Have you ever been happier? With any other man?

DIANA. Never.
     Pause.

DISSON. I make you happy, don't I? Happier than you've ever been . . . with any other man.

DIANA. Yes. You do.
     Pause.
   Yes.
     Silence.

Disson's house. Workroom.
DISSON *at his workbench. With sandpaper and file he is putting the finishing touches to a home-made model yacht. He completes the job, dusts the yacht, sets it on a shelf and looks at it with satisfaction.*

Disson's house. Breakfast room. Morning.
DISSON *and* DIANA *at the table.*
DISSON. Your eyes are shining.
     Pause.
   They're shining.

DIANA. Mmmnnn.

DISSON. They've been shining for months.

DIANA (*smiling*). My eyes? Have they?

DISSON. Every morning.

> *Pause.*

I'm glad you didn't marry that . . . Jerry . . . whatever-
hisnamewas . . .

DIANA. Oh, him . . .

DISSON. Why didn't you?

DIANA. He was weak.

> *Pause.*

DISSON. I'm not weak.

DIANA. No.

DISSON. Am I?

> *He takes her hand.*

DIANA. You're strong.

> THE TWINS *enter the room.*
>
> THE TWINS *mutter,* 'Morning'.
>
> DIANA *and* DISSON *say* 'Good Morning'.
>
> *Silence.* THE TWINS *sit.* DIANA *pours tea for them. They
> butter toast, take marmalade, begin to eat.*
>
> *Silence.*

Would you like eggs?

TOM. No, thanks.

DIANA. John?

> *Silence.*

DISSON. John!

JOHN. What?

DISSON. Don't say what!

JOHN. What shall I say?

DIANA. Would you like eggs?

> *Pause.*

JOHN. Oh.

> *Pause.*

No, thanks.

The boys giggle and eat. Silence.

JOHN *whispers to* TOM.

DISSON. What are you saying? Speak up.

JOHN. Nothing.

DISSON. Do you think I'm deaf?

TOM. I've never thought about it.

DISSON. I wasn't talking to you. I was talking to John.

JOHN. Me? Sorry, sir.

DISSON. Now don't be silly. You've never called me sir before. That's rather a daft way to address your father.

JOHN. Uncle Willy called his father sir. He told me.

DISSON. Yes, but you don't call *me* sir! Do you understand?

Willy's office. Morning.

DISSON *leads* WILLY *in.*

DISSON. Here you are, Willy. This'll be your office. How'd you like it?

WILLY. First rate.

DISSON. These two offices are completely cut off from the rest of the staff. They're all on the lower floor. Our only contact is by intercom, unless I need to see someone personally, which is rare. Equally, I dislike fraternization between the two offices. We shall meet only by strict arrangement, otherwise we'll never get any work done. That suit you?

WILLY. Perfectly.

DISSON. There was a man in here, but I got rid of him.

DISSON *leads* WILLY *through a communicating door into his own office.*

Disson's office.
On a side table coffee is set for two.
DISSON *goes to the table and pours.*
DISSON. I think I should explain to you the sort of man I am.

I'm a thorough man. I like things to be done and done well.
I don't like dithering. I don't like indulgence. I don't like
self-doubt. I don't like fuzziness. I like clarity. Clear intention. Precise execution. Black or white?

WILLY. White, please.

DISSON. But I've no patience with conceit and self-regard. A
man's job is to assess his powers coolly and correctly and
equally the powers of others. Having done this, he can proceed to establish a balanced and reasonable relationship with
his fellows. In my view, living is a matter of active and willing
participation. So is work. Sugar?

WILLY. Two, please.

DISSON. Now, dependence isn't a word I would use lightly,
but I will use it and I don't regard it as a weakness. To understand the meaning of the term dependence is to understand
that one's powers are limited and that to live with others is
not only sensible but the only way work can be done and
dignity achieved. Nothing is more sterile or lamentable than
the man content to live within himself. I've always made it
my business to be on the most direct possible terms with the
members of my staff and the body of my business associates.
And by my example opinions are declared freely, without
shame or deception. It seems to me essential that we cultivate
the ability to operate lucidly upon our problems and therefore be in a position to solve them. That's why your sister
loves me. I don't play about at the periphery of matters. I
go right to the centre. I believe life can be conducted
efficiently. I never waste my energies in any kind of timorous
expectation. Neither do I ask to be loved. I expect to be
given only what I've worked for. If you make a plum pudding,
what do you do with it? You don't shove it up on a shelf.
You stick a knife into it and eat it. Everything has a function.
In other words, if we're to work together we must appreciate
that interdependence is the key word, that it's your job to
understand me and mine to understand you. Agreed?

WILLY. Absolutely.

DISSON. Now, the first thing you need is a secretary. We'll get on to it at once.

WILLY. Can I suggest someone? I know she's very keen and, I'd say, very competent.

DISSON. Who?

WILLY. My sister.

Pause.

DISSON. Your sister? You mean my wife?

WILLY. She told me she'd love to do it.

DISSON. She hasn't told me.

WILLY. She's shy.

DISSON. But she doesn't need to work. Why should she want to work?

WILLY. To be closer to you.

Willy's office.

WILLY *and* DIANA *at their desks, both examining folders intently.*
   Silence.

Disson's office.

DISSON *and* WENDY *at their desks.* WENDY *typing on an electric typewriter.* DISSON *looking out of the window.* DISSON *turns from the window, glances at the door leading to* WILLY'S *office. The intercom buzzes on* WENDY'S *desk. She switches through.*

WENDY. Mr Disson does not want to be disturbed until 3.30.

   DISSON *glances again at* WILLY'S *door.*
   Silence.

Disson's house. Sitting-room. Early evening.

DIANA *and* THE TWINS *are sitting about, reading.*

DIANA. Do you miss your mother?

JOHN. We didn't know her very well. We were very young when she died.

DIANA. Your father has looked after you and brought you up very well.

JOHN. Oh, thank you. He'll be pleased to hear that.

DIANA. I've told him.

JOHN. What did he say?

DIANA. He was pleased I thought so. You mean a great deal to him.

JOHN. Children seem to mean a great deal to their parents, I've noticed. Though I've often wondered what 'a great deal' means.

TOM. I've often wondered what 'mean' means.

DIANA. Aren't you proud of your father's achievements?

JOHN. We are. I should say we are.

    Pause.

DIANA. And now that your father has married again . . . has the change in your life affected you very much?

JOHN. What change?

DIANA. Living with me.

JOHN. Ah. Well, I think there definitely is an adjustment to be made. Wouldn't you say that, Tom?

DIANA. Of course there is. But would you say it's an easy adjustment to make, or difficult?

JOHN. Well, it really all depends on how good you are at making adjustments. We're very good at making adjustments, aren't we, Tom?

    The front door slams. DIANA *and* THE TWINS *look down at their books.* DISSON *comes in. They all look up, smile.*

DISSON. Hullo.

    They all smile genially at him.

    DISSON *looks quickly from one to the other.*

Disson's office. Morning.
Sun shining in the window. DISSON *at his desk.* WENDY *at the*
cabinet. He watches her. She turns.

WENDY. Isn't it a beautiful day, Mr Disson?

DISSON. Close the curtains.

    WENDY *closes the curtains.*

Got your pad?

WENDY. Yes, sir.

DISSON. Sit down.

    WENDY *sits in a chair by the corner of his desk.*

Warwick and Sons. We duly acknowledge receipt of your
letter of the twenty-first inst. There should be no difficulty
in meeting your requirements. What's the matter?

WENDY. Sir?

DISSON. You're wriggling.

WENDY. I'm sorry, sir.

DISSON. Is it the chair?

WENDY. Mmn . . . it might be.

DISSON. Too hard, I expect. A little hard for you.

    Pause.

Is that it?

WENDY. A little.

DISSON. Sit on the desk.

WENDY. The desk?

DISSON. Yes, on the leather.

    Slight pause.

It'll be softer . . . for you.

WENDY. Well, that'll be nice.

    Pause. WENDY *eventually uncrosses her legs and stands. She*
    looks at the desk.

I think it's a little high . . . to get up on.

DISSON. Of course it isn't.

WENDY (*looking at the desk*). Hmmmn-mmmn . . .

DISSON. Go on, get up. You couldn't call that high.

WENDY *places her back to the desk and slowly attempts to raise herself up on to it.*
She stops.

WENDY. I think I'll have to put my feet on the chair, really, to hoist myself up.

DISSON. You can hoist yourself up without using your feet.

WENDY (*dubiously*). Well . . .

DISSON. Look, get up or stay down. Make up your mind. One thing or the other. I want to get on with my letter to Birmingham.

WENDY. I was just wondering if you'd mind if I put my high-heeled shoes on your chair . . . to help me get up.
Pause.

DISSON. I don't mind.

WENDY. But I'm worried in case my heels might chip the wood. They're rather sharp, these heels.

DISSON. Are they?
Pause.
Well, try it, anyway. You won't chip the wood.
WENDY *puts her feet on the chair and hoists herself up on to the desk.*
He watches.
WENDY *settles herself on the desk and picks up her pen and pad. She reads from the pad.*

WENDY. There should be no difficulty in meeting your requirements.

Disson's house. Games room. Day.
DISSON *and* WILLY *are playing ping-pong.* THE TWINS *watch. A long rally.* DISSON *backhand flips to win the point.*

JOHN. Good shot, Dad.

TOM. Thirteen-eighteen.

WILLY. Your backhand's in form, Robert.

JOHN. Attack his forehand.

WILLY *serves. A rally.* WILLY *attacks* DISSON'S *forehand.*
DISSON *moves over to his right and then flips backhand to*
win the point. THE TWINS *applaud.*

TOM. Thirteen-nineteen.

WILLY. Backhand flip on the forehand, eh?

WILLY *serves.*

From DISSON'S *point of view see two balls bounce and leap*
past both ears.

TWINS. Shot!

TOM. Fourteen-nineteen.

DISSON *puts down his bat and walks slowly to* WILLY.

DISSON. You served two balls, old chap.

WILLY. Two balls?

DISSON. You sent me two balls.

WILLY. No, no. Only one.

DISSON. Two.

Pause.

JOHN. One, Dad.

DISSON. What?

TOM. One.

Pause.

WILLY *walks to* DISSON'S *end, bends.*

WILLY. Look.

WILLY *picks up one ball.*

One ball. Catch!

He throws the ball. DISSON *gropes, loses sight of the ball.*
It bounces under the table. He crouches, leans under the table
for it. Gets it, withdraws, looks up. WILLY *and* THE TWINS
look down at him.

Disley's surgery.
Room darkened.
A torch shining in DISSON'S *eyes. First the left eye, then the right*
eye. Torch out. Light on.

DISLEY. There's nothing wrong with your eyes, old boy.

DISSON. Nothing?

DISLEY. They're in first-rate condition. Truly.

DISSON. That's funny.

DISLEY. I'd go as far as to say your sight was perfect.

DISSON. Huh.

DISLEY. Check the bottom line.

>   DISLEY *switches off the light, puts on the light on the letter board.*

What is it?

DISSON. EXJLNVCGTY.

DISLEY. Perfect.

>   *Board light off. Room light on.*

DISSON. Yes, I know . . . I know that . . .

DISLEY. Well, what are you worried about?

DISSON. It's not that . . .

DISLEY. Colour? Do you confuse colours? Look at me. What colour am I?

DISSON. Colourless.

DISLEY (*laughs, stops*). Very funny. What distinguishing marks can you see about me?

DISSON. Two.

DISLEY. What?

DISSON. You have one grey strip in your hair, quite faint.

DISLEY. Good. What's the other?

DISSON. You have a brown stain on your left cheek.

DISLEY. A brown stain? Can you see that? (*He looks in the mirror.*) I didn't know it was so evident.

DISSON. Of course it's evident. It stains your face.

DISLEY. Don't . . . go on about it, old boy. I didn't realize it was so evident. No one's ever noticed it before.

DISSON. Not even your wife?

DISLEY. Yes, she has. Anyway, I'd say your eyes are sharp enough. What colour are those lampshades?

DISSON. They're dark blue drums. Each has a golden rim. The carpet is Indian.

DISLEY. That's not a colour.

DISSON. It's white. Over there, by that cabinet, I can see a deep black burn.

DISLEY. A burn? Where? Do you mean that shadow?

DISSON. That's not a shadow. It's a burn.

DISLEY (*looking*). So it is. How the hell did that happen?

DISSON. Listen . . . I never said I couldn't see. You don't understand. Most of the time . . . my eyesight is excellent. It always has been. But . . . it's become unreliable. It's become . . . erratic. Sometimes, quite suddenly, very occasionally, something happens . . . something . . . goes wrong . . . with my eyes.

    Pause.

DISLEY. I can find no evidence that your sight is in any way deficient.

DISSON. You don't understand.

    A knock at the door. LOIS *appears.*

LOIS. I'm just going out. Wanted to say hullo to you before I go.

DISSON. Hullo, Lois.

    He kisses her cheek.

LOIS. You've been in here for ages. Don't tell me you need glasses?

DISLEY. His eyes are perfect.

LOIS. They look it.

DISSON. What a lovely dress you're wearing.

LOIS. Do you like it? Really?

DISSON. Of course I like it.

LOIS. You must see if the birds are still there.

    She lifts the blind.

Yes, they are. They're all at the bird bath.

    They all look into the garden.

Look at them. They're so happy. They love my bath. They do, really. They love it. They make me so happy, my birds. And they seem to know, instinctively, that I adore them. They do, really.

Disson's house. Bedroom. Night.

DISSON *alone, in front of a mirror.*

He is tying his tie. He ties it. The front end hangs only half-way down his chest.

He unties it, ties it again. The front end, this time, is even shorter.

He unties it, holds the tie and looks at it.

He then ties the tie again. This time the two ends are of equal length.

He breathes deeply, relaxes, goes out of the room.

Disson's house. Dining room. Night.

DIANA, WILLY, DISSON *at dinner.*

DIANA. I'd say she was a real find.

WILLY. Oh, she's of inestimable value to the firm, wouldn't you say, Robert?

DISSON. Oh yes.

DIANA. I mean for someone who's not . . . actually . . . part of us . . . I mean, an outsider . . . to give such devotion and willingness to the job, as she does . . . well, it's remarkable. We were very lucky to find her.

DISSON. I found her, actually.

WILLY. You found me, too, old boy.

DIANA (*laughing*). And me.

 Pause.

She's of course so completely trustworthy, and so very persuasive, on the telephone. I've heard her . . . when the door's been open . . . once or twice.

WILLY. Oh, splendid girl, all round.

DISSON. She's not so bloody marvellous.

 Pause. They look at him.

She's all right, she's all right. But she's not so bloody marvellous.

DIANA. Well, perhaps not quite as accomplished as I am, no. Do you think I'm a good private secretary, Willy?

WILLY. First rate.

Pause. They eat and drink.

DISSON. I don't think it's a good idea for you to work.

DIANA. Me? Why not? I love it.

DISSON. I never see you. If you were at home I could take the occasional afternoon off . . . to see you. As it is I never see you. In day-time.

DIANA. You mean I'm so near and yet so far?

Pause.

DISSON. Yes.

DIANA. Would you prefer me to be your secretary?

DISSON. No, no, of course not. That wouldn't work at all.

Pause.

WILLY. But we do all meet at lunch-time. We meet in the evening.

DISSON *looks at him.*

DIANA. But I like working. You wouldn't want me to work for someone else, would you, somewhere else?

DISSON. I certainly wouldn't. You know what Wendy told me, don't you?

DIANA. What?

DISSON. She told me her last employer was always touching her.

WILLY. No?

DISSON. Always. Touching her.

DIANA. Her body, you mean?

DISSON. What else?

Pause.

DIANA. Well, if we're to take it that that's general practice, I think it's safer to stay in the family, don't you? Mind you, they might not want to touch me in the way they wanted to touch her.

Pause.

But, Robert, you must understand that I not only want to
be your wife, but also your employee. I'm not embarrassing
you, am I, Willy?

WILLY. No, of course you're not.

DIANA. Because by being your employee I can help to further
your interests, our interests. That's what I want to do. And
so does Willy, don't you?

Disson's office. Morning.

DISSON *alone. He stands in the centre of the room. He looks at the
door, walks over to* WENDY'S *desk. He looks down at her desk-
chair. He touches it. Slowly, he sits in it. He sits still.*

The door opens. WENDY *comes in. He stands.*

DISSON. You're late.

WENDY. You were sitting in my chair, Mr Disson.

DISSON. I said you're late.

WENDY. I'm not at all.

> WENDY *walks to her desk.*
>
> DISSON *makes way for her. He moves across the room.*

I'm hurt.

DISSON. Why?

WENDY. I've put on my new dress.

> *He turns, looks at her.*

DISSON. When did you put it on?

WENDY. This morning.

> *Pause.*

DISSON. Where?

WENDY. In my flat.

DISSON. Which room?

WENDY. In the hall, actually. I have a long mirror in the hall.

> *He stands looking at her.*

Do you like it?

DISSON. Yes. Very nice.

Disson's house. Workroom.

DISSON. Hold it firmly. You're not holding it firmly.

> TOM *holds a length of wood on the table.* DISSON *chips at its base.*

Use pressure. Grip it.

JOHN. A clamp would be better.

DISSON. A clamp? I want you boys to learn how to concentrate your physical energies, to do something useful.

JOHN. What's it going to be, Dad?

DISSON. You'll find out.

> DISSON *chips. He straightens.*

Give me the saw.

JOHN. Me?

DISSON. The saw! Give me it! (*To* TOM.) What are you doing?

TOM. I'm holding this piece of wood.

DISSON. Well, stop it. I've finished chipping. Look at the point now.

JOHN. If you put some lead in there you could make a pencil out of it.

DISSON. They think you're very witty at your school, do they?

JOHN. Well, some do and some don't, actually, Dad.

DISSON. You. Take the saw.

TOM. Me?

DISSON. I want you to saw it off . . . from here.

> DISSON *makes a line with his finger on the wood.*

TOM. But I can't saw.

JOHN. What about our homework, Dad? We've got to write an essay about the Middle Ages.

DISSON. Never mind the Middle Ages.

JOHN. Never mind the *Middle Ages*?

TOM. Can't you demonstrate how to do it, Dad? Then we could watch.

DISSON. Oh, give me it.

DISSON *takes the saw and points to a mark on the wood.*

Now . . . from here.

TOM (*pointing*). You said from here.

DISSON. No, no, from here.

JOHN (*pointing to the other end*). I could have sworn you said from there.

Pause.

DISSON. Go to your room.

Pause.

Get out.

JOHN *goes out.* DISSON *looks at* TOM.

Do you want to learn anything?

TOM. Yes.

DISSON. Where did I say I was going to saw it?

He stares at the wood. TOM *holds it still.*

Hold it still. Hold it. Don't let it move.

DISSON *saws. The saw is very near* TOM'S *fingers.* TOM *looks down tensely.* DISSON *saws through.*

TOM. You nearly cut my fingers off.

DISSON. No, I didn't . . . I didn't . . .

He glares suddenly at TOM.

You didn't hold the wood still!

Disson's office.

The curtains are drawn.

DISSON. Come here. Put your chiffon round my eyes. My eyes hurt.

WENDY *ties a chiffon scarf round his eyes.*

I want you to make a call to Newcastle, to Mr Martin. We're still waiting for delivery of goods on Invoice No. 634729. What is the cause for delay?

WENDY *picks up the telephone, dials, waits.*

WENDY. Could I have Newcastle 77254, please. Thank you.

She waits. He touches her body.

Yes, I'm holding.
> *He touches her. She moves under his touch.*

Hullo, Mr Martin, please. Mr Disson's office.
> *Camera on him. His arm stretching.*

Mr Martin? Mr Disson's office. Mr Disson . . . Ah, you
know what it's about (*She laughs.*) Yes . . . Yes.
> *Camera on him. He leans forward, his arm stretching.*

Oh, it's been dispatched? Oh good. Mr Disson will be glad.
> *She moves under his touch.*

Oh, I will. Of course I will.
> *She puts the phone down. He withdraws his hand.*

Mr Martin sends his apologies. The order has been dispatched.
> *The intercom buzzes. She switches through.* WILLY'S *voice.*

Yes?

WILLY. Oh, Wendy, is Mr Disson there?

WENDY. Did you want to speak to him, Mr Torrance?

WILLY. No. Just ask him if I might borrow your services for
five minutes.

WENDY. Mr Torrance wants to know if he might borrow my
services for five minutes.

DISSON. What's happened to his own secretary?

WENDY. Mr Disson would like to know what has happened to
your own secretary.

WILLY. She's unwell. Gone home. Just five minutes, that's
all.
> DISSON *gestures towards the door.*

WENDY. Be with you in a minute, Mr Torrance.

WILLY. Please thank Mr Disson for me.
> *The intercom switches off.*

WENDY. Mr Torrance would like me to thank you for him.

DISSON. I heard.
> WENDY *goes through the inner door into* WILLY'S *office,*
> *shuts it.*
> *Silence.*

DISSON *sits still, the chiffon round his eyes. He looks towards the door.*

He hears giggles, hissing, gurgles, squeals.

He goes to the door, squats by the handle, raises the chiffon, tries to look through the keyhole. Can see nothing through the keyhole. He drops the chiffon, puts his ear to the door. The handle presses into his skull. The sounds continue. Sudden silence.

The door has opened.

A pair of woman's legs stand by his squatting body.

He freezes, slowly puts forward a hand, touches a leg. He tears the chiffon from his eyes. It hangs from his neck. He looks up.

DIANA *looks down at him.*

Behind her, in the other room, WENDY *is sitting, taking dictation from* WILLY, *who is standing.*

DIANA. What game is this?

   He remains.

Get up. What are you doing? What are you doing with that scarf? Get up from the floor. What are you doing?

DISSON. Looking for something.

DIANA. What?

   WILLY *walks to the door, smiles, closes the door.*

What were you looking for? Get up.

DISSON (*standing*). Don't speak to me like that. How dare you speak to me like that? I'll knock your teeth out.

   She covers her face.

What were you doing in there? I thought you'd gone home. What were you doing in there?

DIANA. I came back.

DISSON. You mean you were in there with both of them? In there with both of them?

DIANA. Yes! So what?

   Pause.

DISSON (*calmly*). I was looking for my pencil, which had rolled

off my desk. Here it is. I found it, just before you came in,
and put it in my pocket. My eyes hurt. I borrowed Wendy's
scarf, to calm my eyes. Why are you getting so excited?

Disson's office. Day.
DISSON *at his desk, writing.* WENDY *walks to the cabinet,*
examines a file. Silence.

DISSON. What kind of flat do you have, Wendy?

WENDY. Quite a small one, Mr Disson. Quite pleasant.

DISSON. Not too big for you, then? Too lonely?

WENDY. Oh no, it's quite small. Quite cosy.

DISSON. Bathroom fittings any good?

WENDY. Adequate, Mr Disson. Not up to our standard.
      Pause.

DISSON. Live there alone, do you?

WENDY. No, I share it with a girl friend. But she's away quite
      a lot of the time. She's an air hostess. She wants me to become
      one, as a matter of fact.

DISSON. Listen to me, Wendy. Don't ever . . . dream of
      becoming an air hostess. Never. The glamour may dazzle
      from afar, but, believe you me, it's a mess of a life . . . a
      mess of a life . . .
      He watches WENDY *walk to her desk with a file and then*
      back to the cabinet.
      Were you lonely as a child?

WENDY. No.

DISSON. Nor was I. I had quite a lot of friends. True friends.
      Most of them live abroad now, of course – banana planters,
      oil engineers, Jamaica, the Persian Gulf . . . but if I were
      to meet them tomorrow, you know . . . just like that . . .
      there'd be no strangeness, no awkwardness at all. We'd
      continue where we left off, quite naturally.
      WENDY *bends low at the cabinet.*
      He stares at her buttocks.

It's a matter of a core of affection, you see . . . a core of undying affection . . .

Suddenly WENDY'S *body appears in enormous close-up. Her buttocks fill the screen.*

His hands go up to keep them at bay.

His elbow knocks a round table lighter from his desk.

Picture normal.

WENDY *turns from the cabinet, stands upright.*

WENDY. What was that?

DISSON. My lighter.

She goes to his desk.

WENDY. Where is it?

She kneels, looks under the desk. The lighter is at his feet. She reaches for it. He kicks it across the room.

(*Laughing.*) Oh, Mr Disson, why did you do that?

She stands. He stands. She goes towards the lighter. He gets to it before her, stands with it at his feet. He looks at her. She stops.

What's this?

DISSON *feints his body, left to right*

DISSON. Come on.

WENDY. What?

DISSON. Tackle me. Get the ball.

WENDY. What do I tackle with?

DISSON. Your feet.

She moves forward deliberately.

He dribbles away, turns, kicks the lighter along the carpet towards her. Her foot stops the lighter. She turns with it at her foot.

Ah!

She stands, legs apart, the lighter between them, staring at him.

She taps her foot.

WENDY. Come on, then!

He goes towards her. She eludes him. He grasps her arm.

That's a foul!

He drops her arm.

DISSON. Sorry.

She stands with the lighter between her feet.

WENDY. Come on, come on. Tackle me, tackle me. Come on, tackle me! Get the ball! Fight for the ball!

He begins to move, stops, sinks to the floor. She goes to him.
What's the matter?

DISSON. Nothing. All right. Nothing.

WENDY. Let me help you up.

DISSON. No. Stay. You're very valuable in this office. Good worker. Excellent. If you have any complaints, just tell me. I'll soon put them right. You're a very efficient secretary. Something I've always needed. Have you everything you want? Are your working conditions satisfactory?

WENDY. Perfectly.

DISSON. Oh good. Good . . . Good.

Disson's house. Bedroom. Night
DISSON *and* DIANA *in bed, reading. She looks at him.*

DIANA. You seem a little subdued . . . lately.

DISSON. Me? Not at all. I'm reading the Life of Napoleon, that's all.

DIANA. No, I don't mean now, I mean generally. Is there – ?

DISSON. I'm not at all subdued. Really.

Pause.

DIANA. It's our first anniversary next Wednesday, did you know that?

DISSON. Of course I did. How could I forget? We'll go out together in the evening. Just you and I. Alone.

DIANA. Oh. Good.

DISSON. I'm also giving a little tea party in the office, in the afternoon. My mother and father'll be up.

DIANA. Oh good.

Pause.

DISSON. How have you enjoyed our first year?

DIANA. It's been wonderful. It's been a very exciting year.

Pause.

DISSON. You've been marvellous with the boys.

DIANA. They like me.

DISSON. Yes, they do. They do.

Pause.

It's been a great boon, to have you work for the firm.

DIANA. Oh, I'm glad. I am glad.

Pause.

Be nice to get away to Spain.

Pause.

DISSON. You've got enough money, haven't you? I mean, you have sufficient money to see you through, for all you want?

DIANA. Oh yes. I have, thank you.

Pause.

DISSON. I'm very proud of you, you know.

DIANA. I'm proud of you.

Silence.

Disson's office.

DISSON. Have you written to Corley?

WENDY. Yes, Mr Disson.

DISSON. And Turnbull?

WENDY. Yes, Mr Disson.

DISSON. And Erverley?

WENDY. Yes, Mr Disson.

DISSON. Carbon of the Erverley letter, please.

WENDY. Here you are, Mr Disson.

DISSON. Ah. I see you've spelt Erverley right.

WENDY. Right?

DISSON. People tend, very easily, to leave out the first R and call him Everley. You haven't done that.

WENDY. No. (*She turns.*)

DISSON. Just a minute. How did you spell Turnbull? You needn't show me. Tell me.

WENDY. TURNBULL.

DISSON. Quite correct.

> *Pause.*

> Quite correct. Now what about – ?

> *The screen goes black.*

> Where are you?

> *Pause.*

> I can't see you.

WENDY. I'm here, Mr Disson.

DISSON. Where?

WENDY. You're looking at me, Mr Disson.

DISSON. You mean my eyes are open?

> *Pause.*

WENDY. I'm where I was. I haven't moved.

DISSON. Are my eyes open?

WENDY. Mr Disson, really . . .

DISSON. Is this you? This I feel?

WENDY. Yes.

DISSON. What, all this I can feel?

WENDY. You're playing one of your games, Mr Disson. You're being naughty again.

> *Vision back.*

> DISSON *looks at her.*

> You sly old thing.

Disley's surgery.

A torch shines in DISSON'S *eyes, first right, then left. Torch out.*
Light on.

DISLEY. There's nothing wrong with them.

DISSON. What then?

DISLEY. I only deal with eyes, old chap. Why do you come to me? Why don't you go to someone else?

DISSON. Because it's my eyes that are affected.

DISLEY. Look. Why don't you go to someone else?

> DISLEY *begins to clear away his instruments.*

Nothing worrying you, is there?

DISSON. Of course not. I've got everything I want.

DISLEY. Getting a holiday soon?

DISSON. Going to Spain.

DISLEY. Lucky man.

> *Pause.*

DISSON. Look. Listen. You're my oldest friend. You were going to be the best man at my wedding.

DISLEY. That's right.

DISSON. You wrote a wonderful speech in my honour.

DISLEY. Yes.

DISSON. But you were ill. You had to opt out.

DISLEY. That's right.

> *Pause.*

DISSON. Help me.

> *Pause.*

DISLEY. Who made the speech? Your brother-in-law, wasn't it?

DISSON. I don't want you to think I'm not a happy man. I am.

DISLEY. What sort of speech did he make?

Disson's house. Sitting-room. Evening.

DISSON. Tell me about Sunderley.

WILLY. Sunderley?

DISSON. Tell me about the place where you two were born. Where you played at being brother and sister.

WILLY. We didn't have to play at being brother and sister. We were brother and sister.

DIANA. Stop drinking.

DISSON. Drinking? You call this drinking? This? I used to down eleven or nine pints a night! Eleven or nine pints! Every night of the stinking week! Me and the boys! The boys! And me! I'd break any man's hand for . . . for playing me false. That was before I became a skilled craftsman. That was before . . .

He falls silent, sits.

WILLY. Sunderley was beautiful.

DISSON. I know.

WILLY. And now it's gone, for ever.

DISSON. I never got there.

DISSON stands, goes to get a drink.

He turns from drinks table.

What are you whispering about? Do you think I don't hear? Think I don't see? I've got my memories, too. Long before this.

WILLY. Yes, Sunderley was beautiful.

DISSON. The lake.

WILLY. The lake.

DISSON. The long windows.

WILLY. From the withdrawing-room.

DISSON. On to the terrace.

WILLY. Music playing.

DISSON. On the piano.

WILLY. The summer nights. The wild swans.

DISSON. What swans? What bloody swans?

WILLY. The owls.

DISSON. Negroes at the gate, under the trees.

WILLY. No Negroes.

DISSON. Why not?

WILLY. We had no Negroes.

DISSON. Why in God's name not?

WILLY. Just one of those family quirks, Robert.

DIANA (*standing*). Robert.

Pause.

Come to bed.

DISSON. You can say that, in front of him?

DIANA. Please.

DISSON. In front of *him*?

He goes to her.

Why did you marry me?

DIANA. I admired you. You were so positive.

DISSON. You loved me.

DIANA. You were kind.

DISSON. You loved me for that?

DIANA. I found you admirable in your clarity of mind, your surety of purpose, your will, the strength your achievements had given you –

DISSON. And you adored me for it?

WILLY (*to* DISSON). Can I have a private word with you?

DISSON. You *adored* me for it?

Pause.

DIANA. You know I did.

WILLY. Can I have a private word with you, old chap? (*To* DIANA.) Please.

DIANA *goes out of the room.*

DISSON *looks at* WILLY.

DISSON. Mind how you tread, Bill. Mind . . . how you tread, old Bill, old boy, old Bill.

WILLY. Listen. I've been wondering. Is there anything on your mind?

DISSON. My mind? No, of course not.

WILLY. You're not dissatisfied with my work, or anything?

DISSON. Quite the contrary. Absolutely the contrary.

WILLY. Oh good. I like the work very much. Try to do my best.

DISSON. Listen. I want you to be my partner. Hear me? I want you to share full responsibility . . . with me.

WILLY. Do you really?

DISSON. Certainly.

WILLY. Well, thank you very much. I don't know what to say.

DISSON. Don't say anything.

Disson's office.

WILLY *at the door.*

WILLY. Coming, old chap?

DISSON. Yes.

WILLY (*to* WENDY). Important lunch, this. But I think we'll swing it, don't you, Robert? (*To* WENDY.) Great prospects in store.

> DISSON *and* WILLY *go out.* WENDY *clips some papers together.*

> DIANA *comes in through the inner door.*

WENDY. Oh, hullo, Mrs Disson.

DIANA. Hullo, Wendy.

> *Pause.*

> DIANA *watches* WENDY *clip the papers.*

Do you like being a secretary?

WENDY. I do, yes. Do you?

DIANA. I do, yes.

> *Pause.*

I understand your last employer touched your body . . . rather too much.

WENDY. It wasn't a question of too much, Mrs Disson. One touch was enough for me.

DIANA. Oh, you left after the first touch?

WENDY. Well, not quite the first, no.

> *Pause.*

DIANA. Have you ever asked yourself why men will persist in touching women?

WENDY. No, I've never asked myself that, Mrs Disson.

DIANA. Few women do ask themselves that question.

WENDY. Don't they? I don't know. I've never spoken to any other women on the subject.

DIANA. You're speaking to me.

WENDY. Yes. Well, have you ever asked yourself that question, Mrs Disson?

DIANA. Never. No.

Pause.

Have lunch with me today. Tell me about yourself.

WENDY. I'll have lunch with you with pleasure.

DISSON *comes in. They look at him. He at them. Silence.*

DISSON. Forgotten . . . one of the designs.

DIANA *smiles at him.* WENDY *clips her papers. He goes to his desk, collects a folder, stands upright.*

DIANA *looks out of the window.* WENDY *clips papers. He looks at them, goes out.* DIANA *and* WENDY *remain silent.*

Disson's house. Games room.

DISSON *and* WILLY *playing ping-pong. They are in the middle of a long rally.* THE TWINS *watch.* WILLY *is on the attack,* DISSON *playing desperately, retrieving from positions of great difficulty. He cuts, chops, pushes.*

TWINS (*variously*). Well done, Dad. Good shot, Dad. Good one, Dad.

WILLY *forces* DISSON *on to the forehand. He slams viciously.* DISSON *skids.*

The screen goes black.

Good shot!

DISSON. Aaah!

Vision back.

DISSON *is clutching the table, bent over it.*

WILLY *throws the ball on to the table.*

It bounces gently across it.

Disson's house. Sitting-room. Evening.

DISSON'S *parents.*

MOTHER. Have I seen that mirror before?

DISSON. No. It's new.

MOTHER. I knew I hadn't seen it. Look at it, John. What a beautiful mirror.

FATHER. Must have cost you a few bob.

MOTHER. Can you see the work on it, John? I bet it must be a few years old, that mirror.

DISSON. It's a few hundred years old.

FATHER. I bet it must have cost you a few bob.

DISSON. It wasn't cheap.

FATHER. Cheap?

MOTHER. What a beautiful mirror.

FATHER. Cheap? Did you hear what he said, Dora? He said it wasn't cheap!

MOTHER. No, I bet it wasn't.

FATHER (*laughing*). Cheap!

> *Pause.*

MOTHER. Mrs Tidy sends you her love.

DISSON. Who?

FATHER. Mrs Tidy. The Tidys.

DISSON. Oh yes. How are they?

FATHER. Still very tidy. (*Laughs.*) Aren't they, Dora?

MOTHER. You remember the Tidys.

DISSON. Of course I remember them.

> *Pause.*

How have you been keeping, then?

FATHER. Oh, your mother's had a few pains. You know, just a few.

MOTHER. Only a few, John. I haven't had many pains.

FATHER. I only said you'd had a few. Not many.

> *Pause.*

MOTHER. Are the boys looking forward to their holiday?

DISSON. Yes, they are.

FATHER. When are you going?

DISSON. I'm not.

Disson's office.

DISSON. Tighter.

> WENDY *ties the chiffon round his eyes.*

WENDY. There. You look nice.

DISSON. This chiffon stinks.

WENDY. Oh, I do apologize. What of?

> *Pause.*

You're very rude to me. But you do look nice. You really do.

> DISSON *tears the chiffon off.*

DISSON. It's useless. Ring Disley. Tell him to come here.

WENDY. But he'll be here at four o'clock, for your tea party.

DISSON. I want him now! I want him . . . now.

WENDY. Don't you like my chiffon any more, to put round your eyes? My lovely chiffon?

> *Pause.*
>
> *He sits still.*

I always feel like kissing you when you've got that on round your eyes. Do you know that? Because you're all in the dark.

> *Pause.*

Put it on.

> *She picks up the chiffon and folds it.*

I'll put it on . . . for you. Very gently.

> *She leans forward.*
>
> *He touches her.*

No – you mustn't touch me, if you're not wearing your chiffon.

> *She places the chiffon on his eyes.*
>
> *He trembles, puts his hand to the chiffon, slowly lowers it, lets it fall.*
>
> *It flutters to the floor.*
>
> *As she looks at him, he reaches for the telephone.*

Disson's office.

DISSON *in the same position.*

DISSON. I need a tight bandage. Very tight.

DISLEY. Anyone could do that for you.

DISSON. No. You're my eye consultant. You must do it for me.

DISLEY. All right.

> *He takes a bandage from his case and ties it round* DISSON'S *eyes.*

Just for half an hour. You don't want it on when your guests arrive, do you?

> DISLEY *ties the knots.*

This'll keep you in the dark, all right. Also lend pressure to your temples. Is that what you want?

DISSON. That's it. That's what I want.

> DISLEY *cuts the strands.*

DISLEY. There. How's that?

> *Pause.*

See anything?

Disson's office. Afternoon.

DISSON *sits alone, the bandage round his eyes.*

Silence.

WILLY *enters from his office. He sees* DISSON *and goes to him.*

WILLY. How are you, old chap? Bandage on straight? Knots tight?

> *He pats him on the back and goes out through the front office door.*
>
> *The door slams.*
>
> DISSON *sits still.*

Corridor.

MR *and* MRS DISLEY *approaching the office.*

LOIS. Why didn't he make it a cocktail party? Why a tea party, of all things?

DISLEY. I couldn't say.

Office.
DISSON'S *head.*
Soft clicks of door opening and closing, muffled steps, an odd cough, slight rattle of teacups.

Corridor.
DISSON'S *parents approaching the office.*
MOTHER. I could do with a cup of tea, couldn't you, John?

Office.
DISSON'S *head.*
Soft clicks of door opening and closing, muffled steps, an odd cough, slight rattle of teacups.

Corridor.
THE TWINS *approach, silent.*

Office.
DISSON'S *head.*
Soft clicks of door opening and closing, muffled steps, an odd cough, slight rattle of teacups, a short whisper.

Corridor.
DIANA *and* WILLY *approach.*
DIANA. Why *don't* you come to Spain with us?

WILLY. I think I will.

Office.
DISSON'S *head.*
*Soft clicks of door opening and closing, muffled steps, an odd cough,
slight rattle of teacups, whispers.*

Corridor.
WENDY *approaches.*

Office.
DISSON'S *head.*
*Soft clicks of door opening and closing, muffled steps, an odd cough,
slight rattle of teacups, whispers.*

Office.
A buffet table has been set out. Two ELDERLY LADIES *serve
tea, sandwiches, bridge rolls, buns and cakes. The gathering is
grouped around the table in silence.* DISLEY *whispers to them.*
DISLEY. His eyes are a little strained, that's all. Just resting
    them. Don't mention it. It'll embarrass him. It's quite all
    right.
        They all take their tea, choose edibles, and relax.
JOHN (*choosing a cake*). These are good.
TOM. What are they?
DIANA (*choosing a bridge roll*). These look nice.
LOIS. You look wonderful, Mrs Disson. Absolutely wonderful.
    Doesn't she, Peter?
DISLEY. Marvellous.
LOIS. What do you think of your grandsons?
FATHER. They've grown up now, haven't they?

LOIS. Of course, we knew them when they were that high, didn't we, Tom?

FATHER. So did we.

TOM. Yes.

WILLY. Big lads now, aren't they, these two?

JOHN. Cake, Granny?

MOTHER. No, I've had one.

JOHN. Have two.

FATHER. I'll have one.

MOTHER. He's had one.

FATHER. I'll have two.

WENDY *takes a cup of tea to* DISSON *and puts it into his hands.*

WENDY. Here's a cup of tea, Mr Disson. Drink it. It's warm.

LOIS (*to* DIANA). You're off to Spain quite soon, aren't you, Diana?

DIANA. Yes, quite soon.

DISLEY (*calling*). We'll take off those bandages in a minute, old chap!

LOIS. Spain is wonderful at this time of the year.

WILLY. Any time of the year, really.

LOIS. But I think it's best at this time of the year, don't you?

DIANA. What sun lotion do you use, Lois?

DISSON'S *point of view.*

No dialogue is heard in all shots from DISSON'S *point of view. Silence.*

Figures mouthing silently, in conspiratorial postures, seemingly whispering together.

Shot including DISSON.

TOM. I went into goal yesterday.

WILLY. How did you do?

LOIS. You can get it anywhere. It's perfect.

JOHN. He made two terrific saves.

TOM. The first was a fluke.

LOIS. How do you sun, then?

DIANA. I have to be rather careful.

TOM. Second save wasn't a bad save.

LOIS. How do you sun, Wendy?

WENDY. Oh not too bad, really.

LOIS (*to* MRS DISSON). We go to our little island every year and when we go we have to leave our poor little Siamese with my mother.

MOTHER. Do you really?

LOIS. They're almost human, aren't they, Siamese?

DIANA. I'm sure my Siamese was.

LOIS. Aren't they, Peter, almost human?

DIANA. Wasn't Tiger a human cat, Willy, at Sunderley?

WILLY. He adored you.

DISLEY. They really are almost human, aren't they, Siamese?

DISSON'S *point of view.*
Silence.
The party splits into groups. Each group whispering.
The two ELDERLY LADIES *at the buffet table.*
DISSON'S PARENTS, *sitting together.*
THE TWINS *and the* DISLEYS.
WILLY, WENDY *and* DIANA *in a corner.*

Shot including DISSON.
The gathering in a close group, the PARENTS *sitting.*

LOIS. I'd go like a shot.

WENDY. What, me? Come to Spain?

DIANA. Yes, why not?

    WILLY *leans across* DISLEY.

WILLY. Yes, of course you must come. Of course you must come.

WENDY. How wonderful.

DISSON'S *point of view.*
WILLY *approaches* DISSON. *With a smile, he takes a ping-pong ball from his pocket, and puts it into* DISSON'S *hand.*
DISSON *clutches it.*

DISSON'S *point of view.*
WILLY *returns to* WENDY *and* DIANA, *whispers to them.*
DIANA *laughs (silently), head thrown back, gasps with laughter.*
WENDY *smiles.*
WILLY *puts one arm round* WENDY, *the other round* DIANA.
He leads them to WENDY'S *desk.*
WILLY *places cushions on the desk.*
DIANA *and* WENDY, *giggling silently, hoist themselves up on to the desk. They lie head to toe.*

DISSON'S *point of view. Close-up.*
WENDY'S *face.* WILLY'S *fingers caressing it.* DIANA'S *shoes in background.*

DISSON'S *point of view. Close-up.*
DIANA'S *face.* WILLY'S *fingers caressing it.* WENDY'S *shoes in background.*

DISSON'S *point of view.*
LOIS *powdering her nose.*

DISSON'S *point of view.*
The ELDERLY LADIES *drinking tea, at the table.*

DISSON'S *point of view.*
DISLEY *talking to the boys by the window.* THE TWINS *listening intently.*

DISSON'S *point of view.*
DISSON'S PARENTS *sitting, dozing.*

DISSON'S *point of view.*
The base of WENDY'S *desk.*
A shoe drops to the floor.

Shot including DISSON.
DISSON *falls to the floor in his chair with a crack. His teacup drops and spills.*
The gathering is grouped by the table, turns.
DISLEY *and* WILLY *go to him.*
They try to lift him from the chair, are unable to do so.
DISLEY *cuts the bandage and takes it off.*
DISSON'S *eyes are open.*
DISLEY *feels his pulse.*
DISLEY. He's all right. Get him up.

> DISLEY *and* WILLY *try to pull him up from the chair, are unable to do so.*
>
> JOHN *and* TOM *join them.*

Get it up.

The four of them, with great effort, manage to set the chair on its feet.

DISSON *is still seated.*

He must lie down. Now, two hold the chair, and two pull him.

> JOHN *and* WILLY *hold the chair.*
> DISLEY *and* TOM *pull.*

The chair.
The chair scrapes, moves no farther.

The group around the chair.
They pull, with great effort.

The chair.
The chair scrapes, moves no farther.

The room.
WILLY. Anyone would think he was chained to it!
DISLEY (*pulling*). Come out!
MOTHER. Bobbie!

> *They stop pulling.*
> DISSON *in the chair, still, his eyes open.*
> DIANA *comes to him.*
> *She kneels by him.*

DIANA. This is . . . Diana.

> *Pause.*

Can you hear me?

> *Pause.*

Can he see me?

> *Pause.*

Robert.
Pause.
Can you hear me?
Pause.
Robert, can you see me?
Pause.
It's me. It's me, darling.
Slight pause.
It's your wife.

DISSON'S *face in close-up.*
DISSON'S *eyes. Open.*

The Basement

THE BASEMENT was first presented by B.B.C. Television on 20 February 1967 with the following cast:

STOTT	Harold Pinter
JANE	Kika Markham
LAW	Derek Godfrey

Directed by Charles Jarrott

A stage version of THE BASEMENT, in double-bill with TEA PARTY, opened at the Duchess Theatre, London, on 17 September 1970, directed by James Hammerstein and produced by Eddie Kulukundis for Knightsbridge Theatrical Productions Ltd, with the following cast:

LAW	Donald Pleasence
STOTT	Barry Foster
JANE	Stephanie Beacham

Exterior. Front area of a basement flat.
Winter. Night.
Rain falling.
Short stone flight of steps from street.
Light shining through the basement door.
The upper part of the house is dark.
The back of a man, STOTT. *He stands in the centre of the area,*
looking towards the door.
He wears a raincoat, his head is bare.

Exterior. Front area.
STOTT'S *face. Behind him, by the wall, a girl,* JANE. *She is*
huddled by the wall. She wears a rainhat, clasps her raincoat to
her.

Interior. Room.
The room is large and long. A window at one end looks out to a
small concrete yard. There are doors to bathroom and kitchen.
The room is comfortable, relaxed, heavily furnished.
Numerous side tables, plants, arm-chairs, book-cabinets, book-
shelves, velvet cloths, a desk, paintings, a large double bed. There
is a large fire in the grate.
The room is lit by a number of table and standard lamps.
LAW *is lying low in an arm-chair, reading, by the fireside.*
Silence.

Exterior. Front area.
STOTT *still.*

Interior. Room.
LAW *in arm-chair. He is smiling at his book.*
He giggles. He is reading a Persian love manual, with illustrations.

Exterior. Front area.
JANE *huddled by the wall.*
STOTT *moves to the door.*

Interior. Room.
Doorbell. LAW *looks up from his book. He closes it, puts it on a side table, goes into the hall.*

Interior. Small hall.
LAW *approaches the front door. He opens it.*
Silence.
He stares at STOTT. *From his position in the doorway* LAW *cannot see the girl.*
LAW (*with great pleasure*). Stott!
STOTT (*smiling*). Hullo, Tim.
LAW. Good God. Come in!
    LAW *laughs.*
  Come in!
    STOTT *enters.*
  I can't believe it!

Interior. Room.
LAW *and* STOTT *enter.*
LAW. Give me your coat. You're soaking. Come on. That's it. I'm absolutely flabbergasted. You must be freezing.
STOTT. I am a bit.
LAW. Go on, warm yourself. Warm yourself by the fire.

STOTT. Thanks.

LAW. Sit down by the fire. Go on.

> STOTT *moves to the fire.*
> LAW *takes the coat into hall.*

Interior. Hall.

LAW *comes into the hall, shaking the raincoat. He looks inside it, at the label, smiles. He hangs it on a hook.*

Interior. Room.

STOTT *warming his hands at the fire.* LAW *comes in.*

LAW. You haven't changed at all. You haven't changed . . . at all!

> STOTT *laughs.*

You've got a new raincoat though. Oh yes, I noticed. Hold on, I'll get you a towel.

> LAW *goes to the bathroom.*
> STOTT, *alone, looks up and about him at the room.*

Interior. Room.
The room.

Interior. Bathroom.

LAW *in bathroom, at the airing cupboard. He swiftly throws aside a number of towels, chooses a soft one with a floral pattern.*

Interior. Room.

LAW *comes in with a towel.*

LAW. Here's a towel. Go on, give it a good wipe. That's it.

You didn't walk here, did you? You're soaking. What happened to your car? You could have driven here. Why didn't
you give me a ring? But how did you know my address?
My God, it's years. If you'd have rung I would have picked
you up. I would have picked you up in my car. What
happened to your car?

> STOTT *finishes drying his hair, puts the towel on the arm of
> a chair.*

STOTT. I got rid of it.

LAW. But how are you? Are you well? You look well.

STOTT. How are you?

LAW. Oh, I'm well. Just a minute, I'll get you some slippers.

> LAW *goes to the cupboard, bends.*

You're going to stay the night, aren't you? You'll have to,
look at the time. I wondered if you'd ever turn up again.
Really. For years. Here you are. Here's some slippers.

STOTT. Thanks.

> STOTT *takes the slippers, changes his shoes.*

LAW. I'll find some pyjamas in a minute. Still, we'll have a
cup of coffee first, or some . . . Or a drink? What about
a drink?

STOTT. Ah.

> LAW *pours drinks, brings the drinks to the sofa and sits
> down by* STOTT.

LAW. You're not living at Chatsworth Road any more, are
you? I know that. I've passed by there, numbers of times.
You've moved. Where are you living now?

STOTT. I'm looking for a place.

LAW. Stay here! Stay here as long as you like. I've got another
bed I can fit up. I've got a camp bed I can fit up.

STOTT. I don't want to impose upon you.

LAW. Not a bit, not a bit.

> *Pause.*

STOTT. Oh, by the way, I've got a friend outside. Can she
come in?

LAW. A friend?

STOTT. Outside.

LAW. A friend? Outside?

STOTT. Can she come in?

LAW. Come in? Yes . . . yes . . . of course . . .

> STOTT *goes towards the door.*

What's she doing outside?

Exterior. Front door.
JANE *is standing in the narrow porch outside the door.*
The door opens.

Interior. Room.
LAW. STOTT *brings the girl in.*

STOTT. This is Jane. This is Tim Law.

> *She smiles.*

JANE. It's kind of you.

LAW. How do you do? I . . . must get you a towel.

JANE. No, thank you. My hair was covered.

LAW. But your face?

> STOTT *comes forward.*

STOTT. It's very kind of you, Tim. It really is. Here's a towel.
(*He gives it to her.*) Here.

LAW. But that's your towel.

JANE. I don't mind, really.

LAW. I have clean ones, dry ones.

JANE (*patting her face*). This is clean.

LAW. But it's not dry.

JANE. It's very soft.

LAW. I have others.

JANE. There. I'm dry.

LAW. You can't be.

JANE. What a splendid room.

STOTT. Isn't it? A little bright, perhaps.

LAW. Too much light?

> STOTT *turns a lamp off.*

STOTT. Do you mind?

LAW. No.

> JANE *begins to take her clothes off.*
> *In the background* STOTT *moves about the room, turning off the lamps.*
> LAW *stands still.*
> STOTT *turns off all the lamps but one, by the fireside.*
> JANE, *naked, gets into the bed.*

Can I get you some cocoa? Some hot chocolate?

> STOTT *takes his clothes off and, naked, gets into the bed.*

I was feeling quite lonely, actually. It is lonely sitting here, night after night. Mind you, I'm very happy here. Remember that place we shared? That awful place in Chatsworth Road? I've come a long way since then. I bought this flat cash down. It's mine. I don't suppose you've noticed the hi-fi stereo? There's all sorts of things I can show you.

> LAW *unbuttons his cardigan.*
> *He places it over the one lit lamp, so shading the light. He sits by the fire.*

The lamp covered by the cardigan.

Patch of light on the ceiling.

Patch of light at LAW'S *feet.*

LAW'S *hands on the chair arms.*
A gasp from JANE.
LAW'S *hands do not move.*

LAW'S *legs. Beyond them, the fire almost dead.*

LAW *puts on his glasses.*

LAW *reaches for* The Persian Manual of Love.

LAW *peers to read.*
A long sigh from JANE.
LAW *reads.*

Exterior. Cliff-top. Day. Summer.
Long-shot of STOTT *standing on a cliff-top.*

Exterior. Beach.
The beach is long and deserted. LAW *and* JANE, *in swimming*
costumes. JANE *building a sandcastle.* LAW *watches her.*
LAW. How old are you?
JANE. I'm very young.
LAW. You are young.
　　He watches her work.
　You're a child.
　　He watches her.
　Have you known him long?
JANE. No.
LAW. I have. Charming man. Man of great gifts. Very old
　friend of mine, as a matter of fact. Has he told you?
JANE. No.
LAW. You don't know him very well?

JANE. No.

LAW. He has a connexion with the French aristocracy. He was educated in France. Speaks French fluently, of course. Have you read his French translations?

JANE. No.

LAW. Ah. They're immaculate. Great distinction. Formidable scholar, Stott. Do you know what he got at Oxford? He got a First in Sanskrit at Oxford. A First in Sanskrit!

JANE. How wonderful.

LAW. You never knew?

JANE. Never.

LAW. I know for a fact he owns three chateâux. Three superb châteaux. Have you ever ridden in his Alvis? His Facel Vega? What an immaculate driver. Have you seen his yachts? Huh! What yachts. What yachts.

> JANE *completes her sandcastle.*

How pleased I was to see him. After so long. One loses touch . . . so easily.

Interior. Cave. Day.
STOTT'S *body lying in the sand, asleep.*
LAW *and* JANE *appear at the mouth of the cave. They arrive at the body, look down.*
LAW. What repose he has.
STOTT'S *body in the sand.*
Their shadows across him.

Interior. Room. Night.
LAW *lying on the floor, a cushion at his head, covered by a blanket. His eyes are closed.*
Silence.
A long gasp from JANE.
LAW'S *eyes open.*

STOTT *and* JANE *in bed.*
STOTT *turning to wall.*
JANE *turns to the edge of the bed.*
She leans over the edge of the bed and smiles at LAW.

LAW *looks at her.*

JANE *smiles.*

Interior. Room. Day.
STOTT *lifts a painting from the wall, looks at it.*
STOTT. No.
LAW. No, you're quite right. I've never liked it.
> STOTT *walks across room to a second picture, looks at it. He turns to look at* LAW.
No.
> STOTT *takes it down and turns to look at the other paintings.*
All of them. All of them. You're right. They're terrible. Take them down.
> *The paintings are all similar watercolours.*
> STOTT *begins to take them from the walls.*

Interior. Kitchen. Day.
JANE *in the kitchen, cooking at the stove, humming.*

Exterior. Backyard. Winter. Day.
The yard is surrounded by high blank walls.

STOTT *and* LAW *sitting at an iron table, with a pole for an* *umbrella.*
They are drinking lager.

LAW. Who is she? Where did you meet her?

STOTT. She's charming, isn't she?

LAW. Charming. A little young.

STOTT. She comes from a rather splendid family, actually.

LAW. Really?

STOTT. Rather splendid.

> *Pause.*

LAW. Very helpful, of course, around the house.

STOTT. Plays the harp, you know.

LAW. Well?

STOTT. Remarkably well.

LAW. What a pity I don't possess one. You don't possess a
harp, do you?

STOTT. Of course I possess a harp.

LAW. A recent acquisition?

STOTT. No, I've had it for years.

> *Pause.*

LAW. You don't find she's lacking in maturity?

Exterior. Beach. Summer. Day.
LAW *and* JANE *lying in the sand.* JANE *caressing him.*

JANE (*whispering*). Yes, yes, yes, oh you are, oh you are, oh
you are . . .

LAW. We can be seen.

JANE. Why do you resist? How can you resist?

LAW. We can be seen! Damn you!

Exterior. Backyard. Winter. Day.
STOTT *and* LAW *at the table with lager.*
JANE *comes to the back door.*

JANE. Lunch is up!

Interior. Hall. Day.
LAW *and* JANE *come in at the front door with towels over their shoulders.*

Interior. Room. Day. Summer.
LAW *and* JANE *at the entrance of the room, towels over their shoulders, staring at the room.*
The room is unrecognizable. The furnishing has changed. There are Scandinavian tables and desks. Large bowls of Swedish glass. Tubular chairs. An Indian rug. Parquet floors, shining. A new hi-fi cabinet, etc. Fireplace blocked. The bed is the same.
STOTT *is at the window, closing the curtains. He turns.*
STOTT. Have a good swim?

Interior. Room. Night. Winter. (Second furnishing.)
STOTT *and* JANE *in bed, smoking.* LAW *sitting.*
STOTT. Let's have some music. We haven't heard your hi-fi for ages. Let's hear your stereo. What are you going to play?

Interior. Bar. Evening.
Large empty bar. All the tables unoccupied.
STOTT, LAW *and* JANE *at one table.*
STOTT. This was one of our old haunts, wasn't it, Tim? This was one of our haunts. Tim was always my greatest friend, you know. Always. It's marvellous. I've found my old friend again –
  Looking at JANE.
And discovered a new. And you like each other so much. It's really very warming.
LAW. Same again? (*To* WAITER.) Same again. (*To* JANE.)

Same again? (*To* WAITER.) Same again. The same again, all round. Exactly the same.

STOTT. I'll change to Campari.

LAW (*clicking his fingers at the* WAITER). One Campari here. Otherwise the same again.

STOTT. Remember those nights reading Proust? Remember them?

LAW (*to* JANE). In the original.

STOTT. The bouts with Laforgue? What bouts.

LAW. I remember.

STOTT. The great elms they had then. The great elm trees.

LAW. And the poplars.

STOTT. The cricket. The squash courts. You were pretty hot stuff at squash, you know.

LAW. You were unbeatable.

STOTT. Your style was deceptive.

LAW. It still is.

> LAW *laughs.*

It still is!

STOTT. Not any longer.

> *The* WAITER *serves the drinks.*
> *Silence.* STOTT *lifts his glass.*

Yes, I really am a happy man.

Exterior. Field. Evening. Winter.
STOTT *and* LAW. JANE *one hundred yards across the field.*
She holds a scarf.

LAW (*shouting*). Hold the scarf up. When you drop it, we run.

> *She holds the scarf up.*
> LAW *rubs his hands.* STOTT *looks at him.*

STOTT. Are you quite sure you want to do this?

LAW. Of course I'm sure.

JANE. On your marks!

> STOTT *and* LAW *get on their marks.*

Get set!
> *They get set.*
> JANE *drops scarf.*

Go!
> LAW *runs.* STOTT *stays still.*
> LAW, *going fast, turns to look for* STOTT; *off balance, stumbles, falls, hits his chin on the ground.*
> *Lying flat, he looks back at* STOTT.

LAW. Why didn't you run?

Exterior. Field.
JANE *stands, scarf in her hand. Downfield,* STOTT *stands.*
LAW *lies on the grass.* LAW'S *voice:*
LAW. Why didn't you run?

Interior. Room. Night. Winter. (Second furnishing.)
STOTT. Let's have some music. We haven't heard your hi-fi for ages.
> STOTT *opens the curtains and the window.*
> *Moonlight.* LAW *and* JANE *sit in chairs, clench their bodies with cold.*

Exterior. Backyard. Day. Winter.
STOTT *walking.* LAW, *wearing a heavy overcoat, collar turned up, watching him.* LAW *approaches him.*
LAW. Listen. Listen. I must speak to you. I must speak frankly. Listen. Don't you think it's a bit crowded in that flat, for the three of us?
STOTT. No, no. Not at all.
LAW. Listen, listen. Stop walking. Stop walking. Please. Wait.
> STOTT *stops.*

Listen. Wouldn't you say that the flat is a little small, for three people?

STOTT (*patting his shoulder*). No, no. Not at all.

    STOTT *continues walking.*

LAW (*following him*). To look at it another way, to look at it another way, I can assure you that the Council would object strenuously to three people living in these conditions. The Town Council, I know for a fact, would feel it incumbent upon itself to register the strongest possible objections. And so would the Church.

    STOTT *stops walking, looks at him.*

STOTT. Not at all. Not at all.

Interior. Room. Day. Summer.

The curtains are closed. The three at lunch, at the table. STOTT *and* JANE *are wearing tropical clothes.* JANE *is sitting on* STOTT'S *lap.*

LAW. Why don't we open the curtains?

    STOTT *eats a grape.*

It's terribly close. Shall I open the window?

STOTT. What are you going to play? Debussy, I hope.

    LAW *goes to the record cabinet. He examines record after record, feverishly, flings them one after the other at the wall.*

STOTT. Where's Debussy?

    STOTT *kisses* JANE.

    Another record hits the wall.

Where's Debussy? That's what we want. That's what we need. That's what we need at the moment.

    JANE *breaks away from* STOTT *and goes out into the yard.*

    STOTT *sits still.*

LAW. I've found it!

Interior. Room. Night. Winter.

LAW *turns with the record.*

The room is furnished as at the beginning.
STOTT *and* JANE, *naked, climb into bed.*
LAW *puts the record down and places his cardigan over the one lit lamp.*
He sits, picks up the poker and pokes the dying fire.

Exterior. Backyard. Day. Summer.
JANE *sitting at the iron table.*
STOTT *approaches her with a glass and bottle.*
He pours wine into the glass.
He bends over her, attempts to touch her breast.
She moves her body away from him.
STOTT *remains still.*

LAW *watches from the open windows.*
He moves to the table with the record and smiles at STOTT.
LAW. I've found the record. The music you wanted.

> STOTT *slams his glass on the table and goes into the room.*
> LAW *sits at the table, drinks from the bottle, regards* JANE.
> JANE *plays with a curl in her hair.*

Interior. Cave by the sea. Evening. Summer.
LAW *and* JANE. *He lying, she sitting, by him.*
She bends and whispers to him.
JANE. Why don't you tell him to go? We had such a lovely home. We had such a cosy home. It was so warm. Tell him to go. It's your place. Then we could be happy again. Like we used to. Like we used to. In our first blush of love. Then we could be happy again, like we used to. We could be happy again. Like we used to.

Exterior. Backyard. Night. Winter.
The yard is icy. The window is open. The room is lit.
LAW *is whispering to* STOTT *at the window. In the background* JANE *sits sewing.* (*Second furnishing.*)

Exterior. Backyard. Window.
LAW *and* STOTT *at the open window,* STOTT'S *body hunched.*
LAW (*whispering very deliberately*). She betrays you. She betrays you. She has no loyalty. After all you've done for her. Shown her the world. Given her faith. You've been deluded. She's a savage. A viper. She sullies this room. She dirties this room. All this beautiful furniture. This beautiful Scandinavian furniture. She dirties it. She sullies the room.
     STOTT *turns slowly to regard* JANE.

Interior. Room. Day.
The curtains are closed.
STOTT *in bed.* JANE *bending over him, touching his head.*
She looks across at LAW.
Silence. (*Second furnishing.*)
LAW. Is he breathing?
JANE. Just.
LAW. His last, do you think?
     Pause.
   Do you think it could be his last?
JANE. It could be.
LAW. How could it have happened? He seemed so fit. He was fit. As fit as a fiddle. Perhaps we should have called a doctor. And now he's dying. Are you heartbroken?
JANE. Yes.
LAW. So am I.
     Pause.
JANE. What shall we do with the body?

LAW. Body? He's not dead yet. Perhaps he'll recover.
    They stare at each other.

Interior. Room. Night.
LAW *and* JANE *in a corner, snuffling each other like animals.*

Interior. Room. Night.
STOTT *at the window. He opens the curtains. Moonlight pierces
the room. He looks round.*

Interior. Room. Night.
LAW *and* JANE *in a corner, looking up at the window, blinking.*

Interior. Room. Day.
STOTT *at the window, closing the curtains. He turns into the room.
The room is unrecognizable. The walls are hung with tapestries,
an oval Florentine mirror, an oblong Italian Master. The floor
is marble tiles. There are marble pillars with hanging plants,
carved golden chairs, a rich carpet along the room's centre.*
STOTT *sits in a chair.* JANE *comes forward with a bowl of fruit.*
STOTT *chooses a grape. In the background* LAW, *in a corner,
playing the flute.* STOTT *bites into the grape, tosses the bowl of
fruit across the room. The fruit scatters.* JANE *rushes to collect it.*
STOTT *picks up a tray containing large marbles.*
He rolls the tray. The marbles knock against each other.
He selects a marble. He looks across the room at LAW *playing
the flute.*

LAW *with flute.*
At the other end of the room STOTT *prepares to bowl.*
STOTT. Play!

STOTT *bowls.*

The marble crashes into the wall behind LAW.

LAW *stands, takes guard with his flute.*

STOTT. Play!
    STOTT *bowls.*

The marble crashes into the window behind LAW.

LAW *takes guard.*
STOTT. Play!
    STOTT *bowls. The marble hits* LAW *on the knee.*

LAW *hops.*

LAW *takes guard.*

STOTT. Play!
    STOTT *bowls.*

LAW *brilliantly cuts marble straight into golden fish tank. The tank smashes. Dozens of fish swim across the marble tiles.*

JANE, *in the corner, applauds.*

LAW *waves his flute in acknowledgement.*

STOTT. Play!
    STOTT *bowls.*

Marble crashes into LAW'S *forehead. He drops.*

Interior. Kitchen. Night.
JANE *in the kitchen, putting spoonfuls of instant coffee into two cups.*

Interior. Room. Night.
The room is completely bare.
Bare walls. Bare floorboards. No furniture. One hanging bulb.
STOTT *and* LAW *at opposite ends of the room.*
They face each other. They are barefooted. They each hold a broken milk bottle. They are crouched, still.

LAW'S *face, sweating.*

STOTT'S *face, sweating.*

LAW *from* STOTT'S *viewpoint.*

STOTT *from* LAW'S *viewpoint.*

JANE *pouring sugar from a packet into the bowl.*

LAW *pointing his bottle before him, his arm taut.*

STOTT *pointing his bottle before him, his arm taut.*

JANE *pouring milk from a bottle into a jug.*

STOTT *slowly advancing along bare boards.*

LAW *slowly advancing.*

JANE *pouring a small measure of milk into the cups.*

LAW *and* STOTT *drawing closer.*

JANE *putting sugar into the cups.*

The broken milk bottles, in shaking hands, almost touching.

The broken milk bottles fencing, not touching.

JANE *stirring milk, sugar and coffee in the cups.*

The broken milk bottles, in a sudden thrust, smashing together.

Record turning on a turntable. Sudden music.
Debussy's 'Girl With The Flaxen Hair'.

Exterior. Front area. Night.
LAW *standing centre, looking at the basement door.*
JANE *crouched by the wall. Rainhat. Raincoat.* LAW *wearing*
STOTT'S *raincoat.*

Interior. Room.
Furnished as at the beginning.
STOTT *sitting by the fire, reading. He is smiling at his book.*

Exterior. Front area.
LAW *still.*

Interior. Room.
STOTT *turns a page.*
Doorbell.
STOTT *looks up, puts his book down, stands, goes into the hall.*

Interior. Room.
The room still. The fire burning.

Interior. Hall.

STOTT *approaches the front door. He opens it.*

Silence.

He stares at LAW. *From his position in the doorway* STOTT *cannot see* JANE.

STOTT (*with great pleasure*). Law!

LAW (*smiling*). Hullo, Charles.

STOTT. Good God. Come in!

    STOTT *laughs.*

 Come in!

    LAW *enters.*

 I can't believe it!

Landscape

Landscape was first presented on radio by the BBC on 25th April, 1968, with the following cast:

BETH   Peggy Ashcroft
DUFF   Eric Porter

Directed by Guy Vaesen

The play was first presented on the stage by the Royal Shakespeare Company at the Aldwych Theatre on 2nd July, 1969, with the following cast:

BETH   Peggy Ashcroft
DUFF   David Waller

Directed by Peter Hall

DUFF: a man in his early fifties.
BETH: a woman in her late forties.
The kitchen of a country house.
A long kitchen table.
BETH sits in an armchair, which stands away from the table, to its left.
DUFF sits in a chair at the right corner of the table. The background, of a sink, stove, etc., and a window, is dim. Evening.

NOTE:

DUFF *refers normally to* BETH, *but does not appear to hear her voice.*
BETH *never looks at* DUFF, *and does not appear to hear his voice.*
Both characters are relaxed, in no sense rigid.

BETH

I would like to stand by the sea. It is there.

Pause

I have. Many times. It's something I cared for. I've done it.

Pause

I'll stand on the beach. On the beach. Well ... it was very fresh. But it was hot, in the dunes. But it was so fresh, on the shore. I loved it very much.

Pause

Lots of people ...

Pause

People move so easily. Men. Men move.

Pause

I walked from the dune to the shore. My man slept in the dune. He turned over as I stood. His eyelids. Belly button. Snoozing how lovely.

Pause

Would you like a baby? I said. Children? Babies? Of our own? Would be nice.

Pause

Women turn, look at me.

Pause

Our own child? Would you like that?

Pause

Two women looked at me, turned and stared. No. I was walking, they were still. I turned.

Pause

Why do you look?

Pause

I didn't say that, I stared. Then I was looking at them.

Pause

I am beautiful.

Pause

I walked back over the sand. He had turned. Toes under sand, head buried in his arms.

DUFF

The dog's gone. I didn't tell you.

Pause

I had to shelter under a tree for twenty minutes yesterday. Because of the rain. I meant to tell you. With some youngsters. I didn't know them.

Pause

Then it eased. A downfall. I walked up as far as the pond. Then I felt a couple of big drops. Luckily I was only a few yards from the shelter. I sat down in there. I meant to tell you.

Pause

Do you remember the weather yesterday? That downfall.?

BETH

He felt my shadow. He looked up at me standing above him.

DUFF

I should have had some bread with me. I could have fed the birds.

BETH

Sand on his arms.

DUFF

They were hopping about. Making a racket.

BETH

I lay down by him, not touching.

DUFF

There wasn't anyone else in the shelter. There was a man and woman, under the trees, on the other side of the pond. I didn't feel like getting wet. I stayed where I was.

Pause

Yes, I've forgotten something. The dog was with me.

Pause

BETH

Did those women know me? I didn't remember their faces. I'd never seen their faces before. I'd never seen those women before. I'm certain of it. Why were they looking at me? There's nothing strange about me. There's nothing strange about the way I look. I look like anyone.

DUFF

The dog wouldn't have minded me feeding the birds. Anyway, as soon as we got in the shelter he fell asleep. But even if he'd been awake . . . . .

Pause

BETH

They all held my arm lightly, as I stepped out of the car, or
out of the door, or down the steps. Without exception. If
they touched the back of my neck, or my hand, it was done so
lightly. Without exception. With one exception.

DUFF

Mind you, there was a lot of shit all over the place, all along the
paths, by the pond. Dogshit, duckshit . . . all kinds of shit . . .
all over the paths. The rain didn't clean it up. It made it even
more treacherous.

Pause

The ducks were well away, right over on their island. But I
wouldn't have fed them, anyway. I would have fed the
sparrows.

BETH

I could stand now. I could be the same. I dress differently, but
I am beautiful.

Silence

DUFF

You should have a walk with me one day down to the pond,
bring some bread. There's nothing to stop you.

Pause

I sometimes run into one or two people I know. You might
remember them.

Pause

BETH

When I watered the flowers he stood, watching me, and watched
me arrange them. My gravity, he said. I was so grave, attending

to the flowers, I'm going to water and arrange the flowers, I
said. He followed me and watched, standing at a distance from
me. When the arrangement was done I stayed still. I heard
him moving. He didn't touch me. I listened. I looked at the
flowers, blue and white, in the bowl.

Pause

Then he touched me.

Pause

He touched the back of my neck. His fingers, lightly, touching,
lightly, touching, the back, of my neck.

DUFF

The funny thing was, when I looked, when the shower was
over, the man and woman under the trees on the other side of
the pond had gone. There wasn't a soul in the park.

BETH

I wore a white beach robe. Underneath I was naked.

Pause

There wasn't a soul on the beach. Very far away a man was
sitting, on a breakwater. But even so he was only a pinpoint,
in the sun. And even so I could only see him when I was
standing, or on my way from the shore to the dune. When I
lay down I could no longer see him, therefore he couldn't see
me.

Pause

I may have been mistaken. Perhaps the beach was empty.
Perhaps there was no-one there.

Pause

He couldn't see .. my man .. anyway. He never stood up.

Pause

Sno zing how lovely I said to him. But I wasn't a fool, on that occasion. I lay quiet, by his side.

Silence

DUFF

Anyway . . .

BETH

My skin . . .

DUFF

I'm sleeping all right these days.

BETH

Was stinging.

DUFF

Right through the night, every night.

BETH

I'd been in the sea.

DUFF

Maybe it's something to do with the fishing. Getting to learn more about fish.

BETH

Stinging in the sea by myself.

DUFF

They're very shy creatures. You've got to woo them. You must never get excited with them. Or flurried. Never.

BETH

I knew there must be a hotel near, where we could get some tea.

Silence

DUFF

Anyway . . . luck was on my side for a change. By the time I got out of the park the pubs were open.

Pause

So I thought I might as well pop in and have a pint. I wanted to tell you. I met some nut in there. First of all I had a word with the landlord. He knows me. Then this nut came in. He ordered a pint and he made a criticism of the beer. I had no patience with it.

BETH

But then I thought perhaps the hotel bar will be open. We'll sit in the bar. He'll buy me a drink. What will I order? But what will he order? What will he want? I shall hear him say it. I shall hear his voice. He will ask me what I would like first. Then he'll order the two drinks. I shall hear him do it.

DUFF

This beer is piss, he said. Undrinkable. There's nothing wrong with the beer, I said. Yes there is, he said, I just told you what was wrong with it. It's the best beer in the area, I said. No it isn't, this chap said, it's piss. The landlord picked up the mug and had a sip. Good beer, he said. Someone's made a mistake, this fellow said, someone's used this pintpot instead of the boghole.

Pause

The landlord threw a half a crown on the bar and told him to take it. The pint's only two and three, the man said, I owe you three pence, but I haven't got any change. Give the threepence to your son, the landlord said, with my compliments. I haven't got a son, the man said, I've never had any children. I bet you're not even married, the landlord said. This man said: I'm not married. No-one'll marry me.

Pause

Then the man asked the landlord and me if we would have a drink with him. The landlord said he'd have a pint. I didn't answer at first, but the man came over to me and said: Have one with *me*. Have one with *me*.

Pause

He put down a ten bob note and said he'd have a pint as well.

Silence

BETH

Suddenly I stood. I walked to the shore and into the water. I didn't swim. I don't swim. I let the water billow me. I rested in the water. The waves were very light, delicate. They touched the back of my neck.

Silence

DUFF

One day when the weather's good you could go out into the garden and sit down. You'd like that. The open air. I'm often out there. The dog liked it.

Pause

I've put in some flowers. You'd find it pleasant. Looking at the flowers. You could cut a few if you liked. Bring them in. No-one would see you. There's no-one there.

Pause

That's where we're lucky, in my opinion. To live in Mr Sykes' house in peace, no-one to bother us. I've thought of inviting one or two people I know from the village in here for a bit of a drink once or twice but I decided against it. It's not necessary.

Pause

You know what you get quite a lot of out in the garden? Butterflies.

BETH

I slipped out of my costume and put on my beachrobe. Underneath I was naked. There wasn't a soul on the beach. Except for an elderly man, far away on a breakwater. I lay down beside him and whispered. Would you like a baby? A child? Of our own? Would be nice.

Pause

DUFF

What did you think of that downfall?

Pause

Of course the youngsters I met under the first tree, during the first shower, they were larking about and laughing. I tried to listen, to find out what they were laughing about, but I couldn't work it out. They were whispering. I tried to listen, to find out what the joke was.

Pause

Anyway I didn't find out.

Pause

I was thinking ... when you were young ... you didn't laugh much. You were ... grave.

Silence

BETH

That's why he'd picked such a desolate place. So that I could draw in peace. I had my sketch book with me. I took it out. I took my drawing pencil out. But there was nothing to draw. Only the beach, the sea.

Pause

Could have drawn him. He didn't want it. He laughed.

Pause

I laughed, with him.

Pause

I waited for him to laugh, then I would smile, turn away, he would touch my back, turn me, to him. My nose .. creased. I would laugh with him, a little.

Pause

He laughed. I'm sure of it. So I didn't draw him.

Silence

DUFF

You were a first-rate housekeeper when you were young. Weren't you? I was very proud. You never made a fuss, you never got into a state, you went about your work. He could rely on you. He did. He trusted you, to run his house, to keep the house up to the mark, no panic.

Pause

Do you remember when I took him on that trip to the north? That long trip. When we got back he thanked you for looking after the place so well, everything running like clockwork.

Pause

You'd missed me. When I came into this room you stopped still. I had to walk all the way over the floor towards you.

Pause

I touched you.

Pause

But I had something to say to you, didn't I? I waited, I didn't say it then, but I'd made up my mind to say it, I'd decided I would say it, and I did say it, the next morning. Didn't I?

Pause

I told you that I'd let you down. I'd been unfaithful to you.

Pause

You didn't cry. We had a few hours off. We walked up to the pond, with the dog. We stood under the trees for a bit. I didn't know why you'd brought that carrier bag with you. I asked you. I said what's in that bag? It turned out to be bread. You fed the ducks. Then we stood under the trees and looked across the pond.

Pause

When we got back into this room you put your hands on my face and you kissed me.

BETH

But I didn't really want a drink.

Pause

I drew a face in the sand, then a body. The body of a woman. Then the body of a man, close to her, not touching. But they didn't look like anything. They didn't look like human figures. The sand kept on slipping, mixing the contours. I crept close to him and put my head on his arm, and closed my eyes. All those darting red and black flecks, under my eyelid. I moved my cheek on his skin. And all those darting red and black flecks, moving about under my eyelid. I buried my face in his side and shut the light out.

Silence

DUFF

Mr Sykes took to us from the very first interview, didn't he?

Pause

He said I've got the feeling you'll make a very good team. Do you remember? And that's what we proved to be. No question. I could drive well, I could polish his shoes well, I earned my keep. Turn my hand to anything. He never lacked for anything, in the way of being looked after. Mind you, he was a gloomy bugger.

Pause

I was never sorry for him, at any time, for his lonely life.

Pause

That nice blue dress he chose for you, for the house, that was very nice of him. Of course it was in his own interests for you to look good about the house, for guests.

BETH

He moved in the sand and put his arm around me.

Silence

DUFF

Do you like me to talk to you?

Pause

Do you like me to tell you about all the things I've been doing?

Pause

About all the things I've been thinking?

Pause

Mmmnn?

Pause

I think you do.

BETH

And cuddled me.

Silence

DUFF

Of course it was in his own interests to see that you were attractively dressed about the house, to give a good impression to his guests.

BETH

I caught a bus to the crossroads and then walked down the lane by the old church. It was very quiet, except for birds. There was an old man fiddling about on the cricket pitch, bending. I stood out of the sun, under a tree.

Pause

I heard the car. He saw me and stopped me. I stayed still. Then the car moved again, came towards me slowly. I moved round the front of it, in the dust. I couldn't see him for the sun, but he was watching me. When I got to the door it was locked. I looked through at him. He leaned over and opened the door. I got in and sat beside him. He smiled at me. Then he reversed, all in one movement, very quickly, quite straight, up the lane to the crossroads, and we drove to the sea.

Pause

DUFF

We're the envy of a lot of people, you know, living in this house, having this house all to ourselves. It's too big for two people.

BETH

He said he knew a very desolate beach, that no-one else in the world knew, and that's where we are going.

DUFF

I was very gentle to you. I was kind to you, that day. I knew you'd had a shock, so I was gentle with you. I held your arm on the way back from the pond. You put your hands on my face and kissed me.

BETH

All the food I had in my bag I had cooked myself, or prepared myself. I had baked the bread myself.

DUFF

The girl herself I considered unimportant. I didn't think it necessary to go into details. I decided against it.

BETH

The windows were open but we kept the hood up.

Pause

DUFF

Mr Sykes gave a little dinner party that Friday. He complimented you on your cooking and the service.

Pause

Two women. That was all. Never seen them before. Probably his mother and sister.

Pause

They wanted coffee late. I was in bed. I fell asleep. I would have come down to the kitchen to give you a hand but I was too tired.

Pause

But I woke up when you got into bed. You were out on your feet. You were asleep as soon as you hit the pillow. Your body . . . just fell back.

BETH

He was right. It was desolate. There wasn't a soul on the beach.

Silence

DUFF

I had a look over the house the other day. I meant to tell you. The dust is bad. We'll have to polish it up.

Pause

We could go up to the drawing room, open the windows. I could wash the old decanters. We could have a drink up there one evening, if it's a pleasant evening.

Pause

I think there's moths. I moved the curtain and they flew out.

Pause

BETH

Of course when I'm older I won't be the same as I am, I won't be what I am, my skirts, my long legs, I'll be older, I won't be the same.

DUFF

At least now ... at least now, I can walk down to the pub in peace and up to the pond in peace, with no-one to nag the shit out of me.

Silence

BETH

All it is, you see ... I said ... is the lightness of your touch, the lightness of your look, my neck, your eyes, the silence, that is my meaning, the loveliness of my flowers, my hands touching my flowers, that is my meaning.

Pause

I've watched other people. I've seen them.

Pause

All the cars zooming by. Men with girls at their sides. Bouncing up and down. They're dolls. They squeak.

Pause

All the people were squeaking in the hotel bar. The girls had long hair. They were smiling.

DUFF

That's what matters, anyway. We're together. That's what matters.

Silence

BETH

But I was up early. There was still plenty to be done and cleared up. I had put the plates in the sink to soak. They had soaked overnight. They were easy to wash. The dog was up. He followed me. Misty morning. Comes from the river.

DUFF

This fellow knew bugger all about beer. He didn't know I'd been trained as a cellarman. That's why I could speak with authority.

BETH

I opened the door and went out. There was no-one about. The sun was shining. Wet, I mean wetness, all over the ground.

DUFF

A cellarman is the man responsible. He's the earliest up in the morning. Give the drayman a hand with the barrels. Down the slide through the cellarflaps. Lower them by rope to the racks. Rock them on the belly, put a rim up them, use balance and leverage, hike them up onto the racks.

BETH

Still misty, but thinner, thinning.

DUFF

The bung is on the vertical, in the bunghole. Spile the bung. Hammer the spile through the centre of the bung. That lets the air through the bung, down the bunghole, lets the beer breathe.

BETH

Wetness all over the air. Sunny. Trees like feathers.

DUFF

Then you hammer the tap in.

BETH

I wore my blue dress.

DUFF

Let it stand for three days. Keep wet sacks over the barrels.
Hose the cellar floor daily. Hose the barrels daily.

BETH

It was a beautiful autumn morning.

DUFF

Run water through the pipes to the bar pumps daily.

BETH

I stood in the mist.

DUFF

Pull off. Pull off. Stop pulling just before you get to the dregs.
The dregs'll give you the shits. You've got an ullage barrel.
Feed the slops back to the ullage barrel, send them back to
the brewery.

BETH

In the sun.

DUFF

Dip the barrels daily with a brass rod. Know your gallonage.
Chalk it up. Then you're tidy. Then you never get caught
short.

BETH

Then I went back to the kitchen and sat down.

Pause

DUFF

This chap in the pub said he was surprised to hear it. He said he was surprised to hear about hosing the cellar floor. He said he thought most cellars had a thermostatically controlled cooling system. He said he thought keg beer was fed with oxygen through a cylinder. I said I wasn't talking about keg beer, I was talking about normal draught beer. He said he thought they piped the beer from a tanker into metal containers. I said they may do, but he wasn't talking about the quality of beer I was. He accepted that point.

Pause

BETH

The dog sat down by me. I stroked him. Through the window I could see down into the valley. I saw children in the valley. They were running through the grass. They ran up the hill.

Long Silence

DUFF

I never saw your face. You were standing by the windows. One of those black nights. A downfall. All I could hear was the rain on the glass, smacking on the glass. You knew I'd come in but you didn't move. I stood close to you. What were you looking at? It was black outside. I could just see your shape in the window, your reflection. There must have been some kind of light somewhere. Perhaps just your face reflected, lighter than all the rest. I stood close to you. Perhaps you were just thinking, in a dream. Without touching you, I could feel your bottom.

Silence

BETH

I remembered always, in drawing, the basic principles of

shadow and light. Objects intercepting the light cast shadows. Shadow is deprivation of light. The shape of the shadow is determined by that of the object. But not always. Not always directly. Sometimes it is only indirectly affected by it. Sometimes the cause of the shadow cannot be found.

Pause

But I always bore in mind the basic principles of drawing.

Pause

So that I never lost track. Or heart.

Pause

DUFF

You used to wear a chain round your waist. On the chain you carried your keys, your thimble, your notebook, your pencil, your scissors.

Pause

You stood in the hall and banged the gong.

Pause

What the bloody hell are you doing banging that bloody gong?

Pause

It's bullshit. Standing in an empty hall banging a bloody gong. There's no one to listen. No one'll hear. There's not a soul in the house. Except me. There's nothing for lunch. There's nothing cooked. No stew. No pie. No greens. No joint. Fuck all.

Pause

BETH

So that I never lost track. Even though, even when, I asked

him to turn, to look at me, but he turned to look at me but I couldn't see his look.

Pause

I couldn't see whether he was looking at me.

Pause

Although he had turned. And appeared to be looking at me.

DUFF

I took the chain off and the thimble, the keys, the scissors slid off it and clattered down. I booted the gong down the hall. The dog came in. I thought you would come to me, I thought you would come into my arms and kiss me, even ... offer yourself to me. I would have had you in front of the dog, like a man, in the hall, on the stone, banging the gong, mind you don't get the scissors up your arse, or the thimble, don't worry, I'll throw them for the dog to chase, the thimble will keep the dog happy, he'll play with it with his paws, you'll plead with me like a woman, I'll bang the gong on the floor, if the sound is too flat, lacks resonance, I'll hang it back on its hook, bang you against it swinging, gonging, waking the place up, calling them all for dinner, lunch is up, bring out the bacon, bang your lovely head, mind the dog doesn't swallow the thimble, slam—

Silence

BETH

He lay above me and looked down at me. He supported my shoulder.

Pause

So tender his touch on my neck. So softly his kiss on my cheek.

Pause

My hand on his rib.

Pause

So sweetly the sand over me. Tiny the sand on my skin.

Pause

So silent the sky in my eyes. Gently the sound of the tide.

Pause

Oh my true love I said.

Silence

Silence was first presented by the Royal Shakespeare Company at the Aldwych Theatre on 2nd July, 1969, with the following cast:

ELLEN: a girl in her twenties	Frances Cuka
RUMSEY: a man of forty	Anthony Bate
BATES: a man in his middle thirties	Norman Rodway

Directed by Peter Hall

Three areas.
A chair in each area.

RUMSEY

I walk with my girl who wears a grey blouse when she walks and grey shoes and walks with me readily wearing her clothes considered for me. Her grey clothes.

She holds my arm.

On good evenings we walk through the hills to the top of the hill past the dogs the clouds racing just before dark or as dark is falling when the moon

When it's chilly I stop her and slip her raincoat over her shoulders or rainy slip arms into the arms, she twisting her arms. And talk to her and tell her everything.

She dresses for my eyes.

I tell her my thoughts. Now I am ready to walk, her arm in me her hand in me.

I tell her my life's thoughts, clouds racing. She looks up at me or listens looking down. She stops in midsentence, my sentence, to look up at me. Sometimes her hand has slipped from mine, her arm loosened, she walks slightly apart, dog barks.

ELLEN

There are two. One who is with me sometimes, and another. He listens to me. I tell him what I know. We walk by the dogs.

Sometimes the wind is so high he does not hear me. I lead him to a tree, clasp closely to him and whisper to him, wind going, dogs stop, and he hears me.

But the other hears me.

BATES

Caught a bus to the town. Crowds. Lights round the market, rain and stinking. Showed her the bumping lights. Took her down around the dumps. Black roads and girders. She clutching me. This way the way I bring you. Pubs throw the doors smack into the night. Cars barking and the lights. She with me, clutching.

Brought her into this place, my cousin runs it. Undressed her, placed my hand.

ELLEN

I go by myself with the milk to the top, the clouds racing, all the blue changes, I'm dizzy sometimes, meet with him under some place.

One time visited his house. He put a light on, it reflected the window, it reflected in the window.

RUMSEY

She walks from the door to the window to see the way she has come, to confirm that the house which grew nearer is the same one she stands in, that the path and the bushes are the same, that the gate is the same. When I stand beside her and smile at her, she looks at me and smiles.

BATES

How many times standing clenched in the pissing dark waiting?

The mud, the cows, the river.

You cross the field out of darkness. You arrive.

You stand breathing before me. You smile.

I put my hands on your shoulders and press. Press the smile off your face.

ELLEN
There are two. I turn to them and speak. I look them in their eyes. I kiss them there and say, I look away to smile, and touch them as I turn.

Silence

RUMSEY
I watch the clouds. Pleasant the ribs and tendons of cloud.

I've lost nothing.

Pleasant alone and watch the folding light. My animals are quiet. My heart never bangs. I read in the evenings. There is no-one to tell me what is expected or not expected of me. There is nothing required of me.

BATES
I'm at my last gasp with this unendurable racket. I kicked open the door and stood before them. Someone called me Grandad and told me to button it. It's they should button it. Were I young . . .

One of them told me I was lucky to be alive, that I would have to bear it in order to pay for being alive, in order to give thanks for being alive.

It's a question of sleep. I need something of it, or how can I remain alive, without any true rest, having no solace, no constant solace, not even any damn inconstant solace.

I am strong, but not as strong as the bastards in the other room, and their tittering bitches, and their music, and their love.

If I changed my life, perhaps, and lived deliberately at night, and slept in the day. But what exactly would I do? What can be meant by living in the dark?

ELLEN

Now and again I meet my drinking companion and have a drink with her. She is a friendly woman, quite elderly, quite friendly. But she knows little of me, she could never know much of me, not really, not now. She's funny. She starts talking sexily to me, in the corner, with our drinks. I laugh.

She asks me about my early life, when I was young, never departing from her chosen subject, but I have nothing to tell her about the sexual part of my youth. I'm old, I tell her, my youth was somewhere else, anyway I don't remember. She does the talking anyway.

I like to get back to my room. It has a pleasant view. I have one or two friends, ladies. They ask me where I come from. I say of course from the country. I don't see much of them.

I sometimes wonder if I think. I heard somewhere about how many thoughts go through the brain of a person. But I couldn't remember anything I'd actually thought, for some time.

It isn't something that anyone could ever tell me, could ever reassure me about, nobody could tell, from looking at me, what was happening.

But I'm still quite pretty really, quite nice eyes, nice skin.

BATES *moves to* ELLEN

BATES

Will we meet to-night?

ELLEN

I don't know.

Pause

BATES

Come with me to-night.

ELLEN

Where?

BATES

Anywhere. For a walk.

Pause

ELLEN

I don't want to walk.

BATES

Why not?

Pause

ELLEN

I want to go somewhere else.

Pause

                        BATES
Where?

                        ELLEN
I don't know.

Pause

                        BATES
What's wrong with a walk?

                        ELLEN
I don't want to walk.

Pause

                        BATES
What do you want to do?

                        ELLEN
I don't know.

Pause

                        BATES
Do you want to go anywhere else?

                        ELLEN
Yes.

                        BATES
Where?

                        ELLEN
I don't know.

Pause

BATES

Do you want me to buy you a drink?

ELLEN

No.

Pause

BATES

Come for a walk.

ELLEN

No.

Pause

BATES

All right. I'll take you on a bus to the town. I know a place. My cousin runs it.

ELLEN

No.

Silence

RUMSEY

It is curiously hot. Sitting weather, I call it. The weather sits, does not move. Unusual. I shall walk down to my horse and see how my horse is. He'll come towards me.

Perhaps he doesn't need me. My visit, my care, will be like any other visit, any other care. I can't believe it.

BATES

I walk in my mind. But can't get out of the walls, into a wind.

Meadows are walled, and lakes. The sky's a wall.

Once I had a little girl. I took it for walks. I held it by its
hand. It looked up at me and said, I see something in a tree, a
shape, a shadow. It is leaning down. It is looking at us.

Maybe it's a bird, I said, a big bird, resting. Birds grow
tired, after they've flown over the country, up and down in the
wind, looking down on all the sights, so sometimes, when they
reach a tree, with good solid branches, they rest.

Silence

ELLEN

When I run . . . when I run . . . when I run . . . over the grass
. . .

RUMSEY

She floats . . . under me. Floating . . . under me.

ELLEN

I turn. I turn. I wheel. I glide. I wheel. In stunning light.
The horizon moves from the sun. I am crushed by the light.

Silence

RUMSEY

Sometimes I see people. They walk towards me, no, not so,
walk in my direction, but never reaching me, turning left, or
disappearing, and then reappearing, to disappear into the
wood.

So many ways to lose sight of them, then to recapture sight
of them. They are sharp at first sight . . . then smudged . . .
then lost . . . then glimpsed again . . . then gone.

BATES

Funny. Sometimes I press my hand on my forehead, calmingly, feel all the dust drain out, let it go, feel the grit slip away. Funny moment. That calm moment.

ELLEN *moves to* RUMSEY

ELLEN

It's changed. You've painted it. You've made shelves. Everything. It's beautiful.

RUMSEY

Can you remember . . . when you were here last?

ELLEN

Oh yes.

RUMSEY

You were a little girl.

ELLEN

I was.

Pause

RUMSEY

Can you cook now?

ELLEN

Shall I cook for you?

RUMSEY

Yes.

ELLEN

Next time I come. I will.

Pause

RUMSEY

Do you like music?

ELLEN

Yes.

RUMSEY

I'll play you music.

Pause

RUMSEY

Look at your reflection.

ELLEN

Where?

RUMSEY

In the window.

ELLEN

It's very dark outside.

RUMSEY

It's high up.

ELLEN

Does it get darker the higher you get?

RUMSEY

No.

Silence

ELLEN

Around me sits the night. Such a silence. I can hear myself.
Cup my ear. My heart beats in my ear. Such a silence. Is it
me? Am I silent or speaking? How can I know? Can I know
such things? No-one has ever told me. I need to be told things.
I seem to be old. Am I old now? No-one will tell me. I must
find a person to tell me these things.

BATES

My landlady asks me in for a drink. Stupid conversation.
What are you doing here? Why do you live alone? Where
do you come from? What do you do with yourself? What
kind of life have you had? You seem fit. A bit grumpy. You
can smile, surely, at something? Surely you have smiled, at a
thing in your life? At something? Has there been no pleasant-
ness in your life? No kind of loveliness in your life? Are you
nothing but a childish old man, suffocating himself?

I've had all that. I've got all that. I said.

ELLEN

He sat me on his knee, by the window, and asked if he could
kiss my right cheek. I nodded he could. He did. Then he
asked, if, having kissed my right, he could do the same with
my left. I said yes. He did.

Silence

RUMSEY

She was looking down. I couldn't hear what she said.

BATES

I can't hear you. Yes you can, I said.

RUMSEY

What are you saying? Look at me, she said.

BATES

I didn't. I didn't hear you, she said. I didn't hear what you
said.

RUMSEY

But I am looking at you. It's your head that's bent.

Silence

BATES

The little girl looked up at me. I said: at night horses are
quite happy. They stand about, then after a bit of a time
they go to sleep. In the morning they wake up, snort a bit,
canter, sometimes, and eat. You've no cause to worry about
them.

ELLEN *moves to* RUMSEY

RUMSEY

Find a young man.

ELLEN

There aren't any.

RUMSEY

Don't be stupid.

ELLEN

I don't like them.

RUMSEY

You're stupid.

ELLEN

I hate them.

Pause

RUMSEY

Find one.

Silence

BATES

For instance, I said, those shapes in the trees, you'll find they're just birds, resting after a long journey.

ELLEN

I go up with the milk. The sky hits me. I walk in this wind to collide with them waiting.

There are two. They halt to laugh and bellow in the yard. They dig and punch and cackle where they stand. They turn to move, look round at me to grin. I turn my eyes from one, and from the other to him.

Silence

BATES

From the young people's room – silence. Sleep? Tender love?

It's of no importance.

Silence

RUMSEY

I walk with my girl who wears—

BATES

Caught a bus to the town. Crowds. Lights round—

Silence

ELLEN

After my work each day I walk back through people but I don't
notice them. I'm not in a dream or anything of that sort. On
the contrary. I'm quite wide awake to the world around me.
But not to the people. There must be something in them to
notice, to pay attention to, something of interest in them.
In fact I know there is. I'm certain of it. But I pass through
them noticing nothing. It is only later, in my room, that I
remember. Yes, I remember. But I'm never sure that what
I remember is of to-day or of yesterday or of a long time ago.

And then often it is only half things I remember, half things,
beginnings of things.

My drinking companion for the hundredth time asked me if
I'd ever been married. This time I told her I had. Yes, I told
her I had. Certainly. I can remember the wedding.

Silence

RUMSEY

On good evenings we walk through the hills to the top of the
hill past the dogs the clouds racing

ELLEN

Sometimes the wind is so high he does not hear me.

BATES

Brought her into this place, my cousin runs it.

ELLEN

all the blue changes, I'm dizzy sometimes

Silence

RUMSEY

that the path and the bushes are the same, that the gate is the same

BATES

You cross the field out of darkness.
You arrive.

ELLEN

I turn to them and speak.

Silence

RUMSEY

and watch the folding light.

BATES

and their tittering bitches, and their music, and their love.

ELLEN

They ask me where I come from. I say of course from the country.

Silence

BATES

Come with me tonight.

ELLEN

Where?

BATES

Anywhere. For a walk.

Silence

RUMSEY

My visit, my care, will be like any other visit, any other care.

BATES

I see something in a tree, a shape, a shadow.

Silence

ELLEN

When I run ...

RUMSEY

Floating ... under me.

ELLEN

The horizon moves from the sun.

Silence

RUMSEY

They are sharp at first sight ... then smudged ... then lost ...
then glimpsed again ... then gone.

BATES

feel all the dust drain out, let it go,

feel the grit slip away.

ELLEN

I look them in their eyes.

Silence

RUMSEY

It's high up.

ELLEN

Does it get darker the higher you get?

RUMSEY

No.

Silence

ELLEN

Around me sits the night. Such a silence.

BATES

I've had all that. I've got all that. I said.

ELLEN

I nodded he could.

Silence

RUMSEY

She was looking down.

BATES

Yes you can, I said.

RUMSEY

What are you saying?

BATES

I didn't hear you, she said.

RUMSEY

But I am looking at you. It's your head that's bent.

Silence

BATES

In the morning they wake up, snort a bit, canter, sometimes, and eat.

Silence

ELLEN

There aren't any.

RUMSEY

Don't be stupid.

ELLEN

I don't like them.

RUMSEY

You're stupid.

Silence

BATES

For instance, I said, those shapes in the trees.

ELLEN

I walk in this wind to collide with them waiting.

Silence

BATES

Sleep? Tender love? It's of no importance.

ELLEN

I kiss them there and say

Silence

RUMSEY

I walk

Silence

BATES

Caught a bus

Silence

ELLEN

Certainly. I can remember the wedding.

Silence

RUMSEY

I walk with my girl who wears a grey blouse

BATES

Caught a bus to the town. Crowds. Lights round the market

Long silence

        Fade lights

Revue Sketches

NIGHT
THAT'S YOUR TROUBLE
THAT'S ALL
APPLICANT
INTERVIEW
DIALOGUE FOR THREE

NIGHT was first presented by Alexander H. Cohen Ltd in an entertainment entitled *Mixed Doubles* at the Comedy Theatre on 9th April, 1969, with the following cast:

MAN   Nigel Stock
WOMAN   Vivien Merchant
Directed by Alexander Doré

THAT'S YOUR TROUBLE, THAT'S ALL, APPLICANT, INTERVIEW and DIALOGUE FOR THREE were first presented on B.B.C. Radio on the Third Programme between February and March 1964.

NIGHT

A woman and a man in their forties.
They sit with coffee.

MAN. I'm talking about that time by the river.
WOMAN. What time?
MAN. The first time. On the bridge. Starting on the bridge.

Pause.

WOMAN. I can't remember.
MAN. On the bridge. We stopped and looked down at the river. It was night. There were lamps lit on the towpath. We were alone. We looked up the river. I put my hand on the small of your waist. Don't you remember? I put my hand under your coat.

Pause.

WOMAN. Was it winter?
MAN. Of course it was winter. It was when we met. It was our first walk. You must remember that.
WOMAN. I remember walking. I remember walking with you.
MAN. The first time? Our first walk?
WOMAN. Yes, of course, I remember that.

Pause.

We walked down a road into a field, through some railings. We walked to a corner of the field and then we stood by the railings.
MAN. No. It was on the bridge that we stopped.

Pause.

WOMAN. That was someone else.

MAN. Rubbish

WOMAN. That was another girl.

MAN. It was years ago. You've forgotten.

Pause.

I remember the light on the water.

WOMAN. You took my face in your hands, standing by the railings. You were very gentle, you were very caring. You cared. Your eyes searched my face. I wondered who you were. I wondered what you thought. I wondered what you would do.

MAN. You agree we met at a party. You agree with that?

WOMAN. What was that?

MAN. What?

WOMAN. I thought I heard a child crying.

MAN. There was no sound.

WOMAN. I thought it was a child, crying, waking up.

MAN. The house is silent.

Pause.

It's very late. We're sitting here. We should be in bed. I have to be up early. I have things to do. Why do you argue?

WOMAN. I don't. I'm not. I'm willing to go to bed. I have things to do. I have to be up in the morning.

Pause.

MAN. A man called Doughty gave the party. You knew him. I had met him. I knew his wife. I met you there. You were standing by the window. I smiled at you, and to my surprise you smiled back. You liked me. I was amazed. You found me attractive. Later you told me. You liked my eyes.

WOMAN. You liked mine.

Pause.

You touched my hand. You asked me who I was, and what

I was, and whether I was aware that you were touching my hand, that your fingers were touching mine, that your fingers were moving up and down between mine.

MAN. No. We stopped on a bridge. I stood behind you. I put my hand under your coat, onto your waist. You felt my hand on you.

   Pause.

WOMAN. We had been to a party. Given by the Doughtys. You had known his wife. She looked at you dearly, as if to say you were her dear. She seemed to love you. I didn't. I didn't know you. They had a lovely house. By a river. I went to collect my coat, leaving you waiting for me. You had offered to escort me. I thought you were quite courtly, quite courteous, pleasantly mannered, quite caring. I slipped my coat on and looked out of the window, knowing you were waiting. I looked down over the garden to the river, and saw the lamplight on the water. Then I joined you and we walked down the road through railings into a field, must have been some kind of park. Later we found your car. You drove me.

   Pause.

MAN. I touched your breasts.

WOMAN. Where?

MAN. On the bridge. I felt your breasts.

WOMAN. Really?

MAN. Standing behind you.

WOMAN. I wondered whether you would, whether you wanted to, whether you would.

MAN. Yes.

WOMAN. I wondered how you would go about it, whether you wanted to, sufficiently.

MAN. I put my hands under your sweater, I undid your brassière, I felt your breasts.

WOMAN. Another night perhaps. Another girl.

MAN. You don't remember my fingers on your skin?

WOMAN. Were they in your hands? My breasts? Fully in your hands?

MAN. You don't remember my hands on your skin?

Pause.

WOMAN. Standing behind me?

MAN. Yes.

WOMAN. But my back was against railings. I felt the railings .. behind me. You were facing me. I was looking into your eyes. My coat was closed. It was cold.

MAN. I undid your coat.

WOMAN. It was very late. Chilly.

MAN. And then we left the bridge and we walked down the towpath and we came to a rubbish dump.

WOMAN. And you had me and you told me you had fallen in love with me, and you said you would take care of me always, and you told me my voice and my eyes, my thighs, my breasts, were incomparable, and that you would adore me always.

MAN. Yes I did.

WOMAN. And you do adore me always.

MAN. Yes I do.

WOMAN. And then we had children and we sat and talked and you remembered women on bridges and towpaths and rubbish dumps.

MAN. And you remembered your bottom against railings and men holding your hands and men looking into your eyes.

WOMAN. And talking to me softly.

MAN. And your soft voice. Talking to them softly at night.

WOMAN. And they said I will adore you always.

MAN. Saying I will adore you always.

THAT'S YOUR TROUBLE

Two men in a park. One on the grass, reading. The other making cricket strokes with umbrella.

1. A. (*stopping in mid-stroke*): Eh, look at that bloke, what's he got on his back, he's got a sandwich board on his back.
2. B.: What about it?
3. A.: He wants to take it off, he'll get a headache.
4. B.: Rubbish.
5. A.: What do you mean?
6. B.: He won't get a headache.
7. A.: I bet he will.
8. B.: The neck! It affects his neck! He'll get a neckache.
9. A.: The strain goes up.
10. B.: Have you ever carried a sandwich board?
11. A.: Never.
12. B.: Then how do you know which way the strain *goes*? (*Pause.*) It goes down! The strain goes down, it starts with the neck and it goes down. He'll get a neckache and a backache.
13. A.: He'll get a headache in the end.
14. B.: There's no end.
15. A.: That's where the brain is.
16. B.: That's where the *what* is?
17. A.: The brain.
18. B.: It's nothing to do with the brain.
19. A.: Oh, isn't it?
20. B.: It won't go anywhere *near* his brain.
21. A.: That's where you're wrong.
22. B.: I'm not wrong. I'm right. (*Pause.*) You happen to be talking to a man who knows what he's talking about. (*Pause.*) His brain doesn't come into it. If you've got a strain, it goes down. It's not like heat.

23. A.: What do you mean?

24. B. (*ferociously*): If you've got a strain it goes down! Heat goes up! (*Pause.*)

25. A.: You mean sound.

26. B.: I what?

27. A.: Sound goes up.

28. B.: Sound goes anywhere it likes! It all depends where you happen to be standing, it's a matter of physics, that's something you're just completely ignorant of, but you just try carrying a sandwich board and you'll find out soon enough. First the neck, than the shoulders, then the back, then it worms into the buttocks, that's where it worms. The buttocks. Either the right or the left, it depends how you carry your weight. Then right down the thighs – a straight drop to his feet and he'll collapse.

29. A.: He hasn't collapsed yet.

30. B.: He will. Give him a chance. A headache! How can he get a headache? He hasn't got anything on his head! I'm the one who's got the headache. (*Pause.*) You just don't know how to listen to what other people tell you, that's your trouble.

31. A.: I know what my trouble is.

32. B.: You don't know what your trouble is, my friend. That's your trouble.

MRS. A.: I always put the kettle on about that time.

MRS. B.: Yes. (*Pause.*)

MRS. A.: Then she comes round.

MRS. B.: Yes. (*Pause.*)

MRS. A.: Only on Thursdays.

MRS. B.: Yes. (*Pause.*)

MRS. A.: On Wednesdays I used to put it on. When she used to come round. Then she changed it to Thursdays.

MRS. B.: Oh yes.

MRS. A.: After she moved. When she used to live round the corner, then she always came in on Wednesdays, but then when she moved she used to come down to the butcher's on Thursdays. She couldn't find a butcher up there.

MRS. B.: No.

MRS. A.: Anyway, she decided she'd stick to her own butcher. Well, I thought, if she can't find a butcher, that's the best thing.

MRS. B.: Yes. (*Pause.*)

MRS. A.: So she started to come down on Thursdays. I didn't know she was coming down on Thursdays until one day I met her in the butcher.

MRS. B.: Oh yes.

MRS. A.: It wasn't my day for the butcher, I don't go to the butcher on Thursdays.

MRS. B.: No, I know. (*Pause.*)

MRS. A.: I go on Friday.

MRS. B.: Yes. (*Pause.*)

MRS. A.: That's where I see you.

MRS. B.: Yes. (*Pause.*)

MRS. A.: You're always in there on Fridays.

MRS. B.: Oh yes. (*Pause.*)

MRS. A.: But I happened to go in for a bit of meat, it turned out to be a Thursday. I wasn't going in for my usual weekly on Friday. I just slipped in, the day before.

MRS. B.: Yes.

MRS. A.: That was the first time I found out she couldn't find a butcher up there, so she decided to come back here, once a week, to her own butcher.

MRS. B.: Yes.

MRS. A.: She came on Thursday so she'd be able to get meat for the weekend. Lasted her till Monday, then from Monday to Thursday they'd have fish. She can always buy cold meat, if they want a change.

MRS. B.: Oh yes. (*Pause.*)

MRS. A.: So I told her to come in when she came down after she'd been to the butcher's and I'd put a kettle on. So she did. (*Pause.*)

MRS. B.: Yes. (*Pause.*)

MRS. A.: It was funny because she always used to come in Wednesdays. (*Pause.*) Still, it made a break. (*Long pause.*)

MRS. B.: She doesn't come in no more, does she? (*Pause.*)

MRS. A.: She comes in. She doesn't come in so much, but she comes in. (*Pause.*)

MRS. B.: I thought she didn't come in. (*Pause.*)

MRS. A.: She comes in. (*Pause.*) She just doesn't come in so much. That's all.

APPLICANT

An office, LAMB, a young man, eager, cheerful, enthusiastic, is striding nervously, alone. The door opens. MISS PIFFS comes in. She is the essence of efficiency.

PIFFS: Ah, good morning.

LAMB: Oh, good morning, miss.

PIFFS: Are you Mr. Lamb?

LAMB: That's right.

PIFFS [*studying a sheet of paper*]: Yes, You're applying for this vacant post, aren't you?

LAMB: I am actually, yes.

PIFFS: Are you a physicist?

LAMB: Oh yes, indeed. It's my whole life.

PIFFS [*languidly*]: Good. Now our procedure is, that before we discuss the applicant's qualifications we like to subject him to a little test to determine his psychological suitability. You've no objection?

LAMB: Oh, good heavens, no.

PIFFS: Jolly good.

> MISS PIFFS *has taken some objects out of a drawer and goes to* LAMB. *She places a chair for him.*

PIFFS: Please sit down. [*He sits.*] Can I fit these to your palms?

LAMB [*affably*]: What are they?

PIFFS: Electrodes.

LAMB: Oh yes, of course. Funny little things.

> *She attaches them to his palms.*

PIFFS: Now the earphones.

> *She attaches earphones to his head.*

LAMB: I say how amusing.

PIFFS: Now I plug in.

She plugs in to the wall.

LAMB [*a trifle nervously*]: Plug in, do you? Oh yes, of course. Yes, you'd have to, wouldn't you?

MISS PIFFS *perches on a high stool and looks down on* LAMB.

This help to determine my . . . my suitability does it?

PIFFS: Unquestionably. Now relax. Just relax. Don't think about a thing.

LAMB: No.

PIFFS: Relax completely. Rela-a-a-x. Quite relaxed?

LAMB *nods.* MISS PIFFS *presses a button on the side of her stool. A piercing high pitched buzz-hum is heard.* LAMB *jolts rigid. His hands go to his earphones. He is propelled from the chair. He tries to crawl under the chair.* MISS PIFFS *watches, impassive. The noise stops.* LAMB *peeps out from under the chair, crawls out, stands, twitches, emits a short chuckle and collapses in the chair.*

PIFFS: Would you say you were an excitable person?

LAMB: Not – not unduly, no. Of course, I—

PIFFS: Would you say you were a moody person?

LAMB: Moody? No, I wouldn't say I was moody – well, sometimes occasionally I—

PIFFS: Do you ever get fits of depression?

LAMB: Well, I wouldn't call them depression exactly—

PIFFS: Do you often do things you regret in the morning?

LAMB: Regret? Things I regret? Well, it depends what you mean by often, really – I mean when you say often—

PIFFS: Are you often puzzled by women?

LAMB: Women?

PIFFS: Men.

LAMB: Men? Well, I was just going to answer the question about women—

PIFFS: Do you often feel puzzled?

LAMB: Puzzled?

PIFFS: By women.

LAMB: Women?

PIFFS: Men.

LAMB: Oh, now just a minute, I ... Look, do you want separate answers or a joint answer?

PIFFS: After your day's work do you ever feel tired? Edgy? Fretty? Irritable? At a loose end? Morose? Frustrated? Morbid? Unable to concentrate? Unable to sleep? Unable to eat? Unable to remain seated? Unable to remain upright? Lustful? Indolent? On heat? Randy? Full of desire? Full of energy? Full of dread? Drained? of energy, of dread? of desire?

Pause.

LAMB [*thinking*]: Well, it's difficult to say really ...

PIFFS: Are you a good mixer?

LAMB: Well, you've touched on quite an interesting point there—

PIFFS: Do you suffer from eczema, listlessness, or falling coat?

LAMB: Er ...

PIFFS: Are you virgo intacta?

LAMB: I beg your pardon?

PIFFS: Are you virgo intacta?

LAMB: Oh, I say, that's rather embarrassing. I mean – in front of a lady—

PIFFS: Are you virgo intacta?

LAMB: Yes, I am, actually. I'll make no secret of it.

PIFFS: Have you always been virgo intacta?

LAMB: Oh yes, always. Always.

PIFFS: From the word go?

LAMB: Go? Oh yes, from the word go.

PIFFS: Do women frighten you?

> *She presses a button on the other side of her stool. The stage is plunged into redness, which flashes on and off in time with her questions.*

PIFFS [*building*]: Their clothes? Their shoes? Their voices? Their laughter? Their stares? Their way of walking? Their way of sitting? Their way of smiling? Their way of talking? Their mouths? Their hands? Their feet? Their shins? Their thighs? Their knees? Their eyes?
Their [*Drumbeat*]. Their [*Drumbeat*]. Their [*Cymbal bang*]. Their [*Trombone chord*]. Their [*Bass note*].

LAMB [*in a high voice*]: Well it depends what you mean really—

> *The light still flashes. She presses the other button and the piercing buzz-hum is heard again.* LAMB's *hands go to his earphones. He is propelled from the chair, falls, rolls, crawls, totters and collapses.*

> *Silence.*

> *He lies face upwards.* MISS PIFFS *looks at him then walks to* LAMB *and bends over him.*

PIFFS: Thank you very much, Mr. Lamb. We'll let you know.

INTERVIEW

INTERVIEWER: Well, Mr. Jakes, how would you say things are in the pornographic book trade?

JAKES: I make 200 a week.

INTERVIEWER: 200?

JAKES: Yes, I make round about 200 a week at it.

INTERVIEWER: I see. So how would you say things were in the pornographic book trade?

JAKES: Oh, only fair.

INTERVIEWER: Only fair?

JAKES: Fair to middling.

INTERVIEWER: Why would you say that, Mr. Jakes?

JAKES: Well, it's got a lot to do with Xmas, between you and me.

INTERVIEWER: Xmas?

JAKES: Yes, well what happens is, you see, is that the trade takes a bit of a bashing round about Xmas time. Takes a good few months to recover from Xmas time, the pornographic book trade does.

INTERVIEWER: Oh, I see.

JAKES: Yes, what's got something to do with it is, you see, that you don't get all that many people sending pornographic books for Xmas presents. I mean, you get a few, of course, but not all that many. No, we can't really say that people in our trade get much benefit from the Xmas spirit, if you know what I mean.

INTERVIEWER: Well, I'm sorry to hear that, Mr. Jakes.

JAKES: Well, there you are. We make the best of it. (*Pause.*) I mean I put a sprig of holly . . . here and there . . . I put holly up all over the shop, but it doesn't seem to make much difference. (*Pause.*)

INTERVIEWER: What sort of people do you get in your shop, Mr. Jakes?

JAKES: I beg your pardon?

INTERVIEWER: What sort of people do you get in your shop?

JAKES: I'd rather not answer that question, thanks.

INTERVIEWER: Why not?

JAKES: I should think the security police could tell you a thing or two about that.

INTERVIEWER: Security police?

JAKES: Yes. They've got their dossiers, don't you worry about that.

INTERVIEWER: But we have no security police in this country.

JAKES: Don't you? You'd be surprised. They know all about it, take it from me. I've seen their dossiers.

INTERVIEWER: You've seen their dossiers?

JAKES: Dossiers? I've looked at more of their dossiers than you've had nights off.

INTERVIEWER: I see. Well, perhaps we'd better pass on to another question.

JAKES: Dossiers? I've been there morning and afternoon checking over their dossiers, identifying my customers, identifying their photographs right into the middle of the night, right into the middle of their dossiers.

INTERVIEWER: I had no idea—

JAKES: We've got them all taped in the pornographic book trade, don't you worry about that.

INTERVIEWER: Yes, well—

JAKES: You've no need to become anxious about *that*.

INTERVIEWER: Mr Jakes—

JAKES: Every single individual that passes through my door goes out.

INTERVIEWER: What?

JAKES: Every single dirty-minded individual that passes through my door goes straight out again. As soon as he's chosen his fancy – out he goes.

INTERVIEWER: You don't . . . keep them in?

JAKES: Keep them in! Never! I wouldn't keep one of them

in my own little pornographic bookshop, not me. Not that they haven't begged, mind you. Begged. They've gone down on their bended knees and begged me to allow them to stay the night in the backroom, in the punishment section. Not me. Not since I got the word.

INTERVIEWER: I think perhaps—

JAKES (*confidentially*): You don't think the security police are the only people who've got dossiers, do you?

INTERVIEWER: No, I'm sure—

JAKES: You don't think that, do you? Get out of it. I'm up half the night doing my dossiers! I've got one on every single member of my clientele. And the day's coming, my boy, I can tell you.

INTERVIEWER: Coming?

JAKES: We're going to hold a special exhibition, see? We'll have them all in there, white in the face, peeping, peering, sweating, showing me false credentials to get to the top shelf, and then at a given moment we lock the doors and turn the floodlights on. And then we'll have them all revealed for what they are.

INTERVIEWER: What ... are they?

JAKES: They're all the same, every single one of them. COMMUNISTS.

DIALOGUE FOR THREE

1ST MAN: Did I ever tell you about the woman in the blue dress? I met her in Casablanca. She was a spy. A spy in a blue dress. That woman was an agent for another power. She was tattooed on her belly with a pelican. Her belly was covered with a pelican. She could make that pelican waddle across the room to you. On all fours, sideways, feet first, arseupwards, any way you like. Her control was superhuman. Only a woman could possess it. Under her blue dress she wore a shimmy. And under her shimmy she wore a pelican.

2ND MAN: The snow has turned to slush.

1ST MAN: The temperature must have dropped.

WOMAN: Sometimes I think I'm not feminine enough for you.

1ST MAN: You are.

WOMAN: Or do you think I should be more feminine?

1ST MAN: No.

WOMAN: Perhaps I should be more masculine.

1ST MAN: Certainly not.

WOMAN: You think I'm too feminine?

1ST MAN: No.

WOMAN: If I didn't love you so much it wouldn't matter. Do you remember the first time we met? On the beach? In the night? All those people? And the bonfire? And the waves? And the spray? And the mist? And the moon? Everyone dancing, somersaulting, laughing? And you – standing silent, staring at a sandcastle in your sheer white trunks. The moon was behind you, in front of you, all over you, suffusing you, consuming you, you were transparent, translucent, a beacon. I was struck dumb, dumbstruck. Water rose up my legs. I could not move. I was rigid. Immovable. Our eyes met. Love at first sight. I held your gaze. And in your eyes, bold and unashamed, was desire. Brutal, demanding desire. Bestial, ruthless, remorseless. I stood there magnetised, hypnotised. Transfixed. Motionless and still. A spider caught in a web.

1ST MAN (*to* 2ND MAN): You know who you remind me of? You remind me of Whipper Wallace, back in the good old days. He used to knock about with a chap called House Peters. Boghouse Peters we used to call him. I remember one day Whipper and Boghouse – he had a scar on his left cheek, Boghouse, caught in some boghouse brawl, I suppose – well, anyway, there they were, the Whipper and Boghouse, rolling down by the banks of the Euphrates this night, when up came a policeman ...... up came this policeman ...... up came a policeman ...... this policeman ...... approached ...... Boghouse ...... and the Whipper ...... were questioned ...... this night ...... the Euphrates ...... a policeman ......

Tea Party

(Short Story)

I wrote this short story in 1963, and in 1964 was commissioned by the B.B.C. to write a play for the European Broadcasting Union. I decided to treat the same subject in play form. In my view, the story is the more successful.

H.P.

My eyes are worse.

My physician is an inch under six feet. There is a grey strip in his hair, one, no more. He has a brown stain on his left cheek. His lampshades are dark blue drums. Each has a golden rim. They are identical. There is a deep black burn in his Indian carpet. His staff is bespectacled, to a woman. Through the blinds I hear the birds of his garden. Sometimes his wife appears, in white.

He is clearly sceptical on the subject of my eyes. According to him my eyes are normal, perhaps even better than normal. He finds no evidence that my sight is growing worse.

My eyes are worse. It is not that I do not see. I do see.

My job goes well. My family and I remain close friends. My two sons are my closest friends. My wife is closer. I am close friends with all my family, including my mother and my father. Often we sit and listen to Bach. When I go to Scotland I take them with me. My wife's brother came once, and was useful on the trip.

I have my hobbies, one of which is using a hammer and nails, or a screwdriver and screws, or various saws, on wood, constructing things or making things useful, finding a use for an object which appears to have no value. But it is not so easy to do this when you see double, or when you are blinded by the object, or when you do not see at all, or when you are blinded by the object.

My wife is happy. I use my imagination in bed. We love with the light on. I watch her closely, she watches me. In the morning her eyes shine. I can see them shining through her spectacles.

All winter the skies were bright. Rain fell at night. In the morning the skies were bright. My backhand flip was my strongest weapon. Taking position to face my wife's brother, across the dear table, my bat lightly clasped, my wrist flexing, I waited to loosen my flip to his forehand, watch him (*shocked*) dart and be beaten, flounder and sulk. My forehand was not so powerful, so swift. Predictably, he attacked my forehand. There was a ringing sound in the room, a rubber sound in the walls. Predictably, he attacked my forehand. But once far to the right on my forehand, and my weight genuinely disposed, I could employ my backhand flip, unanswerable, watch him flounder, skid and be beaten. They were close games. But it is not now so easy when you see the pingpong ball double, or do not see it at all or when, hurtling towards you at speed, the ball blinds you.

I am pleased with my secretary. She knows the business well and loves it. She is trustworthy. She makes calls to Newcastle and Birmingham on my behalf and is never fobbed off. She is respected on the telephone. Her voice is persuasive. My partner and I agree that she is of inestimable value to us. My partner and my wife often discuss her when the three of us meet for coffee or drinks. Neither of them, when discussing Wendy, can speak highly enough of her.

On bright days, of which there are many, I pull the blinds in my office in order to dictate. Often I touch her swelling body. She reads back, flips the page. She makes a telephone call to Birmingham. Even were I, while she speaks (holding the receiver lightly, her other hand poised for notes), to touch her swelling body, her call would still be followed to its conclusion. It is she who bandages my eyes, while I touch her swelling body.

I do not remember being like my sons in any way when I was a boy. Their reserve is remarkable. They seem stirred by no passion. They sit silent. An odd mutter passes between them. I can't hear you, what are you saying, speak up, I say. My wife says the same. I can't hear you, what are you saying, speak up. They are of an age. They work well at school, it appears. But at pingpong both are duds. As a boy I was wide awake, of passionate interests, voluble, responsive, and my eyesight was excellent. They resemble me in no way. Their eyes are glazed and evasive behind their spectacles.

My brother in law was best man at our wedding. None of my friends were at that time in the country. My closest friend, who was the natural choice, was called away suddenly on business. To his great regret, he was therefore forced to opt out. He had prepared a superb speech in honour of the groom, to be delivered at the reception. My brother in law could not of course himself deliver it, since it referred to the longstanding friendship which existed between Atkins and myself, and my brother in law knew little of me. He was therefore confronted with a difficult problem. He solved it by making his sister his central point of reference. I still have the present he gave me, a carved pencil sharpener, from Bali.

The day I first interviewed Wendy she wore a tight tweed skirt. Her left thigh never ceased to caress her right, and vice versa. All this took place under her skirt. She seemed to me the perfect secretary. She listened to my counsel wide-eyed and attentive, her hands calmly clasped, trim, bulgy, plump, rosy, swelling. She was clearly the possessor of an active and inquiring intelligence. Three times she cleaned her spectacles with a silken kerchief.

After the wedding my brother in law asked my dear wife to remove her glasses. He peered deep into her eyes. You have

married a good man, he said. He will make you happy. As he
was doing nothing at the time I invited him to join me in the
business. Before long he became my partner, so keen was his
industry, so sharp his business acumen.

Wendy's commonsense, her clarity, her discretion, are of
inestimable value to our firm.

With my eye at the keyhole I hear goosing, the squeak of them.
The slit is black, only the sliding gussle on my drum, the hiss
and flap of their bliss. The room sits on my head, my skull
creased on the brass and loathsome handle I dare not twist, for
fear of seeing black screech and scrape of my secretary writhing
blind in my partner's paunch and jungle.

My wife reached down to me. Do you love me, she asked. I do
love you, I spat into her eyeball. I shall prove it yet, I shall
prove it yet, what proof yet, what proof remaining, what proof
not yet given. All proof. (For my part, I decided on a more
cunning, more allusive strategem.) Do you love me, was my
counter.

The pingpong table streaked with slime. My hands pant to gain
the ball. My sons watch. They cheer me on. They are loud in
their loyalty. I am moved. I fall back on strokes, on gambits,
long since gone, flip, cut, chop, shtip, bluff to my uttermost. I
play the ball by nose. The twins hail my efforts gustily. But
my brother in law is no chump. He slams again, he slams again,
deep to my forehand. I skid, flounder, stare sightless into the
crack of his bat.

Where are my hammers, my screws, my saws?

How are you? asked my partner. Bandage on straight? Knots
tight?

The door slammed. Where was I ? In the office or at home ? Had someone come in as my partner went out ? Had he gone out ? Was it silence I heard, this scuffle, creak, squeal, scrape, gurgle and muff ? Tea was being poured. Heavy thighs (Wendy's ? my wife's ? both ? apart ? together ?) trembled in stilletos. I sipped the liquid. It was welcome. My physician greeted me warmly. In a minute, old chap, we'll take off those bandages. Have a rock cake. I declined. The birds are at the bird bath, called his white wife. They all rushed to look. My sons sent something flying. *Someone?* Surely not. I had never heard my sons in such good form. They chattered, chuckled, discussed their work eagerly with their uncle. My parents were silent. The room seemed very small, smaller than I had remembered it. I knew where everything was, every particular. But its smell had altered. Perhaps because the room was overcrowded. My wife broke gasping out of a fit of laughter, as she was wont to do in the early days of our marriage. Why was she laughing ? Had someone told her a joke ? Who ? Her sons ? Unlikely. My sons were discussing their work with my physician and his wife. Be with you in a minute, old chap, my physician called to me. Meanwhile my partner had the two women half stripped on a convenient rostrum. Whose body swelled most ? I had forgotten. I picked up a pingpong ball. It was hard. I wondered how far he had stripped the women. The top halves or the bottom halves ? Or perhaps he was now raising his spectacles to view my wife's swelling buttocks, the swelling breasts of my secretary. How could I verify this ? By movement, by touch. But that was out of the question. And could such a sight possibly take place under the eyes of my own children ? Would they continue to chat and chuckle, as they still did, with my physician ? Hardly. However, it was good to have the bandage on straight and the knots tight.

OTHER GROVE PRESS DRAMA AND THEATER PAPERBACKS

E487   ABE, KOBO / Friends / $2.45

B415   ARDEN, JOHN / John Arden Plays: One (Serjeant Musgrave's Dance, The Workhouse Donkey, Armstrong's Last Goodnight) / $3.95

E312   ARDEN, JOHN / Serjeant Musgrave's Dance / $3.95 [See also John Arden Plays: One, B415 / $3.95]

B109   ARDEN, JOHN / Three Plays (Live Like Pigs, The Waters of Babylon, The Happy Haven) / $2.45

E610   ARRABAL, FERNANDO / And They Put Handcuffs on the Flowers / $1.95

E486   ARRABAL, FERNANDO / The Architect and The Emperor of Assyria / $3.95

E611   ARRABAL, FERNANDO / Garden of Delights / $2.95

E521   ARRABAL, FERNANDO / Guernica and Other Plays (The Labyrinth, The Tricycle, Picnic on the Battlefield) / $4.95

E532   ARTAUD, ANTONIN / The Cenci / $3.95

E425   BARAKA, IMAMU AMIRI (LeRoi Jones) / The Baptism and The Toilet: Two Plays / $2.45 [See also Grove Press Modern Drama, John Lahr, ed., E633 / $5.95]

E670   BARAKA, IMAMU AMIRI (LeRoi Jones) / The System of Dante's Hell, The Dead Lecturer and Tales / $4.95

E471   BECKETT, SAMUEL / Cascando and Other Short Dramatic Pieces (Words and Music, Eh Joe, Play, Come and Go, Film) / $3.95

        BECKETT, SAMUEL / The Collected Works of Samuel Beckett in Twenty-two Volumes / $85.00

E96   BECKETT, SAMUEL / Endgame / $1.95

E680   BECKETT, SAMUEL / Ends and Odds / $1.95

E502   BECKETT, SAMUEL / Film, A Film Script / $1.95

E623   BECKETT, SAMUEL / First Love and Other Shorts / $1.95

E318   BECKETT, SAMUEL / Happy Days / $2.45

E692   BECKETT, SAMUEL / I Can't Go On; I'll Go On / $6.95

E226   BECKETT, SAMUEL / Krapp's Last Tape and Other Dramatic Pieces (All That Fall, Embers [a Play for Radio], Acts Without Words I and II [mimes]) / $2.45

E33   BECKETT, SAMUEL / Waiting for Godot / $1.95 [See also
      Seven Plays of the Modern Theater, Harold Clurman, ed.,
      E 717 / $6.95]
B411 BEHAN, BRENDAN / The Complete Plays (The Hostage, The
      Quare Fellow, Richard's Cork Leg, Three One Act Plays for
      Radio) / $3.95
B79   BEHAN, BRENDAN / The Quare Fellow and The Hostage:
      Two Plays / $2.95 [See also Seven Plays of the Modern
      Theater, Harold Clurman, ed., E717 / $6.95]
E624 BEHAN, BRENDAN / Richard's Cork Leg / $2.95 [See also
      The Complete Plays, Brendan Behan, B411 / $3.95]
E90   BETTI, UGO / Three Plays (The Queen and the Rebels, The
      Burnt Flower-Bed, Summertime) / $3.95
B60   BRECHT, BERTOLT / Baal, A Man's A Man, The Elephant
      Calf / $1.95 [See also Seven Plays by Bertolt Brecht, GP248 /
      $12.50 and The Jewish Wife and Other Short Plays, B80 /
      $1.95]
B312 BRECHT, BERTOLT / The Caucasian Chalk Circle / $1.95
      [See also Seven Plays by Bertolt Brecht, GP248 / $12.50 and
      Grove Press Modern Drama, John Lahr, ed., E633 / $5.95]
B119 BRECHT, BERTOLT / Edward II: A Chronicle Play / $1.45
B120 BRECHT, BERTOLT / Galileo / $1.95 [See also Seven Plays
      by Bertolt Brecht, GP248 / $12.50]
B117 BRECHT, BERTOLT / The Good Woman of Setzuan / $1.95
      [See also Seven Plays by Bertolt Brecht, GP248 / $12.50]
B80   BRECHT, BERTOLT / The Jewish Wife and Other Short Plays
      (In Search of Justice, The Informer, The Elephant Calf, The
      Measures Taken, The Exception and the Rule, Salzburg
      Dance of Death) / $1.95
B89   BRECHT, BERTOLT / The Jungle of Cities and Other Plays
      (Drums in the Night, Roundheads and Peakheads) / $1.95
B129 BRECHT, BERTOLT / Manual of Piety / $2.45
B414 BRECHT, BERTOLT / The Mother / $2.95
B108 BRECHT, BERTOLT / Mother Courage and Her Children /
      $1.95 [See also Seven Plays by Bertolt Brecht, GP248 /
      $12.50]
GP248 BRECHT, BERTOLT / Seven Plays by Bertolt Brecht (In the
      Swamp, A Man's A Man, Saint Joan of the Stockyards, Mother
      Courage and Her Children, Galileo, The Good Woman of
      Setzuan, The Caucasian Chalk Circle) / $12.50
B333 BRECHT, BERTOLT / The Threepenny Opera / $1.95
E517 BULGAKOV, MIKHAIL / Flight: A Play in Eight Dreams and
      Four Acts / $2.25
B193 BULGAKOV, MIKHAIL / Heart of a Dog / $2.95
B147 BULGAKOV, MIKHAIL / The Master and Margarita / $3.95
E693 CHEKHOV, ANTON / The Cherry Orchard / $2.95

E650	NICHOLS, PETER / The National Health / $3.95
B400	ORTON, JOE / The Complete Plays (The Ruffian on the Stair, The Good and Faithful Servant, The Erpingham Camp, Funeral Games, Loot, What the Butler Saw, Entertaining Mr. Sloane) / $4.95
E393	ORTON, JOE / Entertaining Mr. Sloane / $2.95 [See also The Complete Plays of Joe Orton, B400 / $4.95]
E470	ORTON, JOE / Loot / $2.95 [See also The Complete Plays of Joe Orton, B400 / $4.95]
E315	PINTER, HAROLD / The Birthday and The Room: Two Plays / $2.95 [See also Seven Plays of the Modern Theater, Harold Clurman, ed., E717 / $6.95]
E299	PINTER, HAROLD / The Caretaker and The Dumb Waiter: Two Plays / $2.95
B402	PINTER, HAROLD / Complete Works: One (The Birthday Party, The Room, The Dumb Waiter, A Slight Ache, A Night Out, The Black and White, The Examination) / $3.95
B403	PINTER, HAROLD / Complete Works: Two (The Caretaker, Night School, The Dwarfs, The Collection, The Lover, Five Revue Sketches) / $3.95
B410	PINTER, HAROLD / Complete Works: Three (Landscape, Silence, The Basement, Six Revue Sketches, Tea Party [play], Tea Party [short story], Mac) / $3.95
E411	PINTER, HAROLD / The Homecoming / $1.95
E555	PINTER, HAROLD / Landscape and Silence: Two Plays / $3.95 [See also Complete Works: Three by Harold Pinter, B410 / $3.95]
E432	PINTER, HAROLD / The Lover, Tea Party and The Basement / $2.95 [See also Complete Works: Two by Harold Pinter, B403 / $3.95 and Complete Works: Three by Harold Pinter, B410 / $3.95]
GP604	PINTER, HAROLD / Mac (A Memoir) / $4.50 [See also Complete Works: Three by Harold Pinter, B410 / $3.95]
E480	PINTER, HAROLD / A Night Out, Night School, Revue Sketches: Early Plays / $1.95 [See also Complete Works: One by Harold Pinter, B402 / $3.95 and Complete Works: Two by Harold Pinter, B403 / $3.95]
E663	PINTER, HAROLD / No Man's Land / $1.95
E606	PINTER, HAROLD / Old Times / $1.95
E350	PINTER, HAROLD / Three Plays (The Collection, A Slight Ache, The Dwarfs) / $3.95 [See also Complete Works: One by Harold Pinter, B402 / $3.95 and Complete Works: Two by Harold Pinter, B403 / $3.95]
E497	SHAW, ROBERT / The Man in the Glass Booth / $2.95
E635	SHEPARD, SAM / The Tooth of Crime and Geography of a Horse Dreamer: Two Plays / $3.95

CRITICAL STUDIES